Reimagining Legal Pluralism in Africa

Developments in International Law

VOLUME 80

The titles published in this series are listed at *brill.com/diil*

Reimagining Legal Pluralism in Africa

Balancing Indigenous, State, and Religious Laws

Edited by

Anthony C. Diala and Christa Rautenbach

BRILL | NIJHOFF

LEIDEN | BOSTON

Library of Congress Cataloging-in-Publication Data

Names: Diala, Anthony C., editor. | Rautenbach, C. (Christa), editor.
Title: Reimagining legal pluralism in Africa : balancing indigenous, state, and religious laws / edited by Anthony C. Diala and Christa Rautenbach.
Description: Leiden ; Boston : Brill/Nijhoff, 2024. | Series: Developments in international law, 0924-5332 ; volume 80 | Includes bibliographical references and index. |
Identifiers: LCCN 2024010452 | ISBN 9789004696730 (hardback) | ISBN 9789004696747 (ebook)
Subjects: LCSH: Legal polycentricity–Africa, Sub-Saharan. | Customary law–Africa, Sub-Saharan. | Religion and law–Africa, Sub-Saharan. | Law–Africa, Sub-Saharan. | Indigenous peoples–Legal status, laws, etc.–Africa, Sub-Saharan. | Legal polycentricity–South Africa.
Classification: LCC KQC105 .R45 2024 | DDC 340.90967–dc23/eng/20240317
LC record available at https://lccn.loc.gov/2024010452

Typeface for the Latin, Greek, and Cyrillic scripts: "Brill". See and download: brill.com/brill-typeface.

ISSN 0924-5332
ISBN 978-90-04-69673-0 (hardback)
ISBN 978-90-04-69674-7 (e-book)
DOI 10.1163/9789004696747

This book is printed on acid-free paper and produced in a sustainable manner.

Contents

PART 3
Islamic and Comparative Law in African Legal Pluralism

PART 4
Theoretical Perspectives on African Legal Pluralism

Foreword

Reimagining Legal Pluralism in Africa is a collection of 13 contributions and an epilogue by Justice Sachs, edited by Anthony Diala and Christa Rautenbach. It tackles an ambitious task: how to regulate the complex interactions between state laws imported from Europe and sub-Saharan Africa's many different indigenous legal regimes. Traditionally, the relationship between these various laws has been viewed from a strictly hierarchical point of view, assuming that the latter enjoyed an overriding authority. As a result, courts and lawmakers, whether those operating during the colonial or the current human rights eras have taken what the editors describe as a jurispathic approach. In other words, the application of indigenous laws has had to fall in line with the dominant state regimes on the understanding that they were fundamentally incompatible.

In a series of carefully detailed studies of succession, marriage and traditional leadership, the essays propose a radically different approach based on adaptive legal pluralism. This form of pluralism initially seeks to identify the foundational values of indigenous laws so that they can be used, together with state laws, as primary judicial and legislative standards. It then requires a flexible process of dialogue and negotiation between the different laws so that they can be mutually adapted to find practical solutions to the ever-changing social, economic and political problems that arise from their interactions. The desired outcome is a more just and inclusive legal order.

The authors of this book, who come from a variety of different backgrounds, are to be congratulated for proposing an entirely new solution to conflicts of laws, one that is eminently sensible and long overdue. Indeed, this work is a significant contribution to the remarkably limited scholarship on the subject, and it should become an essential aid to judges, lawgivers, academics and students.

Thomas Bennett
Emeritus Professor, Department of Public Law,
University of Cape Town, South Africa

Acknowledgements

We want to express our deepest gratitude to all the individuals who have contributed to the realisation of this book. First and foremost, we sincerely appreciate the contributors to the insightful chapters in this collection, whose expertise and valuable insights have enriched this work.

We extend our heartfelt thanks to the reviewers and scholars who provided valuable feedback and constructive criticism, which greatly enhanced the quality and depth of this publication. In addition, we extend our sincere appreciation to Alan Brimer for his meticulous language editing, which has significantly improved the clarity and coherence of the manuscript. We are also grateful to Tina Coetzer for her thorough and careful checking of the references, ensuring the accuracy and consistency of the citation style throughout the book.

We extend our recognition to Brill's publishers, dedicated editorial staff, and meticulous production team. Their unwavering belief in the viability of this project and their tireless efforts behind the scenes have been instrumental in bringing this book to fruition.

This book would not have been possible without everyone's collective efforts and support. Their contributions are sincerely acknowledged and deeply appreciated.

Anthony C. Diala and Christa Rautenbach

Notes on Contributors

Anthony C. Diala
is a professor of legal pluralism and director of the Centre for Legal Integration in Africa at the Faculty of Law, University of the Western Cape, South Africa. https://orcid.org/0000-0003-2582-0139.

Bonolo Ramadi Dinokopila
is an Associate Professor in the Department of Law at the University of Botswana. https://orcid.org/0000-0001-6291-4762.

Davinia Gómez-Sánchez
is an Associate Professor of Philosophy of Law (University of Deusto, Spain) and a human rights researcher at the Pedro Arrupe Human Rights Institute (University of Deusto). https://orcid.org/0000-0001-7058-5356.

Reshard L. Kolabhai
is enrolled for an LLM at Yale Law School. He was a Lecturer in Constitutional Law and the Bill of Rights at the Faculty of Law, North-West University (Potchefstroom Campus), South Africa until June 2023. https://orcid.org/0000-0002-7734-1650.

Jennifer H. Mike
is an Assistant Professor of Law at the American University of Nigeria, Director of its Centre for Governance, Human Rights and Development and Chair of its Department of Public Law. She is a Solicitor and Advocate of the Supreme Court of Nigeria. https://orcid.org/0000-0002-1716-9158.

Boitumelo Mmusinyane
is an Associate Professor of Law at North-West University (Mahikeng Campus), South Africa and an admitted Advocate of the High Court of South Africa. https://orcid.org/0000-0001-9397-3159.

Samson Odetayo
is a Lecturer in the Department of Public and International Law at the Faculty of Law, KolaDaisi University, Ibadan.

Philip O. Odiase
is a Senior Lecturer and the Head, Department of Private and Property Law at Adekunle Ajasin University, Akungba-Akoko, Ondo State, Nigeria. https://orcid.org/0000-0002-0823-726X.

Adeniyi Olatunbosun
is a Senior Advocate of Nigeria, a Professor of International Law and the Vice-Chancellor of KolaDaisi University, Ibadan. https://orcid.org/0000-0002-6216-0961.

Fatima Osman
is an Associate Professor in the Private Law Department at the University of Cape Town, South Africa. https://orcid.org/0000-0002-1357-7840.

Rita Ozoemena
is an Associate Professor in the Department of Public, Constitutional and International Law, University of South Africa. https://orcid.org/0000-0002-0437-8858.

Khupi Ramarumo
is an Advocate of the High Court and a Member of the South African Bar Association.

Christa Rautenbach
is a Professor of Law, North-West University (Potchefstroom Campus), South Africa. https://orcid.org/0000-0001-6641-0123.

Rodrigo Ferreira Barros
is an anthropology researcher at the Federal University of Mato Grosso (UFMT), Brazil. https://orcid.org/0000-0002-6100-0800.

Albie Sachs
is a retired judge of the Constitutional Court of South Africa and a human rights activist.

Yüksel Sezgin
is Professor of Political Science at Syracuse University, New York, USA. https://orcid.org/0000-0002-9044-0215.

George Fordam Otieno Wara
is a postdoctoral fellow at the Free State Centre for Human Rights, University of Free State, South Africa.

CHAPTER 1

Introduction

Anthony C. Diala and Christa Rautenbach

1 The Complex Interplay of Legal Systems*

In Sub-Saharan Africa, State laws, customary laws, and to a lesser extent, religious laws co-exist in a tenuous relationship.[1] State laws, also known as common law or laws of general application, are the remnants and adaptations of legal systems that Western Europeans imposed during colonial rule in the 19th and 20th centuries.[2] They encompass statutory laws, codifications, judicial precedents, and the legal culture that accompanied colonial transplants. Religious laws mainly consist of Islamic or Shariah law principles, which have varying degrees of recognition in African legal systems.[3] Customary laws comprise two types: indigenous laws, which are pre-colonial customs observed in their original forms, and adaptations of indigenous practices to globalisation and other socio-economic changes.[4] As we show, most of these socio-economic changes occur alongside coercive pressure exerted on indigenous behaviour by State laws.

This volume investigates legislative and judicial attitudes towards legal pluralism in Africa and the future of indigenous laws in this context. There are three main reasons why this inquiry is significant.

Firstly, State and indigenous African laws emerged in distinct social settings, with State laws being products of European legal systems, specifically

* This work is based on research supported in part by the National Research Foundation of South Africa (NRF Grant Number 136532). However, the opinions, findings and recommendations are not attributable to the NRF.

1 For an overview of the pluralistic characteristics of the South African legal system, see Rautenbach, "Deep Legal Pluralism," 144; and Rautenbach, "Cultural Expertise," 157.

2 In parts of Africa, European colonialism goes way further than the nineteenth century. For example, South Africa was officially colonised in 1652. See Oliver and Oliver, "Colonisation of South Africa," 1–8.

3 We recognise that Africa is a heterogeneous and complex continent, as evident in its staggeringly diverse peoples and cultures. For detailed analysis, see Chazan et al., *Politics and Society in Contemporary Africa*, 14.

4 Diala and Kangwa, "Rethinking the Interface Between Customary Law and Constitutionalism," 191.

 | DOI:10.1163/9789004696747_002

the common and civil law traditions. The common law tradition originated in England during the Middle Ages and was later transplanted to British colonies across America, Australia, New Zealand, Asia, and Africa. On the other hand, the civil law tradition developed in continental Europe and was transplanted to territories colonised by imperial powers such as France, Germany, Spain, Portugal, Belgium, Italy, and the Netherlands. Both legal systems underwent significant evolutionary phases that shaped their unique traits. For instance, they evolved from hunter-gathering societies to subsistence agriculture and then to industrialised societies. With the advent of the First Industrial Revolution in Britain (circa 1760 to 1840), Western laws underwent a radical transformation to adapt to industrialisation.[5]

During the Second Industrial Revolution in the late 19th century, Europe's adoption of technological systems such as the railroad, communication networks, and energy, water, and sewage systems stripped European laws of their processual, communal character. Instead, industrialisation imbued them with an individualist, legal positivist nature that suited Europe's emergent capitalism. This individualism is reflected today in the tone of constitutional bills of rights and in how the common law and civil law traditions centre normative authority on a sovereign with coercive enforcement powers.

In contrast, indigenous African laws emerged in closely-knit, agrarian societies that prioritised the welfare of family members in social organisation. In these societies, communal norms were process-oriented and motivated by foundational values. Studies have shown that pre-colonial adjudication occurred in familial settings, with clan elders serving as presiding officers.[6] These elders typically adopted restorative values that promoted normative flexibility.[7]

Since individual rights and obligations were subject to the interests of the clan or extended family, dispute resolution was consensus oriented. Moreover, wealth was generated collectively through farming and hunting activities. The concept of individual property rights was largely absent, as personal property consisted mainly of items of adornment.[8] Unfortunately, this social setting was disrupted by European colonialism.

---

5 The Industrial Revolution denotes the global transition from subsistence agriculture to new manufacturing processes, in which machine tools; chemicals, water and steam power, and rise of the mechanised factory system resulted in greatly increased output. It also led to advances in medicine, rise in the rate of population growth, and unprecedented socio-economic transformations.

6 See, for example, Murithi, "African Indigenous and Endogenous Approaches," 16–30.

7 Ajayi and Buhari, "Methods of Conflict Resolution," 138–57.

8 Diala and Diala, "Normative Intersectionality," 86–108.

The impact of European colonialism on African societies is so significant that it is impossible to cover all of its consequences in this brief introduction.[9] However, it is worth noting that colonialism is responsible for modernity in Africa. Notably, it brought about urbanisation, Western education, independent income, and commercialised agriculture that served its exploitative economic goals. Before colonisation, women were mainly responsible for subsistence agriculture, which formed the foundation of African economies. However, colonialism severed women's economic relationship with the land, broke the family's wealth from the control of elders, and weakened the strong kinship ties of the extended family.[10]

More importantly, colonialism disrupted the historical continuity of indigenous laws by imposing European legal culture, specifically the common law and civil law systems. In courts, colonisers judged the validity of indigenous laws based on their imported moral standards, adjudication procedures, and philosophical reasoning.[11] They dismantled many indigenous institutions, established new courts and administrative procedures, and introduced new systems of work, food, fashion, and transactions that destroyed the agrarian basis of African political economies. In many ways, the radical socio-economic changes brought about by European colonialism marked the beginning of a new era in Africa – a sort of normative line in the sand for the evolution of indigenous African laws.[12]

Secondly, there is a significant disconnect between indigenous laws and state laws. Even after political independence was granted to Africans, the economic and socio-political structures imposed by the departed European colonisers remained largely intact. The state laws that dominate legal pluralism are individualistic in nature, authoritarian in outlook, and rigid in their judicial application.[13] Adjudication is based on procedures that favour legal certainty and judicial precedents. Due to the enduring, self-replicating nature of colonial institutions in Africa, state laws are essentially European cultural

9 For a sample, see Rodney, *How Europe Underdeveloped Africa*; Snyder, "Colonialism and Legal Form," 49–90; Chanock. *Making of South African Legal Culture,* 243–72; Chaock, "Neither Customary nor Legal," 72–88.

10 Tsikata, "Gender, Land Tenure and Agrarian Production Systems," 1–19.

11 A notorious yardstick is the so-called "repugnancy clause", which demanded that recognisable African customs must be compatible with natural justice, public policy, equity and good conscience. This standard has since been replaced by constitutional values of dignity, equality and non-discrimination in many southern African states.

12 Diala, "Legal Pluralism," 3.

13 This trait reflects the positivist character of colonial legal transplants. For analyses of legal positivism, see Hart, *Concept of Law*; George, *Autonomy of Law*.

constructs. They possess a historical continuity grounded in industrial capitalism, which is at odds with the agrarian nature of indigenous laws. The resulting normative dissonance turns African social fields into remarkable contestation and adaptation sites.

This book's analysis of judicial decisions highlights the stark contrast between indigenous laws and state laws, which has led to conflicts over property rights for groups such as married women, girls, and younger males. These groups are the most affected by the radical changes that have occurred in the agrarian foundations of indigenous laws due to people's insistence on applying customs that are no longer suited to modern conditions. In the pre-colonial past, families lived close together for defence and agricultural purposes. Since ancestral worship was the predominant religion, land held a sacred status as the site of worship. The family produced income jointly through work parties, often accompanied by rituals. In this communal lifestyle, private property rights were scarce, except for items of adornment, and the eldest male member of the family served as its representative in the spiritual and material worlds. He alone inherited the family property with a trustee-like duty to promote the family's best interest.[14]

Furthermore, gender relations were largely complementary rather than binary, as brides joined the welfare-oriented system of their husbands' families in exogamous marriage communities.[15] In the rare event of divorce, they returned to their fathers' houses and were absorbed back into the welfare system. However, this care-based agrarian setting was shattered by urbanisation, western education, individual income, migrant labour systems, and other socio-economic changes. As a result, the application of customs in the face of changed social conditions negatively affected the property rights of women, girls, and younger male children.[16]

Finally, many indigenous customs were misinterpreted or distorted in the courts, while others, such as male primogeniture, were ossified in case law and legislation without regard for changes in social conditions.[17] As one judge observed,[18]

---

14 Diala, "Reform of the Customary Law of Inheritance in Nigeria," 633–54; Mbatha, "Reforming the Customary Law of Succession," 259; Okoro, *Customary Laws of Succession in Eastern Nigeria*, 4.

15 Sudarkasa, "'The Status of Women'," 91–103.

16 *Bhe v Magistrate, Khayelitsha* 2005 (1) SA 580 (CC) paras 82, 83.

17 See for example the KwaZulu Act on the Code of Zulu Law 16 of 1985, the Natal Code of Zulu Law (Proc. R151 of 1987 in GG 10966 of 9 October 1987), and *Bhe v Magistrate, Khayelitsha* 2005 (1) SA 580 (CC).

18 *Agbai v Okogbue* (1991) 7 NWLR (Pt. 204) 390 at 417 per Nwokedi JSC.

> customary laws were formulated from time immemorial. As our society advances, they are more removed from their pristine social ecology. They meet situations which were inconceivable at the time they took root.

Indeed, some African elders allegedly exploited the changes introduced by colonialism to strip customs of their foundational values of welfare.[19] Consequently, hardships occur when customs are applied without their foundational values. So, how should judges and legislators approach indigenous African laws? What does State regulation of indigenous laws portend for the future of personal laws in the continent? We turn to these questions in the next section.

2 Jurispathic Law Reforms

> When a judge faces a question in which legal meaning is contested, therefore, the problem is not, as is usually said, that there is a 'gap' in the law or that the law is 'unclear.' Rather, there is simply too *much* law – a host of meanings competing for recognition. Under this view, the judge does not 'make' law to fill a gap, but rather plucks one existing meaning from the host available. The role of the judge therefore is purely negative. It is 'jurispathic,' or law-killing, in the sense that the judge will select one of the squalling brood of conflicting legal meanings to elevate and to enforce with the violence of the state-and will slay the rest.[20]

The future of personal laws in Africa is evident in how states manage law reforms amidst neo-liberal pressures and the unprecedented socio-economic changes of globalisation in interconnected social fields.[21]

This volume demonstrates that African states are intensifying their judicial and legislative reforms of indigenous laws of inheritance, land tenure, traditional leadership, initiation rites, and marriage laws. They are doing so ostensibly to harmonise these laws with the values enshrined in constitutional bills of rights, but the result is jurispathic. The term "jurispathic" is derived from the Latin words, "jus", meaning law, and "spatha", meaning sword. So, jurispathic reforms can be interpreted as the violent displacement of established legal

19 Chanock, "Neither Customary nor Legal," 76.

20 Snyder, "Nomos, Narrative, and Adjudication," 1624. Footnotes omitted.

21 Diala, "Neoliberal Influences," 81–108.

norms, in other words, "law-destroying" their normative value.[22] Examples range from judicial invalidations of discriminatory customs to legislative impositions of principles such as dignity, equality, and non-discrimination. The mode of operation of these reforms reveals much about the interaction of normative orders in Africa.

The official stance towards indigenous personal laws reveals a discernible pattern: whenever a cultural practice is successfully challenged in court as offensive to constitutional (human rights) values, judges invalidate it, and legislators follow with law reform. Notably, the values employed by judges to strike down indigenous laws are successors of European values of natural justice, equity, fairness, and public policy, which are widely known as the "repugnancy test". Against the backdrop of colonial continuity, State reforms of personal laws fuel long-standing controversy over the status of indigenous laws in Africa's legal pluralism.[23]

While the defenders of indigenous laws justify their preservation with nationalist or cultural relativist arguments about upholding tradition, reform advocates utilise universalist human rights values to champion law reform.[24] However, neither the defenders of indigenous laws nor the reform advocates usually address the discordance between the origins and nature of State laws and indigenous laws.[25] The recognition and integration of religious laws further complicate this intricate web of legal pluralism.

The interaction of religious laws with other normative systems, unlike indigenous laws, is not clearly defined. Generally, in states without a Muslim majority population, the default position of judges and legislators is often to marginalise or ignore Islamic laws. Sezgin's contribution to this book explores the challenges faced by Islamic law in the Ghanaian context. He notes that Ghanian courts have often declined to recognise the customary existence of Islamic law, dismissing Muslim family law claims on procedural grounds. This reluctance raises important questions about the judicial approach to Islamic law and its implication for Ghana's plural legal system. Sezgin delves into the historical backdrop, suggesting that non-recognition of Islamic laws is partly rooted in how the post-independence judiciary inherited the colonial narrative that Islamic law is not a native law of the land. However, the reluctance

22 For analysis, see Cover, "The Supreme Court, 1982 Term," 4; Zenker and Höhne, *The State and the Paradox of Customary Law,* 4.

23 Hellum, "Human Rights and Gender Relations," 635–55; Hellum, "Women's Human Rights," 88–104.

24 Mnisi and Claassens, "Rural Women Redefining Land Rights," 491–516.

25 Diala, "A Butterfly that Thinks Itself a Bird," 383.

could also be influenced by judges' legal positivist inclinations,[26] as seen in cases such as *Akyeampong v Marshall* [1959] D.Ct. (unreported), where a widow's claim under the personal Christian laws of her deceased husband was successful.

The recognition of religious laws is crucial, particularly in countries where a significant portion of the population adheres to such legal systems. In Ghana, where Islamic law is practiced by about 20 percent of the population, the non-recognition of Islamic law raises fundamental questions about the inclusivity and adaptability of the legal system.[27]

In South Africa, the legal landscape concerning the recognition of Islamic personal laws has witnessed notable shifts, presenting both challenges and advancements.[28] A nuanced comparison with Ghana highlights the diverse approaches within African contexts towards the integration of religious laws into the broader legal framework.

Unlike Ghana, where courts have shown reluctance to engage substantively with Islamic laws, South African courts have demonstrated increased tolerance towards Islamic personal laws. However, this tolerance is not without its limitations, often guided by an ethos of legal positivism that leans towards Western values. For instance, in *Amod v Multilateral Motor Vehicle Accident Fund* 1999 (4) SA 1319 (SCA), the court granted relief based on a contract arising from an Islamic marriage but explicitly refrained from recognising the marriage itself, especially its potentially polygynous nature.

The South African Constitutional Court, through cases like *Daniels v Campbell* 2004 (7) BCLR 735 (CC) and *Hassam v Jacobs* 2009 (5) SA 572 (CC), has taken steps to interpret and extend legal recognition to certain aspects of Islamic personal law. For example, in *Daniels v Campbell*, it broadened the definition of "spouse" in the Intestate Succession Act to include surviving partners in monogamous Muslim marriages. Similarly, *Hassam v Jacobs* saw an extension of the meanings of "spouse" and "surviving partner" to polygynous Muslim marriages.

The official scrutiny of Islamic personal law by the South African Law Reform Commission, beginning in the late 1990s, marked a significant turning point. The Commission's 2003 report on *Islamic Marriages and Related Matters*,[29]

---

26 For example, the reluctance to recognise a claim or practice that is not supported by legislation.

27 Ghana Statistical Service's Population and Housing Census 2021.

28 For a detailed discussion, see Rautenbach (ed), *Introduction to Legal Pluralism in South Africa*, 14–5, 67–77 and 375–90; Rautenbach, "Families and Legal Pluralism in South Africa", 61–91.

29 See SALRC, *Project 59: Islamic Marriages and Related Matters.*

followed by a 2010 Bill on Muslim Marriages introduced into parliament,[30] demonstrated a proactive effort to recognise Muslim marriages. Nevertheless, it has not yet been enacted into law. The recognition journey in South Africa has involved numerous legal battles to compel Parliament to enact legislation recognising Muslim marriages. The recent success in *Women's Legal Centre Trust v President of the Republic of South Africa* 2022 (5) SA 323 (CC), where the court ordered the state to enact legislation within 24 months to recognise Muslim marriages, signifies a potential groundbreaking moment.

At the end of 2022, a pivotal development emerged in the form of a Private Member Bill presented to parliament – the "Registration of Muslim Marriages Bill" (B30–2022).[31] This Bill seeks to officially recognise and regulate Muslim marriages in South Africa. If successfully enacted, it holds the potential to integrate Islamic law into the state legal framework, marking a momentous evolution in the accommodation of religious laws within the broader legal pluralism of South Africa.

As noted earlier, African judges, most of whom are orientated in Western culture, tend to invalidate customs that they find to violate human rights. This tendency creates the impression that law reforms are shaping indigenous norms to conform to universalist ideals of dignity, equality, and non-discrimination. This process is particularly evident in South Africa, where judges and legislators are working to address the historical injustices of apartheid. For instance, the Single Marriage Bill, which is still in the planning phase, aims to regulate all forms of marriages and life partnerships under one legislation.[32] Other examples include the Recognition of Customary Marriages Act,[33] which mandates equality in matrimonial relationships, the Reform of Customary Law of Succession and Regulation of Related Matters Act,[34] which

30 Draft Muslim Marriage Bill (BX-2011). A copy of the Bill is available at https://pmg.org.za/bill/235/.

31 The Bill (B30–2022) was introduced by a parliamentary member, MGE Hendricks. He is also a member of the *Al-Jama-ah* community, in terms of s 76(2) of the Constitution of the Republic of South Africa, 1996 ('the Constitution'). The detailed "Memorandum on the Objects of the Registration of Muslim Marriages Bill, 2022" gives an overview of the Muslim community's plight regarding the statutory recognition of its marriages since 1987. For more information see General Notice 1380 of 2022, published in *Government Gazette* 47448 on 4 November 2022.

32 See SALRC, *Project 144: Single Marriage Statute*. The co-editor, Christa Rautenbach, is the chairperson on the Advisory Committee since 2020. The final report was completed in 2022 but has not yet been released to the public because it is awaiting ministerial approval.

33 Act 120 of 1998.

34 Act 11 of 2009. In general, see the discussions in chs. 2 and 3.

approved the judicial abolition of male primogeniture, and the Traditional and Khoi-San Leadership Act of 2019,[35] which mandates equality and non-discrimination in traditional institutions.

The process of transforming indigenous laws into universalist human rights images is most apparent in judicial decisions. For instance, in 2004, the Constitutional Court of South Africa abolished the custom of male primogeniture, a fundamental rule of indigenous succession.[36] In other rulings, the court has established community of property as the default position for all customary law marriages.[37] Similarly, judges and legislators in Nigeria, Kenya, Zimbabwe, and Tanzania have reformed indigenous personal laws to align with State laws.[38] The chapters included in this book analyse some of these reforms.

3 Framework and Layout

The normative orders in Africa interact hierarchically, with State laws occupying the top position. This hierarchy is a legacy of the regulatory power dynamics established by European colonialism.[39] Consequently, despite pre-dating African constitutions, indigenous laws are subordinated to the latter and other statutory laws. The coercive nature of African legal pluralism is consistent with the histories of colonialism in Europe and America, where colonised people

35 Act 3 of 2019. This law was introduced to address the gap in the Traditional Leadership and Governance Framework Act 41 of 2003 that failed to provide for the recognition of Khoi-San leaders. The former Act is the first comprehensive statutory regulation of traditional leadership in South Africa post-apartheid. See Rautenbach, "Mapping Traditional Leadership and Authority," 495.

36 *Bhe v Magistrate, Khayelitsha* 2005 (1) SA 580 (CC).

37 *Ramuhovhi v President of the RSA* (2018), *Gumede v President of the RSA* (2009), and *Sithole v Sithole* (2021).

38 *Onyibor Anekwe v Mrs Maria Nweke* (2014) All FWLR (Pt. 739) 1154, *Ukeje v Ukeje* (2014) 11 NWLR (Pt. 1418) 384–414; *Rebeca Z. Gyumi v Attorney General* (Misc. Civil Cause 5 of 2016) [2016] TZHC 2023 (3 March 2016); *Diana Eunice Kawenda v Minister of Justice, Legal and Parliamentary Affairs and Two Others* (Constitutional Court) Judgment No. CCA 3/22 (24 May 2022) 3. See also Kenya's Matrimonial Property Act of 2013, Marriage Act of 2014, and art. 45(1) and (3) of the 2010 Constitution, which guarantees "equal rights at the time of the marriage, during the marriage, and at the dissolution of the marriage". However, on 27 January 2023, the Supreme Court of Kenya ruled that marital property must be shared based on fairness rather than an automatic ratio of 50:50. See *Joseph Ombogi Ogentoto v Martha Bosibori Ogentoto* (Supreme Court of Kenya) Petition No. 11 of 2020 (27 January 2023).

39 Diala and Kangwa, "Rethinking the Interface Between Customary Law and Constitutionalism," 191.

were compelled to adapt to the laws imposed by their colonisers, leading to the integration of indigenous laws with the imposed laws.[40] History shows that if the colonised people failed to integrate their indigenous laws properly, those laws usually disappeared.[41] Against this historical backdrop, this book is grounded in the idea of adaptive legal pluralism.[42]

Adaptive legal pluralism views the interaction of normative orders in recently colonised societies as essentially imitative. It offers the foundational values of indigenous laws as platforms for legal integration. In his proposal for the convergence of legal orders in Africa, Diala identifies "five overlapping phases", as follows:

> In phase one, customary laws are understood as products of people's adaptations to socioeconomic changes. In two, governments ascertain the foundational values of indigenous laws and respect cultural pluralism by avoiding [needless destruction of] substantive [indigenous] laws. These values, such as bridewealth and succession principles, are generally stable and similar across Africa. In phase three, judges use indigenous values as primary judicial standards. In four, law reforms incorporate these values into statutes. For example, sections 20–21 and Schedule 2 of the 1975 Constitution of Papua New Guinea enshrine customary law as the 'underlying law'. In phase five, indigenous laws transform into customary laws. Thereafter, state laws become indistinguishable from customary laws and both merge into national common laws.

As previously noted, a notable aspect of legal pluralism in Africa is how law reforms compel indigenous laws to conform to universalist human rights standards, a continuation of colonial imposition of industrial legal systems on Africa's agrarian political economies. As a theoretical framework, adaptive legal pluralism addresses the normative challenges posed by this situation. Rather than using a conflict of laws approach, adaptive legal pluralism emphasises dialogue between State and indigenous laws.

Within this framework of dialogue, Sezgin's contribution underscores that the consistent refusal of Ghana's judiciary to recognise Islamic law has deprived nomadic groups of essential feedback for harmonising their legal

40 Nicholas and Metzger, *Introduction to Roman Law*, 2; Zweigert and Koetz, *Introduction to Comparative Law*.

41 Brown, "Customary Law in Modern England," 565–6.

42 For an outline of adaptive legal pluralism, see Diala note 12.

meanings with the State's. He notes that cases like *Giwah v Ladi*[43] reveal that certain elements within the Muslim community may be open to internal reform and reinterpretation. While recognising the complexities of dialogue between State and indigenous laws, it is crucial to acknowledge that various factors can influence this process, with some potentially unsuitable for normative adaptations in specific socio-cultural contexts.

One challenge lies in the paucity of reasoned judgments providing convincing explanations for judicial decisions. This is exemplified in *Ukeje v Ukeje*,[44] where the Nigerian Supreme Court failed to address the preservative philosophy of property rights and its unsuitability to contemporary conditions.[45] Technicality and undue reliance on rules are also influential, with the dismissal of some Islamic law claims on procedural grounds not necessarily influencing the behaviour of claimants. They might continue observing their Islamic laws or push for, in Sezgin's words, internal reform through the adoption of legal principles from court systems into their communities' value systems.

Forum shopping by litigants further complicates dialogue between legal orders. Sezgin's data indicates that Muslims often bypass the formal legal system for family and property disputes, resorting to traditional authorities and alternative dispute resolution forums applying Islamic law and local customs. While cases like *Giwah v Ladi* [2010] showcase moments when the Ghanaian judiciary recognised the existence of Islamic law, there remains an overarching attitude summarised by Ollennu as an "ignorance of the Ghanaian way of life" when Islamic succession is applied over native law.[46]

Additionally, some judges seem to misunderstand the implications of legal pluralism, as seen in cases like *Yahaya v Yakubu* [2012] DLSC 3057, where Ghana's Court of Appeal reversed a trial court decision, holding that Islamic law is not indigenous law.

This book delves into the future of indigenous African laws and, to a lesser extent, religious laws within the context of legal pluralism. It is structured into four main sections, with double blind peer-reviewed chapters that cover the areas of succession, marriage, traditional leadership, and theoretical perspectives.

Part 1, titled "Succession in African Legal Pluralism", focuses on succession, with two contributors examining the topic. In Chapter 2, Rautenbach explores

---

43 *Giwah v Ladi* [2010] DLHC 7067; *Giwah v Ladi* [2011] CA (unreported); *Giwah v Ladi* [2013–2014] 2 GLR 1139.

44 *Ukeje v Ukeje* (2014) 11 NWLR (Pt 1418) 384–414.

45 Diala "A Critique of the Judicial Attitude towards Matrimonial Property Rights", 100–22.

46 Ollennu, *The Law*, 267–68.

South Africa's jurisprudential reforms of customary laws of succession, highlighting how statutory changes are systematically replacing indigenous norms with common law norms, despite the diverse legal environment of South Africa. Meanwhile, Osman, in Chapter 3, presents a case study of a rural South African village to explore the interplay between individualised asset acquisition and the communal nature of the customary law of succession, arguing that it exemplifies the dynamics of normative resistance to State interventions.

Part 2, titled "Marriage in African Legal Pluralism", shifts the focus to marriage issues, with contributions from four authors. In Chapter 4, Ozoemena *et al* use systems theory and social dominance theory to explore the clash between "Western" values and African customary practices in the context of two proposals in South Africa's Single Marriage Bill. They call for a balance between customary practices and human rights obligations and the harmonisation of customary laws with State laws. Olatunbosun and Odetayo, in Chapter 5, examine the functional relevance of woman-to-woman marriage in conditions of legal pluralism in Nigeria. They argue that this form of marriage should not be subjected to the colonial-era test of repugnancy and recommend the harmonisation of customary and statutory marriages to ensure their equal status. Finally, Mmusinyane, in Chapter 6, analyses the impact of constitutional reforms on Batswana customary laws of marriage, highlighting how the judiciary's treatment of these laws is concerning, with the Constitution and Western precedents seemingly applied consistently, making customary law subservient to foreign rules of evidence.

Part 3, titled "Islamic and Comparative Law in African Legal Pluralism", focuses on normative interaction from the perspective of Islamic and comparative law. Sezgin's contribution in Chapter 7 critiques the reluctance of Ghanaian courts to engage with Muslim personal law in substantive terms, arguing that this tendency undermines judicial legitimacy and misses a vital opportunity to influence the future development of legal meanings within the Muslim community. In Chapter 8, Barros discusses how indigenous peoples in Brazil and South Africa are attempting to overcome their inadequate representation in official spaces through community protocols that outline their terms of engagement with the State. These protocols demonstrate how efforts at decolonisation and autonomy are shaping legal pluralism in the global South. Odiase, in Chapter 9, explores the sustainability of customary law arbitration in Nigeria, highlighting the contrast between the rigid procedures of state courts and the organic fluidity of customary law. He argues that customary law arbitration will thrive better if the courts reconcile the need for legal certainty with the flexible nature of customary laws. Finally, Gómez-Sánchez, in Chapter 10, proposes an alternative construction of the right to property based on the worldviews of the indigenous San people, which avoids liberal, positivist concepts of property and instead champions values such as mutual dependence, egalitarianism, redistribution, and reciprocity.

Part 4, titled "Theoretical Perspectives on African Legal Pluralism", concludes the book. In this section, Mike, in Chapter 11, analyses religious and cultural justifications for the criminalisation of adultery in Nigeria, using arguments about cultural relativism and universalism of human rights. In Chapter 12, Dinokopila argues that customary law is being undermined by Botswana's common law and statutory laws. Kolabhai, in Chapter 13, posits that customs can only be understood in their dialectic relationship with State laws, especially in their mutually adaptive roles in constructing a shared system of political economy across space and time.

4 Concluding Words: Towards Legal Integration

Legal pluralism in Africa is unique due to the continent's diverse peoples, cultures, and traditions.[47] It has been shaped by the colonial and post-colonial history of the continent, which has had a significant impact on the development and interaction of different legal systems.

It is certainly true that the colonial imposition of European legal systems on African societies was a significant factor in shaping the legal landscape of many African countries today. As such, the term "colonial legal pluralism" could be used to describe the legal system that emerged from this historical process. However, it is essential to note that legal pluralism in Africa is not solely a product of colonialism but also reflects pre-colonial and post-colonial realities, which is more in line with our use of adaptive legal pluralism. Therefore, the term "African legal pluralism" would be appropriate as long as it acknowledges the complexity and diversity of legal systems across the continent and avoids reducing them to a single, monolithic entity.

We use the idea of adaptive legal pluralism as a framework that recognises the coexistence of different normative orders, such as customary, religious, and State law, in African societies. It emphasises the importance of dialogue, negotiation, and mutual adaptation between these different legal systems, intending to find practical solutions to the regulatory challenges that arise from their interaction.

47 Atuguba, "Three Levels and Seven Types of Law," 17.

This framework recognises that legal pluralism in Africa is not a static or monolithic concept, but is instead constantly evolving and adapting to new circumstances. As such, it requires an approach that is dynamic, flexible, and able to respond to changing social, economic, and political realities.

Overall, adaptive legal pluralism seeks to promote a more just and inclusive legal world that recognises the diversity and complexity of legal traditions in Africa and beyond. The chapters herein offer a representative sample of contemporary legal pluralism in southern Africa, examining its manifestations in other areas of law and contexts. Throughout the book, we see that the interaction between State and indigenous laws is complex, often reflecting the legacy of colonialism and ongoing struggles for autonomy and recognition. However, adaptive legal pluralism offers a way forward, emphasising the importance of dialogue, negotiation, and mutual adaptation between different legal systems. By embracing adaptive legal pluralism, we can move towards a more just and inclusive legal system that recognises the diversity and complexity of legal traditions in Africa and beyond.

The book's unique contribution is that it challenges the dominant conflict of laws approach that tends to emphasise the incompatibility of state and indigenous laws. Instead, the book proposes the adaptive legal pluralism framework that stresses dialogue and engagement between State and indigenous laws. The book highlights how adaptive legal pluralism can help address the challenges that arise from the colonial imposition of industrial legal systems onto Africa's agrarian political economies.

The book is useful for scholars of law, anthropology, sociology, political science, and history, as well as policymakers, legal practitioners, and development practitioners working in Africa. Overall, it provides insights into the complexities of normative interaction in Africa and offer practical solutions for the regulatory challenges that arise from it.

We hope that you find the content stimulating!

Bibliography

Literature

Ajayi, Adeyinka Theresa, and Lateef Oluwafemi Buhari. "Methods of Conflict Resolution in African Traditional Society." *African Research Review* 8, no. 2 (2014): 138–57.

Atuguba, Raymond A. "Legal Pluralism in Africa: Three Levels and Seven Types of Law." In *The Routledge Handbook of African Law,* edited by Muna Ndulo and Cosmas Emeziem, 17–52. London: Routledge, 2022.

Brown, W. Jethro. "Customary Law in Modern England." (1905) 5(8) *Columbia Law Review* 5, no. 8 (1905): 561–83.

Chanock, Martin. "Neither Customary nor Legal: African Customary Law in an era of Family Law Reform." *International Journal of Law and Family* 3, no. 1 (1989): 72–88.

Chanock, Martin. *The Making of South African Legal Culture 1902–1936: Fear, Favour and Prejudice.* Cambridge: Cambridge University Press, 2001.

Chazan, Naomi, et al., eds. *Politics and Society in Contemporary Africa. 3 ed.* Boulder, CO: Lynne Rienner, 1999.

Cover, Robert. "The Supreme Court, 1982 Term – Foreword: Nomos and Narrative." *Harvard Law Review* 97 (1983): 4–68.

Diala, Anthony C. "A Butterfly that Thinks Itself a Bird: The Identity of Customary Courts in Nigeria." *Journal of Legal Pluralism and Unofficial Law* 51, no. 3 (October 2019): 381–405. https://doi.org/10.1080/07329113.2019.1678281.

Diala, Anthony C. "A Critique of the Judicial Attitude towards Matrimonial Property Rights under Customary law in Nigeria's Southern States." *African Human Rights Law Journal* 18, no. 1 (2018): 100–22.

Diala, Anthony C. "Legal Pluralism and the Future of Personal Family Laws in Africa." *International Journal of Law, Policy and The Family* 35, no. 1 (2021): 1–17. doi: https://doi.org/10.1093/lawfam/ebab023.

Diala, Anthony C. "Neoliberal Influences on Legal Pluralist Marriage Reforms in Africa." *Journal of International and Comparative Law* 9, no. 2 (2022): 81–108.

Diala, Anthony C. "Reform of the Customary Law of Inheritance in Nigeria: Lessons from South Africa" *African Human Rights Law Journal* 14, no. 2 (2014): 633–54.

Diala, Anthony C., and Betsheba Kangwa. "Rethinking the Interface Between Customary Law and Constitutionalism in Sub-Saharan Africa." *De Jure* 52, no. 1 (2019): 189–206.

Diala, Anthony C., and Jane C. Diala. "Normative Intersectionality in Married Women's Property Rights in Southern Nigeria." *Law, Democracy and Development* 24 (2020): 86–108.

George, Roger P., ed. *The Autonomy of Law: Essays on Legal Positivism.* Oxford: Clarendon Press, 1994.

Ghana Population and Housing Census 2021, https://census2021.statsghana.gov.gh/.

Hart, H. L. A. *The Concept of Law.* 2 ed. Oxford: Clarendon Press, 1994.

Hellum, Anne. "Human Rights and Gender Relations in Postcolonial Africa: Options and Limits for the Subjects of Legal Pluralism." *Law & Social Inquiry* 25, no. 2 (2000): 635–55.

Hellum, Anne. "Women's Human Rights and African Customary Laws: Between Universalism and Relativism –Individualism and Communitarianism." *European Journal of Development Research* 10, no. 2 (1998): 88–104.

Mbatha, Likhapha. "Reforming the Customary Law of Succession." *South African Journal on Human Rights* 18 (2002): 259–86.

Mnisi, Sindiso, and Anika Claassens. "Rural Women Redefining Land Rights in the Context of Living Customary Law." *South African Journal on Human Rights* 25, no. 3 (2009): 491–516.

Murithi, Tim. "African Indigenous and Endogenous Approaches to Peace and Conflict Resolution." In *Peace and Conflict in Africa*, edited by David J. Francis, 16–30. London: Zed Books, 2008.

Nicholas, Barry, and Ernest Metzger. *Introduction to Roman Law*. Oxford: Oxford University Press, 1962.

Okoro, Nwakamma. *The Customary Laws of Succession in Eastern Nigeria and the Statutory and Judicial Rules Governing their Application*. London: Sweet & Maxwell, 1966.

Oliver, Erna, and Willem H. Oliver. "The Colonisation of South Africa: A Unique Case." *HTS: Theological Studies* 73, no. 3 (2017): 1–8.

Ollennu, N. A. *The Law of Testate and Intestate Succession in Ghana*. London: Sweet and Maxwell, 1966.

Rautenbach, Christa. ed. *Introduction to Legal Pluralism in South Africa*. 6 ed. Durban: LexisNexis, 2021.

Rautenbach, Christa. "Cultural Expertise in Litigation in South Africa: Can the Western World Learn Anything form a Mixed, Pluralistic Legal System?" *Studies in Law, Politics, and Society* 78 (2019): 157–78.

Rautenbach, Christa. "Deep Legal Pluralism in South Africa: Judicial Accommodation of Non-State Law." *Journal of Legal Pluralism* 60 (2010): 143–77.

Rautenbach, Christa. "Mapping Traditional Leadership and Authority in Post-Apartheid South Africa: Decentralisation and Constitutionalism in Traditional Governance." In *Decentralisation and Constitutionalism in Africa*, edited by Charles M. Fombad, and Nico Steytler, 483–519. Oxford: Oxford University Press, 2019.

Rautenbach, Christa. "Families and Legal Pluralism in South Africa: Celebrating Diversity but at what Cost?" In *The Pluralisation of Family forms*, edited by Nina Dethloff, and Katharina Kaesling, 61–91. Intersentia: 2023.

Rodney, Walter. *How Europe Underdeveloped Africa* (London: Bogle-L'Ouverture Publications and Tanzanian Publishing House, 1972).

Snyder, Francis G. "Colonialism and Legal Form: The Creation of 'Customary Law' in Senegal." *Journal of Legal Pluralism and Unofficial Law* 19 (1981): 49–90.

Snyder, Franklin G. "Nomos, Narrative, and Adjudication: Toward a Jurisgenetic Theory of Law." *William & Mary Law Review* 40, no. 5 (1999): 1623–729.

South African Law Reform Commission. Project 59, Report: Islamic Marriages and Related Matters. Pretoria: SALRC, 2003.

South African Law Reform Commission. *Project 144, Discussion Paper 152: Single Marriage Statute*. Pretoria: SALRC, 2021.

Sudarkasa, Niara. "'The Status of Women' in Indigenous African Societies." *Feminist Studies* 12, no. 1 (1986): 91–103.

Tsikata, Dzodzi. "Gender, Land Tenure and Agrarian Production Systems in Sub-Saharan Africa." *Agrarian South: Journal of Political Economy* 5, no. 1 (2016): 1–19.

Zenker, Olaf, and Markus Virgil Höhne, eds. *The State and the Paradox of Customary Law in Africa.* Abingdo: Routledge, 2018.

Zweigert, Konrad, and Hein Koetz (Tony Weir trans.). *Introduction to Comparative Law, Vol. 3.* 3 ed. Oxford: Clarendon Press, 1998.

Case Law

Ghana

Akyeampong v Marshall [1959] D.Ct. (unreported).

Giwah v Ladi [2010] DLHC 7067.

Giwah v Ladi [2011] CA (unreported).

Giwah v Ladi [2013–2014] 2 GLR 1139.

Yahaya v Yakubu [2012] DLSC 3057.

Kenya

Joseph Ombogi Ogentoto vs Martha Bosibori Ogentoto (Supreme Court of Kenya) Petition No. 11 of 2020 (27 January 2023).

Nigeria

Agbai v Okogbue [1991] 7 NWLR (Pt. 204) 390.

Onyibor Anekwe v Mrs Maria Nweke (2014) All FWLR (Pt. 739) 1154.

Ukeje v Ukeje (2014) 11 NWLR (Pt. 1418) 384.

South Africa

Amod v Multilateral Motor Vehicle Accident Fund 1999 (4) SA 1319 (SCA).

Bhe v Magistrate, Khayelitsha 2005 (1) SA 580 (CC).

Daniels v Campbell 2004 (7) BCLR 735 (CC).

Gumede v President of the Republic of South Africa 2009 (3) SA 152 (CC).

Hassam v Jacobs 2009 (5) SA 572 (CC).

Ramuhovhi v President of the Republic of South Africa 2018 (2) SA 1 (CC).

Sithole v Sithole 2021 (5) SA 34 (CC).

Women's Legal Centre Trust v President of the Republic of South Africa 2022 (5) SA 323 (CC).

Tanzania

Rebeca Z. Gyumi v Attorney General (Misc. Civil Cause 5 of 2016) [2016] TZHC 2023 (3 March 2016).

Zimbabwe

Diana Eunice Kawenda v Minister of Justice, Legal and Parliamentary Affairs and Two Others (Constitutional Court) Judgment No. CCA 3/22 (24 May 2022).

Legislation and Government Publications.

Kenya

Constitution of Kenya, 2010.

Matrimonial Property Act, 2013.

Marriage Act, 2014.

South Africa.

KwaZulu Act on the Code of Zulu Law 16 of 1985.

Natal Code of Zulu Law (Proc. R151 of 1987 in GG 10966 of 9 October 1987).

Recognition of Customary Marriages Act 120 of 1998.

Reform of Customary Law of Succession and Regulation of Related Matters Act 11 of 2009.

Traditional and Khoi-San Leadership Act 3 of 2019.

Traditional Leadership and Governance Framework Act 41 of 2003.

PART 1

Succession in African Legal Pluralism

CHAPTER 2

State Intervention in the Customary Law of Succession in South Africa: What Remains of Customary Norms in the "Rainbow Nation"?

Christa Rautenbach

Abstract

The South African customary law of succession had been the subject of human rights debates for a long time, primarily because of the way its inherently patriarchal rules treated women. After a few judicial decisions post-apartheid dealing with the unequal division of property between beneficiaries in customary law, the Reform of Customary Law of Succession and Regulation of Related Matters Act 11 of 2009 came into operation on 20 September 2010 to settle the matter. As the Act declares in its preamble, it aims to "modify the customary law of succession", and it does this by essentially replacing customary law norms with common law norms, albeit allowing a few variations to accommodate customs peculiar to traditional communities. However, whether the adaptations are enough to do justice to the constitutional guarantee of customary law's protection remains a contentious point. This contribution provides an overview of the most crucial state interventions in the customary law of succession and asks whether any customary norms remain after all the statutory changes were made.

1 Introduction

Soon after South Africa transitioned into a new constitutional dispensation, more than 30 years ago, the expression "rainbow nation" became entrenched in South African popular and legal discourses.[1] The slogan invokes images of colour, happiness, reconciliation, unity and diversity; it interlinks with the

1 E.g., see, Møller, Dickow, and Harris, "South Africa's 'Rainbow People'," 246: "Nobel peace laureate Archbishop Desmond Tutu at a celebration commemorating the new nation introduced the rainbow over South Africa as a symbol of reconciliation and unity among all the diverse people in the nation. This spirit of unity is captured in the new identity adopted by South Africa as the nation of the 'rainbow people'. ... South Africans have made the symbol of the rainbow their own. The rainbow is ubiquitous and competes with the flag as a national symbol which signifies pride. The expression 'rainbow nation' has popular appeal as a catch

 | DOI:10.1163/9789004696747_003

constitutional phrase "united in our diversity".[2] Although unity and diversity are contrasting terms, they signify "social cohesion" while simultaneously celebrating differences.[3] Such a viewpoint is commensurate with the dicta in the Constitutional Court's judgment in *MEC For Education, Kwazulu-Natal v Pillay.*[4]

> It does not envisage a society of atomised communities circling in the shared space that is our country, but a society that is unified in its diversity. That unity requires a 'pluralistic solidarity' between our different racial, cultural, religious and linguistic communities. That solidarity, of course, must not be based on domination by a majority culture or group, but on a shared understanding of the human dignity of all citizens and the recognition of our need for solidarity with one another in our common land.

Unity and diversity also denote the South African legal system's plurality, consisting of common and customary laws.[5] Common law, the law of general application, is a mixture of historically transplanted western laws that includes common-law norms,[6] legislation, and case law. On the other hand, customary law consists of traditional communities' customs that apply when – in the Constitution's words – they are "applicable".[7] The term "applicable" appears several times in the Constitution in different contexts. However, in this context it refers to the choice of law or conflict of law rules, which determines the applicable law where more than one system of law – in this case, common and customary laws – coexist. Bennett refers to this process as the "interpersonal conflict of laws".[8] He explains that these rules are mirrored in the choice of

---

phrase, political slogan and source of inspiration for group enterprise." Also see Rautenbach, "Deep Legal Pluralism," 143. "The research for this chapter was concluded in June 2023."

2 The expression is contained in the preamble to the Constitution of the Republic of South Africa, 1996 (hereafter "the Constitution"). It is interesting to note that the transitional Constitution (Constitution of the Republic of South Africa 200 of 1993) did not contain a similar expression in its preamble.

3 *Gumede v President of the Republic of South Africa* 2009 (3) SA 152 (CC), para. 22.

4 2008 (1) SA 474 (CC) para. 155. Footnotes omitted.

5 For an overview of the pluralistic characteristics of the South African legal system, see Rautenbach, "Deep Legal Pluralism," 144; and Rautenbach, "Cultural Expertise," 157.

6 There are many ports of entry to describe the characteristics and reasons for the development of common law in South Africa. For historical reasons, the common law developed into a hybrid mix of predominantly Roman Dutch Law with a good dose of English law. In general, see Rautenbach, "Constitutional Court," 600–01.

7 Section 211(1) reads: "The courts must apply customary law when that law is applicable, subject to the Constitution and any legislation that specifically deals with customary law." "However, see the viewpoint on adaptive pluralism in the introduction."

8 See Bennett, "Interpersonal Conflict of Laws," 127.

law rules in private international law, with the difference that interpersonal conflict of laws is dependent on the law of a person while those in private international law depend on territories. In other words, a person is a connecting factor in the interpersonal conflict of laws. In South Africa a person's race is often the connecting factor. Although race should no longer be the guide to choosing between legal systems to suit a person's lifestyle, as Bennett suggests,[9] it is easier said than done, especially where someone's traditional and modern lifestyles interconnect.

The intersection of various identities is the focus of Amoah's research. She uses the GRACE model (Gender, Race, Age, Culture, Equality) to demonstrate how they intersect to affect African women's access to equality in South Africa.[10] She explores the intersectionality of the fictional person GRACE, who must navigate the plurality laws in South Africa. GRACE is young, a woman and of colour, three characteristics that place her in a marginalised category which complicates the movement between legal systems. Culture is the common denominator that puts her at the intersection of all her identities. At home she lives under a system of customary law with a different value system, and in the city she is subject to the South African common law with yet another value system. She uses Bennett's concept of ubuntu as one of the solutions to GRACE's problem. Since an individual cannot exist in isolation, it is necessary to consider the community when an individual's rights are considered. That does not mean that one must be weighed against the other, but that society must be made to understand why it needs to adapt its customs to the norms and values of human rights.[11]

The application question leads to another issue: which version of customary law must be applied?[12] In the context of this discussion, both the living and official versions of customary law are relevant. The former includes oral tradition, and the latter consists of those customary norms recorded in legislation, case law and textbooks. The courts have confirmed that the Constitution[13]

---

9 Bennett, "Interpersonal Conflict of Laws," 131.

10 See Amoah, "When Grace Met Bennett," 34–35.

11 I have commented on her discussion of the GRACE model in Rautenbach, "In the Shade of an African Baobab," 12.

12 Living and official customary law are often different from each other. Himonga, "Advancement of African Women's Rights," 82, 84.

13 The transitional Constitution commenced on 27 April 1994 and was replaced by the final Constitution on 4 December 1997. Section 181(1) of the transitional Constitution provided for the recognition of a "traditional authority which observes a system of indigenous law", and s. 181(2) provided that "[i]ndigenous law shall be subject to regulation by law". The term "indigenous law" was replaced with "customary law" in the final Constitution. In addition, Constitutional Principle XIII in the transitional Constitution placed customary law on an

elevated the status of customary law, both living and official, to one equal to common law, subject to the Constitution only.[14] In *Alexkor Ltd v Richtersveld Community*,[15] for instance, the Constitutional Court held that

> the Constitution acknowledges the originality and distinctiveness of indigenous law as an *independent source of norms within the legal system*. At the same time the Constitution, while giving force to indigenous law, makes it clear that such law is subject to the Constitution and has to be interpreted in the light of its values. Furthermore, like the common law, indigenous law is subject to any legislation, *consistent with the Constitution*, that specifically deals with it. In the result, indigenous law feeds into, nourishes, fuses with and becomes part of the amalgam of South African law.

Acknowledging the independence and separateness of customary law is one thing, but it is another to own up to this recognition. In contrast to common law, the bulk of customary law is virtually unrecorded and known only to those who live it. That is not to say that an official version of customary law does not exist, but the courts have adopted the view that living customary law is the authentic version that should be applied.[16] Does this mean that one should overlook official customary law entirely? Ignoring it would not make

equal footing with common law and provided: "Indigenous law, like common law, shall be recognised and applied by the courts, subject to the fundamental rights contained in the Constitution and to legislation dealing specifically therewith." The transitional Constitution contained a set of principles in Schedule 4 that had to be considered when the final Constitution was drafted. In terms of s. 71(2) of the transitional Constitution, the Constitutional Court had to testify that all the provisions in the final text complied with these principles. This was done in *In re: Certification of the Constitution of the Republic of South Africa, 1996* 1996 (10) BCLR 1253 (CC). Section 211 of the final Constitution provides in general for the application of customary law though subject to the qualification that it must be "applicable" and "subject to the Constitution and legislation that specifically deals with customary law". For a discussion of the problems with this formulation, see Rautenbach, *Introduction to Legal Pluralism*, 19–25.

14 *Alexkor Ltd v Richtersveld Community* 2003 (12) BCLR 1301 (CC) para. 55: "While in the past indigenous law was seen through the common-law lens, it must now be seen as an integral part of our law. Like all law it depends for its ultimate force and validity on the Constitution. Its validity must now be determined by reference not to common law, but to the Constitution." Footnotes omitted.

15 *Alexkor Ltd v Richtersveld Community* 2003 (12) BCLR 1301 (CC) para. 51. Footnotes omitted, and emphasis added.

16 See Rautenbach, *Introduction to Legal Pluralism*, 5 (footnote 4) for a list of some of the cases.

sense at all. The Constitution clearly states that customary law is subject to the Constitution and legislation "specifically" dealing with it.[17] One can very well imagine that an "official" customary rule has become so embedded in a community's fabric that it is "lived" without its origins being questioned.[18] One example is the operation of traditional courts under the Black Administration Act.[19] They have been functioning within the parameters of state law since 1927, and it would be tough to determine which norms are still "proper" living customary law and which are not. It would also not make sense to say that customary law is subject to legislation, implying that it could be amended by statute but deny the existence of official customary law. Such a viewpoint could create the impression that living customary law would always trump statutory customary law and imply that – contra constitutional instruction – customary law could not be developed by legislation, which we know is not true. Of course, one could carry on with a lengthy discussion about the ossification of and interference in customary law by state intervention, and several debates in this context exist.[20] However, this chapter is not concerned with whether it should happen or not but takes the view that it has already happened in the customary law of succession. The question here is whether state intervention replaced the customary norms, not whether it should.

The judiciary's different approaches to customary law also muddle the waters. As Bennett points out, while customary law in its social setting does not pose insurmountable difficulties, it is a different story in a court that operates according to common-law tradition.[21] Courts apply evidentiary rules

17 Constitution, s. 211(3).

18 There is no way of telling if this is the position in some traditional communities. Only empirical research would be able to discover the truth and I am unaware of any studies that deal with the question. In the 1990s the author was a member of the Traditional Authorities Research Group that did fieldwork in three provinces to determine the role of traditional authorities post 1994. At several communities they followed the Black Administration Act 38 of 1927 and its regulations as the applicable law. The unpublished report is titled *The Administrative and Legal Position of Traditional Authorities in South Africa and their Contribution to the Implementation of the Reconstruction and Development Programme*. Some of the research findings were published as Traditional Authorities Research Group, "Role and Future of Traditional Leaders", 295.

19 38 of 1927. See ss. 12 (civil jurisdiction) and 20 (criminal jurisdiction). These sections have not been repealed yet and legal reform of traditional courts came to a halt when the Traditional Courts Bill (B15–2008) was not taken further in parliament. See Parliamentary Monitoring Group, "Traditional Courts Bill."

20 Rautenbach, *Introduction to Legal Pluralism*, 30–33.

21 Bennett, "Re-Introducing African Customary Law," 2; Rautenbach, *Introduction to Legal Pluralism*, 30–32, and the case law discussed.

unfamiliar to a customary law setting.[22] They must interpret norms usually dissimilar from their own and inevitably transform social practices into law through their decisions.[23] An inescapable consequence of elevating customary law and its living version to the same common law status brings customary norms out into the open, exposing them to constitutional scrutiny and the risk of being struck down. The customary law of succession, the focus of this discussion, is one example of the judiciary replacing customary norms with a common-law statute.[24]

Although many aspects of customary law have been subject to legal reform over the last two and a half decades, this contribution aims to illustrate how the customary law of succession has been developed through case law and legislation in recent years. After all, as Phillips says:[25]

> if legal developments cannot be separated from other historical trends then a sense of history is vital to understanding the law, even (or perhaps because), it tends to highlight the limitations of law.

The overarching aim of the discussion is to determine whether modern-day developments can still be called customary law of succession or if something entirely new has been created. In other words, what remains of customary norms? The first part of the discussion provides an overview of the courts' diverse approaches to customary law to provide context. The focus then shifts to the judicial and statutory reforms in the customary law of succession. Finally, before a conclusion is reached the last part briefly deals with the question posed in this contribution: whether any customary norms remain in the customary law of succession.

---

22 See Rautenbach, "Oral Law," 1–25, for a discussion of the challenges the judiciary face in finding and applying living customary law in court.

23 See Rautenbach, "Case Law," 1–20, for a discussion of the courts' approach to living customary law and the authoritative value of their judgments.

24 See the discussion at 2. The terms "succession" and "inheritance" are used interchangeably in this contribution, as synonyms. I do acknowledge that they have different meanings in customary law. For an explanation of the difference between the two terms, see in general Rautenbach and Du Plessis, "Reform of the South African Customary Law of Succession," 336–37.

25 Phillips, "Why Legal History Matters," 294.

2 Judicial Approaches to Customary Law

The judiciary has a constitutional mandate to develop customary law in line with constitutional rights and values.[26] In *Carmichele v Minister of Safety and Security*,[27] albeit in the context of common law, the Constitutional Court explained its position in terms of this responsibility as follows:[28]

> Before the advent of the IC [interim Constitution], the refashioning of the common law in this area [law of delict] entailed 'policy decisions and value judgments' which had to 'reflect the wishes, often unspoken, and the perceptions, often but dimly discerned, of the people'. A balance had to be struck between the interests of the parties and the conflicting interests of the community according to what 'the (c)ourt conceives to be society's notions of what justice demands'. Under s 39(2) of the [final] Constitution concepts such as 'policy decisions and value judgments' reflecting 'the wishes ... and the perceptions ... of the people' and 'society's notions of what justice demands' might well have to be replaced, or supplemented and enriched by the appropriate norms of the objective value system embodied in the Constitution.

Given the fact that section 39(2) of the final Constitution also applies to customary law, this does not bode well for the continuance of any customary norms that seemingly infringe on constitutional rights and values. Another consequence of constitutional recognition is the judiciary's viewpoint that the "validity" of customary law must now be determined "by reference not to common law, but to the Constitution".[29] Also, in *MM v MN*[30] the Constitutional Court said, "customary law reflects the rights and values of the *Constitution from which it draws its legal force*".[31] Without engaging in the Court's language, it is necessary to emphasise that the "validity" of a customary norm usually depends on community acceptance of the norm and not on an empowering document, even if the document is a supreme constitution such as the South

26 Section 39(2) of the Constitution speaks of the court's development of common and customary law "to promote the spirit, purport and objects of the Bill of Rights".

27 2001 (4) SA 938 (CC).

28 *Carmichele v Minister of Safety and Security* 2001 (4) SA 938 (CC) para. 56 (footnotes omitted).

29 *Alexkor Ltd v Richtersveld Community* 2003 (12) BCLR 1301 (CC) para. 51.

30 2013 (4) SA 415 (CC).

31 *MM v MN* 2013 (4) SA 415 (CC) para. 46. Emphasis added.

African one. Hamnett[32] describes customary law as "a set of norms which the actors in a social situation abstract from practice and which they invest with binding authority". Also, Bennett[33] describes customary law as a legal system that "derives from social practices that the community concerned accepts as obligatory." South African legislation recognises these social features of customary law. For example, the Recognition of Customary Marriages Act[34] defines "customary law" as "the customs and usages traditionally observed among the indigenous African peoples of South Africa and which form part of the culture of those peoples." Thus, a customary norm will be valid and binding if it is regarded as such in the community's eyes, regardless of its constitutional status.

Another aspect already alluded to is the judiciary's different approaches to customary law, which seem to depend on the version of customary law before it. As Saunders says, there are at least three versions of customary law: the official one, the living one and, somewhere in between, the academic one.[35] So far, the judiciary has adopted different approaches to customary law. In some cases it sanctioned the community's development of a customary norm, a process that has been gaining the favour of some scholars.[36] For example, in *Shilubana v Nwamitwa*[37] the Constitutional Court allowed a first-born daughter to take up her father's leadership position without any male siblings, at the royal family's request. Usually the male primogeniture rule allows only the eldest son to ascend to this position, excluding other male and female heirs of the royal family. In essence, the Court acknowledged the adaptability of customary law and the community's right to develop its own rules. While Justice van der Westhuizen acknowledged customary law's equal status to common law, he emphasised that customary law must be interpreted and applied in its contemporary setting to prevent its stagnation.[38]

> Customary law must be permitted to develop, and the enquiry must be rooted in the contemporary practice of the community in question. Section 211(2) of the Constitution requires this. The legal status of

32 Hamnett, *Chieftainship and* Legitimacy, 14.

33 Bennett, *Customary Law*, 1.

34 120 of 1998; see s. 1.

35 Sanders, "How Customary is African Customary Law?" 406. The question as to the different versions of customary law is one that scholars and the judiciary have long been struggling with, and the issue is far from settled.

36 Nhlapo, "Customary Marriage", 275–276.

37 See *Shilubana v Nwamitwa* 2009 (2) SA 66 (CC).

38 *Shilubana v Nwamitwa* 2009 (2) SA 66 (CC), para. 55.

> customary-law norms cannot depend simply on their having been consistently applied in the past, because that is a test which any new development must necessarily fail. Development implies some departure from past practice. A rule that requires absolute consistency with past practice before a court will recognise the existence of a customary norm would therefore prevent the recognition of new developments as customary law. This would result in the courts applying laws which communities themselves no longer follow, and would stifle the recognition of the new rules adopted by the communities in response to the changing face of South African society. This result would be contrary to the Constitution and cannot be accepted.

The Court's bottom-up approach confirms the contention that customary law is living law "rooted in the everyday practices" of communities.[39] However, the judgment also debunks the view that a custom's longevity is crucial to prove the existence of the customary norm, as is required in common-law custom.[40] Although the point is not taken further in this discussion, the absence of a prolonged existence could be a vital difference between customary and common-law customs. It is typically required that the latter have existed over a long time, while the same seems not necessary in the case of a "living" customary norm.[41]

Yet, in *MM v MN*[42] the Constitutional Court followed a top-down approach to developing a customary norm. In this case the majority averred that customary law is "a system of law that is practised in the community" with its values and norms followed by generations and subject to change to "meet the changing needs" of society.[43] The first step would be to find the custom's content to determine the legal norm.[44] The second step necessitates an evaluation of the

39 Nhlapo, "Customary Marriage", 276.

40 The test for a common-law custom to be recognised was formulated in the *locus classicus*, *Van Breda v Jacobs* 1921 AD 330. The requirements are that the custom must have been in existence for a long period, it must be observed in general by the relevant community, it must be reasonable and its content must be certain and clear.

41 For example, see *Shilubana v Nwamitwa* 2009 (2) SA 66 (CC), para. 55, where the Court spoke of the "contemporary practice of the community".

42 2013 (4) SA 415 (CC).

43 *MM v MN* 2013 (4) SA 415 (CC) para. 24. The decision and its forerunners were discussed by various authors. For example, see Bakker, "Validity of a Customary Marriage – Part 1," 233 *et seq.* He provides a list of other scholarly sources in footnote 27.

44 The Court acknowledged that determining its "living" content would require "innovation" to prevent finding only its "stultified" version contained in legislation and court precedent. See *MM v MN* 2013 (4) SA 415 (CC) para. 43.

norm to see if it complies with constitutional values and rights; if it does not, a court has to develop it. Here the question was whether Tsonga law and custom require a husband to obtain his wife's permission to conclude a subsequent valid marriage. There was no consensus between the witnesses as to whether her consent was required or not. The Court did not view the discrepancies as a problem but merely as an illustration of "nuance and accommodation", which did not prevent it from concluding that the first wife's consent was a validity requirement for consecutive marriages.[45] A notable aspect of the judgment is that the Court determined that the first wife's permission was required in Tsonga law. This was found despite its earlier finding that Tsonga law had to be developed to oblige a husband to obtain a first wife's permission for him to enter into a subsequent marriage.[46] It is unclear from the judgment why it still had to develop the norm when it found it to be a requirement.

The third approach to customary law concerns the judiciary's development of official customary law, such as the Recognition of Customary Marriages Act.[47] The Act recognises customary marriages and attempts to reform them according to the constitutional mandate of equality and human dignity. It is noteworthy that the Act refers to customary law to determine the validity of a marriage concluded in terms of the Act.[48] However, section 7(1) regulating the proprietary consequences of monogamous and polygynous marriages before and after the Act's commencement proved controversial.[49] The provision has

---

45 *MM v MN* 2013 (4) SA 415 (CC) para. 61. In reaching this conclusion, the Court ignored the common-law rules of evidence because, in its own words, "[customary law] does not depend on rules of evidence: a court must determine for itself how best to ascertain that content". The minority judgment held an opposite view and emphasised that the rules of evidence cannot be ignored when a court deals with customary law issues. Also see in general the discussion by Rautenbach, "Oral Law," 14–16.

46 *MM v MN* 2013 (4) SA 415 (CC) para. 75.

47 120 of 1998.

48 The Recognition of Customary Marriages Act, s. 3(1) provides: "(1) For a customary marriage entered into after the commencement of this Act to be valid – (a) the prospective spouses – (i) must both be above the age of 18 years; and (ii) must both consent to be married to each other under customary law; and (b) *the marriage must be negotiated and entered into or celebrated in accordance with customary law*." Emphasis added.

49 Section 7(1) reads: "(1) The proprietary consequences of a customary marriage entered into before the commencement of this Act continue to be governed by customary law. (2) A customary marriage entered into after the commencement of this Act in which a spouse is not a partner in any other existing customary marriage, is a marriage in community of property and of profit and loss between the spouses, unless such consequences are specifically excluded by the spouses in an antenuptial contract which regulates the matrimonial property system of their marriage."

been under judicial attack several times, leading to its demise.[50] In *Gumede v President of the Republic of South Africa,*[51] the Constitutional Court declared section 7(1) unconstitutional. It replaced the customary law matrimonial property system with the common law system by stating that monogamous customary marriages concluded before 15 November 2000 were in community of property. In *Ramuhovhi v President of the Republic of South Africa*[52] the Constitutional Court extended this invalidity to polygynous marriages. It suspended the order for 24 months to allow parliament to make legislation and set out the property regime that should apply during the suspension period. Several judicial inroads into the Recognition of Customary Marriages Act led to the Recognition of Customary Marriages Amendment Bill (B12–2019), approved by the cabinet on 24 July 2019. The Bill has been transformed into legislation on 26 May 2021.[53]

The fourth approach to customary law could be regarded as the judiciary's development of a customary norm by replacing it with a common-law statute. Such an example is the well-known case of *Bhe v Magistrate, Khayelitsha,*[54] which dealt with inheritance. The judgment set a series of legislative changes into motion, leading to a drastic transformation of the customary law of succession. In essence, the Constitutional Court struck down the customary rule of male primogeniture and the legislation that embodied the rule.[55] The Court replaced the customary norm with a modified common-law statute, the Intestate Succession Act,[56] an approach with which some scholars do not agree.[57] On face value, the reforms boil down to replacing customary norms with common law ones. Some implications of the judgment for the customary law of succession are explored in more detail in the next section.

---

50 For example, see the detailed analysis by Bakker, "Validity of a Customary Marriage – Part 1," 231; and Bakker, "Validity of a Customary Marriage – Part 2," 357.

51 2009 (3) SA 152 (CC).

52 2018 (2) SA 1 (CC). The Court held that s. 7(1) of the Recognition of Customary Marriages Act is inconsistent with the Constitution because it discriminates on the basis of race and/or ethnic and social origin insofar as women in "old" polygamous customary marriages are excluded from the protection afforded to women in monogamous marriages.

53 See Recognition of Customary Marriages Amendment Act 1 of 2021.

54 2005 (1) SA 580 (CC). A detailed discussion of the case and its implications is given by Himonga, "Advancement of African Women's Rights," 82, 93–97.

55 The relevant provision was s. 23 of the Black Administration Act, as well as its regulations. See the discussion at section 3.

56 81 of 1987.

57 See Himonga, "Reflection on *Bhe*," 4 who argues that the minority viewpoint of Justice Ngcobo better reflects the realities of living customary law than the majority decision that merely replaced the customary law norms with common-law norms.

3 Reform of the Customary Law of Succession

3.1 *Socio-Legal Influences on the Customary Laws*

Legal reform is a natural and necessary occurrence. Law must adapt to changing circumstances, and the customary law of succession is no exception. The general function of the law of succession is to regulate the transfer of a person's property after death. Its rules have always been responsive to changing socio-economic circumstances that include[58]

> the preservation of the social order, the continuation of economic life, the maintenance of the family, the provision of an incentive to socially beneficial conduct and the creation of a mechanism to assert personal freedom.

Considering the importance of property in general and land in particular as family unification and support mechanisms, succession rules in most jurisdictions, especially intestate succession, are geared towards keeping the family's land and wealth for future generations.[59] Some literature in South Africa focusses on land and family formations as reasons for the significant difference between the customary and common law of succession, linking extended families to the customary law and so-called "nuclear" ones to the common law.[60] However, Brenner[61] illustrates that the existence of extended families is not foreign to western communities. They profoundly influenced property and succession development during the Middle Ages. Property "was viewed as property of the extended family and not of its individual members, and the

58 De Waal, "Social and Economic Foundations," 163–64. The role of socio-economic and cultural politics in the shaping of the customary law of succession is also illustrated by Mnisi, "The Interface," 16, 32–44.

59 Bekker and De Kock, "Adaptation of the Customary Law of Succession," 366.

60 De Waal, "Social and Economic Foundations," 165 and 173. The common law idea of a family, consisting of married parents and their children, has been under constant threat. Apart from legislation including polygynous customary marriages (Recognition of Customary Marriages Act 120 of 1998) and same-sex marriages (Civil Union Act 17 of 2006), the judiciary has included polygynous Muslim marriages, which are not yet recognised in South Africa. For more information and a discussion of some of the cases on Muslim marriages, see Rautenbach, *Introduction to Legal Pluralism*, 377–92. For an exposé of the historical meaning of "family" in Tswana law, see Schapera, *Tswana Law*, 12–19. Bennett, *Customary Law*, 180–86 warns against a generalised view of "nuclear" and "extended" families but agrees that socio-economic developments probably led to the transformation of extended families into nuclear families based on conjugal links between family members.

61 Brenner, "Why did Inheritance Laws Change?" 94–99.

father was viewed as the chief caretaker and manager" of the property. Male primogeniture was generally applied to regulate the succession of property in noble families.[62] Changes in the social structures and the eldest son's diminished role in providing for the family when the father died led to new inheritance rules with considerable freedom of testation in western countries.[63]

The common law of succession in South Africa, both testate and intestate, also did not escape the winds of change. The early origins of succession laws are remarkably similar to what we believe the customary law of succession norms to be or previously to have been.[64] Intestate succession dates back to when the family took centre stage, and the only form of ownership was common family ownership. Succession aimed to distribute the family property among the family members. The concept of wills and testate succession developed much later and only concerning a deceased's personal property, as in the customary law, as explained earlier, where a deceased could dispose of only his or her personal property in a will. With the focus shifting from the family to the individual, the common law of succession adjusted to meet the demands of modernity in family dynamics. One of the most drastic changes was abolishing the legitimate portion or universal succession, where certain heirs were entitled to a part of an estate.[65] Instead, the principle of *voluntas testatoris servanda est* (the testator's will must be followed) came to the forefront. Today a testator is generally free to disinherit his family entirely or to favour specific children in his will.[66] Concerning intestate succession, Roman-Dutch law (*Aasdomsrecht* and *Schependomsrecht*) used to apply to property division, but the Intestate Succession Act abolished both systems in 1987.[67]

According to Bekker and De Kock,[68] customary law property is like the concept of common law property in the medieval period and should be understood as follows:[69]

62 Brenner, "Why did Inheritance Laws Change?" 94–99.

63 Brenner, "Why did Inheritance Laws Change?" 99–102.

64 In general, see De Waal, "Law, Society and the Individual," 300–18.

65 Intestate succession includes the close blood relatives and spouses of a deceased. However, the traditional idea of a family has been judicially challenged on several occasions and extended to include spouses not included before. For an overview of some of the constitutional challenges to the meaning of "spouse", see Paleker, "Intestate Succession," 30–33.

66 The so-called "legitimate portion" is no longer part of South African law, and a testator may disinherit his spouse and children. The children have a common law claim for maintenance and spouses have a claim for maintenance in terms of the Maintenance of Surviving Spouses Act 27 of 1990. In general, see Jamneck, "Freedom of Testation," 125–37.

67 Intestate succession is regulated by common law rules and the Intestate Succession Act.

68 Bekker and De Kock, "Adaptation of the Customary Law of Succession," 366.

69 Bekker, *Seymour's Customary Law*, 74.

> Although the property of the house is commonly spoken of as belonging to the family head, because this is a brief and convenient way of describing the matter, it belongs in law to the family as a unit, under his supervision and control; it has also been described as belonging in communal ownership to the family, which, of course, includes the family head.

Customary law recognises the right to ownership, though not as understood under common law. Particularly controversial is communal land tenure, which has two dimensions; the communal one concerning the community as a whole and an individual of a family or an individual. This type of land was passed on under the statutory rules of succession, some of which have been repealed.[70] Unfortunately, land tenure has developed into a complex and highly politicised topic that falls outside this chapter's scope.[71]

Currently more pronounced differences exist between the common and customary law of succession. However, the differences might not be noticeable after legal developments since 2005. One difference is that the common law of succession does not distinguish between heirs based on the age or gender of the beneficiaries. In contrast, the customary law of succession followed male primogeniture and probably still does in living law, favouring the deceased's eldest male descendant. According to the male primogeniture rule, the eldest son succeeds his father in property and status,[72] excluding the deceased's wives and daughters from inheritance. In *Bhe v Magistrate, Khayelitsha,* Justice Langa explains the principle as follows:[73]

> Central to the customary law of succession is the rule of primogeniture, the main features of which are well established. The general rule is that only a male who is related to the deceased qualifies as intestate heir. Women do not participate in the intestate succession of deceased estates. In a monogamous family, the eldest son of the family head is his heir. If the deceased is not survived by any male descendants, his father succeeds

70 For a summary, see Rautenbach, *Introduction to Legal Pluralism*, 125–213.

71 For an introduction to some of the issues, see the chapter on law of property by Pienaar, "Law of Property," 119–53.

72 The general order of succession to the male members in a polygynous household also depended on the status of a wife. However, it is important to note that the application of the rule differed depending on the customs of a particular community. See Rautenbach, *Introduction to Legal Pluralism*, 194–98.

73 *Bhe v Magistrate, Khayelitsha* 2005 (1) SA 580 (CC) para. 77.

> him. If his father also does not survive him, an heir is sought among the father's male descendants related to him through the male line.

Another distinction between the two forms of succession is "what" the beneficiaries inherit. In the case of the common law of succession, it strictly includes only the estate property that the beneficiaries inherit. In the case of customary succession laws, the emphasis was not on the division of property but on the continuation of status, like the position in the Middle Ages. The heir, who figuratively stepped into the deceased's shoes, gained control over the property and the people over whom the deceased had ownership and power during his life.[74] For various reasons, socioeconomic changes in customary law occurred more slowly than in their Western counterpart. One reason is that colonial powers ignored customary norms and were mainly concerned with developing the transplanted western norms.[75]

However, customary law did not escape the winds of change completely. Although outdated and not representative, a sociological study reveals that despite the influence of modernity, male primogeniture and its responsibilities remained relevant in the late 1970s.[76] Brandel-Syrier cites several statements that are representative of this conclusion:[77]

> The first male child is important to us Africans. He has certain privileges. He is the first to be served with food, he is consulted on family matters, he also has, as the eldest, direct contact with his father, and is treated as the future head of the family. Also he is the main heir. He inherits his father's personal belongings and the family relics. The major share of the cattle is his. If the father thinks well of education, or if he wants it himself, it is of course the first-born who is educated first. Furthermore, while he is still young he has special responsibilities. He has to allow others a share of his inheritance. No one should go hungry or be in need. He has to assume responsibility for the other children if the father is dead. He is responsible for their upbringing and well-being. He has to see to their education, pay his younger brother's lobola, find good husbands for his sisters and generally provide for their needs. He is still like that, or should be. He also has a right to be consulted in all family matters, and

74 Rautenbach, *Introduction to Legal Pluralism*, 193.

75 *Gumede v President of the Republic of South Africa* 2009 (3) SA 152 (CC), para. 20. Also see 3.2 below.

76 Brandel-Syrier, "First-Borns and Younger Sons," 42.

77 Ibid.

> that brings burther (sic) responsibilities. In the difficulties and insecurities of cultural change, the role of the eldest has become more important as the advance of the whole sibling group depends largely on the eldest brother's example, leadership and assistance.

Over the years, several factors based on Western values and individuality have gradually deprived male primogeniture of its economic basis. They include the depopulation of rural areas and the loss of kinship values because of increased individual independence, western education, and changes in traditional ways of life.[78] Sibani[79] points out that one should not underestimate the impact of western culture on traditional societies. The cross-pollination of cultures is a natural outflow of contact between communities with different value systems.

Although less critical, another difference between customary and common law lies in the assumption that wills (or testate succession) were unknown in customary law. Because customary law was and still is essentially oral, this belief is not without merit. However, research has revealed that a family head could make oral allocations of property that had to be respected. This indicates that the notion of freedom of testation may well have been known to customary law, albeit not in the common law sense.[80] Even though a testator subject to customary law was free to make a will, his freedom of testation was statutorily limited in the case of specific categories of property, as will be illustrated below.[81]

The application of choice of law rules was another way to ensure that customary and common succession laws never mixed.[82] However, as illustrated in the following section, post-apartheid[83] legal developments have slowly but surely eroded those differences to a point where they are no longer exact.[84]

---

78 See, in general, Sibani, "Impact of Western Culture," 66–69.

79 Sibani, "Impact of Western Culture," 56, 57.

80 Rautenbach, *Introduction to Legal Pluralism*, 193–94. The process of disposing property this way can be compared with the *donatio mortis causa* in common law. See De Waal, "Law, Society and the Individual," 318.

81 See 3.2.

82 For a detailed discussion of the choice of law rules to determine which law had to be applied before 2005, see Bennett, "Conflict of Personal Laws," 50.

83 The year 1994 is the date that signifies the end of apartheid in South Africa. That was when the first democratic elections were held and the transitional Constitution commenced.

84 A discussion of the position in KwaZulu-Natal is excluded since Zulu law of succession has been primarily codified in the two Codes of Zulu Law. The KwaZulu Act on the Code of Zulu Law 16 of 1985 and the Natal Code of Zulu Law, Proclamation R151 of 1987, known as the KwaZulu-Natal Codes or Codes of Zulu Law, contain uniform provisions pertaining to the Zulu law of succession that applies in the KwaZulu-Natal province. The two Acts

3.2 *Setting the Stage for the Reform of Customary Law of Succession*

3.2.1 Judicial Intervention

The judiciary has blamed customary law's "underdeveloped" state on colonisation. In *Gumede v President of the Republic of South Africa,*[85] Deputy Chief Justice Moseneke declared:

> customary law was entirely prevented from evolving and adapting as the changing circumstances of the communities required. It was *recorded and enforced* by those who neither practised it nor were bound by it. Those who were bound by customary law had no power to adapt it. Even when notions of spousal equality and equity and the abolition of the marital power of husbands over wives were introduced in this country to reform the common law, 'official' customary law was left unreformed and stone-walled by static rules and judicial precedent, which had little or nothing to do with the lived experience of spouses and children within customary marriages. With the advent of democratic rule much had to give way.

An early example of the recordings and enforcements was the controlling Black Administration Act commencing in 1927.[86] The British government introduced the Act to establish a separate but unified system of "control and management" of black people.[87] One of the things it aimed to control was customary succession laws. Section 23(1), the "backbone"[88] of the official customary law of succession and the embodiment of male primogeniture, stipulated:

---

stand to be repealed but at the time of the writing of this contribution, they are still on the statute book.

85 2009 (3) SA 152 (CC) para. 20. Footnotes omitted, and emphasis added.

86 In 1910 the four British colonies were unified and formed the Union of South Africa. Although the Union primarily had self-governing powers, the British crown remained involved in the affairs of the country until the Union of South Africa became wholly independent in 1961 with the establishment of the Republic of South Africa. The British followed a policy of not replacing the law of the territories they colonised, and so Roman-Dutch law remained the law of the land. For more information on historical developments, see Zimmermann and Visser, *Southern Cross*; Chanock, *Making of South African Legal Culture*.

87 The preamble of the Act read: "To provide for the better control and management of Black affairs." At that time the laws pertaining to black people were still fragmented among the different provinces, which were based on the boundaries of the former British colonies and the Boer republics.

88 Mnisi, "The Interface," 131.

> All movable property belonging to a Black [African] and allotted by him or accruing under Black law or custom to any woman with whom he lived in a customary union, or to any house, will upon his death devolve and be administered under Black law and custom [emphasis added.]

In essence, this was a choice of law rule that pointed towards applying customary law in inheritance matters. Communal land was treated differently and had to devolve according to the tables of succession provided in the Act.[89] All other properties that did not fall into these two categories could be bequeathed in a will.[90] To prevent the application of common-law rules, the Intestate Succession Act stated that it did not apply to an estate, to which section 23 of the Black Administration Act applied.[91]

Also, regulations promulgated under the Black Administration Act provided for the distribution of customary law estates, where section 23 did not apply.[92] The regulations listed choice of law rules to explain when the common law of succession would be applicable and when the customary law of succession would be the appropriate law. In short, if the matrimonial consequences resembled a common-law marriage, the common law of succession was applicable. Otherwise, the customary law of succession involving male primogeniture had to be used to distribute the estate between the heirs.[93] The regulations did not

---

89 Black Administration Act, s. 23(2) and (10) repealed by the Repeal of the Black Administration Act and Amendment of Certain Laws Act 28 of 2005.

90 Black Administration Act, s. 23(3) repealed by the Repeal of the Black Administration Act and Amendment of Certain Laws Act 28 of 2005.

91 Intestate Succession Act, s. 1(4)(b). The provision was also declared unconstitutional in *Bhe v Magistrate, Khayelitsha* 2005 (1) SA 580 (CC) and repealed in 2010 by the Reform of Customary Law of Succession and Regulation of Related Matters Act 11 of 2009.

92 Black Administration Act and regulation 2 of the Regulations for the Administration and Distribution of Estates of Deceased Blacks (GN R200 in Government Gazette 10601 of 6 February 1987). Section 23 and the regulations was declared unconstitutional in *Bhe v Magistrate, Khayelitsha* 2005 (1) SA 580 (CC) in 2005 and repealed in 2010 by the Reform of Customary Law of Succession and Regulation of Related Matters Act 11 of 2009. Regulation 2 of GN R200 of 1987 provided: "2. If a Black dies leaving no valid will, so much of his property, including immovable property, as does not fall within the purview of subsection (1) or subsection (2) of section 23 of the Act shall be distributed in the manner following: ...".

93 See reg. 2 of GN R200 of 1987 for a detailed list of all scenarios where the common law of succession could be applied. In *Zondi v President of the RSA* 2000 (2) SA 49 (N) the Natal Provincial Division of the High Court (renamed the KwaZulu-Natal High Court, Pietermaritzburg) declared reg. 2 to be unconstitutional to the extent that it distinguished for the purpose of intestate succession between the estate of a person who was a partner in a civil marriage in terms of s. 22(6) of the Black Administration Act on the one hand, and the estate of a person who was a partner in a civil marriage in community of

provide for the situation where the traditional family system no longer existed, which led to difficulties for some women and children if the male heirs were not interested in providing for them. It also did not deal with the situation where a husband had two wives; one married under common law and another under customary law.[94]

The statutory endorsement of the rule of male primogeniture with its concomitant duty to support remained in place for a long time despite socioeconomic changes and evidence that first-born sons often failed to honour their responsibilities. As already pointed out, Brandel-Syrier identified the unwillingness of first-born sons to honour the commitments that accompany the right to inherit already in the late 1970s. The situation is probably much worse nowadays.[95]

As already alluded to, male primogeniture and section 23 were declared unconstitutional and were struck down in *Bhe v Magistrate, Khayelitsha*. Still, the Court did not express any views on the eldest son's concomitant duty to support, nor did the legislative changes. Formally, one must assume that this duty fell away when the judiciary struck down the male primogeniture rule. Mnisi points out that members of traditional societies have approached state courts to recognise a "clear right of ownership" to prevent the application of the concomitant duty of care required by living customary law.[96] In doing this they could ensure that the customary law duty to support was no longer attached to the property because it was no longer regarded as property held under "Black law and custom".

Soon after South Africa adopted a new constitutional dispensation, the South African Law Commission (renamed the South African Law Reform Commission in 2003) launched a large-scale investigation into harmonising common and customary law. Harmonising the common and customary laws of succession was included in its mandate.[97] The Commission conceded that

---

property or a marriage under an antenuptial contract on the other hand. GN R200 of 1987 was later declared unconstitutional in its entirety in *Bhe v Magistrate, Khayelitsha* 2005 (1) SA 580 (CC).

94 Although having two marriages, one in terms of common law and another in terms of customary law, is not allowed, it happens anyway. A recent example is *Ramuhovhi v President of the Republic of South Africa* 2018 (2) BCLR 217 (CC). Also see Rautenbach and Du Plessis, "South African Law Commission's Proposals," 22–23.

95 Brandel-Syrier, "First-Borns and Younger Sons," 41.

96 Mnisi, "The Interface," 138.

97 South African Law Commission, *Project 90: Issue Paper 12*. Although it had been on the agenda of the Commission for a while, the investigation began in all earnest in 1996 when a new project committee was appointed. It had its first meeting in 1996 and issued its first two papers dealing with the conflict of laws and customary marriages. The investigation

succession rules are "inevitably shaped by the type of society in which they are supposed to operate."[98] It acknowledged that socioeconomic influences had a significant impact on succession laws before and after European settlement:[99]

> In the predominantly subsistence economies of precolonial Africa, each family was more or less self-sufficient. Food production, whether herding or farming, was the main activity, and livestock and land were the major assets. Because all members of a family had an immediate concern with the husbandry of these assets, no one person could claim full rights and powers over them. Thus, although the head of a family was overall manager of the family estate, his powers were in practice less important than his responsibilities to care for dependants. ...
>
> When the head of a family died, rules of succession were needed to determine who would take over the powers associated [with] his position, since someone had to take over the responsibility of managing the family estate and caring for surviving dependants.

The person upon whom the responsibility fell to support other family members was the oldest son. The situation was more complicated if he predeceased the deceased and there were no other male offspring or in cases where a polygynous system existed.[100] Although the Commission conceded that very little evidence existed on current trends in the customary law of succession at the time, it also acknowledged that "economic pressures and changes in family structure" had resulted in alternative ways of distributing the deceased's property. One example is the rule of ultimogeniture. The youngest son, the last to leave the family home, inherits the property and the responsibility to care for his aged parents. However, no topical evidence suggests that ultimogeniture is also prevalent in South Africa.[101]

In May 1998 the former Department of Justice introduced a draft Customary Law of Succession Bill in Parliament. In general, the purpose was to extend

into the customary law of succession kicked off in 1998 with the publication of an issue paper (South African Law Commission, *Project 90: Issue Paper 12*). All the documents relevant to the project are available at South African Law Reform Commission, "All Projects."

98 South African Law Commission, *Project 90: Issue Paper 12*, 5.

99 Ibid.

100 South African Law Commission, *Project 90: Issue Paper 12*, 7–8.

101 South African Law Commission, *Project 90: Issue Paper 12*, 8–9. In terms of the rule of ultimogeniture the youngest son of a deceased is entitled to inheritance. It was also contested in one of our neighbouring countries, Botswana. For a discussion, see Rautenbach, "A Family Home", 145.

the common law norms of testate and intestate succession embodied in the Wills Act[102] and Intestate Succession Act to customary law estates. The Bill also provided for the distribution of estates in polygynous households. It was a radical move away from the male primogeniture rule and removed all restrictions on an African testator's freedom of testation. However, traditional authorities fiercely resisted attempts to "westernise" customary norms, and the government decided to shelve the Bill.[103]

In 1999 the South African Law Commission revived the investigation and published a Discussion Paper in 2000.[104] At the time of writing, the *Mthembu* rulings discussed below had gone through three stages of adjudication. However, the Commission was aware of the judiciary's view that the legislature and not the courts should develop the male primogeniture rule.[105] Accordingly, the Commission proposed its version of a Customary Law of Succession Bill, which followed more or less the same pattern as the earlier one submitted by the department to parliament.

All the developments were deemed necessary considering the new constitutional dispensation emphasising equality. While the investigation into the reform of the customary law of succession continued in the background, the courts were asked to rule on the constitutionality of the male primogeniture rule in the *Mthembu v Letsela* trilogy.[106] I will refer to these cases as *Mthembu 1*, *Mthembu 2* and *Mthembu 3*. The facts were as follows:[107] Letsela (the deceased) died intestate in 1993. He lived with Mthembu (the appellant) on a property in which he held a 99-year leasehold title. They had a daughter who was born in 1988. The deceased's father (the first respondent), mother and three sisters also survived him. The appellant alleged that she and the deceased had entered into a customary marriage in 1992.[108] The magistrate involved in the estate distribution (the second respondent) indicated that the estate was to devolve according to customary law. As a result, the first respondent was the only male

102 7 of 1953.

103 A copy of the Draft Bill is available at Government of the Republic of South Africa. "Amendment of Customary Law of Succession Bill.". In general, see Rautenbach and Du Plessis, "South African Law Commission's Proposals," 20, 24–27; South African Law Commission, *Project 90: Discussion Paper 93*, x.

104 South African Law Commission, *Project 90: Discussion Paper 93*.

105 South African Law Commission, *Project 90: Discussion Paper 93*, xii–xiii.

106 *Mthembu v Letsela* 1997 (2) SA 936 (T) (*Mthembu 1*); *Mthembu v Letsela* 1998 (2) SA 675 (T) (*Mthembu 2*); and *Mthembu v Letsela* 2000 (3) SA 867 (SCA) (*Mthembu 3*).

107 For a summary of the facts, see *Mthembu 3* paras. 2–7.

108 She supported this allegation with a copy of a receipt of the first instalment towards her *lobolo* (bride-wealth). However, the deceased had died before the balance had been paid.

who qualified to inherit under the rule of male primogeniture. He claimed the property on which the appellant and Thembi still lived. The appellant contested the rule's constitutionality on various grounds, most notably that it discriminated against her and her daughter.

In *Mthembu 1*, Le Roux J followed a purposive approach to the rule of male primogeniture. He concluded that "even if this rule is *prima facie* discriminatory on the grounds of sex or gender", the unfairness of the discrimination had been "refuted" by the male's concomitant duty to support family members.[109] The Court compared this form of differentiation between men and women to other types of everyday differentiation, such as separate toilet facilities for men and women, which "no right-minded" person would consider discriminatory.[110] It based its decision partly on a legal opinion provided by Bennett, believing that the rule did not discriminate unfairly against women because the appellant retained the right to live at the deceased's homestead even if another male inherited it.[111] However, the Court could not make a final decision because there was no evidence before it regarding the marriage between the appellant and the deceased. Therefore, the matter was postponed for oral evidence.

The second time, in *Mthembu 2*, the case came before Mynhardt J. The parties did not present additional evidence, and the Court held the matter had to be decided on the basis that the appellant and the deceased were unmarried. The implication was that there would be no duty of support on the successor (the first respondent) to maintain the appellant and her daughter.[112] Mynhardt J also considered the constitutionality of the customary rule of primogeniture and came to the same conclusion as was arrived at in *Mthembu 1*. However, the rule was linked to a successor's concomitant duty to support the deceased's widow and children and, in this context, could not be regarded as unconstitutional.[113] Also, the Court believed it should be the legislature's responsibility, not the courts, to develop the customary law of succession.[114]

109 He pointed out that "the devolution of the deceased's property onto the male heir involves a concomitant duty of support and protection of the woman or women to whom he was married by customary law and of the children procreated under that system and belonging to a particular house. … I find it difficult to equate this form of differentiation between men and women with the concept of 'unfair discrimination' as used in section 8 of the [1993] Constitution (945–947)".

110 *Mthembu 1* 946.

111 *Mthembu 1* 945.

112 *Mthembu 2* 680.

113 For a discussion of the grounds see *Mthembu 2* 681–89.

114 At the time, both Kerr and Bennett were of the view that development should take place by means of legislation. According to them, customary law should not be changed through

The wife, Mthembu, appealed against Mynhardt J's decision. In the Supreme Court of Appeal, in *Mthembu 3*, it was argued, among other things, that there had been a valid customary marriage between the deceased and the appellant.[115] In the alternative, the appellant argued that if the daughter were to be regarded as illegitimate, that would be unfair discrimination because an illegitimate son succeeds in the absence of a legitimate son, but an illegitimate daughter never inherits.[116] However, Mapati AJA agreed with the Court *a quo* that the marriage was not valid and that the daughter was illegitimate. Therefore, her exclusion from inheritance was because she was illegitimate and not her gender, and there was no need to engage in a constitutional investigation.[117] Unfortunately, the Court failed to consider the constitutionality of excluding "illegitimate" children from inheritance. It held that the provisions of the transitional Constitution did not apply to the facts because the transitional Constitution had come into effect only after the husband had died.[118] It is interesting to note Mpati AJA's viewpoint of section 23 of the Black Administration Act and its regulations. He said as follows:[119]

> What needs to be stressed from the outset is that the regulation in issue did not introduce something foreign to black persons. ... It merely gave legislative recognition to a principle or system which had been in existence and followed, at least, for decades. It is not inconceivable that many blacks, even to this day, would wish their estates to devolve in terms of black law and custom. Section 23(3) of the Act provides that: 'All other property of whatsoever kind [excluding property referred to in ss (1) and (2)] belonging to a black shall be capable of being devised by will.' The existing law therefore enables blacks to avoid the consequences of the application of the customary law of succession if they so wish. It is therefore within the power of blacks to choose how they wish their estates to devolve. If they take no steps to alter the devolution of their estates (as

---

the courts, but by means of legislation, after commissions on national and provincial level had done extensive research. Until then customary law, as it is, must be applied. See Kerr, "Inheritance in Customary Law," 269; and Bennett, "Equality Clause," 124–25.

115 The appellant argued that there had been an agreement between the deceased and appellant to marry and *lobolo* had been paid in part. This was, according to her, enough to establish a valid customary marriage. See para. 16.

116 *Mthembu 2* para. 19.

117 *Mthembu 2* para. 33.

118 The 1993 Constitution did not operate retroactively.

119 *Mthembu 3* paras. 23–24.

> is their right), the resulting consequences cannot be assumed to be contrary to their wishes.
>
> As the wishes of the deceased are still paramount in our law, it is difficult to see how a regulation which respects that right can be said to the unreasonable and *ultra vires* at common law.

The outcome of the three *Mthembu* cases was disappointing for women's and children's rights. However, the judiciary faced a dilemma. Were it to dismiss a customary rule without careful consideration of the right to culture and the newly acquired status of customary law, it would run the risk of being accused of being paternalistic and biased.

In *Bhe v Magistrate, Khayelitsha,* which followed five years later, section 23 and the customary rule of male primogeniture were viewed in a much less favourable way.[120] The Constitutional Court heard three cases simultaneously since they all dealt with the constitutionality of male primogeniture. In the first case, Ms Bhe applied on behalf of her two minor daughters for an order declaring male primogeniture unconstitutional to allow them to inherit their deceased father's estate. In terms of male primogeniture, the property would have to succeed to the deceased's eldest brother. He intended to sell the property, which would leave the family homeless.

In the second case, Ms Shibi applied for an order to inherit from her deceased brother's estate instead of his cousins, who qualified to inherit according to the male primogeniture rule.

The third case was an application by the Women's Legal Centre and the Human Rights Commission for direct access to the Constitutional Court to attack the constitutionality of male primogeniture and section 23 in general. The Court found that section 23 and male primogeniture boiled down to unfair discrimination resulting in the statutory provision and the customary norm being struck down as unconstitutional. The Court applied a modified version of the Intestate Succession Act to fill the void and accommodate situations unique to customary law.[121]

120 The jurisprudential history of the case spans over a few years before it reached finality in the Constitutional Court. *Shibi v Sithole* TPD Case 7292/01 of 19 November 2003 (unreported) also dealt with the constitutionality of the male primogeniture rule, and it was eventually decided together with *Bhe v Magistrate, Khayelitsha* 2005 (1) SA 580 (CC) in the Constitutional Court. For more information on *Bhe v Magistrate, Khayelitsha* 2005 (1) SA 580 (CC), the other judgments of the courts *a quo*, see Rautenbach, Du Plessis and Pienaar, "Is Primogeniture Extinct," 99.

121 See *Bhe v Magistrate, Khayelitsha* 2005 (1) SA 580 (CC), para. 136 for the order of the Court.

While acknowledging the importance of interpreting customary law in its setting instead of through a common-law lens, the Court pointed out that customary law also changes and can be adapted by legislation.[122] Moreover, as noted by the majority in *Bhe v Magistrate, Khayelitsha*, the setting had changed, at least in urban communities:[123]

> Modern urban communities and families are structured and organised differently and no longer purely along traditional lines. The customary law rules of succession simply determine succession to the deceased's estate without the accompanying social implications which they traditionally had. Nuclear families have largely replaced traditional extended families. The heir does not necessarily live together with the whole extended family which would include the spouse of the deceased as well as other dependants and descendants. He often simply acquires the estate without assuming, or even being in a position to assume, any of the deceased's responsibilities. In the changed circumstances, therefore, the succession of the heir to the assets of the deceased does not necessarily correspond in practice with an enforceable responsibility to provide support and maintenance to the family and dependants of the deceased.

However, no reliable empirical evidence exists to support the contention that urban communities and families are no longer structured "along traditional lines", as suggested by the Court. Statistics about rural families living under a system of customary law are generally based on wild guesses and outdated data, and there is no way of telling the exact figures. While one cannot safely measure in terms of statistical terms, some authors have presented estimates for South Africa's rural population based on statistical results for vulnerable groups and development indicators. It is said that the rural population is about 33% or 16 million of the total national population of 59 million people and that the lives of most of these people are still regulated by customary law.[124]

Setting statistics aside for now, it is trite that many people are still affected by customary law and that it remains a relevant actor in legal discourse. The

122 *Bhe v Magistrate, Khayelitsha* 2005 (1) SA 580 (CC), paras. 42–44.

123 *Bhe v Magistrate, Khayelitsha* 2005 (1) SA 580 (CC), para. 80. Footnotes omitted.

124 Moore and Himonga, "Living Customary Law," 61; Budlender, *Women and Men in South Africa*, 9. The statistics provided by Lehohla in 2002 estimated that about 10 million people lived in rural areas. This was approximately 50% of the population at the time. See Lehohla, *Measuring Rural Development*. However, these numbers are now considerably higher considering that the statistics were based on the 1996 population census.

viewpoints on the decision of the Constitutional Court in *Bhe v Magistrate, Khayelitsha* generally fall into two camps. On the one hand, some regard the decision as a victory for women's inheritance rights, although they caution against using common-law norms instead of developing customary ones.[125] On the other hand, some argue that the judgment will become mere paper law because it does not consider living realities.[126] In hindsight the minority judgment of Justice Ngcobo in *Bhe v Magistrate, Khayelitsha* seems to have followed a better path in the quest to develop customary law in line with constitutional obligations instead of replacing it with a common-law statute.

Nevertheless, he cautioned against the tendency to interpret customary norms through a common-law lens.[127] And said the customary law of succession, including male primogeniture, had to be understood in its social context, which included reciprocal rights and duties for family members.[128] If one evaluated it in context, it was evident that changing circumstances might influence customary norms. Ngcono J explained:

> The rule of male primogeniture might have been justified by the social and economic context in which it developed. It developed in the context of a traditional society which was based on a subsistence agricultural economy characterised by a self-sufficient family organisation. Within this system, an elaborate network of reciprocal obligations between members of a family existed which ensured that the needs of every member for food, shelter and clothing were provided for. The roles that were assigned to men and women in traditional African society were based on the type of social structure and economy that prevailed then.[129] [...]
>
> The role that women play in modern society and the transformation of the traditional African communities into urban industrialised communities with all their trappings, make it quite clear that whatever role the rule of male primogeniture may have played in traditional society, it can no longer be justified in the present day and age. Indeed, there are instances where in practice women have assumed the role of the head of the family.[130]

125 Pieterse, "Relational Socio-Economic Rights," 209; Rautenbach, Du Plessis and Pienaar, "Is Primogeniture Extinct," 113; Himonga, "Advancement of African Women's Rights," 96.

126 See Weeks, "Securing Women's Property Inheritance," 151 and the sources she refers to in note 54.

127 *Bhe v Magistrate, Khayelitsha* 2005 (1) SA 580 (CC) para. 156.

128 *Bhe v Magistrate, Khayelitsha* 2005 (1) SA 580 (CC) paras. 161–78.

129 *Bhe v Magistrate, Khayelitsha* 2005 (1) SA 580 (CC) para. 188.

130 *Bhe v Magistrate, Khayelitsha* 2005 (1) SA 580 (CC) para. 190.

However, it is too late now to embrace the approach of the minority because the legislature adopted legislation in 2010 which had significant implications for the customary law of succession. An overview of the most critical developments follows in the next section.

3.2.2 Statutory Modifications of the Customary Law of Succession

In *Bhe v Magistrate, Khayelitsha* the Court made it abundantly clear that its order was an interim measure; it was the legislature's responsibility to put appropriate legislation in place.[131] The "appropriate" statute followed six years after a lengthy process – the Reform of Customary Law of Succession and Regulation of Related Matters Act (hereafter the Reform Act).[132] As reflected in its long title, the purpose of this Act is to "modify the customary law of succession". It cannot stand alone, and one must read it with the common-law Intestate Succession Act. Section 2(1) of the Reform Act reads:

> The estate or part of the estate of any person who is subject to customary law who dies after the commencement of this Act and whose estate does not devolve in terms of that person's will, must devolve in accordance with the law of intestate succession as regulated by the Intestate Succession Act.

Thus, the Intestate Succession Act will regulate all intestate estates even though the deceased was subject to customary law. However, suppose customary law is the connecting factor. In such a case, the Intestate Succession Act must be interpreted considering the Reform Act, allowing for situations that generally occur in customary law only.[133]

Reading the two Acts in unison is no easy feat, even for one who has a legal background. The legislature tries to harmonise two opposite normative orders by adapting a common-law Act to include exceptions unique to customary law. For example, terminology such as "descendant" and "spouse" in the Reform Act is confusing.[134] The Intestate Succession Act does not define the concept "descendant". The common law refers to blood relations in the descending line

131 *Bhe v Magistrate, Khayelitsha* 2005 (1) SA 580 (CC) paras. 115–16, 136.

132 11 of 2009. It commenced on 20 September 2010. For a summary of the processes leading up to the finalisation of the Act, see Rautenbach and Meyer, "Lost in Translation," 150–51.

133 See s. 3 of the Reform Act. The title of the section reads "Interpretation of certain provisions of Intestate Succession Act".

134 For a more detailed discussion of some of the issues, see Rautenbach and Meyer, "Lost in Translation," 149.

(e.g., the deceased's children, grandchildren, great-grandchildren and so on). On the other hand, the Reform Act defines a descendant to include a broader circle of descendants than in the common law, to include:[135]

a) someone who was accepted by the deceased under customary law as his child;
b) any other woman, excluding the wife or wives of a deceased, with whom he entered into a substitute marriage to provide children for his house (seedraiser or substitute wife);[136] and
c) a woman to whom a female deceased was married to give children for the deceased's house (woman-to-woman) marriage.[137]

Another example is the definition of "spouse" in the Reform Act. Again, the concept is undefined in the Intestate Succession Act, but it is trite that it ordinarily refers to a person married in terms of the general marriage laws.[138] In the Reform Act a spouse is defined as "a partner in a customary marriage [...] recognised in terms of [...] the Recognition of Customary Marriages Act". The latter does not define a spouse but describes a customary marriage as one concluded following customary law. The definition is wide enough to include substitute and traditional woman-to-woman marriages because they are concluded following customary law. So far, so good. However, another provision in the Reform Act muddles the water somewhat. The Act contains an interpretation clause that states that the word "spouse" in the Intestate Succession Act must be interpreted to include seedraiser and woman-to-woman marriages.[139] A reading together of the relevant provisions in the Reform Act has

135 Reform Act, s. 1 read with s. 2(2)(b) and (c). Also see the discussion in Rautenbach and Meyer, "Lost in Translation," 149, 152.

136 Also referred to as the *ukungena* custom, this refers to a situation where a wife dies without bearing children for her husband. The husband may then take a wife to beget children for him and his deceased wife. There are variations to this custom but in general the children are regarded as the children of the predeceased wife and her husband. In general, see Rautenbach, *Introduction to Legal Pluralism*, 113–14.

137 A woman-to-woman marriage occurs where a wife is childless and takes in another woman to bear children for the house.

138 The marriage laws include the Marriage Act 25 of 1961, the Civil Union Act 17 of 2006 and the Recognition of Customary Marriages Act 120 of 1998. Exceptions include the extension of the concept spouse to unrecognised Muslim marriages to provide for the application of the Intestate Succession Act and the Maintenance of Surviving Spouses Act 27 of 1990. See *Daniels v Campbell* 2004 (5) SA 331 (CC) (monogamous Muslim marriage) and *Hassam v Jacobs* 2009 (11) BCLR 1148 (CC) (polygynous Muslim marriage).

139 Reform Act, s. 3(1).

the practical outcome that wives involved in substitute and woman-to-woman marriages are regarded as both spouses and descendants in terms of the Reform Act. Such an outcome would lead to absurd results when the child's portion is calculated because it would result in the customary law wife receiving a double portion instead of her common-law counterpart, who would receive only one portion. Such an outcome could not have been the intention of the Reform Act, but to date the mischiefs have gone unnoticed.[140]

Another aspect worth mentioning is that the Reform Act bestows total freedom of testation upon anyone subject to customary law.[141] Previously the Black Administration Act prevented the testamentary disposition of specific property that had to devolve according to "Black law and custom".[142] Although this restriction no longer applies, the question of whether a testator can revive male primogeniture by utilising the freedom of testation remains.[143] South African testators may make almost any testamentary provision they please. Accordingly, testators may even disinherit their family members entirely. There are very few statutory and common law restrictions to curb this freedom.[144] Strictly speaking, a testator could indirectly "revive" male primogeniture by instituting his eldest son as the only heir. He may even ensure the continuation of male primogeniture by using the legal construct of *fideicommissum* to create a series of senior male heirs, one after the other.[145] He could also burden the legacy to the eldest male with a *modus*[146] to devote the property he received to maintaining the rest of the family members to mirror his customary law duty of support.

A close working relationship between customary and common succession laws might be the way forward. However, scholars are generally set on keeping customary and common law apart. They have not yet embraced the idea that South African law would be much richer if the two systems worked together

140 A child's portion is calculated by dividing the value of the estate by the number of surviving descendants plus the spouse. See Intestate Succession Act, s. 1(4)(f).

141 Reform Act, s. 4.

142 See s. 23(1).

143 For a more detailed discussion of this question, see Rautenbach, "A Few Comments," 132.

144 In general, see Jamneck, "Freedom of Testation," 126–37.

145 A *fideicommissum* is a common-law concept created in a will and is a form of substitution where a testator "directs that a series of beneficiaries are to own his whole estate or part of it, or specific assets one after the other". For example, "I bequeath my property to my eldest son under the condition that it must devolve to his eldest son at his death". In general, see Van der Linde, "Content of Wills," 169–79.

146 A *modus* or obligation is a common-law construct where a testator burdens a bequest with a qualification that it must be used for something specific, such as the payment of other family members. For more detail, see Jamneck, "Content of Wills," 154–56.

instead of being at loggerheads all the time. As expressed by the late Chief Justice Mahomed,[147]

> Southern Africa will be poorer without the sound discipline, effectiveness and historical experience of Roman-Dutch law … [and] will also be poorer without the spiritualising, humanistic and bonding values of Customary law.

However, not everyone similarly sees the merger between customary and common succession laws as the answer. Authors such as Bennett have repeatedly spoken out against the practice of common law as a "superior normative order".[148] The question may be asked whether the merger between the common and customary law of succession achieved unity in diversity as promised in the Constitution and our aspirations to be a "rainbow nation", or did it happen at the cost of customary law norms?

4 What Remains of Customary Norms in the Law of Succession?

The concept of norms has been a focal point in many legal and social scholarship discussions. Scholars in socio-legal theory refer to themselves as "socio-legal scholars" who engage in the intersectionality between legal and social norms.[149] It is often said that lawyers are generally more concerned about legal authority and finding the legal position in a positive norm. They are engaged with questions such as "what does the law say?" and "what does the evidence prove?"[150] Many lawyers view the law as a separate entity removed from society and free from the influence of politics, socioeconomics, and other factors. However, there is no successful denying that law and society are closely interlinked.[151] Therefore, I agree with the observation:[152]

---

147 Mahomed, "Future of Roman-Dutch Law," 363.

148 Bennett, "Re-Introducing African Customary Law," 5.

149 The importance of socio-legal studies is illustrated by – to name only a few – the establishment of interest groups (Socio-Legal Studies Association in Birmingham), law journals dedicated the theme (Social-Legal Review in Bangladore), graduate courses (Society-Legal Studies at the University of Oxford), textbooks (Creutzfeldt, Mason & McConnachie, *Routledge Handbook*; Baier, *Social and Legal Norms*), and so on.

150 Derber, "What the Lawyer can Learn," 145.

151 Baier, "Introduction," 1.

152 Thomas, Van der Merwe, and Stoop, *Historical Foundations*, 6.

> Society and all its aspects form an integral part in the creation of and changes in the law. Law is part of society, created by society and in its turn influences and shapes society, just as the climate or the economic conditions.

The influence of societal changes on the law is also evident in South Africa. Even though the colonial powers in South Africa initially transplanted western laws into the land, those laws barely look the same today. Kelsen's idea that the law should be kept pure from other influences failed in a South African context.[153] It is no longer easy to distinguish between "legal" and "social" norms,[154] especially not in a pluralistic society such as South Africa, where state and non-state normative orderings coexist. South African judges recognise the close link between law and society. They have used "non-legal" (political, cultural, moral, socioeconomic, and historical) arguments several times in their reasoning to right wrongs committed in the past. For example, in *Du Plessis v De Klerk*[155] the Court cited with approval the Canadian case of *R v Salituro*:[156]

> Judges can and should adapt the common law to reflect the changing social, moral and economic fabric of the country. Judges should not be quick to perpetuate rules whose social foundation has long since disappeared.

153 In general, see Kelsen, *Reine Rechtslehre*, 3–9; Knight, *Pure Theory of Law*, 3–10. Kelsen was the originator of the idea that the law should be kept pure from other influences – i.e., that there is a basic norm (*Grundnorm*) from which all different norms are derived. The basic norm is the authoritative source for the validity of all norms that belong to the same order, for example, a constitution, and all other norms can be traced back to it. However, a norm is not valid because of its content but because it is created in a certain way. A specific process begins the norms of a legal order – they are made by a competent organ such as the legislature. Kelsen believed that one must study the law in isolation to eliminate other subject matters such as psychology, sociology, ethics, and political theory. Though he acknowledged the interconnectedness of these matters, he preferred to avoid interdisciplinarity because it could obscure the essence of legal science. Seen in this way, customary norms – closely linked to societal values – will most definitely not be regarded as legal norms because they are rooted in society and not in a "competent" legislature. For a general discussion of the blurred lines between social and legal norms, see Rautenbach, "Thinking about Norms," 107–15.

154 Menski, *Comparative Law*, 82.

155 1996 (3) SA 850 (CC), para. 61.

156 (1992) 8 CRR (2d) 173 ([1991] 3 SCR 654).

This quotation focusses on the Court's power to develop the common law.[157] But, the judiciary has the same power concerning customary law. Therefore, one must assume that it "can and should adapt the [customary law] to reflect the changing social, moral and economic fabric of the country." In South Africa one need not be a socio-legal scholar to realise that norms in law and society are interlinked. However, a problem arises when state intervention does not consider customary norms or culture when making laws.

Returning to the question posed in the beginning, "what remains of customary norms?", I acknowledge that it presupposes that we agree that customary norms are universal and fixed, at least in the geographical area where they apply. They are not. Bennett[158] defines customary law as a legal system that "derives from social practices that the community concerned accepts as obligatory." The societal characteristic of customary law is much more pronounced than in common law, though society is not irrelevant in making common law.[159] South African legislation recognises the social features of customary law. For example, the Recognition of Customary Marriages Act[160] defines "customary law" as "the customs and usages traditionally observed among the indigenous African peoples of South Africa and which form part of the culture of those peoples."[161]

South African society comprises many communities ("peoples") with different languages and cultural features. The communities' values and norms, both social and legal, vary in many respects. These values and norms are also in a constant process of change and development due to social changes. As explained by Mbiti,[162]

> In traditional life the family is the nucleus of both individual and corporate existence, the area where a person really experienes (sic) personal consciousness of himself and of other members of society. Now, the family is the most severely affected part of African life. Within one family or

157 It was handed down in terms of s. 35(3) of the transitional Constitution.

158 Bennett, *Customary Law*, 1.

159 Take for example the way statutes are created. Normally, an issue or need would arise in society, which then triggers the interest of law makers, who initiate the process. In South Africa both the judiciary and the legislature can make laws, though the former makes a judgment and the latter a statute. Also see the discussion by Schiff, "Socio-Legal Theory," 287.

160 120 of 1998. See s. 1.

161 The Customary Law of Succession Act contains a similar definition in s. 1, except that the word "people" is used instead of "peoples".

162 Mbiti, *African Religions*, 213.

> household may be found two totally different worlds coexisting: the children may be attending university studies, while the parents are illiterate and concerned mainly with cultivating their fields with wooden sticks. In such a family, there are two sets of expectations, economic standards, cultural concerns and world views. Some families are obviously more affected than others. The new change shows itself outwardly in many ways such as education, clothing, houses, food and moral behaviour.

The dynamics in society make it difficult to establish the exact content of customary norms and even more difficult to prove those norms in a court of law. Take, for example, the case of *MM v MN,* where there was no consensus between the witnesses on whether the husband required his wife's consent to enter a subsequent marriage. The witnesses came from various backgrounds, all "qualified" to testify about customary norms: advisors to traditional leaders, individuals involved in customary marriages, traditional leaders, anthropologists, and other experts. Yet they all disagreed about the content of the specific norm and whether permission was imperative to constitute a valid second marriage, illustrating how difficult it is to find commonalities in societal norms.[163]

Considering that society is on the move under constant external socioeconomic and other influences, norms are expected to evolve constantly. This phenomenon was described by Schapera, an eminent and well-cited social anthropologist in southern Africa, as "The Evolution of the Kgatla Family" in his well-known book "Married Life in an African Tribe".[164] He considered how marriage and family life in a traditional community changed due to its contact with Western influences and concluded:[165]

> The old tribal culture has in consequence become greatly modified, and in the process of transformation the traditional domestic institutions were also affected.

Considering that his account of traditional family life was given in the late 1930s and the unlikelihood that the evolution has stopped, one can presume that the changes are even more pronounced today.[166] Despite the influence of modernity on family life, the rules of succession resembled the patrilineal bias

163 Rautenbach, "Oral Law," 15.
164 See Schapera, *Married Life*, 333.
165 Schapera, *Married Life*, 7.
166 Also see Truschel, "Nation-Building," 185–93.

of the Kgatla society at the time. There is no evidence (being lawyerly again) to suggest that the situation has changed and no evidence to suggest otherwise. The law is ill-equipped to deal with social changes and differences because legal development typically takes much longer than societal development. A problem usually comes out in the open only when aggrieved members of a community institute court action, followed by legislative change, such as in the case of the customary law of succession.

5 Conclusion

At face value the merger of the common and customary law of succession is unfortunate. For the legal pluralist, perhaps the most curious part of this union between two diverse normative fields is the outward fusion of two opposite sources of law. In hindsight, given that both are considered independent sources of norms in the South African legal system, a different approach to legal reform should probably have been taken to acknowledge this difference instead of imposing one onto the other. Nhlapo asks a valid question regarding the legal reform of customary law: "Assuming that securing the place of customary law in the South African legal system is a legitimate objective, are we going about it the right way?"[167] The question is equally relevant for modifying the customary law of succession: "did we go about it the right way?"

Most customary law of succession rules has been replaced by statutes generally based on common law principles. These changes, however, have not unified the common and customary law entirely. Therefore, under certain circumstances it would still be necessary to determine if a person who died intestate was subject to customary law to apply the modifications prescribed in the Reform of Customary Law of Succession Act. Therefore it is recommended that a person indicates in their will which legal system should apply to the deceased estate.

I commenced with the slogan "rainbow nation" and the constitutional phrase "united in our diversity". Is this what has been forged between the common and customary laws of succession? Can we say there is unity in diversity or was this just a quick fix because the alternative would have taken much longer? Replacing the customary law of succession with a common-law system where inequalities have already been ironed out might be a convenient solution. Still, perhaps it was not the right one. What should have been considered

167 See Nhlapo, "Customary Law," 2.

is developing a brand-new statute for intestate succession that applies to all in South Africa instead of merely modifying common law legislation to accommodate customary norms. Such an approach could have prevented any real or perceived impressions that the common law was preferred to customary law.

Whether this union of diverse normative orders is a rainbow remains to be seen. There is also very little evidence on the content of customary norms in the context of inheritance. So far the issue has not led to published litigation, and as far as I know, no anthropological research exists to reveal the actual position. Therefore, I must concede that the question whether customary norms remain has to be left unanswered. The judiciary and the legislature may be criticised for not developing the customary law of succession but for replacing it with statutes based on common law principles. However, people subject to customary law have gained the power to execute a will, which could be used to their advantage. Nothing prevents a testator living under a system of customary law from applying his newly acquired freedom of testation to revive the rule of male primogeniture, using a will indirectly.[168] Typically such a provision would be considered by a family head who wished to retain the customary law property within the family living under a system of customary law. To ensure continuation, he might even consider applying common law concepts such as substitution and *modus*.[169] One can only begin to imagine the options open to such a testator. All that is needed is an innovative drafter of wills who knows the common and customary succession law. Of course, it seems that making wills has not yet gained popularity among the members of traditional communities. Therefore, it will be necessary to advocate the idea of wills and their advantages to those communities. Considering the traditional authority's role in developing customary law in line with the Constitution and the rights of women and children,[170] it might be necessary to start with them. They play an essential role in educating and empowering their communities. If they are convinced of the advantages of wills, nothing stops them from adapting something typically western to ensure the continuation of customary succession norms, if they are constitutional.

168 See Rautenbach, "A Few Comments," 142–57.

169 A *modus* is an obligation linked to a bequest. For example, where a testator adds a qualification to a testamentary bequest which obliges the beneficiary to do something in return. The father may bequeath his estate to his eldest son with the obligation that he provides for the rest of his siblings. See Jamneck, "Content of Wills," 154–56.

170 Mmusinyane, "Role of Traditional Authorities," 152.

Bibliography

Literature

Amoah, Jewel. "When Grace Met Bennett: An Intersectionality Analysis of Bennett's Commentary on Culture and Legal Pluralism in South Africa." In *In the Shade of an African Baobab: Tom Bennett's Legacy*, edited by Christa Rautenbach, 23–43. Cape Town: Juta, 2019.

Baier, Matthias, ed. *Social and Legal Norms: Towards a Socio-Legal Understanding of Normativity*. London: Routledge, 2013.

Baier, Matthias. "Introduction." In *Social and Legal Norms: Towards a Socio-Legal Understanding of Normativity*, edited by Matthias Baier, 1–12. London: Routledge, 2013.

Bakker, Pieter. "The Validity of a Customary Marriage under the Recognition of Customary Marriages Act 120 of 1998 with Reference to Sections 3(1)(b) and 7(6) – Part 1." *Journal for Contemporary Roman Dutch Law* 79 (2016): 231–47.

Bakker, Pieter. "The Validity of a Customary Marriage under the Recognition of Customary Marriages Act 120 of 1998 with Reference to Sections 3(1)(b) and 7(6) – Part 2." *Journal for Contemporary Roman Dutch Law* 79 (2016): 357–68.

Bekker, J. C. *Seymour's Customary Law in Southern Africa*. 5 ed. Cape Town: Juta, 1989.

Bekker, J. C., and P. D. De Kock. "Adaptation of the Customary Law of Succession to Changing Needs." *Comparative and International Law Journal of Southern Africa* 25, no. 3 (1992): 366–78.

Bennett, T. W. "Re-Introducing African Customary Law to the South African Legal System." *The American Journal of Comparative Law* 57, no. 1 (2009): 1–31.

Bennett, T. W. "The Conflict of Personal Laws: Wills and Intestate Succession." *Journal of Contemporary Roman Dutch Law* 56 (1993): 50–64.

Bennett, T. W. "The Equality Clause and Customary Law." *South African Journal on Human Rights* 10, no. 1 (1994): 122–30.

Bennett, T. W. "The Interpersonal Conflict of Laws: A Techniques for Adapting to Social Change in Africa." *The Journal of Modern African Studies* 18, no. 1 (1980): 127–34.

Bennett, T. W. *Customary Law in South Africa*. Cape Town: Juta, 2004.

Brandel-Syrier, Mia. "First-Borns and Younger Sons: Culture Change and Sibling Relations." *South African Journal of African Affairs* 9, no. 1 (1979): 41–45.

Brenner, Gabrielle A. "Why did Inheritance Laws Change?" *International Review of Law and Economics* 5, no. 1 (1985): 91–106.

Budlender, Debbie. *Women and Men in South Africa: Five Years On*. Pretoria: Statistics South Africa, 2002.

Chanock, Martin. *The Making of South African Legal Culture 1902–1936: Fear, Favour and Prejudice*. Cambridge: Cambridge University Press, 2001.

Creutzfeldt, Naomi, Marc Mason, and Kirsten McConnachie. *Routledge Handbook of Socio-Legal Theory and Methods*. London: Routledge, 2019.

De Waal, Marius. "Law, Society and the Individual: The Limits of Testation." In *Essays on the History of Law*, edited by D. P. Visser, 300–18. Cape Town: Juta, 1989.

De Waal, Marius J. "The Social and Economic Foundations of the Law of Succession." *Stellenbosch Law Review* 8 (1997): 162–75.

Derber, Mlilton. "What the Lawyer can Learn from Social Science." *Journal of Legal Education* 16, no. 2 (1963): 145–54.

Government of the Republic of South Africa. "Amendment of Customary Law of Succession Bill (B109–98)." Accessed April 13, 2021. https://bit.ly/2OK6wyp.

Hamnett, Ian. *Chieftainship and Legitimacy: Anthropological Study of Executive Law in Lesotho*. London: Routledge, 1975.

Himonga, Chuma. "The Advancement of African Women's Rights in the First Decade of Democracy in South Africa: The Reform of the Customary Law of Marriage and Succession." *Acta Juridica* (2005): 82–107.

Himonga, Chuma. "Reflection on *Bhe v Magistrate Khayelitsha*: In Honour of Emeritus Justice Ngcobo of the Constitutional Court of South Africa." *Southern African Public Law* 32, no. 1–2 (2017): 1–18.

Jamneck, Juanita. "Content of Wills: Absolute Bequests, Conditions, the Modus and Estate Massing." In *The Law of Succession in South Africa*, edited by Juanita Jamneck and Christa Rautenbach, 143–162. 3 ed. Cape Town: Oxford University Press, 2017.

Jamneck, Juanita. "Freedom of Testation." In *The Law of Succession in South Africa*, edited by Juanita Jamneck and Christa Rautenbach, 125–37. 3 ed. Cape Town: Oxford University Press, 2017.

Kelsen, Hans. *Reine Rechtslehre, Einleitung in die Rechtswissenschaftliche Problematik*. Leipzig: Verlag Franz Deuticke, 1960. (English translation from the 2nd revised German Edition by Knight, Max, *The Pure Theory of Law*. 2 rev ed. Berkeley: University of California Press, 1970).

Knight, Max, *The Pure Theory of Law*. 2 rev ed. Berkeley: University of California Press, 1970.

Kerr, A. J. "Inheritance in Customary Law under the Interim Constitution and under the Present Constitution." *South African Law Journal* 115 (1998): 262–270.

Lehohla, Pali. *Measuring Rural Development: Baseline Statistics for the Integrated Sustainable Rural Development Strategy*. Pretoria: Statistics South Africa, 2002.

Mahomed, I. "The Future of Roman-Dutch Law in Southern Africa, Particularly in Lesotho" *Lesotho Law Journal* 1, no. 2 (1985): 357–365.

Mbiti, John S. *African Religions and Philosophy*. 2 ed. Oxford: Heinemann, 1990.

Menski, Werner. *Comparative Law in a Global Context*. 2 ed. Cambridge: Cambridge University Press, 2006.

Mmusinyane, B. "The Role of Traditional Authorities in Developing Customary Laws in Accordance with the Constitution: *Shilubana and Others v Nwamitwa* 2008 (9) BCLR

914 (CC)." *Potchefstroom Electronic Law Journal* 12, no. 3 (2009): 136–61. https://doi.org/10.17159/1727-3781/2009/v12i3a2737.

Mnisi, S. "The Interface Between Living Customary Law(s) of Succession and South African State Law." DPhil in Law thesis, Trinity, 2009.

Møller, Valerie, Helga Dickow, and Mari Harris. "South Africa's 'Rainbow People', National Pride and Happiness." *Social Indicators Research* 47 (1999): 245–80.

Moore, Elena, and Chuma Himonga. "Living Customary Law and Families in South Africa." In *South African Child Gauge 2018*, edited by Katharine Hall, Linda Richter, Zitha Mokomane, and Lori Lake, 61–69. Cape Town: Children's Institute, University of Cape Town, 2018.

Nhlapo, Thandabantu. "Customary Law in Post-Apartheid South Africa: Constitutional Confrontations in Culture, Gender and 'Living Law'." *South African Journal on Human Rights* 33, no. 1 (2017): 1–24.

Nhlapo, Thandabantu. "Customary Marriage: Missteps Threaten the Constitutional Ideal of Common Citizenship." *Journal of Southern African Studies* 47, no. 2 (2021): 273–89.

Parliamentary Monitoring Group. "Traditional Courts Bill (B15–2008)." Accessed April 11, 2021. https://pmg.org.za/bill/409/.

Parliamentary Monitoring Group. "Recognition of Customary Marriages Amendment Bill (B12–2019)." Accessed April 11, 2021. https://pmg.org.za/bill/891.

Paleker, Mohamed. "Intestate Succession." In *The Law of Succession in South Africa*, edited by Juanita Jamneck and Christa Rautenbach, 25–45. 3 ed. Cape Town: Oxford University Press, 2017.

Phillips, Jim. "Why Legal History Matters." *Victoria University of Wellington Law Review* 41, no. 3 (2010): 293–316.

Pienaar, J. M. "Law of Property." In *Introduction to Legal Pluralism in South Africa*, edited by Christa Rautenbach, 119–53. 6 ed. Durban: LexisNexis, 2021.

Pieterse, Marius. "Relational Socio-Economic Rights." *South African Journal on Human Rights* 25, no. 2 (2009): 198–217.

Rautenbach, Christa, and Margaret M. Meyer. "Lost in Translation: Is a Spouse a Spouse or a Descendant (or Both) in terms of the Reform of Customary Law of Succession and Regulation of Related Matters Act?" *Journal of South African Law* 1 (2012): 149–60.

Rautenbach, Christa, and Willemien Du Plessis. "Reform of the South African Customary Law of Succession: Final Nails in the Customary Law Coffin?" In *The Future of African Customary Law*, edited by Jeanmarie Fenrich, Paolo Galizzi, and Tracy E. Higgins, 336–360. Cambridge: Cambridge University Press, 2011.

Rautenbach, Christa, and Willemien Du Plessis. "South African Law Commission's Proposals for Customary Law of Succession: Retrogression or Progression." *De Jure* 3 (2003): 20–31.

Rautenbach, Christa, ed. *Introduction to Legal Pluralism in South Africa*. 6 ed. Durban: LexisNexis, 2021.

Rautenbach, Christa, Willemien Du Plessis, and Gerrit Pienaar. "Is Primogeniture Extinct like the Dodo, or is there any Prospect of It Rising from the Ashes? Comments on the Evolution of Customary Succession Laws in South Africa." *South African Journal on Human Rights* 22, no. 1 (2006): 99–118.

Rautenbach, Christa. "A Family Home, Five Sisters and the Rule of Ultimogeniture: Comparing Notes on Judicial Approaches to Customary Law in South Africa and Botswana." *African Human Rights Law Journal* 16 (2016): 145–74.

Rautenbach, Christa. "A Few Comments on the (Possible) Revival of the Customary Law of Male Primogeniture: Can the Common-Law Principle of Freedom of Testation come to Its Rescue?" *Acta Juridica* (2014): 132–59.

Rautenbach, Christa. "Case Law as an Authoritative Source of Customary Law: Piecemeal Recording of (Living) Customary Law?" *Potchefstroom Electronic Law Journal* 22 (2019): 1–20. http://dx.doi.org/10.17159/1727-3781/2019/v22i0a7591.

Rautenbach, Christa. "Cultural Expertise in Litigation in South Africa: Can the Western World Learn Anything form a Mixed, Pluralistic Legal System?" *Studies in Law, Politics, and Society* 78 (2019): 157–78.

Rautenbach, Christa. "Deep Legal Pluralism in South Africa: Judicial Accommodation of Non-State Law." *Journal of Legal Pluralism* 60 (2010): 143–77.

Rautenbach, Christa. "In the Shade of an African Baobab: Thomas W (Tom) Bennett on Custom and Religion." In *In the Shade of an African Baobab: Tom Bennett's Legacy*, edited by Christa Rautenbach, 1–15. Cape Town: Juta, 2019.

Rautenbach, Christa. "Oral Law in Litigation in South Africa: An Evidential Nightmare?" *Potchefstroom Electronic Law Journal* 20 (2017): 1–25. http://dx.doi.org/10.17159/1727-3781/2017/v20i0a3268.

Rautenbach, Christa. "The Constitutional Court of South Africa." In *Comparative Constitutional Reasoning*, edited by András Jakab, Arthur Dyevre, and Giulio Itzcovich, 560–603. Cambridge: Cambridge University Press, 2017.

Rautenbach, Christa. "Thinking about Norms in Pluralistic Societies: Blurred Lines between the 'Legal' and the 'Social' of Pluralist Normative Orders." In *Le droit comparé et … /Comparative Law and …*, edited by Alexis Albarian and Olivier Moréteau, 107–115. Aix-en-Provence: Aix Presses Universitaires d'Aix-Marseille, 2016.

Rautenbach, Christa. "Families and Legal Pluralism in South Africa: Celebrating Diversity but at what Cost?". In *The Pluralisation of Family Forms*, edited by Nina Dethloff and Katharina Kaesling, 61–91. Intersentia: Cambridge, 2023.

Sanders, A. J. G. M. "How Customary is African Customary Law?" *The Comparative and International Law Journal of Southern Africa* 20, no. 3 (1987): 405–10.

Schapera, Isaac. *A Handbook of Tswana Law and Custom*. Oxford: Oxford University Press, 1959.

Schapera, Isaac. *Married Life in an African Tribe*. London: Faber and Faber, 1940.

Schiff, David N. "Socio-Legal Theory: Social Structure and Law." *The Modern Law Review* 39, no. 3 (1976): 287–310.

Sibani, Clifford Meesua. "Impact of Western Culture on Traditional African Society: Problems and Prospects." *International Journal of Religion and Human Relations* 10 (2018): 56–72.

South African Law Commission. *Project 90: Discussion Paper 93 on the Customary Law of Succession*. Pretoria: South African Law Commission, 2000.

South African Law Commission. *Project 90: Issue Paper 12 on Succession: Harmonisation of the Common Law and Indigenous Law*. Pretoria: South African Law Commission, 1998.

South African Law Reform Commission. "All Projects." Accessed March 7, 2021. https://www.justice.gov.za/salrc/projectlist.htm.

Thomas, Ph. J, C. G. Van der Merwe, and B. C. Stoop. *Historical Foundations of South African Private Law*. 2 ed. Durban: LexisNexis, 2000.

Traditional Authorities Research Group. "The Role and Future of Traditional Leaders in South Africa." *Koers* 64, no. 2/3 (1999): 295–324.

Traditional Authorities Research Group. *The Administrative and Legal Position of Traditional Authorities in South Africa and their Contribution to the Implementation of the Reconstruction and Development Programme*. Unpublished, 1996.

Truschel, Louis W. "Nation-Building and the Kgatla; the Role of the Anglo-Boer War." *Botswana Notes and Records* 4 (1972): 185–93.

Van der Linde, A. "Content of Wills: Substitution, Usufruct and Accrual." In *The Law of Succession in South Africa*, edited by Juanita Jamneck and Christa Rautenbach, 163–186. 3 ed. Cape Town: Oxford University Press, 2017.

Weeks, Sindiso Mnisi. "Securing Women's Property Inheritance in the Context of Plurality: Negotiations of Law and Authority in Mbuzini Customary Courts and Beyond." *Acta Juridica* (2011): 140–73.

Zimmermann, Reinhard, and D. P. Visser. *Southern Cross: Civil Law and Common Law in South Africa*. Oxford: Clarendon Press, 1996.

Case Law

Alexkor Ltd v Richtersveld Community 2003 (12) BCLR 1301 (CC).

Bhe v Magistrate, Khayelitsha 2005 (1) SA 580 (CC).

Carmichele v Minister of Safety and Security 2001 (4) SA 938 (CC).

Daniels v Campbell 2004 (5) SA 331 (CC).

Du Plessis v De Klerk 1996 (3) SA 850 (CC).

Gumede v President of the Republic of South Africa 2009 (3) SA 152 (CC).

Hassam v Jacobs 2009 (11) BCLR 1148 (CC).

In re: Certification of the Constitution of the Republic of South Africa, 1996 1996 (10) BCLR 1253 (CC).
MEC For Education, Kwazulu-Natal v Pillay 2008 (1) SA 474 (CC).
MM v MN 2013 (4) SA 415 (CC).
Mthembu v Letsela 1997 (2) SA 936 (T).
Mthembu v Letsela 1998 (2) SA 675 (T).
Mthembu v Letsela 2000 (3) SA 867 (SCA).
R v Salituro (1992) 8 CRR (2d) 173 ([1991] 3 SCR 654).
Ramuhovhi v President of the Republic of South Africa 2018 (2) SA 1 (CC).
Shibi v Sithole TPD Case 7292/01 of 19 November 2003 (unreported).
Shilubana v Nwamitwa 2009 (2) SA 66 (CC).
Van Breda v Jacobs 1921 AD 330.
Zondi v President of the RSA 2000 (2) SA 49 (N).

Legislation

Black Administration Act 38 of 1927.
Civil Union Act 17 of 2006.
Constitution of the Republic of South Africa Act 200 of 1993.
Constitution of the Republic of South Africa, 1996.
Intestate Succession Act 81 of 1987.
KwaZulu Act on the Code of Zulu Law 16 of 1985.
Maintenance of Surviving Spouses Act 27 of 1990.
Marriage Act 25 of 1961.
Natal Code of Zulu Law Proclamation R151 of 1987.
Recognition of Customary Marriages Act 120 of 1998.
Reform of Customary Law of Succession and Regulation of Related Matters Act 11 of 2009.
Repeal of the Black Administration Act and Amendment of Certain Laws Act 28 of 2005.
Wills Act 7 of 1953.

CHAPTER 3

The Communal Nature of the South African Customary Law of Succession: Developments in the 21st Century

Fatima Osman

Abstract

Customary law is generally described as a communal or group-orientated system of law. In the customary law of succession, the communal nature is manifested in norms that provided support to the family rendered vulnerable by the passing of the family head. These norms identified a successor to the status of family head to ensure the stability of the family and community. The collective well-being of the family was emphasised rather than the rights of individual family members. This chapter examines the evolution of the communal nature of succession through a case study conducted in a rural village in South Africa. It draws on findings from a range of interviews with members of the community, traditional leaders, and state officials responsible for the administration of estates. The case study reveals an entrenchment of the pre-constitutional position, which prioritised the individualised acquisition of assets rather than traditional notions that focussed on succession to the position of household head. The individualised acquisition of assets seems to have been in alignment with positivist state law, which, at first glance, extinguishes the group and communal nature of customary law. On the other hand, the chapter reveals how the communal nature of the customary law of succession permeates the current devolution of an estate. The extended family and the community provide invaluable emotional and financial support to the deceased's close family upon the death of a family member. Furthermore, socio-economic considerations in communities, such as poverty and unemployment, and broader country issues such as a lack of access to courts, have in many ways led to a strengthening of communal ties. The persistence of these communal characteristics suggests stronger ideals of legal pluralism that may resist state interventions in this arena. The chapter highlights the significance of this resistance for law reform and the judicial development of customary law.

 | DOI:10.1163/9789004696747_004

1 Introduction*

Customary law in South Africa is generally described as a communal or group-oriented system of law.[1] Its communal characteristics are clearly evident in the customary law of succession, but the colonial and apartheid eras distorted this nature through their focus on the inheritance of property and emphasis on the patriarchal features of the law. In the constitutional era the recognition of customary law, subject to the Constitution and other legislation, has seen a continuation of the distortion of the law.[2] This chapter examines how the state regulation of the customary law of succession – both in the pre- and post-constitutional eras – has impacted on the communal nature of the customary law of succession.

First the chapter provides a historical overview of how the pre-colonial customary law of succession evinced strong communal characteristics. It thereafter discusses how the state regulation of the law in both the pre- and post-constitutional eras distorted the communal nature of the law. The chapter then draws on findings from a case study conducted in the rural Eastern Cape province of South Africa to argue that communal characteristics persist despite state law providing for a much more individualised system of succession.

Finally, it concludes by noting the implications of the state regulation of customary law for legal pluralism and law-making in South Africa. It argues that these empirical findings suggest the existence of a strong pluralistic state which people navigate to achieve the best possible outcome for themselves, and that understanding how individuals view and use the legal system is essential for effective law-making.

2 Historical Overview of the Customary Law of Succession

Historically the customary law of succession was aimed at ensuring minimal disturbance in the family. The death of the family head (the husband) usually

* This chapter is based on my PhD which was supported by the National Research Foundation Sabbatical Grants to complete doctoral degrees (SGD170613240190), and the NRF Chair in Customary Law, Indigenous Values and Human Rights. Nonetheless, all views expressed, and mistakes made are solely my own.

1 Church, "Place of Indigenous Law", 99.

2 Section 211(3) of the Constitution of the Republic of South Africa, 1996 (hereafter "the Constitution") provides: "The courts must apply customary law when that law is applicable, subject to the Constitution and any legislation that specifically deals with customary law."

triggered concerns regarding the family's spiritual and emotional well-being. Thus, the norms of succession provided support to the family at a vulnerable time and identified a successor to the status of family head to ensure the stability of the family and community.[3] The collective well-being of the family – with family understood to be the extended family and not merely the nuclear family – and community was emphasised rather than the rights of individual family members to property.

The identification of a new family head, the central focus of the customary law of succession, was carried out through the principle of male primogeniture. This meant that succession was through the male line and the first-born son was the successor, failing which another male would succeed in a predetermined order.[4] Comaroff, however, notes that rules were never applied rigidly to determine accession to chieftaincy, which occurred on a competitive basis.[5] Similarly, in the context of succession in a family, the principle of male primogeniture provided a guideline for the order of succession but families had a discretion to modify the principle to ensure the overall goal of maintaining the welfare of surviving family members.[6]

In addition, the family head could make dispositions of property in anticipation of death to ensure the family's well-being. These were verbal dispositions of property, akin to death bed wishes, rather than a written will, which was unknown in customary law.[7] Dispositions, usually made within family ties,[8] could be made to younger sons to pay their *lobolo* or to help them establish their homes[9] in accordance with the underlying customary law value of the continuation and well-being of the family.[10] Dispositions in bad faith or which flagrantly contravened the customary law principles of succession[11] or undermined the interests of the family risked not being effected after the

3 For a general discussion of the values underlying the customary law of succession, see Mbatha, "Reforming the Customary Law of Succession," 260–61; and Himonga and Moore, *Reform of Customary Marriage*, 234.

4 Rautenbach and Osman, "Law of Succession and Inheritance," 194–97.

5 Comaroff, "Rules and Rulers," 1.

6 Bennett, *Customary Law*, 334–35.

7 Olivier, Bekker, Olivier, and Olivier, *Indigenous Law*, 147 and 153; Badejogbin, "Interplay of Customary Law," 17; Bekker, *Seymour's Customary Law*, 311; and Mbatha, "Reforming the Customary Law of Succession," 262.

8 Badejogbin, "Interplay of Customary Law," 18.

9 Bekker, *Seymour's Customary Law*, 77; and Olivier, Bekker, Olivier, and Olivier, *Indigenous Law*, 154.

10 Kerr, *Customary Law of Immovable Property*, 148–49.

11 Olivier, Bekker, Olivier, and Olivier, *Indigenous Law*, 153.

head's passing.[12] This is because the successor assumed responsibility for the household[13] and control of the deceased's assets, all of which were aimed at ensuring the well-being of the family. For example, the successor stepped into the shoes of the deceased and assumed responsibility for the maintenance and well-being of the deceased's dependents.[14] The assumption of the deceased's assets enabled him to discharge his responsibilities towards the deceased's dependents.[15] This accords with the understanding that rights in property were always limited by obligations and counterbalanced by the rights and privileges of others.[16] Furthermore, the identification of a single successor meant that an individual could be held responsible and accountable for the well-being of the family.[17] A successor who failed in his responsibilities faced sanction by the family, whose coercive pressure was usually sufficient to ensure compliance,[18] failing which the matter could be escalated to the chief or customary court and the successor stripped of his status and dispossessed of the property.[19]

In summation, customary law of succession was initially premised on the continuation and well-being of the family. The focus was on succession and the identification of an heir to assume responsibility for the family. Typically, the inheritance of property followed succession so that the heir could discharge his responsibilities. However, the family head also had a limited power to dispose of some property. This ensured the well-being of these sons and the establishment of their homes. The family, often represented by the elder males of the family, witnessed the customary dispositions and ignored or enforced dispositions to secure the well-being of the family.[20]

12 Kerr, *Customary Law of Immovable Property*, 128, 148–49.

13 Bekker and De Kock, "Adaptation the Customary Law of Succession," 368. For a good discussion of the principle and how it operates, Rautenbach, "Legal Position of South African Women," 280–86.

14 Kerr, *Customary Law of Immovable Property*, 136; Olivier, Bekker, Olivier, and Olivier, *Indigenous Law*, 160; Bekker and De Kock, "Adaptation the Customary Law of Succession," 368; and Hunter, *Reaction to Conquest*, 122.

15 Church and Church, "Constitutional Imperative," 9.

16 Cousins, "Characterising 'Communal' Tenure," 111.

17 Mbatha, "Reforming the Customary Law of Succession," 260.

18 Kerr, *Customary Law of Immovable Property*, 136.

19 Kerr, *Customary Law of Immovable Property*, 136 and 138; Bekker and De Kock, "Adaptation the Customary Law of Succession," 368.

20 Bennett, *Customary Law*, 351.

3 State Regulation of the Customary Law of Succession

In accordance with the notions of weak legal pluralism, the South African state sought to regulate the customary law of succession. The state regulation of customary law accords with notions of weak legal pluralism and had a distortive effect on the nature of the customary law succession, which is explored below.

3.1 *Pre-Constitutional Era – Pre 1994*

During apartheid the Black Administration Act[21] was the state's central tool in regulating the lives of black people, including the administration of customary law estates.[22] Section 23 of the Act, along with the regulations thereunder, provided a comprehensive framework for the administration of customary law estates.[23] The mere regulation of the law in a statutory form such as the Black Administration Act changed the nature of the law. A key feature in the customary law of succession was the flexibility in the application of norms.[24] The law comprised of principles and norms – rather than fixed and rigid rules – which could be relaxed or applied differently in pursuit of the underlying goal of ensuring the well-being of the family.[25]

The substantive provisions of the Black Administration Act and the regulations thereunder significantly changed the focus of the customary law of succession. The provisions regulated the inheritance of property as opposed to the identification of an heir to assume responsibility for the family. Where the inheritance of property was historically a secondary concern under customary succession, the Black Administration Act elevated it to the primary matter for resolution. The focus was the devolution of the property.[26] This constituted a significant distortion of the law and marked a shift from the family and group orientation of the law to individualised interests.[27]

21 Black Administration Act 38 of 1927 (hereafter "the Black Administration Act").

22 Langa CJ in *Bhe v Magistrate, Khayelitsha; Shibi v Sithole* 2005 (1) SA 580 (CC) para. 61 described the Act as the "cornerstone of racial oppression, division and conflict in South Africa" that had been specifically designed to separate and exclude Africans from the rest of the population.

23 The section detailed the devolution of movable property, land in tribal settlements and all other property. It also regulated the adjudication of disputes and the jurisdiction to administer customary law estates. For a discussion of the provisions see Rautenbach and Osman, "Law of Succession and Inheritance," 200–01.

24 Bekker and Koyana, "Judicial and Legislative Reform," 570–71.

25 Ibid.

26 Weeks, "Customary Succession," 216.

27 Mbatha, "Reforming the Customary Law of Succession," 264.

The Black Administration Act was also silent regarding the heir's responsibility towards the deceased's dependents.[28] As previously discussed, under customary law the heir would be responsible for the deceased's dependents. Initially the courts attached to the inheritance of property an expectation that the heir would provide for the deceased's dependents[29] but this waned over time and "[t]he loose principle of male primogeniture under living law became the rule of oldest male inheritance under official law".[30] The result was that the male heir often inherited the property in his individual capacity without courts enforcing any of the heir's responsibilities to care for the dependents, creating hardship for widows and children.

Furthermore, the devolution of property in accordance with the Black Administration Act changed the nature of property ownership to the individualistic and alienable.[31] Where property devolved in accordance with the Black Administration Act, state officials imposed a common law understanding of ownership on the property. The heir became the owner of the property, as ownership was understood in the common law, with the right to use and dispose of the property as he saw fit.[32] The introduction of the foreign, common-law understandings of concepts such as ownership, absolute rights and alienation arguably distorted the nature of the law and shifted it onto a more individualised basis.[33]

The concomitant socio-economic changes of the time also contributed to changes in the nature of the customary law of succession. Apartheid confined black individuals to the homelands and resulted in a migrant labour system in which men left their homes and families to seek work in urban areas.[34] The prolonged absence of husbands and fathers resulted in marital disharmony and breakdowns, economic insecurity and emotional misery.[35] It had a disastrous impact on the fabric of customary law societies and a general breakdown in the family unit.[36] Migration further transformed the agricultural subsistence economy to a cash economy.[37] The process of individualisation

28 Mbatha, "Reforming the Customary Law of Succession," 263–264.

29 Weeks, "Customary Succession," 216.

30 Ibid.

31 Mbatha, "Reforming the Customary Law of Succession," 264.

32 Himonga and Moore, *Reform of Customary Marriage*, 234.

33 Mamashela, "New Families," 622.

34 Seidman, "Is South Africa Different?" 422.

35 Murray, "Migrant Labour," 140.

36 Ibid.

37 Brown, "Impact of Male Labour Migration," 370. The study was in relation to Botswana, but the findings are arguably applicable to South Africa.

increased as men worked for wages on an individual basis separate from their families.[38] The demand for cash to buy goods and services meant that goods that had been historically shared or exchanged for use on the basis of kinship were bought and sold for cash.[39] This hurt the family group orientation of the past where individuals shared resources and relied upon their family or the greater group in the event of misfortune.[40] Individualism strengthened as cash became the primary means of exchange and wage earners were separated from their families. This change filtered into the customary law of succession as the focus shifted to the inheritance of property and the securing of the interests of an individual heir over the family interests.

In sum, the courts' adherence to the principle of male primogeniture and the omission of any responsibilities of the heir undermined customary law's ability to ensure succession in the best interests of the family. Unscrupulous heirs assumed the property with none of the responsibility. The focus shifted to the inheritance of property and individual interests were secured over the well-being of the family. The distortions in the legal framework along with socio-economic changes at the time arguably created a more individualised system of succession.

3.2 *Constitutional Era – Post 1994*

The state regulation of the succession practices of customary law with all its accompanying distortions was not without contestation. In accordance with Moore's notion of the semi-autonomous social field, individuals resisted state intrusion into the regulation of their lives and developed their own norms.[41] In this regard, Mbatha reported changed practices by families aimed at ensuring the well-being of the family and not the individual heir.[42] Parents concerned about the control of the residential property raised children with the belief that the residential home was family property that should be accessed based on need.[43] For example, "needy children, including single women, women who have returned from broken marriages and disabled people" should have access

38 Brown, "Impact of Male Labour Migration," 370.

39 Brown, "Impact of Male Labour Migration," 378.

40 Ibid.

41 Moore defines a semi-autonomous social field as one that generates its own rules and induces compliance with these rules but is nonetheless subject to the rules and decisions of the outside social matrix. The outside legal system penetrates and influences the social field which also retains a degree of autonomy and the ability to resist outside rules and decisions in some instances. See Moore, "Law and Social Change," 720.

42 Mbatha, "Reforming the Customary Law of Succession," 269.

43 Ibid.

to the home.[44] Similarly, Kingwill found that women are identified as the most suitable caretakers for family property, as they are seen "as better insurance against loss of property, more likely to maintain the property and less likely to evict family members".[45] These stronger entitlements of women to property conflict starkly with the legal framework which saw the devolution of property to a single male heir.

After the adoption of the Constitution and the state recognition of customary law as a system of law, the contestations between the legal framework and changing practices described above played out in the courts.[46] The challenges culminated in the high-profile case of *Bhe v Magistrate, Khayelitsha* where the father of the deceased claimed the deceased's property based on the principle of male primogeniture and indicated an intention to evict the deceased's children and their mother, which would leave them homeless.[47] Under customary law an heir had an obligation to manage property in the best interests of the family, who retained enjoyment of the property.[48] However, the devolution of property under the Black Administration Act allowed the heir – as exemplified in the *Bhe* case – to take ownership of the property and to do with it as he pleased, with no constraints. The Constitutional Court in *Bhe v Magistrate, Khayelitsha* declared section 23 of the Black Administration Act, the regulations thereunder and the principle of male primogeniture unconstitutional. The court ordered, as an interim remedy, that customary law estates would devolve in accordance with the common law Intestate Succession Act[49] modified to accommodate polygamous marriages.

Several years later, the South African legislature brought into force the Reform of Customary Law of Succession Act[50] to regulate the administration

44 Mbatha, "Reforming the Customary Law of Succession," 269 fn 41.

45 Kingwill, "Lost in Translation," 229.

46 *Mthembu v Letsela* 2000 (3) SA 867 (SCA) and *Zondi v President of the Republic of South Africa* 2000 (2) SA 49 (N). In *Moseneke v The Master* 2001 (2) SA 18 (CC) the magistrate's jurisdiction over the estates of Black individuals which devolved in accordance with the common law (and not customary law) was also challenged. While in these cases the litigants challenged the devolution of the property in terms of the law, in some cases the official position may not be challenged but nonetheless may not operate. In her research Kingwill found a discrepancy between legal ownership and that practised in reality and states that there is a shadow land-tenure system beneath the official records: Kingwill, "In the Shadows," 160.

47 *Bhe v Magistrate, Khayelitsha* 2005 (1) SA 580 (CC).

48 Mbatha, "Reforming the Customary Law of Succession," 260–62.

49 Intestate Succession Act 81 of 1987.

50 Reform of Customary Law of Succession and Regulation of Related Matters Act 11 of 2009 (hereafter "the Reform Act").

of customary law estates. The Reform Act provides that customary law estates devolve in accordance with the Intestate Succession Act – again with some accommodation for customary law practices. This, in conjunction with the Administration of Estates Act,[51] creates a uniform system of administration of estates for all races in the country.[52] It also suggests an entrenchment of a weakly pluralistic state in which the state uses positive law to control the application of customary law, which is explored later in this chapter.

4 Current Insights into the Customary Law of Succession

4.1 *Reform Act*

As mentioned previously, the Reform Act as read with the Intestate Succession Act regulates the devolution of customary law estates. The brief Intestate Succession Act sets out the rules for the distribution of assets primarily to the nuclear family, namely the surviving spouse and children.[53] For example, in estates smaller than R250 000 the surviving spouse is the sole heir. In estates larger than R250 000 the estate is shared between the spouses and children. In the presence of a spouse and children, other family members like parents, siblings, nephews or nieces do not inherit from the deceased, regardless of whether they were supported by the deceased.

The Intestate Succession Act is premised on protecting the rights of the nuclear family. While the Reform Act modifies this slightly by accommodating customary practices such as polygamous marriages and adopting a broader definition of "spouse" and "descendant" to capture particular customary law practices, the primary beneficiaries remain spouses and descendants.[54] The Reform Act does not cater for family formations prevalent in customary law,

51 Act 66 of 1965 (hereafter "the Administration of Estates Act"). For a discussion on the administration of estates, see Abrie et al., *Deceased Estates*.

52 The use of the common law to regulate customary law derives from the dominant position of the common law in the South African legal system. A discussion of this is beyond the scope of this chapter, but see Himonga, "Taking Stock," 222–23; and Rautenbach, "South African Common and Customary Law," 129. For a discussion of the dominance of the common law in the field of marriage and succession, see Himonga, "Advancement of African Women's Rights," 82.

53 Section 1 of the Intestate Succession Act. For a discussion of the rules of intestate inheritance, see Jamneck et al., *Law of Succession*, 30; and De Waal and Schoeman-Malan, *Law of Succession*, 20.

54 For a discussion of the accommodations, see Himonga and Nhlapo, *African Customary Law*, 178–82.

such as acknowledging that a grandparent, sibling or even niece or nephew may be considered family by the deceased and thus deserving of an inheritance. Furthermore, the South African Law Commission recommended that once the Intestate Succession Act was made generally applicable, the "customary heir's duty to continue supporting" family members should, in fairness, be abolished as women and children would inherit in their own right.[55] The Reform Act omits the express repeal, but state officials in the case study do not impute customary law responsibilities to the heir. Individual interests are thus secured over those of the family by focussing on the inheritance of property and omitting the responsibilities of the heir. Thus, while the current legislative framework may evince a clear shift from the colonial and apartheid position of securing the interests of a single male heir, the expansion is limited to securing the interests of the slightly modified nuclear family. However, in the customary law discourse, the need to look beyond state regulation – official customary law – to the actual practices of people found in living customary law is well understood. It is examined below.

4.2 *Emerging Practices*

Prompted by the enactment of the Reform Act, I conducted fieldwork over four years from 2015–2018 in the Eastern Cape Province of South Africa as part of my PhD study.[56] The purpose of the case study was to understand the administration of customary law estates in the new dispensation. This chapter draws

55 South African Law Commission, *Discussion Paper 93* (*Project 90*), xvii and 43. It also recommended the repeal of the Natal and KwaZulu codes to ensure the uniform application of the rules throughout South Africa.

56 The Faculty of Law Ethics Committee of the University of Cape Town conferred ethics approval with effect from 8 May 2015. As part of the approval, the confidentiality and anonymity of the village and participants were guaranteed. The village is therefore referred to as Kwelanga, which literally means sunshine, to protect the participants' confidentiality. The informed, oral consent of all parties involved in the study to conduct and record interviews was also obtained. For a comprehensive discussion of the methodology used for the case study, see Osman, "Administration of Customary Law Estates," 11–22.

The Eastern Cape Province is one of the poorest provinces in South Africa. The Province was formed in 1994 with the adoption of the South African Constitution and is constituted predominantly from the areas of the former homelands of Transkei and Ciskei. The homelands, or Bantustans, were separate areas in South Africa to which the apartheid state moved the majority of the Black population to prevent them from living in urban areas. The infrastructure (such as roads, water, and telecommunications) of these areas was never developed and the Province remains one of the most underdeveloped in the country.

on findings from the case study to explain the impact of state interventions on the nature of customary law.

The case study was conducted in the Kwelanga village with an almost exclusive indigenous population. Consonant with the broader municipality, Kwelanga is an impoverished village with high levels of unemployment. Nonetheless, most individuals had at some point worked in the cities, frequently at a mining company in a state office or as a domestic worker, and returned to the village upon losing their job, reaching retirement age or when they were unable to work. Thus, many individuals had financial assets, such as a bank account, insurance policy, pension, or provident fund, which were required to be reported to the state offices as part of the administration process for beneficiaries to access them. As part of the case study I conducted interviews with participants who narrated how relatives' (a spouse's, child's, parent's, sibling's or grandparent's) estates had been wound up. In addition, I conducted focus groups interviews (small group discussions) with members of the community to canvass the general views on the administration of estates. Furthermore, I also interviewed key informants such as the traditional authorities in the village and state officials at the state offices responsible for the administration of estates with the object of understanding the state perspective on administration of estates.[57]

I draw upon my findings from the case study and current literature to illustrate emerging practices in the customary law of succession and the impact of the state regulation of the law.

4.2.1 Devolution of Property

The notions of family property, as well as house and personal property, were constructed during the colonial and apartheid eras to describe the different customary entitlements to property. The classification of property determined the process of its devolution.[58]

"Family property" is traditionally defined as property that has not been allotted or does not accrue to any particular house.[59] It encompasses fields

57 My data were further augmented by an analysis of files from the state offices, but this chapter does not draw significantly upon an analysis of these files.

58 For example, section 23(1) of the Black Administration Act provided that movable property including that accruing to any woman with whom he lived in a customary union, or to any house – generally thought of as house property – would devolve in accordance with Black law and custom.

59 Pienaar, "Law of Property," 126; Bekker, *Seymour's Customary Law*, 71; South African Law Reform Commission, *Report* (*Project 90*), 61. The Reform Act does not define "family property".

and livestock that have a production function and serve family interests.[60] Individuals often define family property, which is frequently land, in terms of its accessibility by the family and the role it plays in maintaining family relations.[61] In this regard, it is important to note that land tenure is often described as social tenure, as people derive their rights from membership in a social group (simply put, membership in a family or a community confers access to land)[62] and land is vital in the creation of relationships.[63] This is because it is not a property right *per se* that is created but rather a set of reciprocal rights and obligations that vest in individuals over the property that explain how the individuals relate to one another and the property.[64] Kingwill explains that rights are maintained through continuous participation in family affairs, maintaining the property and caring for family members.[65] The strength of rights is often determined by how and where one fits into the family,[66] and those with the strongest rights are those who live in the home and maintain contact.[67] Individuals and the group often both have entitlements in the land,[68] as complementary interests could be held simultaneously in the land.[69] The precise nature of the individual and group right will depend on the particular case.[70] Thus even though individuals may exercise individual control and enjoyment of the land in respect of the use and entitlements conferred upon them,[71] there are multiple entitlements to the property, which means that it is not considered an individual asset that can be disposed of or transmitted to an heir.[72]

On the other hand, house property typically consists of the house itself, fields assigned to a particular wife, anything the wife brought into the marriage or the members of the house earned, damages paid for adultery, *lobolo* received for the marriage of a daughter, cattle earmarked for the house, and

60 Mbatha, "Reforming the Customary Law of Succession," 262.
61 Kingwill, "Lost in Translation," 224.
62 Okoth-Ogendo, "Nature of Land Rights," 100. For a more detailed discussion of indigenous land rights, see Okoth-Ogendo, "Nature of Land Rights," 95.
63 Cross, "Alternate Legality," 311.
64 Okoth-Ogendo, "Nature of Land Rights," 100.
65 Kingwill, "Lost in Translation," 229.
66 Kingwill, "In the Shadows," 166.
67 Kingwill, "Lost in Translation," 229.
68 Cross, "Alternate Legality," 312.
69 Cousins, "Characterising 'Communal' Tenure," 111.
70 Cross, "Alternate Legality," 312.
71 Okoth-Ogendo, "Nature of Land Rights," 102.
72 Kingwill, "[En]gendering the Norms of Customary Inheritance," 211.

furniture and household items used in the house.[73] The property forms a separate household estate and if there are three wives, each of them establishes her own house with her own household estate.[74] There is not always a clear distinction between family and house property in monogamous marriages where there is only one house or estate and the property could easily be regarded as either family or house property.[75] Less contentious is personal property, which is typically interpreted as being the clothes, tools and weapons that serve an individual's interests, and which can be disposed of by the individual.[76] This property tends to be of little value and could be distributed to family members.

Despite the dated nature of the terminology of family, house and personal property, it is used in the chapter as it is well-established in the literature and used by the Reform Act – the implementation of which was investigated in the study – to regulate the devolution of property. Furthermore, the Recognition of Customary Marriages Act and the Constitutional Court both employ such terminology in the description of the proprietary consequences of polygynous marriages.[77] The chapter thus presents an understanding of lived realities in the light of the legal framework – but notes difficulties in the analysis thereof – as it may be necessary to invoke such terminology in the assertion of rights in the current legal framework.

Himonga and Moore found that family property is excluded from the official administration of estates process.[78] They define family property as including houses, livestock and gardens.[79] In contrast, the state officials in my case study drew no distinction in the administration of the property based on the classification of the property as family property or the broader interests the property served.[80] Nonetheless, the state officials excluded homes in the village from the Reform Act's ambit though the Act does not provide for such exclusion. The officials applied the exclusion on the practical basis that the homes did

73 Kerr, *Customary Law of Immovable Property*, 160; Coertze, *Bafokeng Family Law*, 245; and Bennett, *Customary Law*, 256.

74 Kerr, *Customary Law of Immovable Property*, 159.

75 Bennett, *Customary Law*, 364.

76 Pienaar, "Law of Property," 129.

77 Section 7(1) of the Recognition of Customary Marriages Act 120 of 1998 and *Ramuhovhi v President of the Republic of South Africa* 2018 (2) SA 1 (CC).

78 Himonga and Moore, *Reform of Customary Marriage*, 256.

79 Ibid.

80 The variation suggests a diversity in practice across indigenous groups and underscores the need for further study to understand the relevance and categorisations of property today.

not have title deeds and could not be transferred.[81] The exclusion is in accordance with the social reality in Kwelanga where homes are not sold and transferred between individuals.

Homes tend to have a spiritual significance as the family's relatives are buried on the property[82] and are thus unlikely to be sold. The family will not leave its deceased nor would another family wish to live on the property. Rituals on significant occasions like death, marriage or birth must be performed by the family on their property, further negating their ability to sell the property. Furthermore, land remains freely available in the village and individuals prefer to obtain their own plots and build their own homes.

Homes in the village that are excluded from the state administration process devolve in accordance with customary law.[83] The exclusion fortuitously addresses Ngcobo J's criticism in *Bhe v Magistrate, Khayelitsha* regarding the inappropriateness of the application of the Intestate Succession Act to small estates. Ngcobo J stated that in some instances, the application of the Intestate Succession Act may result in the family home being sold and the proceeds distributed among the heirs.[84] The distribution of the home may leave family members without a home or livelihood.[85] The exclusion of the homes from the state administration – albeit due to pragmatic considerations of the houses not having title deeds – and the application of customary law to determine its devolution ameliorates such inequity by keeping the home intact.[86]

Customary law regulates the devolution of homes in Kwelanga and thus is critical to analysing the administration of estates. The analysis of findings from the case study reveals that the principle of male primogeniture does not apply

81 This was the position stated by all state officials and confirmed in the analysis of case files in which homes in the village are not reported as part of the estate. The *Policy and Procedure Manual* does not state that immovable property in the village is excluded but states that a municipal valuation of the property is required where the deceased was the owner of immovable property. This suggests it would be hard to report an estate without a municipal valuation; Meyer and Rudolph, *Policy and Procedure Manual*, 29. For a discussion of the devolution of family property through the state structures, see Bolt and Masha, "Recognising the Family House," 147.

82 Bennett notes that the family's relatives are buried on the property with the belief that the deceased join the ancestors and remain with the family in spirit; Bennett, *Sourcebook*, 381.

83 It is unclear how family property located in an urban area would be dealt with as this was not encountered in the case study.

84 *Bhe v Magistrate, Khayelitsha; Shibi v Sithole* 2005 (1) SA 580 (CC), para. 232.

85 Ibid.

86 The inequity may persist with family property situated in an urban area. For a discussion of the devolution of family houses in an urban context, see Bolt and Masha, "Recognising the Family House".

as a rigid rule; that is, the eldest son does not automatically assume control of the home in the village. The home is generally assumed by the widow and administered in the best interests of the family. The composition of the family may differ from just the widow and children to include extended family members like a grandparent or grandchild. Where there is no widow, or she requires assistance in the home, a son or daughter is selected by the family to administer the property in the interests of the family. The selection of the heir is based on who is in the best position to care for the family rather than with reference to a fixed customary law rule. The selected heir would have frequently shouldered responsibility for the family prior to the death of the parent.

These findings accord with Kingwill's earlier findings that it is a "responsible person" who assumes the management of the property.[87] The person, selected by consent, manages the property on behalf of the family and cannot exclude family members from the property.[88] A younger or female family member may be selected to ensure the well-being of the family.[89] Trustworthiness is more important than gender in the determination of who is selected to care for the property.[90] Similarly, I found that daughters were not excluded from managing the property and were often thought to be more responsible than boys. One participant in a focus group with females explained:

> Yes, because the boys they don't [care for the house]. Even on the day of the funeral, even for preparations [for] the funeral. That is the girls who will prepare. Even for preparation before the funeral, it's the girl who will go to town, do the groceries and all that.[91]

The family group orientation of the law is clear in the devolution of the property, which occurs in the best interests of the family rather than according to a fixed rule. In this regard customary law demonstrates its characteristic flexibility to respond to the specific needs of the family. The responsibility for the home depends on the family dynamics and while the eldest son is frequently selected as the heir, it may be another sibling, including a daughter, who is selected. The danger, of course, is that the heir assumes control of the property and fails to discharge his or her duties towards the family. Vesting control of the property in one person poses a risk to the security of the family as individuals

87 Kingwill, "Lost in Translation," 225.
88 Ibid.
89 Kingwill, "Lost in Translation," 226.
90 Kingwill, "[En]gendering the Norms of Customary Inheritance," 227.
91 Focus group with females under 40 years of age, 17 October 2016.

have acted in the past, as in the *Bhe* case, to secure their own interests rather than those of the family.

In summation, the family group orientation of customary law is evident in the devolution of homes in Kwelanga. While these devolutions are not countenanced by state law and operate effectively outside the purview of the state, they play a significant role in maintaining the family and group interests. Homes, and in some instances even livestock, function as family property to serve the broader interests of the family and not an individual heir.

4.2.2 An Heir's Responsibility towards Family Members

As discussed previously, the Reform Act appears to do away with the customary successor's responsibility to care for family members. However, in practice the matter is more nuanced and the group and family orientation of the law continues to manifest itself in subtle forms. My findings in Kwelanga suggest that the heir may or may not take responsibility for the family depending on the nature of the family relationships. In Kwelanga the death of a family head generally leaves behind the widow and her children. There was unanimous agreement among participants that "It's the wife and children who will benefit only."[92] Where the children are young, the widow assumes control of the estate and uses it to care for her children in accordance with a typical parent-child relationship.[93] One woman aptly stated "You [the widow] raise up your children using that money."[94] The widow may go beyond this and share benefits with the deceased's other children or dependent family members, such as parents or siblings. This depends on the family dynamics, particularly the widow's relationship with the deceased's children and family members. Where the deceased supported the children, the widow is more likely to share benefits with them than when the existence is only discovered upon the deceased's death.

Where a child assumes control of the property, there is an expectation amongst individuals in Kwelanga that the child will care for the family. One participant explained that he would leave his sizeable livestock operation to his eldest son "because I can see he's the one who can actually help the members of the family".[95] Himonga and Moore similarly found the inheritance of property to encompass an obligation to use the property on behalf of the family.[96] The obligation may entail consultation with family members

92 Interview with female participant, 2 September 2015.

93 Also noted by Himonga and Moore, *Reform of Customary Marriage*, 265.

94 Interview with female participant, 2 September 2015.

95 Interview with male participant, 10 September 2015.

96 Himonga and Moore, *Reform of Customary Marriage*, 254.

in decision-making, performing marriage rituals with the property, selling livestock when there is a financial need in the family and allowing access to the family home.[97] It extends to a broad category of people as family is defined widely to include grandparents, grandchildren, siblings, nieces and nephews.

In addition, verbal dispositions of property are frequently used and encouraged in the village to prevent the maladministration of the property alluded to above and protect the family interests. The value of these disposals may range from a few livestock to the deceased's entire farming operation and thus may be of really significant value. The family head allots property to the person considered most able to administer it in the best interests of the family. This preventative action is meant to safeguard against property grabbing and the heir shirking his responsibilities towards the family. As one male interviewee explained in an individual interview, he would leave most of his estate, including a sizeable farming operation, to his eldest son, whom he trusted to administer the property and care for the family:

> According to our custom, only one person is the heir, but in our days we have to distribute the property. As a parent you have to do that while you are still alive, just like me. I have a first born, a son, he's the one now who's helping me with all what I'm doing here and the other one, I will actually share with them, but everything or most of the things that I have, it's my first born who will benefit and then I will only share with the other children. I'm solely doing that because he's always by my side, he's supporting me, he's helping me, hence I've decided to actually take that route. It helps a lot too – the other children if they have problems, the other children, they will come to my son and actually say to them, here's the problem, 'I need a sheep, I need a cattle, can you sell one cattle for me? I need to do certain things.'[98]

The interviewee chose the first born as he was confident that the son would assist family members, including members of the extended family, as the son had done in the past. Furthermore, the dispositions are meant to ameliorate inheritance disputes and guard against property grabbing. A family meeting consisting of the spouse and children is usually convened and the allotment of property discussed. The discussion regarding the allotment of property is meant to ensure the acceptance and enforcement of the dispositions by the

97 Himonga and Moore, *Reform of Customary Marriage*, 254–55.
98 Interview with male participant, 10 September 2015.

family. These disposals are generally respected and given effect to upon the individual's death.

In summation, succession to status with a responsibility to care for the family was the central tenet of customary law succession. In a South African context, in which state resources are strained to provide adequate welfare benefits to vulnerable parties,[99] the law served an important social function. Today, the manner in which an heir may care for family members depends on the family dynamics – the new legal framework does not enforce these obligations. Where the obligations are fulfilled, they play an invaluable role in supporting vulnerable parties and ensuring the well-being of the family and community at large.

4.2.3 Financial and Emotional Support

The family group nature of customary law succession is pervasive in the funeral process itself. Upon the death of an individual, the extended family and community are informed and provide invaluable emotional and practical support to the deceased's close family.[100] The burial site is arranged, rituals performed and food prepared by the family and community members. Men typically gather wood and prepare the grave, while women prepare food. A family meeting is convened which typically consists of the widow, the deceased's parents, and other close relatives. The purpose of the meeting is to decide the details of the funeral, such as the day of the funeral, how many cattle will be slaughtered and other logistical arrangements. The meetings are often dominated by elder males in the family, and younger family members though present will frequently not speak. The widow speaks and is commonly positioned as the key decision-maker in these meetings. The widow is typically the only person with knowledge regarding the deceased's financial affairs and generally dictates how the funeral should be conducted. The widow voices her needs and looks to the family for financial support especially where she lacks the funds to conduct the funeral. Moreover, the family provides emotional support to the newly bereaved widow and children upon the death of the family head. With

99 The Old Persons Grant is set at R2 080 per month and R2 100 for those older than 75; see Western Cape Government, "Old Age Pension". The child support grant is set at R500 per month; see Sassa, "Child Support Grant Amount".

100 The findings are consistent with the understanding that communities have an "ethic of mutual obligation and alliance" and that families may be embroiled in an exchange relationship with neighbours in the sharing of labour, food, the undertaking of celebrations and rituals and ensuring the security of the community, see Cross, "Alternate Legality," 316.

the increasing costs of funerals, the family and community are an important source of emotional and financial support for the widow.

The participants agreed unanimously that funerals have developed into elaborate and expensive proceedings. Whereas historically funerals were a quick process with the burial occurring within a day or two, the process may now take several weeks and cost anywhere up to R100 000.[101] During this time the extended family must be fed, which entails the purchase of additional groceries and the slaughter of sheep or cattle. The increase in funeral costs is largely due to societal pressure. This was best expressed by one participant in the focus group who stated: "It's difficult. You need to buy scones, you need to buy juices. On that day you need to buy groceries, you need to prepare tea. In some instances, you'll find out that now the wedding, the funeral now, it's more like a wedding. The expense is too much."[102] Societal pressure to conduct a "proper" funeral often results in large and expensive funerals. The hosting of a large funeral seems to indicate the success or well-being of the family and individuals feel pressurised into this expenditure.

The escalating costs have strengthened communal ties, as the community assists with the expenses. While some individuals interviewed had private funeral policies, almost all were members of the village's burial scheme, demonstrating the inter-dependency of the members of that community.[103] Individuals contribute to the scheme every month, and on the death of an individual the scheme provides the family with groceries and sheep to be slaughtered for the funeral or a monetary amount to cover the funeral costs. Where an individual was not a member of the scheme or there are insufficient funds to cover the funeral costs, family members and neighbours may assist by bringing groceries, food, or an animal to slaughter for the funeral. As one male interviewee explained: "Yes, a family meeting was called and then we have to contribute some money in preparing for the burial. We had to pay the mortuary fee, we bought the coffin, we bought some groceries for the funeral, we bought some sheep then we conducted the funeral – that was it."[104]

---

101 Interviews and focus groups with participants confirmed the costly nature of funerals.

102 Focus group with females under 40 years of age, 17 October 2016.

103 The dependency on neighbours echoed Hammond-Tooke's earlier research on the important role of neighbours in the old Transkei area, in which Kwelanga is located. Hammond-Tooke noted how people depended upon their neighbours in times of emergency, sickness, death, birth and in everyday life. See Hammond-Tooke, *Command or Consensus,* 113.

104 Interview with male participant, 10 September 2015.

4.2.4 Dispute Resolution

The family is the primary body for the resolution of succession and inheritance disputes.[105] While the village is presided over by a resident chief or headman or tribal council and king, succession disputes are rarely taken to the chief or headman, whose involvement is noted in limited instances only.

The family generally refers to the elder males in the husband's family, but some noted that the mother would be involved in resolving the dispute. The family discusses the matter and recommends a solution to restore peace in the family. Generally individuals, both male and female, were confident that the family could resolve the dispute in a fair manner. In an illustration of strong legal pluralism and the semi-autonomous social field, the recommendation is usually followed, reflecting the authority and coercive power vested in the family. The family does not implement beatings or such other punitive measures. Its source of power instead appears to be twofold. First, customary law and its institutions regulate people's lives. It exerts a normative force on people's lives and the family is viewed as a speedy and accessible dispute resolution forum. Secondly, there is the threat of ostracisation from the family. In a community where individuals depend on one another for employment, transport, to act as witnesses to weddings or to provide assistance with a funeral, the threat of ostracisation is real and sufficient to ensure compliance. A participant in a male focus group explained:

> It is important for people to listen to the family because everything … even before we take it to [the courts] we apply the law. Everything must be discussed in the family first. We don't take things to the law. If you have a problem, the family members are the ones who will come and assist or help you. If you don't listen to the family members, if you have any problems … what will happen is that if anything that has happened to your stock, they will say okay it's fine, you take care of it yourself. We will not help you because you did not want to listen to us. For instance, if there are some issues, we won't just go to court to report the case. They will tell you, that you know, this thing we could have resolved it in your family. You don't have to come and discuss these things here.[106]

105 Himonga and Moore also found that very few succession matters are taken to court and that the family remains the most popular forum for dispute resolution; Himonga and Moore, *Reform of Customary Marriage*, 278.

106 Focus group with males under 40 years of age, 18 October 2016.

Solutions ensure the coherence and well-being of the family rather than the realisation of individual rights. The risk, of course is that in a patriarchal society the solutions favour men at the expense of vulnerable parties like women and children. However, there was no indication from the case study that women feared being treated unfairly. Given that women are most likely to have their property rights threatened and to use the dispute resolution forum,[107] its continued popularity speaks to its effectiveness. Family mediation is also more likely to be sensitive to the family needs and congruent with the underlying values of succession.

Where the family cannot resolve the dispute, it is escalated to the police or magistrate's court. However, Burman, Carmody, and Hoffman-Wanderer in their research note that there is a pervasive perception that matters should be resolved within the family and community and the escalation of matters to courts is viewed as an embarrassment to the family.[108]

5 Implications for Legal Pluralism

The state regulation of the customary law succession – both in the pre- and post-constitutional era – evinces weak legal pluralism. Thus, while the customary law of succession was recognised historically, the state regulated the law in accordance with its political agenda of racial segregation and control of the population. Today the Constitution recognises customary law as a valid system of law equal to that of common law,[109] but regulates it to ensure constitutional compliance. In the context of the customary law of succession, regulation through the adoption of the common law Intestate Succession Act to regulate

107 First, state officials stated that it is predominantly women who report estates. Secondly, men do not experience difficulties in succession and inheritance matters.

108 Burman, Carmody, and Hoffman-Wanderer, "Protecting the Vulnerable," 141.

109 Customary law is arguably implicitly recognised in the individual and group right to culture; see sections 30 and 31 of the Constitution which provide that the rights may not be exercised in a manner inconsistent with the Bill of Rights: Bennett, *Customary Law*, 88. Sections 39(2) and (3) recognise customary law alongside the common law in the development and recognition of rights in the law. Section 181(1)(*c*) provides for the establishment of a Commission for the Promotion and Protection of the Rights of Cultural, Religious and Linguistic Communities, section 211(1) recognises the institution of traditional leadership and section 211(2) provides for the functioning of traditional authorities. Also see *Alexkor Ltd v the Richtersveld Community* 2004 (5) SA 460 (CC) para. 51. For a discussion of the constitutional recognition of customary law, see Himonga and Bosch, "Application of African Customary Law," 312–14; Rautenbach, "Mixing South African Common Law," 222; and Rautenbach, "Some Comments," 107.

the devolution of customary law estates has moved South Africa into an almost unitary system of succession – though not quite all the way there, as minor accommodations were made for customary law practices in the Reform Act.[110]

Nonetheless, it is apparent that individuals exhibit greater agency in the administration of an estate than contemplated by the state. For example, the use of verbal dispositions of property – not countenanced by the state – illustrates how individuals navigate the legal framework to achieve their interests. The legal requirement that testamentary dispositions be in writing is rejected, as individuals continue to use oral dispositions and display much stronger ideals of legal pluralism to regulate their lives.[111] Most interviewees in Kwelanga were unaware of the legal ineffectiveness of the verbal dispositions frequently used to dispose of property. But even when informed of it, they maintained that they could effectively dispose of their property in such a manner. In a clear illustration of strong legal pluralism, individuals do not depend on the state for recognition, nor does non-recognition deter their behaviour. They induce compliance with these dispositions without state sanction.

Of course, that is not to say that the law is never determinative and, in many cases, women assert the law to bolster their claims to property. Many female participants asserted that state recognition of them as heirs meant that their rights could not be challenged. Female participants in focus groups explained:

> If we have that letter which says A, B, C, D it belongs to you, there's nothing they [brothers of the deceased] can do. Especially when those brothers, they don't appear on that letter, [they claim] they also have a share of something. Then there's nothing they can do.[112]
>
> The brother can't do that [take her property] because everything that is on that paper it belongs to me, no one can say anything I will just show them that paper.[113]

The women appeared to be referring to the letter of authority issued in terms of section 18 of the Administration of Estates Act, as most estates I encountered

110 The Reform Act also seems to suggest that the Act creates a separate system of succession by providing that the Act applies to a person, who amongst others, is subject to customary law; s. 2 of the Reform Act.

111 Bolt and Masha similarly found the pervasiveness of verbal dispositions in inheritance practices. Individuals see no difference between written dispositions and verbal dispositions explained to kin and were unconcerned with issues of evidentiary proof or the legal weight thereof; see Bolt and Masha, "Recognising the Family House".

112 Focus group with women under 40 years of age, 17 October 2016.

113 Focus group with women under 40 years of age, 18 October 2016.

in the interviews and Master's Office were smaller than R250 000 and fell within the scope of this section. The women claimed that with the state recognition of their status as the surviving spouses, their entitlements to the property could not be challenged. It speaks to how individuals strategically navigate the normative frameworks and will leverage and invoke state law and its institutions to achieve the best possible outcome for themselves.

This nuanced understanding of how individuals view the legal system is essential for the effective regulation of the customary law of succession and the safeguarding of rights. The state should be cognisant that while it may regulate the customary law of succession through legislation and the prism of weak legal pluralism, customary law and people's use thereof is robust. Thus, simply prohibiting a practice or the non-recognition thereof is unlikely to be successful. People demonstrate agency to resist state interventions or may adapt to state laws to further their interests. Thus, state law should not be positioned as "bad" and to be resisted for its intrusions into the customary law sphere. Rather, state law may play a vital role in the realisation of rights as individuals readily embrace and invoke the law to bolster their claims. Understanding the law's important – but not guaranteed – role in the realisation and protection of rights makes for better law-making in pluralistic societies such as South Africa.

6 Conclusion

The customary law of succession was distorted during the colonial and apartheid periods in South Africa. The focus shifted to the inheritance of property with a dilution of the heir's responsibilities. Socio-economic changes at the time also drove change as urbanisation, migration, and the emergence of new forms of property resulted in a more individualised system of succession. Today the Reform Act as read with the Intestate Succession Act regulates the devolution of customary law intestate estates. It substitutes customary law with the common law and emphasises the distribution of assets and the winding up of the estate. Furthermore, there is a blurring of the various forms of property, and individualised notions of ownership are increasingly gaining traction. The positive law seems, at first glance, to have extinguished the group nature of customary law.

Nonetheless, the group nature of customary law manifests itself clearly in the devolution of homes in Kwelanga – excluded from the state administration process. Heirs (generally widows) assume responsibility for the well-being of the family. Moreover, individuals also continue to use verbal dispositions of property to secure the well-being of the family. The family head may select an heir or share property with non-heirs to circumvent disputes regarding the property and fortify the well-being of family members. Furthermore, the family and community at large, provide critical financial and emotional support to the bereaved family during the funeral process. Funerals have evolved into elaborate and protracted proceedings and the family and the larger community assist with the burial, and contribute funds as may be necessary. Finally, the family remains the first port of call for the resolution of succession disputes and offers solutions for the well-being of the family rather than the realisation of individual rights.

Thus, while the state has purported to control the application of customary law through the Reform Act, individuals navigate the legal framework(s) – both customary law and state law – in their own best interests. Individuals may assert state law to bolster their claims to property and simultaneously reject the idea that state law can regulate their lives. In accordance with notions of deep legal pluralism, state law may be asserted, refuted or adapted.

Bibliography

Literature

Abrie, W, et al. *Deceased Estates*. 10 ed. Durban: LexisNexis, 2015.

Badejogbin, Rebecca E. "Interplay of Customary Law of Testacy and Statutory Regulation of Intestacy with Respect to the Transfer of Customary Law Rights in Land in South Africa." *SADC Law Journal* 4 (2014/15): 10–25.

Bekker, Jan C. *Seymour's Customary Law in Southern Africa.* 5 ed. Cape Town: Juta, 1989.

Bekker, Jan C., and Digby Sqhelo Koyana. "The Judicial and Legislative Reform of the Customary Law of Succession." *De Jure* 45, no. 3 (2012): 568–84.

Bekker, Jan C., and Pieter Daniël de Kock. "Adaptation of the Customary Law of Succession to Changing Needs." *Comparative and International Law Journal of Southern Africa* 25, no. 3 (November 1992): 366–78.

Bennett, Thomas William. *A Sourcebook for African Customary Law for Southern Africa.* Cape Town: Juta, 1991.

Bennett, Thomas William. *Customary Law in South Africa.* Cape Town: Juta, 2004.

Bolt, Maxim, and Tshenolo Masha. "Recognising the Family House: A Problem of Urban Custom in South Africa." *South African Journal on Human Rights* 35, no. 2 (2019): 147–68.

Brown, Barbara B. "The Impact of Male Labour Migration on Women in Botswana." *African Affairs* 82, no. 328 (July 1983): 367–88.

Burman, Sandra, Louise Carmody, and Yonina Hoffman-Wanderer. "Protecting the Vulnerable from 'Property Grabbing': The Reality of Administering Small Estates." *South African Law Journal* 125 (2008): 134–56.

Church, Jacqueline, and Joan Church. "The Constitutional Imperative and Harmonisation in a Multicultural Society: A South African Perspective on the Development of Indigenous Law." *Fundamina: A Journal of Legal History* 14, no. 2 (2008): 1–13.

Church, Joan. "The Place of Indigenous Law in a Mixed Legal System and a Society in Transformation: A South African Experience." *Australia and New Zealand Law and History E-journal* (2005): 94–106.

Coertze, Roelof Dewald. *Bafokeng Family Law and Law of Succession.* Pretoria: SABRA, 1990.

Comaroff, John L. "Rules and Rulers: Political Processes in a Tswana Chiefdom." *Man* 13, no. 1 (1978): 1–20.

Cousins, Ben. "Characterising 'Communal' Tenure: Nested Systems and Flexible Boundaries." In *Land, Power and Custom: Controversies Generated by South Africa's Communal Land Rights Act*, edited by Anika Claassens, and Ben Cousins, 109–37. Cape Town: UCT Press, 2008.

Cross, Catherine. "An Alternate Legality: The Property Rights Question in Relation to South African Land Reform." *South African Journal on Human Rights* 8, no. 3 (1992): 305–31.

De Waal, Marius Johannes, and Linda (M. C.) Schoeman-Malan. *Law of Succession.* 5 ed. Cape Town: Juta, 2016.

Hammond-Tooke, William David. *Command or Consensus: The Development of Transkeian Local Government.* Cape Town: D. Philip, 1975.

Himonga, Chuma N. "Taking Stock of Changes to Customary Law in a New South Africa." In *Essays in Honour of AJ Kerr*, edited by Graham Glover, 215–35, Durban: LexisNexis, 2006.

Himonga, Chuma N. "The Advancement of African Women's Rights in the First Decade of Democracy in South Africa: The Reform of the Customary Law of Marriage and Succession." *Acta Juridica* (2005): 82–107.

Himonga, Chuma N., and Craig Bosch. "The Application of African Customary Law under the Constitution of South Africa: Problems Solved or Just Beginning?" *South African Law Journal* 117, no. 2 (2000): 306–41.

Himonga, Chuma N., and Elena Moore. *Reform of Customary Marriage, Divorce and Succession in South Africa.* Cape Town: Juta, 2015.

Himonga, Chuma N., and Ronald Thandabanthu Nhlapo, eds. *African Customary Law in South Africa: Post-Apartheid and Living Law Perspectives.* Cape Town: Oxford University Press, 2014.

Hunter, Monica. *Reaction to Conquest: Effects of Contact with Europeans on the Pondo of South Africa.* 2 ed. London: Oxford University Press, 1961.

Jamneck, Juanita, et al. *The Law of Succession in South Africa.* 2 ed. Cape Town: Oxford University Press, 2012.

Kerr, Alastair James. *The Customary Law of Immovable Property and of Succession.* Grahamstown: Rhodes University, 1976.

Kingwill, Rosalie. "[En]gendering the Norms of Customary Inheritance in Botswana and South Africa." *The Journal of Legal Pluralism and Unofficial Law* 48, no. 2 (2016): 208–37.

Kingwill, Rosalie. "In the Shadows of the Cadastre: Family Law and Custom in Rabula and Fingo Village." In *In the Shadow of Policy: Everyday Practices in South Africa's Land and Agrarian Reform*, edited by Paul Hebinck, and Ben Cousins, 159–72. Johannesburg: Wits University Press, 2013.

Kingwill, Rosalie. "Lost in Translation: Family Title in Fingo Village, Grahamstown, Eastern Cape." *Acta Juridica* (2011): 198–226.

Mamashela, Mothokoa. "New Families, New Property, New Laws: The Practical Effects of the Recognition of Customary Marriages Act." *South African Journal on Human Rights* 20, no. 4 (2004): 616–41.

Mbatha, Likhapha. "Reforming the Customary Law of Succession." *South African Journal on Human Rights* 18 (2002): 259–86.

Meyer, Margaret M., and M. B. E. Rudolph. *Policy and Procedure Manual: Administration of Intestate Deceased Estates at Service Points.* Pretoria: Justice College, 2016.

Moore, Sally Falk. "Law and Social Change: The Semi-Autonomous Social Field as an Appropriate Subject of Study." *Law & Society Review* 7, no. 4 (Summer 1973): 719–46.

Murray, Colin. "Migrant Labour and Changing Family Structure in the Rural Periphery of Southern Africa." *Journal of Southern African Studies* 6, no. 2 (1980): 139–56.

Okoth-Ogendo, Hastings Wilfred Opinya. "The Nature of Land Rights under Indigenous Law in Africa." In *Land, Power and Custom: Controversies Generated by South Africa's Communal Land Rights Act*, edited by Anika Claassens, and Ben Cousins, 95–108. Cape Town: UCT Press, 2008.

Olivier, Nicolaas Johannes Jacobus, Jan C. Bekker, Nicolaas J.J. Olivier (Jnr) and Willem H. Olivier. *Indigenous Law.* Durban: Butterworths, 1995.

Osman, Fatima. "The Administration of Customary Law Estates Post the Enactment of the Reform of Customary Law of Succession Act: A Case Study from Rural Eastern Cape, South Africa." PhD diss., University of Cape Town, 2019.

Pienaar, J. "Law of Property." In *Introduction to Legal Pluralism.* 6 ed, edited by Christa Rautenbach, 123–153. Durban: LexisNexis, 2021.

Rautenbach, Christa. "Mixing South African Common Law and Customary Law of Intestate Succession: 'Potjiekos' in the Making." In JCL *Studies in Comparative*

Law: Mixed Legal Systems at New Frontiers, edited by Örücü, Esin, 222–40. London: Wildy, Simmonds and Hill, 2010.

Rautenbach, Christa. "Some Comments on the Status of Customary Law in Relation to the Bill of Rights." *Stellenbosch Law Review* 14 (2003): 107–14.

Rautenbach, Christa. "South African Common and Customary Law on Intestate Succession: A Question of Harmonisation, Integration or Abolition." *Journal of Comparative Law* 3, no. 1 (2008): 119–132.

Rautenbach, Christa. "The Legal Position of South African Women under the Law of Succession." PhD thesis, Potchefstroomse Universiteit vir Christelike Hoër Onderwys, 2001.

Rautenbach, Christa, and Fatima Osman. "Law of Succession and Inheritance." In *Introduction to Legal Pluralism*. 6 ed, edited by Christa Rautenbach, 191–218. Durban: LexisNexis, 2021.

Sassa, "Child Support Grant Amount to Increase with Effect from 1 April 2017." Accessed December 1, 2018. http://www.sassa.gov.za/index.php/newsroom/239-social-grants-amounts-increase-from-april-2017.

Schapera, Isaac. *A Handbook of Tswana Law and Custom.* 2 ed. London: Oxford University Press, 1955.

Seidman, Gay. "Is South Africa Different? Sociological Comparisons and Theoretical Contributions from the Land of Apartheid." *Annual Review of Sociology* 25 (August 1999): 419–40.

South African Law Commission. *Discussion Paper 93 (Project 90): Customary Law of Succession.* Pretoria: SALC, 2000.

South African Law Commission. Discussion *Paper 95 (Project 90): Customary Law: Administration of Estates.* Pretoria: SALC, 2000.

South African Law Reform Commission. *Report (Project 90): Report on the Customary Law of Succession.* Pretoria: SALRC, 2004.

Weeks, Sindiso Mnisi. "Customary Succession and the Development of Customary Law: The Bhe Legacy: Part III: Reflections on Themes in Justice Langa's Judgments." *Acta Juridica* (2015): 215–55.

Western Cape Government. "Old Age Pension (Old Persons Grant)." Accessed December 30, 2018. https://www.westerncape.gov.za/service/old-age-pension-old-persons-grant.

Case law

Alexkor Ltd v the Richtersveld Community 2004 (5) SA 460 (CC).

Bhe v Magistrate, Khayelitsha 2005 (1) SA 580 (CC).

Moseneke v The Master 2001 (2) SA 18 (CC).

Mthembu v Letsela 2000 (3) SA 867 (SCA).

Ramuhovhi v President of the Republic of South Africa 2018 (2) SA 1 (CC).

Zondi v President of the Republic of South Africa 2000 (2) SA 49 (N).

Legislation and Government Publications.

Administration of Estates Act 66 of 1965.

Black Administration Act 38 of 1927.

Constitution of the Republic of South Africa, 1996.

Intestate Succession Act 81 of 1987.

Recognition of Customary Marriages Act 120 of 1998.

Reform of Customary Law of Succession and Regulation of Related Matters Act 11 of 2009.

PART 2

Marriage in African Legal Pluralism

CHAPTER 4

Balancing Customary Practices and Human Rights in the Proposed Single Marriage Bill

Rita Ozoemena, George Fordam Otieno Wara and Khupi Ramarumo

Abstract

This chapter analyses two proposed legislative options by the South African Law Reform Commission (SALRC) for a Single Marriage Bill to determine whether the legislative options will strike the correct balance between South Africa's international human rights obligations and the customary practices of South African communities. The SALRC has proposed a single marriage Bill either unifying a set of requirements and consequences applying to all marriages (the Protected Relationships Bill) or containing different chapters to reflect the current diverse set of legal requirements for civil marriages, civil unions, customary marriages and other marriages that are not accommodated by current legislation (the Recognition and Registration of Marriages and Life Partnerships Bill). Both proposed legislative options seek to ensure the rights to equality, dignity and non-discrimination for everyone as stated in the Bill of Rights and reiterated in the Preambles of both proposals. At the same time, the two proposed legislative options continue to rely on customary practices or culture to define subsisting monogamous or polygynous marriage relationships recognised under the Recognition of Customary Marriages Act 120 of 1998 (RCMA). The SALRC's goals of promoting rights in the Bill of Rights and rights to culture in the proposed Single Marriage Bill are complicated by the incompatibilities between the Bill of Rights and African customary practices, as will be highlighted by court cases invalidating or developing African customary law. The incompatibilities are rooted in South Africa's history and context because the Bill of Rights was inspired by written international human rights instruments and "Western" cultural values while African customary practices were originally unwritten, based on social practices and tested by social observations. In addition, the dominant voices that shaped the "official" version of African customary law at the time of drafting the Bill of Rights were members of the ruling racial minority intent on protecting the accumulated inequality of generations of suppression, domination and apartheid. In this chapter, we rely on systems theory (as the sum of interactive and interdependent component parts) to model the African communities as systems, and social dominance theory (the tendency of human societies to structure themselves as systems of group-based social hierarchies) to examine the clash

 | DOI:10.1163/9789004696747_005

between "Western" values and African customary practices. We also rely on social dominance theory to interrogate the proposed Single Marriage Bill's attempt to create harmony between an alienating international human rights discourse, dynamic community systems and a failed integration effort through the RCMA.

1 Introduction*

This chapter probes the challenges that multicultural societies face in the local application of international human rights norms. We examine whether South Africa's proposed Single Marriage Bill will strike the right balance between the customary marriage practices of South Africa's communities and South Africa's commitment to international human rights. South Africa's Bill of Rights was guided by the Canadian Charter of Rights and Freedoms and also influenced by international human rights law. In terms of international law, for example, Article 1 of the Universal Declaration of Human Rights (UDHR) provides that all human beings are born free and equal in dignity and rights.[1] Similarly, sections 9(1) and 10 of the Constitution of the Republic of South Africa, 1996, provide for the rights to equality and dignity, respectively.[2] The efforts to create a Single Marriage Bill, as described in the Department of Home Affairs' Green Paper on Marriages in South Africa[3] dated 20 April 2021 (hereafter the Green Paper) and the South African Law Reform Commission's Discussion Paper 152 (hereafter Discussion Paper 152),[4] are an attempt to create harmony between an alienating international human rights discourse, dynamic community systems and a failed integration effort through the Recognition of Customary Marriages Act 120 of 1998 (RCMA).

South Africa's marriage laws are in a state of disharmony because South Africa has a hybrid or mixed legal system underpinned by the Roman-Dutch and English common law systems, customary law, case law and legislation governing marriages. The Green Paper acknowledges that the legislation regulating

* The authors are indebted to anonymous reviewers for their insightful comments on the earlier drafts of this chapter.

1 Universal Declaration of Human Rights (1948) (UDHR), Art. 1.

2 Constitution of the Republic of South Africa, 1996 (hereafter the Constitution), ss. 9(1) and 10.

3 See Green Paper on Marriages in South Africa, Public Consultation Version, 20 April 2021 (GN 412 in GG 44557 of 11 May 2021) (hereafter the Green Paper). A Green Paper is a government policy discussion paper that articulates possible solutions that are yet to be adopted by government. The Green Paper is a precursor for a White Paper which articulates a policy position of government that has been approved by Cabinet.

4 SALRC, *Discussion Paper 152*.

marriages in South Africa – the Marriage Act 25 of 1961, the Recognition of Customary Marriages Act 120 of 1998, the partly repealed Black Administration Act 38 of 1927 and the Civil Union Act 17 of 2006 – are a combination of legacy legislation (from the colonial and apartheid eras) and new law that was introduced post-1994 to redress historical injustices. The Green Paper is meant to create a policy framework eventually leading to a statutory framework that will harmonise all the various marriage regimes in South Africa. The Green Paper itself describes this harmonisation exercise as "the beginning of a crucial public discourse that will re-define the concept of marriage in South Africa"[5] and acknowledges the complexity of this process by stating that "the process will unearth issues that may make some of us uncomfortable but will encourage dialogue within the South African and international communities".[6] Discussion Paper 152 contains the texts of the two proposed legislative options; the Protected Relationships Bill and the Recognition and Registration of Marriages and Life Partnerships Bill.[7] The Protected Relationships Bill proposes the enactment of a single Marriage Act that unifies a set of requirements and consequences applying to all marriages. The Recognition and Registration of Marriages and Life Partnerships Bill proposes omnibus legislation in the form of a single Act that contains different chapters to reflect the current diverse set of legal requirements for civil marriages, civil unions, customary marriages and other marriages that are not accommodated by the legislation.

In coming up with the proposed legislative options, the SALRC relies on international norms and standards as contained in international legal instruments, international courts, and resolutions, statements, and reports of the United Nations and other regional and international bodies that collectively constitute international human rights discourse. Under section 39(1)(b) and (c) of the Constitution of the Republic of South Africa, 1996, a court, tribunal or forum must consider international law and may consider foreign law when interpreting the Bill of Rights.[8] The Preambles of both legislative options proposed by the SALRC begin by reciting the Bill of Rights. In addition, both of them note South Africa's international obligations to take appropriate and reasonable measures to eradicate discrimination against women in relationships and to take appropriate and reasonable measures to prevent child marriages. The two legislative options, therefore, rely on international human rights instruments as enshrined in the Bill of Rights to rationalise and harmonise

5 See Green Paper, Preface.
6 See Green Paper, Preface.
7 See SALRC, *Discussion Paper 152*.
8 The Constitution, s. 39(1)(b) and (c).

the marriage laws and practices of South African communities. Unfortunately, international human rights discourse is too general, too universalistic, and too disconnected from local cultural realities to provide a comprehensive repertoire of values necessary for integrating and harmonising customary marriage practices in South Africa.

International human rights discourse is limited because it perceives a community's cultural values as an integrated and static repertoire of ideas, beliefs, meanings and values held by a discrete, clearly bounded and internally homogenous social grouping.[9] In *Mayelane v Ngwenyama*, the Constitutional Court articulated a different view of cultural values and customs as forming part of "living customary law", which it further defined as "a system of law that is practised in the community, has its own values and norms, is practised from generation to generation and evolves and develops to meet the changing needs of the community".[10] In this chapter, we view the customary marriage practices of South African communities as historical, fluid, dynamic and contested processes of interaction within the communities and with other communities.[11] In a collection of essays entitled *The Invention of Tradition* edited by Eric Hobsbawm and Terrence Ranger in 1983, custom is viewed as not being static but often changing, contested and even sometimes invented.[12]

For centuries before colonial rule, South African communities maintained their customary practices, laws and systems of governance. Central to these community systems was the concept of family and community, where all the members of a particular family and the community at large have defined roles and responsibilities and collectively practice "Ubuntu" or "humanity toward others".[13] When young boys and girls come of age, they are initiated into adulthood and take up roles and responsibilities as adult members of their families and communities. One of those roles and responsibilities is marriage, the primary means for the continuity and survival of the community as a whole.[14] In his article, "Integration of the Bride as a Requirement for a Valid

9 See Universal Declaration on Cultural Diversity (2001) (reaffirming that "culture should be regarded as the set of distinctive spiritual, material, intellectual and emotional features of society or a social group, and that it encompasses, in addition to art and literature, lifestyles, ways of living together, value systems, traditions and beliefs").

10 *Mayelane v Ngwenyama* 2013 (4) SA 415 (CC) (hereafter *Mayelane v Ngwenyama*), para. 44, et seq. (citing *Alexkor Ltd v Richtersveld Community* 2004 (5) SA 460 (CC), para. 51).

11 See Merry, "Changing Rights," 41.

12 Hobsbawm, "Introduction," 2–3.

13 Mahao, "O se re ho Morwa 'Morwa Towe!'," 317–36.

14 See Green Paper on Families: Promoting Family Life and Strengthening Families in South Africa (Gen N 756 in GG 34657 of 3 October 2011), 23 (hereafter Green Paper on

Customary Marriage: *Mkabe v Minister of Home Affairs* [2016] ZAGPPHC 460", Bakker quotes Matlapeng AJ's comments in *Motsoatsoa v Roro* that a customary marriage in true African tradition is not about the bride and the groom but involves the two families.[15] Marriage was therefore a family and a community affair rather than an individual's event. As will be explained using systems theory,[16] marriage practices define the identity of communities and the erosion of these marriage practices through colonial and neo-colonial legislation impacts on the dignity, the complexity and the consciousness of members of these communities. Transformative legislation should provide for continuously changing customary practices that enable communities to better interact with their changing environments and to persist and thrive as communities. The new marriage legislation should, therefore, recognise this dynamism of communities and allow them to practice their customs and traditions or to adopt new marriage practices according to each community system's legal and institutional structures. The proposed Single Marriage Bill continues the failure of the current marriage legislation to integrate unrecognised/ancillary customary marriages and it is this deliberate and systematic erosion of customary practices of communities that undermines African customary practices.

South Africa's RCMA has failed to integrate the customary marriage practices of some South African communities. Some of these unrecognised customary marriages are what Bekker and Buchner-Eveleigh in their article, "The Legal Character of Ancillary Customary Marriages", refer to as "ancillary customary marriages".[17] Examples of these ancillary customary marriages include: (1) a woman marrying another woman to bear children for the *lapa*, house or *kraal*, (2) marriages akin to same-sex marriages (which include true woman-to-woman marriages), (3) the sororate/substitute wife from the bride's family to bear children in place of an infertile or deceased wife, (4) the levirate/a man marrying the widow of his deceased brother and (5) ukungena/where a male relative is given access to the woman in order to father children on behalf of her deceased husband.[18] In addition, customary marriages in some royal families and KhoiSan communities and polygamous marriages with non-citizens

Families) (discussing the importance of marriage for the stability of families and society's wellbeing).

15 Bakker, "Integration of the Bride," 2–3.

16 See Luhmann, *Introduction to Systems Theory*, (containing a collection of Niklas Luhmann's lectures); Jacobson, "Survey of Books," (collectively, "The New Science of Niklas Luhmann").

17 Bekker and Buchner-Eveleigh, "Legal Character," 80–96.

18 Bekker and Buchner-Eveleigh, "Legal Character," 82–92.

still exist in the shadows in South Africa because they are not recognised by the RCMA. Even where customary marriages are recognised by the RCMA, challenges remain as to whether such marriages meet the requirement under section 3(1)(b) of the RCMA that a valid customary marriage "must be negotiated and entered into or celebrated in accordance with customary law".[19] These challenges highlight the failure of the RCMA to recognise the customary marriage practices of all South African communities. Indeed, given the dynamic nature of South African communities, official customary law as it exists in the RCMA may itself be a distortion of the communities' customary laws.[20] These failures of the RCMA are an indication of the challenges that the proposed Single Marriage Bill must address in order to strike the right balance between the Bill of Rights and the customary norms and values of South Africa's pluralist society.

The chapter is divided into three main sections, with the first section being a general discussion of the limitations of international human rights discourse in understanding and transforming South African marriage practices. The second section discusses the existence of customary marriages in South Africa and highlights examples of misconceptions and challenges faced in accepting their legal validity. The third section examines how to strike the right balance between international human rights and South African customary marriage practices by re-conceptualising African customary marriage practices.

2 Limitations of International Human Rights Discourse in Understanding and Transforming South African Marriage Practices

International human rights discourse is limited because it excludes cultural rights of linguistic, religious, and cultural community groups from the outset. The international human rights framework, both in regard to the governing instruments and their implementation, is characterised by a certain blindness about the connection that exists between the possession of human rights and the protection of the cultural rights of community groups. The cornerstone of these founding human rights instruments is the UDHR. The UDHR is a product

19 Recognition of Customary Marriages Act 120 of 1998 (hereafter the RCMA), s. 3(1)(b).

20 See *Bhe v Magistrate, Khayelitsha* 2005 (1) SA 580 (CC), para. 86, where Langa DCJ observes as follows: "What needs to be emphasised is that, because of the dynamic nature of society, official customary law as it exists in the textbooks and in the Act is generally a poor reflection, if not a distortion of the true customary law. True customary law will be that which recognises and acknowledges the changes which continually take place."

of the post-Second World War era. It was adopted by the United Nations General Assembly on 10 December 1948 following a long drafting process that took almost two years. The UDHR has been invoked in international treaties, state constitutions and legislation, and in national and international court and tribunal decisions. All 193 members of the United Nations have signed the United Nations Charter and have thereby underwritten the UDHR. Scholars have argued that the UDHR is now part of customary international law and is binding upon all states.[21]

The UDHR does not expressly provide for the rights of linguistic, religious, and cultural community groups that exist in sub-Saharan Africa. Such rights exist only vaguely in its textual references to the "human family" and the "spirit of brotherhood" in the Preamble and in the individual rights of "everyone" as in Articles 1, 27 and 29.[22] Article 1 of the UDHR states that "[e]veryone is entitled to all the rights and freedoms set forth in this Declaration, without distinction of any kind, such as race, colour, sex, language, religion, political or other opinion, national or social origin, property, birth or other status".[23] Article 27 states that "[e]veryone has the right ... to participate in the cultural life of the community".[24] Article 29 states that "[e]veryone has duties to the community in which alone the free and full development of his personality is possible".[25] These references to "human family", "spirit of brotherhood" and "everyone" may be interpreted to mean individuals within communities and not the community groups themselves.

A second limitation of international human rights discourse that leads to the cultural alienation of African communities is the historical, political and cultural context in which international human rights instruments were drafted. African communities engage in human rights discourse with an inherent sense of alienation because they did not participate in its origin and development. Almost all the countries in sub-Saharan Africa were still under the yoke of colonialism in the 1940s when the UDHR was drafted. Colonialism involved the domination of African communities by colonial regimes linked to European powers. It is these European powers that also participated in the drafting of the UDHR and excluded the African communities. Indeed, the Executive Board of the American Anthropological Association objected in writing to the then proposed UDHR on the basis that it failed to recognize cultural diversity and

21 Hannum, "Status of the Universal Declaration," 287.
22 UDHR, Arts. 1, 27 and 29.
23 UDHR, Art. 1.
24 UDHR, Art. 27.
25 UDHR, Art. 29.

espoused Western values only.[26] The other key international human rights instruments – the International Covenant on Economic, Social and Cultural Rights (1966) and the International Covenant on Civil and Political Rights (1966) – were also drafted mostly by Westerners or Western-trained representatives and before the decolonisation of many African states.[27] The colonial state systems in sub-Saharan Africa generally, including in South Africa, further alienated African communities by using repugnancy clauses in the formal constitutional and statutory frameworks through which African customary laws were not to be enforced if contrary to justice or public morality. The value systems by which to determine that African customary laws were not repugnant to justice or morality were generally those of the colonial powers because colonial administrators determined whether an African customary norm or value was repugnant to justice or morality.[28]

The existing marriage legislation in South Africa – the Marriage Act 25 of 1961, the Recognition of Customary Marriages Act 120 of 1998, the partly repealed Black Administration Act 38 of 1927 and the Civil Union Act 17 of 2006 – are thus based on Western values. These Western values rooted in international human rights discourse continue to cast a shadow over South Africa's marriage legislation even as the state engages in efforts to integrate and harmonize the various African customary marriage practices in accordance with the Constitution.

As a result of these inherent limitations of international human rights discourse, some aspects of African cultural practices have become less visible in the discourse than others. Assumptions about women's victimisation in Africa, for example, have led to misinterpretations and a failure to recognise the aspects of African cultural practices that empower women. African women are often construed as victims of an excessively patriarchal society and any positions of power that they hold are often overlooked and downplayed.[29] In South Africa, marriage legislation does not recognise the cultural practices of "ukuthelwa ngenyongo" and "ukugcagca" (the traditional celebration of marriage), and "ukungena" (once a woman marries into a particular family, she is married into that family for life), which are recognised by the communities as essential elements of solemnising a marriage.[30] A major reason for the invisibility of these customary marriage practices in the human rights discourse

26 See Merry, "Changing Rights," 33–34.
27 Merry, "Changing Rights," 35.
28 Thomas and Tladi, "Legal Pluralism," 354–63.
29 Arnfred, "Re-Thinking Sexualities," 11–12.
30 The Green Paper, 19.

is probably due to the inherent limitations of the discourse itself than to any shortcomings of the African cultural practices.

Despite these textual and contextual limitations of international human rights discourse, African communities should adopt a pragmatic approach to human rights by focussing on their own cultural practices in addition to understanding the human rights norms rooted in the morality of European powers. The world today is very different from the world that existed during the December 1948 adoption of the UDHR. African states are now politically independent and should no longer focus on expropriating their communities' land, labour and capital to create modern economies for European powers. The time may be ripe for a revision of the UDHR to expressly provide for the rights of linguistic, religious, and cultural community groups in keeping with the spirit of the drafters. Even if human rights advocates do not succeed in revising the UDHR, they have an opportunity to influence international human rights discourse in a way that takes account of the rights of cultural communities in sub-Saharan Africa. They should orient the discourse toward a focus on the cultural practices of African communities that are the same or similar to the norms, standards and principles that constitute the international human rights regime. These same human rights norms, standards and principles exist and have existed for years among African communities. In much the same way as we discover an individual's characteristics independently of his name, we can also discover the human rights norms, principles and standards of African communities independently of the terminology used to identify them. In seeking to influence international human rights discourse, the focus should be on identifying similar cultural practices among African communities and injecting them into the discourse. As Sylvia Tamale states in "The Right to Culture and the Culture of Rights: A Critical Perspective on Women's Sexual Rights in Africa", "we must invoke the core values of our societies to engender transformation; [and] find those values that resonate from indigenous cultures that will speak to the rights repertoire."[31] She describes this exercise as "a (re)turn to the positive aspects of culture" and emphasizes that "[i]t is vital that we surface the positive, egalitarian aspects of African culture and use it to our advantage; that we (re)interpret the underlying values within our culture with the changing socioeconomic circumstances".[32]

31 Tamale, "Right to Culture," 161.

32 Tamale, "Right to Culture," 164.

3 Existence and Validity of Customary Marriages in South Africa

In this section, we examine the customary marriage practices of South Africa's communities and the failure to integrate them into the legal framework through the RCMA. We rely on Niklas Luhmann's systems theory (as the sum of interactive and interdependent component parts) to model these communities as systems[33] and to highlight the importance that they attach to their cultural rights. Luhmann describes systems as bodies or groupings of interactive and interdependent elements that are functionally differentiated or structured to self-produce and self-preserve and that use feedback loop mechanisms to maintain their integrity and stability.[34] We conceptualise African communities as not just the individuals making up the community, but also the laws, customs, cultures, ancestors, lands, waters, and other elements that the community system considers essential to its continuity and survival.[35] We view these communities and their cultural practices metaphorically as if they were onions with the practices that we can observe today constituting only the surface that, when peeled, leads to an understanding of older customary practices that themselves need to be peeled back in search of a better historical understanding of the communities' customs and traditions.

We also use social dominance theory (the tendency of human societies to structure themselves as systems of group-based social hierarchies)[36] to examine community struggles to assert their cultural rights. These community systems consider that the loss of their essential elements, including culture and norms and values, would result in their disappearance as a people. The essential elements of community systems, such as customary marriage practices, also have essential requirements for them to exist. In "Integration of the Bride as a Requirement for a Valid Customary Marriage: *Mkabe v Minister of Home Affairs* [2016] ZAGPPHC 460", Bakker argues that there are essential requirements under customary law that must be present for a valid customary

33 See Gillespie, "Towards a Discursive Analysis," 657 (discussing Professor Niklas Luhmann's ideas).

34 Baxter, "Autopoiesis," 1993–2003; Cassuto, "Law of Words," 103–08.

35 See *Love v Commonwealth of Australia* (11 February 2020) B43/2018; *Thoms v Commonwealth of Australia* (11 February 2020) B64/2018 (collectively, *Love v Commonwealth*) (High Court of Australia) 124–25 (the Australian High Court recognised these constituent elements or component parts of a system when it stated that "the people, the ancestral spirits, the land and everything on it are 'organic parts of one indissoluble whole'").

36 See Wilson, "Why Diversity Fails," (for an explanation of social dominance theory); Pratto, Sidanius and Levin, "Social Dominance Theory"; Sidanius et al., "Social Dominance Theory".

marriage to exist.[37] He names the essential requirements as follows: family participation, a lobolo agreement, and integration of the bride into the husband's family. According to him, these essential requirements cannot be waived or done away with by agreement of the parties. A deviation can be allowed only if it can be proved that the living customary law of a certain tribe has evolved to such an extent that the essential requirement can no longer be regarded as an essential requirement for a valid customary marriage.

We focus on customary marriages in this section because marriages are essential for the stability of families and ultimately the wellbeing of the entire community system.[38] Both proposed legislative options have the same definition of a protected relationship or marriage or life partnership entered into in terms of culture as follows: "any subsisting monogamous or polygynous marriage or relationship concluded or entered into in terms of the tenets of any religion or culture before or after the commencement of this Act".[39] This definition perpetuates the failure by the RCMA to integrate unrecognised/ancillary customary marriages such as (1) a woman marrying another woman to bear children for the *lapa*, house or *kraal*, (2) marriages akin to same-sex marriages (which include true woman-to- woman marriages), (3) the sororate/substitute wife from the bride's family to bear children in place of an infertile or deceased wife, (4) the levirate/a man marrying the widow of his deceased brother and (5) ukungena/where a male relative is given access to the woman in order to father children on behalf of her deceased husband.[40]

Even where customary marriages are recognised by the RCMA, challenges remain as to whether such marriages meet the requirement of being "negotiated and celebrated according to customary law" in terms of section 3(1)(b) of the RCMA. In *Mayelane v Ngwenyama*[41] the Constitutional Court was asked to rule on the validity of a customary marriage that was entered into without the consent of the existing wife. In *Tsambo v Sengadi*[42] the Supreme Court of Appeal of South Africa had to determine the validity of a customary marriage where the customary practice of the handing over of the bride was not done in accordance with the customs of the families concerned. In *Mabuza v Mbatha*[43] the High Court of South Africa (Cape of Good Hope Provincial Division) also

37 Bakker, "Integration of the Bride," 2.

38 See Green Paper on Families, 23.

39 SALRC, *Discussion Paper 152*, 135 et seq.

40 Bekker and Buchner-Eveleigh, "Legal Character," 80–96.

41 *Mayelane v Ngwenyama.*

42 *Tsambo v Sengadi* (244/19) [2020] ZASCA 46 (30 April 2020) (hereafter *Tsambo v Sengadi*).

43 *Mabuza v Mbatha* 2003 (7) BCLR 743 (C) (hereafter *Mabuza v Mbatha*).

grappled with the validity of a customary marriage that was entered into without the formal integration of the bride into the bridegroom's family as was required by custom. These are examples of challenges that Courts have had to deal with to determine the validity of customary marriages in South Africa despite the existence of legislation (the RCMA) that is meant to integrate and harmonise the customary marriage practices of South African communities.

3.1 *Prevailing Customary Marriage Practices in South Africa*

South Africa's marriage legislation is based on Western values imported into South Africa during the colonial and apartheid era. In this chapter, we rely on social dominance theory (the tendency of human societies to structure themselves as systems of group-based social hierarchies)[44] to explain colonialism. According to social dominance theory, when social systems interact, they tend to structure themselves hierarchically, thereby resulting in one system's dominating and suppressing the other.[45] In his book, *How Europe Underdeveloped Africa,*[46] Walter Rodney discusses the maintenance of this group-based hierarchical structure through an analysis of power relations. He defines power as the ability to defend one's interests and, if necessary, to impose one's will by any means necessary. The result of the use of colonial power against South African communities was a thriving European minority in South Africa living in the midst of socially and economically marginalised South African communities. The colonial state system then used apartheid to maintain and sustain this hierarchical structure in South Africa. Apartheid ("apartness" in the language of Afrikaans) was a system based on a statutory framework and state policies that segregated non-white citizens from whites in South Africa.[47] To this day, these Western values of a bygone era continue to cast a shadow over South Africa's marriage legislation.

South Africa's colonial and apartheid legacy creates limitations that may impede efforts to accurately identify the customary marriage practices of the communities. However, there are fundamental underlying marriage principles which are uniform among communities in South Africa. Bakker names three essential requirements under customary law that must be present for a valid

44 See Wilson, "Why Diversity Fails," (for an explanation of social dominance theory); Pratto, Sidanius and Levin, "Social Dominance Theory"; Sidanius et al., "Social Dominance Theory".

45 Wilson, "Why Diversity Fails"; Pratto, Sidanius and Levin, "Social Dominance Theory"; Sidanius et al., "Social Dominance Theory".

46 Rodney, *How Europe Underdeveloped Africa*, 224.

47 Posel, "Meaning of Apartheid," 123–26.

customary marriage to exist and that underscore the concept of the union of families in marriage; (1) family participation, (2) a lobolo agreement, and (3) integration of the bride into the husband's family.[48] These requirements truly identify the cultural practices of these communities that have sustained their family relations over generations.

The courts have also dealt with these essential requirements of a valid customary marriage in South Africa. In *Mayelane v Ngwenyama*[49] the Constitutional Court examined the validity requirements for a customary marriage in the Xitsonga community. The Constitutional Court concluded that the RCMA is premised on a customary marriage that is in accordance with the dignity and equality demands of the Constitution and that Xitsonga customary law must be developed, to the extent that it does not yet do so, to include a requirement that the consent of the first wife is necessary for the validity of a subsequent customary marriage. Section 6(4) in both proposed legislation options is consistent with the holding of the Constitutional Court in requiring spousal consent for subsequent customary marriages as follows:

> The male party to a subsisting polygynous [protected relationship] marriage or life partnership who wishes to enter into a further [protected relationship] marriage or life partnership must notify all the female parties to their subsisting relationship in the prescribed form of his intention to enter into a further relationship to obtain the consent of all the female parties who must indicate their consent in the prescribed form, before he may enter into such a further relationship; provided that if he enters into a further relationship without the consent of all the female parties to the subsisting polygynous relationship, that further relationship entered into will be void; and provided further that the registering officer must enquire into the existence of such consent having been sought and granted when the further relationship is registered.[50]

The proposed Single Marriage Bill, therefore, incorporates the spousal consent requirement for subsequent customary marriages that was imposed by the Constitutional Court in *Mayelane v Ngwenyama*. The case is an example of the delicate balance that courts must strike between the rights in the Bill of Rights and customary marriage practices. Section 211(3) of the Constitution requires courts to "apply customary law when that law is applicable, subject to the

48 Bakker, "Integration of the Bride," 2.

49 *Mayelane v Ngwenyama*.

50 SALRC, *Discussion Paper 152*, 135 et seq.

Constitution and any legislation that specifically deals with customary law", while section 39(2) of the same Constitution requires the Courts to "promote the spirit, purport and objects of the Bill of Rights". Given the inconclusive evidence on whether or not Xitsonga customary law requires spousal consent for subsequent customary marriages, the Court held that it should, in order to promote the fundamental rights to equality and human dignity.

Lindiwe Sarah Mabuza vs Frank Mphumeni Mbatha[51] was another case involving questions of the validity of a customary marriage. In *Mabuza vs Mbatha*, the integration of the bride had not been done in accordance with siSwati Customary Law, which required a practice known as "ukumekeza". Ukumeza was a customary practice which involved the bride appearing naked before her in-laws. The Court found that the customary marriage was valid because ukumekeza, like so many other customs, has somehow evolved so much that it is probably practised differently than it was centuries ago.

The changing nature of customary marriage practices also played out in a recent Supreme Court of Appeal ruling, *Tsambo vs Sengadi*,[52] where J. Molemela with the majority concurring held that "having correctly found on the facts of this case that the physical handing over of the bride was waived in favour of a symbolic handing over, a customary marriage was concluded".[53] In *Tsambo v Sengadi* the validity of the customary marriage was questioned because the handing over of the bride had not occurred in accordance with the customs of the community. This was after the female spouse was handed over to the family of the male spouse at the residence of the female's family immediately after the conclusion of the lobola negotiations and the part payment of the lobola. The Supreme Court of Appeal found that the handing over was not a strict requirement for a valid customary marriage and could be waived. It found that there was a tacit waiver of the custom of the handing over of the bride because a symbolic handing over of the respondent to the deceased's family had occurred after the conclusion of the customary marriage. Customary marriage practices are thus not static, definite and uncontested, but are historical, fluid, dynamic and contested processes of interaction within communities and among communities. Even with these changes in customary marriage practices, marriage remains the cornerstone of family and community life in South Africa and the proposed Single Marriage Bill attempts to establish a uniform code that will protect all relationships worthy of the protection of the law. It is our view that this attempt at uniformity will ultimately lead to non-recognition

51 *Mabuza v Mbatha.*

52 *Tsambo v Sengadi.*

53 *Tsambo v Sengadi*, para. 31.

of customary practices of communities in South Africa, thereby putting cultural transformation at risk. It is to this issue of misconceptions of the nature of customary marriages and the future recognition of customary marriage practices under the proposed Single Marriage Bill that we now turn.

3.2 *Misconceptions on African Customary Marriages and the Proposed Single Marriage Bill in South Africa*

The constitutional and legislative framework of South Africa seeks to redress colonial and apartheid era injustices by entrenching equality and non-discrimination, which values are also recognised in international human rights law. Accordingly sections 9, 10, 15 and 31 of the South African Constitution provide for equality, non-discrimination, a right to dignity, a right to freedom of conscience and religion, and a right to culture.[54] Culture also enjoys constitutional recognition and protection by virtue of sections 181(1)(c), 211 and 212 of the Constitution.[55] In other words, principles of equality, non-discrimination, human dignity and unity in diversity are recognised in South Africa. It is to engender these values in a democratic South Africa that the RCMA was enacted. As already alluded to in the previous sections, there has been a number of challenges on the meaning and proper interpretation particularly of section 3(1) of the RCMA.

Section 3 of the RCMA lists the following requirements to be met before a customary marriage is validated under the Act:

> (1) For a customary marriage entered into after the commencement of this Act to be valid-
>
> (a) the prospective spouses-
>
> (i) must both be above the age of 18 years; and
>
> (ii) must both consent to be married to each other under customary law; and
>
> (b) the marriage must be negotiated and concluded into or celebrated in accordance with customary law.

The provision requiring consent to be married according to customary law seemingly does not present challenges but constitutes the basis of numerous misconceptions regarding customary marriages that have gained traction in South Africa. Marriage in indigenous South African communities is generally known to be a decision of the two families, affirming the consent of the

54 The Constitution, ss. 9, 10, 15, and 31.

55 The Constitution, ss. 181(1)(c), 211 and 212.

marriage parties. The requirement of "consent to be married to each other under customary law" should take cognisance of the fact that other persons are also critically involved in this marriage in addition to the couple. In other words, the families that are being joined together through the marriage relationship are also involved. This is different from the individualist concept of consent stipulated in the Marriage Act or in a civil union, for instance. It is important to attempt to understand the nature of African marriages and how they come into existence. Marriage as a process in indigenous African communities relies on the consent of the families for their son and daughter to get married. Thus the questions raised in *Tsambo v Sengadi* should not have arisen. The intentions of the parties are clearly formulated and noted in the process and no one is in doubt as to whether a marriage is contemplated or not.

In terms of the proposed Single Marriage Bill, the consent of the parties remains the only consideration. In other words, the couple can consent to marriage under any circumstances without their families' consent and such will be regarded in terms of the Act as a valid customary marriage where the parties have met the other requirements. The consequence will be a gradual erosion of the community practices of the people regarding customary marriage in South Africa. Another fundamental misconception of customary marriage that underscored its recognition as a valid marriage prior to 1994 is that it is "potentially polygynous". This categorisation characterises customary marriages as morally unreliable and as unlikely to lead to the promotion of equality. Yet the preamble to the RCMA does not specifically refer to polygyny or the regulation of polygynous marriages.

The issue of the consent of the first wife to a subsequent customary marriage was dealt with by the court in *Mayelane v Ngwenyama*. In this case, the Court held that the marriage of the second wife was not valid because she could not show evidence of being married to the deceased.[56] Two aspects of this case that suggest the existence of misconceptions about marriage are, in the first instance, that marriage is a personal and not a family affair. If it was truly so, evidence of the families properly being part of the marriage process would be less contestable. Secondly, the consent of the wife or wives to a subsequent marriage should be part of the process of marriage from the beginning. This suggests that the customary practices of the people are not being taken into consideration or not properly understood. Hence the misconceptions in law, as evident in the decisions of the courts. For most people, the understanding is that the RCMA is a state law or a civil law, as opposed to customs, that are part of the living day-to-day practice of the people that guide their community

56 *Mayelane v Ngwenyama*, paras. 10–11.

and their lives. The spouses in a customary marriage have a duty to ensure that their marriage is registered.[57] Either spouse may apply to the registering officer using the prescribed form and must furnish the prescribed information and any additional information that the registering officer may require to be satisfied about the existence of the marriage. A certificate of registration of a customary marriage issued under the RCMA constitutes *prima facie* proof of the customary marriage. Section 4(3)(b) of the RCMA provides that "a customary marriage must be registered within (3) three months after the conclusion of the marriage or within such longer period as the Minister may from time to time prescribe by notice in the Gazette".[58] However, the same Act at section 4(9) provides that "[f]ailure to register a customary marriage does not affect the validity of that marriage".[59] A marriage officer must satisfy himself or herself of the existence of a customary marriage and then issue a certificate.[60] The nature of customary marriages in South Africa is such that this approach to the registration and ultimately the recognition of the existence of a customary marriage is fraught with inconsistencies. The proposed Single Marriage Bill does not offer adequate measures to address the misconceptions on the nature of customary marriages and how persons, particularly women, ought to be protected in the Act. What the proposed Single Marriage Bill seems to address is the opportunity for traditional leaders to confirm traditional marriages and assist the parties in their registration.[61] The role of traditional leaders in marriage processes are not recognised yet they are given the opportunity to assist with registering the marriage because involving them would be advantageous due to their authority and proximity to the communities that they serve. The challenge that arises from this is that the recognition of customary marriages will mostly affect urban and modern South Africans who practice their culture.

As observed earlier, some customary marriages in South Africa, such as unrecognised/ancillary customary marriages and marriages in some royal families and KhoiSan communities, and polygamous marriages with non-citizens, still exist in the shadows because they are not recognised by the RCMA. Some of these challenges are logistical because the communities live in remote areas where no marriage officers can be found to validate the customary marriages. Even where customary marriages are recognised by the RCMA, challenges

57 RCMA, s. 4(1).

58 RCMA, s. 4(3)(b).

59 RCMA, s. 4(9).

60 RCMA, s. 4(5)(b).

61 SALRC, *Discussion Paper 152*, 135, et seq., Annexure B1, Option 1: Draft Bill: Protected Relationships Bill, s. 8(3)(10).

remain as to whether such marriages meet the requirement of being "negotiated and celebrated according to customary law" in terms of the RCMA.

Since the RCMA came into force on 15 November 2000 it has brought changes to the social institution of marriage for African people who wish to live under customary law. For instance, parties to a customary marriage should register their marriage in terms of section 4 of the RCMA within a specific period of time even though failure to register the marriage does not attract any sanction or render the marriage invalid. Parties to a customary marriage can divorce only by court order and their proprietary rights are protected under the RCMA. The RCMA has succeeded in giving impetus to substantive equality as noted by the Constitutional Court in many of the cases involving customary law. For instance, in the trilogy case of *Bhe v Magistrate, Khayelitsha*,[62] the importance and centrality of equality was advanced to highlight the commitment to ensuring adherence to the constitutional values as guaranteed in the Constitution. Langa DCJ held as follows:[63]

> The centrality of equality is underscored by the Court … s 9 of the Constitution also guarantees the achievement of substantive equality to ensure that the opportunity to enjoy the benefits of an egalitarian and non-sexist society is available to all including those who have been subjected to unfair discrimination.

By drawing on this foundational value and right,[64] the intention of the RCMA is to address the injustices of the past and give effect to the principles of equality, non-discrimination, human dignity and unity in diversity recognised in the Constitution. On the other hand, the misconceptions regarding the nature of customary marriages have resulted in numerous challenges in terms of the interpretation of the RCMA.

Although the RCMA intended to address discriminatory practices and differential treatment based on race, it quickly turned into a contentious piece of legislation. It must be borne in mind that, with the coming into law of the RCMA, there is a tripartite body of laws addressing issues of customary law, namely the constitution, statutory law and customary law. Against this backdrop, challenges to the provisions or import of the provisions of the RCMA came before

62 2005 (1) SA 580 (CC). Three cases were heard simultaneously: *Bhe v Magistrate, Khayelitsha Magistrate, Shibi v Sithole* and *South African Human Rights Commission v President, Republic of South Africa*.

63 *Bhe v Magistrate, Khayelitsha* 2005 (1) SA 580 (CC), para. 50.

64 The Constitution, s. 1(a) and (b).

the Courts for adjudication. In many instances, the main challenge relates to the validity of customary marriages. The contentious issues remain whether a marriage meets the requirement of being "negotiated and celebrated according to customary law".[65] In *Mrapukana v Master of the High Court and Mandia Mirriam Magwaxaza*, Dlodlo J held that the Applicant had indeed concluded a valid customary marriage with the deceased and thus qualified to be the executrix of the deceased's estate and not the second respondent. He stated as follows:

> The Applicant/Plaintiff reaffirmed her assertion that she was married to the deceased by way of customary marriage. She gave minute details as to the steps taken by the deceased's family and her own family prior to, during and after the celebration of this customary marriage. She dealt exhaustively with the payment of lobolo, the agreement between the two (2) families that she and the deceased should enter into this customary marriage, the handing over of herself by her family to that of the deceased, the celebration as well as all other ancillary rituals that form the central part of the coming into being of the customary marriage. Despite grilling and truth searching cross-examination, her evidence did not change its colour. Cross-examination instead served to put her in a position to give further details to improve on her evidence in chief.[66]

The case also touched on the issue of the registration of customary marriages that is provided for in section 4 of the RCMA. The Respondent relied on the non-registration of the marriage of the Applicant to the deceased as the reason for the invalidity of the marriage. The court confirmed that the registration of a customary marriage *per se* is not an essential requirement for the validity of a customary marriage in accordance with section 4(9) of the RCMA.[67] Since the tripartite body of laws plays a crucial role in the determination of issues relating to customary law, it is instructive that the normative standards remain the customs and practices of the people albeit measured against the constitution. In *Machika v Mthethwa*[68] in confirming that lobola forms an integral part of the requirements of section 3(1)(b) of the RCMA and customary law, the court

65 RCMA, s. 3(1)(b).

66 *Mrapukana v Master of the High Court* (6567/2007) [2008] ZAWCHC 113 (21 November 2008) (hereafter *Mrapukana v Master*), para. 27.

67 *Mrapukana v Master*, para. 31.

68 *Machika v Mthethwa* (55842/2011) [2013] ZAGPPHC 308 (24 October 2013) (hereafter *Machika v Mthethwa*).

held that the handing over of the bride is what distinguishes cohabitation from marriage.[69]

The handing over of the bride according to customary law has also been contentious. In recent times there have been deviations from the actual practice, resulting in challenges to the validity of the customary marriage. Although reference is often made to the relevant provision in the RCMA, much evidence is also submitted on the actual practices of the communities. In *Machika v Mthethwa*, Nkosi AJ admonished that "[t]his judgment cannot be read to mean easy deviation to acceptable cultural and customary practices."[70] Some of the reasons given by communities that waive some customary practices is urbanisation and modern ways of life, as held by Molemela J in *Tsambo v Sengadi*:[71] "… the physical handing over of the bride was waived in favour of a symbolic handing over; therefore, a customary marriage was concluded." This decision raises contentious issues as to the actual meaning of the handing over of the bride, although it implies a confirmation that the handing over of the bride or the integration of the bride into the husband's family is a requirement for a valid customary marriage,[72] as also envisaged in section 3(1)(b) of the RCMA.

One of the most critical challenges to the RCMA involves an order of invalidity. In *Gumede v President of the Republic of South Africa*[73] Moseneke DCJ reiterated the value of equality and the role that the RCMA purports to play in giving effect to the right to equality. Mr. Gumede filed for divorce before the High Court and, before the divorce was granted, Mrs. Gumede approached the High Court with a view to procuring an order invalidating the statutory provisions that regulate the proprietary consequences of her customary marriage. She sought invalidation on the grounds that the statutory provisions unfairly discriminated against customary law wives on grounds of gender and race. The RCMA provides that a customary marriage concluded after its commencement on 15 November 2000 (a "new marriage") is ordinarily a marriage in community of property. The RCMA also provides that customary marriages concluded before the cut-off date of 15 November 2000 ("old marriages") such as the Gumedes' customary marriage in 1968 are governed by customary law. Codified customary law in the KwaZulu Act and the Natal Code provides that a wife in an "old marriage" has no claim to the family property during or upon

69 *Machika v Mthethwa*, para. 63.
70 *Machika v Mthethwa*, para. 57.
71 *Tsambo v Sengadi*, paras. 17–18.
72 *Mkabe v Minister of Home Affairs* (2014/84704) [2016] ZAGPPHC 460 (9 June 2016), paras. 36–40.
73 2009 (3) SA 152 (CC).

the dissolution of the marriage because the husband is the family head and the owner of all the family property.[74] The Constitutional Court invalidated section 7(1) of the RCMA insofar as it provides that the proprietary consequences of a marriage entered into before the commencement of the RCMA continue to be governed by customary law. Section 7(2) of the RCMA was also invalidated insofar as it distinguishes between a customary marriage entered into after and before the commencement of the RCMA, by virtue of the inclusion of the words "entered into after the commencement of this Act". The Constitutional Court has thus confirmed that this differential treatment is unconstitutional as it unjustifiably limits the right to human dignity and the right not to be unfairly discriminated against.[75] *Gumede v President of the Republic of South Africa*[76] confined itself to monogamous customary marriages only but the same issues were adjudicated by the court in *Ramuhovhi and the President, Republic of South Africa*[77] relative to polygamous marriages. Consequently section 7(1) and (2) of the RCMA was also declared inconsistent with the Constitution in so far as it discriminated against women in polygamous marriages.

These challenges to the RCMA highlight the point noted in *Bhe* that "given the dynamic nature of society, official customary law as it exists in the textbooks and in the Act [is] generally a poor reflection, if not a distortion of customary law".[78] A core argument remains whether the tripartite body of laws in South Africa provides adequate protection to women as required under South Africa's international human rights obligations. The challenges to the RCMA present a lens through which to view the scope of the changes envisaged in the proposed Single Marriage Bill. The proposed Protected Relationship Bill supported by the SALRC does not recognise customary law. It simply provides basic requirements similar to those in the Marriage Act of 1961, on the understanding that all the nuances of customary law cannot be met in a single Bill. The certainty envisaged in the proposed Bill will be counter-productive to the protection of cultural rights. In the first instance, the RCMA regulates the recognition, validity and registration of customary marriages. The reliance by African people on the RCMA will be eliminated given that there have been challenges in the court to the interpretation of several provisions in the RCMA. Secondly, the Single Marriage Bill will create a lacuna that will further alienate many

74 KwaZulu Act on the Code of Zulu Law 16 of 1985, s. 20; Natal Code of Zulu Law (Proc. R151 in GG 10966 of 9 October 1987), ss. 20 and 22.

75 Rautenbach, ed., *Introduction to Legal Pluralism*, 103.

76 2009 (3) SA 152 (CC); See Rautenbach, ed., *Introduction to Legal Pluralism*, 103.

77 *Ramuhovhi v President of the Republic of South Africa* 2018 (2) SA 1 (CC).

78 *Bhe v Magistrate, Khayelitsha* 2005 (1) SA 580 (CC), para. 86.

people, particularly women in rural African communities. In other words, the Single Marriage Bill will be unable to deal with several issues that the RCMA has been concerned with in recent times. In addition, the amendment to the RCMA promulgated in 2021 to address some of the shortcomings as directed by the court, is instructive but fails to adequately provide important safeguards for the majority of the African people, particularly women. We argue that the proposed Single Marriage Bill might address certainty in laws regarding marriage. It must, however, settle the relegation of community practices and by so doing elevate the status of community rights and human rights.

4 Re-conceptualising African Customary Marriage Practices

In this section, we return to the fundamental question of this chapter: how to create the right balance between the customary marriage practices of South Africa's communities and the state's commitment to international human rights. The right balance between the South African state system and the communities should result in statutory recognition of the customary marriage practices of these communities as a path toward a stable coexistence between the multiple legal systems in South Africa. Such a balance can be struck through a transformative legal framework such as the RCMA. Despite the challenges it has faced, the RMCA is a positive step toward transforming the state system's interface with South African communities from one of dominance and suppression to the recognition of these community systems. The Single Marriage Bill should therefore address the challenges faced by the RCMA by integrating and harmonising the customary marriage practices of the African communities so that rights that are based on the communities' customary practices have equal footing in law with rights granted formally under South Africa's constitutional and statutory frameworks.

The Single Marriage Bill is still in its embryonic phase. As anticipated by the Green Paper itself, the policy document has been submitted to the Cabinet for approval and will be followed by a Marriage Bill to be presented to the Cabinet for approval by 31 March 2023 and to Parliament by 31 March 2024.[79] The drafters of the single marriage legislation, therefore, have over a year to reconceptualize the South African state's interface or interaction with communities. The state will need to pivot away from the tendency to dominate and suppress the community systems and, instead, integrate them into the state's

79 The Green Paper.

socio-economic system, including harmonising their customary marriage practices. The RCMA and the proposed Single Marriage Bill are steps in the right direction and a departure from colonial and apartheid models of interaction.

The South African state should go further and study and understand key aspects of the cultural life of the communities and the communities' resilience by mapping their key structural attributes, essential dynamics, interdependencies and feedback loop mechanisms[80] in order to create a harmonised marriage legislation. The Single Marriage Bill should also embrace the analytical approach to culture as a historical, fluid, dynamic and contested process of interaction in a community. As Sylvia Tamale states in "The Right to Culture and the Culture of Rights: A Critical Perspective on Women's Sexual Rights in Africa", "we must invoke the core values of our societies to engender transformation [and] find those values that resonate from indigenous cultures that will speak to the rights repertoire".[81] The new cultural rights recognition frameworks should therefore recognise this dynamism of communities and allow them to practice their cultures or to adopt new cultural practices according to each community system's legal and institutional structures.

The transformation of African customary marriage practices could also be aided by the judicial system. Section 211(3) of the Constitution provides that "the Courts must apply customary law when that law is applicable, subject to the Constitution and any legislation that specifically deals with customary law".[82] Through the application of customary law the courts create precedents that eventually lead to certainty, predictability, reliability, equality and uniformity about customary marriage practices. According to the Constitutional Court, the role of the courts in creating precedent relating to custom would be "a manifestation of the rule of law itself, which is in turn a founding value of the South African Constitution".[83] Through the courts' allowing customary law to thrive in the South African legal system, the communities' customary marriage practices will be integrated and harmonised over time and be aligned

80 See Baxter, "Autopoiesis," 1993–2003 (discussing a system's use of feedback loop mechanisms to re-generate itself and ensure its own survival as a system. A system is able to use its own negative and positive feedback loop mechanisms to maintain equilibrium among its component parts. A negative feedback loop is self-correcting and self-stabilising; it can correct a systemic imbalance much as a thermostat rectifies a temperature imbalance. A positive feedback loop is self-reinforcing; an initial perturbation to one component of the system is amplified as it propagates around the loop).

81 Tamale, "Right to Culture, 161."

82 The Constitution, s. 211(3).

83 *Camps Bay Ratepayers and Residents Association v Harrison* 2011 (2) BCLR 121 (CC), para. 28.

with the Constitution. The courts could also act as arbiters of disputes that arise in the contestation for power between states and community systems and thereby provide guardianship for the new integration and harmonisation model envisioned by the Green Paper. An arbiter is needed between the state system and the community systems that coexist in South Africa because of the social dominance theory of systems tending to hierarchise whenever they interact. Recall that it was the colonial and neo-colonial state systems that used predatory legislation, compulsory acquisition, unconscionable agreements or treaties, forced eviction and other suppression and domination tactics to push the African communities to the fringes of their socio-economic systems. There is therefore a risk of the state systems continuing to use tools of domination and suppression to continue dominating the African community systems. African communities should use the opportunity provided by the process of developing a single marriage legislation to strengthen and develop their own legal and institutional structures. In this way, transformative law reform through the judicial system could lead to integrated and harmonised marriage laws in South Africa.

Human rights observers and practitioners also need to take a fresh look at South African customary marriage practices even as proposals are made to reform those cultures, as is happening with the proposed Single Marriage Bill in South Africa. The African communities that engage in these local cultural practices are themselves made up of interactive and interdependent individuals, their laws and customs, cultures, ancestors, land, waters, and other essential elements focussed on self-production and self-sustenance of the community as a whole. These communities tend to regenerate and transform themselves to more effectively achieve their self-production and self-sustenance objective. With the passage of time, they develop cultural practices that are more suitable for the environment that they inhabit. The communities themselves remain resilient and continue to resist external disruption for as long as they exist as communities.

The application of international human rights norms should therefore be viewed from the perspective of the local communities that are receiving these norms. All cultures change and traditions change all the time. Western culture, for example, has changed from embracing slavery to prohibiting and eventually criminalising the practice. African cultures are no exception. They are living and are already changing to embrace international human rights norms.[84] There are already shifts, modifications and subtle changes occurring in local

84 Ozoemena, "Living Law," 147–63.

cultural practices, meaning that local cultures are in a trajectory of internal transformation.[85] Achieving the right balance between cultural practices and human rights may therefore depend on learning from, appreciating and further developing these internal transformations of local cultures and not to disrupting or distorting them based on the application of an inaccurate and misleading view of Western discourse. African communities should use their existing, often uncharted cultural transformation potential and build on that instead of weakening their legal and institutional structures in the guise of applying international human rights norms.

5 Conclusion

This chapter has been about the challenges that multicultural societies face in the local application of international human rights norms. We have examined whether South Africa's proposed Single Marriage Bill will strike the right balance between the customary marriage practices of South Africa's communities and South Africa's commitment to international human rights. The proposed Single Marriage Bill represents a new trend in sub-Saharan Africa where the states are taking the lead in remodelling their interfaces or interactions with the African communities from one of dominance to one of recognition. This is a step in the right direction as it demonstrates that the South African state is starting to view cultural values from the perspectives of the communities themselves and not through a colonial or apartheid lens. The South African state should go further and study and understand key aspects of the cultural life of the communities and the communities' resilience by mapping their key structural attributes, essential dynamics, interdependencies and feedback loop mechanisms in order to create an integrated and harmonised marriage legislation for these communities. A harmonised marriage legislation should lead to a rebalancing of the power asymmetries between the state and South African communities and among the communities, thereby creating stable environments where the community systems are able to recover, co-exist and thrive as community systems.

85 Arnfred, "Re-Thinking Sexualities," 11–12.

Bibliography

Literature

Arnfred, Signe. "Re-Thinking Sexualities in Africa: Introduction." In *Re-Thinking Sexualities in Africa*, edited by Signe Arnfred, 7–33. Uppsala: Almqvist & Wiksell Tryckeri AB, 2004.

Bakker, Pieter. "Integration of the Bride as a Requirement for a Valid Customary Marriage: *Mkabe v Minister of Home Affairs* [2016] ZAGPPHC 460." *Potchefstroom Electronic Law Journal* 21 (2018): 1–15. http://dx.doi.org/10.17159/1727-3781/2018/v21i0a1737.

Baxter, Hugh. "Autopoiesis and the 'Relative Autonomy' of Law." *Cardozo Law Review* 19 (July, 1998): 1987–2090.

Bekker, J. C., and Buchner-Eveleigh, M. "The Legal Character of Ancillary Customary Marriages." *De Jure* 50, no. 1 (2017): 80–96. http://dx.doi.org/10.17159/2225-7160/2017/v50n1a5.

Cassuto, David Nathan. "The Law of Words: Standing, Environment, and Other Contested Terms." *Harvard Environmental Law Review* 28 (2004): 79–128.

Gillespie, John. "Towards a Discursive Analysis of Legal Transfers into Developing East Asia." New York University Journal of International Law and Politics 40, no. 3 (Spring, 2008): 657–721.

Hannum, Hurst. "The Status of the Universal Declaration of Human Rights in National and International Law." *Georgia Journal of International and Comparative Law* 25 (1995/96): 287–397.

Hobsbawm, Eric. "Introduction: Inventing Traditions." In *The Invention of Tradition*, edited by Eric Hobsbawm and Terence Ranger, 1–14. Cambridge: Cambridge University Press, 1983.

Jacobson, Arthur J. "Survey of Books Relating to the Law; VII. Legal Theory and Philosophy: Review – Autopoietic Law: The New Science of Niklas Luhmann. Autopoietic Law: A New Approach to Law and Society, (edited by Gunther Teubner, 1988)." *Michigan Law Review* 87, no. 6 (1989): 1647–89.

Luhmann, Niklas. *Introduction to Systems Theory*, edited by Dirk Baecker, and translated by Peter Gilgen. Cambridge: Polity Press, 2013.

Mahao, Nqosa Leuta. "O se re ho Morwa 'Morwa Towe!' African Jurisprudence Exhumed." *Comparative and International Law Journal of Southern Africa* 43, no. 3 (November, 2010): 317–36.

Merry, Sally Engle. "Changing Rights, Changing Culture." In *Culture and Rights: Anthropological Perspectives*, edited by Jane K. Cowan, Marie-Benedicte Dembour, and Richard A. Wilson, 31–55. New York: Cambridge University Press, 2001.

Ozoemena, Rita. "Living Law: A Truly Transformative Tool?" *Constitutional Court Review* 6 (2016): 147–63.

Posel, Deborah. "The Meaning of Apartheid before 1948: Conflicting Interests and Forces within the Afrikaner Nationalist Alliance." *Journal of Southern African Studies* 14, no. 1 (1987): 123–39.

Pratto, Felicia, Jim Sidanius and Shana Levin. "Social Dominance Theory and the Dynamics of Intergroup Relations: Taking Stock and Looking Forward." *European Review of Social Psychology* 17 (2006): 271–320. https://doi.org/10.1080/10463280601055772.

Rautenbach, Christa, ed. *Introduction to Legal Pluralism in South Africa.* 6 ed. Durban: LexisNexis, 2021.

Rodney, Walter. *How Europe Underdeveloped Africa.* Cape Town: Pambazuka Press, 2012.

Sidanius, Jim, et al. "Social Dominance Theory: Its Agenda and Method." *Political Psychology* 25, no. 6 (2004): 845–80.

South African Law Reform Commission (SALRC). *Project 144, Discussion Paper 152: Single Marriage Statute.* Pretoria: SALRC, 2021.

Tamale, Sylvia. "The Right to Culture and the Culture of Rights: A Critical Perspective on Women's Sexual Rights in Africa." *Urgent Action Fund – Africa: Sex Matters* (2007): 149–165. ISBN 9966-7203-4-0.

Thomas, Ph J., and Dire D. Tladi. "Legal Pluralism or a New Repugnancy Clause." *Comparative and International Law Journal of Southern Africa* 32, no. 3 (1999): 354–63.

Wilson, Erika K. "Why Diversity Fails: Social Dominance Theory and the Entrenchment of Racial Inequality." *National Black Law Journal* 26, no. 1 (2017): 129–53.

Case Law

Australia

Love v Commonwealth of Australia (11 February 2020) B43/2018; *Thoms v Commonwealth of Australia* (11 February 2020) B64/2018 (collectively, *Love v Commonwealth*) (High Court of Australia).

South Africa

Alexkor Ltd v Richtersveld Community 2004 (5) SA 460 (CC).

Bhe v Magistrate, Khayelitsha 2005 (1) SA 580 (CC).

Camps Bay Ratepayers and Residents Association v Harrison 2011 (2) BCLR 121 (CC).

Gumede v President of the Republic of South Africa 2009 (3) SA 152 (CC).

Mabuza v Mbatha 2003 (7) BCLR 743 (C).

Machika v Mthethwa (55842/2011) [2013] ZAGPPHC 308 (24 October 2013).

Mayelane v Ngwenyama 2013 (4) SA 415 (CC).

Mkabe v Minister of Home Affairs (2014/84704) [2016] ZAGPPHC 460 (9 June 2016).

Motsoatsoa v Roro [2011] 2 All SA 324 (GSJ).

Mrapukana v Master of the High Court (6567/2007) [2008] ZAWCHC 113 (21 November 2008).

Ramuhovhi v President of the Republic of South Africa 2018 (2) SA 1 (CC).
Shibi v Sithole 2005 (1) SA 580 (CC).
South African Human Rights Commission v President, Republic of South Africa 2005 (1) SA 580 (CC).
Tsambo v Sengadi (244/19) [2020] ZASCA 46 (30 April 2020).
Legislation and Government Publications.

Canada

Canadian Charter of Rights and Freedoms, 1982.
South Africa.
Black Administration Act 38 of 1927.
Civil Union Act 17 of 2006.
Constitution of the Republic of South Africa, 1996.
Green Paper on Families: Promoting Family Life and Strengthening Families in South Africa (Gen N 756 in GG 34657 of 3 October 2011).
Green Paper on Marriages in South Africa, Public Consultation Version, 20 April 2021 (GN 412 in GG 44557 of 11 May 2021).
KwaZulu Act on the Code of Zulu Law 16 of 1985.
Marriage Act 25 of 1961.
Natal Code of Zulu Law (Proc. R151 of 1987 in GG 10966 of 9 October 1987).
Recognition of Customary Marriages Act 120 of 1998.

Treaties and Agreements

International Covenant on Civil and Political Rights (1966).
International Covenant on Economic, Social and Cultural Rights (1966).
Universal Declaration of Human Rights (1948).
Universal Declaration on Cultural Diversity (2001).

CHAPTER 5

Recognition of Woman-to-Woman Marriage under State Laws and African Customary Laws

Adeniyi Olatunbosun and Samson Odetayo

Abstract

The term "woman-to-woman marriage" is treated as a misnomer and a mockery of the word "marriage" by European colonialists and the legal systems they developed as part of their imperial occupation of African territories. Its historical treatment explains why it was subjected to the colonialists' test of repugnancy in order to determine the level of its conformity to Western understanding of what marriage should be. This chapter examines the practice of woman-to-woman marriage in conditions of legal pluralism in Nigeria and its functional relevance in the communities where it is practised. Using a cultural relativist argument, we query the justifications for subjecting this form of marriage to the test of repugnancy. We also argue that a foreign woman-to-woman marriage would be accorded recognition in Nigeria under , going by the rule that the validity of marriage is hinged on the law of the place where it was celebrated (*lex loci celebrationis*). We urge for the harmonisation of customary (African) and statutory (English) marriages in order to ensure parity of status for both forms of marriages.

1 Introduction

In recent years the definition of marriage as a social institution, as well as its nature, has generated so much controversy that it is becoming increasingly difficult to give a universal definition of what it entails. There are opposing schools of thought when it comes to defining the term "marriage".[1] On the one side are those authors who view it as the union of persons of opposite sex. These authors argued that for any union to qualify as a "marriage", such a union must be between "persons of opposite sex" and as such a union of between two men or two women can never qualify as a marriage. This is the "conjugal" school.[2] The scholars in this school believe that the sanctity of the institution

1 Girgis, George and Anderson, "What is Marriage?" 246.

2 Finnis, "Law, Morality, and Sexual Orientation," 1066; also see Finnis, "Marriage," 388–406.

 | DOI:10.1163/9789004696747_006

of marriage will be corrupted and the word "marriage" itself will lose its meaning if same sex unions are to be regarded as marriages. On the other side of the divide are writers who express the view that using a person's sex as the criterion for marriage is "foolishness" because gone are the days when assessing the sex of a party to a marriage was a straight-forward issue.[3] In view of the challenges involved in determining the sex of transsexuals and intersex persons, it has been argued that marriage should not be defined through the lens of sex or gender. Thus, it is said that marriage is the union of two consenting adults irrespective of their sexes. This is the "revisionist" school since its proponents aim to revise the definition of marriage to include same sex union and other non-conventional marital relationships such as woman-to-woman marriage.[4]

This chapter will not delve into the dialectics of what a marriage is *stricto sensu*. Rather, it focusses on the African practice of woman-to-woman marriage, its nature, instances of its practice in certain African societies, and whether this type of marriage will be recognised by virtue of the *lex loci celebrationis* rule under Private International Law. The paper is divided into five major parts. Part 1 examines the African customary practice of woman-to-woman marriage and the practice of lesbianism. The argument here is that woman-to-woman marriage and lesbianism are different, contrary to the assertions of some scholars. Thus, the socio-cultural context of woman-to-woman marriage is discussed under this Part. In Part 2, we discuss manifestations of woman-to-woman marriage in African societies, with particular reference to the Mbaise and Nnobi people of the south-eastern part of Nigeria. We also make cross-cultural references to other African tribes (Kipsigis and Nandis in Kenya and the Lovedu people in South Africa). Here we argue that this marriage performs a functional socio-cultural role in the communities where it is practised. Part 3 examines the reception of the repugnancy doctrine into the legal systems of some common law African countries (with specific references to Nigeria, Kenya and South Africa), while also investigating the attitudes of courts regarding the doctrine of repugnancy. In Part v the paper considers the challenges of the cross-border recognition of woman-to-woman marriage in view of the doctrine of public policy, which allows a forum to refuse recognition to a foreign marriage which runs afoul of a forum's definition of marriage. Finally, the paper concludes that subjecting woman-to-woman marriage to the archaic doctrine of repugnancy is no longer fashionable. Thus, a refusal by the court of a forum to recognise a woman-to-woman marriage is hypocritical

3 Kogan, "Transsexuals, Intersexuals, and Same-Sex Marriage", 371.

4 Girgis, George and Anderson, "What is Marriage?" 246; also see Macedo, "Homosexuality and the Conservative Mind," 279.

where there is a tribe in the forum where such marriage is practised. Finally, the paper recommends that Nigeria and Kenya should emulate the legal development in South Africa, where the test of repugnancy has been expunged from their laws.

2 Woman-to-Woman Marriage and Lesbianism

The phrase "woman-to-woman marriage" is a term of convenience employed to describe an institution that developed in some African tribes in time immemorial. It is easier to describe the concept as it is practised in the various African communities than to define it. Among the Igbo people of south-eastern Nigeria, particularly the Mbaise people[5] of Imo State and the Nnobi people[6] of Anambra State, when a married woman has no children (or has children but no son) and the husband dies, it is culturally allowed for her to marry another woman.[7] When this happens she (the first woman) becomes the husband of the second woman since she (the first woman) is the one who pays her (the second woman's) dowry and fulfils other traditional rites as it is done under a heterosexually contracted marriage. The wife who pays the dowry or bride price is usually referred to as the "female-husband" while the second woman on whom the bride price is paid is referred to as the "bride" or "wife".[8] If the husband of the "female-husband" is dead, a male adult member of the husband's family would be procured to perform the function of having sexual intercourse with the bride while the responsibilities of taking care of the bride fall on the "female-husband". Where the husband of the "female-husband" is alive, it is his duty to engage in sexual intercourse with the bride for the purposes of having children for the female-husband. It is important to note that a wife (in contrast to a wealthy, unmarried woman) does not have the power to marry a bride except where she has sought and obtained the consent of her husband (if the husband is alive) or his relatives (if the husband is dead). Thus, a woman-to-woman marriage is different in purpose, content and

5 Omoteye and Akinlade, "Legal Implications," 36–38.

6 Amadiume, *Male Daughters*, 70–72.

7 There are other instances where a married woman who has sons and daughters may still decide to "marry" another woman for herself. These instances are discussed in Part 2 of this chapter.

8 Oboler, "Is the Female-Husband a Man?" 69 defines a "female-husband" as "a woman who pays bride wealth for and thus marries (but does not have sexual intercourse with) another woman".

structure from the sexual practice of lesbianism, since the African tradition does not permit the two women to have intercourse.[9]

Among the Nandis of Kenya, a woman past the age of child-bearing and who has no son may enter into a form of marriage with another woman.[10] This may be done during the lifetime of her husband, but it is more usual after his death. A marriage consideration is paid, as in a regular marriage, and a man from the woman's husband's clan has intercourse with the girl in respect of whom the marriage consideration has been paid. Any children born to the girl are regarded as the children of the woman who paid the marriage consideration and her husband. The implication of the above analysis is that African customary "woman-to-woman marriage" is totally different in content and objectives from the contemporary practice of lesbianism.

To the Kipsigis (Kenya), woman-to-woman marriage is known as *ketunci toloch*; i.e., "one marries for support". This might refer to the support of the widow herself by prospective sons or to the support of the husband's house by carrying on the family. The widow goes through exactly the same procedure as a man in taking to her a wife. A husband is found for this wife from amongst the relations of the deceased husband of the widow, if possible. Failing that, some other man is found of the girl's choice. The children of this union are the children of the widow and her deceased husband. We see here an attempt to prevent the dying out of a family as a basic unit of the society. The desire of a childless woman to have children in her old age to support her is understandable in a society where old age without children is hard and lonely.[11] Among the Kamba a barren woman is treated as a social pariah and cannot succeed to the property of her husband upon his death.[12] To overcome this challenge, a barren wife can resort to woman-to-woman marriage, through which she will become a female-husband to her wife and the wife bears children who bring joy and honour to the barren female-husband.

Unfortunately, some scholars erroneously equate African woman-to-woman marriage practices with lesbianism as practised in the Western world. Since the union appears to be between persons of the same sex, it is easier for a person who does not have a proper grasp of African culture to equate the practice with lesbianism. For instance, Epprecht expressed the view that woman-to-woman marriages under African customary law accommodate lesbianism,

---

9 Onuorah, "Religious, Socio-Cultural and Moral Implications," 113. Also see Amadiume, *Male Daughters*, 7.

10 Cotran, *Restatement of African Law*, 117.

11 Orchardson, "Notes on the Marriage Customs," 106.

12 Cadigan, "Woman-to-Woman Marriage," 91.

albeit covertly.[13] He argued that these institutions acted to provide cover for lesbian-like sexual practices, including kissing, general touching, and even oral sex. He further observed that because of the high premium placed on children, most African societies worked towards presenting an appearance of universal conformity to a fecund heterosexual norm. Such appearance of universal conformity is, in his view, a facade as the existence of homosexual practices was socially protected by a deeply embedded culture of silence.

In the same vein, some African scholars have argued that the definition of marriage as the union of two (or more) persons of opposite sex raises complicated issues when one considers the existence of "hermaphrodites" and "pseudo-hermaphrodites"[14] and advances in medical science which have made sex-change operations feasible.[15] They were adamant that despite the public disavowal of homosexual practices in Nigeria, same gender relationships have been formalised and even legalised in certain parts of the country from time immemorial.

Epprecht's view of the nature and practice of woman-to-woman marriage in African societies reflects the misconceptions of the practice by the colonialists.[16] Wallowing in the mire of ethnocentrism, the colonial overlords believed, albeit erroneously, that an arrangement where an African woman decides to take a "wife" for the purpose of having offspring through the "wife" for her husband is not only repugnant but also a barbaric and an unjust cultural practice that must be rejected in its entirety. To the colonialists, the one and only way for determining the acceptability of a marriage practice, irrespective of the creativity and the ingenuity of the African society that instituted such practice, is if it conforms to the European standards or understanding of what marriage is. Thus, the African marriage which forms part of the African culture is treated as second-class and therefore inferior to the western culture and matrimonial practices.

In fact, Sir Fredrick D. Lugard, a colonial Governor-General of the Colony and Protectorate of Nigeria, miscategorised woman-to-woman marriage as a form of slavery.[17] He observed that the custom of elderly women procuring young girls, whom they call "wives", and with whom they go through a marriage

13 Epprecht, "'Unsaying' of Indigenous Homosexualities," 635.

14 The term "hermaphrodite" is "an *offensive* word for a *person* with both *male* and *female sex organs*" (see Cambridge Online Dictionary, "Hermaphrodite"). A person with male and female reproductive organs is generally referred to as an "intersex person".

15 Olookoba and Mahmud, "Appraising the Cross-Currents," 368.

16 Epprecht, "'Unsaying' of Indigenous Homosexualities," 631.

17 Lugard, *Dual Mandate*, 387.

ceremony, appears to be prevalent among African tribes. He argued that the purchase money is misnamed "dowry", and the female-husband becomes the absolute owner of the girls. What could be farther from the truth! What is baffling, however, is the fact that the Holy Bible upon which the colonial marriage institution is based recorded instances of woman-to-woman marriages, even though the Bible did not specifically use the concept. We read of the story of Abraham, Sarah and Hagar when Sarah was unable to bear a child for her husband. It was recorded that Sarah "gave" Hagar to Abraham to be his wife with the intent that Sarah "may obtain children by her".[18] In the case of Jacob, "when Rachel saw that she bare Jacob no children" she also gave her maid to her husband so that she (Rachel) "may have children by her".[19] Since these instances were recorded in the Bible, which has the greatest influence on the understanding of marriage in the Western Hemisphere, one begins to wonder where the idea of the repugnancy of African woman-to-woman marriage came from? Irrespective of how the colonialists came about the idea of repugnancy, it suffices to say that it is the misconceived idea of what a woman-to-woman marriage entails that has led to the unjustifiable and perpetual subjection of the African woman-to-woman marriage to the repugnancy test. At this juncture, we will consider instances of woman-to-woman marriage in African societies.

3 Instances of Woman-to-Woman Marriage in African Societies

As stated earlier, the practice of woman-to-woman marriage in Africa is different from that of lesbianism. The concept of woman-to-woman marriage often creates confusion, leading some people who are not familiar with the practice to link it to lesbianism. The African practice of woman-to-woman marriage has nothing to do with woman-to-woman sexual intercourse.[20] Rather, the practice of female-husband is adopted by barren women (and sometimes wealthy, famous and influential women) to produce children when all other options have failed. Although the female-husband pays the bride price, there is always a man in the background who would be performing the duty of a husband, especially the sexual function to make the girl bear children for the female-husband. In fact, Amadiume has strenuously argued that the interpretations of woman-to-woman marriage as lesbianism would be "totally inapplicable, shocking and offensive" to African women, "since the strong bonds

18 The Holy Bible: Genesis 16:2–3.
19 Genesis 30:1–3.
20 Omoteye and Akinlade, "Legal Implications," 35.

and support" which exist between the female-husband and her wife (wives) do not include lesbian sexual practices.[21] She disagrees strongly with those scholars who have cited this African practice to justify their choices of sexual alternatives which have roots and meanings in the West. Thus, a typical African woman-to-woman marriage arrangement involves two women undergoing formal marriage rites; the requisite bride price is paid by one party as in a heterosexual marriage.[22] The woman (female-husband) who pays the bride price for the other woman becomes the sociological "husband" and the "father" of any resulting offspring. The children of such a union belong to the lineage of the husband of the female-husband (where she is married) or to her own lineage (if she is not married), but not to the biological father of the children.[23] The purpose of woman-to-woman marriage in Africa is never for anything concerning sexual intercourse between the female-husband and the girl/woman she marries. We wish to state here that there may be instances where covert sexual or amorous relationship may exist between the female-husband and the wife, but such few instances of amorous or sexual relationship cannot be taken as a general practice among the various African societies.

There are different kinds of female-husband marriage as practiced in Nigeria and other African societies. Such marriages include but are not limited to the following instances.[24]

3.1 *Barren or Sterile Woman*

This is the most common circumstance that leads to the practice of woman-to-woman marriage. In most African societies barren married women are usually stigmatised. A man is at liberty to take a second wife as a result of the infertility of the wife. Thus, it is not strange to see a barren wife or a wife who is unable to have a male child marrying a young girl for her husband as a way of securing her position in her husband's family. Since the marriage is contracted by the barren wife and "forced" on her husband, it is her duty to pay the requisite bride-price in respect of a new wife who is expected to bear children in her place. Paying the bride price gives the wife the authority and control over the new wife as she is regarded as the "female-husband" of the new wife. All the children of such marriage are regarded as the children of the first wife

21 Amadiume, *Male Daughters*, 7.

22 Carrier and Murray, "Woman-Woman Marriage," 255.

23 Omoteye and Akinlade, "Legal Implications," 34.

24 On the reasons for the development of woman-to-woman marriage, see Wairimũ and O'Brien, "Revisiting 'Woman-Woman Marriage'," 8–14; Cadigan, "Woman-to-Woman Marriage," 91–94.

(i.e. the female-husband) since "*she* who pays the piper calls the tune". In these societies married women (who are barren or have no male child) prefer marrying new wives for their husbands to leaving their matrimonial home or allowing their husbands to die without having (male) children.

Some legal authorities argue that since such marriages are, in fact, contracted in the name of the husband, there is no question of one woman being married to another.[25] Though that may be rightly so, the financial support and moral concern of the barren or sonless wife should not be ignored, especially where the woman is the bread-winner of the family and the husband cannot provide the resources needed to afford a second wife by himself. This means that without the agreement and financial support of the old wife (female-husband), it would not be possible for the poor and sonless or childless husband to marry another wife to have children.[26]

3.2 *Married and Unmarried Female-Husband*

Another example of a woman-to-woman marriage is a wealthy woman who may be married or unmarried and with or without children. Achebe told the story of Ahebi Ugbabe, an influential and wealthy female chief in Enugu-Ezike in the south-eastern part of Nigeria.[27] Ugbabe was a female warrant chief and "king" who assumed otherwise male roles, including marrying wives for herself and her brothers. Achebe repeatedly (and rightly so) states that in Igbo land this practice of woman-to-woman marriage is totally unrelated to homosexuality. It is only a mark of wealth and social status. These wives married by women had sexual relations with men.[28]

Also Amadiume told the story of a wealthy, powerful woman – Okenwanyi – who lived in Nnobi town in the present-day Anambra State, Nigeria.[29] Because of her wealth and her influence Okenwanyi (who was not a barren woman as she had two children – a male and a female – for her husband) was able to marry nine wives for herself during the subsistence of her marriage with her husband. This confirms our assertion (and those of other scholars) that the practice of woman-to-woman marriage did not develop wholly as a result of the barrenness or sterility of the female-husband or her inability to have male children. It sometimes happened that rich and powerful women were able to marry other women with a view to recruiting a large labour force who

25 Williamson, "Changes in the Marriage System," 53.
26 Omoteye and Akinlade, "Legal Implications," 40.
27 Achebe, *The Female King*, 206–08.
28 Ezekwem, "Review of *The Female King*".
29 Amadiume, *Male Daughters*, 123–32.

would either work on the farm of the female-husband or help her with her trading activities. The practice of woman-to-woman marriage is known as "igba ohu" among the Igbos. Woman-to-woman marriage is also practised among the Ibibio, Annang, Oron and Efik communities of southern Nigeria. In Nkwa Ibiono in Ibiono Ibom Local Government Area of Akwa Ibom State, one Prophetess Ikwo Idio was said to have married many wives and taken them to her house. She brought young men to work for her as palm fruit harvesters and to service the women to procreate children for her. Prophetess Ikwo Idio was a rich woman. Before she died in 2003 she had through the practice of female-husband "given birth" to many children who now inherit her property and keep her name alive.[30]

The practice of a wealthy female-husband taking a large household of wives is not unique to Nigeria. In Kenya Wangu wa Makeri is another legendary woman of great substance who held sway and became a "headman" at a time when that office was exclusively reserved for men. She was elevated to the position of headman in 1902. When the British colonial authorities began a taxation system, Makeri acted as the go-between for the Kikuyu and these authorities, under which she became a controversial figure to her people.[31] Although she was married to Makeri wa Mbogo, some scholars are of the view that she was barren and therefore married several women through whom she had several children.[32] The above instances reveal that wealthy African women who have the means and the clout, whether married or unmarried, usually engaged in woman-to-woman marriage practices for the purposes of procreation and also as a display of their status and achievement in society.

3.3 *Female Children Marrying for Their Sonless Fathers*[33]

It was and still is common to see some female children of a family collectively pay the bride price of a younger girl after the death of their sonless father in the name of their eldest sister so that the new bride can give birth to male children to preserve their father's lineage and for inheritance purposes. The bride would choose a bed mate from the family of the female-husband so that she would procreate male children. The choice of the bed mate was critically determined,

30 Omoteye and Akinlade, "Legal Implications," 36.

31 Wikipedia, "Wangu wa Makeri".

32 Kareithi, "Wangu wa Makeri".

33 In *Okonkwo v Okagbue* 9 NWLR (Pt. 368) 301 (hereafter *Okonkwo v Okagbue*) it was held that the practice of posthumously marrying a woman to a dead father for the purposes of raising children in the name of the father and with the intent to commit fraud is repugnant.

and the female-husband had, as a matter of compulsion, to assist the bride in choosing her sex partner. There are reasons for the involvement of the female-husband in choosing a bed mate for the girl. These include: (i) to ensure that the bed mate is a blood relation of the female-husband; (ii) to preserve the blood ties of the family; (iii) to ensure that the bride would not pollute the family by raising children fathered by miscreants, thieves or persons with ailments; (iv) to prevent the introduction of undesirable traits into the family; and (v) to prevent the introduction into the family of an Osu (an outcast).[34] Female children can marry for their father while he is still living if he has no male children.

Ultimately, African society did not (and still does not) look down on the practice of woman-to-woman marriage since the essence of such a marriage is procreation, companionship and support. There is at least one decision of the Nigerian Supreme Court to back up the assertion that a woman-to-woman marriage is recognised in Nigeria.[35] We now turn to the question of how the repugnancy test clause found its way into the corpus of African legal systems.

4 Woman-to-Woman Marriage, the Repugnancy Test and African Legal Systems

A convenient point at which to start the examination of how the doctrine of repugnancy was introduced into the corpus of the legal systems of the Anglophone African countries[36] is the 1884/1885 Berlin Conference where African countries were shared and partitioned among the then European powers. Once an African territory was subdued, the colonial overlords made it a point of duty to "persuade" the Africans to relinquish their religions in favour of Christianity and the British notion of civilisation. The colonial governments also set out to undermine traditional authorities by establishing court systems which were fashioned in accordance with the European systems of law that resulted in kings and chiefs losing their judicial powers. Section 24(1) of High Court Law of Lagos State,[37] which has its root in the Supreme Court Ordinance of 1876, provides that the high court shall observe and enforce those aspects of

34 Omoteye and Akinlade, "Legal Implications," 39. Also see Emefiene, *History of Ubulu People*, 218.

35 *Meribe v Egwu* (1976) LPELR-1861 (SC) (hereafter *Meribe v Egwu*).

36 An Anglophone country/state for the purposes of this chapter is a country/state which was formerly colonised by Britain and whose legal system bears resemblance to (or was influenced by) the British legal system.

37 Cap H3, Laws of Lagos State 2015.

customary law which are applicable and are not repugnant to natural justice, equity and good conscience.[38]

In a similar manner, section 3(2) of the Kenyan Judicature Act, Cap 8, 2012 provides that:

> The High Court, the Court of Appeal and all subordinate courts shall be guided by African customary law in civil cases in which one or more of the parties is subject to it or affected by it, so far as it is applicable and is not repugnant to justice and morality or inconsistent with any written law.[39]

In the case of South Africa, the Native Administration Act 38 of 1927 allowed customary law to be applied nation-wide, but only in a separate system of courts constituted by traditional leaders and native commissioners. While the courts of traditional leaders could apply only customary law, the courts of native commissioners (together with their Appeal Court) had a discretion to apply either customary or common law in any "suits or proceedings between Natives involving questions of customs followed by Natives".[40] Although customary law was not entirely excluded from magistrates' courts and the Supreme Court, it had to be proven in each case, as if it were a foreign law or a species of common-law custom.[41] And since it had to be proven in each case, then it had to be shown that such customary law did not violate the test of repugnancy.[42] The application of customary law was subject to a "repugnancy" proviso. In other words, customary law could not be applied if it was contrary to natural justice or public policy.

What is observable from a consideration of the laws of the legal systems above is the requirement that the applicable customary law must not be

38 Also see s. 17(e) of the Supreme Court Act, Cap S15, Laws of the Federation of Nigeria 2004 and s. 18(3) of the Nigerian Evidence Act, 2011.

39 Before 1895, when Kenya was declared a British Protectorate, the country had no structured legal system. The territory was administered through the chartered Imperial British East Africa Company, which carried out all the obligations undertaken by the British Government under any treaty or agreement made with another state. In 1896 the territory became known as the East African Protectorate. It was later renamed Kenya Colony and Protectorate in 1920 and remained so until 1963 when Kenya became an independent state.

40 Section 11(1) of the Native (later Black) Administration Act 38 of 1927.

41 Taiwo, "Repugnancy Clause," 109.

42 Ibid. Also see s. 211 of the Constitution of the Republic of South Africa, 1996, which provides that the courts must apply customary law when that law is applicable, subject to the Constitution and any legislation that specifically deals with customary law.

repugnant to "justice, equity and good conscience". The colonialists believed that African customs were barbaric and uncivilised and as such the customs must be proved to be civilised enough to justify their applicability. To put it bluntly, the custom had to meet the British standards of civility for it to be accepted and applied. While it is conceded that certain aspects of African culture and customary practices may look strange to an outsider, a proper evaluation and appreciation of such cultural practices will reveal that there is justifiable and well-considered reasoning behind the practice. Ethnocentrism is a potent delusion that usually deprives its victim of the ability to appreciate the culture of other people without having to view such appreciation from the lens of his/her own cultural background. For example, some Africans[43] find it strange that the citizens of the Western world could be clamouring for same sex marriage while polygamy is treated as barbaric and backward.[44]

Now, what custom the court will treat as repugnant will depend on the facts of each case and due to the vagueness of the word "repugnant" courts usually exercise restraints in its application. They applied the repugnancy proviso only with regard "to such customs as inherently impress us with some abhorrence or are obviously immoral in their incidence".[45] The rationale behind the introduction of the doctrine of repugnancy for determining the validity of African customs has been questioned.[46] Whose ethics are to be violated if the repugnancy clause is not invoked? While the concept of natural law, equity (not in its technical sense) and good conscience would tend to suggest a universal system, the concept of public policy would suggest a system of values pertaining to a particular society. Since values, standards and principles vary from place to place and from time to time, the concepts of equality, morality and fairness differ from one society to another. It is clear from the legislation and the practice of the courts that customary law is not judged in terms of an African system of

43 Amadiume, *Male Daughters*, 114 while discussing the attitude of the Western world to woman-to-woman marriage and other African marriage practices wondered why "in spite of their monogamous orientation, women are said to be very promiscuous … They shudder at the thought of polygyny, immediately equating it with oppression of women, simply because wives have to share a man sexually".

44 See s. 2 of Zero Tolerance for Barbaric Cultural Practices Act, 2015 (Canada) which amends s. 41 of the Immigration and Refugee Protection Act as follows: "A permanent resident or a foreign national is inadmissible on grounds of practising polygamy if they are or will be practising polygamy with a person who is or will be physically present in Canada at the same time as the permanent resident or foreign national. (2) For the purposes of subsection (1), polygamy shall be interpreted in a manner consistent with paragraph 293(1)(a) of the Criminal Code".

45 Taiwo, "Repugnancy Clause," 109.

46 See generally, Bennett, "Re-Introducing African Customary Law," 1–31.

values but exclusively in terms of European standards, because the very existence of a repugnancy clause indicates that the customary system of law to be applied is subject to another system of law.[47]

In the South African context it is observed that the repugnancy proviso has been jettisoned, having outlived its usefulness (if any). In *Bhe* the South African Constitutional Court stated that:[48]

> Quite clearly the Constitution itself envisages a place for customary law in our legal system. Certain provisions of the Constitution put it beyond doubt that our basic law specifically requires that customary law should be accommodated, not merely tolerated, as part of South African law, provided the particular rules or provisions are not in conflict with the Constitution.

The Court further stated that the South African Bill of Rights does not deny the existence of any other rights or freedoms that are recognised or conferred by customary law as long as they are consistent with the Bill of Rights.[49] It follows from this that customary law must be interpreted by the courts, as first and foremost answering to the contents of the Constitution. It is protected by and subject to the Constitution in its own right. It is for this reason that an approach that condemns rules or provisions of customary law merely on the basis that they are different from those of the common law or legislation or some other foreign laws from a foreign legal system would not be a correct approach.

In *Alexkor Ltd v Richtersveld Community* the court also stated that:

> While in the past indigenous law was seen through the common law lens, it must now be seen as an integral part of our law. Like all law it depends for its ultimate force and validity on the Constitution. Its validity must now be determined by reference not to common law, but to the Constitution.[50]

This approach avoids the mistakes which were committed in the past and which were partly the result of the failure to interpret customary law in its own setting but rather attempting to see it through the prism of the common law

47 Bennett, "Conflict of Laws," 59.

48 *Bhe v Magistrate, Khayelitsha* 2005 (1) SA 580 (CC) para. 41.

49 Section 39(3) of the Constitution.

50 *Alexkor Ltd v Richtersveld Community* 2004 (5) SA 460 (CC) para. 51.

or other systems of law. That approach also led in part to the fossilisation and codification of customary law, which in turn led to its marginalisation. This consequently denied it of its opportunity to grow in its own right and to adapt itself to changing circumstances.

In Nigeria the attitude of courts in subjecting the rules of customary law to the test of repugnancy is different from the attitude of South African courts as described above. In *Meribe v Egwu*[51] the Supreme Court was called upon to pronounce on the validity of one such marriage. The facts of the case are as follows. The land in dispute belonged to one Nwanyiakoli who because she was barren married Nwanyiocha (the plaintiff's/respondent's mother). Nwanyiakoli paid the bride price and bore the other incidental costs of the celebration of the marriage. Although Nwanyiocha was for all intents and purposes meant to be Chief Egwu's wife (Chief Egwu being Nwanyiakoli's husband), the children born by Nwanyiocha would be regarded as the children of Nwanyiakoli since she was the one that "married" Nwanyiocha. Chief Egwu died in 1925 while Nwanyiakoli died in 1937. The defendants/appellants, who were the grandsons of Chief Egwu through a third wife, argued that woman-to-woman marriage was contrary to public policy and good conscience and since the claim of the Plaintiff/Respondent to the land in dispute was based on a woman-to-woman marriage such a claim should not stand. The trial court gave judgment in favour of the plaintiff/respondent, and on appeal the Supreme Court in dismissing the appeal stated that:

> We ... do not think that on a close examination of the facts of this case, there was a 'woman to woman' marriage between Nwanyiakoli and Nwanyiocha. The true nature of the arrangement was appreciated by the learned trial judge when he, rightly in our view, made the following observations: 'The facts disclosed in evidence did not show that Nwanyiakoli married Nwanyiocha for herself, a fact naturally impossible – but that she married in that context is merely colloquial, the proper thing to say being that *she procured Nwanyiocha for Chief Egwu to marry her*. There was no suggestion in evidence that there was anything immoral in the transaction.' (Emphasis supplied).[52]

The court held that considering the particular facts of the case there was nothing "immoral in the transaction" as a woman-to-woman marriage

51 *Meribe v Egwu*; see also *Iweze v Okocha* (1967/68) MSNLR 64.

52 *Meribe v Egwu*, 13.

(involving sexual intercourse between the two women) was "naturally impossible". However, the Court stated *obiter* that where there is evidence of such a woman-to-woman marriage involving sexual intercourse between the two women or where the marriage was procured to commit fraud, the court would not hesitate to declare the marriage as repugnant and therefore invalid.[53] Thus, in the case of *Okonkwo v Okagbue,* where two sisters purported to marry a wife for their deceased brother some 30 years after his death, the court held that a culture that permits a dead man to give birth to children 30 years after his death is repugnant to natural justice, equity and good conscience.[54] The implication of the dictum of Madarikan JSC in *Meribe v Egwu* and the decision of the Supreme Court in *Okonkwo v Okagbue* is that where woman-to-woman marriage is contracted either to commit fraud or as a cover for lesbianism or other forms of a same-sex sexual relationship, the Nigerian courts will not hesitate to strike down such a union as being "immoral", illegal and contrary to the current Nigerian public policy.[55] Thus, parties cannot hide under the traditional practice of woman-to-woman marriage to engage in illicit sexual relationships.

In Kenya the colonial attitude to African customs (particularly African customary marriage) is evidenced in the decision of the court in *R v Amkeyo,*[56] where the matter of the validity of a customary marriage arose in the context of the common law rule that a wife could not be compelled to testify against her husband. In that case the parties had married under African customary law and were living together as husband and wife. The court refused to recognise the validity of the customary marriage, thereby compelling the wife to testify against her husband. Chief Justice Hamilton stated that the use of the word "marriage" to describe the relationship entered into by an African native with a woman of his tribe according to tribal custom was a misnomer. The Chief justice further stated that the elements of a so-called marriage by native custom differ so materially from the ordinary accepted idea of what constitutes a civilised form of marriage that it is difficult to compare the two! This decision illustrates the discriminatory attitude of the Europeans and their court systems to the African Marriage institution.

In post-colonial Kenya it is not clear where the court stands on the issue of woman-to-woman marriage as there are at least two conflicting decisions of the Kenyan High Court on this issue. In *Maria Gisese w/o Angoi v Marcella Nyomenda* a dispute arose over the dissolution of a marriage between a

53 See the cases of *Okonkwo v Okagbue; Ojukwu v Agupusi and Anor* (2014) LPELR 22683 (CA).

54 *Okonkwo v Okagbue.*

55 Section 1(1) and (2) of the Nigerian Same Sex Marriage (Prohibition) Act, 2014.

56 *R v Amkeyo* (1917) 7 EALR 14.

female-husband and her wife performed under Kisii customary law which permits woman-to-woman marriage.[57] The widow, who was the female-husband, identified a man with whom her wife would bear a child, according to their custom, and the children of the marriage were regarded as the female-husband's children. The court held that the lack of choice or consent from the wife in the matter of which man should have sexual intercourse with her was "repugnant to justice and an abuse of an individual freedom of choice". It was further held that woman-to-woman marriages could not be recognised. On the other hand, the court in *Esther Chepkuaui v Chepngeno Kobot Chebet and Johanah Kipsang*[58] took a different approach when it held that, although the practice of woman-to-woman marriage looks repugnant to justice and morality, if it is recognised by the entire community, it should be recognised as customary law of that community.

Unlike in the case in South Africa, African customs (and by extension woman-to-woman marriage) are still subjected to the relics of colonialism as contained in the laws of Kenya and Nigeria. In these two jurisdictions a woman-to-woman marriage would be declared invalid if it failed the test of repugnancy as inherited from the imported legal system of the colonialists, while in South Africa the test for determining the validity of a custom (e.g. woman-to-woman marriage) is not based on a vague repugnancy doctrine but rather on the conformity of such custom to the Constitution of South Africa. This, in our opinion, is a better approach, since the South African Constitution is derived from the people as opposed to English law, which was imposed on Africans. It was in view of this that the makers of the South African Constitution carefully omitted the use of the word "repugnancy" from their Constitution. It is therefore advised that the laws of Kenya and Nigeria be modified with a view to removing the archaic test to ensure that the validity of African marriage is not subject to an arbitrary and unjustifiable foreign standard.

5 Cross-Border Recognition of Woman-to-Woman Marriage

Marriage is a pre-legal, pre-state institution, as it existed prior to the existence of modern states and legal systems.[59] This reality is recognised under international law when the 1948 Universal Declaration of Human Rights,[60] the

57 *Maria Gisese w/o Angoi v Marcella Nyomenda* [1981] Divorce Cause No. 16 of 1980.

58 *Esther Chepkuaui v Chepngeno Kobot Chebet and Johanah Kipsang* Civil App. No. 1 of 1981.

59 Wardle, "Institution of Marriage," 160.

60 Universal Declaration of Human Rights (1948).

foundational document of modern international human rights laws, calls the family the natural and fundamental group unit of society and expressly protects the gender equality of "men and women" in forming the institution of marriage, as a core and essential universal value of human rights in modern legal systems.[61] Similarly, the Cairo Declaration on Human Rights in Islam, adopted in 1990 by the nations belonging to the Organisation of the Islamic Conference, provides that the family is the foundation of society, and marriage is the basis of its formation. Men and women have the right to marriage.[62] This widely respected principle of international law acknowledges and establishes some important facts that bear upon the subject of this chapter. First, it recognises the essentiality of marriage and the family; that marriage and the family are foundational social institutions. Second, it recognises that the concept of marriage is not a mere creation of the state. The state (or more specifically, the law) does not "create" marriage any more than it "creates" children, or air, or land. Rather, it recognises such pre-existing social institutions or realities and regulates them in ways that are intended to preserve and protect society's basic institutional resources and serve the public interest.

As stated in the preceding parts of this work, the general rule under private international law demands that each country must recognise the validity of a marriage which is valid in terms of the law of the place where it was celebrated (i.e. where the marriage contract was made).[63] Under this general rule, often referred to as the *lex loci celebrationis* (place of celebration rule), a marriage is valid everywhere if valid where celebrated and, conversely, void everywhere if void where celebrated.[64] It is therefore the universal practice of civilised nations that the permission or prohibition of particular marriages belongs to the country where the marriage is to be celebrated.[65] Thus, supposing Mrs. A. went through a woman-to-woman marriage ceremony in Kenya and Mrs. A and her *wife*, Mrs. B., then moved to Nigeria and sought to enforce the recognition of their union under the Nigerian law, the implication of the place of celebration rule would be that the woman-to-woman union (since it was valid where celebrated) would be valid in Nigeria.

An important aspect of the *lex loci celebrationis* is that the rule is not carved in stone and certain exceptions have therefore been developed, such that a

61 Ibid. Art. 16(1): "Men and women of full age … have the right to marry and to found a family. They are entitled to equal rights as to marriage, during marriage and at its dissolution."

62 Cairo Declaration of Human Rights in Islam (1990), Art. 5.

63 Section 283 of Restatement (Second) of Conflict of Laws, 1971.

64 Story, *Commentaries*, 103–04.

65 *Haviland v Halstead* (1866) 34 NY 643.

forum or court may refuse recognition to a marriage which is otherwise valid in terms of the law of the place of celebration.[66] These exceptions have been used throughout legal history to refuse recognition to controversial domestic relations ranging from slavery to anti-miscegenation and to marriages within the prohibited degrees, etc.[67] The historical records[68] show that in most cases the recognition of controversial foreign domestic relationships (such as woman-to-woman marriage) came down to a matter of determining if the public policy of the forum strongly opposed it, and the extent to which giving recognition to such a foreign relationship in the particular fact or context of the specific case and the precise issue it raises would undermine that policy. While the specific resolution of these domestic relations conflicts has varied over time and from issue to issue, several prevailing principles have emerged. First, protection of the strong domestic policy of the forum is the dominant, controlling consideration. Second, respect for established relations and presumptions in favour of upholding the validity of established relationships were influential considerations. Third, fundamental human rights or "natural law" or "international law" may occasionally influence the analysis. And finally, when recognition of a novel form of domestic relationship would directly contradict or seriously impair or defy a strong public policy of the forum regarding the domestic relations, that consideration (i.e. the public policy) consistently controlled the outcome.[69] Other legal (or even extra-legal) considerations may clarify the issues, but they almost always give way to strong forum public policy considerations. Thus, cases involving the inter-jurisdictional recognition of slavery,[70] interracial marriage, polygamous marriage,[71] consanguineous marriage etc. show that

66 For exceptions to this rule, see Story, *Commentaries*, 98 and 104.

67 Wardle, "From Slavery to Same-Sex Marriage," 1904.

68 *Somerset v Stewart* (1772) 98 Eng Rep 499 (KB) (hereafter *Somerset v Stewart*); Hulsebosch, "Nothing but Liberty," 650; Wardle, "From Slavery to Same-Sex Marriage," 1872; Cleve, "'Somerset's Case'," 611.

69 Wardle, "From Slavery to Same-Sex Marriage," 1904.

70 *Somerset v Stewart*.

71 The case of *People v Ezeonu* 588 NYS 2d 116 (1992) deals with a man who was criminally charged with the statutory rape of a 13-year-old girl. One of the defences to statutory rape is that the defendant was married to the complainant. Ezeonu attempted to raise this defence but the problem was that the complainant was his second wife. The marriage was lawful where made, in Nigeria. The court held that foreign marriages would be recognised as valid only if they were not contrary to public policy in New York and it considered polygamy to be "repugnant to public policy".

the most important factor predicting and controlling the recognition of such domestic relationships is the strength of the public policy of the forum.[72]

Thus, two refinements should be noted in how the public policy doctrine is used in marriage cases. First, the exception is not employed as an overly blunt tool but is selectively refined in application. Rather than repudiate the place of celebration rule in every case that would, for instance, be incestuous under forum law, many legal systems recognise that some differences are more matters of degree than of fundamental policy.[73] A legal system that permits second cousins to marry may be more willing to recognise a law extending the privilege to first cousins than one extending it to siblings. Similarly, a country that permits sixteen-year-olds to marry may apply another country's law permitting fifteen-year-olds to do so, but not one extending the right to nine-year-olds. Second, many legal systems distinguish between the validity of a marriage and the ability to enjoy its "incidents". There was a time when courts treated marriage as a simple yes-or-no proposition. A marriage was either valid, in which case it was valid for all purposes, or it was not, in which case it was invalid for all purposes. Particularly in modern times, courts have been willing to draw finer lines between the status of marriage and its incidents, applying the place of celebration rule to the question of validity while saving the public policy exception for particular "incidents" of being married. For instance, the right to cohabit is a usual incident of being married but not a necessary one. A man married to two wives in India might be able to move to Michigan without being prosecuted for bigamy, but Michigan law might forbid the three of them from living together as husband and wives. At the same time, the surviving wives may both be permitted to inherit as spouses under the state's law of succession.[74]

The implication of the above analysis of the interplay between public policy and certain foreign domestic relationships is that where a domestic relationship (such as woman-to-woman marriage) appears to offend the public policy of a particular country, such a relationship would be denied recognition on the ground of the policy. The question then is whether a foreign woman-to-woman marriage offends the Nigerian public policy rule such that the marriage would be denied recognition in Nigeria. We are of the opinion that this

72 For instance, the Canadian Supreme Court stated in *Beals v Saldanha* (2003) SCC 72, a foreign judgment, that what the Court was called upon to enforce must not be contrary to "our view of basic morality" and should not be egregious such that it shocked the conscience of the court.

73 Kramer, "Same Sex Marriage," 1970.

74 *Compo v Jackson Iron Co.* (1883) 50 Mich 578.

question should be answered in the negative since the custom of woman-to-woman marriage is not strange to the Nigerian legal system as the Nigerian Supreme Court has been called upon on various occasions to pronounce on its validity. While the Nigerian Supreme Court has, on some occasions, held that woman-to-woman marriage is repugnant (especially where there is an element of fraud), it is worthy of note that the Court's first decision on woman-to-woman marriage in *Meribe v Egwu* has never been overruled. What can be distilled from the available cases is that where a woman-to-woman marriage is contracted for the purposes of committing fraud, the court will not hesitate to strike down such marriage as being repugnant.[75] We therefore hold the opinion that the cross-border recognition of woman-to-woman marriage is possible in Nigeria since the custom is commonly practised particularly in the south-eastern part of the country. However, where the so-called woman-to-woman marriage is a façade for lesbianism or same sex marriage, the Nigerian courts have the power both under the exceptions to the rule of *lex loci celebrationis* and Same Sex Marriage (Prohibition) Act, 2014 to declare such a marriage either as repugnant or contrary to public policy or illegal.[76]

Specifically, woman-to-woman marriage should be accorded recognition for the following reasons. First, the applicable conflict of laws rule in Nigeria is *lex loci celebrationis* and since the marriage is valid by the law of the country where it is celebrated (e.g. Kenya or South Africa), it should be treated as valid in Nigeria. Second, Nigerian local public policy would not be adversely affected by such a recognition since woman-to-woman marriage is in fact a heterosexual marriage and as such, it is not caught within the prohibitive provisions of the Same Sex Marriage (Prohibition) Act, 2014. Refusal to recognise woman-to-woman marriage would bring untold hardships on the children of such a union. The interests of such children would be badly prejudiced, and they would be made to suffer for the "misdeeds" of their parents, for which they are not responsible. To avoid this unwholesome result, it is recommended that:

(i) a foreign woman-to-woman marriage should be recognised in Nigeria;
(ii) the Nigerian courts should have jurisdiction to dissolve such a marriage and to make ancillary orders in respect of the obligations of the parties thereto;
(iii) where there is evidence of same sex sexual intercourse between the parties, the marriage would be treated as a same sex union and

75 See *Okonwo v Okagbue*.
76 Sections 1 and 3 of the Same Sex Marriage (Prohibition) Act.

> the provision of the Same Sex Marriage (Prohibition) Act, 2014 as well as the doctrine of public policy would be activated to deny the recognition to such a union.

Again, both Kenya and South Africa have amended their laws such that a customary marriage is placed on the same footing as statutory marriages. In South Africa section 2 of the Recognition of Customary Marriages Act, 1998 provides that a marriage which is a valid marriage at customary law and exists at the commencement of the Act is for all purposes recognised as a marriage even if polygamous. While the Act does not specifically mention woman-to-woman marriage as practised, for example, among the Lovedu tribe of South Africa, we strongly believe that such marriage is valid in customary law and as such, should be recognised as a valid marriage under the Act.[77] By virtue of Section 43 of the Kenya Marriage Act, 2014, customary marriage is recognised as a marriage celebrated in accordance with the customs of the communities of one or both of the parties to the intended marriage. Under the Marriage (Customary Marriage) Rules, 2017, such a marriage can be registered even if it is actually polygamous. However, a failure to register does not affect the validity of the marriage. One can safely submit that under the Kenyan Marriage Act, 2014 and the Marriage (Customary Marriage) Rules of 2017, a woman-to-woman marriage will be recognised as a marriage in accordance with the customs of the communities where it is celebrated. It is therefore recommended that Nigeria should take a cue from the legal developments both in Kenya and South Africa where both statutory and customary marriages are entitled to registration and the issuance of marriage certificates.

6 Conclusion

The African traditional concept of marriage is teleological in that its primary focus is procreation. Under African culture the death of a man does not necessarily mean the death of his name as long as he has somebody to bear his name. Unfortunately, marriage under African laws and customs has consistently been treated as an aberration, as sub-standard or as second-class by the colonialists and, by extension, the Western world. This position explains why African marriages were (and are) subjected to the colonialists' test of

77 Gumede, "Woman-to-Woman Marriages," 112–22. Note that other requirements as to age, the consent of the parties, etc., must be met before a customary marriage can be recognised as valid. See s. 3 of the Act.

repugnancy in order to determine the level of their conformity to the Western understanding of what marriage should be. The Western approach to marriage as an institution is simplistic, to say the least. Marriage is treated as a union of a man and a woman (or two consenting adults depending on one's view of marriage) to the "exclusion" of all others. Where the husband is infertile or the wife is barren, there are two solutions: either they wait for the death of one of the parties or they file for divorce. However, Africans believe that there are various options open to a childless couple and one of them is the practice of woman-to-woman marriage.

The functional relevance of woman-to-woman marriage to the societies where it is being practised cannot be over-emphasised. Woman-to-woman marriage gives the female-husband a sense of independence as she has the final say over the affairs of her wife. It is also an ingenious solution to the problems associated with barrenness since any offspring from such a woman-to-woman marriage is regarded as the offspring of the female-husband. Finally, it drastically reduces the rate of divorce since infertility is a ground for divorce under customary law. In view of the functional relevance of this marriage, it is suggested that the attitude of the courts especially in Nigeria and Kenya in applying the imported (colonial) test of repugnancy to determine the validity of such a marriage is an insult to African customary practices. A better approach is to examine the rationale behind the development of this practice, the roles it plays in the societies where it is practised and the attitude of the members of such a society to the custom. While it is conceded that there are certain aspects of the custom that need some form of review in order to ensure that the custom is in conformity with constitutional provisions, rejecting this custom as barbaric or repugnant is an echo of the old colonial attitude towards African culture. Suffice to say that such an attitude must be expunged from African legal systems and the time to do it is now.

Bibliography

Literature

Achebe, Nwando. *The Female King of Colonial Nigeria: Ahebi Ugbabe*. Bloomington: Indiana University Press, 2001.

Amadiume, Ifi. *Male Daughters, Female-Husbands: Gender and Sex in an African Society*. London: Zed Books, 1987.

Bennett, Thomas William. "Conflict of Laws: The Application of Customary Law and the Common Law in Zimbabwe." *International and Comparative Law Quarterly* 30, no. 1 (1981): 59–103.

Bennett, Thomas William. "Re-Introducing African Customary Law to the South African Legal System." *American Journal of Comparative Law* 57, no. 1 (2009): 1–31.

Cadigan, Jean R. "Woman-to-Woman Marriage: Practices and Benefits in Sub-Saharan Africa." *Journal of Comparative Family Studies* 29, no. 1 (1998): 89–98.

Cambridge Online Dictionary. "Hermaphrodite." Accessed February 14, 2023. https://dictionary.cambridge.org/dictionary/english/hermaphrodite.

Carrier, Joseph M., and Stephen O. Murray. "Woman-Woman Marriage in Africa." In *Boy-Wives and Female-Husbands: Studies of African Homosexualities*, edited by Murray Stephen and Roscoe Will, 255–66. New York: St. Martin's Press, 1998.

Cleve, George van. "'Somerset's Case' and Its Antecedents in Imperial Perspective." *Law and History Review* 24, no. 3 (2006): 601–45.

Cotran, Eugene. *Restatement of African Law: The Law of Marriage and Divorce: Kenya – Vol. 1*. London: Sweet and Maxwell, 1968.

Emefiene, I. R. *The History of Ubulu People with Special Searchlight on Ubulu-Uno*. Benin City: Floreat Systems, 2006.

Epprecht, Marc. "The 'Unsaying' of Indigenous Homosexualities in Zimbabwe: Mapping a Blind-Spot in an African Masculinity." *Journal of Southern African Studies* 24, no. 4 (1998): 631–51.

Ezekwem, Ogechukwu. "Review of *The Female King of Colonial Nigeria: Ahebi Ugbabe*. (Review no. 1393)." Accessed October 20, 2021. https://reviews.history.ac.uk/review/1393.

Finnis, John M. "Marriage: A Basic and Exigent Good." *The Monist* 91, no. 3/4 (2008): 388–406.

Finnis, John M. "Law, Morality, and Sexual Orientation." *Notre Dame Law Review* 69, no. 5 (1994): 1049–76.

Girgis, Sherif, Robert George, and Ryan T. Anderson. "What is Marriage?" *Harvard Journal of Law and Public Policy* 34, no. 1 (2010): 245–87.

Gumede, P. "Woman-to-Woman Marriages among the Lovedu: The Need for Official Recognition." *Speculum Juris* 1 (2009): 112–22.

Hulsebosch, Daniel J. "Nothing but Liberty: 'Somerset's Case' and the British Empire." *Law and History Review* 24, no. 3 (2006): 647–57.

Kareithi, A. "Wangu wa Makeri". Accessed October 20, 2021. https://www.standardmedia.co.ke/the-standard/article/2000051911/wangu-wa-makeri.

Kogan, Terry. "Transsexuals, Intersexuals and Same-Sex Marriage." *Brigham Young University Journal of Public Law* 18, no. 2 (2003): 371–418.

Kramer, Larry. 1997. "Same-Sex Marriage, Conflict of Laws, and the Unconstitutional Public Policy Exception." *Yale Law Journal* 106, no. 7 (1997): 1965–2008.

Lugard, Frederick D. *The Dual Mandate in British Tropical Africa*. London: William Blackwood and Sons, 1922.

Macedo, Stephen. "Homosexuality and the Conservative Mind." *Georgia Law Journal* 84 (1995): 261–300.

Oboler, Regina Smith. "Is the Female Husband a Man? Woman/Woman Marriage among the Nandi of Kenya." *Ethnology* 19, no. 1 (1980): 69–88.

Olookoba, Saka M., and Adebayo K. Mahmud. "Appraising the Cross-Currents of Law, Religion and Culture on Same Sex Marriage Issue in Nigeria: The Human Rights Approach." *Hungarian Journal of Legal Studies/Acta Juridica Hungarica* 55, no. 4 (2014): 367–83.

Omoteye, Oyedotun. and M. T. Akinlade. "Legal Implications of Same-Sex Marriage (Prohibition) Act, 2013 on Customary Female-Husband Marriage or Woman-to-Woman Marriage in Nigeria." *International Journal of Advanced Legal Studies and Governance* 6, no. 1 (2016): 22–45.

Onuorah, Patricia C. "The Religious, Socio-Cultural and Moral Implications of Same-Sex Sexual Union in Contemporary Nigerian Society." PhD diss., University of Nigeria, 2012.

Orchardson, Ian Q. "Notes on the Marriage Customs of the Kipsigis." *Journal of the East Africa and Uganda Natural History Society* (1931): 99–112.

Story, Joseph. *Commentaries on the Conflict of Laws*. Boston: Billiard, Gray and Co, 1834.

Taiwo, Elijah Adewale. "Repugnancy Clause and its Impact on Customary Law: Comparing the South African and Nigerian Positions: Some Lessons for Nigeria." *Journal for Juridical Science* 34, no. 1 (2009): 89–115.

Wairimũ, Ngarũiya Njambi, and William E. O'Brien. "Revisiting 'Woman-Woman Marriage': Notes on Gĩkũyũ Women." *National Women's Studies Association Journal* 12, no. 1 (2000): 1–23.

Wardle, Lynn D. "From Slavery to Same-Sex Marriage: Comity Versus Public Policy in Inter-Jurisdictional Recognition of Controversial Domestic Relations." *Brigham Young University Law Review* 6 (2008): 1855–926.

Wardle, Lynn D. "The Institution of Marriage and other Domestic Relations." *Amsterdam Law Forum* 3, no. 2 (2011): 160–75.

Wikipedia. "Wangu wa Makeri." Accessed October 20, 2021. https://en.wikipedia.org/wiki/Wangu_wa_Makeri.

Williamson, Kay. "Changes in the Marriage System of the Okrika Ijo." *Africa: Journal of the International African Institute* 32, no. 1 (1962): 53–60.

Case Law

Canada

Beals v Saldanha (2003) SCC 72.

England

Somerset v Stewart (1772) 98 Eng Rep 499 (KB).

Kenya

Esther Chepkuaui v Chepngeno Kobot Chebet and Johanah Kipsang Civil App. No. 1 of 1981.

Maria Gisese w/o Angoi v Marcella Nyomenda [1981] Divorce Cause No. 16 of 1980.

R v Amkeyo (1917) 7 EALR 14.

Nigeria

Iweze v Okocha (1967/68) MSNLR 64.

Meribe v Egwu (1976) LPELR-1861 (SC).

Ojukwu v Agupusi and Anor (2014) LPELR 22683 (CA).

Okonkwo v Okagbue 9 NWLR (Pt. 368) 301.

South Africa

Alexkor Ltd v Richtersveld Community 2004 (5) SA 460 (CC).

Bhe v Magistrate, Khayelitsha 2005 (1) SA 580 (CC).

United States of America.

Compo v Jackson Iron Co. (1883) 50 Mich 578.

Haviland v Halstead (1866) 34 NY 643.

People v Ezeonu 588 NYS 2d 116 (1992).

Legislation and Government Publications

Canada

Immigration and Refugee Protection Act, 2001.

Zero Tolerance for Barbaric Cultural Practices Act, 2015.

Kenya

Judicature Act, Cap 8, 2012.

Marriage Act, 2014.

Marriage (Customary Marriage) Rules, 2017.

Nigeria

High Court Law of Lagos State, Cap H 3, Laws of Lagos State 2015.

Supreme Court Act, Cap S 15, LFN 2004.

Evidence Act, Cap 112, LFN 1990.

Same Sex Marriage (Prohibition) Act, 2014.

Restatement (Second) of Conflict of Laws, 1971.

Supreme Court Ordinance 11 of 1876.

South Africa

Constitution of the Republic of South Africa, 1996.

Native / Black Administration Act 38 of 1927.
Recognition of Customary Marriages Act 120 of 1998.

International Documents

Cairo Declaration of Human Rights in Islam (1990). In UNGA. "Status of Preparation of Publications, Studies and Documents for the World Conference on Human Rights. Addendum: Contribution of the Organisation of the Islamic Conference." A/Conf.157/PC/62/Add.18, June 9, 1993. https://documents-dds-ny.un.org/doc/UNDOC/GEN/G93/140/33/IMG/G9314033.pdf.

Treaties and Agreements

Universal Declaration of Human Rights (1948).

CHAPTER 6

Constitutional Transformation of the Customary Marriage Laws of the Batswana Tribe

Boitumelo Mmusinyane

Abstract

The Batswana tribe is one of the ethnic groups that still conform to their customary laws and practices, sometimes against constitutional values and norms. Considering that the 1996 Constitution requires reform of marriage practices, the Batswana tribe still cling to its old ways of negotiating, organising, and celebrating the marriage of its children and finds constitutional demands as encroaching on its right to practice its culture. To the Batswana tribe, the customary laws of marriage unlock blessings for its children, who need to be the custodians of its marriage culture. Undoubtedly, people ought to adapt to the changing times. While the Batswana tribe continues to embrace modernity in other aspects of life, it nevertheless wants to retain certain customary laws and practices. Constitutional demands such as equality and non-discrimination are seen as threatening the Batswana marriage practices at the behest of the western systems that are seen as assimilating Africans' way of life. This chapter aims to critically evaluate various Batswana customary law and practices governing marriage to show how they are affected by constitutional reforms. The chapter includes a discussion of how these reforms are seen as encroaching on the Batswana's right to freely practice their marriage culture. It argues that the 1996 Constitution and western-inspired judicial precedents seem to be applied consistently, thus making customary laws subservient to western-originated rules of evidence.

1 Introduction

The African way of life during the apartheid regime was restricted, controlled, and arbitrarily suppressed, and western law concepts were imposed on Africans by the apartheid government and enforced by the judiciary in cultural

 | DOI:10.1163/9789004696747_007

disputes/claims as they deemed fit. In *Daniels v Campbell* Moseneke had this to say about the use of a Eurocentric determination of customary law:[1]

> True to their worldview, the judges of the past displayed remarkable ethnocentric bias and arrogance at the expense of those they perceived as different. They exalted their own and demeaned and excluded everything else. Inherent in this disposition ... is inequality, arbitrariness, intolerance, and inequity. The requirements were that the customary law should not be contrary to public morals and such public morals were Eurocentric.

Although Africans have developed a normative system of unwritten customary laws, rules and traditions that govern their affairs, these are not properly understood, applied and interpreted by our higher courts. The 1996 Constitution[2] seems to have an overshadowing influence on the courts' application and interpretation of the customary laws of marriage. What complicates the proper understanding and interpretation of these varying customary laws of marriage are that some scholars seem to conflate the practices and customary laws of these tribes.[3] Finnegan's delineation of the matter is incontrovertible as she writes:[4]

> Africa possesses both written and unwritten traditions, with the latter being far less widely known and appreciated. Such forms do not fit neatly into familiar categories of literate cultures, they are harder to record and present, and for a superficial observer at least, they are easier to overlook than the corresponding written material.

What needs to be noted is that most African communities subscribe mainly to the living customary law, which is transmitted orally from generation to generation. The living customary law is instrumental in protecting the rights of both individuals and groups in a multi-cultural constitutional democracy like South Africa.[5] However, it poses many challenges, particularly regarding the ascertainment of its content. The core strength of the 'living law' approach is

1 *Daniels v Campbell* 2004 (7) BCLR 735 (CC), para. 74.

2 Constitution of the Republic of South Africa, 1996.

3 Manthwa and Ntsoane, "Right to Bury the Deceased," 617; Solway, "'Slow Marriage'," 312; *Tsambo v Sengadi* (244/19) [2020] ZASCA 46 (30 April 2020) (hereafter *Tsambo v Sengadi*); Budlender, "Afterword," 331.

4 Finnegan, *Oral Literature*, 1.

5 Ozoemena, "Living Customary Law," 162.

its democratising function. The law is what the people in the community practise, and it changes according to their needs. But finding the living customary law is no simple matter, precisely because the content of the law evolves and varies in time and in place or community and, inevitably, there will often be contestation about its content.[6]

The Batswana tribe is predominantly found in the North West, Northern Cape, and Gauteng provinces of South Africa, in addition to in the neighbouring country of Botswana. Its language, Setswana, is spoken by over 4 million people.[7] Notably the Batswana tribe, as a functional community both in Botswana and South Africa, does not have a comprehensive or a universal written customary law governing marriage. Its law of marriage is deducible from various case laws, books and a consideration of the living customary law, which is often interpreted in accordance with the constitutional transformations of the law taking place.

Therefore, the purpose of this chapter is to articulate for the first time what constitutes the legal requirements for a valid customary law in the Batswana tribe in the context of the demand for the universalism of rights, cultural relativism, and deference to the constitutional dispensation. Further, the purpose is to critically evaluate the impact of the higher courts' views on the "handing over of the bride" requirement, which is central to the Batswana tribe's legal requirements for a valid customary marriage. The chapter will also critically analyse jurisprudential issues around adjudication and judge's prejudices when dealing with disputes relating to customary marriages.

2 Interplay of Cultural Relativism with Eurocentric Notions of Universal Human Rights

Because we are living with the legacy of colonialism, we need to approach with caution the tendency towards universalism, which is to impose the western context and western concepts on clashing *African* (my emphasis) cultural values. Eurocentric notions of human rights need to take into account the sensitive and varying and unique political, economic, and cultural factors that lie behind even their best-intentioned activities. Undoubtedly ignoring those factors and the imposing Western values (on African cultural values) is likely to be met with understandable suspicion, or even with resistance.[8] Donnelly

6 Rautenbach, "Case Law as an Authoritative Source," 4.

7 *Alexander,* "11 Languages".

8 Donnelly, "Relative Universality of Human Rights," 300.

describes cultural relativity as an undeniable fact; moral rules and social institutions evidence an astonishing cultural and historical variability. Cultural relativism is a doctrine that holds that (at least some of) such variations are exempt from legitimate criticism by outsiders, a doctrine that is strongly supported by notions of communal autonomy and self-determination.[9] Universalism, on the other hand, denotes that each human being possesses certain inalienable rights simply because he or she is a human being, regardless the person's national background, religious or political views, gender, age *or culture* (my emphasis).[10] Therefore, according to Schaumburg-Müller:[11]

> The claim for universality is inherently dangerous because human beings seem to have a built-in propensity for unwarranted generalizations, especially taking one's own culture, law, language etc. as the prototype, not realizing the particularity of one's own affiliation.

Furthermore:

> It is therefore essential that rights – or any other human phenomenon – which claim to be of universal application are scrutinized in order to establish what is truly universal and what is rather contingent particularities, and – more importantly – in order to be able to make norms and regulations that are truly of general interest and application and not merely needs and interests of particular cultures and societies.

The concept of law today is pluralistic in nature, although there is no universally accepted definition of legal pluralism.[12] However, some scholars have justified legal pluralism, in the context of this chapter, to be:[13]

> the approach to law and legal theory that offers the most hope for understanding the role of diverse normative regimes not connected to the State and conceiving them in a language and vocabulary that does not presuppose the State as the stand.

9 Ibid.
10 LawTeacher. "Universalism".
11 Schaumburg-Müller, "In Defense of Soft Universalism," 120.
12 Tamanaha, "Non-Essentialist Version of Legal Pluralism," 296–98.
13 Macdonald, "Metaphors of Multiplicity," 91.

To some extent they are sympathetic with the view that "legal centralism" is the false ideology that "law is and should be the law of the state, uniform for all persons, exclusive of all other law, and administered by a single set of state institutions".[14] On the other hand, Tamanaha believes the following:[15]

> Law (now seen in terms of institutional norm enforcement) – at least state law – is often not a major source of social order ... since there are many sources of social order, including culture, customs, habits, reciprocity, and language, many of which do not entail the institutionalized enforcement of norms. The institutionalized enforcement of norms is seldom the dominant influence on social order, at least in non-totalitarian societies. Moreover, the law often does more things or is used to do more things, than just maintain social order, including, among other functions or purposes, enabling, facilitative, performative, status conferring, defining, legitimative, distributive, power-conferring, and symbolic; or being used as an instrument of harassment, revenge or vindication, or as a resource of raw power. Finally, it should not be assumed that law is always functional – the presence of and resort to law.

The social orders, behaviours, norms and standards governing communities and giving them a feeling of belonging in a legal order that controls, guides, informs and educates them about the need for the development of their values reflects their societal changes and development. Connolly is of the view that:[16]

> World cultures, concept acquisition, and cultural learning *on the part of members themselves* take place within rule-based contexts, including linguistic, educational, ethical, and religious contexts.

Customary laws and practices finds themselves at the centre of controversy of retaining their core component and being measured or being expected to remodel themselves to suit the western concepts of human rights universality and relativism. To Africans, culture is:[17]

> everything in the life of an individual which in the end constitutes his/her cultural identity, it includes all the cultural aspects a person can imagine.

14 Griffiths, "What is Legal Pluralism?" 4.
15 Tamanaha, "Non-Essentialist Version of Legal Pluralism," 301.
16 Connolly, "Legal Pluralism," 40, 47.
17 Pilane, "Analysis of the Construction," 53.

> It helps them to know who they are, where they belong, and what they are capable of. It influences them from the day they are born. Culture cannot be seen but it can be practiced. Again, it helps them to remember where they come from and who they are.

Such accommodation entails that the customary law and practices that most Africans have complied with since time immemorial and that have a deeply significant meaning and value to these communities be now adapted to western concepts. Africans conform to their customary law and practices and subscribe to strictly adhering to them to maintain social order, while obtaining blessing, light and guidance from such observance.

Customary laws have been followed for many years, and despite section 211(3)[18] of the 1996 Constitution many Africans consider that their law has now have been relegated to the status of mere rituals and practices.[19] The law of the State often situates them as running counter to the values that underlie the 1996 Constitution.[20] In this context the 1996 Constitution[21] is the central law that reigns supreme and is universally applicable to everyone and accommodates only that customary law and those practices that subscribe to its own values and principles.[22] This constitutional centralism and universalism is what unsettles the customary law and practices of African communities. Therefore, to Galanter "'Legal centralism' has impaired our consciousness of 'indigenous law'"[23] as an independent law capable of being applied on its own and of being sustained as such. It could also be viewed that considering many social phenomena that contribute to the maintenance of social order (giving rise to concrete behaviour), including customs, habits, language, the complex of social obligations (that is, reciprocity) and the institutionalised imposition of sanctions,[24] courts need to be mindful when evaluating different customary

18 Section 211(3) states that the courts must apply customary law when that law is applicable, subject to the 1996 Constitution and any legislation that specifically deals with customary law.

19 *Tsambo v Sengadi*, paras. 6, 9; also see Budlender, "Afterword," 331; *LS v RL* 2019 (4) SA 50 (GJ) (hereafter *LS v RL*); *Mabuza v Mbatha* 2003 (4) SA 218 (C) (hereafter *Mabuza v Mbatha*); and Bennett, *Sourcebook*, 194.

20 *Ntoagae v Makabanyane* (M420/2015) [2015] ZANWHC 78 (12 November 2015) (hereafter *Ntoagae v Makabanyane*), para. 6.

21 With its (westernised) fundamental rights invoked from the United Nations (UN) Universal Declaration of Human Rights, International Covenant on Civil and Political Rights, and International Covenant on Economic Social and Cultural Rights.

22 Section 2 of the 1996 Constitution.

23 Galanter, "Justice in Many Rooms," 8.

24 Tamanaha, "Non-Essentialist Version of Legal Pluralism," 300–01.

laws and to recognise their uniqueness, relevance, meaning and value because of the constitutional values that underlie the spirit and purpose of the Bill of Rights.

It cannot be denied that cultural rights being part of human rights are now an object of rights claims.[25] In South Africa the right to practice one's culture is entrenched in the 1996 Constitution, with section 31(1) of the 1996 Constitution stating that "persons belonging to a cultural, religious or linguistic community may not be denied the right, with other members of that community – (a) to enjoy their culture, practice their religion and use their language". *The 1996 Constitution reminds our courts to apply customary law i*n terms of section 39(2): "When interpreting any legislation, and when developing the common law or customary law, every court, tribunal or forum must promote the spirit, purport and objects of the Bill of Rights", while section 39(3) of the 1996 Constitution provides that "the Bill of Rights does not deny the existence of any other rights or freedoms that are recognized or conferred by common law, customary law or legislation, to the extent that they are consistent with the Bill of Rights".[26] Lastly, section 211(3) recognises the applicability of customary law on an equal footing when that law is in line with the 1996 Constitution and any other relevant legislation.

Taking all these sections together gives one mixed feelings as to what the 1996 Constitution regards as acceptable customary law and practice, and what is not acceptable. In this sense, while customary law is recognised, as is the well-developed common law, it needs to be consistently applied and tested in line with the Constitution. In the case of *Alexkor Ltd v The Richtersveld Community*,[27] which deals with the interplay between the law of property and the community's use of their land in terms of their customary law, the court found that customary law should not be treated as a stepchild of the South African legal system but as a part of an integrated legal system. This portends that cultural practices, traditions, norms and laws deserve to be approached in

25 Article 15 of the UN International Covenant on Economic, Social and Cultural Rights; also see Cowan, Dembour, and Wilson, *Culture and Rights*, 8.

26 Also see s. 2 of the 1996 Constitution.

27 *Alexkor Ltd v The Richtersveld Community* 2004 (5) SA 460 (CC) para. 51: "While in the past indigenous law was seen through the common law lens, it must now be seen as an integral part of our law. Like all laws, it depends on their ultimate force and validity on the Constitution. Its validity must now be determined by reference not to common law, but to the Constitution. The courts are obliged by section 211(3) of the Constitution to apply customary law when it is applicable, subject to the Constitution and any legislation that deals with customary law … In the result, indigenous law feeds into, nourishes, fuses with, and becomes part of the amalgam of South African law."

a manner similar to any other law, while taking into cognisance the uniqueness of every culture. Customary marriages in SA are regulated by section 3 of the Recognition of Customary Marriages Act (RCMA),[28] which provides that "for a marriage to be considered customary and valid, both parties must have consented to be married to each other under the customary law and the marriage must be negotiated and entered into or celebrated in accordance with customary law". The Act does not prescribe the content, form or process of how these customary marriages need to unfold and the reason for this was to enable the traditional communities themselves to apply their own customs and traditional ways of concluding these marriages. Of course, this has led to our higher courts producing inconsistent orders, which are to be dealt with hereunder.

A question that needs to be asked is whether the 1996 Constitution exists to transform the law (customary law) or to assimilate such law and assert its dominant universalism and relativism. *To Donnelly:*[29]

> Moral rules, including human rights, function within a moral community. Radical universalism requires a rigid hierarchical ordering of the multiple moral communities to which individuals and groups belong. To preserve complete universality for basic rights, the radical Universalist must give absolute priority to the demands of the cosmopolitan moral community over all other 'lower' moral communities.

It is very clear that the adoption of the 1996 Constitution came with a lot of surprising twists and turns, especially to the African traditional communities. While they welcomed the introduction of the Bill of Rights, the Constitution is seen as encroaching on their entrenched way of life, their customary laws, their rich customs and their traditions. The recognition of fundamental rights in any African society entails a denial, rejection or overriding of culture, while the constitutional recognition of culture is seen as prohibiting (potentially in some cases) the pursuit of universal fundamental rights.[30] This tug of war is quite evident in South Africa as we witness both the recognition of rights and the prohibition of culture taking place in relation to customary marriages, such as those of the Batswana tribe.

---

28 Act 120 of 1998.

29 Donnelly, "Cultural Relativism," 402.

30 Cowan, Dembour and Wilson, *Culture and Rights*, 4.

3 Adaptation of the Batswana Law of Marriage to the Bill of Rights

Marriage plays a major role in the formulation of a responsible society. In a case that dealt with the right of married partners to live together irrespective of their nationality, it was found in *Dawood, Shalabi, Thomas v Minister of Home Affairs*[31] that "the institutions of a marriage and the family are considered to be significant in providing security and support to individuals, and play an incremental role in the nurturing of children". To the Batswana tribe, progression through life is also measured through marriage and it is an essential concern of the parents to see that their sons and daughters get married.[32] "Culture therefore needs to be appreciated as a unified arrangement of practices and meanings that is intrinsically valuable and worthy of legal recognition and protection."[33] It is therefore critical to analyse the history of the Batswana marriage in terms of their customary laws and practices.

3.1 *Historical Determination of the Batswana Customary Law of Marriages*

In every African tribe, marriage as a union signifies not just a relationship between two individuals but the cementing of a relationship between two families.[34] In addition to connecting the two families, the process also introduces the new wife to the husband's ancestors[35] to invoke blessings on the marriage.[36] This process involves having the new wife being first brought formally into her new family. The Batswana tribe, like any other African tribes, holds it significant always to be in contact with the spirits of its ancestors (*Badimo*). The life and well-being of the members of the community are centred on the *Badimo,* with whom they need to communicate[37] regularly.[38] *Badimo*'s relationship and connection with the living will be dealt with hereunder in the context of the legal requirements of handing over of the bride. With regard to

31 *Dawood, Shalabi, Thomas v Minister of Home Affairs* 2000 (3) SA 936 (CC), para. 30.

32 Pilane, "Analysis of the Construction," 32.

33 Cowan, Dembour and Wilson, *Culture and Rights*, 8.

34 Mulaudzi, "Cultural Perceptions," 153–54; Matjila, "Some Aspects," 13.

35 Segami and Van Eeden, "Marital Symbols," 38.

36 Matjila and Haire, *Bringing Plaatjie Back Home*, 67–68.

37 Other examples are the ritual perforance of introducing the new wife and or new members (children) to the family graves (Manthwa and Ntsoane, "Right to Bury the Deceased," 616–17) or going to the one place at home where the family throws their rubbish and it is known as *Thothobolo* and taking along home-made sorghum beer, tobacco (ntsu and Boxer tobacco) to introduce the new family members.

38 Matjila and Haire, *Bringing Plaatjie Back Home*, 85–86.

the Batswana culture, being old in terms of age does not make you an adult, but being married means that you are regarded as a man (old enough), as married men/women are charged with certain forms of responsibilities in their tribe.[39] These responsibilities mean that you are considered a husband/wife, a father/mother and a provider/nurturer, and you are also now competent to fully execute certain duties, such as being part of the delegation to negotiate *Bogadi*[40] for the unmarried, being called to resolve conflicts between married couples, and to participate in other tribal matters.

It is to be noted that historically women were respected within the African tribes and central to the consultation before men do anything. In this context the power of a man over a woman can be considerable in a traditional society.[41]

3.2 *The Importance of Bogadi under the Batswana Customary Law of Marriage and the Bogadi Transformative Process*

While section 3(1)(b) of the RCMA provides that for the marriage to be valid it must be negotiated, entered into or celebrated in accordance with customary law, the presence of the words "or celebrated" in section 3(1)(b) does not assist in giving effect to section 3 of the Act. It has been found that a celebration is not a requirement for a valid customary marriage.[42] Notable in section 3 of the Act are also the omissions of an agreement on *Bogadi*, or the payment in part or full or in part of *Bogadi*, or the handing-over of the bride, as requirements for a valid customary marriage.[43] Therefore, it is vital to evaluate the significance of *Bogadi* in the Batswana tribe and its relevance to the conclusion of a valid customary marriage. It needs to be determined to a full extent if *Bogadi* constitutes a core requirement to a valid customary marriage for the Batswana tribe.

Historically, the Batswana adopted a generally applicable slow marriage process[44] as an integral component of a valid marriage within the bounds of their customary law. The process entails:

39 Datta, "In the Eyes of a Child," 101–02.

40 Commonly known as *Lobola*.

41 Matjila and Haire, *Bringing Plaatjie Back Home*, 81.

42 *ND v MM* (18404/2018) [2020] ZAGPJHC 113 (12 May 2020) (hereafter *ND v MM*), para. 9.

43 Ibid.

44 In the past, marriage proceeded slowly, often tentatively, with one ritual act or prestation in the process leading to the next, or perhaps not ... Unions could dissolve or carry on, with informal exchanges taking place intermittently before the potential next formal ritual and prestation. Furthermore, the marital status is indeterminate but gradually gains solidity with public recognition of years of conjugality, exchanges, and rituals. The transfer of Bogadi eliminates ambiguity with respect to the children's social status. See Solway, "'Slow Marriage'," 311.

a) A meeting of two families (the bride-to-be and the groom-to-be), with both families having particularly chosen their representatives in terms of their culture.[45]
b) Before being allowed to gain entry into the yard (signifying the home), the groom's family is required by customary law to pay *Pula molomo,*[46] which is a small fee enabling them to be given permission to enter the bride's family home. *Pula molomo* also recognises the presence of the delegations and once it is paid, the delegates are welcomed and the *Bogadi* negotiations are considered to have been opened.[47]
c) *Bogadi* discussions involve the observance of a number of rituals and practices before the actual price is determined:
   i) In instances where a child has been born between the parties to be married, the bride's family shall demand payment of what they call *Tshenyo*[48] (*go thobela segotlo* or *go roba Mosetsana leoto*),[49] while in Botswana it is called *go tlhaga legora.*[50] *Tshenyo* must be paid by the groom's family before *Bogadi* can be negotiated, and it is paid in the form of a live sheep called *Mathobela Segotlo.*
   ii) In cases where there are no children between the parties but the bride has children from a previous relationship, a discussion ensues to determine if they will be part of the bride's marriage (*O e gapa le Namane*).[51] *O e gapa le Namane* literally translated means: "You lead it with its calf." Stripped of its metaphor, this means that the child follows its mother into the marriage.[52]

45 Uncles and aunts (in Setswana these terms are very broad, to mean the daughters' and sons' uncles and aunts who are the bride's and groom's parents' brothers and sisters) from both sides.

46 *Fanti v Boto* 2008 (5) SA 405 (C) (hereafter *Fanti v Boto*), para. 25.

47 Mmusi, *'A re Bueng Setswana'*, 264.

48 This is also common in other communities where "If the girl is pregnant, the young man is required to pay for the defloration and the pregnancy and this charge is referred to as *inkomo yesisu* (cattle used as payment for the defloration and the pregnancy). Though in Batswana the damage may not necessarily be fixed to be cattle." Mulaudzi, "Cultural Perceptions," 153–54, 155.

49 To impregnate a woman before marriage.

50 Solway, "'Slow Marriage'," 315.

51 In Batswana culture, this has important relevance to the identity and responsibilities of the groom and his family related to the raising of such children.

52 Monye, "Customary Law and Adoption," 3–4.

iii) Once *Tshenyo* has been paid or *O e gapa le Namane* has been dealt with, the actual *Bogadi* price negotiations commence. Traditionally *Bogadi* is paid in kind, in the form of cattle[53] and a full sack of *Mabele*.[54]
iv) *Serwalo* follows only when the bride's family has to take the traditional beer contained in steel containers and food to the groom's family, and it is delivered only by women.
v) Before *Serwalo* can take place, nothing is rushed. According to Solway there is a slow marriage process, leaving a reasonable period of time between each part of the process.[55]

d) Even amongst the Batswana tribe, as a symbolic act *Bogadi* is seen as having a communal and cultural depth and meaning. To Segami and Van Eeden:[56]
Bogadi payment by the groom is an acknowledgment and gratitude to the bride and her family for the upbringing of the bride. In Zulu tradition, similarly to Batswana tribes *Bogadi* is also a symbol lekau (*ubumnumzane*) (manhood) of the *umkhwenyna's* (*baagwe*) (bride-groom's) father, showing that they are not poor. *Bogadi* also serves as a token to the *badimo-amathongo* (ancestors) that the *isibaya* (*kgotla*) (lineage) is growing and, as it grows, it will create a strong *umuzi* (*motse*) (family).

Therefore, *Bogadi* and the values it represents in the Batswana culture may play a role in both the marital and spiritual well-being of Batswana women.[57] It is clear that observance of the rituals and ceremonies of customary marriages by the Batswana tribe is strict, as no marriage subsists between the parties unless and until *Bogadi* has been paid. It is, therefore, entirely up to the parties to agree to meet, request, pay and/or accept payment of Bogadi[58] (Lobola) and to adopt it as part of their laws, rituals or celebrations to conclude their valid

53 To Batswana, cattle symbolise various things, including life, wealth, and communion. Cattle bind the bride and groom and their families together. The ancestors, it is believed, bless the union after *Bogadi* has been presented and a cow is slaughtered (*go tsholola madi*), as a way of establishing a union. Matjila and Haire, "Cattle Motif," 213.

54 A sack was later used for taking *Serwalo* to the groom's family.

55 Solway, "'Slow Marriage'," 311.

56 Segami and Van Eeden, "Marital Symbols," 37.

57 Segami and Van Eeden, "Marital Symbols," 37.

58 To date *Bogadi* continues to be a legal requirement for the recognition of a customary marriage, despite the attempts to do away with it. See Mofokeng, "Lobolo Agreement," 277–88; South African Law Commission, "Project 90," para, 4.3.3.16.

customary marriages. In the Batswana tribe, what determines if it is a customary marriage or not is the content and manner in which the negotiations, the Bogadi payment, *go gorosa ngwetsi* (the handing over of the bride)[59] and the subsequent celebrations are followed. Historically, these are core issues that are deliberated upon by both families in extensive meetings before agreeing to anything.

4 Batswana Customary Law of Marriage under Constitutional Scrutiny

> The Constitutional Court has cautioned courts to be cognisant of the fact that customary law regulates the lives of people and that the need for flexibility and the imperative to facilitate its development must therefore be balanced against the value of legal certainty, respect for vested rights and the protection of constitutional rights. The courts must strive to recognise and give effect to the principle of living, actually observed customary law, as this constitutes a development in accordance with the 'spirit, purport and objects' of the Constitution within the community, to the extent consistent with adequately upholding the protection of rights.[60]

Though the law has dealt with some of the inequalities in customary marriages,[61] some continue to exist, but that does not suggest that the observance of the entire cultural process needs to stop.[62] Some moral values of our customary law still need to be retained and passed on to the next generations. According to Simons:[63]

> People and ideas circulate freely in modern African society. Most men, and many women, move to and from between country and town, and spend much of their lives outside a tribal environment, or what passes as such nowadays. They become members of groups that are not based on kinship or even local ties; their range of relationships is wider than in the tribe but less intensive and personal. Those who wish to do so can escape,

59 In Setswana she is also called *Sego sa Metsi*. See Pilane, "Analysis of the Construction," 39. Herbst and Du Plessis, "Customary Law v Common Law Marriages," 112.

60 *Mbungela v Mkabi* 2020 (1) SA 41 (SCA) (hereafter *Mbungela v Mkabi*), para. 18.

61 By the Recognition of Customary Marriages Act 120 of 1998.

62 Matjila and Haire, *Bringing Plaatjie Back Home*, 81.

63 Simons, "Customary Unions," 325.

> usually without much difficulty, from family and village supervision into the towns, and live among people who know little of their background and circumstances.

It cannot be denied that the Batswana tribe is rapidly adapting/changing in response to societal demands. However, it is still holding on to its old way (customary law, rituals and practices) of doing things. The old way of doing things is regarded by the elders as still being relevant since they see themselves as the custodians of their culture.[64] However, due to urbanisation and migration most married couples find themselves following European values and norms which do not embrace the African cultural worldview.[65] For example, in relation to the traditional ceremonies of marriage, per Pilane, things are no longer the same "today, since the introduction of the Western civilization, and especially Christianity, these ceremonies have in most tribes and also in the Batswana tribe, been considerably modified".[66] It is therefore not surprising that Dube succinctly sums up the heavy criticism of the *Bogadi* customs by various writers using the Christianity standards.[67] But that has not stopped *Bogadi* from being a legal requirement in all customary marriages. The Eurocentric view of the African way of life continues to erode many African traditions and seems to be finding its way through to the youth as they begin to abandon their culture. Simons writes in this regard as follows:[68]

> Town and country do not constitute distinct societies but are bridged by the migrant labour system, which transmits reciprocal influences. Rural populations, even while retaining the original outward form of tribal institutions acquire the characteristics of urban communities. The small, compact groups are being dissolved; the patriarchal family is smaller; the authority of the head has declined; kinship obligations are often resented and enforced, if at all, with difficulty; and the rebellious of both sexes tend to escape into the obscurity and freedom of urban life.

---

64 Mmusinyane, "Role of Traditional Authorities," 137. Also see *Shilubana v Nwamitwa* 2009 (2) SA 66 (CC), para. 5, where the court acknowledged that past practices should not be interpreted as being irrelevant in today's society, since such practices and traditions may still be of considerable importance in customary law, but should be considered together with other important factors.

65 Mulaudzi, "Cultural Perceptions," 157.

66 Pilane, "Analysis of the Construction," 39.

67 Dube, "Translating Cultures," 5–6.

68 Simons, "Customary Unions," 326.

Their involvement in societal development has automatically enabled African communities to adapt to the prevalent changes. The form, content and nature of the culture of the Batswana tribe have evolved. But this evolution has not been without consequences. As Mulaudzi puts it, "Doing away with the customary preliminary steps in the initiation of marriage proposals has left many young women vulnerable."[69] There is a lacuna in relation to identity, cultural values and belonging in today's marriages, as the anchor of traditional culture is cast aside. In particular, the older people in the community, seeing the changes in the customs that they have always relied upon, see themselves as being pressured to part ways with their identity just to conform with this transformative wave. Matjila and Haire appeal to the Batswana tribe not to erode their culture but rather to incorporate modern ideas which respect women and to treat them as equals.[70] Double standards in marriage continue to persist.[71] It is true that customary law is a living law and not static and needs to reflect the changing needs of an evolving community and its societal values. To Donnelly:[72]

> Human nature, at the levels of the individual, the group, and the species alike, is a range of possibilities, varying, in part in response to culture, within apparently fixed psychobiological limits; it is as much a project, and an individual and social discovery, as a given.

However, this evolution should not just be accepted at face value. The development of customary law could be taking place in urban areas may not be the same as the customary law development that is automatically happening in rural areas. That "always evolving" nature of customary law requires a serious re-evaluation as it cannot be used as a one-size-fit-all approach, as done by the Supreme Court of Appeal in *Tsambo v Sengadi*.[73] The case dealt with whether or not a valid customary law marriage came into existence between the deceased, Tsambo, and the respondent, Ms Lerato Rubeta Sengadi. The court had to decide whether or not pursuant to the conclusion of the lobola

69 Mulaudzi, "Cultural Perceptions," 153–54, 157.

70 Matjila and Haire, *Bringing Plaatjie Back Home*, 96.

71 Ibid.

72 Donnelly, "Cultural Relativism," 403.

73 *Tsambo v Sengadi*, para. 17. The case dealt with the question of whether the wife was officially handed over to the Tsambo family in Mahikeng when the couple themselves were residing together in Gauteng. The Tsambo family disputed the existence of a customary marriage since no handing over was done by the Sengadi family.

negotiations, the handing over of the bride ensued in satisfaction of the requirement that the marriage must be negotiated and entered into or celebrated in accordance with customary law in terms of section 3(1)(*b*) of the Recognition of Customary Marriages Act. The Supreme Court of Appeal found that there was a tacit waiver of the custom of the handing over of the bride, because a symbolic handing over of the respondent to the deceased's family had occurred after the conclusion of the customary marriage.[74] Clearly the so-called symbolic handover as upheld by the Supreme Court of Appeal and relying on a western system of precedents, our High Courts are now going to refer to this judgment as a binding precedent, thereby in the development of the handing over requirement across all ethnic groups.[75] What also complicates[76] the Supreme Court of Appeal's generic interpretation of the customary law of the community is the deepening alienation of the court's developed law from those it is meant to serve.[77] There is a danger in using the common law precedent system that, in relation to these cultural rights, claims as a determination of what needs to be cautioned against. This is further evidenced by the *Tsambo v Sengadi* judgment, as follows:[78]

> It is evident from the foregoing passage that strict compliance with rituals has, in the past, been waived. The authorities cited by the respondent, mentioned earlier in the judgment, also attest to that. Clearly customs have never been static. They develop and change along with the society in which they are practised. Given the obligation imposed on the courts to give effect to the principle of living customary law, it follows ineluctably that the failure to strictly comply with all rituals and ceremonies that were historically observed cannot invalidate a marriage that has otherwise been negotiated, concluded or celebrated in accordance with customary law.

It is clear that in terms of the old way of doing things there are quite a number of what the Batswana tribe regard as legal requirements for a valid customary marriage, which are applied together with certain cultural practices or

74 *Tsambo v Sengadi*, paras. 11, 31.

75 Osman, "Precedent, Waiver and the Constitutional Analysis," 80, 83.

76 Himonga and Pope, "*Mayelane v Ngwenyama*,", 318, 322.

77 Goodsell, "Constitution, Custom and Creed," 113–14; Mwambene and Sloth-Nielsen, "Benign Accommodation?" 14; Mwambene and Kruuse, "Marital Rape," 43–45.

78 *Tsambo v Sengadi*, para. 18.

rituals.[79] At the same time, the Batswana customary practices of marriage have also embraced certain reforms, for example, by now allowing women/mothers to be part of the *Bogadi* negotiation process, in particular unmarried mothers,[80] and this is not only in the Batswana tribe. Such cultural practices have now been adapted to individual choices. For example, those who are divorced were previously not allowed to be part of the negotiations, but this practice is gradually eroding, allowing everyone to join in, if that is what the family wishes.

Although cultures, traditions and customary laws differ per tribe, some traits from other African tribes are found to be similar to those of the Batswana tribe. For example, in *Mabena v Letsoala*,[81] which dealt with whether a valid customary marriage existed where no male/father was present at the negotiations, the court acknowledged that a girl's mother is capable of negotiating for the *lobolo* of her daughter's marriage, thereby either applying the living law or developing customary law.[82] Similarly, in relation to a mother's capacity to act as the family head, Judge Dlodlo in *Fanti v Boto* said:[83]

> I want to make it very clear that the mother of a girl whose father died or is for some other acceptable and understandable reason absent and/or unable to discharge duties normally meant for the 'kraalhead', is quite entitled to act as the head of the family. Such a mother becomes the 'father' and legal guardian of the children of her family. I state categorically that such a mother would legitimately negotiate for and even receive *lobolo* paid in respect of her daughter.

While this development is welcomed, the core composition of delegates remains the same. Marriage decisions are collective in nature, and the delegates are to include parents, *bomalome* (mother's brothers), *mmaane/mmangwane* (aunts), *borrangwane/rramogolo* (father's siblings) *borakgadi* (aunts' or father's sisters)[84] and grandparents. These are significant parties in the consultation process. Respect for their elders[85] is vitally important and Batswana children

79 See *Motsepe v Khoza* (South Gauteng High Court) (unreported) case number 15078/2012 of 8 April 2013 (hereafter *Motsepe v Khoza*), and *Fanti v Boto*.

80 Similarly to *Mabena v Letsoalo* 1998 (2) SA 1068 (T) (hereafter *Mabena v Letsoalo*).

81 *Mabena v Letsoala*.

82 In terms of s. 39(2) of the 1996 Constitution.

83 *Fanti v Boto*, para. 21.

84 Matjila, "Some Aspects," 13.

85 Pitso and Carmichael, "Premarital Childbearing," 189.

know that they are expected to inform and consult with them before taking a decision to marry or get married. Since time immemorial, this has been found to be at the centre of the Batswana tribe customary law and practice governing marriage. Despite the existence of this marriage culture and its associated marriage laws, this does not prevent the parties themselves from going to the Department of Home Affairs to get married, and such a marriage would still be valid in accordance with the South African law under the Marriage Act[86] or Civil Union Act.[87] However, Batswana children raised in their culture are mindful that such marriages are likely not to have the blessings of their parents and even their ancestors.[88] They know that by failing to follow the process of the customary law of marriage they would be inviting bad luck and there wold be a dark cloud over their future – *dikgaba.* Solway explained *dikgaba* as an "anger or sadness on the part of the elders/ancestors towards their juniors and can result in any sort of misfortune, from the failure of crops to illness, particularly in children, further exposing the couple and their children to be more vulnerable to *dikgaba* in the absence of these key rituals".[89] This is just one of the repercussions that the Eurocentric court universally applying the constitutional norms may not be aware of when making certain pronouncements about the validity of these customary marriages. The uncertainty in the customary law relating to the existence of a marriage remains is captured by Simons:[90]

> The holding of a ceremony raised a presumption that the family heads had given their consent, that they had agreed on the lobolo, and that the bride had been handed over to her husband's group. Even today it is seldom difficult to prove a union that has been effected with the proper formalities.

At the same time, although the RCMA stipulates that the marriage must be celebrated in accordance with the customs of that community, it has been accepted since as long ago as 1958 that:[91]

86 Act 25 of 1961.
87 Act 17 of 2006.
88 Diala, "Legal Pluralism," 10; Pilane, "Analysis of the Construction," 42, 43, 44.
89 Solway, "'Slow Marriage'," 312.
90 Simons, "Customary Unions," 325.
91 Ibid.

> The omission of a ceremony, as has been suggested, did not invalidate a union, nor would it have given rise to serious doubts. Certainty could be provided by other means.

As for the situation today, the judgment in the *Mbungela v Mkabi* case is a classic assertion that:[92]

> the provisions in section 3 of the RCMA do not restrict parties to a specific list of requirements that ought to be complied with for a valid customary marriage to exist, but rather, the court must consider the flexibility of the customary law systems as well as the present practices and lived experiences of the communities and customs concerned.

The *Mbungela* judgment confirms the notion that every African tribe subscribes to different customs, traditions and customary laws and there can never be a one-size-fits-all solution when these matters are brought before courts. Nevertheless, it must be noted that the contradictory ways in which customary law is being treated and watered down by relying on the Constitution and the frequency with which courts continue to make orders that communities do not subscribe to or fail to regard as their customary laws make such court-imposed laws mute and irrelevant in a constitutional society, as will be shown hereunder. The customary law of marriage exists and should not be misunderstood. It should not be thought that every requirement of this law is or should be seen as being adaptable, which is contrary to what the Batswana tribe have for generations consistently maintained and established as the customary law and practices governing their marriages.

4.1 *Cultural Practices/Rituals Performed during the Batswana Marriage Process*

The Batswana tribe recognises the differences between what it regards as its customary law of marriage and its rituals or cultural practices. This will be evident in the legal requirements mentioned hereafter and what they consider to be its rigid customarypractices/rituals relating to the conclusion of a customary marriage across all groups. These practices/rituals are not universally found or practiced by all the Batswana tribes and in some certain Batswana tribes, they are however believed to be a component of the establishment of a customary marriage. For example, the *Bahurutshe* tribe[93] requires its newlyweds to come

92 *Mbungela v Mkabi, para. 17.*

93 For example, see Monyai and Skosana, "Historical Exposition," 18.

together in a ceremony referred to as *go loma* (to bite meat),[94] where the couple is put in a room with chosen elders of both families, and a special piece of meat from the slaughtered beast, roasted on burning wood, is given to the couple to eat it without touching it with their hands. The elders put the meat in their mouths. This ritual binds them together, cementing them as one couple. Some tribes, such as Batlhaping, also require compliance with a *Serwalo, go tshubela ngwetsi*[95] process. Due to their flexibility and adaptations, these rituals/practices could be interpreted as constituting practices rather than as elements of the customary law of marriage of the Batswana. However, certain principles have been found across the Batswana tribe to have been universally and consistently applied from time immemorial and strict compliance with them is necessary to validate their children's marriage in terms of customs and traditions.

4.2 *Legal Requirements for a Valid Customary Marriage in the Batswana Tribe: Post Constitutionalism*

With the 1996 Constitution in place and the development of the Batswana customary law of marriage, it is abundantly clear that the Batswana tribe have made a very express distinction between what constitutes their customs and traditional practices and what constitutes their customary law of marriage, in that principles similar to those observed in the pre-constitutional era exist today and are consistently applied. There are nine essential customary legal requirements to be complied with in concluding a valid customary marriage in the Batswana tribe, namely:

1. As a form of respect and good upbringing, Batswana children (although regarded as adults when over 18 years old)[96] must consult their elders before getting married.[97] The groom informs his parents and grandparents, who then calls *bomalome, borramogolo, borrangwane* (uncles) and *borakgadi* (aunts) to the said marriage discussion meeting.[98] Most

94 *Leseka* is also another practice of calling upon the newlyweds to be joined by other married couples to come together and share cooked meat in the presence of the elders.

95 The mother-in-law going to the new wife's house to light up the fire for her, as a form of welcoming her in the homestead.

96 Section 17 of the Children's Act 38 of 2005.

97 The mutual consent of the parents to the marriage is necessary, particularly so far as a woman is concerned, and should two parties marry without the consent of the parents on both sides the marriage is not looked upon as valid. See Frylinck, "Casual Notes," 319; Matjila, "Some Aspects," 13.

98 *Borakgadi* are held in high esteem as easing things and are believed to provide luck to the brother's children.

importantly, *bomalome* and *borakgadi*[99] constitute the pillar of the negotiations.[100]

2. A formal notice is then written by the groom's representative and is sent to the bride's family to inform them of their son's intention to marry their daughter and requesting a specific date for them to meet with them.[101] The bride's family responds with a suitable date.
3. The parents from both sides then hold their own meetings to choose in advance those who will form part of the negotiations.[102] Development here have led to a situation where the elders are no longer strict about who forms part of the delegation, but *bomalome and borakgadi* lead the delegation.
4. On the agreed meeting date, the groom's delegates arrive very early at the locked/closed gate of the bride's family, and before the gate is opened they are required to pay *Pula molomo*.[103] This has to be done before the groom's family can be welcomed.
5. Once *Pula molomo* is paid, *Patlo* process follows. *Patlo* process forms a critical part of the *go batla Mosadi/sego sa metsi* process, which is the most important requirement for customary marriage. It is spearheaded by women representatives only-*borakgadi*. The process entails that a marriage agreement is entered into by the parents of the groom and bride, incorporating the giving of gifts[104] by the groom to the bride, before the *Bogadi* process.[105] *Patlo* may take place without the immediate payment of *Bogadi*, but when that happens it is expected that *Bogadi* will be paid later. Social acceptance is crucial for a union to be called a marriage in Botswana.[106] Marriages become socially recognised when *Patlo*

99 They are a critical part of conducting the *Patlo* process.

100 They are important members of the family in the Batswana culture; Ntsoane, "Batswana Indigenous Conflict Resolution Methods," 18, 19.

101 This is also common with the *Tshivenda;* see Mulaudzi, "Cultural Perceptions," 153–54, 155.

102 Ntsoane, "Batswana Indigenous Conflict Resolution Methods," 17–18.

103 Mmusi, *'A re Bueng Setswana'*, 264.

104 The gifts must always include groceries, two traditional shawl-blankets called *Tjale*, one for the wife-to-be and the other for the bride's mother, and a complete set of clothes for the bride.

105 Terms criticised by Sibisi and not relevant to the actual meaning or significance of *Bogadi*. Sibisi, "Juristic Nature of *iLobolo* Agreements," 57.

106 The Batswana in South African and those in Botswana practise more or less the same form of a customary marriage with little or no difference between them. See Pitso and Carmichael, "Premarital Childbearing," 188.

ceremony has occurred.[107] The Batswana tribe are now also prepared to accept money instead of material gifts. *Patlo* can be further explained as:

> the rite that couples have to undergo in order for their marriages to be regarded as lawful and as carrying the rights, duties, and privileges accorded married people by Batswana society.

6. After the *Patlo* process a discussion ensues relating to any child born between the parties before marriage. The groom is required by customary law to present the bride's family with a *Mathobela Segotlo* sheep[108] as an acknowledgment of *go thobela segotlo.*[109] The Batswana are now accepting money for the purpose of convenience and preference instead of actual live sheep as *Mathobela-Segotlo.*
7. In cases where the bride has a child by someone else from a previous relationship, a discussion related to that child must take place so that it can be resolved whether the groom *o e gapa le namane* or not.[110]
8. Once that has resolved, *Bogadi* negotiations can now take place. The groom's family must present a live sheep to the bride's family. This is known as *Nku ya Bogadi.* A bottle of alcohol must also be presented as a gift. The Batswana tribe currently also accepts money instead of the actual sheep and or alcohol. For *Bogadi,* the bride's family dictates if they want cattle or money.[111] The latter has now been widely accepted, meaning that the Batswana tribe have evolved in keeping abreast with modern ways of life.[112] Once agreed, the groom's family pays[113] *Bogadi.*[114] Therefore *Bogadi* remains a critical legal component of marriage for the

107 Pitso and Carmichael, "Premarital Childbearing," 188.

108 It is known as *Mathobela segotlo.*

109 Impregnating a girl before marriage.

110 *Motsepe v Khoza* paras. 14–17.

111 Recently money became the optional method of paying *Bogadi;* see Herbst and Du Plessis, "Customary Law v Common Law Marriages," 111.

112 Sibisi, "Juristic Nature of *iLobolo* Agreements," 58–59.

113 *Malome o gapa Bogad*i (the uncle is expected to take a portion of Bogadi); as Frylinck puts it, *Bogadi* goes to the mother's brother and not to the father or mother. See Frylinck, "Casual Notes," 319. However, this practice has evolved so that now one sees the Uncle taking a smaller portion, but the money is still kept by the mother's family, either as a contribution to the forthcoming marriage celebration or to use in whichever way they see fit.

114 According to the Batswana customary law of marriage, there can never be a marriage between their children until *Bogadi* has been paid. See Pilane, "Analysis of the Construction," 35–36, 37. Dube, "Translating Cultures," 5–6.

Batswana tribe.[115] In other words, *Bogadi*'s significance persists despite transformations in its meaning, the timing and the frequency of its presentation as well as in the society as a whole.[116]

9. Lastly there is the handing over of the bride (*go gorosa ngwetsi*),[117] where the wife is now formally brought to her husband's home in the presence of both parties' representatives. This requirement is a core component of the validity of the customary marriage in the Batswana tribe as it has been consistently maintained and applied to date and thus it cannot be reduced to a mere cultural practice/ritual and thought to be adaptable as found in some court cases and by some scholars.[118]

The Motsepe v Khoza case[119] dealt with whether or not a valid customary marriage existed and whether or not the husband was legally liable to pay maintenance for his wife's two minor children not born of him under the customary law principle *O e gapa le Namane*. The court considered a number of factors in finding that a valid customary marriage existed when:

a) the elders of the families of the two parties met and negotiated a customary marriage for the parties;
b) there was an amount paid by the elders of the respondent to the elders of the applicant;
c) both parties agreed the above was *lobola*;
d) the elders of the applicant handed her over to the elders of the respondent; and
e) the negotiations and payment of *lobola* were followed by a celebration, which both parties acknowledged took place.

These five requirements were found to have satisfied the legal requirements of a customary marriage in line with section 3 of the RCMA.[120] It is argued that this cannot be seen merely as a practice but as a key and essential legal requirement governing the validity of a marriage in the Batswana tribe. Thus it was found in *Fanti v Boto*[121] that certain rituals and ceremonies have to take place and they need to involve the participation of both families as they constitute a concrete, visible way in which a customary marriage is entered into.[122]

115 Sibisi, "Juristic Nature of iLobolo Agreements," 60, 61, 62, 65, 66–67, 68.

116 Solway, "'Slow Marriage'," 309.

117 Diala, "Legal Pluralism," 11.

118 *Tsambo v Sengadi*, para. 69; also see Budlender, "Afterword," 331; *LS v RL*; *Mabuza v Mbatha*; Bennett, *Sourcebook*, 194.

119 *Motsepe v Khoza* paras. 6, 9.

120 *Motsepe v Khoza*, para. 8.

121 *Fanti v Boto*, para. 21.

122 *Fanti v Boto*, para. 23.

Therefore these ceremonies and ritual processes must be viewed as processes in which essential legal requirements have been incorporated.[123]

It needs to be acknowledged that the above legal processes are now capable of being fast-tracked, resulting in what is being called a "fast *Bogadi*" process, whereby the "prestations, events and rituals that have occurred over a lifetime or more now take place within a few days".[124] Despite the tenth requirement, that of handing over, being a legal requirement under the Batswana customary law, it has been demonstrated to be a debatable requirement of a valid customary marriage across tribes in South Africa today, and this needs a further evaluation.

4.2.1 Controversies Surrounding *Go Gorosa Ngwetsi* – The Handing over of the Bride

As in other tribes in South Africa, *go gorosa ngwetsi* in the Batswana tribe is at the heart of the conclusion of a valid marriage. As Simon says:[125]

> The essentials of a customary union in the Cape Province have frequently been defined as: the consent of the contracting parties; the delivery and acceptance of lobolo; and the handing over of the bride to her husband.

The handing over process with its own rules is known in the Batswana tribe as *go gorosa ngwetsi* (handing over) and it takes place at any time after *Bogadi* has been paid. Simons further emphasises that this handing over is a critical part of the marriage:[126]

> Marriage was a well-attested act, preceded by negotiations, accompanied by festivities, and demonstrated by the bride's formal installation in her new home.

Due to the inconsistent way this requirement has been interpreted and applied by our higher courts, the question whether customary law is adaptable and to what extent has arisen. Clearly our courts so far have issued different interpretations of the (in)significance of this requirement, as a mere practice or as constituting a valid customary marriage. *In the case of Mbungela v Mkabi,*[127] two

---

123 Ibid.
124 Solway, "'Slow Marriage'," 311–12.
125 Simons, "Customary Unions," 322–23.
126 Simons, "Customary Unions," 324–25.
127 *Mbungela v Mkabi*, paras. 26, 27.

questions were addressed: whether the ceremony of the handing over of the bride is a key determinant of a valid customary marriage, and whether or not there is a waiver so that the absence of the handing over does not invalidate a customary marriage. The court held that in this instance the bridal transfer ritual had been waived, and that it had to be recognised that there was no inflexible rule that there was no valid customary marriage if just this one ritual had not been observed, even if the other requirements of section 3(1) of the Act had been met. Consequently, our higher courts have entered into the arena of controversy about how to interpret this customary law requirement. On the other hand in the *Ntoagae* case, which also dealt with a dispute about the Batswana customary marriage ritual of the handing over of the bride, the court acknowledged that the handing over process was a key requirement in concluding a valid customary marriage.[128] The court held that a customary marriage is not exclusively about the parties themselves but that it envelopes the families of the respective parties.[129] Significantly, this requirement amongst members of the Batswana tribe is critical to the validity of the marriage, and as it stands it is the law that governs marriage between members of the Batswana tribe or being married into and by members of the Batswana tribe.

It is argued that, according to the Batswana customary law, the performance of formal event of the handing over cannot be taken lightly, as if it were the mere dropping off of the bride, or merely symbolic, as in the *Tsambo v Sengadi* and *Mbungela v Mkabi* matters. The handing over requirement constitutes more than a mere symbolic act or a mere ritual as it goes beyond the meeting of the two families physically meeting. It was found in *Fanti v Boto*[130] that:

> All authorities are in agreement that a valid customary marriage only comes about when the girl has been formerly transferred or handed over to her husband or his family. Once that is done severance of ties between her and her family happens. Her acceptance by the groom's husband and her incorporation into his family is ordinarily accompanied by well-known extensive rituals and ceremonies involving both families.

This therefore entails the involvement of the two families from the inception of the *lobola* negotiations to the ultimate handing over.[131] The significance of

---

128 *Ntoagae v Makabanyane*, paras. 7, 14; it was admitted that no handing over had taken place but claimed that was a technicality, see also *Moropane v Southon* (755/12) [2014] ZASCA 76 (29 May 2014), paras. 39–40, 55.

129 *Ntoagae v Makabanyane*, para. 15.

130 *Fanti v Boto*, para. 22.

131 *Ntoagae v Makabanyane*, para. 15.

the handing over requirement was also outlined in *Motsoatosa v Roro*[132] as follows:

> One of the crucial elements of a customary marriage is the handing over of the bride by her family to her new family, namely that of the groom. As the man's family gained a daughter through the marriage, from her family, the bride is invariably handed over to him at his family's residence. Handing over of the bride (*go gorosa ngwetsi*) is not only about celebration with the attendant feast and rituals. It encompasses the most important aspect associated with the married state namely: *go laya/ukuyala/ukulaya* in the vernacular. There is no English equivalent of this word or process but loosely translated it implies "coaching" which includes the education and counselling of both the bride and groom by the elders of their rights, duties, and obligations which a married state imposes on them. This is the most important and final step in the chain of events and happens in the presence of both the bride's and the groom's families. One can describe this as the official seal of the African context, of the customary marriage.

However, our courts have demonstrated their disagreement with this account, justifying their declaration of the invalidity of this core requirement through their reliance on the modern Constitution.[133] This is particularly based on the fact that the rights of women, equality and dignity are seen as overriding

132 *Motsoatosa v Roro* 2011 (2) All SA 324 (GSJ), paras. 19, 20.

133 In *LS v RL* the high court held that the custom is unlawful as it unfairly and unjustly discriminates against the gender of the applicant as a woman and denies her the constitutional right of dignity and equality "because only women, after consenting to enter into a customary law marriage are subject to this unequal treatment by the custom of handing over"; *LS v RL*, para. 35. Also see *Mabuza v Mbatha,* where the court considered whether non-compliance with the siSwati custom of bridal transfer, *ukumekeza*, invalidated a customary marriage. The court held: "[T]here is no doubt that ukumekeza, like so many other customs, has somehow evolved so much that it is probably practised differently than it was centuries ago ... As De Villiers testified, it is inconceivable that ukumekeza has not evolved and that it cannot be waived by agreement between the parties and/or their families in appropriate cases." *Mabuza v Mbatha* paras. 25–26, while Bennett, *Sourcebook*, 194 states that: "In contrast, customary law was always flexible and pragmatic. Strict adherence to ritual formulae was never absolutely essential in close-knit, rural communities, where certainty was neither a necessity nor a value. So, for instance, the ceremony to celebrate a man's second marriage would normally be simplified; similarly, the wedding might be abbreviated by reason of poverty or the need to expedite matters [because of a pregnancy or elopement]."

several cultural practices/laws.[134] *Clearly, this constitutional interpretation by the courts seems to subjugate the customary law of these communities to the judgments of the courts, as the courts have the sole authority to determine what they call law, a practice and/or ritual has evolved or should be flexible.* Some authors also argue that the handing over of the bride is more of a practice than a customary law.[135] However, considering these laws in the narrow sense as being just cultural practices[136] violates the fundamental rights of a society to run its own affairs in line with sections 31 and 39(3), read with section 211(3) of the 1996 Constitution. Matjila and Haire reiterate the significance of a person's culture as:[137]

> the way a person relates to nature and to his fellow human beings. [This] is passed down from generation to generation. Thus culture is neither a luxury nor 'art's sake' but rather the very substance, the everyday creativity, and resourcefulness of people's lives.

In Setswana culture the handing over of the bride is considered to constitute a core legal requirement determining the validity of a customary marriage. To add to the controversial nature of the court's view, there are those academic analysts[138] who view the requirement of handing over of a bride as simply a means or process of introducing a bride to her new family merely signifying the start of the marital consortium. It is argued that the cultural identity of an African goes beyond mere compliance with a number of rituals but as Mokgoro[139] described it to includes but not limited to cultural artefacts,[140]

---

134 Sections 9 and 10 of the 1996 Constitution.

135 Budlender, "Afterword," 331.

136 Maluleke describes traditional cultural practices to be those that reflect the values and beliefs held by members of a community, that are passed from generation to generation, and are applicable to every social grouping subscribing to its own specific traditional cultural practices and beliefs. See Maluleke, "Culture, Tradition, Custom," 2. This therefore means that certain cultural practices not ingrained or rigid or not consistently practised would be overridden by the equality clause. See Kaganas and Murray, "Contest between Culture and Gender Equality," 417. The customary law will be applied in so far as it does not violate the objectives and purposes of the 1996 Constitution, s. 39(3).

137 Matjila and Haire, *Bringing Plaatjie Back Home*, 61–62.

138 Dlamini, *Juridical Analysis*, 90–93; Bennett, *Customary Law*, 221. The judge also relied upon the said authors in *Mbungela v Mkabi, para. 25.*

139 Mokgoro, "Protection of Cultural Identity," 1549–50.

140 Socially constructed and sanctioned features of the group experience and identity; traditions and customs.

forms of expression,[141] systems of knowing,[142] a world view, a historical understanding[143] and religious experience.[144] Thus the handing over of the bride cannot be reduced to having no legal significance to those most closely involved in the experience. To Ntsoane:[145]

> Unlike the way things are in Western societies, an individual's existence is intertwined with those of others and with the community he or she is from. Family life is most important and should be interpreted contextually to include ancestors.

It is noteworthy that the authors whom the judges have relied on do not belong to the Batswana tribe and cannot be expected to have a deeper knowledge and understanding[146] of the legal and cultural meaning and significance of *go gorosa ngwetsi* as a key requirement to the Batswana valid customary marriage. This is based on the fact that Batswana customary marriages go beyond celebrations. There are laws that have to be complied with and these laws or rules encompass families and the integration with those members of the families who have passed on.[147] *Go gorosa Ngwetsi* enables the family at this time to perform these significant steps in completing the customary marriage. The bride is not just brought to her husband's family home. Culture dictates that she should be brought with her own start-up luggage to establish a new home.[148]

141 Whether through a language medium, ritual, song, dance, art, affection, or other abstract emotional expression, and so forth.

142 This may include western empiricism, superstition, experience, and so forth.

143 Legend, idiom, fable, etc.

144 Including the spiritual as opposed to the material realm, and the religious as opposed to the secular.

145 Manthwa and Ntsoane, "Right to Bury the Deceased," 617.

146 This is true of the *Mvamvu* case that dealt with a rape of his customary wife committed by the accused as against the *Jezile* case that dealt with human trafficking and three counts of the rape of a 14-year-old girl. A cultural defence was not considered in the Western Cape Province, as opposed to the situation in the *Jezile* judgment, where a cultural defence (in a case of marital rape) was used as mitigation based on the customary practice of *ukuthwala*. Mwambene and Kruuse, "Marital Rape," 38–39. Also see *Jezile v Jezile* 2015 (2) SCR 452 (WCC); *S v Mvamvu* 2005 1 SACR 54 (SCA).

147 An individual in an African law context should be understood to be part of a community made up of three sub-communities, described succinctly by Ramose as follows: "the community in African culture is an ethical entity comprising the living, the living dead and the yet to be born. The critical ethical concern is to recognize and abide by the obligation to maintain and preserve harmonious relations within these three dimensions of the community"; Ramose, "In Memoriam," 323.

148 The necessary furniture and household utensils to be used in her new home.

The handing over process is unique in the sense that the newlyweds are counselled and given advice on the duties of a wife and husband and their custodianship of moral values, with all family representatives contributing their wisdom to the new family life. The said process is not taken lightly and cannot be done "symbolically" before or without *Ngwetsi* being formally handed over to her husband's family. Customary law has an intrinsic connection to African identity, practices, values and norms and cannot be easily understood by judges and courts.

5 Judicial Attitude to Batswana Customary Law and Practices

The discretions exercised by courts and the judicial notice of customary law are not without criticism and their reliance on the Constitution alienates members of traditional communities from it, as they see the Constitution as a threat to their existence. It is argued that due to the court's developmental approach, customary law is gradually losing its value, credibility and relevance as the law governing various communities in South Africa. The application of the 1996 Constitution so far has given rise to the notion that no customary law can be left to apply within the constitutional provisions of section 211. The handing over requirement has never been a practice or a ritual and the SCA as the highest court in the land seems to have confirmed it to be a mere ritual, as in the *Tsambo* case. It has always been the law and failing to comply with it invalidates the marriage conducted in terms of the Batswana customary law. Thus, the content and context used in previous cases and books cannot be universally applied across cultures. Every culture has its own meaning, uniqueness, value and purpose that it purports to serve and must be individually assessed against its own merits, yet there are similarities among these systems of customary law that must not be overlooked. Judges reliance on the Constitution and the precedent system suggests that they conceive of themselves as the only ones, together with some scholars, with the authority to dictate what is the law under customary law and what is a ritual or practice – and this is done to communities who have practised these laws and fully understand their repercussions. To Knoetze:[149]

> It is difficult to envisage how the court 'can create rules which are not fully observed by the community' by utilising active development of the

149 Knoetze, "Fathers Responsible," 49.

> law. The court runs the risk of merely creating 'paper law', which would be difficult to enforce in a community where that version of the law is neither favoured nor practised.

To Bekker:[150]

> Society will (not) change by legal decree. The living law will probably for a long time to come differ from the law on paper. The so-called common law may in fact distort customary law and practice to the extent that the enacted version becomes meaningless in society.

A community governed by court orders seems unrealistic considering to manage or dismantle an established customs that these communities fully subscribe to, the consequence of their own laws, is something beyond what is written or known by outsiders. In fact, the number of cases going to court is insignificant in comparison with the number of instances in which the same community still applies and enforces its customary law. Through their attempts at development, the courts appear to be attempting to transforming the customary law so that it prohibits and rejects the ancestral connection, including communication with, acceptance by, the protection of and the blessings of the ancestors. The deeper meaning and relevance of *Badimo*/ancestors in people's lives and the form of retribution invoked through *dikgaba* are things that our courts and some scholars cannot see with a naked eye or deeper understanding. As far back as in 1958 the judiciary was already criticised by Simons for lacking an understanding and knowledge of customary laws in that:[151]

> Judges often make broad statements, usually without adequate or reliable supporting information, on the nature of change in tribal custom; but insufficient attention has been given to its legal and sociological implications.

It is argued that the way in which the courts are dealing with customary law cases seems to confirm what Knoetze, Donnelly and Simons say about the misconceptions about the principles of customary law when they are examined through a Eurocentric lens, which misconceptions lead to an unconscious desire to make a ruling in terms of the said Eurocentric and or constitutional

150 Bekker, "Official Status of Customary Law," 129–30.
151 Simons, "Customary Unions," 322.

standards. It is clear that our courts continue to fail to face the reality of what the community[152] deems to be its customary law and continues to impose what they view as the reformed customary law governing these tribes. Donnelly is of the view that:[153]

> There is no logical or inescapable moral reason why people cannot accept or choose it as their principal form of social organization and the primary locus of their extra-familial moral and political commitments. Once we allow the moral validity of such commitments, we are bound to accept at least certain types of substantial moral variability, including variability in human rights practices.

A rule of recognition should arise which identifies the procedural requirements for validity within both the non-indigenous and the indigenous legal regimes as well as the scope of application of valid laws, and which provides a mechanism for the distribution of adjudicative responsibilities and the resolution of conflicts between the two regimes. It is very clear that the inconsistent research, application and interpretation of customary law prior to the constitutional era, has to some degree a negative impact on the manner in which parts of that law have been or are being interpreted, applied and developed by our courts.

The misconception of customary law by the courts and some authors may be understood in the context of Lewis' statement that individual rights always connect with communal rights, and although we are individualistic in nature, we are inter-connected as members of a community.[154] The 1996 Constitution intends to serve communal rights, but the manner in which they are dealt with under the Constitution has resulted in the adoption of an individualistic approach by the courts in terms of which they reject and deny customary law claims. According to Diala:[155]

> Adaptive legal pluralism regards the interaction of legal orders in sub-Saharan Africa as essentially imitative. A striking feature of this interaction is how law reforms mould indigenous norms into universalist images of the rights to dignity, equality, and non-discrimination. The jurisprudence of cultural contestations indicates that whenever an indigenous

152 Mmusinyane, "Demanding Equal Rights," 152, 153–56.

153 Donnelly, "Cultural Relativism," 402.

154 Lewis, "Judicial Translation," 1126, 1133, 1144, 1147.

155 Diala, "Legal Pluralism," 2.

> norm is constitutionally challenged as offensive to human rights values, judges invalidate it and legislators support the invalidation with law reform.

Courts need to be mindful that the traditions and customs of the different tribes that exist in South Africa are diverse and require an individualistic approach when interpreting them, as it would be dangerous to assume that the rules of one tribe are applicable to the others.[156] In instances where the parties before courts are from the same community, then section 211 of the Constitution dictates that the court must apply customary law, subject to the 1996 Constitution. It remains to be seen if the handing over requirement of the Batswana tribe is going to survive constitutional scrutiny, taking into cognisance the approach the courts have already taken on a similar issue. The law is meant to be understood, interpreted, and applied by lawyers and judges and as agents of the law they ought to have enough comprehension of what they purport to develop and transform. A classic example is found in the case of *Motsepe v Khoza,* where Thulare J said:

> By the whim and paradox of history, I am called upon to not only interpret, but also to be equal to the task of developing customary law.

To this end, Monye notes that in terms of the Constitution, it is not required of a judge to develop customary law in terms of the judge's personal indulgence or whims,[157] but to interpret and develop the custom before him in accordance with section 211(3) read with section 39(2) of the Constitution. Reading from the same page, Connolly is of the view that:[158]

> the capacity and limits of interpretation may depend not so much on an abstract concept of law as on a more localized operative notion of what it is to be a Judge or Tribunal member or bureaucrat. In relation to a cross-cultural interpretive encounter at an Indigenous rights hearing, for example, the question we would most likely be concerned with is the extent to which a presiding Judge could come to an understanding of evidence of Indigenous law without losing his/her identity as a Judge.

156 Osman, "Precedent, Waiver and the Constitutional Analysis," 80, 83.

157 Monye, "Customary Law and Adoption," 13.

158 Connolly, "Legal Pluralism," 29–30, 33, 34.

Given the fact that the conceptual scheme differs, for a judge who does not belong[159] to a community practicing that kind of culture to be called upon to adjudicate cultural disputes, that judge would have to first undertake a process of concept acquisition in order to be able to interpret these groups and cultures.[160] It is on this premise that the more the judge's conceptual scheme is shared with that of the indigenous claimants relating to their law, the more conducive it will be for him/her to successfully interpret those agents and their law.[161]

On the other hand, in instances where counter interpretive legal factors have appeared over the course of a hearing, it may be difficult for a judge to acquire relevant indigenous concepts and be able to adequately interpret evidence in the context of indigenous law. This means that extensive interpretation will be required for them to succeed.[162] In this regard Connolly argues that the thought and practice of a judge before such a case, including his/her capacity to interpret and understand the evidence of a culturally different law and society, will always be influenced by a number of internal and external factors. Such factors are the positive legal rules regulating judicial practice, the rules of evidence and judges' beliefs about the nature of law and the nature of their own adjudicative role.[163] Being a judge involves, for them, doing what judges do, as dictated by their operative concept of a judge.[164] Therefore, there is no single customary law of marriage in South Africa. These laws are diverse and should not be categorised by courts as one law governing all communities. Thus Osman expresses the opinion that:[165]

> Flexible, developing notions of customary law are likely to be overlooked in favour of certain and easily ascertainable law. It is thus argued that judgments on customary law, particularly those that pronounce on the requirements of a customary marriage, should not be applied as precedent in subsequent cases. Section 3 of the Recognition Act obliges courts to determine the customary-law requirements of a marriage of the community concerned and courts should fulfil this legislative obligation. In

159 In the form of his/her being a white person in a dispute involving black people, or a Zulu judge in a dispute involving Xhosa people, or a Venda judge in a case involving Batswana people.

160 Connolly, "Legal Pluralism," 32, 33.

161 Connolly, "Legal Pluralism," 34.

162 Connolly, "Legal Pluralism," 35.

163 Connolly, "Legal Pluralism," 51.

164 Ibid.

165 Osman, "Precedent, Waiver and the Constitutional Analysis," 83.

> doing so, courts should have regard to official customary law, such as precedent, as a source of law rather than treating it as a binding rule to be applied. The application of judgments as precedent risks distorting the law and giving effect to official customary law at the expense of the constitutionally recognized living customary law.

Without a proper understanding of their roles, judges' approaches are likely to diminish customary laws that practically govern the affairs of a particular tribe and introduce the kind of laws that the same community views as toothless. Thus, despite the *Bhe* decision invalidating the primogeniture principle,[166] the issue remains contentious as the courts continue to be inundated with similar succession issues from various communities.[167] Mmusinyane notes that there are many other customs and traditions that continue to offend the Constitution and clearly until such time as they are challenged, they would continue to be applied and practised by various communities across South Africa.[168] Accordingly, an understanding of constitutional law should not be seen as a catalyst enabling one to deal with any other law, as such laws are also recognised by the Constitution[169] and must be applied by all courts in South Africa. This is because that customary laws governing the majority of black people in South Africa also need to be understood properly and interpreted adequately to maintain their own unique identity in a constitutional framework. In relation to Batswana marriage, courts need to rather focus on what Diala regards as their ultimate purpose in dealing with such cases:[170]

> Realistically, the test is whether a change has occurred in the custom of handing over the bride. If there is no change, the custom is indigenous law; if a change has occurred, it is customary law – without the appellation of 'living' or 'official'.

This means that the time has come for our courts to abandon the categorisation of all customary law as the same law equally impacted in a similar manner by the universalistic constitutional development and transformation of the law.

166 *Bhe v Magistrate, Khayelitsha* 2005 (1) SA 580 (CC).

167 *Shilubana v Nwamitwa*; *Mphephu-Ramabulana rv Mphephu* 2022 (1) BCLR 20 (CC); Maunatlala and Maimela, "Implementation of Customary Law of Succession," 40, 42; Tshikota, "Game of Thrones," 60, 63, 67.

168 Mmusinyane, "Role of Traditional Authorities," 136.

169 Section 211 of the 1996 Constitution.

170 Diala, "Legal Pluralism," 11.

6 Conclusion

It is evident that the Batswana customary law of marriage has evolved, although a number of core legal requirements continue to be retained and consistently observed, despite some having been overruled by the courts in terms of the values of the 1996 Constitution. In every marriage that takes place or that has led to the parties being married in terms of civil law, those parties have without fail first subjected themselves to certain areas of the customary law governing them. Over and above complying with the legislation governing a civil marriage, the Batswana tribe still invoke/comply with their customary law processes to ensure compliance with their way of life. Clearly, the constitutional transformation of customary law is and should not be meant to erode, diminish or distract from their customary law, as such law unquestionably continues to govern these traditional communities. This is a classic example of what the court purports to create as the law not being followed or observed by these communities, because they are of the view that their customary law so provides. Tamanaha states that it should not be assumed that the law is always functional.[171] It has been affirmed by Solway that:[172]

> Not only is marriage itself on the decline, but there is a contraction in the scope of kin and generations involved in marital activities and a contraction in time, with rituals and exchanges that once occurred over decades now collapsed into a narrow time frame.

It also needs to be acknowledged that the Batswana tribe has embraced the transformation of their culture by sometimes not insisting on compliance with particular customs and traditions, such as allowing the registration of parties' marriage under the Recognition of Customary Marriages Act, or the Civil Union Act, or the acceptance of money instead of cattle and sheep, and in general the waiving of certain practices and rituals. At the same time, the Batswana tribe requires adherence to and respect for what they deem to be their own customary laws, even when the degree of compliance is questionable. Recognition of the Batswana customs would give marriage laws value and legitimacy in traditional communities, unlike law that is imposed on them by a court that does not fully understand nor value their identity as a distinct cultural community.

171 Tamanaha, "Non-Essentialist Version of Legal Pluralism," 301.

172 Solway, "'Slow Marriage'," 309.

From the above analysis, it seems clear that the courts and some scholars struggle to understand certain aspects (legal requirements, rituals/customs and traditions) of customary laws. This opinion is based on the fact that the impact or effect of overruling these laws is often felt (beyond court orders) by the parties themselves when couples (*Badimo*) reveal certain challenges (*dikgaba*) troubling their union or children later in life. While our courts will continue to be the final arbiter of customary law disputes, it seems clear that the customary law of the Batswana tribe will always have a way of mending itself in its own time, despite what the court has overruled, rejected, or abolished in terms of the 1996 Constitution.

Bibliography

Literature

Alexander, Mary. "The 11 Languages of South Africa." Updated October 31, 2022. https://southafrica-info.com/arts-culture/11-languages-south-africa.

Bekker, Jan Christoffel. "The Official Status of Customary Law: Ten Years Later." *Anthropology Southern Africa* 26, no. 3–4 (2003): 124–30.

Bennett, Thomas William. *A Sourcebook of African Customary Law for Southern Africa.* Cape Town: Juta, 1991.

Bennett, Thomas William. *Customary Law in South Africa.* Cape Town: Juta, 2004.

Budlender, Geoff. "Afterword: Searching for the Constitutional Living Customary Law." *Journal of Southern African Studies* 47, no. 2 (2021): 327–32. https://doi.org/10.1080/03057070.2021.1893514.

Connolly, Anthony Williams. "Legal Pluralism and the Interpretive Limits of Law." In *Culture in the Domains of Law*, edited by René Provost, 23–53. Cambridge: Cambridge University Press, 2017. https://doi.org/10.1017/9781316681060.002.

Cowan, Jane, Marie-Benedicte, Dembour, and Richard Wilson, eds. *Culture and Rights: Anthropological Perspectives.* Cambridge: Cambridge University Press, 2003.

Datta, Kavita. "In The Eyes of a Child, a Father is Everything: Changing Constructions of Fatherhood in Urban Botswana." *Women's Studies International Forum* 30, no. 2 (2007): 97–113. https://doi.org/10.1016/j.wsif.2007.01.005.

Diala, Anthony Chima. "Legal Pluralism and the Future of Personal Family Laws in Africa." *International Journal of Law, Policy and The Family* 35, no. 1 (2021): 1–17. doi: https://doi.org/10.1093/lawfam/ebab023.

Dlamini, Robinson Mandlenkosi. "A Juridical Analysis and Critical Evaluation of Ilobolo in a Changing Zulu Society." PhD thesis, University of Zululand, 1983.

Donnelly, Jack. "The Relative Universality of Human Rights." *Human Rights Quarterly* 29, no. 2 (2007): 281–306.

Donnelly, Jack. "Cultural Relativism and Universal Human Rights." *Human Rights Quarterly* 6, no. 4 (1984): 400–19. https://doi.org/10.2307/762182.

Dube, Musa. "Translating Cultures: The Creation of Sin in the Public Space of Batswana." *Scriptura* 114, no. 1 (2015): 1–11.

Finnegan, Ruth. *Oral Literature in Africa*. Oxford: Oxford University Press, 1976.

Frylinck, J. P. "Casual Notes on Native Marriage Laws and Customs in Bechuanaland." *South African Law Journal* 34 (1917): 319–21.

Galanter, Marc. "Justice in Many Rooms: Courts, Private Ordering, and Indigenous Law." *Journal of Legal Pluralism and Unofficial Law* 19, no. 1 (1981): 1–47. https://doi.org/10.1080/07329113.1981.10756257.

Goodsell, Erin. "Constitution, Custom and Creed: Balancing Human Rights Concerns with Cultural and Religious Freedom in Today's South Africa." *Brigham Young University Journal of Public Law* 21, no. 1 (2007): 111–54.

Griffiths, John. "What is Legal Pluralism?" *Journal of Legal Pluralism and Unofficial Law* 24, no. 1 (1986): 1–56.

Herbst, Marissa, and Willemien Du Plessis. "Customary Law v Common Law Marriages: A Hybrid Approach in South Africa." *Journal of Comparative Law* 3 (2008): 105–18.

Himonga, Chuma, and Anne Pope. "*Mayelane v Ngwenyama and Minister for Home Affairs*: A Reflection on Wider Implications." *Acta Juridica* (2013): 318–38.

Kaganas, Felicity, and Christina Murray. "The Contest between Culture and Gender Equality under South Africa's Interim Constitution." *Journal of Law and Society* 21, no. 4 (1994): 409–33.

Knoetze, Elmarie. "Fathers Responsible for the Sins of their Children? Notes on the Accessory Liability of a Family Head in the Customary Law of Delict." *Speculum Juris* 2 (2012): 47–65.

Law Teacher. "Universalism and Cultural Relativism in Human Rights." Accessed June 16, 2022. https://www.lawteacher.net/free-law-essays/international-law/universalism-and-cultural-relativism-in-human-rights-international-law-essay.php?vref=1.

Lewis, Liz. "Judicial Translation and Contextualisation of Values: Rethinking the Development of Customary Law in Mayelane." *Potchefstroom Electronic Law Journal* 8, no. 4 (2015): 1126–60. http://dx.doi.org/10.4314/pelj.v18i4.11.

Macdonald, Roderick. "Metaphors of Multiplicity: Civil Society, Regimes and Legal Pluralism." *Arizona Journal of International and Comparative Law* 15 (1998): 69–91.

Maluleke, Mikateko Joyce. "Culture, Tradition, Custom, Law and Gender Equality." *Potchefstroom Electronic Law Journal* 15, no. 1 (2012): 2–22.

Manthwa, Aubrey, and Lefa Ntsoane. "The Right to Bury the Deceased in Terms of Customary Law: Whose Right is It?" *Tydskrif vir Hedendaagse Romeins-Hollandse Reg* 83, no. 4 (2020): 611–21.

Matjila, Sekepe, and Karen Haire. "The Cattle Motif in Sol T. Plaatje's Publications in English Re-Storying the African and Batswana Sensibilities." *Journal of Black Studies* 41, no. 1 (2010): 207–17.

Matjila, Sekepe, and Karen Haire. *Bringing Plaatjie Back Home: Ga e Phetsolele Nageng – 'Re-Storying' the African and Batswana Sensibilities in his Qeuvre.* Trenton: Africa World Press, 2015.

Matjila, Sekepe. "Some Aspects of Batswana Traditional Beliefs as Reflected by an Intertextual Analysis of Mothoagae's Poetry." *South African Journal of African Languages* 27, no. 1 (2007): 6–21. https://doi.org/10.1080/02572117.2007.10587282.

Maunatlala, Kgopotso, and Charles Maimela. "The Implementation of Customary Law of Succession and Common Law of Succession Respectively: With a Specific Focus on the Eradication of the Rule of Male Primogeniture." *De Jure* 53, no. 1 (2020):36–53. http://dx.doi.org/10.17159/2225-7160/2020/v53a3.

Mmusi, Sheila. *'A re Bueng Setswana': A Multidimensional Approach to the Teaching and Learning of Setswana as a Foreign Language.* Madison: NALRC Press, 2005.

Mmusinyane, Boitumelo. "Demanding Equal Rights and Treatment of Husbands/ Partners in Paternity Disputes: A South African Perspective." *African Journal of Legal Studies* 9, no. 3 (2016): 147–76. https://doi.org/10.1163/17087384-12340009.

Mmusinyane, Boitumelo. "The Role of Traditional Authorities in Developing Customary Laws in Accordance with the Constitution: *Shilubana and Others v Nwamitwa* 2008 (9) BCLR 914 (CC)." *Potchefstroom Electronic Law Journal* 12, no. 3 (2009): 136–61.

Mofokeng, Lesala. "The Lobolo Agreement as the Silent Requisite for the Validity of a Customary Marriage in Terms of the Recognition of Customary Marriages Act." *Tydskrif vir Hedendaagse Romeins-Hollandse Reg* 68 (2005): 277–88.

Mokgoro, Yvonne. "The Protection of Cultural Identity in the Constitution and the Creation of National Unity in South Africa: A Contradiction in Terms." *SMU Law Review* 52, no. 4 (1999): 1549–61.

Monyai, Reginald Botshabeng, and Peter Skosana. "A Historical Exposition of the Dominance of Western Culture on the Batswana People." *International Journal of Humanities and Social Science Invention* 2, no. 9 (2013): 13–22.

Monye, Stephen. "Customary Law and Adoption: The 'O e Gapa le Namane' Custom as a Reflection of Customary Law Development in South Africa." *Journal of Law, Society and Development* 4, no. 1 (2017): 1–19.

Mulaudzi, Phalandwa Abraham. "Cultural Perceptions and Linguistic Terminology Regarding Traditional Marriage within Indigenous South African Communities." *South African Journal of African Languages* 33, no. 3 (2013): 153–58. https://doi.org/10.1080/02572117.2013.871456.

Mwambene, Lea, and Helen Kruuse. "Marital Rape and Cultural Defence in South Africa." *Stellenbosch Law Review* 29, no. 1 (2018): 25–47.

Mwambene, Lea, and Julia Sloth-Nielsen. "Benign Accommodation? Ukuthwala, 'Forced Marriage' and the South African Children's Act." *African Human Rights Law Journal* 11, no. 1 (2011): 1–22.

Ntsoane, Otsile. "Batswana Indigenous Conflict Resolution Methods: A Narrative." *African Journal of Indigenous Knowledge Systems* 2, no. 2/3 (2003): 15–25.

Osman, Fatima. "Precedent, Waiver and the Constitutional Analysis of Handing Over the Bride [Discussion of *Sengadi v Tsambo* 2018 JDR 2151 (GJ)]." *Stellenbosch Law Review* 31 (2020): 80–90.

Ozoemena, Rita. "Living Customary Law: A Truly Transformative Tool?" *Constitutional Court Review* 6 (2014): 147–63. https://doi.org/10.2989/CCR.2014.0008.

Pilane, Gabaitsiwe Elizabeth. "An Analysis of the Construction of Tswana Cultural Identity in Selected Tswana Literary Texts." PhD thesis, Potchefstroomse Universiteit vir Christelike Hoër Onderwys, 2002.

Pitso, Joseph, and Gordon Carmichael. "Premarital Childbearing in Thamaga Village, Botswana." *Journal of Population Research* 20, no. 2 (2003): 187–202.

Ramose, Mogobe. "In Memoriam: Sovereignty and the 'New South Africa'." *Griffith Law Review* 16, no. 2 (2007): 310–29.

Rautenbach, Christa. "Case Law as an Authoritative Source of Customary Law: Piecemeal Recording of (Living) Customary Law?" *Potchefstroom Electronic Law Journal* 22 (2019): 1–21. http://dx.doi.org/10.17159/1727-3781/2019/v22i0a7591.

Schaumburg-Müller, Sten. "In Defense of Soft Universalism: A Modest, yet Presumptuous Position." *Cuadernos Constitucionales de la Cátedra Fadrique Furió Ceriol* 62, no. 63 (2007): 113–26.

Segami, Victoria, and Chrizanne van Eeden. "Marital Symbols and the Marriage Satisfaction and Spiritual Well-Being of BaTswana Married Women." *Journal of Psychology in Africa* 30, no. 1 (2020): 37–43. https://doi.org/10.1080/14330237.2020.1722363.

Sibisi, Siyabonga. "The Juristic Nature of *iLobolo* Agreements in Modern South Africa." *Obiter* 42, no. 1 (2021): 57–69.

Simons, Jack. "Customary Unions in a Changing Society." *Acta Juridica* (1958): 320–41.

Solway, Jacqueline. "'Slow Marriage', 'Fast Bogadi': Change and Continuity in Marriage in Botswana." *Anthropology Southern Africa* 39, no. 4 (2016): 309–22. http://dx.doi.org/10.1080/23323256.2016.1235980.

South African Law Commission. "Project 90: The Harmonisation of the Common Law and the Indigenous Law: Report on Customary Marriages." Accessed October 20, 2022. https://www.justice.gov.za/salrc/reports/r_prj90_cstm_1998aug.pdf.

Tamanaha, Brian. "A Non-Essentialist Version of Legal Pluralism." *Journal of Law and Society* 27, no. 2 (2000): 296–321.

Tshikota, Gudani. "Game of Thrones: The Battle of the Mphephus", *Pretoria Student Law Review* 14, no. 2 (2020): 54–67.

Case Law

Alexkor Ltd v The Richtersveld Community 2004 (5) SA 460 (CC).
Bhe v Magistrate, Khayelitsha 2005 (1) SA 580 (CC).
Daniels v Campbell 2004 (7) BCLR 735 (CC).
Dawood, Shalabi, Thomas v Minister of Home Affairs 2000 (3) SA 936 (CC).
Fanti v Boto 2008 (5) SA 405 (C).
Jezile v Jezile 2015 (2) SCR 452 (WCC).
LS v RL 2019 (4) SA 50 (GJ).
Mabena v Letsoalo 1998 (2) SA 1068 (T).
Mabuza v Mbatha 2003 (4) SA 218 (C).
Mbungela v Mkabi 2020 (1) SA 41 (SCA).
Moropane v Southon (755/12) [2014] ZASCA 76 (29 May 2014).
Motsepe v Khoza (South Gauteng High Court) (unreported) case number 15078/2012 of 8 April 2013.
Motsoatosa v Roro 2011 (2) All SA 324 (GSJ).
Mphephu-Ramabulana v Mphephu 2022 (1) BCLR 20 (CC).
N D v M M (18404/2018) [2020] ZAGPJHC 113 (12 May 2020).
Ntoagae v Makabanyane (M420/2015) [2015] ZANWHC 78 (12 November 2015).
S v Mvamvu 2005 1 SACR 54 (SCA).
Shilubana v Nwamitwa 2009 (2) SA 66 (CC).
Tsambo v Sengadi (244/19) [2020] ZASCA 46 (30 April 2020).

Legislations and Government Publications

Children's Act 38 of 2005.
Civil Union Act 17 of 2006.
Constitution of the Republic of South Africa, 1996.
Marriage Act 25 of 1961.
Recognition of Customary Marriages Act 120 of 1998.

Treaties and Agreements

International Covenant on Civil and Political Rights (1966).
International Covenant on Economic Social and Cultural Rights (1966).
Universal Declaration of Human Rights (1948).

PART 3

Islamic and Comparative Law in African Legal Pluralism

CHAPTER 7

The Past, Present, and Future of Muslim Personal Law in Ghana: A Judicial Analysis

Yüksel Sezgin

Abstract

Ghana has inherited colonial legislation that recognises and regulates the consequences of Muslim personal law. However, in practice courts almost never recognise the normative existence of Islamic marriages, divorces or succession claims and systematically dismiss the cases on procedural grounds without discussing their merits. What explains the judiciary's attitudes toward Islamic law? Why do Ghanaian courts refuse to engage with Muslim personal law in substantive terms? How does this judicial policy affect Ghana's plural-legal system and multireligious democracy? Drawing on Robert Cover's insights and concepts from "Nomos and Narrative", the present chapter suggests that Ghanaian courts methodically engage in undignified jurispathic killing against Islamic law claims. This occurs because the post-independence judiciary internalised the colonial narrative that Islamic law was not a native law of the land. In doing so, however, courts miss a vital opportunity to influence the future development of legal meanings of nomic groups in the Muslim community, which, in turn, increases the risk of marginalisation among Ghanaian Muslims and undermines the legitimacy of the judiciary and the constitutional order in their eyes.

1 Introduction

Fifty-three countries formally integrate Muslim family laws (MFLs) into their legal systems. Regarding the manner and extent to which they integrate MFLs, one can speak of two ideal-typical models: direct and indirect integration. In the former model, written or uncodified religious family laws are applied by state-appointed judges in state-operated civil or religious family courts. In the latter model, the state does not directly incorporate religious laws or courts

 | DOI:10.1163/9789004696747_008

into the national system. Instead, it recognises and regulates the consequences of MFLs, which are applied by traditional/religious authorities.[1]

A prime example of indirect integration is found in Ghana. The Marriage of Mohammedans Ordinance (MMO), enacted by the British colonial administration in 1907, established the regulatory framework for indirectly integrating "Mohammedan" law. The ordinance, which is still in force as part of the Marriages Act of 1985, required the registration of all "Mohammedan" (Muslim) marriages and divorces to be legally valid. Section 10[2] of the ordinance also provided that upon the death of a Muslim whose marriage was duly registered, succession to his property would be regulated by "Mohammedan" law.

The MMO of 1907 did not codify the applicable religious law or designate any authority to apply it. Instead, under British indirect rule, traditional authorities (chiefs, *sheiks*, *malam*s) were left to implement the MFL. When officiating at marriages or mediating divorces or inheritance disputes, these authorities would apply their interpretation of Islamic law following local customs. Courts would then recognise and regulate the consequences of Islamic marriages/divorces duly registered after a licensed "Mohammedan priest" (imam) had confirmed their validity according to Islamic law.[3]

In national jurisdictions where MFLs are directly integrated, the authority to apply and interpret MFLs lies with state courts. However, in countries with indirect integration the courts' role is primarily limited to ascertaining the validity of religious/traditional authorities' legal acts according to Islamic and civil laws and recognising their consequences. However, this "limited" role does not mean that courts in the latter countries play a lesser role in regulating MFLs than their counterparts in the former countries. As they ascertain the validity of legal acts in MFL cases, civil courts in indirect integration systems may establish the criteria for "valid" Islamic marriages/divorces or review the constitutionality of instant divorces (i.e., *talaq*).[4] In other words, in jurisdictions with indirect integration, the judiciary's "limited" supervisory role is broad enough for willing judges to intervene in the MFLs to bring about legal reforms or engage in activism to "contain, tame, and mitigate the resurgence of sacred law in their respective polities".[5]

1 Sezgin, "Undignified Jurispathy," 1303–33.
2 PNDCL 111 repealed s. 10 of the MMO in 1985 (more on this later).
3 Anderson, *Islamic Law*, 249; Aziz, "Muslim Family Law," 21.
4 Sezgin, "Undignified Jurispathy," 1303–4.
5 Hirschl, "Constitutional Courts," 312.

As Hirschl demonstrates in *Constitutional Theocracies*,[6] constitutional courts, even in the least likely settings, have stood against expansionist interpretations of religious laws and consistently tried to limit their reach. Considering the 1992 Constitution's emphasis on liberal rights, the strong tradition of secular government and the legacy of MMO against this backdrop, Ghana seems an ideal setting to observe Hirschlian judicial secularism in action. However, the Ghanaian judiciary's track record suggests otherwise. Ghanaian courts have been reluctant to engage with Islamic law substantively. In most cases brought by Muslim litigants, courts have declined to recognise the nomic existence of Islamic law and dismissed MFL claims on procedural grounds. Despite frequent regime changes, the Ghanaian judiciary's dismissive attitude toward Islamic law has been surprisingly consistent since independence in 1957. What explains the judiciary's attitudes toward Islamic law? Why are Ghanaian courts reluctant to engage with Islamic law in substantive terms? What does this judicial approach mean regarding Ghana's plural legal system and multireligious democracy?

The present chapter will answer these questions utilising Robert Cover's[7] concept of jurispathic law-killing. According to Cover, non-state nomic groups (e.g., tribal, religious) challenge the state's normative claims by engaging in jurisgenerative activity that leads to the creation of alternative legal meanings in society.[8] The fecundity of the jurisgenerative process creates a multiplicity of legal meanings on almost every question. The primary purpose of state courts, Cover argues, is to solve this very problem of "too much" law by committing "jurispathy" (law-killing) against the legal meanings of non-state groups.[9] Among competing legal meanings, state courts pick one and elevate it to the status of official law by backing it with the state's violent apparatus while destroying all other meanings.[10]

By expanding Cover's theoretical framework, the present chapter will argue that there are two types of law-killing: dignified and undignified. The difference is akin to that between capital punishment and summary execution. Dignified killing allows the court to engage with religious law-based claims in substantive terms and provide nomic groups with feedback to harmonise their legal meanings with those of the state. Harmonisation is essential to jurisgenesis

6 Hirschl, *Constitutional Theocracy*, 1–20.

7 Cover, "The Supreme Court"; Cover, "Violence and the Word".

8 Cover, "The Supreme Court," 11.

9 Cover, "The Supreme Court," 41; Cover, "Violence and the Word," 1609–16.

10 Cover, "The Supreme Court," 47; Cover, "Violence and the Word," 1609–16.

and the de-escalation of normative tensions. Through its feedback loop, dignified law-killing allows reformist elements within nomic groups to push for internal reform and offer new legal meanings by drawing on the courts' judgments and integrating legal principles therein into their communities' value systems.[11]

In cases of undignified killing, the state courts reject the legal meanings of nomic communities on procedural grounds without discussing what is at stake. The claim is refused on procedural grounds because someone failed to follow formalities, filed the wrong form, or missed the deadline to register a legal act duly. Because courts do not engage with legal meanings of nomic groups in substantive terms, no feedback is provided either. This means that the cycle of normative violence will probably continue as the legal meanings of the state and nomic groups grow further apart. Moreover, suppose courts repeatedly reject claims by a particular cultural group on procedural grounds. In that case, this will undermine their legitimacy among the members of that group and potentially weaken the latter's commitment to the rule of law.[12] This is precisely what is happening in Ghana.

Ghanaian courts systematically engage in undignified killing against Islamic law claims. This occurs partly because the post-independence judiciary inherited the colonial narrative that Islamic law was not a native law of the land. In doing so, however, the courts miss a vital opportunity to influence the future development of the legal meanings of nomic groups in the Muslim community, which in turn increases the risk of marginalisation among Ghanaian Muslims and undermines the legitimacy of the judiciary and the constitutional order in their eyes.

This chapter proceeds in five parts. Section I will provide the historical background to the British colonial narrative that continues to dictate post-colonial bureaucracy and the judiciary's dismissive approach toward MFL claims. Section II will analyse the postcolonial state's understanding of secularism and demonstrate that the judiciary has been willing to recognise claims of traditional African religions while denying the nomic existence of putatively non-native religious laws (i.e., Islamic law). Section 3 will demonstrate how the bureaucracy and judiciary have acted harmoniously to dismiss Islamic nomic groups' legal meanings. The subsequent section (4) will compare and contrast the judiciary's attitudes toward customary and Islamic marriages and succession claims. Finally, the last section (5) will discuss the political cost of

11 Sezgin, "Undignified Jurispathy," 1323.

12 Tyler, "Procedural Justice," 283–357.

the Ghanaian courts' reluctance to engage substantively with Islamic law or the MFL – used interchangeably in the Ghanaian context.

The chapter utilises the data from fieldwork I carried out in May–July 2017. Eighty-two semi-structured interviews were conducted in Accra, Tamale and Kumasi. The informants (45 women and 37 men) included clerics, academics, teachers, taxi drivers, students, judges, lawyers, hawkers, and vendors. The findings also rest on historical documents and extensive analysis of superior court decisions that I obtained from law reports, electronic databases, and individual lawyers and litigants.

2 The British Colonial Policy toward the MFL and the 1907 Ordinance

2.1 *Historical and Political Considerations that Led to the 1907 Ordinance*

The area that makes up modern Ghana was divided into three regions under British rule: the Gold Coast in the south, the Northern Territories in the north, and the Ashanti in the middle. British colonial administration began in 1821 in the coastal areas and gradually expanded into the hinterland.

According to the 2021 census, about 6.1 million Muslims – 19.9 per cent of the population – live in Ghana.[13] Although a Muslim presence in the hinterland can be traced back to as early as the 15th Century,[14] their arrival in large numbers in the coastal regions (Accra and its vicinity) began in the 19th Century. Under colonial rule Muslims from West African colonies (Nigeria, etc.) immigrated to the Gold Coast and lived in settlements called "*zongos*". The British considered Muslims "more civilised" than indigenous pagan tribes.[15] As a result, they brought Muslims from nearby regions and enlisted them in the colonial military, police force and bureaucracy. Regardless of their ethnic origins, the colonial administration widely referred to these Muslim immigrants as "Hausa".[16] Even though, over the following decades, many local groups (Fanti, Ga, etc.) also converted and became Muslim, due to Islam's initial association with the

13 Christians make up 71.3 per cent, and adherents of traditional religions constitute 3.2 per cent of the population (Ghana Statistical Service, *Ghana 2021*). Compared to the 2010 census, the Muslim population increased from 17.6 per cent to 19.9 per cent in 2021. Nearly half of the Muslim population is concentrated in the Greater Accra, Ashanti and Northern regions.

14 Clarke, *West Africa and Islam*, 37–40; Weiss, *Between Accommodation*, 43.

15 Weiss, *Between Accommodation*, 230.

16 Ibid.

Hausa and their separate settlements (*zongos*), the colonial state came to consider Muslims "aliens"[17] and their customs foreign imports.[18]

Although there were various Muslim dynasties in precolonial Ghana (especially in the north), Islamic law was never imposed in a top-down manner as the official law in any part of the country.[19] In the absence of state enforcement of Islamic law, Islamic precepts and norms, especially concerning marriage, divorce, and succession, were amalgamated into the African customary law applied by native authorities in Muslim communities. This situation remained unchanged until 1907, when the British formally recognised MFL by enacting the MMO. The MMO was initially enacted to cover only the Muslim population on the Gold Coast. However, it was extended to Ashanti in 1919 and the Northern Territories in 1931.[20]

The colonial government introduced the Mohammedan Marriages Bill, which aimed to provide a registration system for Muslim marriages and divorces to the Legislative Council in October 1906.[21] The bill was debated in the Legislative Assembly on December 9, 1907. In support of the bill, the Attorney General claimed that the legislative effort was the outcome of questions concerning "the status of Mohammedans in the West African colonies generally".[22] In other words, political and geostrategic considerations had given rise to the bill. Some assembly members undoubtedly spelled out these considerations. For instance, Mensah Sarbah criticised the bill and warned the government against unnecessarily provoking the Muslim community and politicising Muslim marriage by failing to obtain the community's consent to the bill. Quoting extracts from a whitepaper[23] by the Colonial Office that discussed the rising dangers of "Mohammedanism" in Central Africa, Sarbah cautioned that given the "troubles with professing natives with regard to the Christian Marriage Ordinance", the government should obtain "full information

17 Such views also influenced post-colonial governments' policy toward the Muslim minority. For instance, in 1969 the Ghanaian government passed the Aliens Compliance Order, which required all "aliens" without proper documentation to leave the country. About 200,000 people (primarily Nigerian Muslims – Yoruba and Hausa who had lived in the country since colonial times but could not document their status) were forced to leave within two weeks; see Eades, *Strangers and Traders,* 55; Peil, "Expulsion of West African Aliens," 205–29.

18 Josiah-Aryeh, *An Outline,* 5–15.

19 Weiss, *Between Accommodation,* 268; Anderson, *Islamic Law,* 249; Hiskett, "Commissioner of Police," 130.

20 Anderson, *Islamic Law,* 249–52.

21 Hiskett, "Commissioner of Police," 131.

22 Government Gazette, January 11, 1908, 33.

23 Colonial Office, *Colonial Report,* 26.

concerning the customs and usages of Mohammedans in West Africa ... so that any law ... passed to regulate Mohammedan marriages may not create similar difficulties".[24]

Weiss argues that perceptions of the British administration in Accra toward local Muslims were shaped by developments in the broader West Africa region.[25] That is to say, policy toward Muslims in the Gold Coast was not independent of British experience (or that of other colonial powers) with Islam in Bilad al-Sudan. During the first decade of the 20th Century a revolutionary Islamist movement (Mahdism) swept through West Africa. In 1905–1907 Mahdist uprisings took place in French Niger and British Nigeria with overtly anti-colonial tones. Mahdist agents also infiltrated the Northern Territories.[26] After the Indian mutiny in 1857 and the fall of Khartoum in 1885, British administrators considered Mahdism a serious security problem.[27] Against this backdrop the rising Mahdist threat in adjacent areas caused much anxiety among the colonial officials in Accra and led to the consolidation of colonial rule in the region.[28] As a result, British policy in the Gold Coast and surrounding areas began to change – leading to gradual securitisation of the question of Islam and Muslims – especially those who originally came from Nigeria (i.e., Hausa), as they were considered more likely to fall under Mahdism's spell.[29]

As shown, while the legislative process that resulted in the enactment of the MMO was underway, the British policy toward Muslims in the colony transformed and was increasingly characterised by suspicion and security concerns. Against this background the ordinance's enactment probably had less to do with what Hiskett calls administrative tidying up than with the fight for the hearts and minds of law-abiding Muslim subjects.[30] Perhaps it was a politically expedient move by some colonial officials who may have come to view the MMO as a valuable tool in the ideological battle against Mahdism. They may have seen recognition of Islamic law in the colony as a means of diminishing the appeal of Mahdism and rewarding the loyalty and acquiescence of mainly the Hausa Muslims on whom the colonial administration was overwhelmingly dependent for staffing the military and police force.[31]

---

24 Ibid.
25 Weiss, "Variations," 74.
26 Goody, "Reform, Renewal and Resistance," 143–56.
27 Weiss, "Variations," 78.
28 Lovejoy and Hogendorn, "Revolutionary Mahdism," 219.
29 Weiss, "Variations," 79.
30 Hiskett, "Commissioner of Police," 132.
31 Weiss, *Between Accommodation*, 229–37.

2.2 *The Colonial Narrative and the Beginning of the Jurispathic Policy*

Although the British colonial policy in the juridical field "was full of variations, inconsistencies and reversals of course",[32] the approach toward MFL was relatively consistent. Throughout the colonial period, British officials subscribed to the view that local Muslim communities had never possessed an "ancient civilization or organized system ... based on the Koranic law".[33] As a result, they opposed the institutionalisation of Islamic law and courts in any part of the Gold Coast. In the eyes of the colonial administrators, "shari'a" was the custom of an alien people who came to the Gold Coast from elsewhere. This view of Islamic law does not seem to have changed much, even after the enactment of the MMO in 1907. For example, a 1928 communique issued in response to an (ultimately rejected) application by Hausas for the recognition of Islamic tribunals bluntly stated: "They have voluntarily come into the territory of another people ... [they should] be subject to the laws of that territory even if their own law differs materially."[34]

Evidence suggests that most colonial officials remained sceptical of Islamic law.[35] Many people in the colonial bureaucracy and judiciary probably regarded the MMO as an administrative blunder and worked in tandem to let it lapse. Bureaucrats undermined the administrative machinery to register Muslim marriages/divorces, while the colonial judiciary denied the normative existence of Islamic law in the few cases that came before it.

The ordinance authorised the governor to grant licences to "Mohammedan priests" to officiate at marriages/divorces. Colonial records are patchy, so it is impossible to say how many licences were issued to imams in each locality, but the available evidence suggests that they were insufficient.[36] The MMO required the names of licensed imamsto be published in the Government Gazette (GG). My survey of the GG archives shows that only forty-nine imams were licensed from 1907 to 1957 – an average of less than one imam per year for the entire country.[37] Weiss blames this on the fact that colonial authorities placed restrictions on who could apply to the government for a licence.[38]

32 Goldman, "Fallible Justice," 586.
33 Weiss, *Between Accommodation*, 200.
34 Hiskett, "Commissioner of Police," 130.
35 Hiskett, "Commissioner of Police," 130–34.
36 Weiss, *Between Accommodation*, 272.
37 GG archives show that all imams were appointed following the extension of the MMO to the Northern Territories in 1931. It is unclear if there were any licensed imams before 1931 anywhere on the Gold Coast – probably there were some, but no official record of them seems to exist.
38 Weiss, *Between Accommodation*, 272.

Moreover, most imams were not eager to apply. To obtain a licence they had to pay a 1-pound fee but, in turn, would collect only 5 pence per registered marriage/divorce.[39] To recuperate his cost an imam had to officiate a minimum of twenty marriages/divorces. This did not make much financial sense for many imams since very few registered marriages/divorces took place in their localities.[40] As a result, many towns lacked licensed imams.

Even worse, local authorities were unaware of the ordinance's existence.[41] Most Muslims did not care about registering marriages under it, either. After all, a traditional marriage ceremony conducted by an ordinary imam or *malam* was already regarded as "valid" in the community's eyes.[42] They did not need the colonial authority's approval for their unions' validity. Moreover, those few Muslims who wanted to register their marriages faced several hurdles. First, they had to locate a licensed imam, which was challenging. Second, they needed to find authorities knowledgeable about the ordinance and who had the required registration forms in hand. Many commentators note that most offices did not carry them and instead asked people to register under the Marriage Ordinance (MO) of 1884.[43]

The biggest hurdle was logistical. The MMO required all "Mohammedan" marriages/divorces to be registered with the district commissioner's office for legal validity. To register a marriage the bridegroom, the bride's *wali* (guardian), two witnesses and the licensed "priest" (imam) had to report to the district commissioner's office in person within one week of the celebration of the marriage.[44] Divorces were to be registered in the same manner within one month. Given the cost and difficulty of getting all these people together and transporting them to the nearest town centre in a very short time, the whole registration process was an ordeal. Acknowledging the logistical obstacles, the district commissioner of Bole noted in 1932 that "[t]he main Mohammedan centres ... are respectively seventy, fifty and fifty-five miles from District

39 Ibid.

40 For instance, in Tamale in 1931–39 only one Muslim marriage was registered. During the same period nine marriages were registered in Gushiegu and 157 in Yendi. More than half of the marriages in Yendi were conducted by three imams in 1932–34; rates for other years varied significantly (two in 1931, ten in 1939); see: Weiss, *Between Accommodation*, 273.

41 Anderson, *Islamic Law*, 250.

42 Weiss, *Between Accommodation*, 273.

43 Weiss, *Between Accommodation,* 270–75; Hiskett, "Commissioner of Police," 132–34; Anderson, *Islamic Law*, 249–52.

44 The MMO allows for late registrations with the approval of a divisional court. But it is a complex process that must be initiated within a "reasonable" time after the expiration of the seven-day deadline. See *Ex Parte Ali* [1980] GLR 872.

Headquarters. The [imams] are in most cases far from young and to ask them after every marriage to proceed to headquarters within a week, for registration would … be considered a hardship and have the reverse effect to that intended by the ordinance".[45]

Besides subversive colonial practices that undermined the registration machinery, colonial judges also played a critical role in derailing the application of the MMO. Colonial judges were poorly trained and often appointed with nonmeritocratic considerations.[46] Their judicial preferences and worldviews were closely shaped by those of the colonial administration. In this respect, the judiciary's negligence and ignorance[47] toward the MMO reflected the government's policy to let the MMO fall into disuse.[48] My survey of existing court decisions from the colonial era affirms that British courts almost never recognised MFL claims based on the MMO. I have come across only one decision[49] in which an MMO-based divorce claim was brought to and eventually rejected by colonial courts.[50]

In short, the colonial bureaucracy and judiciary acted in unison to derail the application of the MMO, hence preventing the normative recognition of Islamic law in the Gold Coast. Authorities were well aware of the bureaucratic hurdles and shortcomings of the ordinance, yet they refused to fix them. According to Hiskett, in the 1930s the colonial administration deliberately turned down opportunities to resuscitate the ordinance and give more support to the administration of Islamic law in the colony.[51] Perhaps colonial officials

45 Hiskett, "Commissioner of Police," 133.

46 Goldman, "Fallible Justice," 590.

47 Anderson reports that there were widespread confusion and ignorance about the status and contents of the ordinance among members of the colonial judiciary. He claims that the MMO was defective from its inception. While it provided for recognition of Islamic marriages/divorces, it gave colonial justices no clear guidance as to what constituted a valid marriage or what types of divorce (*khul'*, *talaq*, *faskh*) were allowed – hence leading to bewilderment in the ranks of the judiciary; see Anderson, *Islamic Law*, 251, 76.

48 Anderson, *Islamic Law*, 249–52; Weiss, *Between Accommodation*, 270–75; Hiskett, "Commissioner of Police," 132–34.

49 *Huzaifeh v Saba* [1939] 5 WACA 181.

50 It seems that other scholars could not find much evidence of the application of the MMO by colonial courts either. For instance, Ollennu, *The Law*, 261, in his seminal study on succession law in Ghana, mentions only one (unreported) case (*Blankson v Hausa* [1953] WACA (unreported)) where the West African Court of Appeal applied Islamic succession-rules to the estate of a Fanti man who had registered his marriage in compliance with the MMO. In three other cases, "Mohammedan law" was cited without any reference to the ordinance: *Ali v Hadiza* [1913] Renner 771; *Ali v Ali* [1939] 5 WACA 94; *Buzu v Shardow* [1929] F. Ct. 1926–1929 357.

51 Hiskett, "Commissioner of Police," 132–34.

lacked a genuine understanding of the practical challenges of requiring registration at district headquarters,[52] or maybe some officials opposed the ordinance because they thought it undermined the powers of non-Muslim tribal authorities.[53] Both issues were probably factors in the weak implementation of the MMO,[54] but the main reason appears to be that both the colonial judiciary and bureaucracy likely considered the ordinance a mistake as it contradicted the long-held view that Islamic law, being a foreign importation, had no official status in the colony or the surrounding areas. Hence, the British seem to have deliberately let the ordinance lapse and left the narrative of "alien" Islamic law for the modern Ghanaian state to inherit upon its independence in 1957.

3 Law and Religion in Postcolonial Ghana

3.1 *Bureaucratic Hurdles that Derailed the Enforcement of the 1907 Ordinance*

"In the area of religion-state relations," Lerner writes, "political leaders of newly independent and still-fragile polities … [usually adopted] a conservative, rather than a revolutionary, approach to stabilize the political system and achieve other, more urgent … goals [of nation-building]."[55] This was also the case in Ghana following independence. The country's founding father, Kwame Nkrumah, wanted to create a centralised state with a strong national identity. The new government banned all political activities based on religious or ethnic affiliation to avoid divisive, inflammatory conflicts. It also maintained the colonial status quo in religious matters, which entailed preserving the 1907 ordinance.[56]

To this day, the 1907 ordinance remains the law of the land (as part of the Marriages Act of 1985 or CAP 127). However, just as during the colonial period, in practice, the ordinance has again been let to lapse by the judiciary and derailed by bureaucratic hurdles that have effectively broken down the machinery to register Muslim marriages and divorces.

52 Ibid.

53 Many Muslims lived under non-Muslim chiefs. The ordinance's requirement to register marriages with the government simply meant that Muslims had to bypass the jurisdiction of their local chiefs. This, some officials believed, was wrong, as it undermined the legitimacy of non-Muslim chiefs vis-à-vis their Muslim subjects – which in their eyes violated colonial policy; see Hiskett, "Commissioner of Police," 134.

54 Hiskett, "Commissioner of Police," 132–34.

55 Lerner, "Critical Junctures," 391.

56 Austin, *Politics in Ghana*, 377.

There are three types of valid marriages recognised by Ghanaian law: (1) customary marriage, (2) ordinance[57] marriage under the MO of 1884, and (3) Islamic marriage under the MMO. According to the Legal Resources Centre (LRC), 95.9 per cent of the Ghanaian Muslims surveyed said that the type of marriage they celebrated was a Muslim marriage.[58] 96.2 per cent indicated that they had not registered their marriages; 80.2 per cent were not familiar with the process of registration.[59] Likewise, a 2015 report by the Ghana Statistical Service (GSS) found that no registration records of Mohammedan marriages existed and attributed this primarily to the widespread lack of knowledge among the public and the failure of the government to provide effective institutions to facilitate registrations.[60]

> The findings reveal that the Mohammedan Marriage has never taken effect due to the very short time frame (seven days) … within which it is to be registered; otherwise, it becomes void. Muslims are therefore compelled to register under the Christian [or customary] marriage … in spite of its conflict with their religious practice.[61]

The registration of marriages is conducted by officials at metropolitan, municipal, and district assemblies. The GSS study revealed that while officials at the assemblies had a fair understanding of the registration of customary and civil marriages, they generally had little or no knowledge of the procedures involved in Muslim marriages. This is precisely what I observed during my visits to metropolitan assemblies in Accra, Tamale and Kumasi in May–June 2017. When I inquired about registering Muslim marriages, all the officials I encountered told me that Muslims could register only a civil or a customary marriage. They had no information about Muslim marriages. One Accra official told me, "There were practically no licensed imams in the country". She probably assumed I was a foreigner who wanted to marry a Ghanaian Muslim woman. She continued, "even if we allow you to register a Mohammedan marriage here in the office, you cannot find a licensed imam to officiate it".[62]

57 Most people refer to ordinance marriage as "Christian marriage" due to its association with British rule and Christian values (e.g., monogamy) informing the legislation.

58 Atuguba, *Registration of Islamic Marriages*, 3.

59 Atuguba, *Registration of Islamic Marriages*, 3.

60 Ghana Statistical Service, *Civil Registration*, 25.

61 Ghana Statistical Service, *Civil Registration*, 25.

62 Personal interview with Naomi Afidzitze, the Office of Registrar General, Accra, May 2017.

I heard similar comments from many other informants in Ghana. They all told me that there were no licensed imams. I could not find one in Kumasi or Tamale, but one afternoon in May 2017, I met one in Nima, near Accra. His name was Sheikh Abubakar Shuaib. Sheikh Shuaib proudly told me that he had been licensed as an imam by Nana Akufo-Addo, the sitting president of Ghana, then the Attorney General and Minister of Justice. Sheikh Shuaib gave me a copy of his letter from Mr. Akufo-Addo, dated December 24, 2002. The MMO requires the names of licensed imams to be published in the GG. Although I did not see Sheikh Shuaib's name in the GG, the issue of the gazette dated December 20, 2002 listed the mosque Sheikh Shuaib founded as a place of worship licensed to celebrate marriages.[63]

Sheikh Shuaib also provided copies of recent marriage certificates registered under the MMO. They carried the names and signatures of grooms, brides, the district commissioner, the licensed imam (Sheikh Shuaib himself) and witnesses. He also showed me official correspondence from courts and various ministries as evidence that the government officially recognised his certificates. He told me that he had not received too many requests for "CAP 129[64] [MMO] marriages". He said people who sought to register their marriages under MMO were "educated, or rich people who travelled or had business abroad".[65]

A few days later, I met with a Muslim official at the Ministry of Justice in Accra. When I told the official that I had met a licensed imam she was amazed, as if I had discovered an extinct species. Unfortunately, Sheikh Shuaib passed away in March 2018. I am not sure if his species is now totally extinct or if a few others are still out there but my experience confirms that the machinery for registering marriages under the MMO has long been broken. Like its colonial predecessor, the government is aware of this but takes no action to repair it. The memorandum to the Intestate Succession Law in 1985 (PNDCL 111) was like an official confession by the government: "The MMO ... is hardly ever enforced. Its registration provisions are probably not known to many Muslims ... and [are] even less common knowledge ... to the legal profession". The PNDCL 111

63 A quick review of available GG records between 1970 and 2021 shows that in the last fifty years the government has not appointed any licensed imams as marriage officers. For electronic copies of GG, see GhaLII. "Gazettes".

64 Some people refer to the MMO as CAP 129, in reference to Chapter 129 of *The Laws of the Gold Coast* (an official compilation of laws in force as of December 31, 1951) by McElwaine (1954). Before that, it was referred to as CAP 107, in reference to Chapter 107 of the 1936 edition of the same collection by McCarthy (1937). In 1985 the MMO was subsumed under Part II of the Marriages Act of 1884–1985 (CAP 127).

65 Personal interview with Sheikh Abubakar Shuaib, Accra, May 2017.

repealed section 10 of the MMO, which authorised Islamic succession rules for people married under the ordinance, and imposed a uniform succession law on all citizens regardless of religion or custom. Many commentators viewed this as the last nail in the coffin of the already dead ordinance.[66]

3.2 *Non-native Religions and the Non-recognition of Their Normative Claims*

As in the colonial period, post-independence courts have worked in tandem with the bureaucracy and collectively derailed the application of the MMO. They frequently refused to acknowledge the nomic existence of Islamic law. They have done so not because they serve as Hirschlian bulwarks of secularism against the expansion of Islamic law but because they have internalised the British colonial narrative about the MMO and continue to view it as an import or as non-native law. Moreover, the lack of licensing and registration machinery in many areas has allowed courts to refuse to recognise Islamic marriages, divorces and succession claims on procedural grounds (i.e., due to parties' failure to duly register the said acts under the 1907 ordinance).

Ghana was founded as a secular state. This characteristic of the regime was expressed in different wordings in the 1957, 1969, 1979 and current (1992) constitutions.[67] The colonial administration distinguished between "traditional" and "modern" religions in Ghana.[68] The former category consisted of traditional African religions that the British derogatorily called "fetishism". The latter included Christianity and Islam.[69] These categories survived into the postcolonial era. In the early days of independence, however, thanks to rising nationalism and anti-colonialism, political leaders "espoused a markedly critical attitude toward Christianity, which was dismissed as the 'white man's religion,' colonizing Africans' minds",[70] while exalting native religions. Native religions were considered part of the national heritage and integrated into official ceremonies. Although not considered a native religion, due to its non-western origins Islam was viewed as a diplomatic and cultural asset.[71] Against this backdrop, the Ghanaian secular state disassociated itself from Islam and Christianity. At the same time, traditional religions were elevated in political

66 Ammah and Alhassan, *Academic and Practical Analyses*, 29.

67 Dovlo, "Religion in the Public Sphere," 634.

68 Meyer, "Religious and Secular," 90.

69 Kallinen, "Christianity, Fetishism," 153–68.

70 Meyer, "Religious and Secular," 90.

71 Dumbe, *Islamic Revivalism*, 13–28; Weiss, *Between Accommodation*, 323.

and judicial fields by incorporating customary laws and native institutions (i.e., chieftaincy) into the public administration. As shown below, the postcolonial state's differentiated approach to native vs. non-native religions also extended into Ghanaian courtrooms.

The global secularist trends that Hirschl describes in relation to the jurisprudence of many national high courts never occurred in Ghana.[72] Until recently, the Ghanaian Supreme Court did not even bother to define what secularism entailed in terms of the constitution. In *Bomfeh v Attorney-General* [2019] GHASC 2 the court observed that the government's support for constructing a national cathedral in Accra or setting up a Hajj (Islamic pilgrimage) Board did not amount to the "excessive entanglement" of the state in religion. In contrast, justices interpreted the government's support for the projects as an innocent attempt to foster national unity. They unanimously stated that the constitution, while secular in nature, did not "prohibit the government from supporting, assisting or cooperating with religious groups". They declared that secularism in the context of the constitution "must be understood to allow, and even encourage state recognition and accommodation of religion and religious identity". From this point of view, Ghanaian secularism does not erect a wall of separation. Instead, like its Indian counterpart, it maintains a principled distance that allows a disconnection between religion and state at the institutional level while not making a fetish of it at the policy level.[73] Yet at the level of the law, the Ghanaian judiciary distinguishes the traditional religion on the one hand and Christianity and Islam on the other.

Ghana has a dualistic legal system in which customary law is recognised as one of the primary sources of law under the constitution (Article 11). Customary law contains practices and elements of traditional African religions. This means that when courts apply the customary law of native communities, they indirectly recognise the nomic existence of traditional religions. For instance, in *Boampong v Aboagye* [1980] GLR 927[74] the Supreme Court approved the application of native religious rituals and rules to a destoolment (the removal

72 Hirschl, "Constitutional Courts," 311–34.

73 Bhargava, "States, Religious Diversity," 8–22.

74 "The answer perhaps is to be found in the traditional concept of the chief as the father of his subjects ... and a spiritual head ... Through the chief's ritual acts ... the ancestral spirits are invoked to protect the community from misfortunes ... and to usher in a season of plenty, good fortune in national affairs ... The slaughtering of the sheep is ... to cleanse the abdicating chief; purify the stool; and propitiate the ancestral guardian spirits." For another case where elements of native religions are similarly invoked, see *Hansen v Ankrah* [Supreme Court, Accra] [1987–88] 1 GLR 639.

of a chief) dispute between traditional authorities, and invoked elements of native religion.

However, in cases dealing with non-native religions (Christianity, Islam), the courts have systematically declined to recognise claims based on religious law. For instance, in *Akyeampong v Marshall* [1959] D.Ct. (unreported) a widow applied to the court to succeed in her deceased husband's estate. She based her claim on the rules of the Presbyterian Church, to which both she and her late husband had belonged. These rules stipulated that a widow was entitled to one-third of her deceased husband's property. The Divisional Court rejected the application, stating that church rules were "not part of the law of the land".[75] Instead, it distributed the deceased's estate according to the husband's personal law (i.e., the customary law of his tribe), which did not allow a widow to succeed to her deceased husband's intestate property.[76] As said earlier, customary law is imbued with elements of traditional religion. In this respect, the court's rejection of the succession rules of the church was not a secular reflex. It simply privileged one form of religiously inspired law over another. At the time, the deceased's personal law regulated intestate succession in Ghana. As Kludze argues, the court could have expanded the meaning of "personal law" and allowed the devolution of the property according to the church's rules, but the justices chose not to do so.[77]

One can argue that the justices in *Akyeampong v Marshall* were correct to dismiss the church rules, as there was no legislation authorising their application by Ghanaian courts. In the case of Islamic law, however, such legislation exists. The MMO of 1907 allows the courts to recognise and regulate the consequences of MFL. Still, the Ghanaian judiciary has been equally dismissive of claims based on Islamic law. They have been unwilling to acknowledge its nomic existence, thereby rejecting most MFL claims on procedural grounds due to the parties' failure to register their marriages per the 1907 ordinance.

4 The Postcolonial Judiciary's Jurispathic Stance on Islamic Law

During my field research in Ghana, many informants said that Muslims did not use the formal legal system, especially for their family and property disputes. Instead, they resorted to traditional authorities and a growing number of ADR

75 Ollennu, *The Law*, 95–97.

76 Bankas, "Problems of Intestate Succession," 436.

77 Kludze, *Modern Law*, 232.

forums utilising Islamic law and local customs. However, this does not mean that Muslims were utterly absent from the formal juridical field. Searching through two novel databases,[78] I identified 25 superior court[79] cases from 1961 to 2019 that dealt with "Mohammedan" marriage, divorce, and succession. My analysis of the case law suggests that many disputes were property related. Who inherited what depended on the type and validity of the marriage in question. Before 1985, if the marriage in question were Islamic and registered under the MMO, the heirs were to receive their shares according to Islamic law. In those cases, relatives who would have inherited a greater share of the estate under customary (tribal) succession rules if the marriage in question had been customary (tribal) came to courts to challenge the validity of the Islamic marriages. In other cases, some litigants even alleged that there had been no valid marriage (Islamic or otherwise) between the deceased and the surviving spouse to exclude the latter from inheritance. Similar dispute patterns were also observable after 1985, with slight variations.[80] In all these cases the justices were presented with the same questions: Was there a valid marriage? And what kind of marriage was it: Mohammedan, customary (tribal), or civil?

The first case where the postcolonial judiciary answered these questions was *Kwakye v Tuba* (1961). This was a succession case in which the defendants argued that the deceased was a Muslim and that succession to his estate should be governed by Islamic law. Citing *Akyeampong v Marshall* [1959] Justice Nii Amaa Ollennu declared that succession in Ghana was not based upon a person's religion as a general rule. The only exception was section 10 of the MMO. It stated that succession to a deceased Muslim's estate would be governed by Islamic law if he had registered his marriage under the ordinance. If he died unmarried or without having registered his marriage, then his estate, Ollennu argued, would devolve according to his personal law (i.e., the customary law of his tribe). Ollennu also suggested that unregistered "Mohammedan" marriages should be treated as customary law marriages. A year later, in another Muslim succession case, *Brimah v Asana* (1962), he reiterated the same position.

---

78 *Digital Attorney*, and *Dennislaw*.

79 The Supreme Court, the High Court, the Court of Appeal.

80 Evidence suggests that Muslim traditional/religious authorities often did not abide by the PNDCL 111 and continued applying Islamic law in inheritance cases. Some heirs, however, challenged inheritance rulings by religious authorities and asked courts to redistribute the estates in question according to PNDCL 111; see *Salley v Brimah* [2016] DLCA 8161; *Giwah v Ladi* [2010] DLHC 7067; *Mohamadu v Adamu* [2014] DLCA 4415; *Agbeshie v Amorkor* [2009] GHASC 2.

Justice Ollennu was a highly respected jurist, judge and politician. He served on the High Court and the Supreme Court of Ghana. After retiring from the judiciary, he served as the speaker of the parliament and the acting president of Ghana. His rulings, articles and books on customary law and succession law are considered among the most authoritative sources and widely cited by the judiciary. Given Justice Ollennu's influence, his rulings in the two cases above became landmark decisions shaping the dominant narrative on Islamic law in the ranks of the modern judiciary.

Although some justices who came after Justice Ollennu occasionally issued rulings that declared unregistered Muslim marriages (and divorces)[81] null and void,[82] the general trend has been to consider them customary marriages. Sometimes Muslim couples celebrate their marriages under customary (tribal) and Islamic law. If the marriage was not registered in compliance with the MMO, justices treated it exclusively as a customary marriage because the parties had already contracted it according to their customs.[83] However, if parties contracted only an Islamic marriage and failed to register it, it was unclear what kind of a customary marriage this could be considered, as there was no readily available fallback option. Were they customary marriages, as per the tribal law of the parties, or customary Islamic marriages? The distinction matters because customary law is one of the primary sources of law in the Ghanaian legal system. Suppose the courts recognise the nomic existence of customary Islamic law. In that case, it would mean that some aspects of Islamic law could be considered a primary source of law as far as Ghanaian Muslims are concerned. But such recognition would also challenge the long-established governmental policy and judicial narrative that Islamic law is not a native law of the land.

Many scholars argue that in some parts of Ghana elements of Islamic family law have long been incorporated into customary law.[84] According to this view, apart from Muslim marriages contracted under the 1907 ordinance, there are also unregistered Muslim marriages that have been contracted according to Islamic customs. The High Court delivered the only decision that categorically

81 In several cases the validity of Muslim divorces was contested on the grounds that parties had failed to register their marriages in the first place. One cannot dissolve a marriage that does not legally exist. See *Esseku v Inkoom* [2013] DLCA 4021; *Salifu v Sofo* [2018] DLCA 5149; *Bawa v Gariba* [2019] DLHC 8724.

82 For instance, see *Jebeille v Ashkar* [1977] GLR 458.

83 For instance, see *Esseku v Inkoom* [2013] DLCA 4021. Also see *Lamptey v Lamptey* [2009] DLHC 5591 for a similar discussion.

84 Aziz, "Muslim Family Law," 41–44; Josiah-Aryeh, *An Outline*, 81–90.

recognised the existence of customary Muslim marriage in *Barake v Barake* [1993–94] 1 GLR 635. Justice Brobbey ruled that there were two types of Muslim marriage: marriage registered under the 1907 ordinance and unregistered customary marriage. Justice Brobbey identified the "essential requirements" of customary Muslim marriages as "offer, acceptance, the fact of the proposal and acceptance taking place at one meeting, two witnesses, and the fact that they were Muslim witnesses". Although this was the courts' boldest attempt to recognise customary Muslim marriages to date, my analysis suggests that the judiciary has completely disregarded Justice Brobbey's "essential requirements" test and continues to deny the nomic existence of customary Islamic marriages. The prevailing trend still seems to be that when there is no proper registration under the MMO, following Ollennu's formulation in *Kwakye v Tuba*, justices consider the subsisting marriage a customary marriage under the parties' tribal customs. For instance, *Bawa v Gariba* (2019) ruled that the non-registration of a Muslim marriage reduced it to a customary marriage under the tribal law of the parties.[85]

Similar patterns of rejection are also observed concerning customary Islamic succession rules. As noted, until PNDCL 111 repealed section 10 of the MMO in 1985, Islamic successionrules "technically" applied to the devolution of deceased Muslims' property if they had duly registered their marriages. In practice, however, the post-independence judiciary almost never allowed the application of Islamic successionrules. Nearly all cases[86] were rejected due to the failure to comply with the registration requirements.[87] However, there are two scenarios under which deceased Muslims' estate may still be allowed to devolve according to Islamic law. First, according to the Wills Act of 1971, any Muslim can make a will to request that upon his death his estate be distributed according to Islamic law.[88] Second, although the PNDCL 111 abolished customary intestate succession law, it still made an exception[89] for residual property

85 The position in this 2019 case was not very different from the position observed in *Hausa v Haruna* [1963] 2 GLR 212, in which, upon the plaintiff's failure to show evidence of registration of her Muslim marriage to her late husband, the court decided that it was a marriage under the Gonja tribal law. Although nearly 60 years separate the two cases, the judiciary has firmly maintained its unwavering stance on non-recognition of Muslim customary marriages.

86 For instance, see *Kwakye v Tuba* [1961] GLR 720; *Brimah v Asana* [1962] 1 GLR 118; *Hausa v Haruna* [1963] 2 GLR 212.

87 Kludze, *Modern Law*, 234.

88 Aziz, "Muslim Family Law," 56.

89 For instance, see *Agyekum v Bio* [2016] GHASC 7.

to devolve according to customary law.[90] In the case of Ghanaian Muslims whose customary succession rules are based on Islamic law, the courts may technically allow the residual property to devolve according to those rules. However, this almost never happens in practice. Justice Ollennu, who viewed Islamic succession rules as foreign law, argued that native customs based on Islamic law must be proven to the court's satisfaction.[91] Otherwise the property must devolve according to the deceased's personal (tribal) law.[92] Having internalised this position, Ghanaian superior courts have systematically rejected Islamic succession claims.

In *Hausa v Hausa* (1972) the Court of Appeal refused to recognise customary Islamic succession rules, even though, as Justice Bentsi-Enchill put it, "the applicable customary law [was] deeply modified by Mohammedan law". In the following years the superior courts continuously denied the nomic significance of customary Islamic succession rules. They staunchly struck down decisions[93] of lower courts which occasionally softened their rejectionist stance, ensuring that Islamic succession rules were not acknowledged as the law of the land. For instance, in the case *Yahaya v Yakubu* [2012] DLSC 3057, it was claimed that Alhaji Yahaya, a devout Muslim, left an oral will to distribute his property according to Islamic law. Some of his relatives legally challenged the will. The trial judge upheld the oral will and ordered the devolution of the property according to Islamic rules that he directly cited from the Quran. The Court of Appeal reversed the decision, arguing that the trial judge erred in applying Islamic testamentary rules instead of the parties' customary law.

> [A]ll the parties to this case are Wala people ... So obviously it was Wala customary law that ought to have been used in deciding the issues ... [A]mong the Wala ... Islamic law and customary practice are so intertwined that it is difficult to separate the two. That is why there was no

90 Fenrich and Higgins, "Promise Unfulfilled," 259–341; Hammond, "Towards an Inclusive Vision," 124–60.

91 Ollennu, *The Law*, 262–63.

92 Kludze argues that this is an outdated position. He proposes a new interpretation following s 49(2) of the Courts Law of 1971, which states that "In the absence of intention to the contrary, the law applicable to ... the devolution of a person's estate shall be the personal law" (Kludze, *Modern Law*, 233). A person's embrace of Islam, Kludze claims, constitutes a contrary intention within the meaning of s 49(2). That is to say, a Ghanaian Muslim's estate should devolve according to Islamic law, not the customary law of his tribe (Kludze, *Modern Law*, 233). However, this position has not yet gained the support of the superior courts.

93 For example, see *Agbeshie v Amorkor* [2009] GHASC 2; *Hawa v Agyarko* [2010] DLCA 3610.

> basis for the learned trial judge to say that Islamic, rather than Wala customary law, was the applicable law (*Yahaya v Yakubu* [2012] DLSC 3057).

In brief, as with Islamic marriage, the Ghanaian judiciary has denied recognising and applying Islamic succession rules. During my interviews some Ghanaian judges articulated two specific objections to using Islamic succession rules. First, they said that Islamic law was not native law and the PNDCL 111 had removed the only valid grounds for its application (by repealing section 10 of the MMO). Second, they also argued that Islamic law's underlying notion of property was markedly different from those of native communities in Ghana.[94] Their second objection closely echoed Justice Ollennu's main criticism of Islamic succession rules. He opposed Islamic law due to its individualistic approach to property. He believed that while the Ghanaian customary law made a provision for family property, the Islamic succession law ignored the family as a unit and allocated the deceased's property exclusively among individuals. The application of Islamic succession, a foreign system, at the expense of native law, Ollennu claimed, was "ignorance of the Ghanaian way of life".[95] This position seems to have profoundly influenced the Ghanaian judiciary's attitudes toward Islamic law.

5 Comparison of the Judicial Policy toward Islamic and Customary Marriages

The judiciary has consistently denied the nomic existence of Islamic marriages, divorces and succession claims due to individuals' failure to register their marriages in compliance with the MMO. To date there has been only one case in which the judiciary recognised the validity of Islamic marriage because it was duly registered under the MMO.[96] In some cases people did not care about registration because unregistered marriages were still legitimate in the community's eyes.[97] However, in many other cases people could not register because the legal infrastructure was lacking, just as during the colonial period. There were no licensed imams. The seven-day limit was too restrictive. The requirement

94 Personal interviews; the informants declined to be identified. Accra, May 2017.

95 Ollennu, *The Law*, 267–68.

96 See *Ramia v Ramia* [1981] GLR 275.

97 99.2% of Muslims surveyed by LRC indicated that their "unregistered" marriages were recognised by chiefs and members of their communities; see Atuguba, *Registration of Islamic Marriages*, 3.

that the imam, witnesses, the groom, and the bride's guardian attend in person was too burdensome. The registration offices did not have knowledge of the MMOor simply were too far away from where most Muslims resided.

A male informant in Accra who tried to register his marriage but could not find an imam to do so told me that he felt "betrayed or tricked by the state" because "as a good citizen, [he] wanted to follow the law" yet was unable to do so.[98] As a result, if he or his wife ever goes to court, their Muslim marriage will be considered "non-existent". In other words, they will be penalised by the judiciary because the government has failed to enable them to register their marriage. The judiciary has long been aware of the problems that prevent people from registering their marriages under the MMO but it still has not taken corrective action.

There are two types of customary law in Ghana: the living customary law that people practise regulating their everyday lives and the judicial customary law defined by the courts.[99] Before the Customary Marriage and Divorce (Registration) Law (PNDCL 112)[100] of 1985, customary marriages were not required to be registered. In the absence of documentary evidence the courts had to establish the validity of customary marriages. In an attempt to solve the problem, Justice Ollennu defined the essential elements of customary marriage in *Yaotey v Quaye* [1961] 2 GLR 573 as follows: 1) the agreement by the parties to live together as husband and wife; 2) the consent of the man's family; 3) the consent of the woman's family (indicated by their acceptance of drinks – rum, gin, whiskey, etc. – from the man); and 4) consummation. The essentials defined by Justice Ollennu have become a standard test exercised by the judiciary to establish the validity of customary marriages. However, as Adinkrah notes, some jurists[101] have come to treat these elements (e.g., the acceptance of drinks) as strict requirements, as a "*sine qua non* to the conclusion of a customary marriage".[102] The judiciary's growing dependence upon such standards for the validity of a customary marriage has caused much resentment, as denials resulted in the deprivation of property rights.[103]

98 Personal interview; the informant declined to be identified. Accra, June 2017.

99 Josiah-Aryeh, "Customary Law's Unsteady Stride Forward," 157–68.

100 Which is now part of the Marriage Act of 1985 or CAP 127.

101 In *Badu v Boakye* [1975] 1 GLR 283, due to the rigid application of the essential requirements test the judge refused to recognise the validity of a customary marriage, calling it "concubinage" instead. Similarly, in an earlier case, *Asumah v Khair* [1959] GLR 353, the existence of a customary marriage was denied because the man had not sent drinks to the woman's family.

102 Adinkrah, "Essentials of a Customary Marriage," 45–46.

103 Akamba and Tufuor, "Future of Customary Law," 218.

The PNDCL 112 added insult to the injury. It required the registration of customary marriages within three months and, in section 15, disqualified spouses of unregistered customary marriages from inheriting under the "gender egalitarian" PNDCL 111. Instead it left them at the mercy of customary succession rules that traditionally discriminated against women and children.[104] Despite PNDCL 112's draconian registration requirements, the registration of customary marriages remained extremely rare.[105] As a result, many women (and their children) in unregistered customary marriages were prevented from enjoying the equal property rights promised by the new intestate succession law.

The judiciary was aware of the registration-related problems under customary marriage and succession. In several landmark decisions superior courts intervened and took corrective action. *Bentil v Pratt* [1989–90] 2 GLR 476 ruled that registration was not essential to the validity of a customary law marriage. In *Adade v Dade* [1989] 1 DLCA 248 it was decided that "it would be absurd to deprive a spouse of his or her rights under PNDCL 111 simply because such marriage has not been registered". In *Essilfie v Quarcoo* [1991] DLHC 2010 Justice Lutterodt wrote, "the strict, literal, grammatical approach cannot be right; it does not harmonize with the social consideration". She arrived at the same conclusion as the two earlier rulings regarding the validity of customary marriages and the extension of PNDCL 111 to spouses whose customary marriage had not been registered.

Furthermore, she also challenged the prevailing essentials of the customary marriage doctrine and instead offered a flexible alternative. After criticising the requirement of the acceptance of drinks etc. as superfluous, she wrote, "once it has been proved … that the parties have agreed to and have lived together in the sight of the world as man and wife … the court should hold that the parties are married according to native custom". This new approach seems to have been accepted in many decisions as the new standard for recognising customary marriages.[106] Moreover, the position articulated in the three decisions mentioned above on PNDCL 111 and 112 led the parliament to amend these two laws[107] in 1991 by making the registration of customary marriages optional and allowing customary spouses to inherit under PNDCL 111 regardless of their registration status.

104 Woodman, "Ghana Reforms," 120; Freeman, "Ghana," 159–62.

105 Fenrich and Higgins, "Promise Unfulfilled," 292.

106 See *Baidoo v Baidoo* [2019] GHASC 91; *Buckman v Ankumayi* [2012] DLCA 6486; *Mahama v Awuni* [2004] DLCA 6783.

107 The Customary Marriage and Divorce Registration (Amendment) Law, 1991, (PNDCL 263), and the Intestate Succession (Amendment) Law, 1991, (PNDCL 264).

Ghanaian courts have taken the lead in fixing the registration-related problems of customary marriages. They have softened the criteria for establishing the validity of customary marriages and expanded the inheritance rights of widows and children.[108] The government has followed the courts' lead and amended the relevant legislation to provide a lasting solution. These legislative and judicial responses have helped ease the marital and property-related injustices people experienced due to the non-recognition of their customary marriages.[109] However, the judiciary has failed to take a similar interest in the predicament of Muslim Ghanaians or to show any sensitivity to their registration and succession-related troubles. On the contrary, they have consistently invalidated Muslim marriages,[110] turned a blind eye to the broken machinery, and subjected widows and children to native succession laws, even when Islamic law would have better protected their property rights.[111]

Ghanaian Muslims are significantly underrepresented in the judiciary. Several of my informants[112] told me that as of 2017, of about 170 judges in superior courts, only six were Muslims. In comparison a Muslim member of parliament reported that the Muslim caucus had 46 members in the 275-seat national parliament.[113] That is to say, an overwhelming majority of judges who deal with Muslim cases historically have been non-Muslims. They have not been trained in Islamic law and are not familiar with Muslim communities' cultural practices and customs. However, their attitudes toward Islamic law cannot be explained simply by a lack of familiarity with Muslim culture or traditions. As a former senior state attorney in Ghana told me, "Not a single Ghanaian judge or state attorney will ever consider 'shari'a' native law of the land … It is a foreign law. It was brought to Gold Coast by the colonial administration."[114] In other words, Ghanaian judges are dismissive of Islamic law not because they are unfamiliar with Islamic law or culture but because they inherited the colonial narrative that Islamic law was not a native law of the land.

---

108 Woodman, "Ghana Reforms," 120.

109 Fenrich and Higgins, "Promise Unfulfilled," 294.

110 For an example, see *Hausa v Hausa* [1972] 2 GLR 469.

111 Dankwa, "Property Rights," 1–24.

112 Personal interviews with Rahmata Issahaq-Pelpuo, Legal Advisor, the Federation of Muslim Woman Associations of Ghana (FOMWAG), Accra, June 2017, and Dr. Abdul Baasit Aziz Bamba, Senior Lecturer, the University of Ghana School of Law, Accra, May 2017.

113 The seventh parliament of the fourth republic (2016–2020).

114 Personal interview with David O. Asare, Accra, May 2017.

6 The Social and Political Cost of Undignified Jurispathy

The state courts' consistent denial of MFL claims on procedural grounds and the government's refusal to fix the broken machinery contribute to the growing sense of procedural injustice among Ghanaian Muslims. There are no representative studies that survey Ghanaian Muslims' attitudes toward legal authorities or the state in general. However, nearly three-quarters of my interviewees said they did not trust the courts – especially regarding family and property matters. One taxi driver said: "Courts are not for Muslims. I am a Muslim. They do not represent us. They do not accept our law. My law is shari'a."[115] Likewise, a university student remarked: "We, Muslims in Ghana, do not have a state of our own. The Christian majority owns the state and courts … [which] have no respect for our culture … Why should we obey their law?"[116] Tyler states that individuals' perception of legitimacy is "rooted in the judgment that … the courts are acting fairly".[117] If the courts are perceived to be acting unfairly their legitimacy erodes, making individuals less willing to comply with the law. In this respect one can claim that this is precisely what is happening among some of my Ghanaian informants. The courts' perceived injustice seems to have undermined their trust in the judiciary and eroded their commitment to the rule of law.

Murphy, Cherney and Teston report a positive correlation between procedural injustice and social exclusion among religious minorities.[118] Similarly Renström, Bäck and Knapton find that socially excluded individuals are more prone to identify with extremist groups and resort to political violence.[119] That is to say, the Ghanaian court's systematic denial of Islamic law and the perceived procedural injustice could contribute to a sense of social exclusion and even the radicalisation of some Ghanaian Muslims. In recent years, pointing to the growing influence of Ahlu Sunnah Wal Jama'a (ASWAJ, a home-grown Salafi/Wahhabi movement with strong Saudi/Egyptian connections), some scholars have warned about the increasing danger of Islamic radicalisation and violence in Ghana.[120] I cannot say whether Islamic radicalism is on the rise or if there is a direct correlation between radicalisation and procedural injustice.

115 Personal interview; the informant declined to be identified. Accra, May 2017.
116 Personal interview; the informant declined to be identified. Accra, May 2017.
117 Tyler, "Procedural Justice," 286.
118 Murphy, Cherney, and Teston, "Promoting Muslims' Willingness," 594–619.
119 Renström, Bäck, and Knapton, "Exploring a Pathway," 1204–29.
120 Iddrisu, *Contesting Islam*, 3–21; Dumbe, "Islamic Polarisation," 177–80; Aning and Abdallah, "Islamic Radicalisation," 150–64.

Still, during my field research I encountered several individuals who were enthusiastic supporters of ISIS (Daesh) and loudly criticised the Ghanaian court's handling of "shari'a" cases. One individual who helped arrange my meetings at a local shari'a court said: "I am proud of Daesh and Khalifa al-Baghdadi … I would like to see shari'a fully implemented in Ghana."[121] Another person who reportedly had friends who travelled to Syria to join Daesh was very angry that Ghanaian courts did not recognise Islamic law. When I asked him about their dismissal of Islamic marriages, he said, "Shari'a is the law of God … When courts [do not recognize it], they disrespect Muslims. A state that disrespects Islam is [a] state of *kufr* [disbelief]. It is OK to make *jihad* [against such a state]."[122]

Although radicalisation may be an indirect outcome of perceived procedural injustice, most Muslims do not respond to the courts' undignified jurispathy by adopting extremist views. Instead, they turn to religion-based ADR forums.[123] "There is no uniform Muslim community in Ghana." Muslims are deeply divided along ethnic, tribal and sectarian lines.[124] This plurality has given rise to several ADR forums with competing narratives and legal meanings. Some of these organisations include the Islamic Judicial Committee (IJC) at the Office of the National Chief Imam, the Islamic Research and Reformation Centre (IRRC), the Ghana Muslim Mission (GMM) and the Arbitration and Complaints Section (ACS) at ASWAJ.[125]

There is considerable divergence of legal meanings across these forums. For instance, when I inquired about the minimum age for marriage for a woman, an imam in Accra affiliated with ASWAJ told me: "According to shari'a, as soon as a girl reaches puberty, she can marry. This could be nine, ten, eleven, or twelve."[126] On the other hand, a representative of the GMM told me they would not allow anyone under eighteen to marry.[127] I also observed a similar diversity

121 Personal interview; the informant declined to be identified. Tamale, June 2017.

122 Personal interview; the informant declined to be identified. Tamale, June 2017.

123 Personal interview with Dr. Yunus Dumbe, Senior Lecturer in Islamic Studies, Kwame Nkrumah University, Accra, May 2017.

124 Weiss, *Between Accommodation*, 348; Pellow, "Muslim Segmentation," 423–25.

125 The ACS at ASWAJ is the only ADR forum that provides statistics about its activities. According to the information I obtained from their Accra office, between 2013 and 2015 they handled about 450 cases per year. About 70% of the cases were marital disputes, and 15% were succession-related. About 80% of the cases were filed by female clients. Each year they refer about 30 cases to family tribunals, which are state courts with jurisdiction over matters involving children (custody, etc.).

126 Personal interview with Al-Hajj Umar, Accra, June 2017.

127 Personal interview with Mahmoud Bill (GMM), Accra, May 2017.

of communal legal meanings regarding spousal duties and what it meant to be a "good" husband/wife or even a "good" Muslim. However, legal meanings that I would call "friendlier to women's or children's rights" were often a minority opinion.

Such intragroup differences are relatively minor fractures compared to the significant fault lines that divide the legal meanings of the state and the Muslim community in general. Since the restoration of democratic rule in 1992 the Ghanaian judiciary has become an active defender of human and women's rights.[128] It has shown a growing willingness to hold domestic law and institutions to international standards.[129] However, some nomic groups in the Muslim community have moved in the opposite direction. For instance, I interviewed several women who were the victims of domestic violence. One woman, Asma, sought the help of a local ASWAJ imam. The imam reportedly said: "According to Quran, your husband has a right and duty to discipline you."[130]

In contrast the Domestic Violence Act of 2007 calls for the imprisonment of offenders for up to two years. When Asma asked if she should have reported her husband to the police, the imam allegedly said: "You should avoid involving the police. This is an Islamic matter, not a matter for the state."[131] Asma was not only upset with how the imam handled her case but also disenchanted with the promise of equal rights under the constitution. "This is how Muslim women are treated in this country. I am trapped. Where is the equality or democracy that everybody speaks of?" Nearly half of the women (and some men) shared similar frustration when using religion-based ADR services. Many reported feeling betrayed by the state and its "empty promises of equality" and freedom. The burgeoning gap between the legal meanings of the state and Muslim groups has weakened some Muslim citizens' trust in democratic institutions and the promise of equal citizenship.

---

128 Buamah, "Legal Pluralism," 132–75; Kunbor, "Epistolary Jurisdiction," 2–28.

129 For examples, see *Mensah v Mensah* [2012] GHASC 8; *New Patriotic Party v Inspector General of Police* (1993–94) 2 GLR 459.

130 Personal interview with Asma Asante (pseudonym), Accra, June 2017.

131 Issaka-Toure, who conducted an extensive study of dispute resolution forums operated by Tijaniyya- and ASWAJ-affiliated religious figures, reports that while some *malams* advised against involving the police, others helped their clients report their cases to the authorities. She notes that even among religious figures affiliated with the same movement, there were considerable personal differences in terms of how each *malam* handled domestic violence cases and how they approached the question of whether to involve the state; see Issaka-Toure, "Islamic Construction," 151–58; Issaka-Toure, "Application of Muslim Family Law," 241.

The undignified killing also has a very high opportunity cost for the Ghanaian state. As noted, in this type of jurispathy the courts do not dignify normative claims of non-state groups with a substantive response. They instead brush them away on procedural grounds. By doing so they lose an opportunity to engage with Islamic law in a meaningful and respectful manner and give reform-minded elements in the Muslim community feedback and guidance to harmonise their legal meanings with the state's. As discussed earlier, harmonisation is not the only outcome of dignified law-killing, but it is the most likely one. In many jurisdictions from Malaysia to Morocco civil courts' substantive engagement with religious law-based claims has led to their moderation, as reform-minded groups have been able to harmonise their religious meanings with human/women's rights and the associated norms and values.[132] In the long term this brings the state courts' and the minority communities' legal meanings closer.

There has been only one case so far in which the Ghanaian judiciary has come very close to recognising the existence of Islamic law through the substantive treatment of the normative claims at stake. In *Giwah v Ladi* [2010] the plaintiff contested a ruling by the IJC at the Office of the Chief Imam, which distributed a deceased Muslim woman's estate according to Islamic law, explicitly citing verse 4:11 of the Quran. As the court of original jurisdiction, without dodging the issue on procedural grounds the High Court stated that the IJC should have applied PNDCL 111 instead of Islamic law to the distribution of the estate, thereby setting aside the Islamic ruling, but the High Court then did something entirely unexpected and examined at considerable length Islamic inheritance law as stated in the Quran. It judged that the ICJ ruling had misinterpreted verse 4:11. It also ruled that the ICJ's decision violated the 1992 Constitution's clauses concerning equality before the law, Article 17(1), and non-discrimination, Article 17(2). The High Court's decision was later upheld by the Court of Appeal[133]and the Supreme Court.[134]

Giwah v Ladi [2010] was unprecedented. For the first time superior courts engaged with Islamic law in substantive terms and challenged its commitment to the constitutional principles of gender equality and non-discrimination. Although some officials at the Office of the Chief Imam resented the ruling that set aside their jurisdiction,[135] the official response was somewhat positive: "The

---

132 Shachar, "Privatizing Diversity," 573–607; Sezgin, "Muslim Family Laws," 235–73; Hirschl, *Constitutional Theocracy*, 162–205; Moustafa, *Constituting Religion*, 49–90.

133 *Giwah v Ladi* [2011] CA (unreported).

134 *Giwah v Ladi* [2013–2014] 2 GLR 1139.

135 Personal interview with Seidu H. Nasigri, Legal Adviser, Office of the Chief Imam, Accra, May 2017.

Chief Imam understands the democratic dispensation and believes that the law of the land (Constitution) overrides all other laws in the country."[136] When I asked the legal adviser at the Office of the Chief Imam about the case, he reiterated the supremacy of the constitution over his community's legal meaning. He reportedly did not see a contradiction between the two because human rights and "gender justice [were] the pillars of Islam".[137] Some women's rights activists I interviewed supported the court's ruling in *Giwah v Ladi* and said they welcomed a gender-sensitive reinterpretation of Islamic inheritance rules.[138] This is a clear sign that some nomic groups in the Muslim community are willing to work with the state courts and recognise the state's law as the supreme law by harmonising their legal meanings if/when courts recognise the nomic existence of Islamic law and engage with it substantively.

7 Conclusion

Ghanaian courts have repeatedly engaged in undignified jurispathy against Islamic law by refusing to recognise the validity of Muslim marriages, divorces, and inheritance claims. In doing so they have erected a procedural firewall between the MMO and the official nomos. They have indirectly destroyed the legal meanings built around Islamic law without discussing what was at stake. The authorities often have not cared whether there were feasible registration systems or licensed imams to officiate in "Mohammedan" marriages. The judiciary and the rest of the government blindly followed the colonial narrative that Islamic law was not the native law of the land. The rest was a mere detail.

The judiciary's consistent refusal to recognise Islamic law has deprived nomic groups of critical feedback for harmonising their legal meanings with the state's. The Muslim community in Ghana is an integral part of the socio-economic and political fabric of the country. They are vested in democratic and peaceful co-existence with the political majority. *Giwah v Ladi* has shown that some elements in the Muslim community may be open to internal reform and reinterpretation. In a democratic, multireligious society where religious and customary laws are formally integrated into the state legal system, the harmonisation of divergent legal meanings is critical to de-escalating normative

136 Quoted in the case file, *Giwah v Ladi* [2010] DLHC 7067.

137 Personal interview with Seidu H. Nasigri, Legal Adviser, Office of the Chief Imam, Accra, May 2017.

138 Personal interview with two FOMWAG members who declined to be identified, Accra, May 2017.

tensions, the political inclusion of minorities, and the preservation of their commitment to the rule of law. In this respect the Ghanaian judiciary makes a critical mistake by not facilitating the harmonisation process. This could pose a long-term threat to the survival of Ghana's fragile democracy.

Speaking of the future of MFL in Ghana, there is a need for new legislation to replace the MMO and fix the broken machinery.[139] But this will not be enough. The legal reality is socially constructed through the agency of narrative. To change the world and thereby the reality, the narrative must change too. To enact a new vision, one must break free from the old way of doing things.[140] In other words, the Ghanaian judiciary and the bureaucracy must replace the old colonial narrative about Islamic law. The new narrative must acknowledge the indigeneity of the Muslim community, recognise its internal nomic diversity and emphasise constitutional equality and non-discrimination. Only then can it be ensured that there is a viable future for the MFL in Ghana.

The theoretical and empirical insights drawn from the Ghanaian case are relevant to pluri-legal societies worldwide. The chapter has shown that there are different types of jurispathy with different consequences for state-religion relations and the development of multi-ethnic/religious democracies. Civil courts from Israel to India and Greece to Kenya regularly commit the undignified killing of religious laws, but they are often ignored by current scholarship, which tends to emphasize landmark cases with substantive meat (i.e., dignified killings). In other words, cases of undignified killings are not part of the existing empirical or theoretical models. To remedy this, scholars need to move beyond the binaries of separation/entanglement and religious/secular and examine instances of undignified jurispathy and their implications for majority-minority relations and democratic institutions in pluri-legal societies.

139 The Ghanaian government prepared a new Muslim Marriage and Divorce Bill in 2017. At the time of writing, it has not been yet submitted to the parliament. Some of my informants indicated that the bill's chances of success were slim. However, even if it is passed, the new law would be only a slight improvement over the existing MMO. The most important change would be in the number days (from 7 to 30) within which a marriage must be registered. It would also authorise a wider application of Islamic succession law.

140 Hansen, *Narrative Change*, 1–5.

Bibliography

Literature

Adinkrah, Kofi Oti. "The Essentials of a Customary Marriage: A New Approach." *Review of Ghana Law* 12 (1980): 40–52.

Akamba, Joseph B., and Isidore Kwadwo Tufuor. "The Future of Customary Law in Ghana." In *The Future of African Customary Law*, edited by Jeanmarie Fenrich, Paolo Galizzi, and Tracy E. Higgins, 202–24. New York: Cambridge University Press, 2011.

Ammah, Rabiatu, and Salman M. Alhassan. *Academic and Practical Analyses of the Law Regulating Islamic Marriages in Ghana: Marriage of Mohammedans Ordinance [Cap 129]*. Accra: WILDAF, 2013.

Anderson, J. N. D. *Islamic Law in Africa*. London: HMSO, 1954.

Aning, Kwesi, and Mustapha Abdallah. "Islamic Radicalisation and Violence in Ghana." *Conflict, Security & Development* 13, no. 2 (2013): 149–67.

Atuguba, Raymond A. *The Registration of Islamic Marriages in Ghana's Plural Legal System-Challenges and Strategies for Improvement*. Accra: Legal Resources Centre, 2003.

Austin, Dennis. *Politics in Ghana, 1947–1960*. London: Oxford University Press, 1966.

Aziz, Abdul Baasit Abdul. "Muslim Family Law in Ghana: Resolving the Paradoxes of Its Integration within a Liberal Legal Regime." LLM thesis, Harvard Law School, 2004.

Bankas, Ernest K. "Problems of Intestate Succession and the Conflict of Laws in Ghana." *The International Lawyer* 26, no. 2 (1992): 433–65.

Bhargava, Rajeev. "States, Religious Diversity and the Crisis of Secularism." *The Hedgehog Review* 12, no. 3 (2013): 8–22.

Buamah, Christine. "Legal Pluralism and the Implementation of International Human Rights Law in Africa: The Case of the Convention of the Rights of Persons with Disability (CRPD) in Ghana." SJD thesis, Fordham Law School, 2018.

Clarke, Peter B. *West Africa and Islam: A Study of Religious Development from the 8th to the 20th Century*. London: Edward Arnold, 1982.

Colonial Office. *Colonial Reports – Annual. No. 537. British Central Africa Protectorate*. London: Darling, 1907.

Cover, Robert. "The Supreme Court, 1982 Term – Foreword: Nomos and Narrative." *Harvard Law Review* 97 (1983): 4–68.

Cover, Robert. "Violence and the Word." *Yale Law Journal* 95, no. 8 (July 1986): 1601–29.

Dankwa, E. V. O. "Property Rights of Widows in Their Deceased Husbands' Estate." *University of Ghana Law Journal* 16 (1982–1985): 1–24.

Dovlo, Elom. "Religion in the Public Sphere: Challenges and Opportunities in Ghanaian Lawmaking, 1989–2004." *Brigham Young University Law Review*, no. 3 (2005): 629–58.

Dumbe, Yunus. "Islamic Polarisation and the Politics of Exclusion in Ghana: Tijaniyya and Salafist Struggles over Muslim Orthodoxy." *Islamic Africa*, no. 10 (2019): 153–80.

Dumbe, Yunus. *Islamic Revivalism in Contemporary Ghana.* Stockholm: Södertörns University Press, 2013.

Eades, J. S. *Strangers and Traders: Yoruba Migrants, Markets, and the State in Northern Ghana.* Trenton, N. J.: Africa World Press, 1994.

Fenrich, Jeanmarie, and Tracy E. Higgins. "Promise Unfulfilled: Law, Culture, and Women's Inheritance Rights in Ghana." *Fordham International Law Journal* 25, no. 2 (2001): 259–360.

Freeman, Michael D. A. "Ghana: Legislation for Today." *Journal of Family Law* 27, no. 1 (1988–1989): 159–62.

GhaLII. "Gazettes." Accessed February 13, 2023. https://ghalii.org/gazettes.

Ghana Statistical Service. *Civil Registration and Vital Statistics System in Ghana.* Accra: Ghana Statistical Service, 2015.

Ghana Statistical Service. *Ghana 2021 Population and Housing Census: Background Characteristics.* Accra: Ghana Statistical Service, 2021.

Goldman, Neal M. "Fallible Justice: The Dilemma of the British in the Gold Coast, 1874–1944." PhD diss., Graduate Center, CUNY, 2016.

Goody, Jack. "Reform, Renewal and Resistance: A Mahdi in Northern Ghana." In *African Perspectives: Papers in the History, Politics and Economics of Africa Presented to Thomas Hodgkin*, edited by Christopher Allen and R. W. Johnson, 143–56. New York: Cambridge University Press, 1970.

Hammond, Ama Fowa. "Towards an Inclusive Vision of Law Reform and Legal Pluralism in Ghana." PhD diss., University of British Columbia, 2016.

Hansen, Hans. *Narrative Change: How Changing the Story Can Transform Society, Business, and Ourselves.* New York: Columbia University Press, 2020.

Hirschl, Ran. "Constitutional Courts as Bulwarks of Secularism." In *Consequential Courts: Judicial Roles in Global Perspective*, edited by Diana Kapiszewski, Gordon Silverstein, and Robert A. Kagan, 311–34. Cambridge: Cambridge University Press, 2013.

Hirschl, Ran. *Constitutional Theocracy.* Cambridge, Mass.: Harvard University Press, 2010.

Hiskett, Mervyn. "Commissioner of Police v. Musa Kommanda and Aspects of the Working of the Gold Coast Marriage of Mohammedans Ordinance." *Journal of African Law* 20, no. 2 (1976): 127–46.

Iddrisu, Abdulai. *Contesting Islam in Africa: Homegrown Wahhabism and Muslim Identity in Northern Ghana, 1920–2010.* Durham, N. C.: Carolina Academic Press, 2013.

Issaka-Toure, Fulera. "Application of Muslim Family Law as a Form of Customary Law in Accra, Ghana." *Islamic Africa* 11 no. 2 (2020): 232–51.

Issaka-Toure, Fulera. "Islamic Construction of Gender in Accra the Role of Islamic Religious Authorities in Mediating Marital Conflicts." PhD diss., University of Bayreuth, 2017.

Josiah-Aryeh, Nii Armah. "Customary Law's Unsteady Stride Forward." *University of Ghana Law Journal* 20 (1996–1999): 157–68.

Josiah-Aryeh, Nii Armah. *An Outline of Islamic Customary Law in Ghana*. Accra: Icon Publishing, 2015.

Kallinen, Timo. "Christianity, Fetishism, and the Development of Secular Politics in Ghana: A Dumontian Approach." *Anthropological Theory* 14, no. 2 (2014): 153–68.

Kludze, A. K. P. *Modern Law of Succession in Ghana*. Dordrecht: Foris Publications, 1988.

Kunbor, Ben "Epistolary Jurisdiction of the Indian Courts and Fundamental Human Rights in Ghana's 1992 Constitution: Some Jurisprudential Lessons." *Law, Social Justice & Global Development* 2 (2001): 1–30.

Lerner, Hanna. "Critical Junctures, Religion, and Personal Status Regulations in Israel and India." *Law & Social Inquiry* 39, no. 2 (Spring 2014): 387–415.

Lovejoy, Paul E., and Jan S. Hogendorn. "Revolutionary Mahdism and Resistance to Colonial Rule in the Sokoto Caliphate, 1905–6." *Journal of African History* 31, no. 2 (1990): 217–44.

McCarthy, Leslie Ernest Vivian. *The Laws of the Gold Coast (1936)*. 4 vols. Vol. 2. Accra: Gold Coast Government Printer, 1937.

McElwaine, Sir Percy A. *The Laws of the Gold Coast (1951)*. 5 vols. Vol. 3, Accra: Gold Coast Government Printer, 1954.

Meyer, Birgit. "Religious and Secular, 'Spiritual' and 'Physical' in Ghana." In *What Matters? Ethnographies of Value in a Not So Secular Age*, edited by Courtney Bender, and Ann Taves, 86–118. New York: Columbia University Press, 2012.

Moustafa, Tamir. *Constituting Religion: Islam, Liberal Rights, and the Malaysian State*. Cambridge: Cambridge University Press, 2018.

Murphy, Kristina, Adrian Cherney, and Marcus Teston. "Promoting Muslims' Willingness to Report Terror Threats to Police: Testing Competing Theories of Procedural Justice." *Justice Quarterly* 36, no. 4 (2019): 594–619.

Ollennu, N. A. *The Law of Testate and Intestate Succession in Ghana*. London: Sweet and Maxwell, 1966.

Peil, Margaret. "The Expulsion of West African Aliens." *The Journal of Modern African Studies* 9, no. 2 (1971): 205–29.

Pellow, Deborah. "Muslim Segmentation: Cohesion and Divisiveness in Accra." *The Journal of Modern African Studies* 23, no. 3 (1985): 419–44.

Renström, Emma A., Hanna Bäck, and Holly M. Knapton. "Exploring a Pathway to Radicalization: The Effects of Social Exclusion and Rejection Sensitivity." *Group Processes & Intergroup Relations* 23, no. 8 (2020): 1204–29.

Sezgin, Yüksel. "Muslim Family Laws in Israel and Greece: Can Non-Muslim Courts Bring About Legal Change in Shari'a?". *Islamic Law and Society* 25, no. 3 (2018): 235–73.

Sezgin, Yüksel. "Undignified Jurispathy: Muslim Family Law at Ghanian Courts." *Law & Social Inquiry* 48, no. 4 (2023): 1303–1333.

Shachar, Ayelet. "Privatizing Diversity: A Cautionary Tale from Religious Arbitration in Family Law." *Theoretical Inquiries in Law* 9, no. 2 (2008): 573–607.

Tyler, Tom R. "Procedural Justice, Legitimacy and the Effective Rule of Law." *Crime and Justice* 30 (2003): 283–357.

Weiss, Holger. *Between Accommodation and Revivalism: Muslims, the State and Society in Ghana from the Precolonial to the Postcolonial Era.* Helsinki: Finnish Oriental Society, 2008.

Weiss, Holger. "Variations in the Colonial Representation of Islam and Muslims in Northern Ghana, Ca. 1900–1930." *Journal of Muslim Minority Affairs* 25, no. 1 (2005): 73–95.

Woodman, Gordon R. "Ghana Reforms the Law of Intestate Succession." *Journal of African Law* 29, no. 2 (1985): 118–28.

Case Law

Adade v Dade [1989] 1 DLCA 248.

Agbeshie v Amorkor [2009] GHASC 2.

Agyekum v Bio [2016] GHASC 7.

Akyeampong v Marshall [1959] D.Ct. (unreported).

Ali v Ali [1939] 5 WACA 94.

Ali v Hadiza [1913] Renner 771.

Asumah v Khair [1959] GLR 353.

Badu v Boakye [1975] 1 GLR 283.

Baidoo v Baidoo [2019] GHASC 91.

Barake v Barake [1993–94] 1 GLR 635.

Bawa v Gariba [2019] DLHC 8724.

Bentil v Pratt [1989–90] 2 GLR 476.

Blankson v Hausa [1953] WACA (unreported).

Boampong v Aboagye [1980] GLR 927.

Bomfeh v Attorney-General [2019] GHASC 2.

Brimah v Asana [1962] 1 GLR 118.

Buckman v Ankumayi [2012] DLCA 6486.

Buzu v Shardow [1929] F. Ct. 1926–1929 357.

Esseku v Inkoom [2013] DLCA 4021.

Essilfie v Quarcoo [1991] DLHC 2010.

Ex Parte Ali [1980] GLR 872.

Giwah v Ladi [2010] DLHC 7067.

Giwah v Ladi [2011] CA (unreported).

Giwah v Ladi [2013–2014] 2 GLR 1139.

Hansen v Ankrah [Supreme Court, Accra] [1987–88] 1 GLR 639.

Hausa v Haruna [1963] 2 GLR 212.

Hausa v Hausa [1972] 2 GLR 469.
Hawa v Agyarko [2010] DLCA 3610.
Huzaifeh v Saba [1939] 5 WACA 181.
Jebeille v Ashkar [1977] GLR 458.
Kwakye v Tuba [1961] GLR 720.
Lamptey v Lamptey [2009] DLHC 5591.
Mahama v Awuni [2004] DLCA 6783.
Mensah v Mensah [2012] GHASC 8.
Mohamadu v Adamu [2014] DLCA 4415.
New Patriotic Party v Inspector General of Police (1993–94) 2 GLR 459.
Ramia v Ramia [1981] GLR 275.
Salifu v Sofo [2018] DLCA 5149.
Salley v Brimah [2016] DLCA 8161.
Yahaya v Yakubu [2012] DLSC 3057.
Yaotey v Quaye [1961] 2 GLR 573.

Legislation and Government Publications

Aliens Compliance Order, 1969.
Customary Marriage and Divorce (Registration) Law, (PNDCL 112), 1985.
Customary Marriage and Divorce Registration (Amendment) Law, (PNDCL 263), 1991.
Government Gazette, January 11, 1908.
Intestate Succession (Amendment) Law, (PNDCL 264), 1991.
Intestate Succession Law, (PNDCL 111), 1985.
Marriage Act, 1985.
Marriage of Mohammedans Ordinance, 1907.
Marriage Ordinance, 1884.
Muslim Marriage and Divorce Bill, 2017.

CHAPTER 8

Community Protocols as Self-Determination Strategies in the Global South: Indigenous Experiences of Legal Pluralism in Brazil and South Africa

Rodrigo Ferreira Barros

Abstract

In Brazil and South Africa, the struggles of self-declared indigenous communities are some of the most iconic and dramatic of democracy itself, since these groups account for up to one per cent of their national populations and demand specific recognition as beneficiaries of rights. These rights are recognised and protected to some extent by national and international legislation in both of these countries, but implementing the legislation is still often challenging for governments and indigenous communities. Despite the legal recognition of some of their institutions, it has been markedly difficult for the communities to achieve proper representation in the formal spaces and deliberative stances of politics. To address these issues, indigenous peoples draft, translate and try to execute pieces of self-legislation such as community protocolsas an exercise in decolonisation and autonomy, establishing the "terms of engagement" that must guide the dialogue and relationships of the communities with externalagents. These documents aim to regulate national and international legal devices that deal with self-determination and free, prior and informed consent. The efforts made by these two recent democracies on indigenous-related matters are exemples of how national states deal with sociocultural diversity, presenting key factors and strategies of legal pluralism in the global South.

1 Introduction

This chapter analyses through comparative lenses the development of legal pluralism in matters related to self-declared indigenous communities in two democracies of the Global South, specifically in South Africa and Brazil. We understand legal pluralism as the coexistence and interaction of different systems of justice, a phenomenon always present in the exercise of law, especially

 | DOI:10.1163/9789004696747_009

since this present analysis is dedicated to the interaction of state law with indigenous groups. Although we benefit from analyses and interpretations of different situations related to legal pluralism, we focus here on the nature and production of community consultation protocols, which we interpret as pieces of self-legislation created to establish the terms of engagement that should guide the dialogue, negotiations and any collective relationships that the communities might have with external agents in an attempt to regulate their self-determination. After observing the national and international legal frameworks that apply to both countries pertaining to indigenous rights and legal pluralism, we will compare the situations, the content and the objectives of community protocols in both states.[1]

As will become evident during the text, Brazil and South Africa share characteristics that enable a fruitful comparison of their implementation of indigenous rights and self-determination in state environments. Both are democracies in the Global South with multicultural constitutions and have self-declared indigenous populations that amount to about one per cent of their gross populations,[2] but they are signatories to different international treaties. Through this analysis we intend to highlight the main elements that influence these documents, observing the role of international and national state law in the making and application of these protocols and trying to interpret what kind of legal pluralism is being developed in these cases. The final considerations in this chapter explore the possible contributions of an intercultural approach and interpretation of both countries' state-legal and customary legal orders. Our attempt here is to critically analyse the possibility of utilising the so-called universal human rights, conceived and drafted by hegemonic institutions, in a counter-hegemonic way[3] that in fact enforces the indigenous decision-making processes.

1.1 *Indigenous People, Constitutionalism and Globalisation: The Right to Self-Determination*

Since the beginning of the colonisation processes in the global south, the social systems of indigenous peoples have clashed with colonial rule in the process of attempting to guarantee or recover sovereignty over their communities and territories. The fight for self-determination, that is the right to decide how to

1 All of the references published originally in Portuguese and quoted throughout the text were translated by the author.

2 According to the last published official national census of both countries, which have the year of 2022 as reference.

3 Santos, "Human Rights," 17.

live and how to organise collectively as people, is still a struggle for indigenous groups and traditional communities, even in political systems and regimes that are labelled and see themselves as democratic, plural and multicultural. In the cases of Brazil and South Africa indigenous people were initially deprived of any civil rights, only gradually achieving citizenship in these post-colonial states, even after the advent of independence and democracy.

Nonetheless, with the installation of democratic regimes some countries became participants in and contributors to international forums dedicated to the development of human rights, incorporating into their own legislative frameworks legal devices for the judicial protection of native or aboriginal groups, and enabling new and different policies guided by humanitarian and universalist principles applicable to indigenous groups. Some of these documents, most notably the Declaration of Indigenous Rights of the United Nations, the 169 International Labour Organisation Convention, and the Nagoya Protocol of the International Convention on Biological Diversity, determine guidelines for national states' behaviour regarding the rights to self-determination and autonomy of indigenous groups and several other rights that consequentially derive from these. Other documents such as the International Covenant on Civil and Political Rights and the African Charter on Human and Peoples' Rights do not refer specifically to indigenous groups but use the term "Peoples" when affirming the right to self-determination. These devices can be reinforced by national legislation and are often invoked by indigenous communities informed of their rights and the obligations of their national states.

Despite the legal recognition of some indigenous institutions and some degree of acknowledgment of their presence in national policies, it has been markedly difficult for them to achieve proper representation in the formal spaces and deliberative bodies of politics. In several situations that involve the development of government-sanctioned enterprises such as infrastructure projects, agribusiness, mining sites, scientific research, game farms, nature reserves and national parks, they seem to have little participation in the making of decisions about what should or should not be done in what is considered to be their original territory, or with their ancestral heritage.[4] Consultations and negotiations have historically been conducted in a fashion that ignores or

4 For references to Brazilian situations of the sort, see Fanzeres and Jakubaszko, "Barragens e Violações," who expose the sabotaging of indigenous participation in the dynamics of environmental permits for enterprises in indigenous lands; Almeida, *Ancient Landscapes*, on the struggle of the Kawaiweté, Manoki and Enawenê-Nawê indigenous peoples against the environmental impacts of hydroelectric powerplants in the state of Mato Grosso; and the reports produced by CIMI – Conselho Indigenista Missionário (Feitosa and Brighenti, *Empreendimentos*; CIMI, *Violência Contra os Povos Indígenas*) for general listing of indigenous

delegitimises the communal deliberative stances and traditional representative bodies of these communities. Co-opting and bribing communal leaderships is a colonial technique of indirect rule still applied against indigenous groups by private enterprises interested in indigenous territories and resources. However, some indigenous peoples draft and translate self-legislation principles in written documents to address that process in the hope that if they do so external actors will respect their organisation and inform themselves at least minimally about where they are going and who they are talking to before interfering with their communities and territories.[5] As we will argue during this chapter, this constitutes a claim for the authority of the indigenous representatives, demanding their right to take part in the decision-making process of what affects their own lives and resources.

1.2 *Community Protocols and Legal Pluralism: An Analytical Perspective*

One clear challenge in the application of these universal rights to self-determination is the incredible diversity attached to the concept "indigenous". This global category is locally translated, interpreted and absorbed in different contexts and conditions, but in general it constitutes a category which requires the specific recognition of rights, thus often demanding differentiated judicial recognition. As we will observe later in this text, although there are legal dispositions directed towards indigenous communities, applying these legal instruments can be a very complex task from the state legal point of view. Even though this category is quite instrumentalised and serves as a defence mechanism for the rights of communities that claim it, there is not much that indigenous people have in common globally besides being native to the geographical areas where nations have established their state territories, and having survived the process of colonisation while still maintaining some of their own institutions. Other than that, the term "indigenous people" makes reference to a large variety of peoples and cultures speaking different languages, sharing different customs and therefore having very different institutions which have to be considered and respected. Even in the specific cases that we will observe in this chapter, it is very clear that the indigenous categories are unified constructions of the national states that actually represent several different societies.

---

rights violations in Brazil. For South African examples, see Chan, "Richtersveld Challenge," and Huizenga (Huizenga, "Documenting 'Community',"; Huizenga, "Governing Territory") on the removal of San people from their traditional lands and the attempts of mining companies to operate in the Nama, Khomani San, and Amadiba territories. See Jenkins, "When it Flows," for an indigenous territorial dispute in an urban setting.

5 Rede de Cooperação Amazônica, "Contribuições da RCA," 7.

This means that when their traditional institutions are considered by the state legal system, there is not one over-arching instruction manual, one standard procedure or one judicial formula that can be applied. Until universal ideals can become actual rights they must first be transformed by local perspectives.

The documents that we will analyse in this chapter are central to the issue, being the result of the appropriation of international instruments by local communities to guarantee the right to free, prior and informed consultation (FPIC).[6] How to consult a community might not be a very simple question, especially if we recognise that their stances regarding their representation and their political organisation can be quite different from those of the state. With this in mind, "consultation" and "community" can become tricky concepts if simply brought from somewhere else to be applied in a specific local context. If the right to indigenous self-determination and diversity is to be materialised, the only possibility is for the states to respect each and every indigenous group on its own terms.[7] The right to consultation demands an internal decision-making process from the communities, each of which will have its particular form of social organisation and deliberative and representative stances. This could be of vital importance if we consider that "the closest legal form of recognising the autonomies of traditional groups is recognising the autonomy or willingness of the parties involved when establishing agreements".[8]

If each group makes its decisions in its own ways, there would be no option for a state obliged to consult them other than to follow each of the indigenous requirements for negotiation. Considering that these indigenous forms of organisation are mostly unwritten oral traditions and conform with principles that state law does not recognise, it has arguably been impossible for state authorities to perform proper consultation with indigenous communities because of officialdom's somewhat justifiable ignorance of the internal procedures of decision making among the indigenous people with whom it is negotiating.

To address such situations, indigenous people have therefore been encouraged to draft, translate and produce written documents in which they state

6 In this analysis we make use of the critical Brazilian perspective on FPIC, "*Consulta Livre, Prévia e Informada*". From this perspective we understand that consent (*consentimento*) is a possible result from consultation (*consulta*), but it is not the only possible outcome. Consultation must be done, but consent might not be reached.

7 "The universal character of fundamental indigenous rights implies that: a) they are distinct from other rights; b) that they might be claimed by all social groups and not some of them, meaning that fundamental rights apply to all Indians in Brazil." Gomes da Silva, "Os Direitos dos Índios," 290.

8 Souza Filho, *Protocolos de Consulta Prévia*, 33.

who they are and how they must be consulted, who can make their decisions, how they make their decisions, on what terms and in what time frames they are willing to talk, who must attend or not attend meetings, and any other information they deem necessary. These documents try to set the "terms of engagement" that must guide the dialogue, negotiations and relationships of the communities with the government, private companies, entrepreneurs, researchers, or any other external actors that may have the obligation to consult them. In a general way we can consider the consultation protocols as the "written translations of the internal consensus of each group on how to engage with national states".[9]

With some of the first initiatives emerging in Latin America and Africa, motivated by the international covenants mentioned above, community protocols are being produced and applied in different contexts involving indigenous and traditional communities with the intention of preventing land dispossession, environmental impacts, biopiracy and other violations of their rights.[10] Working groups of the United Nations and civil society organisations have dedicated themselves to monitoring, debating and developing methodologies that can facilitate the drafting of community consultation protocols.[11] These have become guidelines for communities in the exercise of self-determination. In Brazil and South Africa indigenous and traditional communities have received the support of government agencies and non-governmental organisations. These initiatives are on the radar of international organisms:

> Many indigenous peoples, with the support of civil society organizations, have brought elements for the development of guiding principles and procedures, through their own consultation protocols. Brazil sees it as an important contribution to better implement free, prior and informed consultation, in good faith and as a democratic instrument of indigenous protagonism.[12]

9 Souza Filho, *Protocolos de Consulta Prévia*, 39.

10 Delgado, "Community Protocols," 396.

11 As examples of the methodologies already being utilised in South Africa one could observe the Community Protocol Toolbox organised by the NGO Natural Justice (Natural Justice, "Community Protocols Toolbox"), and for a Brazilian example one could check Rede de Cooperação Amazônica, "Protocolos Autônomos".

12 Human Rights Council, "Universal Periodic Review", A/HRC/WG.6/27/BRA/1.

2 Indigenous People's Lives and Rights in Brazil

2.1 *The Road from Colonial Rule to Citizenship*

Since the arrival of the Portuguese different legal systems have determined how the Brazilian administration have behaved towards indigenous communities, with different institutions leading the elaboration and implementation of these policies from time to time. For more than 300 years authority over indigenous communities in Brazil was granted by the Portuguese crown to the Catholic church, which implemented an evangelising mandate through the establishment of "missions" where indigenous groups would be forcibly stripped of their lands and cultures.

It was only in 1910, almost twenty years after the proclamation of the Republic in 1889, that the responsibility for indigenous communities became a matter for the state with the founding of a specific government department dedicated to these groups, the Serviço de Proteção aos Índios (Indian Protection Service) (SPI) headed by the famous Marechal Cândido Rondon. Rondon was a military man from Mato Grosso, of indigenous ancestry himself, deemed the patron of Brazilian communications for the expansion of a system of telegraph lines in the Centre-West and Amazon regions, famous mostly for his defence of indigenous groups and attempted peaceful (but often still deadly) first contacts with then uncontacted communities. Rondon's motto on approaching uncontacted and possibly hostile indigenous groups was: "To die if it is necessary. To kill, never."[13]

Indigenous personnel were hired to serve as auxiliary workers for the SPI services, and a few territories were delineated by the agencies and granted to indigenous groups for their exclusive benefit. Nonetheless, the legal basis and the guidelines of the SPI were of territorial expansion and the incorporation of indigenous communities as labour workers for the Brazilian state, and its activities were characterised by the expropriation of the territories of indigenous peoples. This era was marked by a decline in the population of indigenous communities due to their extermination by massacres and biological warfare involving the use of poison and the intentional distribution of contaminated material to spread smallpox, measles, flu and other diseases. In the words of the Brazilian anthropologist, Alcida Ramos:[14]

13 Ribeiro, "The Soldier Who Wouldn't Shoot", 9.

14 Ramos, *Seduzidos e Abandonados*, 16.

> The Indian Protection Service lasted for 57 years. In this period several *sertanistas* were formed to continue the relentless search for stubborn wildlings that needed to be tamed so that Brazilian society could expand in peace. However, the heroic tone of Rondon disappeared and this tutelary agency was filled with dishonest bureaucrats until 1967, when the SPI was shut down in the midst of a scandal of corruption and violations of indigenous rights. The serious accusations of crimes against peoples and heritage were never legally tried, partly because of a fire that destroyed its files in Brasília. To replace the SPI, the National Indian Foundation (FUNAI) was created, inheriting the same ideology, the same habits and even some of the employees of its predecessor.

In 1967, during the Brazilian military dictatorship, this state organ was somewhat reformed and transformed into the Fundação Nacional do Índio (FUNAI) or National Indian Foundation. This institution has adopted a more progressive approach with the passage of time, mostly through the influence of a change in the required qualifications of its professionals, gradually moving from a colonial perspective based on "acculturation" theories to a more anthropologically based "*indigenista*" approach.[15] This was another shift in the policies relating to indigenous peoples in Brazil, and the growing participation of anthropologists in the government influenced changes in the organisation's basic principles that eventually introduced professional ethics into the government agencies. Also, the founding of different civil society organisations dedicated to the defence of indigenous rights dates from this period; organisations such as OPAN (Operação Amazônia Nativa), CIMI (Conselho Indigenista Missionário), Anaí (Associação Nacional de Ação Indigenista) and others.[16] These organisations have, amongst other things, supported indigenous communities in conducting the process of the autonomous demarcation of their lands, in a collective movement directed to the recovering of lost indigenous territory, and in the maintenance of the territory still occupied.[17] There have been cases of success in the indigenous territorial struggle during this time but

15 *Indigenista* in Brazil makes reference to professionals who work in or out of the government, directly with indigenous groups. Even though the basic principles of anthropology are required, *indigenistas* can have diplomas of different areas such as history, biology, law, business, etc. For Alcida Ramos: "In the specific case of Brazil, Indigenism is clearly an ideological apparatus which includes not only state policies, but especially the vast repertoire of images, attitudes, and actions that both non-Indians and Indians have produced along the history of the country's interethnic front." Ramos, *Pulp Fictions*, 2.

16 Baniwa, "A Conquista da Cidadania Indígena," 209.

17 Fanzeres et al, "A Experiência das Autodemarcações," 165.

also several cases of illegal displacement, land expropriation and literal acts of war such as the bombing of the Waimiri-Atroari villages of Amazonas, and the indigenous prisons in the Krenak territory. At least eight thousand indigenous people were murdered by the Brazilian state during this era, and some of these cases are presented in the 5th text of the Second Volume of the final report of the Brazilian National Truth Commission:[18]

> it was possible to estimate that at least 8.350 indigenous were killed during the period of time investigated by the CNV, as a direct result of the actions or the omissions of government agents. This number includes only the cases observed here, from which it was possible to draw an estimate. The real number of indigenous killed during that period must be exponentially higher, since only a very small part of the affected indigenous groups was analysed, and there are cases in which the number of deaths is high enough to discourage projections.

A major change would come, decades later in 1988, with the promulgation of the so-called "Citizen's Constitution", that established democracy in Brazil after more than 20 years of military capitalist dictatorship. This Constitution is frequently situated in the tradition of what has been called New Latin American Constitutionalism, having as its guiding principles the supremacy of the constitution and the recognition of social rights and cultural diversity, with dispositions dedicated to indigenous communities, self-governance and the administration of justice. These recognitions are relative, since they are always accompanied by restrictions and incompatibility clauses that disallow any contradiction of constitutional law.[19] Nonetheless, this was the first time that a person with an indigenous identity was considered to be a legitimate holder of citizens' rights in Brazil. Previously such a person had still been considered in law[20] to possess a transitory identity, a status that a person could "grow out of" or change gradually if the person could be properly "integrated" in modern society.

Indigenous groups from different regions of Brazil were active participants in the constituent assembly. Assisted by civil society organisations committed to their struggle, they were able to make themselves present in Brasília during the political demonstrations and debates that gave rise to this current legal order and succeeded in including a specific chapter in the Constitution dedicated to

18 Brasil, Comissão Nacional da Verdade, *Relatório Final*, Vol. 2, Text 5, 205.
19 Macedo Moreira and Zema, "Proteção Constitucional," 44.
20 Estatuto do Índio, 1973.

the recognition of their rights. This Brazilian Federal Constitution of 1988 and some of its subsequent supplementary legal regimens specific to indigenous issues compose the Brazilian state legal order that we will consider in this study.

2.2 *Indigenous Brazil: The Current Legal Order*

With more than three hundred different indigenous groups speaking more than one hundred different languages amongst themselves, Brazil has an indigenous population that amounts to nearly one million and seven hundred thousand people dispersed in all regions of the country, representing roughly 0,83 per cent of the gross national population.[21] Since 1988 Brazil has described itself in the foreword to its Constitution as a plural nation, and an entire chapter of the Constitution is dedicated exclusively to the rights of indigenous people. In article 231 of the Brazilian Federal Constitution they are recognised as the original indigenous people of Brazil, entitled to the use of the lands that they occupy, and the Union assumes the duty of protecting them and all of their assets. They are also granted the right to maintain their culture, traditions and social organisation, which intrinsically means that the state recognises their authorities and their traditional political institutions as legitimate:[22]

> Indians shall have their social organisation, customs, languages, creeds and traditions recognised, as well as their original rights to the lands they traditionally occupy, it being incumbent upon the Union to demarcate them, protect and ensure respect for all of their property.
>
> 1. Lands traditionally occupied by Indians are those on which they live on a permanent basis, those used for their productive activities, those indispensable to the preservation of the environmental resources necessary for their well-being and for their physical and cultural reproduction, according to their uses, customs and traditions.

In article 232 they are now considered able to enter judicial litigation in pursuit of their own rights, which officially dismantles the state's tutelage over indigenous people. They are granted the right to the support of the Federal Public Prosecution,[23] an independent state organ that has among its institutional missions the duty of protecting the rights of indigenous communities.

---

21 According to the last published National Brazilian Populational Census from 2022.

22 Constitution of Federal Republic of Brazil, 1988, art. 231.

23 The Federal Public Prosecution (Ministério Público Federal) is an independent state institution with the mandate of carrying out litigation in causes related to collective rights

> The Indians, their communities and organisations have standing under the law to file suits to defend their rights and interests, the Prosecution Office intervening in all the procedural acts.[24]

These dispositions therefore recognise the right to the collective existence of indigenous people, not simply as individuals adhering to the constitutional texts, but as distinct societies with their own particular social organisation and institutions.

In regard to international legislation, Brazil became a signatory of the 169 Convention on Indigenous and Tribal Peoples of the International Labour Organisation in July of 2002, when the Covenant was ratified, and it was incorporated into the legal regimen in 2004 through the Decree n° 5.051. A profoundly updated version of its predecessor (the 107 ILO Convention), this international covenant is probably the most influential legal disposition related to indigenous people in South America, and for Brazil it is certainly the international document that marks the shift towards ethnic and cultural pluralism.[25] Amongst its anti-discriminatory principles it states that indigenous people (and individuals) shall have access to all regular national citizens' rights, and may also maintain their own legal systems. The chapter dedicated to land issues states that governments shall identify, recognise and protect indigenous territories, and the text prohibits their removal from their lands. Most importantly for this present analysis, the 169 Convention in its sixth article affirms the duty of national governments to consult indigenous communities:[26]

> 1. In applying the provisions of this Convention, governments shall:
>   – (a) consult the peoples concerned, through appropriate procedures and in particular through their representative institutions, whenever consideration is being given to legislative or administrative measures which may affect them directly;

Having been ratified into the Brazilian legal regimen it has the force of law and it is, as we will see, frequently invoked by indigenous groups conscious of their government's obligation to consult them.

---

and public goods. In its structure there is an exclusive department dedicated to the rights of indigenous and traditional communities (6 CCR). In this department there is a sector composed by anthropology experts who are required to produce technical reports on judicial cases that require deeper analysis of the cultural or indigenous element present in civil or criminal inquiries.

24 Constitution of Federal Republic of Brazil, 1988, art. 232.

25 Duprat, "Convenção 169 da OIT," 76.

26 169 ILO Convention, ch. 6.

Brazil has also reacted favourably to the United Nation's Declaration of Indigenous Rights, which carries "soft-law" status and serves largely as ideal guidelines on the treatment of indigenous communities by their sovereign states, upholding the rights to self-determination, autonomy and self-government, from which other more specific rights will derive. It also builds legal ground for the institution of free, prior and informed consultation when governments propose to take decisions affecting indigenous communities:

> Indigenous peoples have the right to participate in decision-making in matters which would affect their rights, through representatives chosen by themselves in accordance with their own procedures, as well as to maintain and develop their own indigenous decision-making institutions.[27]
>
> States shall consult and cooperate in good faith with the indigenous peoples concerned through their own representative institutions in order to obtain their free and informed consent prior to the approval of any project affecting their lands or territories and other resources, particularly in connection with the development, utilization or exploitation of mineral, water or other resources.[28]

Although it is subject to the national supreme law, it also compels member states, each in terms of its own capacity, to undertake measures to materialise these rights and principles.

In August of 2020 through the Legislative Act 136/2020 the Brazilian government also ratified the Nagoya Protocol of the Convention on Biological Diversity, that regulates genetic resources and access to traditional and indigenous knowledge, amongst other things. This was somewhat surprising considering that most of the stands taken by the Brazilian government in this period had been in opposition to indigenous rights in general, even those stated in the Constitution. It is still unclear how this disposition will be applied towards indigenous groups in Brazil, but there is a clear legal basis in the text for the recognition of community protocols, with more mature experiences already happening in South Africa, as we shall see in the next section.

These international legal instruments also partially inform the general guidelines of both the state "indigenist" policies and the indigenous communities' internal policies through the autonomous protocols. Our argument is that

27 United Nations Declaration of Indigenous Rights, art. 18.

28 United Nations Declaration of Indigenous Rights, art. 32.2.

while governments use these treaties to legitimate themselves in international diplomacy, committing partially to their premises, indigenous peoples instrumentalise these pieces of legislation and incorporate their premises into their own legal instruments.

2.3 *"Índio", Citizen? – Challenges to Implementation, Participation and Resistance Strategies in 21st Century Brazil*

In terms of state public policy, the current disposition in effect is the PNGATI (Política Nacional de Gestão Territorial e Ambiental de Terras Indígenas), or the Brazilian Policy for Territorial and Environmental Management of Indigenous Lands.[29] Drafted by government employees, civil society and the indigenous movement, this policy is also based on the ILO 169 Convention and incorporates the right to FPIC into the national regimen as an essential tool of dialogue and the partnered management of indigenous lands. This legal arrangement was seen as the consolidation of important principles of indigenous policy, prioritising respect for indigenous decision-making processes, for their traditional ways of life and for their future projects, aiming to support them in their activities related to sustainable development. Guided by this policy, indigenous communities elaborate the Territorial and Environmental Management Plans (Plano de Gestão Ambiental e Territorial) for their indigenous lands, which are documents in which they present themselves, the current situation of their lands, and their plans for the future of these territories. They frequently do this with the support of different organisations (such as FUNAI and NGO's) and using participative methodologies and mapping techniques.

In 2015, during a political conference dedicated to indigenous policy, the huge number of delegates being composed of a vast majority of indigenous representatives, government authorities, academic experts and civil society organisations, a collective organisation was created to assist the government in drafting and developing indigenous policies – the organisation then being called the Conselho Nacional de Política Indigenista, created by Decree n° 8.593. With the objective of informing, participating in and influencing the making and execution of any government actions that affected indigenous groups, this Counsel was instituted as a consultative organ. It had no deliberative mandate, contrary to the expectations of the indigenous movement.[30]

29 Promulgated by the Decree n° 7.747, from 5 June 2012.

30 "Even though the Council is not the ideal one that we claim, we will keep demanding that it be approved in the National Congress with deliberative power." – Sonia Bone Guajajara, APIB's Coordinator during pronouncement in the Ministry of Justice during the installation of the CNPI in 2015 (Carneiro, "Conselho Nacional de Política Indigenista").

After it had languished for two years without receiving any funds for its activities, the Counsel was disestablished in 2019 by a monocratic decision taken by the president of the Republic (Decree n° 9.759/2019) that put an end to several popular counsels dedicated to the direct participation in government of civil society organisations.

Indigenous rights have always been a polemical theme in Brazil, and these legal dispositions, despite being largely accepted by law practitioners and society in general, face wide-ranging criticism. From the moment it was ratified the 169 ILO Convention was the target of criticism by congressmen and high-ranking military officers who suggested that Brazil should re-evaluate its position on these treaties, voicing somewhat exaggerated concerns regarding national sovereignty as opposed to indigenous territorial policies.[31]

The provisions of the indigenous chapter of the Brazilian Constitution have also given rise to other crucial debates regarding the details and procedures of the application of its articles. The statement that indigenous peoples are entitled to their land rights implies the existence of a duty to pursue the realisation of this right, and as one could reasonably expect, that is no simple task. The Decree 1.775 of 1996 determines the basic procedures for the recognition of Indigenous Land, establishing deadlines and conditions for the process of receiving an Indigenous Land claim, the forming of specific technical working groups to identify and delineate the areas of the territorial occupation of indigenous communities, and presenting a draft proposal. The working group shall be led by an anthropologist of recognised qualification, who must present an anthropological study, complemented by other studies of an ethnohistorical, sociological, legal, cartographic and environmental nature, that proposes geographical limits to that territory, the map being drawn with the active participation of the indigenous community. If the study is approved by FUNAI, theoretically the next steps involve its officialisation in the government gazette, its contestation by possible land owners, and later the removal of any non-indigenous occupants from that area, by force if necessary. It is not unusual that some of these occupants will present land deeds issued by the government in ignorance of the indigenous presence or purely as a result of the corruption and malpractice of property officials. If these deeds date from before the publishing of the anthropological report, the occupants might be considered as being of "good faith" and might be entitled to compensation, but any land title dating after that is automatically nullified and its presentation gives rise to no compensation at all.

31 Duprat, "Convenção 169 da OIT," 76; Baniwa, "Autonomia Indígena no Brasil," 121.

There have been very fruitful and relevant projects for demarcating some of these lands funded by programmes such as the PPTAL (Programme of Territorial Protection of the Legal Amazon) and the PDPI (Demonstrative Projects of Indigenous People).[32] A considerable area of nearly thirteen per cent of the national territory has entered the legal category of Indigenous Lands, which is the denomination of an official protected area. It is alarming, though, that a lot of these land claims, especially the older ones, materialised during the military dictatorship era, are clearly incomplete and the outcome of flawed processes, with several involving the illegal displacement of communities. These land delineations are sometimes reviewed and new studies determine the actual perimeter of these territories. Contestations and the judicialisation of the demarcation processes by non-indigenous proprietors of real estate inside indigenous areas can also paralyse the procedures, litigating the processes and in several cases impeding the conclusion of the land claims. Needless to say, while these processes continue the integrity of the territory is continually compromised through ongoing dispossession, while the purported proprietors develop activities that clash with the traditional use of the land. The progressive undermining of indigenous and environmental policies creates a difficult situation for rural environments and indigenous lands, fuelling land conflicts that often result in violence towards indigenous communities.

This is a clear example of how the amendments and jurisprudence associated with the theme are often marked by dispute between the pluralist dispositions of indigenous rights and the Brazilian civil property law. These cases might be appealed to higher courts, and some cases have reached the Supreme Court, creating jurisprudence to be applied nationally.

The reason why we dedicate so much attention to these legal settings of indigenous lands in Brazil is because these conditions drastically affect the ability of indigenous people to exercise the right to administrate justice in their own communities. As Santamaría[33] observes, the geographical/territorial element is important when it comes to legal disputes involving indigenous

---

32 It is noteworthy that the official indigenous agency and policies have never received funding proper to the execution of the enormous task of something we could consider to be indigenous land reform, even if most of it is based purely on recognising current land arrangements. Since the Constitution, the official governmental budget for FUNAI, the agency responsible for leading these land claims, has only decreased throughout the years, and most of the successful projects of indigenous territorial protection have been funded chiefly by global and international agencies. These international funding dynamics for environmental protection have proved to be vulnerable to political shifts in government since the 2018 elections (INESC and INA, "Anti-Indigenous Foundation," 3).

33 Santamaría, "De la Autonomía," 24.

people. Any incident happening on indigenous land, and especially if it does not involve outsiders, is much more likely to be resolved by the community itself through its own authorities. This becomes even more important when the element in dispute is the territory itself, or resources contained in it. As we will observe, the indigenous community protocols in Brazil are strongly linked to their territorial rights and the environmental integrity of their land. Deciding what happens on indigenous land is the main point of intersection and conflict between state and indigenous law and authority.

2.4 *Indigenous Protocols in Brazil: Examples*

In this section we will analyse two indigenous community protocols in Brazil, observe some of the main elements common to them, and describe the specific strategies deployed in each of them according to their specific sceneries. Both of them are recorded in self-explanatory documents, in clear and simple Portuguese, and both documents are available online. We will select the parts of each protocol that are most relevant to our present analysis, briefly providing some context to aid understanding:

2.4.1 The Wajãpi Community Protocol[34]

As our first example we will analyse the Protocolo de Consulta Prévia do Povo Wajãpi, the first one to be published in Brazil. It is didactic and self-explanatory, and has served as an inspiration for other communities. It was published in 2014 with the objective of officially establishing negotiation procedures that had already been in place for years and were affecting indigenous communities. Before giving any further information, it opens with a definition of what a consultation protocol is:

> Consultation protocols are initiatives to officialise towards the State the diversity of adequate proceedures of dialogue with each indigenous people, in which there is an honest intention that they participate actively in the decisions that might affect their lives, rights or territories …
>
> Prior Consultation is an obligation of the Brazilian State. It requires the State to respectfully ask indigenous people their opinion on executive and legislative measures capable of affecting their lives and rights.[35]

34 Conselho das Aldeias Wajãpi, "Protocolo de Consulta e Consentimento Wajãpi".

35 Apina, *Protocolo de Consulta e Consentimento Wajãpi*, front page.

Then follows the title: "Wajãpi kõ omõsãtamy wayvu oposikoa romõ ma'e – Agyvo tã age´e jaiko japosiko karai rovijã gwerãkõ reve ky`y", meaning "Consultation Protocol of the Wajãpi People – This is the way in which we, the government and the Wajãpi, will work from now on". Then the Wajãpi explain why they produced this document, who they are and how they arrive at decisions:

> We, the Wajãpi, have a very different way of life from you. We have a very strong culture and we don't forget a single thing. We know how to paint ourselves, we know how to sing, how to raise and teach our kids, and how to care for our bodies.
>
> We, the Wajãpi, inhabit our lands in a different way from non-Indians. Since very long ago, we have always been moving our houses.[36]

We may observe here the differentiation of their own particular organisation, described as their "way of life", and the development priorities set by the Wajãpi, since these distinctions will in fact affect the consultation process. The second paragraph makes reference to where and how they live and their semi-nomadic way of life. If they cannot always be found at the same "address" this is because they migrate seasonally. Any intention to consult them must take these conditions into account. They also clarify the proper time to consult them when justifying the creation of the document:

> We decided to make this document because often we see that the government wants to do things for the Wajãpi, but they don't ask us what we actually want and need. Sometimes the government does things in the surroundings of the Indigenous Land Wajãpi affecting our rights, but also not asking our opinion. The government has never consulted the Wajãpi people.
>
> We think that the government must listen to our worries, our priorities and our opinions before making its plans. We don't think it is good when the government arrives with finished projects for us, with money to spend on things that are not our priorities. …
>
> The right time to consult us: We want to choose our priorities and participate in the elaboration of the government's work plans before the decisions are made. Consultation must be done when the decisions about the making of a project can still be changed.[37]

36 Apina, *Protocolo de Consulta e Consentimento Wajãpi*, 6.
37 Apina, *Protocolo de Consulta e Consentimento Wajãpi*, 7, 17.

As we observe, the Wajãpi claim that if they are to be consulted in an honest manner, the consultations must be held prior to the decision-making process, as is clear in the phrase "prior consultation". Then, they present themselves:

> We, the Wajãpi, live on the state of Amapá, between the municipalities of Pedra Branca do Amapari and Laranjal do Jari, in an Indigenous Land of 607.017 ha that was delimited and approved in 1996. In 2014 our population is approximately 1100 people living in 81 villages spread through the Indigenous Land Wajãpi.
>
> There is no general cacique of the Wajãpi. We are not a single group. We are several groups. Each family group has a chief, and a chief does not order another chief.
>
> No chief represents all the Wajãpi. Decisions that affect all the Wajãpi are taken by the collective of representatives of all of the villages consulting one another.[38]

Here the Wajãpi are sharing the dynamics of their political organisation and internal processes. They make it very clear that there is no centralised body to be engaged in deliberations, and that the larger forum of the representatives of all of their villages is the body to be officially consulted. Later in the document they establish that in cases in which an internal consensus cannot be reached they might use a voting system where an effective majority must be three-fourths of the total number of participants.

When explaining how the government must consult the Wajãpi, the document stresses the need for the proper translation of both parties' statements to be recorded and registered by Wajãpi secretaries, especially when debating the positive and negative impacts of any possible intervention on their territory. Meetings with government officials must happen inside their territories, must have been previously scheduled, and must make allowance for sufficient time for questioning and debating. They warn the government that in order to guarantee one full day of consultation they must be prepared to spend at least two nights with them in the village. They stress that they will never take a decision at the first meeting, and that Wajãpi civil organisations are not authorised to convey their final decisions by themselves, even if they have participated in all the events necessary to the process of consultation. They also demand that government representatives who attend their meetings must themselves be prepared to take decisions and answer their questions:

---

38 Apina, *Protocolo de Consulta e Consentimento Wajãpi*, 11.

> The government representative must have authority to make decisions and be responsible for the topic of the consultation. The government cannot send representatives without power or responsibility over the theme of the consultation.[39]

After explaining how their initial, internal and final meetings will happen, they recognise the distinction between their way of doing things and that of the national state and affirm:

> This work of consulting, explaining and reaching agreements collectively takes a very long time if compared to the non-indigenous way of taking care of things. But it is our way, and it must be respected. If the government doesn't respect our ways of organising, it cannot say that it has consulted our people.[40]

They attach the 6th Chapter of the ILO Convention (No. 169) to the end of the document and a brief description of the process of making the protocol. The final credits observe the participation of two NGO's RCA (Rede de Cooperação Amazônica) and Iepé (Instituto de Pesquisa e Formação Indígena), and the financial support of the Norwegian Rainforest Foundation.

Even though the document is quite clear and self-explanatory, the process of its making by the Wajãpi was also analysed by the anthropologist Bruno Caporrino, who considers that those agreements "already existed long before they were formalised: it [the protocol] is the fruit of the establishment of standards and criteria for the decision-making process that the Wajãpi have been developing and perfecting for decades".[41] His proposed interpretation is that the motivation for the drafting of this document is to reduce the power of harassment of the Brazilian state, in an attempt to tame or domesticate the "*karai kõ*" (Wajãpi word for white or non-indigenous people).[42]

2.4.2 The Munduruku Consultation Protocol[43]

The Munduruku Consultation Protocol was published in 2015 when the Munduruku people was being pressured by the building of hydroelectric dams that destroyed their sacred places, including a complex of waterfalls and

39 Apina, *Protocolo de Consulta e Consentimento Wajãpi*, 23.
40 Apina, *Protocolo de Consulta e Consentimento Wajãpi*, 32.
41 Caporrino, *Dos que Flecham Longe*, 18.
42 Caporrino, *Dos que Flecham Longe*, 39.
43 Movimento Munduruku Ipereg Ayu, "Protocolo de Consulta Munduruku".

ancient cemeteries with funerary urns dating back thousands of years. A series of dramatic events linked to their ancestral territory occurred. The incidents involved the killing of a Munduruku in an explosive helicopter raid over their official territory by the state National Force, and demonstrations suppressed with tear gas and rubber bullets. As they were facing strong repression of their demonstrations and claims for participation in decision making, the publication of the community protocol was important to expose the untruthfulness of the governmental allegations that the Munduruku were not open to dialogue, causing the suspension of the environmental permit of the UHE São Luis do Tapajós.[44] The document starts with the following:

> We, the Munduruku people, want to listen to what the government has to say. But we don't want any false information. For the Munduruku people to be able to decide, we must know what is actually going to happen. And the government must listen to us. Before anything else, we demand the demarcation of the Indigenous Land Sawré Muybu. Under no circumstances will we accept being removed.
>
> We also demand that the government protect the indigenous people that live in our lands in isolation and the right to consultation of the other indigenous people affected by projects, such as the Apiaká and the Kayabi. Finally, we demand that riverine communities that will be affected by the dams in the Tapajós River (such as the Montanha and Mangabal, Pimental and São Luiz communities) have their right to consultation guaranteed in accordance with their specific realities. Just like us, riverine people also have the right to their own consultation.[45]

From this first paragraph we can see that the Munduruku people felt that they had been lied to and ignored by the government in the past. The territorial issue was important enough for them to condition any other negotiations on the recognition of their ancestral lands. In the second paragraph we can see a strong element of solidarity not only with other indigenous communities, but also with the traditional fishermen and *quilombola*[46] communities neighbouring them, strategically incorporating them in the consultation process to get more actors to side with them.

44 Souza Filho, *Protocolos de Consulta Prévia*, 128.

45 Movimento Munduruku Ipereg Ayu, "Protocolo de Consulta Munduruku," 3.

46 The term *Quilombos* makes reference to communities of African ascendancy in Brazil who can trace their origins and the occupation of their territories to the slavery era.

> Who must be consulted? The Munduruku of all of the villages in the Tapajós must be consulted, including the ones located in Indigenous Lands not yet demarcated. We don't want the government to consider us divided: there is only one Munduruku people.
>
> How do we, Munduruku, make our decisions? When a project affects us all, our decision is a collective one. ... No Munduruku association decides for the Munduruku people, no organisation speaks for us all. The decisions of our people are made in general assemblies summoned by our caciques.[47]

This part is a clear response to the government strategies of co-opting indigenous leaderships or organisations, presenting themselves as a unified collective represented by a general assembly called by their *caciques*.

> The government cannot consult us when they have already made a decision. Consultation must be done before anything. All of the meetings must be done in our territory – in the village of our choosing – and not in the city.
>
> When the federal government come to consult us in our village, they must not arrive in the landing track, spend a day and return. They must be patient with us. They must live like we do, eat what we eat. They must listen to our conversation. Meetings must be in the Munduruku language and we'll choose the translators. In these meetings, our knowledge must be considered on the same level as the knowledge of the *pariwat* (non-Indians) because we are the ones who know about the rivers, the forest, the fish and the earth. We are the ones who will coordinate the meetings, not the government.[48]

Here the Munduruku not only highlight the importance of the consultation being "prior", but also present their understanding of how an intercultural dialogue must happen. They demand that outsiders engage for at least a short period in their Munduruku way of life, possibly in the hope that they might understand what it means to live as they do in their environment. This might be a response to several cases in which we saw attempts by the State to organise events and circumstances on its own, in its own state logic and language, such as public hearings in urban environments and closed meetings in government

47 Movimento Munduruku Ipereg Ayu, "Protocolo de Consulta Munduruku," 4, 8.
48 Movimento Munduruku Ipereg Ayu, "Protocolo de Consulta Munduruku," 5, 6.

offices, as if they alone could constitute the consultations with indigenous communities.[49]

> For the consultation to be really free, we won't accept armed *pariwat* in our meetings. ... The government already comes with a camera but they cannot record our images without authorisation.[50]

Having experienced repression by the police on more than one occasion, even in their own territories, the Munduruku people stress their rejection of dialogue with armed people. At the conclusion of the document they make clear what they expect from this document and as an outcome of such consultations:

> What do the Munduruku people expect from consultation? We expect the government to respect our decision. We have veto power. *Sawê!*[51]

Below this there is a signification of the support of the Prosecutor's Office in the making of the document, endowing it with legal state authority. Although the claim of having the power to veto might seem very bold, the right to refuse any proposal presented is only logical in a consultation process, otherwise we would be not talking about consulting a community but of informing them of decisions that have already been taken. This clearly differentiates the concept of consultation from that of seeking consent, adapting the significance of "universal human rights" to their local (and national) perspective. Oliveira analyses the protocol and the process of the Munduruku appropriation of the right to prior consultation, identifying differences between the government's legal sensibility and the Munduruku legal sensibility.[52] While the Munduruku see the river and the flora and fauna as part of the same living entity, the government separates each species and its specific impacts. While the Munduruku see all of themselves as part of a group, the government would try to consult only those that they consider to be "directly" affected. In terms of the government's legal sensibility, prior consultation is not a space to decide on whether or not the power plants (in this instance) were to be constructed but a negotiation of compensation policies, while the Munduruku refused to see the matter as concluded. Oliveira considers that the protocol built a consolidated document of legal orientation envisioned by the Munduruku since the beginning of the

49 Pontes Júnior, "Audiência Pública," 111.

50 Movimento Munduruku Ipereg Ayu, "Protocolo de Consulta Munduruku," 6.

51 Movimento Munduruku Ipereg Ayu, "Protocolo de Consulta Munduruku," 8.

52 Oliveira, "'Respeitem a Forma de a Gente Ser'," 2631.

conflict and was essential in altering the course of negotiations in favour of the Munduruku.[53] Even if a complex of smaller hydroelectric dams were built along the Tapajós river, the environmental permit for the construction of the main planned power plant, the UHE São Luís do Tapajós, was denied and archived in 2016, constituting an important victory for the Munduruku in the justice system.

3 Indigenous Peoples' Rights and Lives in South Africa

3.1 *Khoi-San: Indigenous Identity and Recognition in South Africa*

Since the promulgation of its democratic constitution in 1996 South Africa has affirmed itself to be a plural nation, recognising the injustices committed in the past, invoking the values of universal suffrage and non-discrimination, and setting the goal of promoting the full citizenship of all South Africans.[54] With the country having a population of approximately sixty two million people,[55] the number that self-identify themselves as indigenous people, the Khoi and San communities, would amount to less than one per cent of the total population.[56] It is relevant to point out that unlike the situation in the case of Brazil there isn't a specific category in the national census to identify indigenous groups, and they variably fit into the categories "coloured", "black African" or mostly "other". [57] The last South African census included a field for "Khoi, Nama and San Languages", marked by 0,01% of the national population.

The "Khoisan" category itself is a construction, allegedly coined by a German anthropologist named Leonard Schultze in the 1920's, assembling under the same term the ethnic groups of hunter-gatherers, such as the different San groups, and the pastoralist Khoi-khoi communities, despite the significant cultural and linguistic distinctions between them. Even Khoi-khoi and San are not necessarily the terms they actually call themselves. They might recognise more specific denominations such as *khoena* (meaning a khoe person), or terms designating each specific group such as Gorinhaicona, or /Xam, for example. Maybe even less respectful of these differences was the apartheid classification of "coloured". As is well known, these racial categories had the force of law and

53 Oliveira, "'Respeitem a Forma de a Gente Ser'," 2635.
54 Constitution of the Republic of South Africa, 1996.
55 According to the 2022 national Census.
56 IWGIA, *Indigenous World 2019*, 544.
57 As an example we can observe the data from Platfontein-NC, with 86% self-declaring as "other"; Firth, "Platfontein."

were developed on the basis of scientific racism, where we observe the significant participation of anthropology or *volkekunde* departments.[58] It is quite clear that these categorisations produced long-term effects that still operate in the aftermath of apartheid.[59] While on this specific theme, some authors consider that "one cannot fully comprehend this new phenomenon of Khoisan recognition without speaking about Coloured identity".[60] A strongly symbolic situation is described by Sharon Gabie.[61] In completing questionnaires during field research with the Koranna people, researchers would mark the "Coloured" box, and would be required by the interviewee to cross that out and write "Khoisan" on top of it. As a strategic representative category, "Khoisan" might frequently be evoked by specific communities in several contexts, but might also be rejected in favour of the self-denomination of each group, such as !Xun, +khomani, Koranna, etc.

The other possible category for Khoi and San groups to fit into, that of "black African", would in their view not address their specific needs. Most ethnic groups in South Africa of Bantu origin, despite being native to the land and despite having their own specific indigenous languages, indigenous customs and indigenous legal systems, do not exactly claim an indigenous identity in the same terms as indigenous people in Brazil. These groups might benefit from a pluralist legal disposition that protects indigenous traditions and languages but do not often subscribe to the broad global category of "indigenous people," even though the interpretation of the terms traditional or tribal can create converging political spaces shared by those identities.

In this sense the category "indigenous people" is claimed almost exclusively[62] by the Khoi and San groups, which are broadly recognised internationally and partially recognised nationally. San people, for example, are considered to have the oldest records of occupying the same territory, making them arguably the ethnic group most worthy of the classification "indigenous".[63] Rock art found in Blombos Cave points to human occupation dating to more than seventy thousand years ago and interpretations of the genetic data mark them as one of the oldest human populations in the world, genetically speaking. Not surprisingly

58 Gordon, "Apartheid's Anthropologists," 548.

59 Posel, "What's in a Name?" 69.

60 Gabie, "Khoisan Ancestry," 31.

61 Gabie, "Khoisan Ancestry," 7.

62 Kuper, "O Retorno do Nativo," 217 notes that the only other claim to the indigenous category in South Africa was a provocative claim made by the Boer nation, which was ignored by all relevant institutions for obvious reasons.

63 "The San are believed to have lived longer on one area of land than any other group in human history." – Huizenga, "Documenting 'Community'," 147.

this has also made them a "hotspot" for scientific research. Their communities, lands and heritage are therefore the target of genetic, archaeological, anthropological and all sorts of scientific investigations, actually reaching the point of harassment, as we will observe in the next section of this chapter. Although it is illustrative, this concept of San and Khoi people as pure strains of original humanity is quite essentialist and dangerous, presenting them as isolated cultures and groups, as if they would have not engaged in significant trade with other populations. Although there are San and Khoi communities that live in rural territories, follow ancient traditions and speak their mother languages, there is also a cultural presence in the urban spaces of Cape Town, for example, in the "coloured" communities, where it is possible to find oral knowledge, rituals and cultural practices of Khoi origin coexisting with elements of different cultures such as Malay, Muslim, Xhosa and other African cultures that have been present in Cape Town throughout its history.[64]

Although the colonial project of land dispossession of their territories and heritage started with the arrival of the first settlers on their lands and drastically developed during the apartheid regime, the achievement by the State of a democratic constitution shoul mean improvement in the quality of the citizenship of the indigenous people, but to this day Khoi and San people still face challenges in attempting to benefit from their own heritage. After the democratisation of the Republic of South Africa the Khoi and San people appear to occupy a rather more dignified position as their symbols are presented on the national coat of arms, which displays figures inspired by San rock art and sayings written in the /Xam language. This brings us to an important question frequently asked by indigenous people – to what extent do these popular representations in the iconography of the national identity correspond to the actual recognition of specific rights for these communities?

3.2 *Indigenous People – The Legal Setting in South Africa*

To start answering this question let us observe the instances of the use of the words "indigenous" and "customary" in the supreme legal disposition of South Africa, the Constitution of the Republic of South Africa of 1996. It is common knowledge that the South African constitution is internationally recognised as a pluralist and progressive legal document, being influenced by most of the same global debates that influenced the Brazilian Constitution, such as the UDHR, and having itself served as a strong influence on other nations' legal orders. Universalist international premises have a strong influence in this post-apartheid legal order, and "... the legislative framework of legal pluralism in

64 Bam, *Ausi Told Me*, 82.

South Africa cannot be explained outside the influence of globalisation".[65] Even though it is geographically distant from South America, some aspects follow some of the same premises observed in the aforementioned New Latin-American Constitutionalism although, as we will see, the indigenous element might be considerably more latent in the American states. The Constitution's preamble affirms that South Africa belongs to all who live in it, united in its diversity. Displayed in the national flag in the same saying in /Xam language: "!ke e:/xarra //ke".

The 6th paragraph of the first chapter of the Constitution, "Founding Provisions", pertains to "Languages". It recognises the diminished status of indigenous languages in the recent history of the country and states that South Africa must take measures to elevate their status.[66] The paragraph initially makes reference to the Bantu idioms that are currently recognised as official national languages. The Pan South African Language Board, established by an amendment eight years after the enactment of the Constitution is responsible for creating conditions for the use and development of all the official languages, plus the Khoi, Nama and San languages and also the sign languages, although except for signing these are still not recognised as official. It is clear that despite their being displayed on the national flag, the Khoi and San languages still occupy a secondary (to say the least) position in South Africa.[67]

Let us then observe another section in the South African Constitution that makes reference to customary law and could be of interest to our present analysis. Chapter 2 states that when interpreting the Bill of Rights courts must observe that:[68]

> (3) The Bill of Rights does not deny the existence of any other rights or freedoms that are recognised or conferred by common law, customary law or legislation, to the extent that they are consistent with the Bill.

Further, the dispositions on the roles of traditional leaders, as set out in Chapter 12, recognise (and also limit to the boundaries of the Constitution) the authority of traditional courts of customary law and determine the establishment of houses and councils of traditional leaders. These dispositions on

65 Diala, "Our Laws are Better than Yours," 8.

66 Constitution of the Republic of South Africa, 1996, s. 6(2).

67 A noteworthy initiative on this subject is the creation of a fully recognised Khoekhoegwab course offered by the San and Khoi Unit of the Centre for African Studies at the University of Cape Town in 2019.

68 Constitution of the Republic of South Africa, 1996, s. 39(3).

traditional courts and leaders have produced a long series of legislative debates that resulted in the Traditional Courts Bill, which was highly controversial and was criticised by different sectors of the public for several different reasons, such as the lack of legal protection for women in traditional courts, the lack of accountability for the legal systems, and arguably the reflection of influences from the Bantustan dispensation. Nevertheless, the Bill has undergone several alterations during the legislative construction process, and points to the making of a significant (even if maybe insufficient) effort by the South African state to address these issues.

Of greater interest to the Khoi and San communities were the debates regarding the Traditional and Khoi-San Leadership Act (TKSL) signed by the president of South Africa in November 2019, which provides for the recognition, functions and roles of traditional and Khoi-San leaders. Its former versions, the White Paper on Traditional Leadership and Governance and the Traditional Leadership and Governance Framework Act of 2003 received serious criticism, since they simply stated that they would be applicable to Khoi-San claims to traditionality without observing any Khoi or San specificities. The model of the National House of Traditional Leaderships (NHTL) was for some time considered by some Khoi and San representatives as unfit to incorporate their indigenous modes of deliberation, and for some time leaders of the Koranna Royal House even envisioned a parallel Indigenous Department to properly represent them. They initially refused to participate in the NHTL for considering that it would mean accepting categorisation under the "black African" umbrella term in the same way that they had had to adopt the "Gricqua" umbrella term in the past. Now there is the risk of a dispute over whether to adopt a "traditional" over an "indigenous" status.[69] According to Sharon Gabie:[70]

> They argue that there is a clear differential distinction; those who are traditional leaders and those that are indigenous to a place. Their understanding of indigenous is linked to the geographical area their ancestors occupied before contact with the colonisers and that people who are traditional are those Black chiefs that lived in the former Bantustans or homelands where they could practise their different cultures such as paying lobola for a man to take a wife.
>
> Khoisan Ancestry and Coloured Identity

69 Gabie, "Khoisan Ancestry," 61, 67.

70 Gabie, "Khoisan Ancestry," 64.

The bill was signed into law by President Cyril Ramaphosa in 2019, having being accepted by some national Khoi-San organisations, despite large criticism and opposition. The TKSL Act was seen as an act of restorative justice in the sense that Khoi-San organisations were specifically recognised by the South African state. This pleased the Khoi and San representatives to some extent, but due to the lack of consultation and social participation, the act was nullified by the Constitutional Court of South Africa in 2023.

We can observe that legal dispositions and political spaces that were initially rejected and considered to be too "Bantu-oriented" or to be too like the colonial structures are still of interest and can be claimed by the Khoi and the San. Nonetheless, one of the main criticisms of the Act was the lack of any mention of the land dispossession still suffered by most Khoi and San communities.

Most other instances of the use of the word "indigenous" in the constitutional text or its amendments refer to indigenous biological resources or indigenous knowledge. Examples include the National Environmental Management: Biodiversity Act 10 of 2004 (NEMBA) and the Bioprospecting, Access and Benefit Sharing Regulations (BABS) of 2008, as amended. The latter includes guidelines for benefit-sharing agreements, basic ethical protection for the communities that retain knowledge on the use of indigenous species, and a Bioprospecting Trust Fund. Besides this, there is the listing of areas of concurrent national and provincial legislative competence, which include the administration of indigenous forests, also without any reference to the recognition of indigenous land or its tenure. This lack of provisions and guarantees for indigenous territorial arrangements is one of the main challenges for indigenous or traditional communities.

With no specific process in place for the recognition of their territories, the Khoi and San do not consider the common instruments of land reform in South Africa to have adequate principles. The Restitution of Land Rights Act of 1994 aims mainly for the restitution of territorial rights to land expropriated since the enactment of the Natives Land Act of 1913, the main colonial disposition that alienated the lands of native groups in South Africa. It happens that land dispossession for the Khoi and the San started long before that with the arrival of the first settlers in the Cape Colony, and they demand specific treatment of that issue.[71]

Still, some cases of reterritorialisation were made possible through this disposition, such as in the case of the ǂKhomani San of the Kalahari, who were able to recover parcels of their original territory from farmers, and a larger

71 Stavenhagen, "Report of the Special Rapporteur," E/CN.4/2006/78/Add.2, 11.

shared area through the "!Ae!Hai Kalahari Heritage Park Agreement"[72] concluded in 2002. Although the ethnic element might have drawn the external support of institutions and influenced the general mobilisation it didn't influence the deliberation of the claim itself,that happened by means of common justice dispositions.[73] This led to further legislative discussion especially because these claims would had to be lodged before 1999, setting another burden in the path to restitution. In a 2014 amendment this date was extended to the 30th of June of 2019 and Khoi-San exceptions to the cut-off date of 1913 would be specifically analysed, although still with no clear decision on the procedures to be followed.

Although the constitutional references to traditionality could be taken to imply the legal recognition of the Khoi-San indigenous groups as such, this recognition is somewhat marginal, being only gradually incorporated into the legal order. In the words of the South African Human Rights Commission:[74]

> The result is the Constitution gives significant reference to and recognition of traditional leadership bodies of Bantu-speaking peoples, whilst almost no recognition is given to indigenous persons.

For our present purposes, one could argue the following on the basis of a simple comparison of the constitutional texts:[75]

> In contrast to their American counterparts, African groups, as well as many Asian groups who identify themselves as indigenous, face a different set of issues. First and foremost, while most groups are recognized as 'indigenous' on the international scale, they are still struggling for similar recognition by their national governments.

We can partially agree with that view, noting that our previous section on the Brazilian case made it evident that this national recognition of indigenous rights also materialises only partially. Also, despite being guided by some of the same premises of the universalist project on human rights, South Africa is not a participant in all the same international covenants that Brazil is. South Africa voted in favour of the UNDIR but it hasn't so far signed the 169 ILO Convention, despite the recommendation of the Committee on the Elimination of Racial

72 Anon, *!Ae!Hai Kalahari Heritage Park Agreement.*

73 Huizenga, "Documenting 'Community'," 152.

74 SAHRC, *National Hearing Report*, 56.

75 Hodgson, "Comparative Perspectives," 1042.

Discrimination (CERD) that it do so.[76] On the other hand, South Africa ratified the Nagoya Protocol of the Convention on Biological Diversity in 2013, which regulates the procedures for access and benefit sharing associated with genetic resources and traditional knowledge, recognising and stimulating the production of community protocols to guarantee free, prior and informed consent to guide negotiations with indigenous and traditional communities. Then the BABS regulations were amended in 2015 and the main premises of the Nagoya Protocol were reiterated in the Protection, Promotion, Development and Management of Indigenous Knowledge Act 6 of 2019, which notes the obligation of the State to observe the relevant international treaties and covenants and establishes the National Indigenous Knowledge Systems Office, which is a governmental organ dedicated to defending and facilitating the access of indigenous communities to benefit-sharing rights, and to aiding in the communication of external agents with community holders of indigenous knowledge in cases of bioprospection.

A consideration of these factors accords with the impression that South African consultation protocols focus not as much on their territories as on the communities themselves and on compensating them for the use of their knowledge, resources and heritage, as will be shown in the following pages.

4 Community Protocols and the Right to FPIC in South Africa

4.1 *Khoi-khoi Rooibos Biocultural Protocol*[77]

The first document that we will analyse is the Khoi-khoi Rooibos Biocultural Protocol, published in 2019 with the acknowledged support of the ABS Capacity Development Initiative, the Heinrich Böll Stiftung, the Open Society Initiative for Southern Africa, and Natural Justice. It contains several elements that enable a comparative analysis of the influence of Brazil's and South Africa's legislative contexts over these documents. The drafting of the document was motivated mostly by Nestlé's intention to obtain a patent for the commercial use of the *rooibos* plant (*Aspalathus linearis*), and the communities' claim to ancestral knowledge regarding the use of this plant.

As in our previous examples, the document begins by explaining what a community protocol is:

76 CERD, "Concluding Observations on the Combined Fourth to Eighth Periodic Reports of South Africa," CERD/C/ZAF/CO/4–8, s. D.31.

77 National Khoisan Council, "Khoikhoi Peoples' Rooibos Biocultural Community Protocol".

> Community protocols is a term that covers a broad array of expressions, articulations, rules and practices generated by communities to set out how they expect other stakeholders to engage with them. They may reference customary as well as national or international laws to affirm their rights to be approached according to a certain set of standards.
>
> Communities have always had a set of written, but mostly unwritten, rules about how to interact with outsiders and how they want outsiders to interact with them. … Specifically, it requires external parties to obtain prior, informed consent (PIC) and to take into consideration customary laws and local procedures for interacting with the communities and their resources. [78]

In a section entitled "The Rooibos Restitution Journey", and later in a section dedicated to the ancestral knowledge and use of the rooibos, they explain how the plant, endemic to their native territories, was traditionally used by their people, shared in good faith with Europeans, and misappropriated:

> As an antioxidant, the plant has numerous health benefits and uses. A national and international industry has formed around rooibos tea, cosmetics and other rooibos products. However, the industry did not acknowledge us as its traditional knowledge holders and engaged in the commercialisation of Rooibos without our consent, nor were any benefits shared with us. Our knowledge was misappropriated over 200 years ago.
>
> The use of Rooibos is linked to our ancestors who roamed Southern Africa for many centuries. Our knowledge was passed down from one generation to another generation. We desire that this knowledge continues to be passed down to our future generations. …
>
> Our ancestors taught us the aspects related to the knowledge through largely an oral tradition, storytelling and teaching-by-doing. … The Rooibos cultivation was small-scale, and the popularity of the tea was historically limited to our communities. Rooibos remained unknown to the rest of the world until 1772, when our knowledge of the uses of the plant was appropriated by a Swedish botanist. Although he took some Rooibos to Europe and wrote about it, the real potential for the plant was

78 National Khoisan Council, "Khoikhoi Peoples' Rooibos Biocultural Community Protocol," 2, 4.

> not recognised until 1904. That year, a Russian immigrant to South Africa became interested in Rooibos tea and started trading with us.[79]

There is an explanation of how the document was made, there are diagrams representing those involved in its creation, including the communities represented by the protocol and the National Khoisan Council (NKC), and there is a specific section dedicated to the stakeholders involved in the BCP, including the institutions involved in their proposed 50/50 benefit sharing model. There is also an explanation of how the internal debates happened inside the Khoi-San community and why this protocol, despite its being organised by the NKC, represents only Khoi groups:

> In 2010, the South African San Council initiated the process of advocating for the recognition of their indigenous knowledge to the uses of Rooibos and other plants found in South Africa. In 2012, we, the Khoikhoi, as represented by the National Khoisan Council, joined the San community in fighting for our recognition as traditional knowledge holders to the uses of Rooibos, with the support of Natural Justice.
>
> For the purposes of the Rooibos ABS negotiations, the San communities were represented by the South African San Council. This is due to the fact that the San Council initiated the conversation and has been concluding benefit-sharing contracts on behalf of the San communities over the last decade since the first Hoodia case broke.[80]

An interesting passage alludes to the pressure felt during their internal debates on the Rooibos negotiations, and how their intention was initially to produce a more extensive community protocol covering a wider range of themes:

> That same year (2012), we, the National Khoisan Council, decided to develop a Community Protocol (CP) with the objective of articulating who the Khoisan communities are as non-recognised African indigenous communities in South Africa. By 2013, we had identified the priority issues of our CP as non-recognised indigenous communities in South Africa. These included, amongst others:

79 National Khoisan Council, "Khoikhoi Peoples' Rooibos Biocultural Community Protocol," 6, 60.

80 National Khoisan Council, "Khoikhoi Peoples' Rooibos Biocultural Community Protocol," 6, 48.

> – Constitutional recognition; Recognition of our languages; Land rights; Intellectual property & Access and Benefit-sharing; Women & youth; and Healing & economic development.
>
> But, as the struggle for recognition as knowledge holders to the uses of Rooibos intensified, we decided to put the broader CP process on hold. We had entered into ABS negotiations for Rooibos and decided to focus on this process. [81]

Therefore, the timeline of this BCP starts in 2010 with the Nestlé patent case and follows from there to the development of negotiations. It is evident, though, that the document is more than simply a negotiation tool, since most of the negotiations had already been happening since 2014 when NKC and Nestlé signed an agreement. It is a document in which they officially record and present their agreements but also their history and the history of the political recognition of the Khoi-San in South Africa, their identity and their demands. A specific section is dedicated to the process of land dispossession suffered by the Khoi-San, and another very interesting section presents traditional Khoi-San art and drawings, its meanings, and how it describes their values, possibly as a way of letting stakeholders know that Khoi-San ancestral knowledge can be more profound than what is expressed in written words.

It is only after reading some of these basic "lessons" on the Khoi-San people and the *rooibos* case that the reader will encounter a section on how consent is given by them. They deal with the issues of bioprospection, academic research and other contacts with other parties who must enter in contact with the NKC, and in the cases of bioprospection, parties who must also contact the South African Department of Environment, Forestry and Fisheries. Another section is dedicated to benefit sharing, explaining the process of Khoi recognition and of Khoi individuals obtaining their benefits with their community leaders.

We can understand from this analysis that, although motivated mostly by ABS necessities and economic compensation, the protocol still makes strong demands regarding territorial issues and political recognition, not so differently from the cases analysed previously.

4.1.1 San Code of Research Ethics[82]

Our last case is a much shorter document and is not exactly labelled as a community protocol, but it is very like one and is still useful to our present study

81 National Khoisan Council, "Khoikhoi Peoples' Rooibos Biocultural Community Protocol," 6.

82 South African San Institute, "San Code of Research Ethics".

since it addresses the theme of self-determination. Much like the last document we observed, this document is motivated mostly by the theft of San traditional knowledge, the misuse of Khoi-San images in the media, and other events which led the San to produce this specific document, which is aimed at researchers in different areas of interest who might wish to engage with them for scientific purposes. Authored by the South African San Institute (SASI), it relied on the support of the project Trust – Equitable Research Partnerships and financial support from the European Union. Unlike the other documents considered so far, this one doesn't attach or make any explicit reference to any national or international state legislation.

After explaining very simply, clearly and objectively what FPIC is, the document is divided into five sections: Respect, Honesty, Justice and fairness, Care, and Process. As individuals and as communities they demand fair acknowledgment of their contributions and respect for their culture and history. They say that they feel that they have been lied to in the past and that outsiders approached them in an invasive and disrespectful manner, avoiding their traditional authorities and offering them bribes:[83]

> We have encountered lack of respect in many instances in the past. In Genomics research, our leaders were avoided, and respect was not shown to them. Researchers took photographs of individuals in their homes, of breastfeeding mothers, or of underage children, whilst ignoring our social customs and norms. Bribes or other advantages were offered.

Therefore they require honesty from possible researchers and an open exchange between them and their leaders:[84]

> Open exchange should not patronise the San. Open exchanges implies that an assessment was made of possible harms or problems for the San resulting from the research and that these possible harms are honestly communicated. Prior informed consent can only be based on honesty in the communications, which needs to be carefully documented. Honesty also means absolute transparency in all aspects of the engagement, including the funding situation, the purpose of the research, and any changes that might occur during the process.

83 SASI, "San Code of Research Ethics," 2.

84 Ibid.

In the section on Justice and fairness they state that they must be informed of any benefits arising from research involving their knowledge, even if non-monetary, but demand active participation in the research process to guarantee that the communities will benefit in some way or other from these enterprises. They say that they will do their best to enforce compliance with the Code and might blacklist unethical researchers.

In the Care section they explain that not only must the research aim for the improvement of the living conditions and local needs of the San communities, but it must also be carried out to a standard of excellence, or it might result in bad interaction with the community.

Finally, in the Process section the San Council, who will manage the research process, commits to engaging fairly with the researchers and with the different San structures in the relevant collective deliberations. In a very telling passage the San close their document with a plea for respect for their traditional methods of decision-making, a plea common to all of the cases analysed here:[85]

> Andries Steenkamp, the respected San leader who contributed to this Code of Ethics until he passed away in 2016, asked researchers to come through the door, not the window. The door stands for the San processes. When researchers respect the door, the San can have research that is positive for us.

5 Comparative Analysis

In this analysis we observed the points of view of the states of Brazil and South Africa on indigenous community protocols, focussing on interactions of the official or positive legal systems with the indigenous customary systems. A deeper understanding of interactions such as these could possibly be achieved by extending the analysis to the perspective of the economic/capitalist normative systems that also operate in this social arena and dedicating more attention to the interactions they maintain with both the state and the indigenous legal systems – and their behaviour in regard to community protocols. Observations focussed on the application of single specific community protocols could also reveal details of the political and legal behaviour of traditional and state institutions.

85 SASI, "San Code of Research Ethics," 4.

Another topic that deserves deeper analysis and comparison is the influence and participation of anthropologist professionals in judicial matters involving indigenous groups, since we could observe that despite experiencing some resistance from local law practitioners, anthropological reports have sometimes proved to be very fruitful for a deeper understanding of the indigenous context by the state law system in Brazil. South African anthropology has a history significantly different from Brazil's, and the legacy of specific ethnic policies from the colonial and apartheid era could partly explain the resistance to the more meaningful involvement of anthropologists in government spaces.[86]

There is also a methodological limitation regarding the possibility of field research that could enable a deeper observation of strategic actors, through the perspectives of individuals or selected representatives, to analyse their response to these situations. There is much in the exercise of law that can be profoundly affected by the particular conditions and positions of those who make it, apply or contest it, and this present text certainly cannot address the matter.

The intention of this chapter was mainly to present the theme of indigenous community protocols as a rich field of research for legal pluralism, with a focus on the influences and interventions of international and state law in the self-determination documents constructed by indigenous peoples. The political relationships between the authorities of different societies can help us identify the dynamic spaces, moments and breaches in which these legal systems (international/national state law and indigenous law) find each other in the role of negotiators of arrangements for their own societies. We conclude that a progressive shift from colonialism would demand from the state not a validation of their communal decisions but rather a more diplomatic perspective on these negotiations with traditional communities.

Indigenous protocols from both countries have as a central element the right to self-determination and recognition in the broad perspective. When we analyse which rights derivative from self-determination they address, we find distinct orientations guiding them. In the Brazilian case, due to the existence of constitutional articles influenced by the 169 ILO Convention, indigenous protocols have a stronger legal basis to focus mainly on territorial and legislative matters. Nonetheless, they have been used as negotiation tools in a financial context as well. Influenced more by the Nagoya Protocol, South African indigenous protocols seem to focus mainly on the defence of other rights such

86 Kuper, "South African Anthropology", 97.

as the use of traditional knowledge, genetic material, or archaeological and cultural heritage, and they therefore have substantially different objectives such as guiding benefit-sharing agreements,[87] but we still find several common demands between the Brazilian and South African protocols, such as ancestral land claims and demands for political recognition.

It is relevant to note that we have focussed here on specific cases of self-recognised indigenous communities, but this type of analysis could also be extended to and reach other traditional communities, thus raising different questions. We found that despite the complexity of indigenous identity in both countries and despite situations in which the "traditional" and "indigenous" categories might be in opposition, the legal dispositions analysed, especially the international ones regarding FPIC, are applicable not only to communities self-declared as indigenous but also to peoples that have traditional or indigenous legal systems. In South Africa another Biocultural Community Protocol was developed in 2017 by the Kukula Traditional Health Practitioners Association from the Bushbuckridge Area,[88] representing the Sepedi and Tsonga communities. In Brazil community protocols are also being produced by *quilombola* communities and other traditional groups. Even if the national legal setting might differ in some respects when specific indigenous dispositions are compared, the interpretation in Brazil is that the 169 ILO Convention also applies to traditional groups and therefore enforces this movement of documentation of these customary guidelines of diplomacy. Due to the enormous diversity of the traditional communities in the country, we can expect the number of community protocols to keep on growing in the next years, being that more than 20 indigenous community protocols had already been published by 2021.[89] Researchers and law practitioners are monitoring their production and application in academic spaces such as the Observatory of Community Protocols for Free Prior and Informed Consultation and Consent,[90] a network which collects protocols, jurisprudence, specific and comparative analysis on these communal pieces of legislation.

In South Africa a very significant case is recorded among the traditional Amadiba community of Xolobeni, in the Eastern Cape. In the process of demanding the right to FPIC regarding the installation of a mining company on their traditional lands, they were able to arrive at and publish the collective

87 Natural Justice, "Community Protocols in Africa," 45.
88 Kukula Traditional Health Practitioners Association and Natural Justice, "Biocultural Protocol".
89 Nummer et al, "Protocolos de Consulta Prévia," 351.
90 Observatório de Protocolos Autônomos, "Home".

decisions reached in Komkhulu, their general communal assembly, instead of monocratic decisions by their leaders partnering with the state and the companies. Their general assembly has claimed the right to veto the enterprise or, as it has been put, the right to say no, and has won judicial landmarks and avoiding the advance of the enterprise, at least for some time.[91] Even though there was not a written community protocol, this situation demonstrates the possibility of recognising indigenous or traditional institutions, pointing to the legal possibilities of validating communal decisions in preference to economic interests. These results were possible when the community's defence invoked a national legislation, the Interim Protection of Informal Land Rights Act, or IPILRA, which states that no person may be deprived of any informal right to land without his or her consent.[92]

We can understand that not only the South African Constitution enables legal pluralism but that there are growing efforts towards the recognition of rights for indigenous and traditional communities and the creation of formal spaces of political influence dedicated to their representatives. There have been efforts to recognise their courts, their languages and their heritage, but there is still an absence of territorial and heritage recognition that has a significant influence on the development of their own justice administration systems.

Other possibilities that could also be of interest in both cases are the regional international institutions with continental reach that can hold countries accountable for violations of human rights, such as the Interamerican Court of Human Rights, to which Brazil is bound, having signed the American Declaration on the Rights of Indigenous People, and the African Court on Human and Peoples' Rights, to which South Africa is bound, having ratified the African Charter. Despite the absence of the specific word indigenous in the African Charter, it affirms the right to the self-determination of peoples and it has been used by indigenous groups in Kenya to invoke the collective right to FPIC regarding land restitution, creating a precedent for other cases regarding indigenous communities.[93]

In the Brazilian case we observed that such territorial rights have been materialised mostly through national constitutional law, and that the international dispositions incorporated by indigenous groups in their protocols are taking much longer to be incorporated by official courts in Brazil. The protocols are

91 Huizenga, "Governing Territory," 719.

92 Interim Protection of Informal Land Rights Act 31 of 1996, "Deprivation of informal rights to land".

93 See Claridge, "Landmark Ruling"; and Claridge "Victory for Kenya's Ogiek".

often produced or observed by courts only when enterprises have already materialised in the indigenous territories.[94] One could argue that the discretionary power of Brazilian judges when dealing with matters of legal pluralism is responsible for the fact that the decisions of the indigenous authorities often do not have a binding effect, since there is still a general lack of sensibility and knowledge by law practitioners of the particularities of the indigenous universes.[95] This is comparable to the South African situation, in which there is the "state's tendency to interpret indigenous laws 'through the prism of the common law'".[96]

The South African experiences, on the other hand, show that the mechanism of FPIC can uphold indigenous rights even for communities that are reclaiming benefits from knowledge expropriated hundreds of years ago. As stated earlier, Brazil has only recently ratified the Nagoya Protocol, but the Khoi-khoi and San experiences could inspire similar claims in Brazil since there are several cases of irregular bioprospection and traditional knowledge appropriation that could possibly be interpreted similarly, such as the cases of *erva-mate* and *ayahuasca* (to limit our comparison to beverages, arguably the form in which *rooibos* is most popularly consumed). Most of the protocols of Brazilian indigenous communities do not in their texts so far include sections dedicated to benefit-sharing, traditional knowledge or genetic resources, but these are still themes of relevance for them.

It is a fact that most community consultation protocols are being made in response to the pressure of incoming enterprises and conflicts that require their production, with the result that the documents are often motivated by external agents who have their own agendas.[97] It is also a fact that the legal systems of these two national states are the products of colonisation and not law systems that developed naturally from the continuity of the customs and ideals of the people that they represent. Therefore, although we are talking about multicultural democracies, their laws are still imposed law and will always be perceived as such until interaction with other legal systems, especially those of indigenous communities, are treated in the respectful manner proposed by their own current legal mandates.

94 Nummer et al, "Protocolos de Consulta Prévia," 349.

95 Duprat, "Convenção 169 da OIT," 77.

96 Diala, "Our Laws are Better than Yours," 18.

97 Nummer et al, "Protocolos de Consulta Prévia," 357.

6 Conclusions

From this analysis we argue that there is a common aspect of observable state behaviour when dealing with indigenous legal systems in cases related to criminal law, traditional knowledge and consultation procedures, which may possibly pose a question to the claims to legal pluralism made in the global south. We are referring to the partial validation of indigenous legal systems, which preserves the universalist principles of international treaties but also leaves room for and grants procedural responsibility to the national judges to issue the last word in any matter by choosing whether or not to validate the decisions of indigenous communities, enabling the state to retain control over what it finds "tolerable" to its values and territory.[98] In most cases the state will recognise the indigenous decisions when they are not in conflict "with the interests of national development".[99]

For the state legal systems to achieve the proposed levels of plurality claimed in their policy documents it is necessary for them to invest in critical intercultural dialogue on judicial matters related to indigenous groups. In situations of legal pluralism involving indigenous communities, the question of which law will decide, the law of the white man or the law of the indigenous group, will often have a more complex answer than simply one or the other.[100] Only a critical approach towards interculturality can prevent it from blurring lines and bending them to fit hegemonic interpretations and keeping national states in colonial inertia. A critical perspective must enable us to reach a deeper level of understanding and develop legal behaviours that recognise diversity beyond the incorporation of symbols and names, and actually incorporate indigenous perspectives, principles and ethics.

After observing the indigenous documents from both countries, it is quite clear that the international dispositions mentioned above are incorporated and enforced by the counter-hegemonic groups themselves, being appropriated and internalized in their protocols. The biggest challenge presented seems to be not that of whether indigenous communities around the world agree fully or critically with the definitions of who is indigenous or not, or with what is proposed in these conventions, since they can clearly interpret

98 Silveira and Macuxi, "Direito do Estado e Jurisdição Indígena," 163.

99 Macedo Moreira and Zema, "Proteção Constitucional," 69.

100 Oliveira and Castilho, "Introdução," 2.

and instrumentalise them,[101] but with whether national states can uphold their commitment to the treaties they sign, and how they can actually implement them.

To categorise the kind of legal pluralism happening in these cases, both countries have previously been characterised as subscribing to a rather weak legal pluralism, which characterisation seems to be appropriate when we observe that most of their indigenous decision-making processes must eventually be sanctioned by the state system. Both of them could be considered as unitary formal legal pluralist systems, since other legal systems must be recognised by an "official" legal system, which has the prerogative of conferring or not conferring legitimacy on the other law systems and limiting the scope of their agency.[102] Community protocols can be categorised as living customary law, since they are the current dispositions being applied by the communities and are products of their traditional forms of organisation, but they are also influenced by national and international law and are therefore the hybrid productions of dialogue procedures based on both indigenous principles and global humanitarian dispositions.

We understand after this analysis that, when dealing with the clash of systems inherent in legal pluralism involving indigenous communities, plural and multicultural states would increasingly have a role of a mediator of dialogue and guardian of basic rights rather than that of the bearer of the final decisive interpretation, or in one word, the judge. We understand also that the exercise of the administration of justice is linked to a degree with the material conditions of a community, the territorial element being highly significant in both cases. In regard to the development of future relations between states and indigenous legal systems, proper indigenous participation could be promoted, when it is available, by honouring the request for respect made by the indigenous peoples themselves in their protocols, which seems to be a productive possibility of intercultural legal dialogue.

101 "Indigenous people demonstrated a remarkable awareness of the differences in norms and processes between the various coexisting legal systems.": Tamanaha, "Understanding Legal Pluralism," 385.

102 "It is what happens in Brazil regarding law produced by indigenous people. The Federal Constitution makes reference to customs, not indigenous law, or consuetudinary law. In turn, the 169 ILO Convention clearly subjugates these laws when stating that they must be 'compatible with the national justice systems and with internationally recognized human rights." Castilho, "Indígenas na Prisão," 130.

Bibliography

Literature

Almeida, Juliana. *Ancient Landscapes of the Juruena.* Cuiabá: OPAN, 2019.

Anon. *!Ae!Hai Kalahari Heritage Park Agreement*, 29 May 2002. Accessed February 24, 2023. https://www.xauslodge.co.za/media/aehai-heritage-park-land-settlement.pdf.

Apina, Conselho das Aldeias Wajãpi, et al. *Protocolo de Consulta e Consentimento Wajãpi.* Macapá: Instituto de Pesquisa e Formação Indígena, Iepé, e Rede de Cooperação Amazônica, 2014. Acessed February 24, 2023. https://observatorio.direitosocioambiental.org/protocolo-de-consulta-e-consentimento-wajapi-2014/.

Bam, June. *Ausi Told Me: Why Cape Herstoriographies Matter.* Cape Town: Jacana, 2021.

Baniwa, Gersem. "A Conquista da Cidadania Indígena e o Fantasma da Tutela no Brasil Contemporâneo." In *Constituições Nacionais e Povos Indígenas*, edited by Alcida Rita Ramos, 206–27. Belo Horizonte: Editora UFMG, 2012.

Baniwa, Gersem. "Autonomia Indígena no Brasil: Desafios e Possibilidades" In *Convenção 169 da OIT e os Estados Nacionais*, edited by Deborah Duprat, 117–38. Brasília: ESMPU, 2015.

Brasil, Comissão Nacional da Verdade. *Relatório Final da Comissão Nacional da Verdade.* Brasília: Comissão Nacional da Verdade, 2014.

Caporrino, Bruno. *Dos que Flecham Longe: O Protocolo de Consulta e Consentimento Wajãpi.* Manaus: UFAM, 2019.

Carneiro, Monica. "Conselho Nacional de Política Indigenista é Instalado Durante Ato no Ministério da Justiça." Accessed February 24, 2023. https://www.gov.br/funai/pt-br/assuntos/noticias/2016/conselho-nacional-de-politica-indigenista-e-instalado-durante-ato-no-ministerio-da-justica.

Castilho, Ela Wiecko V. de. "Indígenas na Prisão: O Déficit de Perspectiva Intercultural." In *Lei do Índio ou Lei do Branco: Quem Decide? Sistemas Jurídicos Indígenas e Intervenções Estatais*, edited by Assis da Costa Oliviera and Ela Wiecko Volkmer de Castilho, 127–56. Rio de Janeiro: Lumen Juri, 2019.

Chan, T. M. "The Richtersveld Challenge: South Africa Finally Adopts Aboriginal Title." In *Indigenous Peoples' Rights in Southern Africa*, edited by Robert Hitchcock and Diana Vinding, 114–33. Copenhagen: IWGIA, 2004.

Claridge, Lucy. "Landmark Ruling Provides Major Victory to Kenya's Indigenous Endorois: *Centre for Minority Rights Development and Minority Rights Group International* (MRG) *on Behalf of the Endorois Community v The Republic of Kenya*." Accessed February 16, 2023. https://minorityrights.org/publications/landmark-ruling-provides-major-victory-to-kenyas-indigenous-endorois-august-2010/.

Claridge, Lucy. "Victory for Kenya's Ogiek as African Court Sets Major Precedent for Indigenous Peoples' Land Rights: *African Commission on Human and Peoples' Rights v the Republic of Kenya.*" Accessed February 16, 2023. https://minorityrights.org/publications/victory-kenyas-ogiek-african-court-sets-major-precedent-indigenous-peoples-land-rights/.

Conselho Indigenista Missionário (CIMI). *Violência Contra os Povos Indígenas no Brasil. Dados de 2020.* Brasília: Conselho Indigenista Missionário, 2020.

Delgado, Natalia Aguilar. "Community Protocols as Tools for Resisting Exclusion in Global Environmental Governance." *Revista de Admministração de Empresas* 56, no. 4 (2016): 395–410.

Diala, Anthony. "Our Laws are Better than Yours: The Future of Legal Pluralism in South Africa." *Revista General De Derecho Público Comparado* 26 (2019): 1–23.

Duprat, Deborah. "A Convenção 169 da OIT e o Direito à Consulta Prévia, Livre e Informada." In *Convenção 169 da OIT e os Estados Nacionais*, edited by Deborah Duprat, 53–78. Brasília: ESMPU, 2015.

Fanzeres, Andreia and Andrea Jakubaszko. "Barragens e Violações dos Direitos Indígenas na Bacia do Rio Juruena." In *Ocekadi: Hidrelétricas, Conflitos Socioambientais e Resistência na Bacia do* Tapajós, edited by Daniela Fernades Alarcon, Brent Millikan, and Maurício Torres, 323–37. Brasília-DF: International Rivers Brasil, 2016.

Fanzeres, Andreia, et al. "A Experiência das Autodemarcações." In *Novas Reflexões Indigenistas*, edited by Andreia Fanzeres, and Ivar Busatto e João Dal Poz, 163–87. Cuiabá: OPAN, 2021.

Feitosa, Saulo Ferreira, and Clóvis Antônio Brighenti. *Empreendimentos que Impactam Terras Indígenas.* Brasília: Conselho Indigenista Missionário, 2014.

Firth, Adrian. "Platfontein." Accessed February 17, 2023. https://census2011.adrianfrith.com/place/383004.

Gabie, Sharon. "Khoisan Ancestry and Coloured Identity: A Study of the Korana Royal House under Chief Josiah Kats." Masters diss., University of the Witwatersrand, 2014.

Gomes da Silva, Paulo Thadeu. "Os Direitos dos Índios: Paradoxos e Colonialismos Internos." In *Convenção 169 da OIT e os Estados Nacionais*, edited by Deborah Duprat, 287–306. Brasília: ESMPU, 2015.

Gordon, Robert. "Apartheid's Anthropologists: The Genealogy of Afrikaner Anthropology." *American Ethnologist* 15, no. 3 (1988): 535–53.

Hodgson, Dorothy Louise. "Comparative Perspectives on the Indigenous Rights Movement in Africa and the Americas." *American Anthropologist* 104, no. 4 (2002): 1037–49.

Huizenga, Daniel. "Documenting 'Community' in the ≠khomani San Land Claim in South Africa." *Political and Legal Anthropoloty Review* 37, no. 1 (2014): 145–61.

Huizenga, Daniel. "Governing Territory in Conditions of Legal Pluralism: Living Law and Free, Prior, and Informed Consent (FPIC) in Xolobeni, South Africa." *Extractive Industries and Society* 6, no. 3 (2019): 711–21.

Instituto de Estudos Socioeconômicos (INESC), and Indigenistas Associados (INA). "Anti-Indigenous Foundation: A Portrait of FUNAI Under the Bolsonaro Administration." Accessed February 17, 2023. https://www.inesc.org.br/wp-content/uploads/2022/06/release-funai_atualizado_EN.pdf.

IWGIA. *The Indigenous World 2019*. Copenhagen: IWGIA, 2019.

Jenkins, Tauriq. "When it Flows, it Floods." *New Agenda. South African Journal of Social and Economic Policy* 79 (2021): 36–41.

Kukula Traditional Health Practitioners Association and Natural Justice. "Biocultural Protocol of the Kukula Traditional Health Practitioners Association." Accessed February 17, 2023. https://za.boell.org/sites/default/files/bcp-kukula-traditional-health-practitioners-association-english.pdf.

Kuper, Adam. "O Retorno do Nativo." *Horizontes Antropológicos* 8, no. 17 (2002): 213–37.

Kuper, Adam. "South African Anthropology. An Inside Job." *Paideuma* 45 (1999): 83–101.

Macedo Moreira, Erika, and Ana Catarina Zema. "Proteção Constitucional da Jurisdição Indígena no Brasil." In *Lei do Índio ou Lei do Branco: Quem Decide? Sistemas Jurídicos Indígenas e Intervenções Estatais*, edited by Assis da Costa Oliviera and Ela Wiecko Volkmer de Castilho, 43–74. Rio de Janeiro: Lumen Juris, 2019.

Movimento Munduruku Ipereg Ayu, et al. "Protocolo de Consulta Munduruku, 2014." Accessed February 24, 2023. https://acervo.socioambiental.org/acervo/documentos/protocolo-de-consulta-munduruku.

National Khoisan Council. "The Khoikhoi Peoples' Rooibos Biocultural Community Protocol." Accessed February 17, 2023. https://absch.cbd.int/api/v2013/documents/BAF781F0-5952-1178-E665-AD78748E6743/attachments/611555/NJ%20Rooibos%20BCP_Web_72ppi.pdf.

Natural Justice. "Community Protocols Toolbox." Accessed February 17, 2023. https://naturaljustice.org/publication/community-protocols-toolbox/.

Natural Justice. "Community Protocols in Africa: Lessons Learned for ABS Implementation." Accessed February 17, 2023. https://naturaljustice.org/wp-content/uploads/2018/11/2018_Community-Protocols-in-Africa_Lessons-Learned_Natural-Justice.pdf.

Nummer, Fernanda Valli, et al. "Protocolos de Consulta Prévia Para a Defesa de Territórios e Direitos Indígenas: Desafios à Pluralidade de Direitos." *Aceno – Revista de Antropologia do Centro-Oeste* 8, no. 17 (2021): 345–62.

Observatório de Protocolos Autônomos. "Home." Accessed February 17, 2023. https://observatorio.direitosocioambiental.org/#.

Oliveira, Assis da Costa; and Ela Wieko Volkmer de Castilho. "Introdução: Sobre Conflitos Jurídicos, Direitos Indígenas e Indagações," In *Lei do Índio ou Lei do Branco: Quem Decide? Sistemas Jurídicos Indígenas e Intervenções Estatais*, edited by Assis da Costa Oliviera and Ela Wiecko Volkmer de Castilho, 1–10. Rio de Janeiro: Lumen Juris, 2019.

Oliveira, Rodrigo Magalhães de. "'Respeitem a Forma de a Gente Ser': Protocolo de Consulta Munduruku e Pluralismo Jurídico." *Revista Direito e Práxis* 12, no. 4 (2021): 2628–57.

Pontes Júnior, Felício. "Audiência Pública, Oitiva Constitucional e Consulta Prévia: Limites e Aproximações." In *Convenção 169 da OIT e os Estados Nacionais*, edited by Deborah Duprat, 79–116. Brasília: ESMPU, 2015.

Posel, Deborah. "What's in a Name? Racial Categorisations under Apartheid and their Afterlife." *Transformation* 47 (2001): 50–74.

Ramos, Alcida. *Pulp Fictions of Indigenism*. Brasília: Universidade de Brasíla, 2001.

Ramos, Alcida. *Seduzidos e Abandonados, ou, Como Amansar Índios Rebeldes*. Brasília: Universidade de Brasíla, 2019.

Rede de Cooperação Amazônica. "Contribuições da RCA Sobre o Direito de Consulta e Consentimento Livre Prévio e Informado para Estudo Temático do Mecanismos de Expertos sobre Direitos dos Povos Indígenas da ONU." Accessed February 17, 2023. https://www.ohchr.org/sites/default/files/Documents/Issues/IPeoples/EMRIP/FPIC/AmazonCooperationNetwork_SP.pdf.

Rede de Cooperação Amazônica. "Protocolos Autônomos de Consulta e Consentimento: Guia de Orientações." Acessed February 24, 2023. https://observatorio.direitosocioambiental.org/wp-content/uploads/2020/12/Protocolos-autonomos-de-consulta-e-consentimento-Guia-de-Orientacoes.pdf.

Ribeiro, Darcy. "The Soldier Who Wouldn't Shoot." *UNESCO Courier* 8–9 (1954): 8–13.

Santamaría, Rosembert Ariza. "De la Autonomía y el Derecho de Administración de Justicia Indígena en Latinoamérica." In *Lei do Índio ou Lei do Branco: Quem Decide? Sistemas Jurídicos Indígenas e Intervenções Estatais*, edited by Assis da Costa Oliviera and Ela Wiecko Volkmer de Castilho, 13–42. Rio de Janeiro: Lumen Juris, 2019.

Santos, Boaventura de Sousa. "Human Rights: A Fragile Hegemony". In *Human Rights and Diverse Societies: Challenges and Possibilities*, edited by Crépeau, Françoisande Sheppard, 17–25. Newcastle: Cambridge Scholars, 2013.

Silveira, Edson Damas, and Júlio Macuxi. "Direito do Estado e Jurisdição Indígena: Casuisticas Amazônicas de Pluralidade, Jusdiversidade e Interlegalidades." In *Lei do Índio ou Lei do Branco: Quem Decide? Sistemas Jurídicos Indígenas e Intervenções Estatais*, edited by Assis da Costa Oliviera and Ela Wiecko Volkmer de Castilho, 157–80. Rio de Janeiro: Lumen Juris, 2019.

South African Human Rights Commission (SAHRC). *Report of the South African Human Rights Commission: National Hearing Relating to the Human Rights Situation of the Khoi-San in South Africa*. Pretoria: SAHRC, 2018.

South African San Institute (SASI). "San Code of Research Ethics." Accessed February 17, 2023. https://www.globalcodeofconduct.org/wp-content/uploads/2018/04/San-Code-of-RESEARCH-Ethics-Booklet_English.pdf.

Souza Filho, Carlos Frederico Marés, et al. *Protocolos de Consulta Prévia e o Direito à Livre Determinação.* São Paulo: Fundação Rosa Luxemburgo, 2019.

Stats SA. "Census 2022 Statistical Release" Accessed February 17, 2023. https://census.statssa.gov.za/assets/documents/2022/P03014_Census_2022_Statistical_Release.pdf.

Tamanaha, Brian Z. "Understanding Legal Pluralism. Past to Present, Local to Global." *Sydney Law Review* 30, no. 3 (2008): 375–411.

Legislation and Government Publications

Brazil

Constitution of Federal Republic of Brazil, 1988.

Decreto nº 1.775, de 8 de janeiro de 1996.

Decreto nº 5.051, de 19 de abril de 2004.

Decreto nº 7.747, de 5 de junho de 2012.

Decreto nº 8.593, de 17 de dezembro de 2015.

Decreto nº 9.759/2019, de 11 de abril de 2019.

Estatuto do Índio, 1973.

Legislative Act 136/2020.

South Africa

Amendments to the Regulations on Bio-Prospecting, Access and Benefitsharing (Gen N 447 in GG 38809 of 19 May 2015).

Bioprospecting, Access and Benefit-Sharing Regulations, 2008 (GN R138 in GG 30739 of 8 February 2008).

Constitution of the Republic of South Africa, 1996.

Interim Protection of Informal Land Rights Act 31 of 1996.

National Environmental Management: Biodiversity Act 10 of 2004.

Natives Land Act 27 of 1913.

Protection, Promotion, Development and Management of Indigenous Knowledge Act 6 of 2019.

Restitution of Land Rights Act 22 of 1994Traditional and Khoi-San Leadership Act 3 of 2019.

Traditional Courts Bill, B1–2017.

Traditional Leadership and Governance Framework Act 41 of 2003.

White Paper on Traditional Leadership and Governance (Gen N 2336 in GG 25438 of 10 September 2003).

International Documents

Committee on the Elimination of Racial Discrimination (CERD). "Concluding Observations n the Combined Fourth to Eighth Periodic Reports of South Africa."

CERD/C/ZAF/CO/4–8. 5 October 2016. https://tbinternet.ohchr.org/_layouts/15/treatybodyexternal/Download.aspx?symbolno=CERD%2fC%2fZAF%2fCO%2f4-8&Lang=en.

Stavenhagen, Rodolfo. "Report of the Special Rapporteur on the Situation of Human Rights and Fundamental Freedoms of Indigenous Peoples: Mission to South Africa." E/CN.4/2006/78/Add.2. 15 December 2005. https://documents-dds-ny.un.org/doc/UNDOC/GEN/G05/167/46/PDF/G0516746.pdf?OpenElement.

Human Rights Council (HRC) Working Group on the Universal Periodic Review. "Universal Periodic Review – National Report: Brazil." A/HRC/WG.6/27/BRA/1. 27 February 2017. https://documents-dds-ny.un.org/doc/UNDOC/GEN/G17/046/89/PDF/G1704689.pdf?OpenElement.

Treaties and Agreements

African Charter on Human and Peoples' Rights (1981).

American Declaration on the Rights of Indigenous Peoples (2016).

ILO Convention 107 on Indigenous and Tribal Populations (1957).

ILO Convention 169 on Indigenous and Tribal Peoples (1989).

International Covenant on Civil and Political Rights (1966).

Nagoya Protocol on Access to Genetic Resources and the Fair and Equitable Sharing of Benefits Arising from their Utilization to the Convention on Biological Diversity (2014).

UN Declaration on the Rights of Indigenous Peoples (2007).

CHAPTER 9

Sustainability of Customary Law Arbitration within the Nigerian Legal System: Judicial Rigidity versus the Organic Fluidity of Customary Law

Philip O. Odiase

Abstract

Arbitration in recent times has become a more popular choice of dispute resolution in Nigeria. In line with the plural configuration of the Nigerian legal system, there are two broad forms of arbitration. These are arbitration conducted in line with the state law and secondly indigenous (customary and Islamic) law-regulated arbitration. Before colonisation, arbitration was the commonest mechanism for dispute resolution. However, colonisation had a profound impact on all pre-existing modes of dispute resolution, particularly on customary law arbitration. In impacting customary arbitration, the English-styled courts acting as the normative custodians and interpreters of state law, fashioned universally applicable ingredients required for binding customary arbitration without strict reference to a particular customary law. This chapter queries the formulation and petrification of these ingredients by the regular courts. In providing a comprehensive insight into this quandary of customary arbitration, it examines some selected landmark cases and questions the propriety of applying the doctrine of *stare decisis* to customary law. It concludes that customary law arbitration would thrive better if the courts could fit the quest for predictability within the dictate of the peculiarity and inherent organic nature of the different Nigerian customary laws.

1 Introduction

Among the most pertinent characteristics of the Nigerian constitutional order since independence is the tremendous impact of colonialism. One of such enduring vestiges is the retention of a plural legal order, which subjects the enforcement of pre-colonial indigenous legal orders to the whims and caprices of transplanted colonialist's law "masquerading as state law,"[1] a

1 Diala, "A Butterfly that Thinks Itself a Bird," 384.

 | DOI:10.1163/9789004696747_010

by-product of indirect rule.[2] This phenomenon is entrenched by implication in the Constitution of the Federal Republic of Nigeria 1999 (the CFRN).[3] While the CFRN did not expressly employ the term legal pluralism or similar terminology, it can be deduced from some of its provisions that the CFRN permits and endorses the coexistence of multi-legal orders in the Nigerian legal system; particularly in the area of personal law.[4] The plural legal constellation supported by the CFRN is broadly made up of state law, customary law and Islamic law. These streams of law have distinctive substantive and procedural rules. To a degree, each legal system has distinct justice administrative mechanisms (at least at the trial level). These are either created[5] or recognised by state laws. In the former case, in addition to English-styled courts, subject to the religious inclinations of the major groups in a state, provisions are made for the establishment of sharia courts or customary courts or both in the state.[6] These supposedly indigenous courts, Diala argues, are "Anglicised courts purporting to be indigenous courts".[7] They are anglicised because, the normative behaviour of the adjudicators, litigants and procedures of these courts have been altered and influenced by the state law.

Taking into consideration cost, accessibility and efficiency, the availability of multiple legal dispute resolution forums presents parties in disputes with several options to select from. Conversely, the recognition of non-state justice actors in the process of dispute resolution provides a fertile environment for non-state justice actors to operate in Nigeria's plural system. One of the prominent non-state justice administration forums is arbitration. Others include mediation and conciliation in their different forms. Due to its plural legal system configuration, different forms of arbitration exist in the Nigerian legal milieu. These may be conveniently divided into two broad groups; state

2 Balonwu, "Growth and Development of Indigenous Nigerian Laws," 31–33.

3 Cap C 23, LFN 2004 (as amended) (hereafter the CFRN).

4 See CFRN, s. 315. The section, subject to the provisions of the CFRN, saved all "existing law" before the promulgation of the CFRN. Personal customary and Islamic laws being laws in existence before the promulgation qualify as existing laws. Also see *Agu v Ikewibe* [1991] 3 NWLR (Pt. 180) 385 (hereafter *Agu v Ikewibe*), 407, where the Supreme Court on the authorities of *Giwa v Inspector-General of Police* (1985) 6 NCLR 369 and *Enyinnaya v Commissioner of Police* (1985) NCLR 464 held that ss. 274(3) and 4(b) of the Constitution, 1979 (*impari material* with s. 315, CFRN), saved customary law as one of the existing laws.

5 Section 6 of the CFRN vests judicial powers in the courts; among the courts listed are the Sharia Court of Appeal and Customary Court of Appeal.

6 States in the southeast and south-south have predominantly customary courts; states in the southwest and north-central have both sharia and customary courts; core northern states have predominantly sharia courts.

7 Diala, "A Butterfly that Thinks Itself a Bird," 382.

law regulated arbitration, on the one hand, and indigenous (customary and Islamic) arbitration, on the other.[8]

Incidentally, owing to the inordinate delay associated with the Nigerian court system, coupled with other commendable social-economic benefits associated with arbitrating, in recent times the settlement of disputes through arbitration has become a more popular choice. On the other hand, resort to customary law-regulated arbitration (customary arbitration or customary law arbitration),[9] which before the arrival of the colonials was the commonest mode of dispute resolution,[10] has lost its prime position. It is in response to this development that this chapter discusses the sustainability of customary law arbitration in Nigeria (with intermittent references to Islamic arbitration). The chapter identifies some aspects of the ingredients of valid customary arbitration *suo motu* developed by the courts as some of the factors militating against the popularity and sustainability of customary arbitration in Nigeria. It also questions the application of the common law doctrine of *stare decisis* to customary law *qua* customary law arbitration and finally makes recommendations to enhance the practice of customary arbitration in Nigeria.

2 Plural Legal Order and the Hierarchy of Laws in Nigeria

Legal pluralism is an integral part of the Nigerian legal system. Although from the literature the term legal pluralism appears to be a relatively recent concept,[11] there are shreds of evidence suggesting that the phenomenon predates most modern states. Countries with a plural legal order usually adopt the practice primarily to manage and balance the competitive normative interests within their constituent cosmopolitan societies.[12] Nigeria is a multi-ethnic state with 3 major ethnic groups, an estimated 370 tribes and more than 500 languages.[13] In other words, Nigeria is a socially and culturally fragmented

8 Akanbi, Abdulrauf and Daibu, "Customary Arbitration," 202.

9 These phrases are used interchangeably in this work. Nwauche, "Customary Law Arbitration," 63–72 tried to distinguish between them. He argued that customary law arbitration is an arbitration conducted by a panel of recognised customary authorities vested with judicial functions, (e.g. a body of chiefs and elders of a community) on the one hand and customary arbitration is an arbitration whose panel does not have a recognised judicial function or recognised customary authority (e.g. an oral submission to the Market Association or a neutral third party, etc.).

10 Ornguga and Orhange, "Law, Legal Theory and Practice," 36.

11 Von Benda-Beckmann and Turner, "Legal Pluralism," 255–56.

12 Von Benda-Beckmann and Turner, "Legal Pluralism," 256–57.

13 Batic, "Future of Minority Languages," 218; Brann, "Language and Ethnicity," 122.

cosmopolitan country, with multiple languages, traditions, religions and independent political histories.[14] Like most cosmopolitan countries it operates a constitutionally supported plural legal system. Historically, before the arrival of the colonists, the indigenous people of Nigeria maintained rich social orders controlled and supported by relatively complex indigenous laws developed over several generations. Following colonisation the colonial authorities transplanted and imposed political institutions and laws on the country.[15] But in order to maximise revenue, legitimise the new superimposed institutions and laws and prevent unwarranted religious and cultural conflicts and revolt, among other reasons, the colonial government strategically introduced the indirect rule method of governance.[16] The system allowed the application of pre-existing indigenous laws subject to the oversight of the new state's institutions.[17] In doing this, the application of customary law was restricted to well-defined areas of personal law,[18] with a caveat that under such circumstances, any applicable customary law must conform to the British notion of law, justice, fairness and equity.[19] This stipulation marked the entrenchment of the spatial and scalar arrangement between the subsisting legal systems in Nigeria. The arrangement made state law the dominant law and placed indigenous law below it and by implication, it empowers the state law in the course of interaction between the two normative orders to either reject or accept any particular customary law as applicable to the facts in issue.

Chief among the possible explanations for the retention of a plural legal system after attaining independence in 1960 was the cosmopolitan nature of the country, coupled with the fact that the political class that took over the reins of government after independence either failed or deliberately refused to understand the history of the country. The state law was the pedestal upon which the new political authority rested. To consolidate their authority, the political

14 Batic, "Future of Minority Languages," 218.

15 Awolowo, *Thoughts on Nigerian Constitution*, 9–10; Uweru, "Repugnancy Doctrine," 292.

16 Gerring et al., "Institutional Theory," 377–80, 399–400.

17 Udoma, *History and Law*, 104–05.

18 Merriam-Webster Dictionary defines personal law as "law that applies to a particular person or class of persons only wherever situated". Merriam-Webster Dictionary. "Personal Law".

19 Section 19 of the Supreme Court Ordinance, 1876, provides: "Nothing in this ordinance shall deprive the Supreme Court of the right to observe and enforce the observance, or shall deprive any person of the benefit of any law or custom existing in the said colony and territories subject to its jurisdiction, such Law or Custom not being repugnant to natural justice, equity and good conscience, nor incompatible either directly or by necessary implication with any enactment of the Colonial Legislature."

class retained the immediate pre-existing constitutional order. In other words, toward consolidation of political power, post-independence political leaders avoided deviations from and retained the colonial superimposed plural legal system order.[20] To date, the subordination of indigenous law to state laws remains the norm and the relationship between them has been predatory, promoting the near exclusiveness of the state laws. The inferior configuration of customary law and its complementary role question the aptness of referring to it as one of the sources of law in Nigeria. Despite the controversies, viewed through the prism of the CFRN[21] and other relevant legislation it is clear that customary law or custom may be considered as the law regulating a given fact or relationship only if the court can find a convergence between the customary law in issue and the underlying interest or principles of the makers of the state law.[22]

The court is the primary constitutional pedestal for the interface between state law and customary law. It functions as the sieve engaged by state law to filter out the supposedly undesirable aspects of customary law and as the binoculars for identifying the points of convergence between customary law and state law. In the performance of these responsibilities, the courts are expected to act objectively. But on the contrary, they have not remained neutral. The courts have been overtly hostile to customary law; sometimes engaging state law to neutralise customary law. Some commentators, such as Abrahams, argue that in the determination of the validity of customary law, the courts usually uphold or reject a customary law using trajectory dictate of values foreign to the customary law under review.[23] Accordingly, "[M]orality and justice must of course mean British and not African conceptions of those attributes."[24] In other words, in deciding whether a particular customary law is repugnant to equity and natural justice, such subjective decisions for or against the custom are invariably based on considerations not necessarily backed by the express provisions of the state law but more often than not backed by values imported from foreign customs and developed in other contexts external to the indigenous custom under review. For instance, the Supreme Court in *Okonkwo v Okagbue,*[25] relying on the opinion of foreign

20 Udoma, *History and Law,* 1–10.

21 For instance, ss. 245 and 282 of the CFRN; s. 16 of the Federal Capital Territory Customary Court Act, Cap F39, LFN and others.

22 Evidence Act, 2011, s. 18(3).

23 Abrahams, "Colonial Legal Service," 8.

24 Abrahams, "Colonial Legal Service," 8.

25 *Okonkwo v Okagbue* [1994] 9 NWLR (Pt. 368) 301.

authors[26] came to the conclusion that the Onitsha native law and custom that allows a sister or sisters to marry a wife for their deceased brother and that the children of that marriage are legitimate children of the deceased is repugnant to natural justice, equity and good conscience and is against public policy. Over time the practice of upholding the repugnancy test using potentially truncating interpretative tools sourced from contexts incompatible with indigenous custom has not only resulted in erecting barriers to the seamless growth of customary law but has in many ways reshaped customary law to fit into the colonial notion of law, which lacks a claim to customary legitimacy.[27]

3 Definition and Nature of Customary Law and Customary Arbitration

Constitutionally customary law, in line with section 315(1) and (4)(b) of the CFRN is one of the "existing laws" in Nigeria; being a body of rules of law in force immediately before the coming into force of the CFRN. By extension customary arbitration, being part of customary law was also saved by the provisions.[28] But the CFRN did not define what the terms "customary law" or "customary law arbitration" mean, though it presumes the existence of customary law and made copious provisions for its administration. In this regard, the CFRN contains provisions that direct the establishment of Customary Court of Appeal[29] and made it a superior court of record;[30] the appointment of at least three persons learned in customary law to the Court of Appeal;[31] the need to have persons learned in customary law on the Supreme Court bench;[32] and so forth. While there is no constitutional definition of the term there is a plethora of statutory definitions of the term "customary law". One of the finest legislative definitions of customary law is that given by the Imo State Customary Court Law 1984.[33] The law defines customary law as

26 Among the authors cited by the court are Keay and Richardson, *Native and Customary Courts*; Megarry and Baker, *Snell's Principles of Equity*.

27 Merry, "Legal Pluralism," 869–70, 875–76.

28 *Agu v Ikewibe*, 407.

29 CFRN, ss. 265 and 280.

30 CFRN, s. 6.

31 CFRN, s. 237.

32 CFRN, s. 288.

33 Edit No. 7.

> [A] rule or body of customary rules, which obtain and is fortified by established usage and which is appropriate and applicable to any particular cause, matter, dispute, issue or question.[34]

This view of customary law as deriving its legitimacy from the people pervades most legislation and case law definitions of the term.

One of the best post-independence definitions of the term was given by Elias C.J.N., in *Kharie Zaidan v Fatima K. Mohssen*.[35] The case in issue centred on the determination of the applicable law to a deceased intestate. While holding that Islamic law applies to the facts of the case, His Lordship held that customary law was "any system of law not being the common law and not being a law enacted by any competent legislature in Nigeria but which is enforceable and binding within Nigeria as between the parties subject to its sway".[36]

This definition re-echoes the approach of Nigerian courts, of treating a non-state normative rule governing a particular set of circumstances as customary law.[37] In applying and enforcing non-state law normative rules, the Nigerian courts divide the plural legal order into two; state laws and other normative systems. That is, to the extent that the rules of a non-state legal system (customary or Islamic) have not been directly legislated on, the courts treat the rules as if they were customary law.[38] Thus, a yet-to-be-domestically codified Islamic law is by implication included in the scope of customary law. The result is that although Islamic Law is widely believed to be of divine origin, it is usually treated as customary law for the purposes of application and enforcement by regular courts.[39] Among the justifications for this approach is that there is a plethora of schools of thought in the Islamic religion and many divergent views among the followers of a particular school of thought.[40] Thus, because

34 Imo State Customary Court Law, 1984, s 1(1).

35 *Kharie Zaidan v Fatima K. Mohssen* (1973) 11 SC 1 (hereafter *Zaidan v Mohssen*).

36 *Zaidan v Mohssen*, 21.

37 *Timothy Tanloju Adesubokan v Rasaki Yunusa* [1971] ANLR 227.

38 The Evidence Act, 2011 does not make provision for the reception and application of Islamic law. In such circumstances, the courts rely on ss. 16–19, which were designed for the reception and application of customary law as the rule governing a particular set of facts.

39 Oba, "Islamic Law as Customary Law," 826–29; Elias C. J. N. in *Zaidan v Mohssen*, 21, held that Islamic was the applicable law. He placed it in the pigeonhole of customary law, however. In support of this, he defined customary law as "any system of law not being the common law and not being a law enacted by any competent legislature in Nigeria but which is enforceable and binding within Nigeria as between the parties subject to its sway".

40 Oba, "Judicial Practice in Islamic Family Law," 276.

of the existence of such divergent views, any aspect of Islamic law of which the court is yet to take judicial notice must be proven before it may be enforced by the court. The Supreme Court has taken judicial notice of the fact that the Islamic law of the Maliki[41] School of Islamic jurisprudence is applicable.[42] Secondly, critics believe that despite the claim of divine origin, the prevailing Islamic law of the Maliki School has been heavily soaked in customs.[43] In Nigeria some aspects of Islamic laws have been modified to such an extent that they have been transformed and reinvented to a level on which some of its normative characteristics may be at variance with what is obtainable in other Islamic jurisdictions.[44]

With regard to customary law *stricto sensus*, the courts accept it as a mirror of accepted usage,[45] prescribing rules of conduct.[46] In the words of Obaseki JSC, in *Oyewunmi v Ogunsesan*,[47] customary law is

> the organic or living law of the indigenous peoples of Nigeria regulating their lives and transactions. It is organic in that it is not static. It is regulatory in that it controls the lives and transactions of the community subject to it. It is said that custom is a mirror of the culture of the people. Customary law goes further and imports justice to the lives of all those subject to it.[48]

---

41 Named after the founder of the school (Malik ibn Anas, d.795), who developed the jurisprudence by interpreting the Quran and *Sunna* using three techniques; *ijtihad, ijma* and *qiyas* in connection with Muslim life, including dispute resolution.

42 *Rabiu v Adamu* [2013] 1 NWLR (Pt. 1337) 36; *Alkamawa v Bello* [1998] 8 NWLR (Pt. 561) 173, 182; Oba, "Judicial Practice in Islamic Family Law," 275.

43 Qureshi argued in his blog that like all Sunni schools in Sharia, the Maliki School uses the Quran as its primary source, followed by the sayings, customs, traditions and practices of Prophet Muhammad, transmitted as hadiths. The tradition includes not only the recorded hadiths but also the four supposedly directed by caliphs (Khalifa) – notably the legal rules of Umar. This source, according to Malik, sometimes supersedes the hadith, as the practice of the people of Medina was considered the living Sunnah. Qureshi, "Muslim Law".

44 In *Zaidan v Mohssen*, the Supreme Court applied the Moslem law of Lebanon. See Oba, "Judicial Practice in Islamic Family Law," 273 and 277–78. In the words of Oba, in Northern Nigeria "Traces of ... customs survived the jihad and new ones emerged subsequently."

45 *Owoniyi v Omotosho* (1961) 1 All NLR 304 (hereafter *Owoniyi v Omotosho*), 309; *Zaidan v Mohssen; Kindey v Military Governor of Gongola State* [1988] 2 NWLR (Pt. 77) 445 and a host of others.

46 *Zaidan* v *Mohssen*, 21.

47 *Oyewunmi v Ogunsesan* [1990] 3 NWLR (Pt. 137) 183 (hereafter *Oyewunmi v Ogunsesan*).

48 *Oyewunmi v Ogunsesan*, 207.

This definition has been adopted without reservation in virtually all cases touching on the meaning and application of customary law.[49] In sum, the courts consider customary law to be "... the customs, rules, traditions, ethos and cultures which govern the relationship of members of a community."[50]

Despite judicial recognition of customary law as one of the sources of law in Nigeria, the disturbing aspect is that in line with the statutory provisions the English courts treat customary law (including Islamic law) and its existence as a matter of fact, and as such its existence must be established by evidence like every other matter of fact.[51] To this end, in proving its existence the burden of proof lies on the person alleging the existence of the custom.[52] This onerous burden may be dispensed with only if judicial notice of the existence of such a customary law has been taken by a superior court of record. These two pre-independence common law principles (judicially noticed or proof in the absence of judicial notice) were first applied by the Privy Council in the Ghanaian case of *Angu v Attah*[53] as far back as 1940.[54] Unfortunately the Nigerian courts made them part of Nigerian case law in *Buraimo v Gbambgboye*.[55] The two principles of law were first incorporated into Nigeria's statutes in 1956 by section 14 of the Evidence Act 1956.[56] Subsequently, the section was split into sections 16, 17, 18 and 19 of Evidence Act 2011. Under the Evidence Act 2011 a custom is said to have been judicially noticed if it has been positively applied at least once by a superior court of record.[57] These requirements become justifiable and more meaningful when viewed against the backdrop that Nigeria has several ethnic groups with over 317 tribes having their various customary laws; though sometimes with some similarities.[58] Moreover, when a superior

49 See *Whyte v Jack* [1996] 2 NWLR (Pt. 431) 407, 420; *Mashuwareng v Abdu* [2003] 11 NWLR (Pt. 831) 403, 415–16; others.

50 *Odoemena Nwaigwe and 2 Ors v Nze Edwin Okere* [2008] 13 NWLR (Pt. 1105) 445, 481, per Tobi JSC.

51 Evidence Act, 2011, ss. 16(1) and 18(1).

52 Evidence Act, 2011, s. 16(2); *Egbuta v Onua* [2007] 10 NWLR (Pt. 1042) 298, 315.

53 *Angu v Attah* (1921) PC 1874–1926, 43.

54 This case has since been repealed in Ghana by the Chieftaincy Act, 1961, which provides for the assimilation of customary law into the common law of Ghana. The implication is that proof of customary law is now a matter of law in Ghana. Asiedu-Akrofi, "Judicial Recognition," 571–93.

55 *Buraimo v Gbambgboye* (1940) 15 NLR 139.

56 Evidence Act, 1956, LN 47 of 1955; Cap 14 LFN 2004. See Park, *Sources of Nigerian Law*, 83–97.

57 Evidence Act, 2011, s. 17.

58 Editor, "Full List of All 371 Tribes".

court acts upon it at least once, it becomes a binding precedent (concerning the custom in issue) on all inferior courts.

Customary law arbitration is recognised as an integral part of customary law under Nigeria's *corpus juris*. Though there are no express statutory provisions regulating customary arbitration, there are a few that impliedly acknowledge its existence. Among the many statutory provisions is section 35 of the Arbitration and Conciliation Act[59] (the national statute regulating commercial arbitration in Nigeria). In recognition of the continuous parallel existence of customary law (*ipso facto* customary law arbitration), the section provides "[T]his Act shall not affect any other law by virtue of which certain disputes: (a) may not be submitted to arbitration; or (b) may be submitted to arbitration only in accordance with the provisions of that or another law". Since customary law is one of the extant sources of law in Nigeria,[60] it is safe to conclude that the reference to "the provisions of that or another law" in the section includes customary law, since under customary law a dispute "may be submitted to arbitration". And thus rather than stultify the growth of customary arbitration, the basic arbitration statute expressly exempts from its ambit arbitration conducted in line with customary law.

Other statutes in support of the practice of customary arbitration are laws setting up the various courts in Nigeria. These laws enjoin the courts[61] to observe and enforce the observance of every customary law which applies to a given set of facts and is neither repugnant to natural justice, equity and good conscience nor incompatible either directly or by implication with any law for the time being in force.[62] Under provisions of this nature and similar provisions, the courts have been able to contribute to the growth of modern customary law arbitration in Nigeria by giving recognition to and enforcing customary law arbitration awards.[63] In *Eugene Nnaekwe Egesimba v Ezekiel Onuzuruike*,[64] while acknowledging that customary law arbitration is deeply rooted in Nigerian customs, the Supreme Court posited that

59 Arbitration and Conciliation Act, 1988, Cap A 18, LFN 2004.

60 *Esuwoye v Bosere* [2017] 1 NWLR (Pt. 1546) 256, 325–26.

61 See for instance s. 13(1) of the High Court Law, Laws of Bendel, 1976, applicable in Edo State.

62 Evidence Act, 2011, s. 18(2); Federal Capital Territory Customary Court Act, 2007, s. 16(a). Section 17(e) of the Supreme Court Act, 1960, Cap S 15, LFN 2004, provides that "the Supreme Court shall observe and enforce the observance of customary law to the same extent as such law is observed and enforced in the Nigerian courts".

63 Nwauche, "Customary Law Arbitration," 62–65.

64 *Eugene Nnaekwe Egesimba v Ezekiel Onuzuruike* [2002] 15 NWLR (Pt. 791) 466 SC (hereafter *Egesimba v Onuzuruike*).

> Customary arbitration by elders of the community is one of many African customary modes of settling disputes and once it satisfies the necessary requirements indicated above as in the case, its decision shall have a binding effect, and has the same authority as the judgment of a judicial body having binding effect on the parties and thus create an estoppel.[65]

Customary arbitration is thus a form of a private traditional arrangement, regulated by the custom of the parties or any custom agreed by the parties, whereby they submit their dispute to a customary arbitration panel selected by them to adjudicate on the dispute, with an underlying understanding that the parties will abide by the final award issued by the arbiter(s).

In addition to the adjudicatory type of customary arbitration, a second type of customary law arbitration devoid of adjudicatory procedure recognised by Nigerian courts exists and is known as the customary law arbitration of oath-taking.[66] This method of customary law is more common among the Igbos of Eastern Nigeria than among other tribes in Nigeria.[67] According to Oba, the commonest form of this type of customary arbitration involves swearing on a dreaded Juju by the swearer, who invokes on himself a conditional curse to be punished by the juju if he lies. It is believed that if the swearer lied, he would be smitten within a specified period of taking the oath, and he is therefore considered the loser. However, if he survives he is considered the winning party.[68] It follows that where the parties to a dispute in accordance with relevant customary law decide to be bound by customary law arbitration resulting in oath-taking and the oath is accordingly administered, the principles of any other law (including state laws) in respect of the subject matter of the dispute will no longer apply and parties are not allowed to rescind or renege from the same once the oath has been taken in line with the agreement of parties.[69] In such a situation, the applicable law is as set forth by the applicable customary rule relating to the oath-taking. However, the parties must be shown to believe in the efficacy of a juju which resulted in the oath-taking to settle the dispute.[70]

---

65 *Egesimba v Onuzuruike*, 513.
66 *Umeadi v Chibunze* [2020] NWLR (Pt. 1733) 405 (hereafter *Umeadi v Chibunze*).
67 Oba, "Juju Oaths in Customary Law," 139.
68 Oba, "Juju Oaths in Customary Law," 141.
69 *Onyenge v Ebere* [2004] 13 NWLR (Pt. 889) 20 (hereafter *Onyenge v Ebere*).
70 *Ume v Okoronkwo* (1996) 12 SCNJ 404.

4 History of Customary Law Arbitration

In relating every existing phenomenon to the primordial time, King Solomon declared that "What has been will be again, and what has been done will be done again; and there is nothing new under the sun."[71] Records show that arbitration's primordial origin predates most human civilizations and that the practice cuts across virtually every clime. Recounting Nigeria's experience Tobi JSC observed

> that before the British brought their system of administration of justice we had our traditional system that worked. It worked and still works better for the indigenes because it is faster and cheaper and they understand it, not being bogged down by the unnecessary and avoidable technicalities that beset the English.[72]

4.1 *Pre-colonial Nigeria*

Historically, the use of arbitration in Nigeria predates its colonial experience. Parties to such matters in the interest of pacific resolution would often refer the dispute to third parties for resolution.[73] The panels were usually made up of family heads, elders, leaders of communities or rulers, sometimes with the ruling chiefs or elders' council in attendance and advising.[74] In northern Nigeria where Islamic law was the predominant source of law,[75] Islamic arbitration known as *Tahkim* was in practice long before the arrival of colonists.[76] The Holy Quran, which contains the precepts of the Islamic religion, encourages the use of *Tahkim* in the settlement of disputes.[77] For instance, the Quran states that "If two parties among the believers fall into quarrel make you peace between them … make peace with justice and be fair for God loves those who are fair (and just)."[78] In matrimonial matters the couple is enjoined to exhaust all available internal aid in resolving a dispute. Where that fails they may employ arbitration. The Holy Quran states that "… if you fear a split between the two of them, then appoint an arbiter from his relatives and an arbiter from

71 Ecclesiastes 1:9, *The Holy Bible* (New International Version, 2011).

72 *Onyenge v Ebere*, 42.

73 Akpata, *Nigeria Arbitration Law*, 1–2.

74 Igbokwe, "Law and Practice of Customary Arbitration," 201–02.

75 Oba, "Islamic Law as Customary Law," 818.

76 Ladapo, "Where does Islamic Arbitration Fit," 123–24.

77 Verses 59 and 128 *Sura Nisa* (*Women*); Verse 9 *Sura AlHujurat* (*The Chambers*). Also see El-Ahdab, *Arbitration with the Arab Countries*, 16.

78 Quran 4 verse 35.

her relatives. If they desire reconciliation, Allah shall reconcile them".[79] In non-Muslim communities in the north (particularly around the middle belt area) where the Islamic law system of arbitration was not practised, the community or district or family heads played the role of arbitrators in accordance with the prevailing customs. In the southern part of Nigeria the mode of arbitration varied from one community to another.[80] As part of the common features and subject to the parties' choice and the subject matter, the arbitrators were either family heads or elders of the community or chiefs,[81] subject to whether the society was cephalous (had a central authority) or an acephalous (egalitarian; controlled through collective leadership).[82]

Whether in the north or south the system was supported by the various indigenous laws and the procedures at the forums were similar to modern arbitration procedures; particularly in terms of parties' autonomy, freedom to submit or not to submit to the jurisdiction of the arbitration panel, and freedom to select the forum to submit their dispute to, and the binding nature of the outcome.[83] Commenting on the pre-colonial type of dispute resolution in West Africa, Webster and Bouhen observe that

> Quarrels between individual of different families in the ward were settled before the people in the ward, elders acting as arbiter. Quarrels between wards come before the full assembly ... A man might attempt to settle with the individual who had aggrieved him, if this failed he could ask respectable elders to intervene or call members of the family together, he could also ask the ward or village head to solve the case.[84]

The system was characterised by a simple and fast but informal process known to the parties, and the resolution of conflict rather than the passing of judgment was the main aim of the process. Explaining the pre-colonial origin of customary law arbitration in Nigeria, Ezediaro described customary arbitration as follows:

> as a method of settling dispute [it] is a tradition of long standing in Nigeria. Referral of a dispute to one or more laymen for decision has

79 Quran 49:35.
80 Oluduro, "Customary Arbitration," 312–15.
81 Elias, *Nature of African Customary Law*, 212.
82 Oluduro, "Customary Arbitration," 314.
83 Elias, *Nature of African Customary Law*, 212.
84 Webster and Boahen, *Revolutionary Years*, 102–03.

deep roots in the customary law of many Nigerian communities. Such a method of dispute resolution was the only reasonable one, for the wise men or the chiefs who were the only accessible judicial authorities. This tradition still persists in certain villages and communities, despite the centralized legal system and the attendant efforts at modernizing and reform of legal system.[85]

4.2 *Colonial Period*

The advent of colonial rule in Nigeria ushered in new laws and a new justice delivery system alien to the indigenous people. The colonial authorities did not adopt most of the pre-existing adjudicatory structure but introduced theirs.[86] English laws which were in force in England on 1st January 1863 were introduced into Lagos Colony by Ordinance 3 of 1863 with effect from March 4th 1863 while the Supreme Court Ordinance 11, of April 9th 1863, provided for the administration of justice in the colony. The new justice delivery institutions dealt with civil disputes between Europeans (merchants and settlers) on the one hand and between Europeans and Africans on the other hand.[87] The other lower courts were introduced to try lesser crimes and misdemeanours.[88] A Supreme Court was established to administer English Common Law and the doctrine of Equity, pre-1863 Statutes of General application in England,[89] later pre-1874 Statutes of General application in England[90] and pre-1900 Statutes of General application in England. As mentioned earlier, subject to the repugnancy rule the colonial government allowed pre-existing indigenous laws to exist side by side with the new state laws in areas of personal law. This development marked the beginning of combative and competitive legal pluralism in Nigeria (the rivalry between "state law" and indigenous laws). The application of the repugnancy rule by the new English courts resulted in some pre-existing customary law dispute resolution forums being either declared illegal or their decisions not being accorded the required judicial recognition, or being refused the aid of public coercive instruments to enforce them.[91] And

---

85 Ezediaro, "Guarantee and Incentives," 775.
86 Diala, "A Butterfly that Thinks Itself a Bird," 384.
87 Obilade, *Nigerian Legal System*, 17–52.
88 Obilade, *The Nigerian Legal System*, 18.
89 Ibid. See Application of English Law to the Settlement of Lagos, Ordinance 3 of 1863; the Supreme Court Ordinance 11 of 1863.
90 The Supreme Court Ordinance 11 of 1876.
91 *Nnaji and Ors v Inspector General of Police* (1957) 2 FSC 18.

in few instances where such decisions were recognised, they must first have been subjected to the rigours of the notorious validity test.

4.3 *Post-Independence*

Contrary to the constitutionally entrenched plural order, the era immediately preceding Nigerian independence witnessed attempts by the state justice sector (in the face of existential threats from non-state justice actors) to monopolise the justice system, increase its acceptability, legitimise its authority and consolidate its effectiveness relative to the pre-existing non-state justice system. To this end, the state justice sector continued in its colonial-era posture of combative interpretation and unwittingly adopted repression strategies[92] to undermine and eliminate non-state justice actors such as customary law arbitration and others.[93] Despite the subtle resentment, hostility and the near non-recognition of customary law arbitration awards by the English-styled courts, customary law arbitration survived. It survived simply because Nigerians, particularly rural people, traders, artisans and other key actors in the informal sector continued to submit their civil disputes to the forum.[94] The rationale for this choice was not farfetched. The practice was developed by the people, rooted in their history, and culture, and formed part of the indigenous justice system.[95] Holdsworth's explanation of a similar attitude on the part of the English fits the Nigerian context perfectly well. He explains that

> the practice of arbitration, therefore, comes so to speak, naturally to primitive bodies of law, and after Courts have been established by the State and a recourse to them has become the natural method of settling disputes, the practice continues because the parties to a dispute want to settle them with less formality and expense than is involved in a recourse to court.[96]

To date, only an infinitesimal proportion of the total volume of disputes in Nigeria is referred to the regular courts and other Western-styled dispute resolution forums. The majority of the people still patronise the indigenous forums.[97] Basically, "custom-based systems … have the advantages of sustainability and

92 For further understanding of the repression strategies, see Swenson, "Legal Pluralism," 438–62.

93 *Okpuruwu v Okponkan* [1988] 4 NWLR (Pt. 90) 554 (hereafter *Okpuruwu v Okponkan*).

94 Oluduro, "Customary Arbitration," 313.

95 Ajayi, "Interaction of English Law," 47–48.

96 Holdsworth, *Holdsworth's History of English Law*, 187.

97 Albrecht and Kyed, "Justice and Security," 1.

legitimacy".[98] On the other hand, the referral of disputes to the regular courts or other western dispute resolution forums is generally frowned upon and in most cases is considered as taboo or an inappropriate response to conflict situations. To date, subject to the parties' agreement, most disputes are still resolved at the level of the family, the village, the clan, the tribe, and the market traders or artisans guild.[99] In other words, in the search for pacific resolution most Nigerians deliberately opt for customary law arbitration.

5 Developing Parameters for Binding Customary Arbitration

Generally, one major snag in the use of arbitration (whether state or customary law regulated) is that the process lacks coercive power to compel obedience to its orders. Consequently, where exigency dictates that an arbitral award be coercively enforced or set aside, the only option open to parties is to engage the aid of the regular courts.[100] The controversy over what constitutes valid customary law arbitration has elicited much debate in the legal literature.[101] The answer to this controversy becomes very important, because, where a customary law arbitration award is adjudged valid, the award will have the same force as the judgment of a regular court, being binding on the parties and creating estoppel.[102] The process requires the party relying on the award to prove the validity of the customary arbitration.[103] Incidentally, the process

98 UNDP, UNICEF and UN Women, *Informal Justice Systems*, 19.

99 Ezediaro, "Guarantee and Incentives," 775.

100 Whytock, "Domestic Courts," 112–14.

101 See Allott, *Essays in African Law*, 126; Igbokwe, "Law and Practice of Customary Arbitration," along with a host of others.

102 *Umeadi v Chibunze*; *Okala v Udah* [2019] 9 NWLR (Pt. 1678) 562 (hereafter *Okala v Udah*); *Nruamah v Ebuzoeme* [2013] 13 NWLR (Pt. 1372) 474; *Agala v Okosin* [2010] 10 NWLR (Pt. 1202) 412; *Okoye v Obiaso* [2010] 8 NWLR (Pt. 1195) 145; *Okereke v Nwankwo* [2003] 9 NWLR (Pt. 826) 592; *Egesimba v Onuzuruike*; *Odonigi v Oyeleke* [2001] 6 NWLR (Pt. 708) 12; *Eke v Okwaranyia* [2001] 12 NWLR (Pt. 726) 181; *Uzoewulu v Ezeaka* [2000] 14 NWLR (Pt. 688) 679; *Obioha v Akukwe* [2000] 5 NWLR (Pt. 658) 699; *Oparaji v Ohanu* [1999] 9 NWLR (Pt. 618) 290 (hereafter *Oparaji v Ohanu*); *Ume v Okoronkwo* [1996] 10 NWLR (Pt. 477) 133; *Akpan v Otong* [1996] 10 NWLR (Pt. 476) 108; *Anyabunsi v Ugwunze* [1995] 6 NWLR (Pt. 401) 255; *Igwego v Ezeugo* [1992] 6 NWLR (Pt. 249) 561 (hereafter *Igwego v Ezeugo*); *Awosile v Sotumbo* [1992] 5 NWLR (Pt. 243) 514 (hereafter *Awosile v Sotumbo*); *Ohiaeri v Akabeze* [1992] 2 NWLR (Pt. 221) 1 (hereafter *Ohiaeri v Akabeze*); *Agu v Ikewibe*, 385; and others.

103 See *Oparaji v Ogidereji* (1999) 70 LRCN 1822; *Idika and Ors v Erisi and Ors* (1988) NSCC 977, 986; [1988] 2 NWLR (Pt. 78) 563; *Mogo Chikwendu v Mbamali and Anor* (1980) 3/4 SC 31, 48; *Joseph Larbi and Anor v Opanin Kwasi and Anor* (1950) 13 WACA 81; *Ahiwe Okere and Ors v Marcus Nwoke and Ors* [1991] 8 NWLR (Pt. 209) 317.

represents one of the dynamics in the chains of interaction between state law and customary normative order that is usually engaged in by the courts to filter, modify, adapt and harmonise the customary law in issue (the arbitration outcome) with the core value of state law. The observation of Paul J. in *Ashogbon v Oduntan*[104] gives credence to this view:

> I regard this court in its equity jurisdiction as in some measure by virtue of the jurisdiction sections of the Supreme Court Ordinance 'the keeper of the conscience' of native communities in regard to the absolute enforcement of alleged native customs.

This statement affirms that the courts do sometimes modify and reshape the rules of customary law in the course of interpreting and applying it. It also amplifies the pivotal dominance of state law over customary law.

A classic example of the court's embarking on modifying customary law may be found in *Agu v Ikewibe*.[105] Operating from the standpoint of the keepers of the conscience of customary law and without strict reference to the particular custom in issue in the case, the Supreme Court developed the indices which are now uniformly applied to all indigenous law-regulated arbitration. Deducible from the decision is that a customary arbitration award would be considered binding by the court if it is proven that:

a) the parties voluntarily submitted the dispute to the customary arbitration;
b) the submission was to a person or persons traditionally recognised as having judicial authority by the custom of the parties;
c) the parties indicated before submission their willingness to be bound by the decision of the customary arbitration or freedom to reject the decision where not satisfied;
d) the arbitration was conducted in line with the custom of the parties;
e) none of the parties withdrew from the arbitration before the publication of the award by the arbitration panel;
f) the arbitration award was published;
g) the arbitration award was accepted by the parties and neither of the parties has resiled from the decisions so pronounced.

104 *Ashogbon v Oduntan* (1935) 12 NLR 7, 10.
105 [1991] 3 NWLR (Pt. 180) 385.

In developing these ingredients the Supreme Court placed reliance on a number of cases from other jurisdictions decided by the West African Court of Appeal and the Privy Council (both presided over by Englishmen).[106] The court also placed reliance on a statement credited to Elias[107] to hold that parties can resile from customary arbitration after the award has been published. Oba argues and rightly so that Elias was inadvertently misquoted in the said passage.[108] The statement in issue was a query and not a conclusion. The Court cited the passage thus:

> [R]eferring a dispute to the family head or an elder of the community for a compromise solution based upon subsequent acceptance by both parties of the suggested award, which becomes binding only after such signification of its acceptance and from which either party is free to resile at any stage of the proceedings up to that point.[109]

In the above quotation, the court ended the passage with a full stop instead of a question mark. Through this inadvertent replacement, the court came to a conclusion different from that reached by Elias, which is "it seems also that neither party can lawfully resile after the award has been made".[110]

Different rules appear applicable to customary arbitration of oath-taking. A decade after *Agu's case*, the Supreme Court in *Umeano Achiakpa v Nduka*[111] enumerated some peculiar conditions for the valid customary arbitration of oath-taking. In the words of the court, it must be established that

> the party who swore the juju implicitly irretrievably and religiously believed in the excruciating and definitive potency and finality of the juju, and that, in addition, once the Oath is taken the Party taking the Oath had no means of thwarting or placating its Wrath – were the party to have deliberately and misleadingly sworn falsely on the Oath.[112]

106 *Assampong v Mensah* (1932) 1 WACA 192; *Kwasi v Larbi* (1952) 13 WACA 76 (*Kwasi v Larbi*); *Mensah v Takyiampong* 6 WACA 118.

107 Elias, *Nature of African Customary Law*, 212.

108 Oba, "Juju Oaths in Customary Law," 143.

109 *Agu v Ikewibe*, 414.

110 Elias, *Nature of African Customary Law*, 213.

111 *Umeano Achiakpa v Nduka* [2001] 14 NWLR (Pt. 734) 623 (hereafter *Achiakpa v Nduka*).

112 *Achiakpa v Nduka*, 649.

In addition, the "… form, nature and effect of the Oath must be strictly proved and the records must show that the Oath refers unequivocally to the subject matter of the Oath".[113] This remained the situation until three years later when another panel of the Supreme Court in *Onyenge v Ebere*[114] adopted a more egalitarian approach devoid of the usual perception of customary law through the prism of common law. After reaffirming that customary arbitration of oath-taking is recognised in Nigerian jurisprudence, Nike Tobi JSC posited that "I think it is good law that in arbitration under customary law, the applicable law is customary law and not common law principles with their characteristic certainty and ossification."[115]

A perusal of law reports from the penultimate and apex courts reveals that the preponderance of customary arbitration cases originated from south-East Nigeria; with an infinitesimal fraction coming from the Middle-belt states and other parts of Nigeria. Whether or not the appellate courts will apply the stringent conditions developed in *Agu's case* to Islamic arbitration when the opportunity presents itself is uncertain. However, worthy of note in this regard is the conclusion reached by Ladapo that "only three out of the seven identified judicially recognised ingredients of customary arbitration are in tandem with the practices and procedures of Tahkim – Islamic customary arbitration of the Maliki School's interpretation".[116]

In defence of the courts' position, Uwaifo JSC in *Eke v Okwaranyia*[117] relying on the dictum of Akpata JSC[118] in *Ohiaeri v Akabeze*, insisted that the courts needed to be circumspect in granting recognition to customary law arbitration, because in his words

> It is a common feature of customary arbitration in a closely-knit community that some of the arbitrators if not all, not only have prior knowledge of the facts of the dispute, but also have their prejudices and varying interests in the matter, and are therefore sometimes judges in their own cause and are likely to pre-judge the issue. Prior knowledge and pre-judging issues are more pronounced in land disputes having bearing with the founding of the village and how families migrated to the village and come to occupy parcels of land. The arbitrators are well informed on

113 Ibid.
114 *Onyenge v Ebere*, 20.
115 *Onyenge v Ebere*, 41.
116 Ladapo, "Where does Islamic Arbitration Fit," 125.
117 *Eke v Okwaranyia* (2001) 86 LRCN 1403, 1428–29.
118 *Ohiaeri v Akabeze*.

> these matters. The position however is that traditional history is sometimes transmitted, received or construed with a slant by the person using it for a purpose. Hence it is essential before applying the decision of a customary arbitration as an estoppel for the court to ensure that parties had voluntarily submitted to the arbitration, consciously indicated their wilingness to be bound by the decision and had immediately after the pronouncement of the decision unequivocally accepted the award.[119]

While some of these fears may appear reasonable, the paranoid preoccupation of the courts along with the resulting guidelines do not in themselves guarantee just outcomes or validate the powers of the court to rewrite, amend, modify or make customary law.

6 Effect of *Stare Decisis* on Customary Arbitration

Flowing from the decision in *Agu v Ikewibe*,[120] a party who wishes to rely on a customary law arbitration award in addition to proving its existence is required to plead and prove to the satisfaction of the court that (a) the parties voluntarily submitted the matter in dispute for resolution, (b) the parties agreed either expressly or by implication that the decision of the arbitration would be accepted as final and binding, (c) the arbitration was conducted in line with the custom of the parties, (d) the arbitrators reached a decision and published an award, and (e) the decision or award was accepted at the time it was published.[121]

In line with the common law doctrine of *stare decisis* (a doctrine underlying the Nigerian judicial system),[122] lower courts are bound by the theory of judicial precedent to follow the decisions of superior courts.[123] Thus, all other

119 *Ohiaeri v Akabeze*, 24.

120 *Agu v Ikewibe*, 407.

121 *Okoye and Anor v Obiaso and Ors* (2010) 186 LRCN 181, 185. See also *Igwego v Ezeugo*; *Anyabunsi v Ugwunze* [1995] 6 NWLR (Pt. 401) 255; *Egesimba v Onuzuruike*; and *Eke v Okwaranyia* (2001) 86 LRCN 1403, 1428–29.

122 *Olagbemiro v Ajagunbade III* [1990] 3 NWLR (Pt. 136) 37.

123 Also known as judicial precedent; a basic principle of the law which states that once a decision (a precedent) on a certain set of facts has been made, other courts of concurrent jurisdiction or lower jurisdiction must apply that decision in cases presenting the same set of facts. Thus, the decision of a superior court forms a precedent and becomes binding and must be followed by courts of like or lower jurisdiction. See *Ibrahim v APC (No. 2)* [2019] 8 NWLR (Pt. 1674) 269; *Aghedo v Adenomo* [2018] 13 NWLR (Pt. 1636) 264; *Amaechi v INEC* [2008] 5 NWLR (Pt. 1080) 227; *Adetoun Oladeji (Nig.) Ltd v Nigerian Breweries* [2007]

courts in the country are required scrupulously to endorse and apply the position of the Supreme Court on every issue, unless the Supreme Court is yet to pronounce on same. Consequently, the superior courts generally frown on a departure by a lower court from the reasoning of a superior court. A refusal by a lower court to be bound by the decision of the superior courts is considered gross insubordination.[124] In *Integrated Realty Ltd. v Odofin*[125] Augie JSC reiterated the obligation of all subordinate courts to adhere to the doctrine. He explains that

> Where from the facts of a case, the principle of law stated by the Supreme Court is applicable, it is unconstitutional, unlawful and a violation of the principle of *stare decisis* for a subordinate court to make rules or conditions for the application of that principle of law.[126]

Accordingly, the parameters developed by the apex court with regard to the validity of customary arbitration awards represent the position of the law on the issue. The lower courts are obliged by the doctrine of *stare decisis* to apply it willy-nilly irrespective of whether or not the lower court considers the view to be the correct position on the issue.[127] Recently, in *Iwu v Ogu*[128] the Court of Appeal had no option but to follow the position of the Supreme Court when it held that a party to customary arbitration may withdraw from the process even after the award has been published. Consequently, lower courts lack the discretion "to add to, modify, qualify or make additional rules"[129] on the parameters of binding customary arbitration. Should the unimaginable happen, the decision of the lower court would be adjudged to be unconstitutional, unlawful and a violation of the principle of *stare decisis*. In line with the doctrine, in *Okala v Udah*, the Supreme Court upheld the decisions of the two lower courts (the High Court and Court of Appeal) because according to the Supreme Court,

---

5 NWLR (Pt. 1027) 415; *Chief of Air Staff v Iyen* [2005] 6 NWLR (Pt. 922) 496; *Idoniboye-Obu v NNPC* [2003] 2 NWLR (Pt. 805) 589.

124 *Bashir Mohammed Dalhatu v Ibrahim Saminu Turaki* [2003] 7 SC 1.

125 *Integrated Realty Ltd v Odofin* [2018] 3 NWLR (Pt. 1606) 301 (hereafter *Integrated Realty v Odofin*).

126 *Integrated Realty v Odofin*, 317.

127 *Ibrahim v APC (No. 2)* [2019] 16 NWLR (Pt. 1699) 469.

128 *Iwu v Ogu* [2020] 9 NWLR (Pt. 1730) 608.

129 See *Dalhatu v Turaki and Ors* [2003] 15 NWLR (Pt. 843) 310; *Olufeagba v Abdur-Raheem* [2009] 18 NWLR (Pt. 1173) 384, 442–44.

"All ... five ingredients presented themselves which impelled the lower court to enforce the customary arbitration".[130]

One of the effects of the application of the doctrine of *stare decisis* to any particular issue of customary law is to petrify the development of that aspect of customary law by establishing a rigid set of common law principles on the issue. Instead, it should be noted that customary law is not a frozen or rigid system of law as it develops from time to time, accommodating the changes in the prevailing social conditions. This core quality of Nigerian customary law was given judicial recognition by Osborn C.J. in *Lewis v Bankole*[131] when he said:

> One of the most striking features of West African native custom ... is its flexibility; it appears to have been always subject to motives of expediency, and it shows unquestionable adaptability to altered circumstances without entirely losing its character.[132]

Thus, the effect of the Supreme Court's parameters, reinforced by the application of the doctrine of *stare decisis cum* judicial notice is the petrification of the organic quality of customary law arbitration.

Closely connected to the stultifying effect of the application of the principle of *stare decisis* to customary law arbitration is the threat posed by some commentators who aver from the theoretical proposition of the legal realists (that the true content or scope of the law is determined by the interpretation given by the court in real situations)[133] that customary arbitration is a valid form of arbitration because the court says it is. The conclusion from this supposedly realistic perspective is that the set of rules developed by the court for testing the validity of a customary law arbitration award[134] represents the current state of the customary law regulating customary arbitration and not the custom of the people.

130 *Okala v Udah*, 581. Also see Ikeyi and Maduka, "Binding Effect of a Customary Arbitration Award," 334–49, who on the contrary argue that the current predominant indication from the Supreme Court is that post-award consent is not necessary to establish a binding customary arbitration award in Nigeria.

131 *Lewis v Bankole* (1909) 1 NLR 81 (hereafter *Lewis v Bankole*).

132 *Lewis v Bankole*, 100–01.

133 Holmes, "Path of Law," 461.

134 Igbokwe, "Law and Practice of Customary Arbitration," 213–14.

7 Critique of the Uniform Set of Parameters Defining Customary Law Arbitration

Surprisingly, despite an avalanche of disapproval of these judge-made customary law rules in legal literature,[135] the Supreme Court continues to endorse them as constituting the basic tool for measuring the validity of customary law arbitration awards. Recently, in *Okala v Udah*,[136] the Supreme Court reiterated "[A]nything short of these conditions will make any customary arbitration award risky to enforce. In other words, unless the conditions are fulfilled, a customary arbitration award is unenforceable."[137] This position has far-reaching implications for the future of customary law arbitration in Nigeria.

The universal application of the set of parameters developed by the court in regard to all customs in Nigeria, as though Nigerian customs were homogenous, is tantamount to judicial dictatorship and a denial of the core quality of customary law, which is that its validity derives from the assent of the people. Another criticism of the uniform set of parameters developed by the Supreme Court is that lawmaking is inconsistent with the constitutional functions of the courts and therefore *ultra vires* the powers of courts.[138] Juxtaposed with the court's constitutional functions, its power is limited to recognising the existence of any custom that has been proven to exist through evidence or has been judicially noticed, to apply the same as binding or to reject the same on grounds of repugnancy. Thus, the power of the courts is limited to observing and enforcing the observance of customs or rejecting them where the custom is contrary to public policy or is not in accordance with the rules of natural justice, equity and good conscience.[139] Under the CFRN, courts lack the power to modify or adjust any customary law. The act of developing universal ingredients for binding customary arbitration is contrary to the well-settled principle of law that the court in the discharge of its interpretative function should avoid judicial legislation.[140] In *FBN Plc v Maiwada*[141] the same Supreme Court observed that

135 Oluduro, "Customary Arbitration," 322–26. Also see Amucheazi, "Validity of Customary Law Arbitration," 515.

136 *Okala v Udah*.

137 *Okala v Udah*, 580–81.

138 Evidence Act, 2011, ss 16–19.

139 Evidence Act, 2011, s. 18(3); also see the dictum of Lord Atkin in *Eleko v Government of Nigeria* [1931] AC 662 (hereafter *Eleko v Government*), 678, where his lordship held that courts cannot transform customs.

140 *Olowu and 3 Ors v Abolore and Anor* (1993) 6 SCNJ (Pt. 1) 1, 19–20.

141 *FNB Plc v Maiwada* [2013] 6 NWLR (Pt. 1348) 444 (hereafter *FNB Plc v Maiwada*).

> judge should be firm and pungent in the interpretation of the law but such should be short of a judge being a legislator. This is because, it is the duty of the legislature to make the law and it is the assigned duty of the judge to interpret the law as it is, not as it ought to be. That will be flouting the rule of division of labour as set out by the 1999 Constitution.[142]

Assuming that some customs conform with the parameters laid down by the Supreme Court, it would still be inappropriate to apply them as universal customary rules to all customary arbitration in Nigeria without first proving in line with statutory requirements that the indices as enunciated by the court apply to the particular customary arbitration in issue. This is so because no customary law in Nigeria has universal application and applies throughout the country. Consequently, each case must be treated separately and the validity determined on the basis of the requirements of the particular customary law in issue.

Agreed that there may be some common features, yet this does not dispense with the statutory requirement that each custom determines the scope and content of its procedural and substantive law. Consequently, where a particular customary arbitration is governed by a valid customary law, the court-formulated parameters ought to be jettisoned. It is a truism that every custom has rules regulating its customary arbitration and that the rules are known to the people.

Among the core issues calling for review in the parameters developed by the court are the requirements of (i) the post-award consent of the parties and (ii) that customary arbitration must be conducted by a traditionally recognised institution for dispute resolution.

7.1 *Post-Award Consent Requirement*

The most controversial aspect of the judicial formulation of parameters for assessing the validity of a customary law arbitration award is the assertion that customary arbitration is binding only if none of the parties reject the award after it is made. Scrutiny of legal literature and previous judicial authorities reveals that the trajectory of the notorious post-award consent laid down in *Agu v Ikewibe* is alien to virtually all known customary laws in Nigeria. Contrary to the notorious post-award consent requirement, among the underlying attractions in submitting disputes to arbitration are the finality of the award and the sanctity of the contract to arbitrate. As a general rule, the courts would

142 *FNB Plc v Maiwada*, 484.

not allow a party who voluntarily submits to arbitration to subsequently resile from the process or the decision reached. Thus, where parties to a dispute voluntarily submit the dispute to arbitration, the decision of such arbitration would be accepted as final and binding on them and it is not open to either party to subsequently back out of the agreement or renege from being bound by the final award of the arbitration panel.[143]

Similarly, there is no customary law in Nigeria that allows a party who voluntarily submits to customary arbitration to subsequently resile from the decision reached.[144] The rule regulating customary arbitration varies from one community to another; each tribe or community has a unique form of customary arbitration, which is well suited to their local circumstances.[145] The law is that where two parties to a dispute voluntarily submit the issue in controversy between them to arbitration according to customary law and agree expressly or by implication that the decision of such arbitration will be accepted as final and binding, then once the arbitrator(s) reach a decision it will no longer be open to either party to subsequently back out of or resile from the decision so pronounced.[146] If a contrary custom exists, in line with the repugnancy doctrine it is incumbent on the court to hold that it is repugnant to good sense and equity. Consequently, courts should in line with good sense and equity refuse the losing party the right to reject the decision of the arbitration to which he voluntarily submitted.[147] The correct position is that submission to customary arbitration is irrevocable. Historically, this was the position in the early days of regular courts in Nigeria. Betuel P.J., in *George Onwusike v Patrick Onwusike*[148] observed that

> The decisions given by the elders, authorized by custom to settle such disputes, and exercising their customary functions, as a result of the submission of the parties to their jurisdiction, unless clearly wrong in principle, is binding on them ... I apprehend that it would be contrary to common sense to allow persons who have voluntarily submitted their dispute to an independent body of their own choosing to render nugatory

143 *Okala v Udah*, 576–77.

144 *Oparaji v Ohanu*, 309.

145 Akanbi, Abdulrauf and Daibu, "Customary Arbitration," 199, 205.

146 *Kwasi v Larbi*; *Oline v Obodo and Ors* (1958) SCNLR 298; *Philip Njoku v Felix Ekeocha* (1972) 2 ECSLR 199; *Eguere Inyang v Simon Essien* (1957) 2 FSC 39 (hereafter *Inyang v Essien*) 1.

147 See *Agu v Ikewibe*, 385.

148 *George Onwusike v Patrick Onwusike* (1926) 6 Eastern Nigerian Law Report 10 (hereafter *Onwusike v Onwusike*).

> the decision arrived at, merely because it does not favour the interest they assert or in some other way is regarded by them as unsatisfactory.[149]

As far back as in 1958 the Federal Supreme Court of Nigeria in *Oline v Obodo*[150] rejected the contention that customary arbitration was merely a form of settlement that allows a party to withdraw at any stage. The court found that

> where parties submitted their dispute for settlement by arbitration in accordance with Native Customary Law and one party withdrew from the arbitration before it was completed, the award of the arbitration was nevertheless binding on all the parties. In the present case, there is a finding of fact against the appellants that they attended the arbitration and that they agreed to be bound by the award of the arbitrator.[151]

The Supreme Court maintained this salutary position[152] until 1992 when *Agu's case* introduced the controversial requirement of the non-withdrawal of a party mid-stream or immediately after the award is issued. Soon after *Agu's case*, in a welcome effort to obliterate the obnoxious requirement, the Supreme Court in *Awosile v Sotunbo*,[153] in an *obiter dictum*, attempted to exclude the requirement by reducing the indices to four. These are: 1) voluntary submission to arbitration by the parties; 2) implied or express agreement to be bound by the decision of the arbitrators; 3) conduct of the arbitration under a particular customary law, and; 4) publication of a final award. Another gallant attempt was made by the court in *Igwego v Ezeugo*.[154] In unequivocal terms the court upgraded its earlier *obiter dictum* in the *Sotunbo case* to *ratio decidendi*. This was the enviable position of customary law arbitration until the Supreme Court once again reintroduced post-award consent as one of the parameters for measuring the validity of a customary arbitration award in *Eke v Okwaranyia*.[155] This remains the position to date.

While conceding that a party to customary arbitration possesses an inherent constitutional right to set aside an arbitral award which is not in harmony with the relevant customary law, it would amount to a negation of the

149 *Onwusike v Onwusike*, 14.
150 *Oline v Obodo* [1958] 3 FSC 84 (hereafter *Oline v Obodo*).
151 *Oline v Obodo*, 86.
152 *Ohiaeri v Akabueze*.
153 *Awosile v Sotunbo*.
154 *Igwego v Ezeugo*.
155 *Eke v Okwaranyia* (2001) 86 LRCN 1403.

underlying principles of customary arbitration to allow one of the parties to unilaterally withdraw from the process after the final award is pronounced. It is patently obvious that the courts are erroneously viewing customary arbitration through the lens of Western non-adjudicatory settlement mechanisms such as conciliation.[156] Consequently, it must be concluded that the court has failed to appreciate that customary arbitration is not conterminous with conciliation or negotiation for settlement or other non-adjudicatory peaceful resolution modes. It is the failure of the courts to see the dividing line between these different modes of private dispute resolution that has resulted in the present state of uncertainty. In practice, under most customary law a party has no power to reject the award of the customary arbitration; unless there is credible evidence showing that the particular custom permits such conduct. As mentioned before, in pre-colonial Africa coercive sanctions (in the form of ostracism) were usually attached to a failure to abide by the outcome of a customary arbitration process. The sanctions would be suspended only where there is an appeal to a high tribunal. The removal of the finality of customary award by the addition of the right to resile at any stage, even after the award has been published, is tantamount to the removal of the fundamental architecture underpinning customary arbitration.

7.2 *Conduct of Customary Arbitration under Customary Law*

Another nagging controversy arising from the parameters developed through case law is the requirement that the arbitration must have been conducted in line with the custom of the parties to the arbitration. This has led to an artificial dichotomy between arbitrations conducted by a traditionally recognised panel with a judicial function and those conducted by a panel without a traditional judicial function. Most Nigerians – particularly rural dwellers, traders and artisans – still submit their disputes to private arbitration. In most of these instances, the disputes are submitted to persons who are not chiefs, elders or traditionally recognised institutions for dispute resolution. A perusal of the cases reveals two types of arbitration purporting to be customary law arbitration. The first type consists of arbitration conducted by traditional institutions such as chiefs and elders considered as possessing customary power to resolve disputes. For instance, in *Ohiaeri v Akabeze*[157] the customary arbitration was conducted by a traditional ruler and his cabinet; in *Agu v Ikewibe* it was the chief and the elders of the town. The second type involves arbitration

156 Arbitration and Conciliation Act, 1988, s. 42.

157 *Ohiaeri v Akabeze* (1992) 7 LRCN 163.

conducted by persons who possess no traditional authority recognised by customary law. Such was the case in *Iyang v Essien*,[158] where councillors of a District Council acted as arbitrators. In *Okere v Nwoke*[159] Parents/Teachers Association body played the role of arbitrators. Uwaifo JCA in *Okpuruwu v Okponkan*, referring to this type of arbitration, noted that

> it may be that in practical life when there is any dispute in any community the parties involved may sometimes decide to refer it to a third disinterested party for settlement ... Admittedly, there can be arbitration in a loose sense of the word here in Nigeria quite apart from that recognised under various statutes.[160]

An excursion into the cases establishes that courts are dogmatically adhering to the line suggested in *Inyang v Essien*,[161] where the persons who acted as arbitrators under customary arbitration were not traditionally recognised justice actors, but councillors of a District Council. The court held that the panel had no authority to make a binding order.[162] Earlier, invoking the parameters listed in the *Agu case* and subsequent decisions, Nwangwu believed that the distinction between chiefs and elders on the one hand and other persons who conduct customary arbitration is that the former have recognised judicial function.[163] In his opinion, the actions of those who are not chiefs or elders can at best be described as peace settlement or conciliation.[164] It is difficult to agree with this reasoning because what is referred to as peace settlement or conciliation is known to customary law as arbitration. Customary law allows the parties to choose the forum to submit their dispute to. This is a common practice in Nigeria, one that can be regarded as a uniform custom and common law of Nigeria.

---

158 *Iyang v Essien* (1957) 2 FSC 39.

159 *Okere v Nwoke* [1991] 8 NWLR (Pt. 209) 317.

160 *Okpuruwu v Okponkan*, 572.

161 *Inyang v Essien* (1957) 2 FSC 39.

162 This is the interpretation given to this case by the Supreme Court in *Agu v Ikwewibe*, 413. Also see the case of *Obasi v Onwuka* (1987) 2 NSCC 981, where the Supreme Court disregarded the arbitration because the parties did not accept the award.

163 Nwangwu, "Is Customary Arbitration Part," 64. Also see *Kwasi v Larbi*, 79, where the Privy Council said "in native customary law, the elders have a recognized judicial function and are in fact a tribunal before which native can bring their disputes for judicial decision".

164 Nwangwu, "Is Customary Arbitration Part," 64–65. Also see Elombi, "Customary Arbitration," 803–24.

It is a negation of customary law to assert that if the parties to a dispute submit their dispute to a group of people for settlement and satisfy all of the prerequisites of relevant custom or the custom of trade except that the submission is not before a recognised traditional authority or is in an urban setting, such a submission is a peace settlement or conciliation. It is difficult to urge the court not to accept such decisions as customary arbitration because parties cannot relate the source of the arbitral tribunal authority to any Nigerian customary law. The authority of the arbitral tribunal lies simply in the parties' voluntary submission of their dispute to the tribunal and agreement, express or implied, to be bound by the decision reached by the tribunal, and it does not lie with the class or choice of arbitrators. Reemphasising parties' autonomy to choose a forum or arbitrators under customary law, Oguntade, J.C.A., while expressing a dissenting view in *Okpuruwu v Okponkan* observed that

> In pre-colonial time and before the advent of regular courts, our people certainly had a simple and inexpensive way of adjudicating over disputes between them. They referred them to elders or a body set up for that purpose. This practice has over the years become so strongly embedded in the system that they survive today as customs … I do not share the view that natives in their own communities cannot have a custom which operates on the same basis of voluntary submission. The right to freely choose an arbitrator to adjudicate with binding effect is not beyond our native communities.[165]

On the whole, the development of a set of rules defining valid customary arbitration contravenes the cardinal rules of interpretation and the primordial principles of the binding effect of a final arbitration award.[166] The statutory power to accept or reject a custom as customary law is without dispute an awesome power, which gives the courts wide latitude of discretion. Despite the wide latitude, it has known limits. In the words of Lord Atkin in *Eleko v. Officer Administering the Government of Nigeria*, "the court cannot itself transform a barbarous custom into a milder one. If it still stands in its barbarous character it must be rejected as repugnant to natural justice, equity and good conscience".[167] Thus, the exercise of the power must be kept within the bounds of the rule of law and the principle of the separation of powers between the different arms of government, which underlies the Nigerian constitutional order.

165 *Okpuruwu v Okponkan*, 587.
166 Jain, "Pathological Arbitration Clauses," 442.
167 *Eleko v Government*, 673.

Without mincing words, the parameters outlined by the court are tantamount to judicial legislation, a function that is clearly outside the traditional adjudicatory interface of the courts and reserved for the legislature. Further, the position of the courts is faulty, because as shown in the preceding sections, the basis of enunciating the parameters is predicated on wrong assumptions that are inconsistent with the fundamental characteristics of customary law and the CFRN. Faced with the permeating effect of judicial precedent, unless the Supreme Court expressly overrules all its previous decisions on the issue, the prevailing state of uncertainty in the law and practice of customary arbitration will persist. This may potentially lead to a gradual obliteration of customary law arbitration in Nigeria. It is hoped that the Supreme Court will think again and adjust its position to reflect the organic nature of customary law when the opportunity presents itself.

8 Future Policy Measures for the Sustainability of Customary Law

Generally, customary law remains a significant part of the Nigerian constitutional order. Though its influence is gradually waning, it is certain that it will not disappear from Nigerian *corpus juris* in the foreseeable future as a significant proportion of the Nigerian population accepts it as their personal law. However, considering the speed of the socio-economic sophistication in modern Nigeria vis-à-vis pre-colonial Nigeria, customary law may fall into oblivion faster than expected unless steps are taken to develop it and enhance its growth to satisfy the proclivity of modern Nigeria. Sadly, there has not been any deliberate policy (save for some failed efforts by some State governments in the past)[168] to pursue a systematic reform of customary laws.

Specifically, the chapter finds on the basis of the arguments presented above that customary law *qua* customary arbitration is by reason of section 315 of CFRN an existing law in Nigeria. In line with the colonial policy of indirect rule, the English court was the institution vested with the responsibility of systematically weeding out any customary law considered repugnant or incompatible with state laws. It has been argued above that the powers vested in the court by the CFRN do not include the authority to legislate or amend customary law,[169] yet in the course of adjudicating on matters touching on customary arbitration the courts have developed rules (procedural or adjectival customary law) for

168 There are records of the official compilation of customary laws of Anambra and Imo States. See Obi, *Customary Law Manual.*

169 *Eleko v Government.*

binding customary arbitration. It has been shown that against the backdrop of dogmatic adherence to the doctrine of judicial precedent by Nigerian courts[170] these apparently innocuous components of binding customary arbitration developed by the regular courts are gradually eroding the organic, flexible, dynamic and self-amending nature of customary law.[171] And as the society becomes more and more sophisticated, the stringent posture adopted by the courts may in the near future expunge customary law arbitration from among the many adjudicatory forums available to Nigerians, leaving other forums whose outcomes are more certain and reliable.[172] It is against this backdrop that this chapter makes the following recommendations:

- First, to balance the desire for certainty in the practice of customary arbitration with the core characteristics of customary law, there is a need to jettison the onerous requirement that a party relying on customary arbitration award should establish to the satisfaction of the court that "neither of the parties has withdrawn from the decision" of the arbitration. Instead, the party seeking to enforce a customary arbitration award should be required to establish in evidence only the requirements prescribed by the applicable customary law for a valid customary arbitration under the particular custom. In adhering to this suggestion, the courts should apply present-day custom and not outdated customary law. In this regard, the court should take cognisance of the totality of the elements which characterise the custom in issue.
- Secondly, it is recommended that customary arbitration presided over by a tribunal made up of person(s) lacking a traditional judicial function, which in recent times has become prevalent in Nigeria due to urbanisation,[173] should be accorded judicial recognition. The standard for according recognition to this type of arbitration could be premised on accepted practice (one of the core characteristics of valid customary law) and the fact that the parties voluntarily submitted their dispute to the process. It is trite that customs undergo changes and modifications subject to the needs of society and Nigerian customary law has exhibited this fine self-modifying quality to a great degree, which is why customary law is described as a mirror of accepted usage,[174] possessing the dynamic quality of being able to adapt

170 *Eze v UNIJOS* (2021) 2 NWLR (Pt. 1760) 208, 223.

171 *Lewis v Bankole*.

172 UNDP, UNICEF and UN Women, *Informal Justice Systems*, 8.

173 Nwauche, "Customary Law Arbitration," 62–65.

174 *Lewis v Bankole*, 84.

seamlessly to changing social circumstances.[175] As an aspect of customary law, customary arbitration also possesses these inherent qualities.

- In the cases examined above there is overwhelming evidence of the practice of submitting disputes to customary arbitration lacking a traditional judicial function in Nigeria, particularly in cosmopolitan urban settings, where the traditional customary institutions of the parties having traditional judicial function may not be present or where the dispute is between persons from two different ethnic backgrounds. It is suggested that such arbitration should be considered as forming part of Nigerian national ethos and be accorded recognition, thereby endorsing a dispute settlement mechanism that is simple, less formal and fast. The use of the term customary arbitration seems acceptable because it signifies that it is an arbitration that does not fall under statutorily regulated arbitration and its validity is premised on social acceptance. After all, the principles of English Common law were largely developed by the courts who took judicial notice of prevailing practices and usages.[176]
- Legislatively, since a binding arbitration award ranks *pari-pasu* with a judgment of a court, it is recommended that only a competent court of law should be empowered to set aside a customary arbitration award. Provisions should be inserted in the laws setting up courts, stipulating that until a customary arbitral award is set aside (within a stipulated timeline), the award is binding and a party cannot resile from it after the award has been made or published.

These recommendations should not be thought to suggest that a customary arbitration award-debtor must accept whatever decision rendered against him hook, line and sinker; far from that. The point being made is that while he has no power whatsoever to reject unilaterally the award so made, he has the right to take steps to challenge the award and to apply for it to be set aside by a competent body or court within a reasonable time.

While the above suggestions are in the interim desirable for sustaining the practice of customary arbitration, for the purposes of entrenching customary law (*qua* customary arbitration), it is imperative that its rules be made more certain and more easily ascertainable in line with the proclivity of modern societies. While having a universal customary law for the entire country (as projected by the parameters formulated by the Supreme Court for binding customary arbitration) may be ideal, it is near impossible because Nigeria is an ethnically heterogeneous country.[177] At this stage of the nation's development,

175 *Owoniyi v Omotosho*, 309.

176 Farrar and Dugdale, *Introduction to Legal Method*, 33–34.

177 Elegido, *Jurisprudence*, 124–40.

it would be more pragmatic to evolve a general local government area customary law, since most local government areas in Nigeria are homes to near homogenous ethnic groups. Consequently, it would be more realistic to restrict the development of a common customary law to a particular local government area. Towards this end, a workable policy would be a systematic compilation in the form of a restatement, and where striking divergence exists, for the purposes of unification there would be a need to codify the areas of divergence for each local government area. In this regard, the appropriate step for each state in Nigeria to take would be to set up a customary law review committee for each local government area in the state, to be headed by a serving or retired judicial officer, with representatives from the Ministry of Justice and elders of the different clans or wards in the local government area. The scope of reference would be to make a scientific and systematic study and recording of the laws of the local government area covering every branch of known customary law and where there exist divergence customary laws, to make recommendations harmonising them. The recommendations of the committee should thereafter be forwarded to the appropriate local government legislative authority for a possible codification of the customs. Once codification is effected in the manner herein suggested, adequate publicity should be given to it in the affected local government area. It follows that given adequate publicity, coupled with the fact that the customary laws in issue were initially based on the assent of the people concerned, there would be no question of divergence between the official customary law (as administered by the courts) and the living customary law (what is practised by the people).[178] In addition, to sustain the core characteristics of customary law (that it is organic and dynamic), the respective local government legislative authority must be proactive. At regular intervals it should review any customary law so codified and amend it in line with the prevailing socio-economic reality and cultural development whenever the need arises.

Until the above suggestions are effected, courts should be wary of applying the common law doctrine of *stare decisis* to customary laws *qua* customary arbitration. Should the courts adhere to this suggestion, it presupposes that the existence of every customary law before a British-style court would remain a matter of fact to be proven. This would also put an end to the application of the principle of judicial notice and prevent the petrification of customary law. It would in turn grant customary law greater freedom to develop.

178 Diala, "Concept of Living Customary Law," 143–65.

9 Conclusion

There is a consensus that if arbitration were to be effectively utilised it would greatly assist in decongesting judicial dockets and enhance justice delivery in Nigeria. Sadly, the uncertainty surrounding customary law arbitration resulting from the judicially created right to withdraw from the process even after an award has been published, coupled with the non-recognition of customary arbitration conducted by persons who are not traditionally vested with judicial functions, have *stricto sensus* declassified customary arbitration as a form of arbitration and have stultified its growth. Furthermore, these impediments are gradually eliding customary arbitration from the list of available forums for dispute resolution in Nigeria. Despite the apparent decrease in the volume of referrals of disputes to customary arbitration, to date it continues to be the forum of choice for many Nigerians, particularly those in the informal sector of the country, being a process rooted in the peoples' history and ethos. It follows that if the parties intending to resort to it are assured of the enforceability of its final awards (notwithstanding any purported withdrawal by a party after an award has been published), this would enhance its sustainability and would aid in preserving it as one of the most preferred fora for dispute resolution in Nigeria.

Bibliography

Literature

Abrahams, Sidney. "The Colonial Legal Service and the Administration of Justice in Colonial Dependencies." *Journal of Comparative Legislation and International Law* 30, no. 3/4 (1948): 1–11.

Ajayi, F. A. "The Interaction of English Law with Customary Law in Western Nigeria." *Journal of African Law* 4, no. 1 (Spring 1960): 40–50.

Akanbi, Muhammed Mustapha, Lukman Adebisi Abdulrauf, and Abdulrazaq Adelodun Daibu. "Customary Arbitration in Nigeria: A Review of Extant Judicial Parameters and the Need for Paradigm Shift." *Journal of Sustainable Development Law and Policy* 6, no. 1 (2016): 199–221.

Akpata, Ephraim. *The Nigeria Arbitration Law in Focus*. Lagos: West African Book, 1997.

Albrecht, Peter, and Helene Maria Kyed. "Justice and Security: When the State isn't the Main Provider". Copenhagen: Danish Institute for International Studies Policy Brief, 2010. Accessed February 21, 2023. https://www.files.ethz.ch/isn/128385/2010_PB-Justice-and-Security_web.pdf.

Allott, Antony. *Essays in African Law*. London: Butterworth, 1960.

Amucheazi, Offonze D. "Validity of Customary Law Arbitration in Nigeria: A Review of *Egesimba v.* Onuzuruike." *Nigerian Bar Journal* 1, no. 4 (2003): 515.

Asiedu-Akrofi, Derek. "Judicial Recognition and Adoption of Customary Law in Nigeria." *American Journal of Comparative Law* 37, no. 3 (1989): 571–93.

Awolowo, Obafemi. *Thoughts on Nigerian Constitution*. Ibadan: Oxford University Press, 1966.

Balonwu, Moses Onuora. "The Growth and Development of Indigenous Nigerian Laws as Part of Our Heritage from the British Colonial Policy of Indirect Rule." In *African Indigenous Laws*, edited by Taslim Olawale Elias, Samuel N. Nwabara, and Chuma O. Akpangbo, 31–67. Lagos: Government Press, 1975.

Batic, Gian Claudio. "The Future of Minority Languages in Nigeria." In *Language and Identity Theories and Experiences in Lexicography and Linguistic Policies in a Global World*, edited by Ilaria Micheli, et al., eds., 217–30. Trieste: EUT Edizioni Università di Trieste, 2021.

Brann, Conrad Max Benedict. "Language and Ethnicity in Nigeria." *International Review of Sociology* 2, no. 1 (1991): 122–144. https://doi.org/10.1080/03906701.1991.9971078.

Diala, Anthony C. "A Butterfly that Thinks Itself a Bird: The Identity of Customary Courts in Nigeria." *Journal of Legal Pluralism and Unofficial Law* 51, no. 3 (October 2019): 381–405. https://doi.org/10.1080/07329113.2019.1678281.

Diala, Anthony C. "The Concept of Living Customary Law: A Critique." *Journal of Legal Pluralism and Unofficial Law* 49, no. 2 (2017):143–65. https://doi.org/10.1080/07329113.2017.1331301.

Editor. "Full List of All 371 Tribes in Nigeria, States Where They Originate." *Vanguard* (Lagos), May 10, 2017. https://www.vanguardngr.com/2017/05/full-list-of-all-371-tribes-in-nigeria-states-where-they-originate/#:~:text=Nigeria%20is%20made%20up%20of,Igbo%2C%20Hausa%20and%20the%20Yoruba.

El-Ahdab, Abdul Hamid. *Arbitration with the Arab Countries*. Hague: Kluwer Law International, 1999.

Elegido, J. M. *Jurisprudence: A Textbook for Nigerian Students*. Ibadan: Spectrum, 1994.

Elias, Taslim Olawale. *The Nature of African Customary Law*. Manchester: Manchester University Press, 1956.

Elombi, George. "Customary Arbitration: A Ghanaian Trend Reversed in Nigeria." *African Journal of International and Comparative Law* 5, no. 4 (1993): 803–24.

Ezediaro, Samuel Oduh. "Guarantee and Incentives for Foreign Investment in Nigeria." *The International Lawyer* 5, no. 4 (October 1971): 770–83.

Farrar, John H., and Anthony M. Dugdale. *Introduction to Legal Method*. 2 ed. London: Sweet & Maxwell, 1984.

Gerring, John, et al. "An Institutional Theory of Direct and Indirect Rule." *World Politics* 63, no. 3 (July 2011) 377–433.

Holdsworth, William Searle. *Holdsworth's History of English Law, Vol. XIV*, edited by Arthur L. Goodhart, and Harold Greville Hanbury. London: Methuen, 1964.

Holmes, Oliver Wendell, Jr. "The Path of Law." *Harvard Law Review* 10 (1897): 457–78.

Igbokwe, Virtus Chitoo. "The Law and Practice of Customary Arbitration in Nigeria: *Agu v Ikewibe* and Applicable Law Issues Revisited." *Journal of African Law* 41, no. 2 (1997): 201–14.

Ikeyi, Nduka, and Tochukwu Maduka. "The Binding Effect of a Customary Arbitration Award: Exorcizing the Ghost of *Agu v Ikewibe*." *Journal of African Law* 58, no. 2 (2014): 328–49.

Jain, Alok. "Pathological Arbitration Clauses and Indian Courts." *Journal of International Arbitration* 25, no. 4 (2008): 433–48.

Keay, Elliot Alexander, and Sam S. Richardson. *The Native and Customary Courts of Nigeria*. Lagos: African Universities Press, 1966.

Ladapo, Oluwafemi A. "Where does Islamic Arbitration Fit into the Judicially Recognized Ingredients of Customary Arbitration in the Nigerian Jurisprudence?" *African Journal on Conflict Resolution* 8, no. 2 (2008): 103–30.

Megarry, Robert, and Paul Vivian Baker. *Snell's Principles of Equity*. 27 ed. London: Sweet & Maxwell, 1973.

Merriam-Webster Dictionary. "Personal Law." Accessed February 5, 2023. https://www.merriam-webster.com/dictionary/personal%20law.

Merry, Sally Engle. "Legal Pluralism." *Law and Society Review* 22, no 5 (1988): 869–96. https://doi.org/10.2307/3053638.

Nwangwu, U. "Is Customary Arbitration Part of Nigerian Jurisprudence?" *Global Journal of Politics and Law Research* 2, no. 7 (1989): 62–83.

Nwauche, Enyinna S. "Customary Law Arbitration and Customary Arbitration in Nigeria." *Nigeria Law and Practice Journal* 3, no. 1 (1999): 63–72.

Oba, Abdulmumimi A. "Islamic Law as Customary Law: The Changing Perspective in Nigeria." *International and Comparative Law Quarterly* 51, no. 4 (2002): 817–50.

Oba, Abdulmumimi A. "Juju Oaths in Customary Law Arbitration and their Legal Validity in Nigerian Courts." *Journal of African Law* 52, no. 1 (2008): 139–58.

Oba, Abdulmumimi A. "The Judicial Practice in Islamic Family Law and Its Relation to *Urf* (Custom) in Northern Nigeria." *Islamic Law and Society* 20, no. 3 (2013): 272–318.

Obi, Samuel Nwankwo Chinwuba. *The Customary Law Manual*. Enugu: Government Printer, 1977.

Obilade, Akintu Olusegun. *The Nigerian Legal System*. Ibadan: Spectrum, 2009.

Oluduro, Olubayo. "Customary Arbitration in Nigeria: Development and Prospects." *African Journal of International and Comparative Law* 19, no. 2 (2011): 307–30.

Onyenge v Ebere [2004] 13 NWLR (Pt. 889) 20.

Ornguga, Kwaghkehelerkwagh Yangien, and N. Ayia Orhange. "Law, Legal Theory and Practice of Customary Arbitration in Nigeria." *International Journal of Law* 6, no. 4 (2020): 36–41.

Park, Andrew Edward Wilson. *The Sources of Nigerian Law*. London: Sweet & Maxwell, 1963.

Qureshi, Javed Ahmed. "Muslim Law." April 4, 2020. Accessed February 24, 2023. http://www.jiwaji.edu/pdf/ecourse/law/MALIKI%20SCHOOL.pdf.

Swenson, Geoffrey. "Legal Pluralism in Theory and Practice." *International Studies Review* 20, no. 3 (2018): 438–62.

Udoma, Egbert Udo. *History and Law of the Constitution of Nigeria*. Lagos: Malthouse Press, 1994.

UNDP, UNICEF and UN Women. *Informal Justice Systems: Charting a Course for Human Rights-Based Engagement*. New York: United Nations Development Program, 2012. Accessed February 21, 2023. https://www.unwomen.org/sites/default/files/Headquarters/Attachments/Sections/Library/Publications/2013/1/Informal-Justice-Systems-Charting-a-Course-for-Human-Rights-Based-Engagement.pdf.

Uweru, Bethel Chuks. "Repugnancy Doctrine and Customary Law in Nigeria: A Positive Aspect of British Colonialism." *African Research Review* 2, no. 2 (2008): 286–95.

Von Benda-Beckmann, Keebet, and Bertram Turner. "Legal Pluralism, Social Theory, and the State." *Journal of Legal Pluralism and Unofficial Law* 50, no. 3 (2018): 255–74. https//doi/10.1080/07329113.2018.1532674.

Webster, James Bertin, and A. Adu Boahen. *The Revolutionary Years of West Africa Since 1800*. London: Longman, 1967.

Whytock, Christopher A. "Domestic Courts and Global Governance." *Tulane Law Review* 84 (2009): 67–123.

Case Law

Adetoun Oladeji (Nig.) Ltd v Nigerian Breweries [2007] 5 NWLR (Pt. 1027) 415.

Agala v Okosin [2010] 10 NWLR (Pt. 1202) 412.

Aghedo v Adenomo [2018] 13 NWLR (Pt. 1636) 264.

Agu v Ikewibe [1991] 3 NWLR (Pt. 180) 385.

Ahiwe Okere and Ors v Marcus Nwoke and Ors [1991] 8 NWLR (Pt. 209) 317.

Akpan v Otong [1996] 10 NWLR (Pt. 476) 108.

Alkamawa v Bello [1998] 8 NWLR (Pt. 561) 173.

Amaechi v INEC [2008] 5 NWLR (Pt. 1080) 227.

Angu v Attah (1921) PC 1874–1926.

Anyabunsi v Ugwunze [1995] 6 NWLR (Pt. 401) 255.

Anyabunsi v Ugwunze [1995] 6 NWLR (Pt. 401) 255.

Ashogbon v Oduntan (1935) 12 NLR 7.

Assampong v Mensah (1932) 1 WACA 192.

Awosile v Sotumbo [1992] 5 NWLR (Pt. 243) 514.
Bashir Mohammed Dalhatu v Ibrahim Saminu Turaki [2003] 7 SC.
Buraimo v Gbambgboye (1940) 15 NLR 139.
Chief of Air Staff v Iyen [2005] 6 NWLR (Pt. 922) 496.
Dalhatu v Turaki and Ors [2003] 15 NWLR (Pt. 843) 310.
Egbuta v Onua [2007] 10 NWLR (Pt. 1042) 298.
Egesimba v Onuzuruike; Odonigi v Oyeleke [2001] 6 NWLR (Pt. 708) 12.
Eguere Inyang v Simon Essien (1957) 2 FSC 39.
Eke v Okwaranyia (2001) 86 LRCN 1403.
Eke v Okwaranyia [2001] 12 NWLR (Pt. 726) 181.
Eleko v Government of Nigeria [1931] AC 662.
Enyinnaya v Commissioner of Police (1985) NCLR 464.
Esuwoye v Bosere [2017] 1 NWLR (Pt. 1546) 256.
Eugene Nnaekwe Egesimba v Ezekiel Onuzuruike [2002] 15 NWLR (Pt. 791) 466 SC.
Eze v UNIJOS (2021) 2 NWLR (Pt. 1760) 208.
FNB Plc v Maiwada [2013] 6 NWLR (Pt. 1348) 444.
George Onwusike v Patrick Onwusike (1926) 6 Eastern Nigerian Law Report 10.
Giwa v Inspector-General of Police (1985) 6 NCLR 369.
Ibrahim v APC (No. 2) [2019] 16 NWLR (Pt. 1699) 469.
Ibrahim v APC (No. 2) [2019] 8 NWLR (Pt. 1674) 269.
Idika and Ors v Erisi and Ors (1988) NSCC 977.
Idika and Ors v Erisi and Ors [1988] 2 NWLR (Pt. 78) 563.
Idoniboye-Obu v NNPC [2003] 2 NWLR (Pt. 805) 589.
Igwego v Ezeugo [1992] 6 NWLR (Pt. 249) 561.
Integrated Realty Ltd v Odofin [2018] 3 NWLR (Pt. 1606) 301.
Iwu v Ogu [2020] 9 NWLR (Pt. 1730) 608.
Iyang v Essien (1957) 2 FSC 39.
Joseph Larbi and Anor v Opanin Kwasi and Anor (1950) 13 WACA 81.
Kharie Zaidan v Fatima K. Mohssen (1973) 11 SC 1.
Kindey v Military Governor of Gongola State [1988] 2 NWLR (Pt. 77) 445.
Kwasi v Larbi (1952) 13 WACA 76.
Lewis v Bankole (1909) 1 NLR 81.
Mashuwareng v Abdu [2003] 11 NWLR (Pt. 831) 403.
Mensah v Takyiampong 6 WACA 118.
Mogo Chikwendu v Mbamali and Anor (1980) 3/4 SC 31.
Nnaji and Ors v Inspector General of Police (1957) 2 FSC 18.
Nruamah v Ebuzoeme [2013] 13 NWLR (Pt. 1372) 474.
Obasi v Onwuka (1987) 2 NSCC 981.
Obioha v Akukwe [2000] 5 NWLR (Pt. 658) 699.
Odoemena Nwaigwe and 2 Ors v Nze Edwin Okere [2008] 13 NWLR (Pt. 1105) 445.

Ohiaeri v Akabeze [1992] 2 NWLR (Pt. 221) 1.
Ohiaeri v Akabeze (1992) 7 LRCN 163.
Okala v Udah [2019] 9 NWLR (Pt. 1678) 562.
Okere v Nwoke [1991] 8 NWLR (Pt. 209) 317.
Okereke v Nwankwo [2003] 9 NWLR (Pt. 826) 592.
Okonkwo v Okagbue [1994] 9 NWLR (Pt. 368) 301.
Okoye and Anor v Obiaso and Ors (2010) 186 LRCN 181.
Okoye v Obiaso [2010] 8 NWLR (Pt. 1195) 145.
Okpuruwu v Okponkan [1988] 4 NWLR (Pt. 90) 554.
Olagbemiro v Ajagunbade III [1990] 3 NWLR (Pt. 136) 37.
Oline v Obodo and Ors (1958) SCNLR 298.
Oline v Obodo [1958] 3 FSC 84.
Olowu and 3 Ors v Abolore and Anor (1993) 6 SCNJ (Pt. 1) 1.
Olufeagba v Abdur-Raheem [2009] 18 NWLR (Pt. 1173) 384.
Onyenge v Ebere [2004] 13 NWLR (Pt. 889) 20.
Opanin Kwasi and Ors v Joseph Larbi (1952) 13 WACA 76.
Oparaji v Ogidereji (1999) 70 LRCN 1822.
Oparaji v Ohanu [1999] 9 NWLR (Pt. 618) 290.
Owoniyi v Omotosho (1961) 1 All NLR 304.
Oyewunmi v Ogunsesan [1990] 3 NWLR (Pt. 137) 183.
Philip Njoku v Felix Ekeocha (1972) 2 ECSLR 199.
Rabiu v Adamu [2013] 1 NWLR (Pt. 1337) 36.
Timothy Tanloju Adesubokan v Rasaki Yunusa [1971] ANLR 227.
Ume v Okoronkwo (1996) 12 SCNJ 404.
Ume v Okoronkwo [1996] 10 NWLR (Pt. 477) 133.
Umeadi v Chibunze [2020] NWLR (Pt. 1733) 405.
Umeano Achiakpa v Nduka [2001] 14 NWLR (Pt. 734) 623.
Uzoewulu v Ezeaka [2000] 14 NWLR (Pt. 688) 679.
Whyte v Jack [1996] 2 NWLR (Pt. 431) 407.

Legislation

Ghana

Chieftaincy Act, 1961.

Nigeria

Application of English Law to the Settlement of Lagos, Ordinance 3 of 1863.
Arbitration and Conciliation Act, 1988, Cap A 18, LFN 2004.
Constitution of the Federal Republic of Nigeria, 1979.
Constitution of the Federal Republic of Nigeria, 1999, Cap C 23, LFN 2004.
Evidence Act, 1956, LN 47 of 1955; Cap 14, LFN 2004.

Evidence Act, 2011.
Federal Capital Territory Customary Court Act, 2007, Cap F39, LFN.
High Court Law, Laws of Bendel, 1976.
Imo State Customary Court Law, 1984.
Supreme Court Act, 1960, Cap S 15, LFN 2004.
Supreme Court Ordinance 11 of 1863.
Supreme Court Ordinance 11 of 1876.

CHAPTER 10

"Our Human Rights are Our Land": Reconceptualising the Right to Property from an Indigenous Perspective

Davinia Gómez-Sánchez

Abstract

Legal orders rooted in western hegemonic legal paradigms are proving limited in addressing historical discrimination, structural inequalities and current human rights challenges. Pointing at the ideological coloniality in the legal realm, this presentation aims at recapturing the validity and meaning of indigenous peoples' perspectives in an attempt to contest and expand the prevailing human rights discourse. Against the dominant values underpinning the mainstream conceptualisation of rights (secularism, autonomy, anthropocentrism, economic growth), the basis for an alternative construction will be advanced here.

Building on epistemically neglected legal worldviews and cultural traditions, this piece explores and identifies valuable aspects stemming from indigenous peoples in Southern Africa to put forward a reformulation of rights. In opposition to liberal concepts of property epitomised in positive laws, this contribution will present an alternative conceptualisation of property, ownership and the non-exclusive uses of land based on the San, highlighting aspects such as mutual dependence, egalitarianism, sharing, redistribution and reciprocity.

1 Introduction[1]

> If the global problem today is defined as terrible human suffering consequent to limited individual rights against abusive state powers, then

1 This research was set within the framework of the DIRS-COFUND European Union's Horizon 2020 Research and Innovation Programme under the Marie Skłodowska-Curie grant agreement Nº 665959. The author thanks Prof Jennifer Hays for her support and guidance, Prof Alan Barnard for his generosity, as well as the Centre for Legal Integration in Africa (CLIA) and the anonymous reviewers for their insightful comments and suggestions that contributed to improve the initial manuscript. All errors remain the author's.

 | DOI:10.1163/9789004696747_011

> human rights may be the best tactic against this problem. But if it is diagnosed as the relatively unchecked globalization of capital, postcolonial political deformations, and superpower imperialism combining to disenfranchise peoples in many parts of the first, second and third worlds from the prospects of self-governance to a degree historically unparalleled in modernity, other kinds of political projects, including other international justice projects, may offer a more appropriate and far-reaching remedy for injustice defined as suffering and as systematic disenfranchisement from collaborative self-governance.[2]

Legal orders rooted in Western hegemonic legal paradigms are proving to be limited in addressing historical discrimination, structural inequalities and current human rights challenges. New scenarios and common problems at the planetary level[3] demand new paradigms to address them, which include political, economic and environmental solutions. However, the normative domain should also adjust to confront those challenges by considering traditionally marginalised paradigms and knowledges. In an exercise in epistemic justice and pointing at the ideological coloniality of the international legal realm, this chapter aims at presenting an alternative conceptualisation of rights (to property) rooted in unconventional sources, specifically in the values and relationships of indigenous peoples. Recapturing the validity and meaning of historically omitted indigenous peoples' perspectives, the purpose is to challenge and expand the prevailing human rights discourse. Against the dominant values underpinning the mainstream conceptualisation of rights (secularism, autonomy, anthropocentrism, economic growth), the basis for an alternative construction will be advanced here: "Our human rights are our land."[4]

In drawing the contours of a new map, this piece will explore and identify valuable aspects stemming from indigenous peoples in Southern Africa as foundations for devising an alternative normative legal formulation that challenges the legal right to property.

The analysis that follows is rooted in critical theories, Third World Approaches to International Law (TWAIL) and decolonial thinking. These approaches question Eurocentric narratives and power asymmetries, aiming

---

2 Brown, "'The Most We can Hope for'", 145.

3 Following Dipesh Chakrabarty, he distinguishes two perspectives in looking at the current crisis we are confronting, a global one (human centric), and a planetary perspective (decentring the human).

4 Statement by Roy Sesana, one of the founders of the First People of the Kalahari organisation in Botswana. In Hitchcock and Vinding, *Indigenous Peoples' Rights*, 11.

at contesting the colonial world order established by European empires. In the case of TWAIL, the role of international law in maintaining a global unjust order despite its pretended "neutrality" is critiqued.[5]

Challenging Western-centric sources of knowledge, the overall purpose of this chapter is therefore to contest the Western epistemic canon that underlies the language of rights with regard to property and land rights. In what follows, salient elements from epistemically neglected legal worldviews are put in dialogue with liberal conceptions of property that sustain the dominant legal paradigm in order to address some of the shortcomings that the latter seem unable to redress. Consequently, in opposition to those concepts of property epitomised in positive laws, this contribution presents elements for an alternative conceptualisation of property, ownership and non-exclusive uses of land based on the San (indigenous peoples from Southern Africa), highlighting aspects such as mutual dependence, egalitarianism, sharing, redistribution and reciprocity. Therefore, beyond the ontological limitations and fragmentation that characterise the Western apprehension of the world, a more holistic approach is proposed, one that puts in dialogue the individual, the community,[6] the environment, nature and culture, the present, the future and the past, entitlements and reciprocity (mutual aid that responds to strategies of both material and social well-being).[7]

The process of indigenous peoples' gaining visibility resulting from their struggles against oppression and domination has been accompanied by a progressive recognition of their rights, their cultural significance and their agency, also within the law.[8] Indigenous demands and realities are no longer invisible

5 "With the rise of positivism in the 19th century, the legal policy and jurisprudence advanced in the line of positivist fabric systematically deprived indigenous people' rights under international law. First, by rejecting the natural law construct of law of nations as universal" and secondly, with the focus on state in international law, the idea of sovereignty and the connection between the notion of statehood and civilisation. Shrinkhal, "Evolution of Indigenous Rights," 14.

6 Communitarism implies recognition of the individuality and the self as autonomous and as a communal being. Coetzee and Roux, *African Philosophy Reader*, 361.

7 Barnard, "Mutual Aid".

8 There are voices that are critical of such appreciation of certain attributes of indigenous peoples. Lindroth and Sinevaara-Niskanen "Colonialism Invigorated?" for instance, claim that describing indigeneity as resilient (and adaptative) might contribute to cementing the marginalised position of indigenous peoples, given that this global narrative demands that they adapt in the face of current struggles, minimising the fact that such resilience is necessary to their actual survival. The political rhetoric transforms victimhood into resourcefulness (Lindroth and Sinevaara-Niskanen, "Colonialism Invigorated?" 247), while the reality is frightful when it is seen in terms of the difficulties, deprivation and struggles it involves.

and attention has turned to the difficult situation indigenous peoples endure.[9] Despite commonalities among indigenous groups that have helped to conform a strong international movement to advance their claims,[10] the situation of indigenous peoples is also diverse in different regions. Those differences do not lie only in the particular difficulties they face while striving for protection and respect, but also in the recognition of their idiosyncrasy. In the case of African indigenous peoples, there is a gap in acknowledging and highlighting the significance of those peculiarities and (valuable) traits.

Against the privilege of ignorance, this research responds to a valorisation of cultures that have been marginalised through epistemic violence and the ontological difference they encompass, worldviews considered not worthy of creating valid "universal" knowledge.[11]

In the African context, besides the epistemological neglect of certain endogenous knowledges, the issue of indigenous peoples is a controversial one already when it comes to the term indigenous and what it means to be indigenous. The general understanding is that indigeneity refers to being first in the land, to nativeness, in opposition to later arrivals such as European settlers. Thus, most of the literature dealing with indigenous peoples does not specifically delve into indigenous peoples as the category protected under the United Nations Declaration on the Rights of Indigenous Peoples (UNDRIP) and in line with the African Commission of Human and Peoples' Rights (ACHPR).[12] Against the everyday use of this word, which connects the term indigenous with the idea of aboriginality and being prior in time, the term indigenous peoples here mirrors

9 Discrimination, marginalisation and under-representation, impoverishment, land grabbing and dispossession (resulting in internal displacements, loss of livelihoods, endangered cultures, identity and heritage), inequalities, low levels of basic formal education, high levels of unemployment and economic dependency (on government welfare services and pensions, charity and others), poor basic health, food insecurity, a sense of alienation from the rest of society, stern assimilationist policies, recurring violence and a lack of agency (in the public space, with regard to the implementation of development projects and sometimes, in connection to research activities).

10 The seed of the indigenous international movement grew from the synergies, mobilisation and lobby efforts initiated by indigenous groups (First Nations, Canadians, American and Nordic) and supporting organisations dating back to the 60s and 70s. The involvement of representatives of African indigenous peoples in the international arena started only in the 80s and 90s.

11 As Semali and Kincheloe put it, the focus on indigenous knowledge aims at decolonising thoughts and minds; reclaiming cultural values and traditional heritages; validating indigenous epistemologies; protecting against new forms of colonisation and exploitation; and promoting the sacred and spiritual as valid ways of knowing. Kubow, "Exploring Western and Non-Western Epistemological Influences," 354.

12 ACHPR, *Report of the African Commission's Working Group*; (see section 2.3 below).

the working definition of the UN Special Rapporteur, José Martínez-Cobo,[13] and the defining characteristics summarised by Erica Irene Daes,[14] namely: prior in time or having historical continuity, and having a special attachment to the traditional land for collective survival, having experienced domination, marginalisation[15] and dispossession, being culturally distinct from the dominant group, self-identifying as a group, and being determined to preserve and transmit to future generations their ancestral territories and ethnic identity (cultural patterns, social institutions, legal systems etc.).

In an attempt to highlight the particularities and value of indigenous peoples' worldviews in Africa (understood in the sense just explained), the present work focusses on contributions from the San that could challenge the conventional understanding of legal categories, their underlying notions and the dominant conceptualisation of rights.

The term San is used as a construct to collectively refer to groups that share a common history and present conditions of deprivation and poverty, despite their different cultural and linguistic peculiarities.[16] These traditional hunter-gatherer groups, who live in contexts of scarcity, risk and uncertainty, have nowadays mixed subsistence livelihoods (foraging, food production, income generating activities such as trade, tourism, hunting, crafts, mining, road building, domestic work, being recipients of aid or food handouts). Despite the fact that the fluidity and transformation of values and practices are intrinsic to all cultures, including that of the San, there are distinctive elements that remain, also with regard to their specific understanding of property. Those aspects

13 Special Rapporteur of the Sub-Commission on Prevention of Discrimination and Protection of Minorities (1981–1984), which is in line with the approach of the Working Group on Indigenous Populations and Communities and Minorities in Africa of the ACHPR.

14 Chairperson-Rapporteur UN Working Group on Indigenous Populations (1984–2001).

15 Marschke, Szablowski, and Vandergeest. "Engaging Indigeneity," 486 identifies four forms of marginalisation: lack of knowledge (resulting in lack of attention), negative or paternalistic stereotypes, disregard for their specificities (leading to programmes that do not account for their peculiar needs) and deliberate assimilationist policies.

16 Cook and Sarkin, "Who is Indigenous?" 96. Within the general term of San population, different ethnic groups prefer to be identified by the name of their own group identity or language family such as: Ju/'hoansi (Ju meaning a person), Bugakhwe, Khwe-ǁAni, Ts'ixa, ǂX'ao-ǁ'aen,!Xóõ (within the Taa branch of the!Ui-Taa language group; a southern Khoe-San language family), ǂHoan, ‡Khomani (or N|u), Naro, G/ui, G//ana, Tsasi, Deti, Shua, Tshwa, Cuaa, Kua, Danisi y /Xaise (IWGIA, *Indigenous World*); South Africa San Institute website – SASI, "Written in the Sand". According to Barnard, "'Bushmen' only came to be defined by that collective term (or by 'San' or 'Basarwa') in relation to outsiders" (Barnard, *Hunters and Herders*, 238). The San are currently present in Botswana, Namibia and South Africa as well as in Zimbabwe (to a lesser extent).

arise from their socio-cultural systems and rules, resulting in an understanding of property in terms of its social function. They further manifest practices such as alternative forms of tenure and uses of land, based on communal tenure, re-distribution, the delayed-exchange rule, demand sharing and reciprocity, as will be developed below. These patterns involve an approach that closely connects the autonomy of the individual with the communal (and a close relationship of belonging), the personal with the collective. Besides, they presuppose the integration of the human and nature (a non-dualistic understanding of nature), an intertemporal dimension of human solidarity (inclusive of future generations) as well as rights tied to social obligations and responsibilities.

The San have been characterised as immediate return societies that promote equality and have egalitarian common property regimes with extended kinship networks of distribution. Rights and obligations are thus formalised in reciprocal exchange mechanisms that function as levelling mechanisms or creative strategies for forging social ties[17] to cope with and reduce risks, while providing them with a sense of belonging and comfort.

Therefore, critical focus on the San aims at identifying elements from their epistemologies, socio-legal orders and worldviews[18] that could contribute to expanding the dominant conceptualisation of human rights as it is enshrined in the corpus of international human rights law.[19] Giving voice to marginalised peoples and enriching international human rights law with input from the historically excluded Third World are among the foci and concerns of TWAIL scholars.[20] If the human rights regimen is reframed by alternative understandings, this could counter coloniality and imperialism, consolidating legitimate claims of other, more inclusive aspirations. "Africa must not just be taken as a problem to be solved but must also be seen as a contributor to positive global development. It has values that could give meaning to the fullness of human society."[21]

17 "Fictive kinship or genealogical bonds" (Hitchcock, "Sharing the Land," 198). To increase the network of people with mutual rights and obligations.

18 Or rather "worlds of vision", following Viveiros de Castro, "Zeno and the Art of Anthropology," 133. Differentiation is placed on the concepts of analysis and understanding rather than on the representations.

19 Against the "essentialising propensity of IHRL" (international human rights law) Esterling, "Looking Forward Looking Back," 282. For a more detailed account of the ideological underpinnings of the dominant human rights conceptualisation, see Gómez-Sánchez, "Transforming Human Rights".

20 Ramina, "TWAIL – 'Third World Approaches'"; Badaru, "Examining the Utility".

21 Ndlovu-Gatsheni, *Giving Africa Voice*, 7.

Some questions around the complex topic of indigenous peoples in the African context are addressed in what follows. First, the category of indigeneity is examined in relation to issues such as cultural traditions, ethnicity, authenticity and the shaping of identity. This analysis is followed by an exploration of the ramifications of the indigenous categorisation through the lens of coloniality. Having discussed those preliminary aspects that shape the indigenous question in Africa, a more concrete description of the meaning of the term in this region is presented, together with some notes on the controversy this notion poses in this context. To conclude, several ideas about African indigenous peoples' views on land, property and law will be advanced as a preamble to section 3 on property rights.

2 The Indigenous Question in Africa

2.1 *Identity Making: Markers of Authenticity and Essentialism*

The complexity of the indigenous realities mentioned above has been exacerbated by the focus on identity brought by global discourses on the topic of indigenous peoples and discussions about their genuine features. There is a risk of essentialising indigenous identity by putting the emphasis on ethnic differences and cultural authenticity (re-indigenising;[22] ideology turns into "IDology").[23] This results from a manipulation of the idea of culture that transforms socio-economic and political claims into demands for cultural preservation.[24] Linking rights to a strict notion of those entitled to them forces the discussion into adjusting the criteria in order to narrow down the category of the legitimate beneficiaries and "authentic" holders of rights provided by the given classification. Furthermore, the symbolic acknowledgement and

---

22 The revalorisation of indigeneity risks falling into the "fetishization of alterity" (Dalglish, "What is the Ontological Turn,") or a "new form of neoliberal governmentality, cynically manipulating critical, postcolonial and ecological sensibilities for its own ends" (Chandler and Reid, "'Being in Being'," 251).

23 Comaroff and Comaroff, "Ethnicity, Inc.: On the Affective Economy" reflect on the dialectic between the commodification of culture and the assertion of corporate identity and marketing/productions (as the self-construction) of ethnicity, reaching the domain of cultural being. "But the assertion of intellectual property – coupled, significantly, with the land claim that preceded it – reanimated San 'identity.' And gave it ever 'thicker', more dense substance; a symptom of this, interestingly, being a sudden increase in people accusing each other, on biological grounds, of 'not being real San'"; SASI Annual Review in Comaroff and Comaroff, *Ethnicity, Inc.: On Indigeneity*, 28.

24 Hodgson, "Introduction," 1042; Sylvain, "Disorderly Development".

political recognition of excluded groups has been misused to confer legitimacy on processes that have resulted in the appropriation of their land by other groups or governments. However, even though at times tradition (in connection with identity) has been used as a cultural commodity, it has also contributed to recovering social memory and pride.

Identity issues pose challenges to the legitimacy, representativeness and entitlements attached to it (including land claims and access to resources). The intricacy of belonging and identity is often diminished, and simplifications are often used by a diverse range of actors (community members, NGOs, academics) in order to advance heterogenous projects and prerogatives. Beyond emplacement and a "relationship to the place and people of the homeland, belonging encompasses the more elusive senses of connection and acceptance".[25] This complexity is illustrated in the case of the San by the vast literature, anthropological scholarly work and discussions on indigenous peoples in the African continent. Existing literature proves that the issue is more nuanced than mere self-identification or the presence of clear-cut identities based on ethnic origin and background, language and attire, but rather encompasses broader aspects involving issues of economic power and leadership.[26] Essentialist accounts of indigenous peoples that omit non-cultural components in the formation of identity and neglect historical and contextual factors that also define indigenous realities are not fair descriptions.

Economic insecurity exacerbated by historical, structural and political factors led to the diversification of traditional livelihoods, as mentioned above. In the case of Botswana,[27] the impact of economic changes and the demand among ethnic minorities for labour during the first half of the past century led to constructed identities that "rarely conformed to a people's prior self-identification".[28] After independence in 1966 the government's priority was to

25 Gressier, *At Home in the Okavango*, 16.

26 Leadership is a notion based on attitudes and skills gained through life, for decision-making and advice to achieve consensus, that confers respect towards "leaders" rather than authority. "Leaders aid in group decision-making, but they do not hold power. Indeed, the act of seeking power is discouraged, and it would weaken their prestige if it became apparent"; Barnard, "Foraging Mode of Thought," 9.

27 Botswana is one of the few African countries where the minority-majority classification in terms of group dominance in society (and also in politics) is applicable – one of the "single-group-dominated states, where the majority group enjoys an established dominant position and hence is generally in effective control of the state. In these states, minority groups are generally in a precarious situation, faced with the danger of discrimination, assimilation and domination"; Dersso, *Taking Ethno-Cultural Diversity Seriously*, 39.

28 Wilmsen, "Mutable Identities," 830.

foster unity and non-racialism to avoid discrimination by promoting Batswana identity (Tswanisation) around the idea of citizenship rather than ethnicity.[29] According to Werbner, the process of indigenisation of the San has tested "the very limits of social justice and democracy in Botswana".[30] Rather than ethnic homogeneity, "a hallmark of Tswana tribal development is the capacity to incorporate strangers as tribal citizens,[31] while allowing for ethnic difference, redefined within certain terms of rank and unequal subjection".[32] Ethnicity is politically constructed and "arises in the exercise of power … [The identities of members of] the dominant group are never ethnicities".[33]

In this same vein, Sylvain warns about the danger of stimulating stereotypical images of indigenous groups and the risk of manipulating cultural ideas "as a tool for securing political, economic, and development resources".[34] She argues that essentialised notions of indigenous cultures come about as a result of the combination of the socio-economic situation of indigenous peoples, the politics of identity, and development ventures. This positioning of peoples as ethno-political groups[35] is based on a configuration of collective self-identification that contributes to consolidating security in a context of inequality[36] and injustice. These categorisations have resulted in involuntary and unequal ethnic ascriptions that continue today, and which have contributed to

29 "In 2006, the CERD Committee expressed its concern that Botswana's objective to build a nation based on the principle of equality for all has been implemented in a way detrimental to the protection of ethnic and cultural diversity, and urged the State to respect and protect the existence and cultural identity of all ethnic groups within its territory"; ILO and ACHPR, *Overview Report,* 68.

30 Werbner, "Challenging Minorities," 680.

31 Mafeje's explanation of the ideology of tribalism is worth noting. He argues that tribalism was the European colonial way of reconstructing the African reality that lived on and the way to understand African societies. However, the ideology of tribalism "over-simplifies, mystifies, and obscures the real nature of economic and power relations", a category with low explanatory power; Mafeje, "Ideology of 'Tribalism'," 261.

32 Werbner, "Challenging Minorities," 680. The standardisation of the features of dominant cultures was often used as a proxy for national integration.

33 Wilmsen, "Introduction," 4.

34 Sylvain, "Disorderly Development," 355.

35 "As class interests of the peoples labelled Basarwa become more explicitly aligned with those of other of Botswana's rural poor, these ethnic labels are likely to become submerged and ultimately replaced by self-designated terms of more meaningful content to the bearers." Wilmsen, "Introduction," 8.

36 For a detailed analysis of ethnicity as "a consciously crafted ideological creation" that encapsulates different forms of consciousness related to factors such as economic, migration and parochial loyalties, psychological satisfaction and other matters, see Vail, *Creation of Tribalism.*

operationalising discrimination and dispossession against stigmatised groups. They further explain, for example, current land tenure schemes (as well as language trends to a certain extent) that reproduce former allocation patterns. These involuntary ethnic classifications are facilitated by relations of structured inequality[37] and the power of cultural hegemonic groups. As a result, disempowered groups are faced with the quandary of aligning themselves with ethnic enclaves to obtain security and a collective sense of identity, or with the mainstream to escape marginality (while remaining a minority).[38]

Members of these groups see the value of reinforcing a collective identity based on ethnicity and livelihood strategies (often mirroring tradition). It allows them to position themselves in broader society as well as in international debates in order to pursue common goals. However, this ambivalence has also brought about tensions and conflicts in the communities.

2.2 *Consequences of Indigenism and the Colonial Logic*

The tendency to situate the indigenous debate within the tension of the binary thinking tradition/modernity[39] (which lies in the background of the approach of many NGOs, donors and governments) is according to Robins[40] one of the reasons for the intensification of the tension and complexity around authenticity, identity and cultural continuity. It contributes to reinforcing essentialist discourses that result in "target categories" or target populations. However, strategic essentialism can work in different ways: as a means to access economic resources as well as to reinforce an endangered culture and secure cultural survival.

Following Ndlovu-Gatsheni, in rescuing the oral history of non-hegemonic groups strategic essentialism "is positively subversive of dominant discourses

---

37 Comaroff, "Ethnicity, Nationalism," 166.

38 This dilemma is further intensified by the equal and fair treatment approach of the Government of all citizens of Botswana, for example, aiming at integration and levelling development standards as explained above. According to Cook and Sarkin "it seems as though non-racial policies are a guise for marginalizing racial issues in a Tswana-dominated society". Cook and Sarkin, "Who is Indigenous?" 129.

39 A useful concept to overcome the dichotomy of western classification between tradition and modernity can be found in Sahlins's notion of "indigenous modernities" (Sahlins, "What is Anthropological Enlightenment?") or indigenisation of modernity. Robins speaks about the hybridised conditions of the San people as opposed to the categorisation in the dichotomy modern-traditional (Robins, "NGOs, 'Bushmen' and Double Vision'," 844).

40 Robins, "NGOs, 'Bushmen' and Double Vision'," 835, 844.

and is a useful weapon for the subaltern[41] whose voice is rarely listened to or even captured."[42] It foregrounds valuable traits and rescues from silence those who have been muted and erased in favour of hegemonic and powerful discourses (such as the universal human rights discourse).[43] As Sylvain and Solway point out, those essentialising representations have brought their situation to the attention of researchers and donors. They have also contributed to resignifying their cultural universes and assisted towards their self-identification (to the point of leading to a partial cultural revival among the San, even if this has been strategic at times). However, they have also resulted in divisions and conflict in the communities themselves, as already mentioned. Besides, as Sapignoli affirms, "rights can sometimes produce the very subjectivities, social relations, and identities that they [legal processes] claim merely to recognize".[44] Some authors also warn about the corporate-sponsored cultural revitalisation of indigenous peoples. Dombrowski documents the abusive nature of corporate support of indigenous peoples in Alaska as a strategy to circumvent governmental restrictions and laws that were detrimental to their corporate goals.[45]

The different factors mentioned above (identity, tradition, essentialism) influence the assumptions and theoretical constructions pertaining to indigenous peoples motivating government and non-governmental development interventions and technical solutions (relocations, aid programmes, etc.).[46] In the case of the San, government development strategies aligned to national interests, which claimed to address inequality and promote social justice, have been assessed as having detrimental effects on the San's self-sufficiency and

---

41 Aware of Spivak's caveat "that the colonized subaltern subject is irretrievably *heterogeneous*" (emphasis added); Spivak, "Can the Subaltern Speak?" 79.

42 Ndlovu-Gatsheni, *Giving Africa Voice*, 13.

43 Engle, "On Fragile Architecture," 151 argues that in the early decades in the discussion of indigenous peoples human rights were seen as inseparable from the civilising mission of colonialism and the liberalising mission of neo-colonialism.

44 Sapignoli, "'Bushmen' in the Law," 211. In relation to the high court case in Botswana (*Sesana v The Attorney General* (52/2002) [2006] BWHC 1 (13 December 2006); see footnote 134), Sapignoli asserts that "A contingent Bushmen identity was created, and evidence of continuity with the past was projected as a claim of land and resource rights into the future." Sapignoli, "'Bushmen' in the Law," 223.

45 Dombrowski, "Praxis of Indigenism," 1067.

46 Interventions that often make little sense to the targeted groups' "values and practices (socially and environmentally"; Ninkova, *"Now that We have Development"*, 232). For a contextualised account of how development institutions create discourses that shape the objects of their knowledge that inform and give form to their interventions, see Ferguson, *Anti-Politics Machine*.

autonomy. They have created a dependency that has placed them in a more vulnerable situation than before, making them reliant on the assistance of the government and various other organisations.[47] Suzman adds the failure of governments' initiatives to lead to meaningful changes in the economic situation of the San as another factor exacerbating this dependency and economic vulnerability,[48] while the San's expectations vis-à-vis the government increase. Hitchcock and Holms refer to the "bureaucratic domination" intended to overturn pre-existing economic and cultural domination (in the case of Botswana).[49] According to the authors, it comes with the demand that the San settle in one place as a precondition for their participation in decision making and further political power. They warn about the actual drivers of transformation and about the direction social change will take among the San.[50]

These approaches are informed by opposing understandings of the nature of a good life: "For the government the relocation was necessary for the creation of the citizen/human, while for the San and Bakgalagadi the relocation was a process of dehumanisation and the extinguishment of their citizenship and basic human rights."[51] As a result, the roles played not only by government but also by transnational and human rights NGOs have been questioned in relation to their legitimacy, their goals, their efficacy and their consequences (including their "representations and conceptions of culture and identity").[52] In the case of Botswana[53] the perverse and disempowering effects of foreign aid interventions (namely cultural insensitivity, not setting a self-driven agenda, diminishing state capacity, fostering dependency, decisions regarding priorities being marked by the need to secure funding) have not affected the country.[54] However, a different dimension in this connection and dependency relates to how it works at the ideological level in relation to mainstream ideas and concepts (such as human rights and development)[55] that might

47 Sapignoli, "Dispossession in the Age of Humanity," 291.

48 Suzman, *Regional Assessment*, 3, 11, 30.

49 Hitchcock and Holm, "Bureaucratic Domination," 307.

50 "We must recognize that the critical force in producing change in hunter-gatherer communities is now the post-independence state, and it need not, indeed probably will not, lead to San empowerment"; Hitchcock and Holm, "Bureaucratic Domination," 332.

51 Sapignoli, "Dispossession in the Age of Humanity," 293.

52 Solway, "Human Rights and NGO 'Wrongs'," 325.

53 Given its economic situation and autonomy as a middle-income country featuring relatively good records, thus, not being a client state at the mercy of foreign actors.

54 Solway, "Human Rights and NGO 'Wrongs'," 326.

55 "In Botswana, by the late twentieth century, 'development' became the state's method of taming" [the margins] … "Bringing the Bushmen within the ambit of the state, ready to take their place in the modern world." Solway, "Human Rights and NGO 'Wrongs'," 332.

influence what is perceived as the correct way of living and being, the legitimacy bestowed on the dominant concepts of human rights and development being highly debatable.

The same can be argued in relation to paradigms of human culture, conservation models and the preservation of natural wilderness, which are often regarded as conflicting with indigenous claims and interests. A paradox arises when these initiatives are contextualised in indigenous peoples' situations, against their claims and interests. Whereas environmental protection is often given priority in areas inhabited by indigenous peoples, the damaging effects, degradation and exploitation of nature and resources on other territories of the pursuit of economic and investment interests goes unmarked. This inconsistency arises from the colonial logic in terms of which the interests and rights of the "native" are trampled on and disregarded in privileging those of the coloniser (with superior goals and priorities, entitlements and rights), as well as the specific economic and development model they entail.

Opposing perspectives relating to conflicting interests intermingle with the broader agendas of the actors involved in national economic, social and development plans[56] and projects. Concerns pertaining to labour resources, land allocation and concessions for wildlife protection areas, nature conservation, ecological preservation and economic activities (agriculture, livestock herding, mining or tourism ventures) are seemingly incompatible with the interests of indigenous peoples. Balancing and managing those clashing interests has profound consequences on their ways of life. However, these conflicts also create tensions vis-à-vis other communities that regard the differential treatment provided to indigenous peoples' groups with suspicion. Tensions may also be created in the given indigenous group, in which case quarrels are often framed along generational lines, gender divisions, in relation to disparate levels of income, life supporting alternatives and so on.

Different strategies have been suggested to address this situation and map out a better path for the future. William Ellis speaks about three different agendas that inspire the different approaches taken by researchers, policy makers and NGO practitioners:[57] revivalism and nostalgia for tradition; access to land

56 "Egalitarianism and discouragement of personal promotion remain deeply embedded in their social structure. The contemporary development schemes that permeate the management and running of the resettlement policy in Namibia run counter to these very same principles ... The contemporary development projects expect cooperation, encourage accumulation, and reward personal advancement, all of which undermine the Ju|'hoan values of a 'good life'." Ninkova, *"Now that We have Development"*, 226.

57 In his analysis of the land question in the context of South Africa.

for grazing livestock; and poverty alleviation alternatives addressing the root causes of alienation. These approaches lead to prioritising different specific goals, defining concrete actions and privileging a particular standpoint as the basis for supporting the claims made by different actors for specific rights, namely cultural survival and the preservation of traditional practices,[58] access to rights in equal terms, assimilation policies aimed at countrywide progress, and affirmative actions[59] and positive discrimination acknowledging their historic and structural marginalisation.

In the case of NGOs and donors, Robins[60] refers to their strategic prioritisation of certain goals which often have little to do with social transformation. They pit culturalist approaches against other strategies that put the accent on alternative livelihood strategies aimed at protecting their needs as historically marginalised groups. The former is connected with ethnic aspects, cultural traits and authenticity questions that imply the holding of essentialist views that can lead to a reification of culture (an authentic authenticity). "The 'protection of human dignity' can lead us in various directions, many of which are paternal and conservative."[61]

2.3 *Understanding Indigenous Peoples in Africa: The Term and the Peoples*

The controversial classification of indigenous as against non-indigenous people in the African context goes back to the first encounters between the local population and European explorers, missionaries and colonial settlers. That context gave rise to the widespread assertion that all Africans are indigenous to Africa. Albert Barume[62] refutes this claim:

58 "International models of indigenism have colluded with essentialist conceptions of culture and ethnicity to obscure the contemporary complexity of San cultural identity and to distort representations of San claims for social and economic justice into demands for 'cultural preservation.'" Hodgson, "Introduction," 1042. The politicisation of cultural identity. Mamdani, *Neither Settler nor Native*, 18.

59 Expressly recognised in several African constitutions, although they rarely refer expressly to indigenous peoples, but rather to minorities, vulnerable groups, historically marginalised groups or communities. The Republic of Congo gives constitutional recognition to "peuples autochtones" (indigenous peoples) (art. 16). In addition, it adopted Law No. 5–2011 on the Promotion and Protection of the Rights of Indigenous Populations. Indigenous populations are also granted protection in the preamble of Cameroon's constitution.

60 Robins, "Whose 'Culture'," 235–236.

61 Hopgood, *Endtimes of Human Rights*, 159.

62 Former African representative to the Expert Mechanism on the Rights of Indigenous Peoples (EMRIP 2015–2018) and independent expert member of the ACHPR Working Group on Indigenous Peoples (2007–2018).

> Someone is indigenous in relation to a given, well-identified area of land. This implies that an African community cannot be indigenous to the entire continent, not even to an entire country, but instead to a precise land that can be demarcated and seen as culturally important. There has to be a land to which a claimant community is culturally strongly attached.[63]

The official conceptualisation of the ACHPR, based on the 2003 report by the Working Group on Indigenous Populations and Communities and Minorities in Africa of the Commission (WGIPC),[64] summarises the main characteristics of indigenous groups as follows: self-identification, dependence on their traditional land and its natural resources for their own survival and way of life, having a culture distinct from that of the majority, often living in inaccessible regions endowed with natural resources, suffering from political and social marginalisation, and being subject to domination and exploitation in national political and economic structures.

In the African context, the recent history of colonial domination and the even more recent history of the struggle for independence have conditioned the way in which the question of indigeneity has been dealt with. Prominence was given to the construction of the nation state, territorial integrity, building national unity and fostering economic progress. Mirroring the liberal democracies in the West, the idea of a single national identity and the supremacy of citizenship over ethnic and cultural differences and issues of belonging prevailed, relegating issues like religion and culture to the private sphere.[65] Any emphasis on ethnic differentiation was seen with suspicion and apprehension, and still is.

---

63 Barume, *Land Rights of Indigenous Peoples*, 49.

64 The ACHPR has not defined the markers of peoplehood. However, the term peoples can be seen to signify the following: those subject to colonial domination, the population of a state as a whole, the people of Africa more generally, in relation to the state as the entity that can exercise the rights of peoples, and lastly, a section of the population subject to discrimination (sub-state groups). The notion of people used in the African Charter on Human and Peoples' Rights (Banjul Charter) is connected to the legal concept of the state, whereas the term populations (and communities) used by the ACHPR and the WGIPC relate to the idea of ethnic affiliation, in which case the right to self-determination does not imply political secession but control of self-development. The ACHPR decided to expand the mandate of the Working Group in 2020 to include the rights of minorities. ACHPR, "Resolution on the Renewal of the Mandate," ACHPR/Res. 455 (LXVI).

65 Kymlicka, "Nation-Building and Minority Rights," 54–96.

As a result, governments have privileged particular social goals, livelihoods, regulatory and legal forms, economic models (market rather than subsistence) and related industrial or agricultural practices (logging, extractive industries), tourism and conservation models. Indigenous peoples' nomadic, pastoralist systems are often overlooked and disregarded as invalid options. Their lifestyles have led many to consider them as uncivilised, caught in a primitive stage of human evolution, and in need of development. Recently independent African countries were not willing to accept within their national boundaries a group that seemed to lag "behind" or to stray away from the path of progress and modernity. After independence, with the national and regional priorities being set on sovereignty, political autonomy and economic growth (against the historical background of colonialism and economic dependency), indigenous peoples' lifestyles resonated with under-development.[66] In the case of the San their marginalisation was fuelled by: "Widespread perceptions of San social inferiority ... taken to justify racial abuse. In Botswana and Namibia in particular, San social and economic marginalisation is not popularly understood to be a consequence of the actions of others, but instead is constructed as a direct consequence of San social inferiority."[67] Deprecation of these groups has led to the provision of "assistance" where the "beneficiaries" are overlooked in the decision-making processes affecting them.

In addition, in order to avoid ethnic-driven conflicts, national unity was built on a narrative of the equality of all citizens rather than on ethnic differentiation. This approach was privileged in Botswana, a country named after the dominant ethnic group, the Tswana (in line with the post-colonial one-nation consensus). According to Cook and Sarkin: "efforts to promote nationalism in many countries often came at the expense of protecting the unique cultures that comprised the citizenry of each nation".[68] Despite Namibia's also following a policy of non-tribalism,[69] it accommodates multiculturalism. San groups have been partially recognised by the government as traditional authorities ("an indigenous homogeneous group" with a common background, culture and area that they inhabit). The government instituted the San Development Programme in 2005[70] "dedicated to the development of San communities so

66 Not only among African states. The ILO Convention 107 (still in force in seventeen countries, six of which are African) refers to populations "at a less advanced stage" (art. 1.a), "not yet integrated" in an integrationist and assimilationist orientation.

67 Suzman, *Regional Assessment*, 9.

68 Cook and Sarkin, "Who is Indigenous?" 118.

69 Suzman, *Assessment of the Status*, 73.

70 Cabinet decision No. 25/29.11.05/001.

that they can be integrated into the mainstream society and economy"[71] as they are considered to be previously disadvantaged, vulnerable and marginalised communities. In South Africa "African Indigenous San and Khoikhoi peoples are not formally recognised in terms of national legislation; however, this is shifting with the Traditional and Khoisan Leadership Act enacted in 2021".[72] This intention of avoiding social division for the sake of national unity is further sustained, to a certain degree, by the refusal to confer special rights on indigenous groups, which would result in greater obligations on the part of the state.

The implementation of this policy has contributed to disagreements around the notion of indigenous peoples and their lack of recognition. How indigenous peoples are seen by outsiders influences their own perceptions, as well as the strategies adopted to further their interests, often involving the re-appropriation of those alien views. At the core of the lack of support and acknowledgment is a general governmental perception of indigenous peoples as backward, non-modern and under-developed (as just explained). On the one hand this has deterred some governments from acknowledging indigenous peoples in their own right.[73] On the other, it has led to the adscription, by members of indigenous groups, to a different grammar in their self-identification, which varies depending on the setting and the interlocutors they are dealing with. At international level they relate to the term indigenous peoples. However, when strategising their claims at domestic level they often opt for less contested categories[74] to accommodate their claims to the government's preferred language.[75] Rather than the label "indigenous" other ethnic, livelihood-related or language-based categorisations are more commonly being used: terms such as pastoralists, herders, hunter-gatherers, foragers, forest people, etc. Preferring categories such as these marks what Kenrick considers to be a political intent, "to assert that these peoples have a right to their way of life".[76]

---

71 Anaya, "Report of the Special Rapporteur," A/HRC/24/41/Add.1, 6.

72 IWGIA, *Indigenous World*, 123.

73 The notion of disagreement between different cultures (the question of alterity), entails perceiving the others' interpretation as wrong; Holbraad, in Carrithers et al, "Ontology," 184.

74 "There are indications that neoliberal ideals underpinning advocacy for recognition of indigenous rights in Africa overshadow any contrary views expressed by those uneasy with this particular concept or legal framework"; Mukwiza Ndahinda, *Indigenousness in Africa*, 347.

75 See Hodgson, *Being Maasai*, 157.

76 Kenrick, "Present Predicament," 42.

However, not acknowledging the social processes and relationships that cause the acute poverty and disempowerment they endure is a severe limitation, as has been shown in the previous section. A definition aimed at encompassing a category of indigenous peoples based on certain components of their identity and ethnicity[77] needs to be complemented by an understanding of indigeneity as a term indicating a relation between a group and the nation state.[78] According to Saugestad, if one attempts to be culturally neutral there is a danger of ending up being culturally blind.[79]

Identity is thus a subjective attribute that encompasses ethnic affiliation as one among various markers (as seen in section 2.1). Acknowledging that language has political connotations and that cultural orientations are fluid and dynamic, the use of the term indigenous peoples can yield both positive and less beneficial outcomes when pursuing goals such as development, increasing visibility and increasing awareness. An emphasis on narrow characteristics that are indicators of one's identity might lead to overlooking certain specificities and losing valuable elements of a culture for the sake of adaptation or incorporation into mainstream society and the national economy, thereby preventing the revitalisation of cultural elements that could reinforce the cohesion and social fabric of the community.

2.4 *The Value of Indigenous Worldviews*

Zips-Mairitsch correctly states that "the reciprocal translation of indigenous and Western legal systems, understandings and terms is problematic",[80] and not much (or not enough) is known about some African indigenous peoples' legal worldviews, especially not about those of the San. Attention has focussed on aspects related to their economies and livelihoods (traditional subsistence hunter-gatherer practices). Many studies have concentrated on their social systems, kinship organisation, education systems, language, technical and artistic expressions (musical instruments, healing practices, dancing, initiation

77 Quoting Wilmsen, "Mutable Identities," 841: "ethnicity is an objective position in an arena of social power, while identity is subjective positioning on a stage of social practice … languages of ethnicity, nationalism and religion draw upon normative images of primordial associations and identification". He reminds us to acknowledge the economics and politics that lead to the creation of the social and cultural traits that define ethnicity. The notion of ethnicity simplifies the complex social and unequal world. Wilmsen and McAllister, *Politics of Difference.*

78 Saugestad, "Dilemmas". Zenker proposes a conceptualisation of indigeneity as "a variant of collectivized-autochthonous-ethnicity". In Gressier, *At Home in the Okavango*, 9.

79 Saugestad, "Dilemmas," 219.

80 Zips-Mairitsch, *Lost Lands?* 177.

rituals), as well as their history, adaptation patterns and cultural characteristics more generally. Encapsulated in those expressions of their socio-cultural orders are values that inspire notions and practices related to resource use, social patterns, their way of life, as well as their relationship with land (and property).[81] Some sketches of those ideas can be drawn from the accounts of anthropologists as well as San individuals' own stories narrated in existing literature.[82]

The foraging mode of thought of hunter-gatherers (immediate-return economies and relatively equal societies) is premised by Barnard to be more resilient than the mode of production and accumulation of delayed-return societies. Sharing as a redistribution practice[83] as well as generalised reciprocity operate among kin in hunter-gatherer societies. Barnard defends the idea of universal kin among foraging peoples and of balanced reciprocity (rather than generalised reciprocity dependant on the closeness of the kinship). Reciprocity "equalise(s) access both to movable property and to natural resources" (water, firewood, game).[84] Redistribution is the result of a social organisation with little social stratification, in which social security is connected to the kin/tribe/family adscription.[85]

Woodburn affirms that egalitarism is characteristic of hunter-gatherer societies with immediate-return economies. This egalitarian quality has implications for authority and sharing[86] as well as for other aspects such as gender relationships and the upbringing of children. However, Woodburn considers sharing not as a form of exchange or reciprocity but as a political phenomenon to avoid "inequalities of power, wealth and status".[87] When it comes to personal possessions, "property is put to work explicitly to develop symmetrical ties of friendship between people" beyond the kin.[88] He understands the

81 "Pre-colonial and present-day African indigenous land tenure is unique and struggles to fit into the common law notion of 'property' and 'ownership.'" Du Plessis, "African Indigenous Land Rights," 63.

82 According to Vermeylen, "stories and narratives act indeed as normative 'lawmaking' sources". Vermeylen, "Nagoya Protocol," 190.

83 Disputed by Woodburn, "'Sharing is Not a Form of Exchange'," on meat sharing among the Hamza in Tanzania.

84 Barnard, "Foraging Mode of Thought," 8.

85 Howard, "Evaluating Human Rights," 176.

86 "In sharing it is not supposed to make a difference that you got this item from me rather than from someone else or directly from the environment. As I have tried to show above, this is by no means a trivial cultural achievement since it is a specific way of creating and determining value." Widlok, "Sharing," 24.

87 Woodburn, "'Sharing is Not a Form of Exchange'," 61.

88 Woodburn, "'Sharing is Not a Form of Exchange'," 57.

practice of demand sharing not as being derived from generosity but based on donor obligation and the entitlement of the recipient. Gift-giving reciprocation among certain kin "hxaro partners"[89] among the!kung is seen as "gestures of friendly intent" to perpetuate relationships and bonds: "simple, voluntary, non-competitive, symmetrical, contractual ties ... they do not mark out or confirm the status of participants".[90]

However, demand sharing can be also explained as a complex behaviour that can be either a testing behaviour or an assertive one. Peterson suggests that: "If moral obligation and commitment to others is construed not in terms of giving freely, but in terms of responding positively to demands, the morality of demand sharing is as positive as that of generosity."[91] Based on the ability to demand from those who have more, it is a practice shaped by legal, political and affective dimensions,[92] but also by uncertainty, mistrust and fear.

Other theorisations construct this rationale differently. Bird-David hypothesises that hunter-gatherers' common view of the environment is that it is giving, from which he derives the notion that their economic system is "constructed in terms of giving".[93] "They (hunter-gatherers) view their environment as giving" and thus their distribution systems and property relations "are constructed in terms of giving", not reciprocity.

Resources are understood as entities to which one can relate in ways different than something one can use or something that is a source of economic wealth. "Land is regarded not simply as an economic or environmental asset, but as a social, cultural and ontological resource. Land remains an important factor in the construction of social identity, the organization of religious life and the production and reproduction of culture."[94]

A reformulation of rights that accounts for these views is due.

89 Hxaro is "a delayed-return system of reciprocity linking people as exchange partners over extensive areas" and allowing for temporary access to resources and land. Hays and Hitchcock, "Land and Resource Rights," 202.

90 Woodburn, "'Sharing is Not a Form of Exchange'," 58.

91 Peterson, "Demand Sharing," 870.

92 Laws, *All Things being Equal*, 225. She extensively analyses the role of "experiences of uncertainty" and vulnerabilities in how egalitarianism is pursued (by Ju|'hoansi of the Nyae conservancy in Namibia). In this line of analysis and anthropology of ethics, see also Peterson, "Demand Sharing".

93 Bird-David, "Giving Environment," 189.

94 AUC, AfDB, and UNECA Consortium, *Framework*, 8.

3 Property Rights and the Land Question

3.1 *Reimagining Human Rights: Feeding the Discourse with an Alternative Formulation*

> The power of Indigenous thinking to change 'our' legal imagination and, therefore, its unquestionable condition as a key ally in the decolonization of international law and in the invigoration of the counter-hegemonic dimensions of international law.[95]

The Western epistemological order has been dominant in constructing the grammar and corpus of human rights. This order has inspired and permeated discourses all over the world, resulting in a homogenous narrative that has been encapsulated in the main human rights instruments. Inspiration from alternative sources of law and legal discourses is limited. As a result, this exchange has often been unidirectional, limited to a particular framework deemed neutral and universal – the Western one and its particular features (secularism, autonomy, anthropocentrism) – while indigenous peoples' worldviews, world-senses and perspectives on the fulfilment of their own ideas of a good life have remained largely without resonance beyond their own communities. The flow of legal ideas should also take place from the local (indigenous peoples) to the global in order to influence the hegemonic discourse and contribute to addressing current planetary challenges. "The challenge is to make sense of the ways in which the forces of the African vernacular and those of liberal democracy are confronting one another at the present moment; how, in ongoing, often strident struggles, both are being transformed – thereby altering the very shape and substance of postcolonial politics, of citizenship, of democracy."[96]

With a few exceptions, current legal systems have not only failed to acknowledge and recognise the specific rights and governing approaches of indigenous peoples, but also to resort to their orders as reference and inspiration. It is for these reasons that the current analysis seeks to contribute towards decolonising the current legal order, to embrace the validity and sense of indigenous philosophies and legal ideas in relation to land tenure[97] regulation. The African

---

95 Bacca, "Double Bind and the Reverse Side," 99.

96 Comaroff and Comaroff, *Theory from the South*, 80. They speak about the shift from ideology to ID-ology (a term encapsulating difference and diversity – the ology of identity). They accredit the term to R. Tabane and F. Haffajee's 2003 newspaper article entitled Ideology is dead, long live ID-ology (Tabane and Haffajee, "Ideology is Dead," 6).

97 Relationship between land and people (individually or collectively).

Union's framework and guidelines on land policy in Africa recognises the need to "blend tradition and modernity in land rights regimes,"[98] acknowledging the importance of building on indigenous tenure arrangements.[99]

In unravelling certain elements from the San past and present worldviews, this chapter aims at identifying valuable aspects that can assist in reconfiguring the idea of property as a legal right and overcoming the West-centrism of the dominant conceptualisation. The San-specific approaches to fellow beings, nature and the environment, their understanding of social ordering and value systems, and their adaptative livelihood strategies are elements that deserve being recaptured to expand narrower understandings of property. Furthermore, "their perspectives and experiences 'from the margins' offer key theoretical and political insights into this complicated place we call 'Africa' by challenging grand narratives of modernization, of 'Africa rising,' of supposedly 'universal' ideas of progress and justice".[100]

TWAIL correctly holds that "The historical model of human rights cannot respond to the needs of the Third World except if there is a radical rethinking and restructuring of the international order, abandoning the efforts to universalize an essentially European corpus of human rights."[101] The new grammar has to express existing multicultural and plural understandings of rights that reflect alternative visions of societies and priorities that can contribute to a more just world. In addition to constructive criticism, a more pragmatic approach connected to the production of alternative human rights knowledge has to be introduced.[102]

3.2 *Property in Dispute: Preliminary Ideas on Differing Conceptualisations*

The aim of this section is to examine ideas around property[103] in two different legal orders, namely property rights law in Western legal systems and an indigenous perspective on property among the San people of Southern Africa.

---

98 AUC, AfDB, and UNECA Consortium, *Framework*, 14.

99 "Even though transhumance is an important adaptive technique for African climates and ecosystem maintenance, this is not reflected in land tenure laws, which are for the most part based on colonial legislation and norms." Crawhall, "Africa and the UN Declaration," 18.

100 Hodgson, "Africa from the Margins," 38.

101 Ramina, "TWAIL – 'Third World Approaches'," 261.

102 Badaru, "Examining the Utility," 385.

103 According to Widlok "Introduction," property is the field of social relations and practices that leads us to understand society and institutions.

It will delve into the relationship between people and resources[104] and the underlying values inspiring their understanding and practices around property in general and with regard to land more specifically. Different types of engagement between human beings and the non-human result in diverse arrangements to regulate and organise those relationships between people and resources. By looking into the different uses of what is owned (disposal, possession, consumption, commodification, sharing) and the related dimensions of the interaction (power, socialisation, identity, ideology, religion/spirituality, time/space, geo-political, economic), certain defining characteristics will be identified of the conceptualisation of rights both by the West and by the San.

As a normative order that recognises rights, establishes binding obligations and imposes penalties by prescribing conflict resolution processes that are enforceable and institutionalised, law can have enormous implications in the social, economic, cultural and political arenas. It can be an enabler of change, empowering and emancipatory, and a tool for resistance, but it can also be limiting, oppressive and conducive to marginalisation. The inherent value of "things" (broadly understood) is protected through rights vested on them, or on the users of those things. Those values might range from utilitarian aspects to intrinsic ones and broader ecological and socio-cultural appreciations. The values and logic behind a given practice (based on its capacity to address societal practices and accommodate expectations, purposes, needs and conceptualisations of life) become legitimised by legal means. Different choices are shaped by particular conditionings and are solved differently, unveiling a spectrum of preferences and priorities based on a variety of meanings, purposes and merits.

Property has been regulated as a legal right. It is contemplated in the United Nations Universal Declaration of Human Rights (UDHR Art. 17, right to own property and not be deprived of it arbitrarily). The two binding covenants reinforcing the UDHR, the International Covenant on Civil and Political Rights (ICCPR) and the International Covenant on Economic, Social and Cultural Rights (ICESCR) do not include this right. At the time of their drafting, the gradual decolonisation process of former colonies together with the ideological divide among democratic and capitalist countries, communist and socialists systems and authoritarian states led to opposition to the inclusion of property rights. In that context it was highly controversial to consider private

104 "What appears from a modernist perspective as 'resources' are entities to which indigenous and other place-based peoples are related in diverse ways. And I stress that the relations are diverse rather than assume that the notion of property can encompass those relations." Blaser, "Political Ontology," 891.

property (linked to individual freedom) as a fundamental right in relation to the common good and collective ownership. ILO Convention 169[105] refers to the rights of ownership and possession instead. The UNDRIP refers to the right to: "Own, use, develop and control the lands, territories and resources that they possess by reason of traditional ownership or other traditional occupation or use, as well as those which they have otherwise acquired" (Art. 26.2).

At continental level The Banjul Charter (adopted in 1981) does mention the right to property in Art. 14, which shall be guaranteed. In its judgment of Application no. 006/2012 (*Ogiek* case) the African Court provides for a broader interpretation, stating that: "Although addressed in the part of the Charter which enshrines the rights recognised for individuals, the right to property as guaranteed by Article 14 may also apply to groups or communities" (para. 123).[106]

There are authors who defend its consideration as a human right[107] (and further regulation in a protocol) based on the understanding of the right to "own" property as intrinsic to human dignity[108] (not just as a strategic right that enables the enjoyment of other rights). Some movements and authors articulate the possibility of a right to land specifically (land rights) in connection with property rights, equality and social justice.[109]

The right to property refers to associations between persons and things most generally, but also extends to non-tangible elements and other persons: "One which involves a measure of socially recognized control over the 'thing' and which necessitates some restrictions on other people's control of the same 'thing'. So, in fact, property rights (whether held individually or jointly) are held in opposition to those who do not hold such rights."[110]

---

105 Ratified by only one African country; Central African Republic. The Banjul Charter has been ratified by all AU members states but Morocco.

106 Also see *Sudan Human Rights Organisation and Centre on Housing Rights and Evictions* (COHRE) *v Sudan*, ACHPR Communication No. 279/03–296/05, 28th ACHPR AAR Annex (Nov 2009–May 2010), para. 205: "It doesn't matter whether they had legal titles to the land, the fact that the victims cannot derive their livelihood from what they possessed for generations means they have been deprived of the use of their property"; finding the Republic of Sudan in violation of art. 14, among others.

107 Commission on Legal Empowerment of the Poor, *Making the Law Work*, cochaired by economist Hernando de Soto (the author of disputed theories around formal property rights system).

108 Howard, "Reconsidering," debates the negative or positive qualities of such a right (to have property or to 'own' it), implying that the state should provide and fulfil versus forbearance.

109 See Gilbert, "Land Rights".

110 Ingold, Riches, and Woodburn, *Hunters and Gatherers*, 13.

Thus, my right over something implies the recognition of such by others who are excluded or restricted in their entitlements towards the thing I am associated with in such a way (to use, possess, dispose of). Furthermore, ownership comes with rules that define that association, sanctions to enforce it and an ideology to justify and legitimise it.[111]

The content of the terms "rights" and "property" varies depending on the grounds on which ownership and landholding are classified, namely modes of governance, tenure systems, entitlements (rights against another person who is excluded), enforceability, and the basis of the interests and values served by property. On the basis of the governance of property, it can be regulated by statutory law or common law. Civil law places ownership at the centre (entailing sovereignty – *dominium* – and legal control as the prime arrangement with limited exceptions over this exclusive model) over factual control or other limited entitlements. Common law stresses the idea of relative title whereby "any given property conflict will be won by the stronger of the conflicting claims on possession".[112] Rights can be governed by customary regimes involving traditional leaders and community-based authorities instead of by the state apparatus. On the basis of landholding and tenure systems, property can be public (state owned), private (communal, family or individual),[113] or freehold. As per the type of prerogatives conferred, right holders may qualify to use, possess, lease, inherit,[114] occupy, transfer or sell. In addition, there are numerous related rights to property: housing[115] (dwelling, shelter), subsistence rights (food and access to resources: water, hunting, gathering, grazing), the development of economic activities, commercial rights over wild plants,[116] cultural rights, religion, development, and so forth. Lastly, depending on its enforceability property rights can be divided into formal or not justifiable rights. Property can

111 Ingold, Riches, and Woodburn, *Hunters and Gatherers.*

112 Van der Walt, *Property in the Margins*, 35.

113 The centrality of "individual or private property because of its importance for economic liberalism as a social system"; Van der Walt, *Property in the Margins*, 37. Protecting individual autonomy and the free market.

114 "What actually is inherited is a set of status positions binding an individual to a network of obligations owed between persons with respect to land." Wilmsen, *Land Filled with Flies*, 53.

115 The ACHPR has implied other rights (housing) from the right to property (in *Social and Economic Rights Action Center and the Center for Economic and Social Rights v Nigeria*, ACHPR Communication No. 155/96 (May 27, 2002)).

116 "The legal regime that has been created with access and benefit sharing agreements has been one that sits uncomfortable with some San peoples who do not believe in the value of protecting their biocultural rights through a property rights framework." Vermeylen, "Nagoya Protocol," 199.

also be seen in connection with the values/interests served by property (based on the aptitude and virtues that can be derived from it: human autonomy, self-realisation, well-being,[117] or the function it performs – the allocation of resources). Property and land are important not only for economic subsistence, but they have cultural, identity and religious significance as well. They can also be approached from different dimensions relating to power and to poverty (or wealth), in that they enable the empowerment of individuals and communities and the sustenance of life (livelihoods).

Following Menski,[118] African worldviews revolve around ideas of togetherness, a never-ending continuum of past, present and future, temporal balance and harmony, the importance of social/cosmic harmony, and self-controlled order. Religion, law and morality are interlinked,[119] holistic nature and interconnectedness order philosophy: the environment, society and religion.[120] There are checks and balances, and different authorities on the same level without pre-eminence: king (the living), the ancestors, supernatural forces, the supreme being, and individual consciousness (internal balancing). Other characteristics are the relevance of the obligations of a person rather than a person's entitlements, the balance between group expectations and individual ambition, public interest and the common good, cooperation[121] and solidarity with regard to groups (the family, the band, the clan, the kinship group), the orality of legal systems and the flexibility of customary law (official and unofficial). These characteristics challenge mainstream understandings of property and entitlements. Even the idea of rights can entail broader meanings beyond individual prerogatives: "The assertion of a right of a human being therefore is not a claim possessed by an atomist individual, but a reflection and an embodiment of social relations in the language of rights."[122]

3.3 *Property Ideas in Western Legal Systems*

According to the Encyclopaedia Britannica, the term "property" is used of:

> An object of legal rights, which embraces possessions or wealth collectively, frequently with strong connotations of individual ownership

117 Alexander and Peñalver, *Introduction to Property Theory*.
118 Menski, *Comparative Law*.
119 Right action (orthopraxis) guiding religions, rather than right belief (orthodoxy).
120 Sky (the un-born, the spirits of the living, natural phenomena), earth (ancestors, the death, peoples' dwelling place), and the world. (Ayittey, *Indigenous African Institutions*, 10).
121 Rather than collectivism, given that cooperation leaves some room for individual volition.
122 Shivji, "Constructing a New Rights Regime," 268.

> ... The extraordinary diversity of the property systems of non-Western societies, however, suggests that any concept of property other than the descriptive one is dependent on the culture in which it is found. Because property law deals with the allocation, use, and transfer of wealth and objects of wealth, it must reflect the economy, family structure, and politics of the society in which it is found.[123]

The general use of the term in Western legal orders entails the right to own, possess, enjoy and dispose of something. It allows for its transferability and enforceability, claims that are closely related to personal liberty, where the value of the individual and his/her connection to the thing are privileged over the group's connection with it. The right to property is considered a civil liberty, a marker of individual freedom. It entails an agglomeration of prerogatives and power vested on an individual upon what is owned (material or immaterial), from which others are excluded (except if the owner permits).[124] Property is conceived in property rights law as a legal construct based on the expectation of attaining the exclusive right to own.

This version of a property right has its roots in the agglomerative tendency of Roman Law that consolidated ownership at the expense of others: *proprietas* and ownership (legal possession and exclusive rights) were separated from the limited privilege of use (*usufructus*). In addition, the legal systems conceived as conflict resolution mechanisms led to the reinforcement of that agglomerative system by virtue of which evidence of ownership had to be produced to solve disputes about who possessed a given thing (possession implies physical apprehension). Later developments consolidated the state's sanctioning of private individual property, occupation (physical possession) and protection of the labour added to the thing/object, considered as an extension of someone's will that had to be respected. Commercial interests favoured tying land to an owner for a long period to preserve its ownership through the generations.

Property theory consolidated from the consideration of property as instrumental to welfare and well-being (utilitarianism). Libertarian theory emphasised the protection of the labour put into things, resulting in the protection of rights (and duties) to use things for self-preservation. According to personality theory, property is linked to the freedom to identify needs and wants, and to achieve a personal end (that of self-realisation and self-development), through

123 Encyclopaedia Britannica, "Property".

124 "Property rights consist in a complex of multital 'claim-right/duty', 'privilege/no-right', 'power/liability' and 'immunity/disability' relations." (Carter, *Philosophical Foundations*, 129).

affirmative actions. Property rights law, being rights-based, has to do with entitlements from which property originates.

Individual property ownership is therefore understood as a "bundle of rights" (a term signifying a set of rights over different objects) which enables the holder of rights to use, dispose, sell or divide the property and above all to exclude others. Further prerogatives that this configuration of property entails would be to prevent opportunism, misuse, and reduce the costs and risks of transactions.

According to the evolutionary theory of land rights, the right to property emerges from the following process: an increase in population pressure, plus market integration, resulting in rising individualisation, and rights holders pressing for the creation of duly formalised private property rights by the state. Land is scarce and therefore an increase in regulation occurs, leading to the emergence of private property, which would be economically justified. Land can be then organised for collective use (at a high governance cost)[125] or divided upon individual rights (stemming from the holding of title). Based on the assumption that formal title provides tenure security, private property is seen to lead to the more productive use of resources, an efficient market, prosperity and wealth, despite the fact that the empirical evidence in that regard is not conclusive.[126] Subsequently land becomes a market asset, but as a result of this commodification those with low purchasing and social power can be put at a disadvantage, causing the further loss of derived rights.

Land tenure and property registration through individual titling and ownership, as against communal and customary land uses and occupation systems, have been privileged and supported by international organisations and government schemes. The underlying assumptions behind this preference have been questioned, "especially the validity of framing economic development on a paradigm derived from western European experience".[127] According to Kingwill, the relationships between groups are sometimes more relevant for ownership purposes than a title deed.[128] The Special Rapporteur on the right

125 The theory of the commons (Elinor Ostrom) argues that those resources under the commons can be governed collectively without their inevitably being endangered.

126 See Platteau, "Evolutionary Theory".

127 Griffiths, "Engaging with the Global," 114.

128 In Du Plessis, "African Indigenous Land Rights," 64. Only 10% of land estate in Africa is subject to formal entitlement, whereas almost 80% is customary domain (with various degrees of *de facto* legal protection outside state-registered property). Alden Wily, "'The Law is to Blame'," 735. This reinforces the idea of customary land as non-market land; Chimhowu and Woodhouse, "Customary vs Private Property Rights?" 352. "Overall, the constitutional recognition of rights deriving from African customary tenure as property interests is still partial or non-existent." Alden Wily, "Compulsory Acquisition," 97. The

to food, Olivier De Schutter, asserted in his 2010 report that "individual titling appears to matter less to the poor than security of tenure".[129] Among the recommendations to ensure the enjoyment of the right to food, the report advised states to encourage communal ownership systems rather than individual titling (42.c).

Privileging and consolidating land tenure registration resulted from the choices adopted by newly independent countries in their aim of strengthening their national unity, and followed the notion of the state held by the former colonial powers,[130] in connection with regional and global economic patterns. In addition, changes in the nature of labour, migration and consumption patterns affected land uses and led to the commodification of land on the basis of its capital value. Among those different purposes were subsistence activities, agriculture, cattle grazing, tourism ventures, environmental conservation,[131] wildlife protection, securing housing etc. Some of these strategies were

---

following countries distinguish customary or community lands in their constitutions as a property ownership category: Angola, DRC, Equatorial Guinea, Ethiopia, Ghana, Kenya, Mozambique, South Sudan, Eswatini, Uganda, Zambia (and South Africa in an indirect way). According to Alden Wily, "no African constitution fails to recognize the *existence* of private landed property and only Guinea Bissau's Constitution offers no protection. To be precise, most African constitutions do not acknowledge private property itself but the right *to* property" (emphasis in the original); Alden Wily, "Compulsory Acquisition," 97.

129 De Schutter, "Access to Land," UNGA A/65/281, 11.

130 Chimhowu and Woodhouse, "Customary vs Private Property Rights?" 352 note that despite accounts "the non-market nature of customary tenure in Africa, to the extent that it exists, is as much a colonial construction as it is rooted in any essentially African value system". They dispute the idea of the communal character ascribed to customary land tenure as an idealised construction from colonial times even though they acknowledge that the commodification of land occurs in customary lands (vernacular market), and it does result in the individualisation of land control leading to the privatisation of land, which is currently more common due to land scarcity, resource management, population growth and mobility, labour markets, and so on. Joreiman points at the strategy of the indirect rule and regimes of land implemented in common law Africa that led to privileging commonly held property of land and giving no recognition to indigenous peoples (this time indigenous understood broadly, in opposition to settlers), arguing that local people were against the absence of land markets and private ownership for native arrangements. Thus [customary law and tenure systems] were applied to people "as members of ethnic groups and not as citizens". Joireman, *Where There is no Government*, 41. In this same vein, Home views the lack of recognition of traditional patterns in the use of land as a legacy of colonialism: "External colonial rule created a dual system of land tenure that restrained private property rights in the tribal/communal areas." Home, "'Culturally Unsuited'," 403.

131 "In 2010, State Parties to the Convention on Biological Diversity (CBD) committed to conserve at least 17 percent of terrestrial areas through protected area management; however, this has led to devastating consequences for the indigenous and local communities whose lands overlap with areas earmarked for protection under that target. Despite this,

adopted as components of the development plans of these states. The privatisation of land for different uses (tourism, conservation, commercial uses, the cattle industry etc.) has ultimately deprived people (mainly in rural areas and in poor households) of their means of subsistence, which were traditionally connected with the natural resources they can no longer reach. "This notion of private property rights in international development policy is based on the model of a rational, autonomous, profit-maximizing, efficient individual who works to better herself. Existing property conceptions are based on narrow, individualist, economistic notions of absolute rights to exclude, use, and transfer."[132]

3.4 *The San Understanding of Land and Property*

> The issue of land rights is apparently neglected in African studies on ethics, culture, and religion. The reason is that land is understood as a matter to be exploited to satisfy human needs. Studies on land, from the perspective of the existing literature, have been left to geographers, lawyers, historians, and sociologists who present land-related issues in terms of reports that lack critical analyses, hermeneutical insights, ethical questions, and transformative suggestions.[133]

The lack of critical analysis that includes alternative insights in the study of land issues results, as Tarimo's statement above indicates, in an absence of proposals that can enable change. This section will explore the specific conceptualisations of land and property among the San, which will shape the conceptual basis for an alternative formulation of the right to property.

During the Botswana High Court case *Sesana v. The Attorney General*[134] an applicant was asked by one of the judges to explain what the San did at the

---

the 'zero' draft of the CBD's post-2020 Global Biodiversity Framework, which is currently being negotiated, contemplates increasing the protected areas target to cover 30 percent of the planet without adequate safeguards for indigenous peoples and local communities." ACHPR WGIPC. "Inter-Session Activity Report," 6. This again shows the complexity of balancing the different interest at stake.

132 Rajagopal, *International Law from Below*, 264.

133 Tarimo, *African Land Rights Systems*, v.

134 This important case dealt with resettlements and the withdrawal of government services to San members living in the Central Kalahari Game Reserve (CKGR) in Botswana. The CKGR was created in 1961 to protect the welfare of the so-called Bushmen. Constitutional recognition of their freedom of movement in the reserve was granted in art. 14.3. However, this guarantee was removed the constitution in 2003 for being discriminatory towards

graves of their forefathers in the land under dispute. "Mongwegi Thobogelo stood silently, opened her shirt and performed the gesture of gathering soil, rubbing it on her bare chest, and standing in a posture of spiritual supplication. ... Thobogelo's one act of wordless testimony removed all doubts about the applicants' attachments to the land – and to their ancestors – from which they had been forcibly relocated."[135]

This case illustrates the different narratives informing the opposing meanings of land. On the one hand the government discourse was that of equality, integration (assimilation), fairness, development, conservation and the cost of services, whereas for the San the issue had to do with forced relocations, the denial of basic rights, and diversity.[136]

According to Barnard, while movable resources might be owned individually, for foragers land is a matter of (collective) knowledge and ownership. Rights to land and its resources are "vested in descendants of the original ancestors"; "they see people as innately free and the state as the usurper",[137] not the guarantor of their inalienable rights to land. Barnard classifies the relationship with land in four ways: ritual association, economic association, notions of ownership and knowledge, and perceptions of power and rights.

For the San the significance of land therefore goes beyond its materiality. Its sacred nature is connected to the territory[138] (of known but unmarked borders), autonomy, culture and identity, (a sense of belonging, as a group and as citizens), and to the ancestors. It derives from a holistic comprehension of life, nature and the universe, as well as from the interconnection between the human and the non-human. A relational understanding is favoured. Rather than "owning land – as a moral capitalist value – [they are] in favour of culturally connecting to it". Their social connectivity is vested on the land.[139]

Ownership can be enjoyed in different ways: communally, collectively, domestically (family), or individually, and the distinctions between private and public, personal and collective (the group), individual and communal

non-San and in order to make the constitution tribally neutral. The verdict was issued in 2006 that the San were in lawful possession of the land.

135 Sapignoli, "'Bushmen' in the Law," 218.

136 The San's attachment to land is thus understood to be not as a commodity or in terms of market value, but more like attachment to a homeland. On the idea of property as homeland, see Ankersen and Ruppert, "Defending the Polygon," 684.

137 Barnard, "Foraging Mode of Thought," 15 and 13.

138 Understood as the area within which one has access rights and the right to the use of resources, as in a homeland – "the units of stewardship and management in both spiritual and material sense." Hitchcock, "Sharing the Land," 193.

139 Blatman-Thomas, "Reciprocal Repossession," 1404.

(jointly used)[140] are entangled. However, within this understanding, holding property does not encompass an alienation right. There is no right to sell the territory they have access to or occupy, nor to give it away.[141]

The patterns, dynamics and practices that direct their interactions with others, as well as the discourses around property that underpin such ritualised behaviour, will define more egalitarian or individualistic relationships. The different types of engagement with human and non-human resources and things will characterise different types of relationships between people and resources and persons among themselves. Different arrangements around "property" challenge the assumption of exclusivity that is central in a liberal system, especially in contexts of scarcity and within the horizon of what is just.[142] "Hunter-gatherer territories are not 'property' in quite the same sense as property is defined in Western legal systems ... The right which they lack – crucial to 'ownership' and 'property' as more narrowly defined – is the right of alienation."[143] Property "rights" generally pertain to the associations between persons and material things (resources, food, land), thus allowing for use, possession (physically holding or occupying), disposal, accumulation, redistribution and exchange. Among the San, the following applies: "People in societies with immediate-return systems are regarded as being born, or naturally endowed, with rights of direct personal access to land and ungarnered resources of the area with which they are associated. These rights are not formally bestowed, nor can they be withheld."[144]

However, property can also refer to less tangible resources, non-material resources, things that one knows ("intellectual property") or skills that one has. It can be bestowed with symbolic value (social, religious or economic, like communications, art, medicine, rituals, harvested food) and held over other persons (their labour, reproductive capacity etc.).

A view of human nature built on the notion of collective priority would imply that such land belongs primarily to some clan or family. The individual has a claim to such land by virtue of membership of the clan or family owning

140 Bodenhorn, "It's Good to Know," differentiates between individual and personal property, the latter referring to the social persona (embedded in his/her role in society), while the former highlights the autonomy of the individual in an equal relationship.

141 Barnard, *Hunters and Herders*, 242.

142 "Property rights grant so much respect for a person's attachments as to disregard completely those in dire need." Carter, *Philosophical Foundations*, 137. That is, irrespective of its having been voluntarily endorsed by society to render it morally legitimate and lawful.

143 Barnard, *Hunters and Herders*, 241.

144 Ingold, Riches, and Woodburn, *Hunters and Gatherers*, 15.

the relevant land.[145] The communities concerned, therefore, do not believe in the collective ownership of land only because their land is their primary source of food supply and income but also because it is the source of their identity and political status as well as a source of fundamental significance for their culture.[146]

The idea of ownership related to property is not unambiguous. Different meanings of the term ownership can be distinguished, such as host, guardian, master or proprietor.[147] Lorna Marshall identifies different types of ownership: no one's, local groups (requiring permission from those groups), belonging to a band/family, and communal. Following Widlok, property regimes in egalitarian societies (such as those of the "Bushmen", where there is equal access to resources) are "made up of individual property rights in combination with 'communal' obligations".[148] For example, "sources of food and water are owned by the headman for the band",[149] the tools and other artefacts which are exchanged, lent and gifted are privately owned,[150] as well as the meat distributed after a hunt. The cooperation in the hunt (production) is translated into the sharing of the game hunted (consumption), to ensure the food supply and thus to reduce the fluctuation in food intake that would otherwise be dependent on the success of each person's catch, but it does not earn respect or prestige.[151] As documented in the ethnographic work of anthropologists studying the dynamics of hunter-gatherers, including the San, the owner of the meat produced by the hunt is the owner of the tool used to successfully kill the prey, not the hunter himself. This "remote control ownership" guarantees an orderly distribution of the meat, diffusing the responsibility in the sharing and distributing.[152] At the same time, sharing the tools contributes to increasing the chances of a successful killing, and therefore the likelihood of ensuring that there is a meal.

Other major features among San societies are social equality, individual autonomy and personal freedom (to move, live, work and associate with

145 Oyowe, "African Conception of Human Rights?" 344.

146 Paul, "Participatory Approaches," 218f, in Zips-Mairitsch, *Lost Lands?* 62.

147 Ichikawa, "Food Sharing," 154. As the owner of a financial asset or a commodity.

148 Widlok, "Introduction," 9.

149 Marshall, "Sharing, Talking, and Giving," 243.

150 Also fruit. Widlok, "Sharing by Default?" 63. According to Widlok, exclusive property rights are conditioned by spatial proximity.

151 Ichikawa, "Food Sharing," 161.

152 Ichikawa, "Food Sharing," 160.

others), and sharing.[153] There is a moral obligation to share or a moral inadmissibility to accumulate,[154] with or without an expectation of return or reciprocation. This transfer (sharing) can take the form of giving gifts, unsolicited giving or reciprocal exchange.[155] Widlok studied the moralities of different forms of transfer: sharing, gift giving (which is closer to altruistic sharing), and reciprocity (which is understood as a two-way transfer), setting them apart from a market rationale and commodity exchange.

Widlok argues that if the time frame or the agency of actors is altered, sharing could be described as a two-way transfer as well. He conceptualises sharing as an act that creates a group who share a "moral base of mutual engagement",[156] away from a monetised logic or a reciprocal exchange (converted value).[157] Widlok identifies three aspects (cultural conditions) that influence sharing, namely relatedness (kin relations), modes of conversation (linguistic pragmatics) and modes of bodily presence (corporeal movements), the main characteristic being sharing in rather than sharing out:

> What sharing adds to our theory of value is that it reminds us that desirability is not merely a function of social relations (what others want tends to become desirable to me, too) but also a function of *inherent affordances of objects in the human environment that lend themselves to become desirable* (what lends itself to human life becomes desirable) and of my ability to recognize this for myself and for fellow human beings.[158]

---

153 A distinction can be made here depending on the emphasis being on the object being shared (and thus divided) or on the subject who shares (the joint experience or performative relationship).

154 According to Woodburn, "Egalitarian Societies Revisited," 23, in immediate return societies, access rights to subsistence resources are taken for granted and restrictions apply to accumulation (and self-aggrandisement). However, sharing is often viewed by members of the communities as "an obstacle to escaping poverty". Dieckmann et al., *"Scraping the Pot"* 514. Failing to share according to Barnard is "an act of bad faith … anti-social". Barnard, "Foraging Mode of Thought," 7.

155 "Where demand sharing entails supporting those who, in the immediate encounter, have less, gift-giving entails supporting those who, in the future, may need someone to 'think for' them … Demand sharing can involve taking or it can involve demanding. These can self-regulate, or they can become exploitative. Giving can foster ongoing relationships of care, or it can become a draining relationship of debt." Laws, *All Things being Equal*, 114.

156 Widlok, "Sharing by Default?" 61.

157 Widlok, "Sharing by Default?" 66.

158 Widlok, "Sharing," 27, emphasis added.

Anthropologist Lorna Marshall highlights meat-sharing (of the big game hunted) and gift-giving among the San social customs[159] connected with their understanding of belonging and the ownership of resources that help describe their cooperation practices within and between band structures. These contribute to avoiding jealousy and mitigating tensions (due to deprivation or hunger), secure friendly relationships, reciprocating and securing living conditions, and an abundant life, despite the lack of certain material possessions. The motives behind sharing are: "to measure up to what is expected of them, to make friendly gestures, to win favour, to repay past favours and obligations, and to enmesh others in future obligations".[160]

In their account of the traditional (low-impact) environmental/land management systems of Ju|'hoansi in the Nyae Nyae and diverse San groups in the N‡a Jaqna conservancies in Namibia, Hays and Hitchcock show how they are "inextricably connected to exchange systems" through the "n!ore" (the "area over which local people have rights of access and resource use"),[161] as well as the "hxaro partnerships". 'kxa/ho' means the landscape of home, "(literally 'sand surface') ... signifies all of the land inhabited in the past and present by the Ju|'hoansi and all of its water, bush foods, game, grazing, wood, minerals and other natural resources, as well as places of historic and cultural significance".[162] The degree of territoriality is based on group membership: "group solidarity played out in spatial terms".[163]

In the context of immediate-return societies, egalitarian systems are not the result of "oppositional solidarity"[164] but are sustained through institutional procedures that promote equality and resist inequality.[165] This reveals that a straight-forward correlation between property and inequality is more nuanced than it can at first appear to be. Anthropological work of the last 50–60 years has provided evidence that such a causality (between property and inequality)

159 She specifically refers to the !Kung Bushmen of the Nyae Nyae region in South Africa. Marshall, "Sharing, Talking, and Giving".

160 Marshall, "Sharing, Talking, and Giving," 239.

161 Hays and Hitchcock, "Land and Resource Rights," 185.

162 Hays and Hitchcock, "Land and Resource Rights," 199.

163 Barnard, *Hunters and Herders*, 242.

164 Developed in opposition to domination by outsiders. Woodburn, "Egalitarian Societies Revisited," 19.

165 It would be necessary to study to what extent the interventions of distant entities and logics such as those of NGOs and development actors working with the San have influenced or will alter these egalitarian dynamics in future, when introducing certain rhetoric and expectations that arise from outsiders' settings, customs, welfare systems, rules, authorities and ideas either contributes to their preservation or influences their transformation into something different.

builds on several assumptions that have been challenged by ethnographic work and subsequent debates. Other factors such as power relationships and control, the division of labour and social differentiation, the dynamics of dependency, structural discrimination and domination contribute to inequality as well as property ownership or the lack thereof.

By way of conclusion, this conceptualisation of ownership and the non-exclusive uses of land stems from the San's arrangements to organise the relationship between people and resources, which is shaped by different dimensions (identity, socialisation, spirituality, time, space, and geo-political aspects). The literature about the San is full of recurring accounts describing an ethos based on egalitarianism, mutual dependence and sharing, rather than on a regime of exclusive property rights. As a result of their understanding of solidarity, of the connection between human beings and nature, and the correlation between rights and responsibilities; communal tenure, exchange, redistribution and reciprocity characterise their property regimes.

"The idea of land as property, whether common or divided, belongs to a language of occupation. But hunter-gatherers do not occupy the land, they *inhabit* it."[166]

4 Conclusion: "'A' is for Apple",[167] "M" for Mongongo[168]

> Una política cosmopolita insurgente de derechos humanos debe hacer frente directamente al individualismo posesivo de la concepción liberal de la propiedad.[169]

This contribution has discussed the right to property and its connection to land, focussing on the different ways they are conceptualised in Western legal orders and from the perspective of an indigenous people in Southern Africa, the San. The different accounts from both perspectives make explicit the values, characteristics and merits of each logic. The focus on an indigenous

166 Ingold, "Time, Memory and Property," 172. Emphasis in the original.

167 Ezeanya-Esiobu, "*How Africa can Use*," minute 01:29.

168 The mongongo tree is found in Southern Africa, in sandy soils. It has been used by the San for centuries, its wood and fruits (mongongo nuts) as a staple diet (the kernel, oil) as well as a body rub and for other uses.

169 De Sousa Santos, *Para Descolonizar Occidente*, 111. An insurgent cosmopolitan politics of human rights must directly confront the possessive individualism of the liberal concept of property. Translation by the author.

conceptualisation responds to an intent to redress epistemic injustice, the privilege of ignorance behind Eurocentric predominance, as well as the enduring indifference towards peripheral knowledges that have been disregarded especially in the construction of a global rights discourse. By exploring and identifying primary characteristics of the San's understanding of property and land (mutual dependence, egalitarianism, non-exclusive uses, sharing, redistribution and reciprocity), the conceptual basis for an alternative formulation of the right to property can be advanced.

This proposal seeks to transcend the shortcomings of the mainstream hegemonic paradigm of human rights by contributing towards a new narrative inclusive of those omitted worldviews and knowledges and highlighting the potential influence and role of indigenous peoples as agents in the making of human rights law beyond the traditional state-centred international law-making.

The aim of this chapter has not been to design an alternative discourse from an indigenous peoples' perspective with an emancipatory purpose for the holders of those alienated knowledges. To assert such a goal as part of an argumentative framework against exclusion would undermine the agency of the indigenous groups. Such an ideological-political presumption would be contrary to the critical foundations of this proposal, which is rooted in decolonial and TWAIL approaches. Thus, the revalorisation of indigenous perspectives in this analysis does not respond to a theorisation as "a new form of colonisation of indigeneity for Western consumption"[170] in the way in which critics of the onto-political turn view the recent attention and emphasis given to indigenous peoples. Rather, it attempts to contribute towards an epistemic shift in the rights discourse and conceptualisation in order to challenge the epistemic hegemony underpinning the grammar of rights. In doing so it has examined anthropological accounts of indigenous land and property conceptualisations vis-à-vis western models of property rights, the latter responding to a monetary logic, consumption and individualistic rationales that disregard inequalities and fairer distribution.

As has been said, there are diverse systems regulating the relationships between people and resources, as well as different understandings of what property is and what it implies. Those arrangements distinguish between the ways of accessing resources (tangible and intangible things, skills, abilities, capacities and knowledge) and the ways that access is regulated with regard to

170 Chandler and Reid, "Becoming Indigenous," 486. According to these authors, onto-political anthropology not only essentialises the indigenous ("'exoticising' indigenous practices"), but also objectifies its subject matter.

other persons, groups or entities (who might claim prerogatives towards those resources). Property paradigms result in concrete property regimes that define socio-economic structures.[171] The centrality of property for the individual and society is largely assumed, as well as its importance for economic liberalism.[172] Unfortunately, this assumption prevails even when measured against existing inequalities, as well as social and economic injustices (partly stemming from such property regimes). Thus the importance of devising alternative formulations rooted in different legal imaginaries whose premises can bring new insights, opportunities and change.

In addition, prominence has been given to the association between tenure and title.[173] The anthropocentric property laws of Western legal systems regulate human-to-human relationships, protecting against interferences on an individual private right while posing restrictions and duties on non-owners. However, beyond the protection of individual autonomy they neglect the conditions of what is owned (earth resources), which is treated as a tradeable commodity. Ownership is connected to rights and entitlements conferring power and a personal choice upon the thing owned (endorsed by the state under state laws). Redefining property entails bringing into the equation the "thing/self-interest of the owner", the implications for others, responsibilities and obligations that broadly understood extend towards the whole of humanity, future generations and the natural world (the ecological conceptions of property).[174] This view brings together the responsibility that arises from an ecological perspective as well as the human/social dimensions of solidarity and fairness in addition to the value of non-human life forms and a wide understanding of harm.

On the other hand, the San understanding of property that emanates from the practices and rules embodied in their socio-cultural systems is

171 "The law is the culpable hand-maiden or enabler of policies which foster capitalist transformation through conventional dispossessory routes." Alden Wily, "'The Law is to Blame'," 752.

172 Van der Walt, *Property in the Margins*, 37. Liberal institutions "do disfavour groups whose survival and flourishing rely on their members' deference to tradition or to authorities within the group. Taylor is right, then, to reject the idea that liberalism can be neutral with respect to basic values that are, in some degree, culturally inflected". Lyshaug, "Authenticity," 307.

173 According to Okoth-Ogendo this "explains why the doctrine of ownership rather than of property became the focal point of much of the land tenure literature". Okoth-Ogendo, "Some Issues of Theory," 7.

174 "Interspecies and intergenerational accountability is a vital antidote to human self-centredness and power." Burdon, *Exploring Wild Law*, 26.

characterised by other foundations: minimised internal social differentiations of power, wealth and status, and social relationships based on sharing and mutuality. Property is seen in its social function, resulting in communal tenure and users' rights and obligations (as opposed to individual tenure and ownership as an alienation right). Even though different categories of ownership can be identified, depending on the objects at stake, this does not immediately imply excluding others. With regard to personal items, for example, (consumable goods, clothes, cooking tools), the San have developed forms of tenure and possession marked by re-distribution and the delayed exchange rule that enable establishing a social security network. Sharing and demand-sharing operate as redistribution practices of the fruits of activities such as hunting, gathering plants, food, honey, firewood and water. This sharing can be read as generosity, in the sense of responding positively to demands. "Ownership" corresponds to those who use it and share it.[175] In addition, generalised reciprocity among kin (of resources such as drinking water, travel freely, game from the hunt) allows them to develop symmetrical ties of friendship between people and lasting relationships, and to equalise access to resources. Access rights to resources necessary to subsistence are taken for granted. Accumulation is not associated with status or self-aggrandisement.[176] For that reason, restrictions to personal promotion and accumulation apply, and the obligation to share prevails, which is exemplified by practices such as gift-giving reciprocation among certain kin.

Despite the complexity of the task of extracting general assertions from a given culture, and the awareness that some of these specificities, being connected to particular realities, might not be readily translatable into different contexts, some of the elements stemming from this alternative understanding of property can be taken to suggest the possibility of developing a more nuanced general interpretation of rights and obligations, a more holistic approach to nature and natural resources, a comprehension of community not as aggregated individuals but as something like an extended kinship with an emphasis on a sense of belonging, responsibility, mutual dependency and solidarity towards other human beings and future generations, an idea of stewardship rather than one of the exploitation of nature and its resources.

All of these are aspects from which we can reformulate and transform the right to property, orienting it towards solidarity. By building on an understanding and logic alternative to that which underpins the current mainstream

---

175 Barnard, *Hunters and Herders*, 141.

176 "The accumulation of objects has not become associated with status." Marshall, "Sharing, Talking, and Giving," 244.

conceptualisation of rights, we could consequently expand the dominant rights discourse. Rather than focussing on the privatisation of land, marketisation, deregulation or re-regulation,[177] those alternative elements could inspire property legislation, governmental policies, development projects and land reforms that are more sustainable and consistent with own ideas and expectations of a good life.

The statement by Roy Sesana incorporated in the title of this text, "Our human rights are our land", suitably exemplifies the contrast in understanding of the meaning of land and of rights more generally. This difference at the core of the diverse conceptualisations of rights has been concealed behind the proclaimed universalism of the received regimen of human rights. However, the hegemonic rights discourse rests in specific ideas of justice, of the human and the world, which are grounded in Eurocentric premises. Its ideological underpinnings can be traced to western traditions and ideals. The crafting of the core instruments of the corpus of human rights follows that pattern, while alternative worldviews are subjugated and appear as scarcely to exist. That dominant grammar has eclipsed alter-native perspectives such as those of the indigenous peoples in Africa. By exploring the San ethos and understanding of land and property, important aspects have been put forward that could lay the foundation for a different concept of property, thus enriching the dominant discourse with an alternative conceptualisation of the right to property. "A" has stood for apple everywhere in the world. It is time to include mongongo nuts as a staple of our diet.

Bibliography

Literature

ACHPR. *Report of the African Commission's Working Group of Experts on Indigenous Populations/Communities*. Copenhagen: ACHPR and IWGIA, 2005.

Alden Wily, Liz. "'The Law is to Blame': The Vulnerable Status of Common Property Rights in Sub-Saharan Africa." *Development and Change* 42, no. 3 (2011): 733–57. https://doi.org/10.1111/j.1467-7660.2011.01712.x.

Alden Wily, Liz. "Compulsory Acquisition as a Constitutional Matter: The Case in Africa." *Journal of African Law* 62, no. 1 (2018): 77–103. https://doi.org/10.1017/S0021855318000050.

177 The incorporation of customary land into state law, for the creation of added value as collateral or surplus.

Alexander, Gregory S., and Eduardo S. Peñalver. *An Introduction to Property Theory*. New York: Cambridge University Press, 2012.

Ankersen, Thomas T., and Thomas K. Ruppert. "Defending the Polygon: The Emerging Human Right to Communal Property." *Oklahoma Law Review* 59, no. 4 (2006): 681–757.

AUC, AfDB, and UNECA Consortium. *Framework and Guidelines on Land Policy in Africa. Land Policy in Africa: A Framework to Strengthen Land Rights, Enhance Productivity and Secure Livelihoods*. Addis Ababa: African Union, 2010.

Ayittey, George B. N. *Indigenous African Institutions*. 2 ed. Ardsley, N.Y.: Transnational Publishers, 2006.

Bacca, Paulo Ilich. "The Double Bind and the Reverse Side of the International Legal Order." *Third World Approaches to International Law Review* 1 (2020): 93–120.

Badaru, Opeoluwa Adetoro. "Examining the Utility of Third World Approaches to International Law for International Human Rights Law." *International Community Law Review* 10, no. 4 (2008): 379–87.

Barnard, Alan. "Mutual Aid and the Foraging Mode of Thought. Re-Reading Kropotkin on the Khoisan." 2004. Accessed February 14, 2023. https://theanarchistlibrary.org/library/alan-barnard-mutual-aid-and-the-foraging-mode-of-thought.

Barnard, Alan. "The Foraging Mode of Thought." *Senri Ethnological Studies*, 60 (2002): 5–24.

Barnard, Alan. *Hunters and Herders of Southern Africa: A Comparative Ethnography of the Khoisan Peoples*. Cambridge: Cambridge University Press, 1992.

Barume, Albert Kwokwo. *Land Rights of Indigenous Peoples in Africa: With Special Focus on Central, Eastern and Southern Africa*. Copenhagen: IWGIA, 2010.

Bird-David, Nurit. "The Giving Environment: Another Perspective on the Economic System of Gatherer-Hunters." *Current Anthropology* 31, no. 2 (1990): 189–96.

Blaser, Mario. "Political Ontology: Cultural Studies without 'Cultures'?" *Cultural Studies* 23, no. 5–6 (2009): 873–96. https://doi.org/10.1080/09502380903208023.

Blatman-Thomas, Naama. "Reciprocal Repossession: Property as Land in Urban Australia." *Antipode* 51, no. 5 (2019): 1395–415. https://doi.org/10.1111/anti.12570.

Bodenhorn, Barbara. "It's Good to Know Who Your Relatives are but We were Taught to Share with Everybody: Shares and Sharing among Inupiaq Households." *Senri Ethnological Studies* 53 (2000): 27–60.

Brown, Wendy. "'The Most We can Hope for …': Human Rights and the Politics of Fatalism." In *Wronging Rights? Philosophical Challenges for Human Rights*, edited by Aakash Singh Rathore, and Alex Cistelecan, 132–48. Abingdon: Routledge, 2011.

Burdon, Peter, ed. *Exploring Wild Law. The Philosophy of Earth Jurisprudence*. Kent Town: Wakefield Press, 2011.

Carrithers, Michael, et al. "Ontology is just another Word for Culture: Motion Tabled at the 2008 Meeting of the Group for Debates in Anthropological Theory, University of Manchester." *Critique of Anthropology* 30, no. 2 (2010): 152–200.

Carter, Alan. *The Philosophical Foundations of Property Rights*. New York: Harvester Wheatsheaf, 1989.

Chandler, David, and Julian Reid. "'Being in Being': Contesting the Ontopolitics of Indigeneity." *The European Legacy: Toward New Paradigms* 23, no. 3 (2018): 251–68. https://doi.org/10.1080/10848770.2017.1420284.

Chandler, David, and Julian Reid. "Becoming Indigenous: The 'Speculative Turn' in Anthropology and the (Re)Colonisation of Indigeneity." *Postcolonial Studies* 23, no. 4 (2020): 485–504. https://doi.org/10.1080/13688790.2020.1745993.

Chimhowu, Admos, and Phil Woodhouse. "Customary vs Private Property Rights? Dynamics and Trajectories of Vernacular Land Markets in Sub-Saharan Africa." *Journal of Agrarian Change* 6, no. 3 (2006): 346–71. https://doi.org/10.1111/j.1471-0366.2006.00125.x.

Coetzee, Pieter H., and Abraham P. J. Roux, eds. *The African Philosophy Reader*. 2 ed. London: Routledge, 2003.

Comaroff, John L. "Ethnicity, Nationalism, and the Politics of Difference in an Age of Revolution." In *The Politics of Difference: Ethnic Premises in a World of Power*, edited by Edwin N. Wilmsen, and Patrick A. McAllister, 162–84. Chicago: University of Chicago Press, 1996.

Comaroff, Jean, and John L. Comaroff. "Ethnicity, Inc: On the Affective Economy of Belonging." In *Corporations and Citizenship*, edited by Greg Urban, 249–66. Philadelphia: University of Pennsylvania Press, 2014.

Comaroff, Jean, and John L. Comaroff. *Ethnicity, Inc.: On Indigeneity and its Interpellations*. Chicago: University of Chicago Press, 2009.

Comaroff, Jean, and John L. Comaroff. *Theory from the South: Or, how Euro-America is Evolving Toward Africa*. Boulder, CO: Paradigm, 2012.

Commission on Legal Empowerment of the Poor. *Making the Law Work for Everyone*. New York: UNDP, 2008.

Cook, Amelia, and Jeremy Sarkin. "Who is Indigenous? Indigenous Rights Globally, in Africa, and among the San in Botswana." *Tulane Journal of International and Comparative Law* 18, no. 1 (2009): 93–130.

Crawhall, Nigel. "Africa and the UN Declaration on the Rights of Indigenous Peoples." *The International Journal of Human Rights* 15, no. 1 (2011): 11–36. https://doi.org/10.1080/13642987.2011.529687.

Dalglish, Cian. "What is the Ontological Turn, and to what Extent are 'Ontological' Approaches relevant for the Anthropological Study of Development? – An Anthropological Essay." Accessed February 14, 2023. https://medium.com/@ciandalglish/what-is-the-ontological-turn-and-to-what-extent-are-ontological-approaches-relevant-for-the-b7bb0af7f2f1.

De Sousa Santos, Bouaventura. *Para Descolonizar Occidente. Más Allá Del Pensamiento Abismal.* Buenos Aires: CLACSO, Prometeo Libros, 2010.

Dersso, Solomon A. *Taking Ethno-Cultural Diversity Seriously in Constitutional Design: A Theory of Minority Rights for Addressing Africa's Multiethnic Challenge.* Leiden: Martinus Nijhoff, 2012.

Dieckmann, Ute, et al., eds. 2014. *"Scraping the Pot": San in Namibia Two Decades After Independence.* Windhoek: Legal Assistance Centre and Desert Research Foundation of Namibia, 2014.

Dombrowski, Kirk. "The Praxis of Indigenism and Alaska Native Timber Politics." *American Anthropologist* 104, no. 4 (2002): 1062–73.

Du Plessis, Elmien. "African Indigenous Land Rights in a Private Ownership Paradigm." *Potchefstroom Electronic Law Journal* 14, no. 7 (2011): 45–69.

Encyclopaedia Britannica. "Property." Last modified February 03, 2024, 2021. https://www.britannica.com/topic/property-legal-concept.

Engle, Karen. "On Fragile Architecture: The UN Declaration on the Rights of Indigenous Peoples in the Context of Human Rights." *European Journal of International Law* 22, no. 1 (2011): 141–63. https://doi.org/10.1093/ejil/chr019.

Esterling, Shea. "Looking Forward Looking Back: Customary International Law, Human Rights and Indigenous Peoples." *International Journal on Minority and Group Rights* 28, no. 2 (2021): 280–305.

Ezeanya-Esiobu, Chika. *How Africa can Use its Traditional Knowledge to Make Progress.* TED Global, 2017. Accessed February 25, 2023. https://www.ted.com/talks/chika_ezeanya_esiobu_how_africa_can_use_its_traditional_knowledge_to_make_progress?utm_campaign=tedspread&utm_medium=referral&utm_source=tedcomshare.

Ferguson, James. *The Anti-Politics Machine: "Development", Depoliticization, and Bureaucratic Power in Lesotho.* Minneapolis, MN: University of Minnesota Press, 1994.

Gilbert, Jeremie. "Land Rights as Human Rights: The Case for a Specific Right to Land." *SUR – International Journal on Human Rights* 10, no. 18 (2013): 115–35.

Gómez-Sánchez, Davinia. "Transforming Human Rights through Decolonial Lens." *The Age of Human Rights Journal* 15 (2020): 276–303.

Gressier, Catie. *At Home in the Okavango. White Batswana Narratives of Emplacement and Belonging.* New York: Berghahn Books, 2018.

Griffiths, Anne. "Engaging with the Global: Perspectives on Land from Botswana." In *Framing the Global: Entry Points for Research,* edited by Hilary E. Kahn, 112–36. Bloomington: Indiana University Press, 2014.

Hays, Jennifer, and Robert Hitchcock. "Land and Resource Rights in the Tsumkwe Conservancies – Nyae Nyae and N‡a Jaqna." In *"Neither Here nor There": Indigeneity, Marginalisation and Land Rights in Post-Independence Namibia*, edited by Willem Odendaal, and Wolfgang Werner, 183–214. Windhoek: Legal Assistance Centre, 2020.

Hitchcock, Robert K. "Sharing the Land: Kalahari San Property Rights and Resource Management." In *Property and Equality. Volume II: Encapsulation, Commercialization, Discrimination*, edited by Thomas Thomas, and Wolde Gossa Tadesse, 191–207. New York: Berghahn, 2007.

Hitchcock, Robert K., and Diana Vinding, eds. *Indigenous Peoples' Rights in Southern Africa*. Copenhagen: IWGIA, 2004.

Hitchcock, Robert K., and John D. Holm. "Bureaucratic Domination of Hunter-Gatherer Societies: A Study of the San in Botswana." *Development and Change* 24, no. 2 (1993): 305–38.

Hodgson, Dorothy L. "Africa from the Margins." *African Studies Review* 60, no. 2 (2017): 37–49.

Hodgson, Dorothy L. "Introduction: Comparative Perspectives on the Indigenous Rights Movement in Africa and the Americas." *American Anthropologist* 104, no. 4 (2002): 1037–49.

Hodgson, Dorothy Louise. *Being Maasai, Becoming Indigenous. Postcolonial Politics in a Neoliberal World*. Indianapolis: Indiana University Press, 2011.

Home, Robert. "'Culturally Unsuited to Property Rights?': Colonial Land Laws and African Societies." *Journal of Law and Society* 40, no. 3 (2013): 403–19.

Hopgood, Stephen. *The Endtimes of Human Rights*. Ithaca: Cornell University Press, 2013.

Howard, Rhoda. "Reconsidering the Right to Own Property." *Journal of Human Rights* 12, no. 2 (2013): 180–97.

Howard, Rhoda. "Evaluating Human Rights in Africa: Some Problems of Implicit Comparisons." *Human Rights Quarterly* 6, no. 2 (1984): 160–79.

Ichikawa, Mitsuo. "Food Sharing and Ownership among Central African Hunter-Gatherers: An Evolutionary Perspective." In *Property and Equality. Volume I: Ritualisation, Sharing, Egalitarianism*, edited by Thomas Widlok, and Wolde Gossa Tadesse, 151–64. New York: Berghahn, 2007.

ILO, and ACHPR. *Overview Report of the Research Project by the International Labour Organization and the African Commission on Human and Peoples' Rights on the Constitutional and Legislative Protection of the Rights of Indigenous Peoples in 24 African Countries*. Geneva: ILO, 2009.

Ingold, Tim, David Riches, and James Woodburn. *Hunters and Gatherers*. Oxford: Berg, 1995.

Ingold, Tim. "Time, Memory and Property." In *Property and Equality. Volume I: Ritualisation, Sharing, Egalitarianism,* edited by Thomas Widlok, and Wolde Gossa Tadesse, 165–74. New York: Berghahn, 2007.

IWGIA. *The Indigenous World 2022*. Copenhagen: IWGIA and DANIDA, 2022.

Joireman, Sandra Fullerton. *Where There is no Government: Enforcing Property Rights in Common Law Africa*. Oxford: Oxford University Press, 2011.

Kenrick, Justin. "Present Predicament of Hunter Gatherers and Former Hunter Gatherers of the Central African Rainforests." In *Africa's Indigenous Peoples: 'First Peoples' or 'Marginalized Minorities'?*, edited by Alan Barnard and Justin Kenrick, 39–60. Edinburgh: University of Edinburgh, Centre of African Studies, 2001.

Kubow, Patricia K. "Exploring Western and Non-Western Epistemological Influences in South Africa: Theorising a Critical Democratic Citizenship Education." *Compare: A Journal of Comparative and International Education* 48, no. 3 (2018): 349–61.

Kymlicka, Will. "Nation-Building and Minority Rights: Comparing the West and Africa." In *Ethnicity and Democracy in Africa*, edited by Bruce Berman, Will Kymlicka, and Dickson Eyoh, 54–72. Woodbridge: Boydell & Brewer, 2004.

Laws, Megan. *All Things being Equal: Uncertainty, Ambivalence and Trust in a Namibian Conservancy*. London: London School of Economics and Political Science, 2019.

Lindroth, Marjo, and Sinevaara-Niskanen, Heidi. "Colonialism Invigorated? The Manufacture of Resilient Indigeneity." *Resilience: International Policies, Practices and Discourses* 7, no. 3 (2019): 240–54. https://doi.org/10.1080/21693293.2019.1601860.

Lyshaug, Brenda. "Authenticity and the Politics of Identity: A Critique of Charles Taylors Politics of Recognition." *Contemporary Political Theory* 3 (2004): 300–20. https://doi.org/10.1057/palgrave.cpt.9300125.

Mafeje, Archie. "The Ideology of 'Tribalism'." *The Journal of Modern African Studies* 9, no. 2 (1971): 253–61.

Mamdani, Mahmood. *Neither Settler nor Native. The Making and Unmaking of Permanent Minorities*. Cambridge: Belknap Press of Harvard University Press, 2020.

Marschke, Melissa, David Szablowski, and Peter Vandergeest. "Engaging Indigeneity in Development Policy." *Development Policy Review* 26, no. 4 (2008): 483–500.

Marshall, Lorna. "Sharing, Talking, and Giving: Relief of Social Tensions among !Kung Bushmen." *Africa: Journal of the International African Institute* 31, no. 3 (1961): 231–49.

Menski, Werner. *Comparative Law in a Global Context: The Legal Systems of Asia and Africa*. Cambridge: Cambridge University Press, 2006.

Mukwiza Ndahinda, Felix. *Indigenousness in Africa: A Contested Legal Framework for Empowerment of "Marginalized" Communities*. The Hague: T. M. C. Asser Press, 2011.

Ndlovu-Gatsheni, Sabelo J. *Giving Africa Voice within Global Governance: Oral History, Human Rights and the United Nations (UN) Human Rights Council*. Leiden: African Studies Centre, 2007.

Ninkova, Velina. *"Now that We have Development": Change, Resilience and Education for the Omaheke Ju/'hoansi*. Tromsø: UiT, the Arctic University of Norway, 2017.

Okoth-Ogendo, H. W. O. "Some Issues of Theory in the Study of Tenure Relations in African Agriculture." *Africa: Journal of the International African Institute* 59, no. 1 (1989): 6–17. https://doi.org/10.2307/1160760.

Oyowe, Oritsegbubemi Anthony. "An African Conception of Human Rights? Comments on the Challenges of Relativism" *Human Rights Review* 15, no. 3 (2014): 329–47.

Paul, James S. N. "Participatory Approaches to Human Rights in Sub-Saharan Africa." In *Human Rights in Africa. Cross-Cultural Perspectives*, edited by Abdullahai Ahmed An-Na'im, and Francis M. Deng, 213–39. Washington: The Brookings Institution, 1990.

Peterson, Nicholas. "Demand Sharing: Reciprocity and the Pressure for Generosity among Foragers." *American Anthropologist* 95, no. 4 (1993): 860–74.

Platteau, Jean-Philippe. "The Evolutionary Theory of Land Rights as Applied to Sub-Saharan Africa: A Critical Assessment." *Development and Change* 27, no. 1 (1996): 29–86.

Rajagopal, Balakrishnan. *International Law from Below: Development, Social Movements, and Third World Resistance*. Cambridge: Cambridge University Press, 2004.

Ramina, Larissa. "TWAIL – 'Third World Approaches to International Law' and Human Rights: Some Considerations." *Revista De Investigações Constitucionais* 5, no. 1 (2018): 261–72.

Robins, Steven. "Whose 'Culture', Whose 'Survival'? The ≠Khomani San Land Claim and the Cultural Politics of 'Community' and 'Development' in the Kalahari." In *Africa's Indigenous Peoples: 'First Peoples' or 'Marginalized Minorities'?*, edited by Alan Barnard and Justin Kenrick, 229–254. Edinburgh: University of Edinburgh, Centre of African Studies, 2001.

Robins, Steven. "NGOs, 'Bushmen' and Double Vision: The P Khomani San Land Claim and the Cultural Politics of 'Community' and 'Development' in the Kalahari." *Journal of Southern African Studies* 27, no. 4 (2001): 833–53.

Sahlins, Marshall. "What is Anthropological Enlightenment? Some Lessons of the Twentieth Century." *Annual Review of Anthropology* 28 (1999): i–xxiii.

Sapignoli, Maria. "'Bushmen' in the Law: Evidence and Identity in Botswana's High Court" *PoLAR: Political and Legal Anthropology Review* 40, no. 2 (2017): 210–25.

Sapignoli, Maria. "Dispossession in the Age of Humanity: Human Rights, Citizenship, and Indigeneity in the Central Kalahari." *Anthropological Forum* 25, no. 3 (2015): 285–305. https://doi.org/10.1080/00664677.2015.1021293.

SASI. "Written in the Sand." Accessed February 14, 2023.

Saugestad, Sidsel. "Dilemmas in Norwegian Development Assistance to Indigenous Peoples." *Forum for Development Studies* 27, no. 2 (2000): 205–34.

Shivji, Issa G. "Constructing a New Rights Regime: Promises, Problems and Prospects." *Social and Legal Studies* 8, no. 2 (1999): 253–76. https://doi.org/10.1177/096466399900800205.

Shrinkhal, Rashwet. "Evolution of Indigenous Rights Under International Law: Analysis from TWAIL Perspective." *The Oriental Anthropologist* 19, no. 1 (2019): 7–24.

Solway, Jacqueline. "Human Rights and NGO 'Wrongs': Conflict Diamonds, Culture Wars and the 'Bushman Question'." *Africa* 79, no. 3 (2009): 321–46. https://doi.org/10.3366/E0001972009000849.

Spivak, Gayatri Chakravorty. “Can the Subaltern Speak?” In *Colonial Discourse and Post-Colonial Theory: A Reader*, edited by Patrick Williams, and Laura Chrisman, 66–112. New York: Columbia University Press, 1994.

Suzman, James. *An Assessment of the Status of the San in Namibia. Regional Assessment of the Status of the San in Southern Africa.* Windhoek: Legal Assistance Centre, 2001a.

Suzman, James. *Regional Assessment of the Status of the San in Southern Africa. An Introduction to the Regional Assessment of the Status of the San in Southern Africa.* Windhoek: Legal Assistance Centre, 2001b.

Sylvain, Renèe. “Disorderly Development: Globalization and the Idea of ‘Culture’ in the Kalahari.” *American Ethnologist* 32, no. 3 (2005): 354–70.

Tabane, Rapule, and Ferial Haffajee. “Ideology is Dead, Long Live ID-ology.” *Mail and Guardian*, June 27, 2003. https://mg.co.za/article/2003-06-27-ideology-is-dead-long-live-idology/.

Tarimo, Aquiline. *African Land Rights Systems*. Bamenda: African Books Collective, 2014.

Vail, Leroy, ed. *The Creation of Tribalism in Southern Africa*. Berkeley: University of California Press, 1989.

Van der Walt, Andries Johannes. *Property in the Margins*. Oxford: Hart, 2009.

Vermeylen, Saskia. “The Nagoya Protocol and Customary Law: The Paradox of Narratives in the Law.” *Law, Environment and Development Journal* 9, no. 2 (2013): 185–201.

Viveiros de Castro, Eduardo. “Zeno and the Art of Anthropology: Of Lies, Beliefs, Paradoxes, and Other Truths.” *Common Knowledge* 17, no. 1 (2011): 128–45.

Werbner, Richard. “Challenging Minorities, Difference and Tribal Citizenship in Botswana.” *Journal of Southern African Studies* 28, no. 4 (2002): 671–84. https://doi.org/10.1080/0305707022000043467.

Widlok, Thomas. “Introduction.” In Property and Equality. Volume I: Ritualisation, Sharing, Egalitarianism, edited by Thomas Widlok, and Wolde Gossa Tadesse, 1–17. New York: Berghahn, 2007.

Widlok, Thomas. “Sharing by Default? Outline of an Anthropology of Virtue.” *Anthropological Theory* 4, no. 1 (2004): 53–70. https://doi.org/10.1177/1463499604040847.

Widlok, Thomas. “Sharing: Allowing Others to Take what is Valued.” *HAU Journal of Ethnographic Theory* 3, no. 2 (2013): 11–31. https://doi.org/10.14318/hau3.2.003.

Wilmsen, Edwin N. “Mutable Identities: Moving Beyond Ethnicity in Botswana.” *Journal of Southern African Studies* 28, no. 4 (2002): 825–41. https://doi.org/10.1080/0305707022000043539.

Wilmsen, Edwin N. *Land Filled with Flies: A Political Economy of the Kalahari*. Chicago: University of Chicago Press, 1989.

Wilmsen, Edwin N. “Introduction: Premises of Power in Ethnic Politics.” In *The Politics of Difference: Ethnic Premises in a World of Power*, edited by Edwin N. Wilmsen, and Patrick A. McAllister, 1–24. Chicago: University of Chicago Press, 1996.

Wilmsen, Edwin N., and Patrick A. McAllister, eds. *The Politics of Difference: Ethnic Premises in a World of Power*. Chicago: University of Chicago Press, 1996.

Woodburn, James. "'Sharing is Not a Form of Exchange': An Analysis of Property Sharing in Immediate-Return Hunter-Gatherer Societies." In *Property Relations: Renewing the Anthropological Tradition*, edited by Christopher M. Hann, 48–63. Cambridge: Cambridge University Press, 1998.

Woodburn, James. "Egalitarian Societies Revisited." In *Property and Equality. Volume 1: Ritualisation, Sharing, Egalitarianism*, edited by Thomas Widlok, and Wolde Gossa Tadesse, 18–31. New York: Berghahn, 2007.

Zips-Mairitsch, Manuela. *Lost Lands? (Land) Rights of the San in Botswana and the Legal Concept of Indigeneity in Africa*. Copenhagen: IWGIA, 2009.

Case Law

African Commission on Human and Peoples' Rights v Republic of Kenya, ACtHPR, Application No. 006/2012 (May 26, 2017) (*Ogiek* case).

Social and Economic Rights Action Center and the Center for Economic and Social Rights v Nigeria, ACHPR Communication No. 155/96 (May 27, 2002).

Sudan Human Rights Organisation and Centre on Housing Rights and Evictions (COHRE) *v Sudan*, ACHPR Communication No. 279/03–296/05, 28th ACHPR AAR Annex (Nov 2009–May 2010).

Botswana

Sesana v The Attorney General (52/2002) [2006] BWHC 1 (13 December 2006).

Legislation

Republic of Cameroon Constitution, 1972 (amended by Law No. 96/06 of 18 January 1996 and Law No. 2008/001 of 14 April 2008).

Republic of Congo Constitution, 2015.

Republic of Congo Law No. 5–2011 on the Promotion and Protection of the Rights of Indigenous Populations.

International Documents

ACHPR. "Resolution on the Renewal of the Mandate, Appointment of the Chairperson, Reconstitution and Expansion of Mandate of the Working Group on Indigenous Populations/Communities." ACHPR/Res. 455 (LXVI). September 18, 2020. https://achpr.au.int/index.php/en/adopted-resolutions/455-resolution-renewal-mandate-appointment-chairperson-recons.

ACHPR WGIPC. "Inter-Session Activity Report of Honourable Commissioner Alexia Gertrude Amesbury, Chairperson of the Working Group on Indigenous Populations/

Communities and Minorities in Africa. 67th Ordinary Session of the African Commission on Human and Peoples' Rights (13 November–3 December 2020)."
Anaya, James. "Report of the Special Rapporteur on the Rights of Indigenous Peoples on the Situation of Indigenous Peoples in Namibia." A/HRC/24/41/Add.1. June 25, 2013. http://unsr.jamesanaya.org/wp-content/uploads/2008/03/2013-report-namibia-a-hrc-24-41-add1-en.pdf.
De Schutter, Olivier. "Access to Land and the Right to Food: Report of the Special Rapporteur on the right to food." UNGA A/65/281. August 11, 2010. http://www.srfood.org/images/stories/pdf/officialreports/20101021_access-to-land-report_en.pdf.

Treaties and Agreements

African Charter on Human and Peoples' Rights (1981).
United Nations Declaration on the Rights of Indigenous Peoples (2007).
Universal Declaration of Human Rights (1948).
International Covenant on Civil and Political Rights (1966).
International Covenant on Economic, Social and Cultural Rights (1966).
ILO Indigenous and Tribal Peoples Convention, 1989 (No. 169).
ILO Indigenous and Tribal Populations Convention, 1957 (No. 107).

PART 4

Theoretical Perspectives on African Legal Pluralism

CHAPTER 11

Penalising Passion: A Reflection on the Offence of Adultery in the Context of Cultural Relativism and Human Rights

Jennifer H. Mike

Abstract

Marriage, a socially desirable institution, is a union that requires fidelity, trust, harmony and mutual confidence. Adultery and all forms of infidelity in marriage are therefore considered destructive vices for the institution of marriage, even if they are private acts between consenting adults. To guarantee a stable and unimpaired system of marriage, the state may legally intervene to require a husband and wife to be mutually bound to each other by a duty of faithfulness. Many justifications have been given for the entrenchment of these laws. The prominent support for laws intruding in the personal space of individuals is rooted in cultural relativism and a strong attachment to religious ideologies. In this light, the extant laws and jurisprudence in Nigeria also support the moral, religious and social indignation against the act of adultery. On the other hand, it has been argued that any activity between two consenting adults is not a matter of state regulation. As the world evolves and new legal orders take shape, it is imperative to review and question existing norms, behaviours and cultures to determine if they conform to the standards of human rights as guaranteed to all humans, or whether they constitute an infringement of those rights, directly or indirectly. This chapter essentially reflects on the religious and cultural justification for the criminalisation of adultery in Nigeria. It examines whether the criminalisation of non-harmful consensual acts between two (or more) people could in effect interfere with the constitutional rights to private and family life, liberty, freedom of association, right to human dignity and even the right to life. It calls for the re-examination of the legal effect of the law from a human rights perspective. The paper consequently makes a case for the decriminalisation of adultery laws on the basis of human rights protections.

1 Introduction

Criminal law essentially aims to maintain public order and peace. In doing so it also regulates people's affairs that are deemed detrimental to the values and

 | DOI:10.1163/9789004696747_012

morals of society. In this respect, criminal statutes exist to ensure that there is as little harm as possible to society and that citizens are protected from conduct that is considered "offensive and injurious" or will damage the fabric of society, in addition to protecting lives and properties. Butler,[1] during the parliamentary consideration of the Wolfenden Report, observed that "there is a sphere of conduct in which the behaviour of individuals must be controlled by the sanctions of the law, in their own interests, in the interests of others, and in the interests of society at large".[2] However, in doing so, the question is whether there is "a sphere which it is proper to leave to the dictates of the individual conscience".[3] In other words, what kinds of conduct are so contrary to the public's interests that the law should intervene to prevent, punish or make a bold statement against it? Should the law interfere in all matters that are generally perceived as wrong, especially from a moral perspective or should it leave some conduct to the dictates of personal freedom, autonomy and private conscience?

Put more succinctly, is there a difference between social, religious, and cultural sin and crime? Crime, as Fuller puts it, is any act that is "more than the violation of group morality and customs".[4] A crime is differentiated from a moral wrong due to the legal consequences of the former. A crime is prescribed and determined by the state and is thus seen to be definite and direct. However, a moral wrong is relative to different people; it is rooted in the beliefs and values that are relative to the norms of an individual, society or culture. While it is trite that legal rules and morality are not conterminous, there is no denying that the law often relies on underlying moral standards to ensure that they are easy to enforce.[5]

The Nigerian criminal legal system offers an example of state regulation that controls the private acts of its citizens, given that it criminalises several sexual acts, including adultery in the Northern part of the country.[6] The law on adultery, being the main focus of this chapter, finds justification in the moral, cultural and religious abhorrence of the act. The penalisation, however, raises issues with respect to the rights bestowed on humans such as the right

1 Butler, R. A. "Homosexual Offences," cc365–508.

2 Butler, R. A. "Homosexual Offences".

3 Butler, R. A. "Homosexual Offences". Also see Mattachine Society, *Mattachine Review,* 51.

4 Fuller, "Morals and the Criminal Law," 624.

5 For more on the relationship between law and moral, see Scheller, "Law and Morality," 319; Kodama, "Bentham's Distinction".

6 Other morality offences include same sex relations, bestiality, sex against the order of nature (unnatural offences), soliciting prostitution, incest, acts of gross indecency, etc. It also regulates deviant human behaviours such as bigamy, abduction and enticement.

to privacy, personal autonomy, freedoms and liberty, which no one should interfere with without just cause. Sometimes the law, in a bid to protect society and its values, has pried too far into the private lives of individuals.[7] Some also argue that adultery is a private act between two consenting adults, and as such, adultery laws are tantamount to policing private affairs that occur in the bedroom.[8]

This chapter examines the criminalisation of adultery through the lens of human rights. In doing so it objectively examines the legal effect of the law in the context of the universalist nature of human rights. Most Nigerians (and Africans in general) may hold the opinion that adultery is an immoral act. The question, however, is what part this opinion should play in the legal regulation of the act as a crime. When does a socially objectionable sexual act cross from being unsavoury to being criminal? Does criminalisation result in a significant decrease in the rate of adultery in society? Should the decision of the majority be weighed against the opinion of the minority? Another factor that is often discounted in the decision to criminalise adultery is the consequential impact on women's rights, the marriage and family in general. Does criminalisation of adultery actually protect a marriage? These questions and many more have continually trailed the penalisation of conduct of a more personal nature.[9]

The first part of this chapter sets the scene with an introductory discussion of adultery and the law on adultery in Nigeria. The second part delineates the argument in support of penalisation and the underlying support for the law. The third part subjects the criminalisation of adultery to human rights scrutiny – essentially an examination of whether criminalising non-harmful consensual acts between adults, could in effect, interfere with the fundamental and constitutional rights to private and family life, liberty, freedom of association, human dignity and even, the right to life. The last part of the chapter concludes with a recommendation for the repeal of adultery laws in Nigeria in the light of the collateral consequences to human rights and the family unit. It is most important at the outset to make it clear that questions or appropriateness of religious ideals and moral norms on adultery are outside the contemplation of

7 Miller, "Punishing Passion," 435.

8 See Miller, "Punishing Passion," 433, 447; Rundel, "Decisions Between Consenting Adults," 878.

9 It is most important at the outset to make it clear that this chapter is concerned with the extent to which socio-cultural and religious norms influence changes in the law as the issue of adultery is largely rooted in moral and religious ideals. It is also worth stating that the author of this chapter is not advocating adultery or undermining the socio-cultural and religious abhorrence of it. The focus of this chapter is on the criminalisation of the act.

this chapter, although references will be made to them as the issue of adultery is largely rooted in moral and religious ideals.

2 Perceptions of Adultery

Adultery being the "sexual intercourse between two persons of whom one or both are married, but who are not married to each other"[10] has been questioned, condemned and even criminalised in certain parts of the world.[11] Adultery is perceived as one of the worst things that could happen to a marriage as it violates the very sanctity of the marriage institution and its vows.[12] As one of the gravest turpitudes and sins of a marriage, its disapproval is backed up by religious texts and socio-cultural considerations.[13] Nevertheless, the act has been committed throughout history and many more affairs are still recorded today. The Infamous Bill Clinton and Monica Lewinsky affair readily comes to mind.[14] Even the great Julius Caesar, conqueror of many nations, could not resist the exciting allure of an illicit affair with the scheming Cleopatra.[15]

While there are no official statistics on the cause of divorce in Nigeria, infidelity, especially on the part of the woman, has led to the breakdown of many homes.[16] Equally, although Nigerian women seldom divorce their husbands for the sole reason of adultery, cheating can have a profound emotional impact on all involved. Indeed, the resulting emotional distress of a spouse's adultery has been acknowledged by the law as evidence that the marriage has broken down irretrievably for the purposes of a divorce in section 15(2)(b) of the Matrimonial Causes Act (MCA).[17] The discovery of an affair can also lead to an acrimonious divorce and affect alimony, child custody[18] and other spousal support after a

10 Sagay, "Adultery," 156.

11 Adultery is a ground for divorce in civil cases. This will be applicable only for couples married under the Marriage Act, Cap 218, LFN 1990, as provided for in s. 15(2)(b) of the Matrimonial Causes Act, Cap 220, LFN 1990 (MCA).

12 Chowbe, "Adultery," 3–24; Barman, "Concept of Hindu Marriage," 5, 9.

13 Chowbe, "Adultery," 3–24; Barman, "Concept of Hindu Marriage," 5, 9.

14 Posner, *Affair of State*; CNN, "A Chronology"; Miller, "Punishing Passion," 447.

15 See more at Roller, *Cleopatra*; Hölbl, *History of the Ptolemaic Empire*; Jones, *Cleopatra*.

16 Although there are no official statistics, this can be inferred from several reports of adultery. See for example, Bello, "My Wife Cheats on Me".

17 This will be applicable only for individuals married under the Marriage Act as provided for in s. 15(2)(b) of the MCA.

18 For example, in *Hanby v Hanby* 158 So. 727 (Ala. 1935). Adultery raised a presumption of parental unfitness in a custody proceeding. The opinion was that "the decree of divorce ... for the wife's adultery was a conclusive adjudication between the parties of her relative

divorce.[19] For women who are dependent on their husbands, this leaves them in an economically disadvantaged position. According to Miller, it could affect the division of marital property and cast the adulterer as a bad and morally unfit parent in child custody proceedings.[20] In the Nigerian case of *Adam v Adam*,[21] for example, the court took into account the unsuitability of the wife due to her adulterous ways in a custody proceeding and further reasoned that her frequent gallivanting and leaving the child behind showed she was unable to bring up the child in the love and security of a home.

An affair can also lead to devastating effects not only for the persons involved but for everyone else too – the other spouse, the children, both extended families and the social connections. Even the reputation of the wife of an adulterer can be tainted.[22] Divorce could also lead to enormous stress for the children and affect their ability to trust future partners if they are aware of the adulterous reason for the breakdown of their parents' marriage.[23] Reputations can be shattered, especially where the adulterer/adulteress occupies a prominent public position.[24] News reports are filled with stories of men and women who

---

unfitness to have the custody of children". Also see *White v White* 166 So. 3d 574 (Miss. Ct. App. 2015), 586–87.

19 Miller, "Punishing Passion," 433. Accordingly, if a mother's life is "dominated by the carnal desires of the flesh," it would influence the child's life and character. In *Ex parte Pankey* 848 So. 2d 963 (Ala. 2002), 973 for example, Moore, C. J., dissenting, expressed the opinion that adultery creates a "presumption of [parental] unfitness" (*Hanby v Hanby* 158 So. 727 (Ala. 1935), 728); also see *Ex parte Pankey* 848 So. 2d 963 (Ala. 2002), 973 (Moore, C. J., dissenting) (saying that adultery creates a "presumption of [parental] unfitness").

20 Miller, "Punishing Passion," 433. See e.g., *Bower v Bower* 758 So. 2d 405 (Miss. 2000), 412 where it was said that adultery was a factor to consider when the conduct "manifests itself into the moral fitness of a parent to raise a child" ; *Bamburg v Bamburg* 386 S.W. 3d 31 (2011), 38 held that "evidence of an extramarital affair is but one factor the trial court is to consider in deciding what custody arrangement serves the best".

21 *Adam v Adam* 3 PLR 1971, SUIT NO. M/196/1970.The woman was described as being of "weak character and easy virtue, who has completely ground down to the last indignity the sanctity of her matrimonial home". Also see *Ajayi v Ajayi and Anor* (HD/27/67) [1970] 10 (18 December 1970).

22 A classic example is Hilary Clinton. As a presidential candidate in 2016 she was subjected to severe criticism, ridicule and several commentaries, especially by political opponents, about her ability to run the country as a result of her husband's act of infidelity. Shire, "How Monica Lewinsky Could Haunt Hillary Clinton"; Crowley, "Lewinsky Scandal"; BBC, "Interview with Hillary Clinton"; Timm, "Monica Lewinsky Jokes". See more discussion at Miller, "Punishing Passion," 448.

23 Emery, *Cultural Sociology of Divorce.*

24 The case of the Clintons offers another example in this respect. Miller, "Punishing Passion," 448.

battered or killed their partners on the grounds of infidelity.[25] Many are languishing in prisons or jail for the harm they inflicted on their cheating spouses. In July 2018, for example, a man was arrested for allegedly butchering his wife to death over a suspected adulterous lifestyle.[26] Similarly, in February 2020 a woman brutally stabbed her husband for keeping a mistress.[27]

While it is still commonly accepted that infidelity is wrong, the social disapproval and sympathy for the underlying causes of infidelity are changing slightly. It is no longer strange to find couples in open relationships, where they willingly agree to engage in romantic sexual relationships outside of their marriage. In Nigeria women have been known to allow their husbands to openly engage in marital relations with other women when they are unable to bear children for them.[28] Some scholars have questioned the concept of fidelity in marriage. Hakim, a British sociologist, controversially advocates adopting a fresh approach to marriage and adultery in her book.[29] She argues, for instance, that the opposition to infidelity is condemning people to live a frustrated "celibate" life and that "sex is no more a moral issue than eating a good meal".[30] Accordingly, "the fact that we eat most meals at home with spouses and partners does not preclude eating out in restaurants to sample different cuisines and ambiences, with friends or colleagues". Sharing a similar view, Perel in her book, *The State of Affairs: Rethinking Infidelity*, argues for a sympathetic understanding of unruly sexual desires in marriage.[31] These unpopular views, however, fly in the face of the fact that illicit sexual affairs outside marriage can destroy the very essence of marriages, kill relationships, rob couples of happiness and have devastating effects on all the parties and their offspring. This, however, is not the focus of this chapter.[32] The issue is whether or not this censure is worth a criminal sanction and the effect of such a law on human rights.

---

25 See the report of men and women who killed their spouses on grounds of suspected infidelity. Folarin and Hanafi, "Man Kills Wife in Benue".

26 Enyioha Opara, "I Killed My Wife".

27 Daily Independent, "Woman Stabs Husband".

28 Igwe and Longjohn, "*Actus Reus*," 77, 82. The writers made a list of some communities in Nigeria where this practice is obtainable, particularly in Rivers State.

29 Hakim, *New Rules*.

30 Ibid.

31 Perel, *State of Affairs*.

32 This chapter will not address the rationale or propriety of criminalising consensual sexual relations.

3 Criminal Liability of Adultery in Nigeria

As stated earlier in the introduction, the Nigerian criminal justice system contains multiple provisions that are in place to regulate deviant and "immoral" sexual behaviours, including adultery.[33] According to section 387 of the Penal Code, which applies to nineteen northern states:[34]

> Whoever, being a man subject to any customary law in which extra-marital sexual intercourse is recognised as a criminal offence, has sexual intercourse with a person who is not and whom he knows or has reason to believe is not his wife, such sexual intercourse not amounting to the offence of rape, is guilty of the offence of adultery and shall be punished with imprisonment for a term which may extend to two years or with fine or with both.

Following this, section 388 makes the same provision that applies to women. These provisions spell out adultery to be a criminal offence, albeit this is subject to a custom or native law that recognises it as an offence in the Northern part of Nigeria. The provisions go further to imply how serious the crime is by giving the punishment of "imprisonment for a term which may extend to two years or with fine or with both".[35]

In a related manner, the Nigerian penal code also punishes wife enticement thus:

> Whoever takes or entices away a woman, who is and whom he knows or has reason to believe to be the wife of any other man, from that man or from a person having the care of her on behalf of that man with intent that she may have illicit intercourse with a person or conceals or detains with that intent any such woman, shall be punished with imprisonment for a term which may extend to two years or with fine or with both.[36]

---

33 The criminal law punishes several sexual behaviours such as same sex relations, sodomy, bestiality, sex against the order of nature (unnatural offences), incest, acts of gross indecency etc.

34 In the southern part of the country, adultery is not expressly stated as an offence.

35 Sections 387 and 388 of the Penal Code Act, LFN 1960. (This provision applies only to the Northern part of Nigeria where the Penal Code Act is applicable).

36 Section 389 of the Penal Code Act, LFN 1960.

In the twelve northern states of Nigeria, adultery (*Zina*) is also a criminal act.[37] The Sharia Penal Laws of these states punish voluntary premarital or extramarital sexual intercourse.[38] The punishment includes caning with one hundred lashes and an imprisonment term of one year if unmarried. The punishment for a married person is death by stoning (Rajm). Since pregnancy outside of marriage constitutes sufficient evidence to enable a woman to be convicted of adultery,[39] more women than men, double the number of their male counterparts, have been convicted of the offence.[40] Amina Lawal and Safiya Husseini are examples of women that were accused of adultery and sentenced to death by stoning by a state Sharia court for conceiving children out of wedlock. The alleged fathers of the children denied any involvement and were released without conviction for lack of evidence.[41]

4 Punishing Infidelity: Arguments in Support of Penalisation

Several arguments have been put forth to justify the penalisation of infidelity. Some of the arguments are based on socio-cultural abhorrence of infidelity, traditional values and protection of the family as an institution, while others are largely rooted in religious and moral ideals. Some of the arguments will be examined.

---

37 Although the penal law on adultery applies to the northern states in Nigeria, it is worth noting that many cultures and traditional norms in the southern part of the country informally punish adultery. For example, adultery among married women is considered a grievous sin and considered as a sacrilege among the Igbos, though it is not a criminal offence in the Criminal Code, Cap C38, LFN 2004 that applies to the southern region or the criminal laws of the states in that region. See more on this at Okorie, "Assessment of the Traditional Penal Code for Adultery," 33–45.

38 For example, see ss. 126 and 127 of the Sharia Penal Code Law of Zamfara State of Nigeria 10 of 2001.

39 This is largely due to the fact that in many interpretations of the sharia law, women are guilty if they are caught having sexual intercourse during the marriage, found pregnant outside a marriage or during a divorce period (Iddah), or a divorcee has sex before remarrying. Within the Maliki school of thought, there is a provision that a baby conceived within five years of a woman's marriage can be considered as fathered by the husband, even if the couple are divorced. Human Rights Watch, "Political Shari'a'?".

40 Weimann, *Islamic Criminal Law*, 177.

41 See Baobab for Women's Human Rights, *Baobab for Women's Human Rights and Shari'a Implementation*, ch. 3; Human Rights Watch, "Political Shari'a'?".

4.1 *Religious Views*

The punishment of adultery is rooted in culture and religion. The law on adultery cannot be divorced from its religious underpinning, particularly by the two dominant religions of Christianity and Islam, which have influenced many statutes in Nigeria including the Criminal Code Act and the Penal Code Act. Their views on marital affairs and fidelity have also had huge roles to play in the statutory prescription of the act as a crime in Nigeria.

In Islam, for instance, adultery, which is known as "*Zina*", is a grave sin and a disgraceful act that is severely punished.[42] Adultery is condemned in *Suratul Isra*, under Chapter 17: 32, and Chapter 24:2. Several other Islamic texts not only condemn *Zina* but also warn against all avenues and means leading to the act. The Qur'an expressly despises the act as follows: "Do not go near to fornication (Zina). Surely it is a shameful deed and evil, opening roads (to other evils)." [Qu'ran 17:32]. This religious injunction clarifies the degree of abhorrence of the act as one of the most heinous, deadliest and greatest of sins imaginable, in addition to being an evil deed that attracts spiritual damnation.[43] Several other verses in the Holy Quran and Hadith prescribe punishments for adultery to include a hundred lashes for fornicators and the death penalty for adulterers on the testimony of four eyewitnesses.[44] The offenders must have also acted of their own free will and must be adults, Muslim and married.

The desire to preserve the Islamic way of preserving marriage fidelity, shunning sexual immorality and religious piety has led to the codification of adultery as an offence in many countries.[45] For this reason, also, the Penal Code and Sharia criminal legal system of the predominately Muslim states in Nigeria adhere strictly to the religious injunction on illegal sexual relations. For example, section 127 of the Sharia Penal Code of Zamfara state punishes this offence with stoning to death (*rajm*).

---

42 *Zina* refers to "an Islamic term of unlawful sexual intercourse" which includes "adultery (married parties), fornication (unmarried parties), prostitution, bestiality, and rape". Semerdjian, "Zinah".

43 Meri, *Medieval Islamic Civilization*, 16–17; Islam Online, "How Islam Views Adultery".

44 Peters, "Zinā or Zinā," 63.

45 Adultery (infidelity) is a criminal offense punishable with severe penalties in several countries including Saudi Arabia, Iran, Thailand, Taiwan, Brunei, Philippines and Syria. In Pakistan the Hudood Ordinance No. VII of 1979 (the Offence of Zina (Enforcement of Hudood) Ordinance VII of 1979) sets a death penalty for the offense of adultery; Quaraishi, "Her Honor," 287. In the United States the Minnesota law on adultery, states: "… when a married woman has sexual intercourse with a man other than her husband, whether married or not, both are guilty of adultery". Minnesota Legislature, "Minnesota Statutes".

In Christianity, the seventh commandment of the Bible in Exodus 20:12 expressly directs that "thou shall not commit adultery". This is buttressed by Leviticus 20:10, which pronounces a death sentence for both the adulterer and adulteress. In the New Testament, Hebrews 13:4 prescribes adultery as an immoral act punishable by God. The text enjoins the believers to hold marriage in high honour and "let the marriage bed be undefiled, for God will judge the sexually immoral and adulterous". Adultery, therefore, conceptually lies within the realm of a grave mortal sin that incurs damnation of the spirit, soul and body. It is not only an offence against a spouse, but it also crosses into the realm of divinity as an offence against the Almighty God, which is hard to challenge. To add credence to the spiritual dimension of the act, Christ emphatically condemns the act when he says "behold, it is written by them of old time, that thou shalt not commit adultery". Christ goes further to warn against adulterous thoughts and feelings, which are the starting point for the eventual act. Supporters of the criminalisation of adultery would therefore argue that the law legally protects and offers an enforceable platform for the religious ethos, and of course the religious text offers a great degree of authoritative guidance for the punishment of adultery.

4.2 *Cultural Relativism, Customary Norms, and Social Values*

Cultural relativism is the notion that the cultural beliefs, norms, practices and traditions of a people are distinctive and particular to that culture. Consequently, any interrogation of this culture should be understood in relation to the cultural context from which it originates. Centrally, cultural relativism holds the belief that the customary norms, moral principles and values of a culture should be examined through the lens of the proponents of that culture and not the standards, practices and beliefs of a different culture.[46] Accordingly, the determination of whether or not a moral value is "right" or "wrong" should be determined in accordance with the "ethical standards of the society within which the action occurs".[47] Cultural relativism creates a customary space for the criminalisation of adultery in Nigeria. Indeed, adultery is subject to customary prescriptions and the penal code makes express reference to this when it stipulates that "whoever, being a man subject to any *customary law* in which extra-marital sexual intercourse".[48]

In many African communities, adultery is an abominable act, although the consequences vary according to societal values, exposure to foreign influence,

46 Younkins, "Why the World is the Way It is".

47 Carnegie Council for Ethics in International Affairs. "Cultural Relativism".

48 Emphasis added. See s. 387 of the Nigerian Penal Code Act.

prevailing ideology and the overarching influence of local tradition. It is regarded as a taboo and "a breach of societal and religious norms" as it "breeds the unhealthy and unwholesome relationship in society, a relationship that can ruin the total well-being of the people".[49] That is to say, it is a social infraction that is capable of affecting trust, peace and joy that are the basic foundations of a happy family life, and of undermining the sanctity of marriage. It corrodes the tranquility of a home and is a violation that society will not tolerate and seeks to deter. As such, a popular argument for penalising adultery is that it protects and maintains the sanctity of matrimony in addition to safeguarding the values of society.[50] The law is essentially a state-imposed sexual discipline and coerces people into being faithful to their marriage vows. Allowing adultery to thrive would lead to a breakdown of marriages as it violates the essence of fidelity and the marriage contract. It would cause couples to drift apart or neglect their duties to the union.[51] Indeed, the paramour might subtly or directly encourage a divorce, leading to the collapse of the marriage, rancour in the married couple's relationship, or worse – abuse. This would invariably affect the wellbeing of the children.[52] Moreover, since adultery embodies dishonesty, it is socially objectionable.[53] Thus, the desire to protect public morality and safeguard the people against corruption is at the root of the law on adultery.

Another reason for adultery's social abhorrence, especially on the part of women, is the risk of passing off the children of other men to the husband as his own and deceiving him into raising children that are not his and invariably passing on properties and inheritance to them.[54] The concern, therefore, is that men will raise children who are not theirs. These children would, in turn, inherit from the men who are not their fathers. This concern about the effect of adulterous conduct by a married woman relates to the danger of imposing illegitimate "offspring upon her unsuspecting husband and bringing an illegitimate heir into his family".[55] Adultery is thus seen as "an outrageous crime,

49 Ojo, "Magun," *Antropologija*, 113.

50 Chowbe, "Adultery"; Viator, "Validity of Criminal Adultery Prohibitions," 837–39.

51 Hermann, *Dominance and Aggression*, 139–57.

52 Okon, "Psychological Effects of Divorce".

53 Ibid.

54 Viator, "Validity of Criminal Adultery Prohibitions," 839, 841–42. Also see Ashaolu, "Man Beats Wife Up"; Miller, "Punishing Passion," 429; Viator, "Validity of Criminal Adultery Prohibitions," 841.

55 Viator, "Validity of Criminal Adultery Prohibitions," 839, 840–41.

striking at the norm of the society and when it results in conception, it inflicts a spurious offspring on the husband".[56]

To ensure that such despiteful acts are not committed, married couples are made to go through certain rituals to ensure faithfulness and full commitment to their spouses alone. For instance, a married woman in the Benin tradition is "made to swear in the husband's ancestral shrine (called *Erimwin Owa*) to be faithful to her husband"[57] to ensure full commitment to the marital relationship. The Yorubas use "*Magun*" (Thunderbolt), a black magic *juju* which is placed in a married woman without her noticing either by her husband or his family so that if she commits adultery her lover could end up losing his life or getting stuck while in the act.[58] In the traditions of many cultures of the Southern Region of the country, the strong belief is that a woman who engages in adultery brings doom to her husband and children or she will become insane.[59] The Northern part of the country mirrors the same rejection of the act. In the Fulani culture, for instance, severe penalties are imposed on an adulterous party, especially an adulterous wife. In many other cultures adultery is forbidden and it is a strong ground for divorce.[60]

In fact, it is for this cultural reason that the ingredients of the offence of adultery as contained under the Penal Code subject the prosecution of adultery to customary or native law in which extra-marital sexual intercourse is recognised as a criminal offence. This customary law is a recognition of the fact that adulterous behaviour is adjudged to be an infraction of customary principles by the framers of the Penal Code. When adultery is punished, the desire to protect social or public morality and prevent the corruption of its virtuous ideals is weighed against an individual's "deviant" sexual conduct. Consequently, sexual acts and "illicit" relationships are measured by a scale of public moral evaluation. Suffice it to say that the law is an agent of social control of the act.

The criminalisation of adultery effectively replaces individual rights with collectivism by assuming that a man/woman's personal choices and values are derived from the cultural values of their society. It presumes that what is important is not what a person does as an individual, but rather what some members of his cultural/social group currently uphold as standards of behaviour. It follows that an individual's private actions incur the public's ire, even

56 Eweka, "Crime in Traditional Society".

57 Adewale, "Benin Crime".

58 Omotosho, "6 Weird Traditions".

59 I Reporter Online, "Meet the Nigerian Tribe"; Nigerian Bulletin, "Igbo Culture and Tradition".

60 Mbosowo, "Extent and Rate of Divorce," 147–70.

if the act does not directly affect the society in question. This approach effectively subjects an individual's personal autonomy and inner conviction to the widely held beliefs and moral norms of their society (unless they wish to be ostracised).

4.3 *Health Justifications*

Another popular support for criminalising adultery as an offence is the high likelihood of contracting sexually transmitted diseases (STDs) and HIV, especially for adulterous married couples who do not use protection during intercourse.[61]

4.4 *Adultery Laws, Cultural Relativism and Human Rights*

The issue of cultural relativism often comes up when discussing human rights and its relationship with customs, traditions and religions.[62] Cultural relativism makes a good case for the preservation and protection of cultures which are sacred to a group of people. However, what happens when the practice of these supposed cultures and customs constitutes violations of human rights?

5 Criminalising Adultery: The Human Rights Debate

While adultery is a breach of the trust, commitment and expectation of fidelity in a marriage, the criminalisation of the act touches upon certain constitutional issues. Arguably the law could in effect impact on constitutionally guaranteed human rights such as those to a private and family life, liberty, freedom of association and even the right to life. These rights are personal rights that relate to how an individual lives his/her life and what the person does with his/her liberty, freedom and dignity, including the persons they wish to associate with. In effect, these rights are very important because they allow individuals to be self-determinant in their daily decisions, and they also ensure that the individual is protected from the excesses of the government or its agencies, the public and even incompatible laws.

61 Smith, "Modern Marriage," 997–1005; Parikh, "Political Economy of Marriage and HIV," 1198–208; Langen, "Gender Power Imbalance," 188–97; Hirsch et al., "Social Constructions of Sexuality,"1227–37.

62 Ibhawoh, "Cultural Relativism," 44.

5.1 *Adultery and the Right to Privacy*

The "privacy of citizens" is a broad concept which encompasses unwarranted interferences in and attacks on the physical, emotional, psychological and personal spheres of all citizens' lives.[63] The basis for the right to privacy laws in Nigeria is section 37 of the 1999 Constitution, which provides that "The privacy of citizens, their homes, correspondence, telephone conversations and telegraphic communications is hereby guaranteed and protected." This law guarantees Nigerians the right to a protected private life, free from public and governmental unlawful intrusion. This right may also mean that persons are granted the right and protection of the law to do private acts in the confines of their homes.[64] The right to privacy further presupposes protection from prying into the private affairs of individuals.[65] A related right to privacy is the right to the home, family and marital life – to order one's private family affairs.[66] The marital right crucially guarantees the marital privacy to marry and raise a family without undue interference. To add credence to this, section 17(3)(h) of the Constitution has to do with encouraging the evolution and promotion of family life.

Although the right to family life is not clearly enunciated in the Nigerian Constitution as a part of the right to privacy, the marginal note to the Section makes mention of the right to a "private and family life".[67] The lack of clarification in the main text on whether or not the right to privacy includes family life leaves a huge gap in construing the extent and scope of the right to privacy in Nigeria. More so, the right to privacy is not an area that has been frequently challenged in Nigeria. Thus, few cases have clarified the scope of this right. Comparatively, Article 8 of the European Convention on Human Rights expressly protects the "right to family life" in addition to privacy. This wider classification concerns a sphere in which everyone can freely pursue the development and fulfilment of their personality, including the protection of their sexual lives and personal relationships.[68] In the case of *X and Y v the Netherlands*[69] the European Court of Human Rights (ECHR) held that private

---

63 A right to privacy is explicitly stated under Art. 12 of the 1948 Universal Declaration of Human Rights.

64 Glenn, *Right to Privacy*, xix, xxix.

65 Olomojobi, *Human Rights and Civil Liberties in Nigeria*, 160.

66 See the discussion on this at O'Reilly "Marital Privacy," 8.

67 Ogbu, *Human Rights Law*, 277.

68 European Court of Human Rights, *Guide on Article 8*, 31; Inter-Parliamentary Union and United Nations Office of the High Commissioner for Human Rights (UN OHCHR) *Human Rights* 146–47.

69 See the *Case of X and Y v the Netherlands* (Application no. 8978/80) March 26, 1985.

life is a concept which covers the physical and moral integrity of the person, including his or her sexual life.[70] In the same vein, some courts in the United States of America have proactively interpreted the right to privacy in the context of a person's personal consensual and non-harmful sexual relations.[71] The right to privacy and family life, including the home, is protected from unlawful interference and attacks on one's honour and reputation as provided under several international human rights laws, such as Article 17 of the International Covenant on Civil and Political Rights (ICCPR) and Article 12 of the Universal Declaration of Human Rights (UDHR).

Privacy in the broader sense means a state in which one is not unduly observed or disturbed by other people – a central notion of freedom and autonomy.[72] It covers a wide range of freedom to plan and order one's life, maintain confidential information, emails and data use, and protect personal medical information, and it extends to other issues such as sexual orientation and personal lifestyles, among other things.[73] Commentators widely interpret this right to imply the freedom of thought, and the freedom of control over one's body and image, reputation, and personality.[74] Another crucial aspect of the right

70 The ECHR has held in a number of other cases that sexual life is an important element of the personal sphere protected by Article 8. See *Dudgeon v the United Kingdom* (Application no. 7525/76) October 22, 1981; *P. G. and J. H. v the United Kingdom* (Application no. 44787/98) September 25, 2001. It was also ruled in some cases that legislation criminalising sexual acts between consenting adults was found to breach Article 8 (*A. D. T. v the United Kingdom* (Application no. 35765/97) July 31, 2000).

71 For example, in the case of *State v Smith* So. 2d 648 (La. App. 4th Cir. 1999), the Lousinana Fourth Circuit Court of Appeal struck down sodomy laws and expanded the protection of the right to privacy in areas affecting the personal autonomy of the individual. In *Stanley v George* (1969) 384 US 557, the United State Supreme Court ruled that a state law which punishes the possession of adult films was a violation of privacy laws. In the US case of *Eisenstadt v Baird* 405 US 438 (1972). the Court emphasised that a marriage is a union of two individuals, and that "it is the right of the individual, married or single, to be free from unwarranted governmental intrusion into matters so fundamentally affecting a person as the decision whether to bear or beget a child". Also see *Lawrence v Texas* 539 US 558 (2003), where the US Supreme Court in a landmark decision reaffirmed the concept of a "right to privacy" and ruled that American laws prohibiting private sexual activity between consenting adults are unconstitutional. While this author is mindful of the cultural and social differences between Nigeria and these countries, their case law is illustrative of a modern approach to privacy lights.

72 Cornell Law School, "Privacy"; Inter-Parliamentary Union and UN OHCHR, *Human Rights*, 145.

73 Inter-Parliamentary Union and UN OHCHR, *Human Rights*, 146–47; Olomojobi, *Human Rights and Civil Liberties in Nigeria*, 160; Solove, "Understanding Privacy," 1–2.

74 Solove, "Understanding Privacy," 1–2; Olomojobi, *Human Rights and Civil Liberties in Nigeria*, 160.

entails protection from an invasion of one's private acts in the home, domestic privacy, unlawful searches and interrogations. In the US case of *Campbell v Sundquist*,[75] for instance, the Tennessee Court of Appeal pronounced that adults' right to engage in consensual and non-commercial sexual acts in the privacy of their homes is at the heart of privacy rights.[76] Fundamentally this is premised on the concept of the personal autonomy of an individual[77] or as Justice Louis D. Brandeis puts it in the case of *Olmstead v US*, "the right to be left alone".[78] Similarly, the right to privacy was described by Lord Hope of the Supreme Court of the United Kingdom in the case of *Re: Diane Pretty*[79] as respect for a person's "private life" and the way the person lives.[80]

Several scholars have made efforts to delineate the scope of this right. In explaining privacy, Solove identified multiple components of the right as follows; personal autonomy, limited access to the self, management of personal information, and the rights to individuality, confidentiality and relationships.[81] Thus, privacy is a fundamental right that is germane to freedom, liberty, democracy, individuality and self-expression.[82] Using the words of Olomojobi, "the right to privacy lies within the realm of self-ownership. It is the moral liberty of doing what an individual deems fit to be done with his/her individualism and keeping others outside the sphere of his/her own ownership".[83] Other scholars explain that this right is vital "to the ability to create and maintain different sorts of social relationships with different people" and is essential for "permitting and protecting an autonomous life", and. significantly, ensuring "emotional and psychological tranquillity".[84] In other words, the right to privacy extends to an opportunity to exert one's independence or individuality, to share private confidences and intimacies.[85] To buttress this point, the ECHR conceived the right to privacy as "the right to establish and develop relationships with other human beings",[86] thus establishing a right to nurture a relationship with others

75 *Campbell v Sundquist* 926 S.W. 2d 250 (Tenn. Ct. App. 1996).

76 Rundel, "Decisions Between Consenting Adults," 888.

77 Inter-Parliamentary Union and UN OHCHR, *Human Rights*, 146–47; Rundel, "Decision Between Consenting Adults," 878.

78 *Olmstead v US* 277 US 438 (1928).

79 *Diane Pretty v Director of Public Prosecutions* [2001] UKHL 61 (HL).

80 Olomojobi, *Human Rights and Civil Liberties in Nigeria*, 165.

81 Solove, "Understanding Privacy," 1–2.

82 Solove, "Understanding Privacy," 1.

83 Olomojobi, *Human Rights and Civil Liberties in Nigeria*, 160.

84 Warren and Brandeis, "Right to Privacy," 193.

85 Wang, *Protecting Privacy in China*, 1–12.

86 *Niemietz v Germany* (72/1991/324/396) December 16, 1992. See more on this at Martin et al., *International Human Rights*, 757.

to a certain extent. This understanding of the notion of private life may be taken to include private sexual and emotional connections with others.

There is a general debate about this core aspect of the right as it applies to Nigeria. Scholars such as Ogbu argue that the constitutional guarantee of privacy does not extend to individual autonomy in the broader sense of freedom of action.[87] He adopts a restrictive interpretation of the right to privacy having regard to the meaning of the associated words in section 37. In his opinion, the right should be viewed within the context of homes, correspondence, telephone conversations and telegraphic communications, essentially the confidentiality of information. This restrictive definition of the right does a disservice to the core principles of human rights that fundamentally protect freedoms and liberty. Accordingly, a wider definition of the right in section 37 of the Constitution is preferred, one that is supported by constitutional guarantees of similar rights such as the right to freedom of thought, conscience and religion (section 38),[88] the right to personal liberty (section 35), the right to freedom of movement (section 41), the right to freedom of expression (section 39), the right to the dignity of human persons (section 34), the right to peaceful assembly and association (section 40), and freedom from discrimination (section 42) on the basis of one's status as a married person.[89] Supporting this wider interpretation, Nwauche favours a definition of privacy that permits an individual to live a life free from intrusion beyond informational privacy.[90] In explaining the definition of privacy, Nwauche argues that the use of the word "home" in section 37 extends to human autonomy and how the subject "lives in his home", exercises this autonomy, and has the right not to have the home invaded.[91] This interpretation touches upon the individual's personal life, sexual life and other aspects of family life.[92] This definition is plausible in the contemplation of the Constitution as the fundamental prescription expressly mentioned protection for the home, meaning it safeguards a person's private

87 Ogbu, *Human Rights Law*, 278.

88 Nigeria Constitution, 1999.

89 Since the law (Penal Code) does not criminalise fornication *per se*, the criminalisation of married people may be discriminatory to their marital status.

90 Nwauche, "Right to Privacy in Nigeria," 63–90. Amnesty International, "Afghanistan: Reject Stoning,"; Amnesty International, "My Life, My Health". Nwauche adopts a definition that is premised on a dignitary interest that recognises the human personality of individuals and protects their individual autonomy that flows from this dignity. Accordingly, the conceptualisation of privacy permits an individual to live a life free from intrusion. Nwauche, "Right to Privacy in Nigeria," 65.

91 Nwauche, "Right to Privacy in Nigeria," 85.

92 Ibid.

activities from interference from the law, the public or the government and its authorities. The Nigerian Supreme Court supported this progressive interpretation of privacy in the case of *Medical and Dental Practitioners Disciplinary Committee v Okonkwo.*[93] The court, per Ayoola, J. S. C., held that the right to privacy encompasses the freedom to choose the course of one's life, fashioned on what one believes, and the right not to be coerced into acting contrary to one's belief, unless of course there is cogent overriding state interest to justify the contrary. Perhaps it is time for the Nigerian courts and lawmakers to adopt a more progressive approach to protecting privacy rights, to increase the protection and broader individual rights of their citizens.

Germane to this privacy law and the issue of adultery is the guarantee to live a private life that is free from the government's intrusion through its criminal justice system or criminal sanction of the affairs of one's life, including ordering one's intimate affairs. Arguably, criminalising the act is tantamount to regulating human sexuality and touches on the right to regulate one's personal sexual lifestyle. A more radical interpretation of the right to privacy would argue that this goes against the essence of privacy laws – the protection of an individual's freedom to make and follow his private sexual affairs – however morally reprehensible the act may be.[94] In a bid to protect society and its values the law has pried into the private lives of individuals. Adultery is a private consensual act between consenting adults. Supporters of decriminalisation may therefore argue that making criminal laws to delve into such matters would be an infringement of the right to order one's privacy and family life, one's liberty and one's dignity. Amnesty International adopts this view and has lamented criminal legislation that breaches privacy rights by targeting consensual sexual relations between adults with harsh punishments.[95] International human rights bodies have affirmed that adult consensual sexual conduct is covered by the concept of privacy.[96] Campaigners also argue against criminal laws used to coerce, control and punish people for making private choices

---

93 *Medical and Dental Practitioners Disciplinary Committee v Okonkwo* (1968) 1 All NLR 306.

94 In Australia for example, the Human Rights (Sexual Conduct) Act, 1994 provides that sexual conduct involving only consenting adults (18 years or over) acting in private would not be subject to arbitrary interference by law enforcement within the meaning of Art.17 of the International Covenant on Civil and Political Rights.

95 Amnesty International, "Afghanistan: Reject Stoning."

96 Accordingly, "autonomy gives rise to a right to one's own body, including in relation to sexuality and sexual conduct ... Central to the concept of privacy is the ability of individuals to make decisions about the most intimate spheres of their lives, including whether, with whom and when to have sex." Inter-Parliamentary Union and UN OHCHR, *Human Rights*, 147.

about their sexual and reproductive lives, bodies and health.[97] If the state can guarantee one's privacy to marry and live in peace, why interfere where a party goes against the vow of marriage, even where the other party has recourse to a divorce court? Although one cannot ignore the fact that the state has long retained sovereignty over marriage and possesses the power to regulate and control entrance into it and exit from it, as a free and adult citizen of Nigeria an individual should be entitled to conduct his/her private affairs without being surveilled by the prying eyes of criminal laws.

5.2 *Adultery and the Right to Personal Liberty*

The right to personal liberty is also one of the most quintessential individual rights of a human being. Justice Oputa writes that personal liberty is premised on the "freedom from external coercion in the use of one's good or faculties. It is the status of not being the property or chattel of another".[98] An extensive definition of this right views it as the freedom to live as one chooses without undue restrictions or constraints from the state or its agencies and third parties.[99] The legal scholar, Blackstone, offers a wider definition of the right as the freedom to think as one thinks fit, without any restraint or control, although this right can be restricted by the state.[100] Crucially, the right relates to the freedom to exercise a wish in tandem with the moral and legal principles of society. It is connected to the essentialist rudiments of an individual's physical freedom and arguably even the individual's mental autonomy and freedom.[101] The libertarian conceptualisation of this right seeks to maximise the freedom of choice, voluntary association, individual autonomy and personal judgment embedded in this right.[102] Section 35(1) of the Nigeria Constitution states that "Every person shall be entitled to his personal liberty and no person shall be deprived of such liberty save in the following cases and in accordance with a procedure permitted by law."[103] The law goes on to provide lawful instances and remedies for the physical deprivation of liberty. The UDHR (Article 3),

97 Amnesty International, "My Life, My Health".

98 Oputa, *Human Rights in the Legal and Political Culture of Nigeria*, as cited in Olomojobi, *Human Rights and Civil Liberties in Nigeria*, 83.

99 See the definition adopted in the case of *Adewole v Jakande* [1981] 1 NCLR 262.

100 Jones, *Selections from Blackstone's Commentaries*, 59.

101 Möller, "Two Conceptions of Positive Liberty," 757–86.

102 Van der Vossen, "Libertarianism".

103 Similarly, the UDHR provides in Art. 3 that "Everyone has the right to life, liberty and security of person." The ICCPR provides in Art. 9(1) that "Everyone has the right to liberty and security of person. … No one shall be deprived of his liberty except on such grounds and in accordance with such procedure as are established by law." The law goes on to provide lawful instances and remedies for physical deprivation of liberty.

ICCPR (Article 9 (1)) and African Charter (Article 6) make similar provisions on the right to liberty and human security. The issue of whether this right is to be interpreted in the restrictive limits of freedom from physical restraint and control, or whether it encompasses individual choices and freedom of action, was touched on in the case of *Adewole v Jakande*.[104] In interpreting the right as contained in section 32 of the 1979 Constitution (now section 35), the court held that it extends to freedom of action, including privileges, immunities and other rights of a personal nature, including "privileges recognised at law for the happiness of free men".[105] The court ruled in this case that the closure of private schools by the Lagos State government was a violation of the personal liberty of parents to train their children where and how they deem fit. The court particularly stated that "personal liberty ... denotes not merely freedom from bodily restraint, but rights to contact, to have an occupation, to acquire knowledge, to marry, have a home, children, to worship, enjoy and have privileges recognised at law for the happiness of free men".[106] The court further approved the definition of personal liberty by Blackstone as encompassing "... the right or power of locomotion; of changing situation or moving one's person to whatsoever place one's own inclination may direct, without imprisonment or restraint, unless by due course of law".[107] The Nigerian Jurist, Ogbu, has rejected this broad view of the provision in favour of a narrow view of physical constraint.[108] According to Ogbu, the provision of that law should be construed as a whole within the contemplation of freedom from undue physical restrain by arrest or detention.

On the contrary, any interpretation of the law should be done in the light of the fundamental objective of that area of law.[109] Human rights law fundamentally aims to safeguard, guarantee and promote the development of human dignity and human freedoms. When the right to liberty is approached from the overall perspective of personal freedom, an enhanced view of liberty as one that is inclusive of emotional, mental and physiological liberty is preferred. Indeed, human rights law echoes this interpretation by guaranteeing the freedom of thought, conscience and human dignity.[110] On the issue at hand, the

---

104 *Adewole v Jakande* [1981] 1 NCLR 262, 278.

105 Ibid.

106 Ibid. The court adopted the definition of personal liberty in *Meyer v Nebraska* 262 US 390 (1923), 399.

107 Ibid.

108 Ogbu, *Human Rights Law*, 191.

109 Marshall, *Personal Freedom*, 13.

110 Berlin, for example, makes a distinction between negative and positive freedom that leads to an enhanced understanding of justice and of the right to liberty. Berlin describes

proponents of decriminalising could argue that a law guaranteeing personal liberty envisages the freedom and liberty to order the affairs of one's life. Any unjustifiable encroachment would amount to a restraint on this right to liberty. Consequently, individuals should have the autonomy to make their own choices (however morally harmful) and plans, to influence and fashion their destinies as a matter of personal interest and not be imprisoned for doing so.

5.3 *Adultery and the Freedom of "Intimate" Association*

The criminalisation of adultery touches upon another human right issue, the freedom of association as guaranteed by section 40 of the Constitution and Article 10(1) of the African Charter. Freedom of association means the liberty to freely associate with others and also to share your opinions, ideas and thoughts with them. The right to associate is one of the fundamental freedoms legally guaranteed in Article 20 of the UDHR and Articles 21 and 22 of the ICCPR. This right principally entails that Nigerians are free to join and maintain associations for the protection of their interest. Following this line of argument, it could be said that individuals should not be criminalised for maintaining "harmless" associations. In the case of *AG Federation v Atiku Abubakar*,[111] for example, the Supreme Court affirmed that an individual have the right to freely assemble and associate and no one should not be denied the constitutional right to "form or belong to any political party, trade union or any other association for the protection of his interests".[112] The point can also be made that this indispensable right to association enables citizens to maintain intimate associations and close relationships of a personal nature.

The intimate and personal aspect of this right is key, but it is often neglected in Nigerian jurisprudence. This right presents a constitutional basis for maintaining private/personal and sexual associations free from state interference.[113]

negative freedoms as the unfettered right of individuals not to be prevented from doing what they want or be obstructed by others. Positive freedom on the other hand is characterised by an unfettered autonomy to make one's own choices and plans, and to influence and fashion one's destiny as a matter of personal interest. It entails an element of internal autonomy to be and do as one decides. Takala, "Concepts of 'Person' and 'Liberty'," 225–28.

111 *AG Federation v Atiku Abubakar* (2008) 2 CCLR SC 483.

112 In *Roberts v United States Jaycees* 468 US 609 (1984) 617–18, for example, the Supreme Court, addressing state action forcing the inclusion of women in an all-male organisation identified two types of protected associations: (1) the First Amendment right to associate for the purposes of free speech, assembly, and the exercise of religion; and (2) the freedom of choice "to enter into and maintain certain intimate human relationships" on the other.

113 Karst, "Freedom of Intimate Association," 624; Shaman, *Equality and Liberty*, 215–16, 227–29; Marcus, "Freedom of Intimate Association," 269.

Beyond the rights of political, group and work association, this right protects intimate relationships, marriage, family relationships, the choice whether or not to procreate, seclusion from others and even the maintenance of relationships outside the traditional family structure.[114] It follows that the criminalisation of private sexual acts could infringe on the right to form and maintain intimate associations.

5.4 *Adultery and the Freedom of Thought, Conscience and Religion*

This right simply means that all persons have the right to think freely, to entertain ideas and hold positions based on conscientious, religious or other beliefs without undue interference.[115] Article 18 of the UDHR, Article 18 of ICCPR, and Article 8 of the African Charter provide for the right to a religious belief and the freedom of conscience and thought of one's choosing, either individually or in community with others in a public and private setting. This right also protects theistic and nontheistic beliefs, including the right not to profess or follow the doctrines of any religion.[116] Section 38(1) of the Nigerian Constitution also guarantees all Nigerians the right to maintain and believe in their own consciences, thoughts and religious preferences. This includes the right to demonstrate or manifest their thoughts, religious or other beliefs by way of worship, observance, practice and teaching in harmony with others or individually.[117] This aspect is significant in permitting people to follow the dictates of their beliefs, values and conscience. Notably, this right complements the freedom of association and assembly by creating the conditions to develop one's values and manifest them as one pleases, albeit within the restraints placed by the law. Implicit in this right is the freedom to hold a personal opinion and belief in what is moral or immoral. Section 42 of the Nigerian Constitution reaffirms this right by providing that no persons shall be discriminated against on the basis of their religious beliefs. Section 10 further aims to ensure that there is equality of all religions and underscores the liberty to freely choose a

---

114 Karst "Freedom of Intimate Association," 624–25; Marcus, "Freedom of Intimate Association," 269–75. The US courts have proactively asserted the right to intimate association. See for example, cases such as *Grisworld v Connecticut* 381 US 479 (1965); *Laurence v Texas* 539 US 558 (2003); *Roberts v United States Jaycees* 468 US 609 (1984); *Loving v Virginia* 388 US 1 (1967).

115 Olomojobi, *Human Rights and Civil Liberties in Nigeria*, 186–87; Swaine, "Freedom of Thought," 405–25.

116 UN Human Rights Committee, "CCPR General Comment No. 22," CCPR/C/21/Rev.1/Add.4, para. 2.

117 Ogbu, *Human Rights Law*, 300–01.

religion by prohibiting the adoption of a particular state religion by the state or federation.

While religion is easy to define and understand, thought and conscience are vague concepts that are harder to adequately delineate and identify. Unfortunately, judicial pronouncement in Nigeria on this right has been on the religious aspect. This leaves open the issue of whether Section 38 protects independent thoughts, conscience, or religion separately, or if thought, religion and conscience merely reinforce religious freedom.

A pertinent question for the abolition of criminal sanctions against adultery is whether the law is contrary to the spirit of the constitutional protection of one's right to develop a moral sense of right and wrong and manifest the dictates of one's conscience in matters of fundamental truth and one's sense of morality? Put more simply, does this right grant one the capacity to be one's own person and to live one's life according to the desires and motives of one's sense of reasoning, thought and moral inclination?

On the principles of freedom, equity and justice that guide the Nigerian Constitution, it is probably fair to argue that these rights grant individuals the freedom to hold or consider opinions, perspectives, ideas and viewpoints that are independent of others' views. This framework for understanding the scope of the right to freedom of thought, conscience and religion was set out by the Nigerian Supreme Court in *Medical and Dental Practitioners Disciplinary Tribunal v Okonkwo.*[118] Ayoola J. S. C., who read the unanimous judgment of the Court, stated that the right to freedom of thought, conscience or religion implies a right not to be prevented without lawful justification from choosing the course of one's life, fashioned on what one believes, and the right not to be coerced into acting contrary to one's belief. The UN's General Comment No. 22 distinguishes freedom of thought, conscience and belief from religion and reiterates support for all aspects of this right.[119] Paragraph 1 of the Comment No. 22 states that the right to freedom of thought, conscience and religion is a far-reaching right that "encompasses the freedom of thought on all matters, personal conviction and commitment to a religion or belief", to be exercised individually or in a group with others.[120] The Comment further enjoins states to ensure that the right to thought and conscience receives equal protection as freedom from religion and belief.[121]

118 *Medical and Dental Practitioners Disciplinary Tribunal v Okonkwo* (2001) JELR 33516 (SC).

119 UN Committee on Economic, Social and Cultural Rights, "General Comment No. 22", E/C.12/GC/22 (General Comment No. 22). Also see Domingo, "Restoring Freedom of Conscience," 176–93.

120 General Comment No. 22.

121 Para 1, General Comment No. 22.

Accordingly, supporters of decriminalisation may argue that this right can be relied on to defend a concept of one's moral obligation, conviction and identity and to promote the autonomy to conduct one's self in a particular manner, even if it is contrary to popular belief. The freedom of expression, as provided for in section 39 of the Constitution, which guarantees the right to hold an opinion and to receive and impart ideas reinforces this point. Bearing in mind that this right is not absolute, the germane issue is whether a criminal punishment is an adequate limitation to this right in the case of a non-violent consensual act.

5.5 *Adultery and the Right to Freedom from Discrimination*

The right to freedom from discrimination is internationally recognised as a human right in several human rights instruments and treaties.[122] Article 2(1) of the ICCPR and Article 2(2) of ICESCR prohibit discrimination of any kind based on race, colour, sex, language, religion, political or other opinions, national or social origin, property, birth and other status. State parties are to respect and guide against discrimination and ensure equal protection of the law in their territories and jurisdictions.[123] Articles 2 and 7 of the UDHR further express the guiding principle of human rights on the values of equality and non-discrimination. Looking at the Preamble to the UDHR, words like "equal and inalienable rights of all members of the human family", "inherent dignity", and "equal rights of men and women and of nations large and small" indicate the approach of human rights to the core issue of equality and non-discrimination.

In Nigeria the freedom and autonomy of an individual are further guaranteed by the constitutional promotion of equality and non-discrimination. The principles of equality and non-discrimination are premised on section 42(1) of the Nigerian constitution, which requires that people are not treated differently on the basis of their social construction.[124] The constitutional provision essentially prohibits discrimination based on a person's ethnicity, community, religious belief, sex, place of origin, political opinion or the circumstances of

122 See UN Human Rights Committee, "CCPR General Comment No. 28", CCPR/C/21/Rev.1/Add.10; UN Human Rights Committee, "CCPR General Comment No. 19", 1990 (paragraph 6 states that 'States parties shall take appropriate steps to ensure equality of rights and responsibilities of spouses as to marriage, during marriage and at its dissolution'); UN Human Rights Committee. "CCPR General Comment No. 18", 1989.

123 UN Committee on the Rights of Persons with Disabilities. "General Comment No. 6 on Equality and Non-Discrimination", CRPD/C/GC/6.

124 Olomojobi, *Human Rights and Civil Liberties in Nigeria*, 300.

the person's birth. In terms of this provision, denying persons on the basis of the groups to which they belong their rights or the possibility of developing their full potential as individuals is a grave injustice and a negation of their right to equality and dignity. It is enshrined in the principle of egalitarianism – the doctrine that all people are equally valuable and deserve equal rights and opportunities.[125] Although the Nigerian Constitution does not expressly protect its citizens from discrimination in all areas of life, the African Charter in Article 2 expansively guarantees the equal enjoyment of the rights and freedoms enshrined in the Charter without distinction as to race, religion, language, political or any opinion, national and social origin, fortune, birth or any status. The provision of Article 2 has a further-reaching effect on discrimination than the stipulated grounds for non-discrimination in section 42(1) of the Constitution. Therefore Nigerians can rely on the African Charter as an enforceable legal instrument to use in seeking redress for infringements of their human rights.[126] The right not to be penalised because one simply holds a contrary opinion to public view may be inferred under this provision.

The law on non-discrimination applies to direct and indirect discrimination. Direct discrimination occurs when individuals are treated less favorably than others in a similar situation and this treatment cannot be objectively and reasonably justified.[127] In the *locus classicus* case of *Mojekwu v Mojekwu*,[128] a discriminatory patrilineal custom was declared unconstitutional and contrary to democratic values. That case dealt with the fact that only male children can inherit their father's property in the Olu Ekpe custom of Anambra State. When a man dies leaving no male child behind, his brother inherits his property and

125 Long, "Egalitarianism"; Wolff, "Fairness, Respect, and the Egalitarian Ethos," 97–122.

126 The African Charter has been duly domesticated into the corpus of Nigerian law by virtue of the African Charter on Human and Peoples' Rights (Ratification and Enforcement) Act, Cap A9, Vol. 1, LFN 2004. Thus the provisions of the Charter have a binding effect on Nigeria's jurisprudence. In a number of cases, the courts have held that the African Charter and all its provisions are indeed directly enforceable in Nigeria. In *Ogudu v State* (1994) 9 NWLR (Pt. 366) 1 (the case is also reported as *Peter Nemi v A. G. of Lagos* [1994] ILRC 376 in some reports), the Supreme Court held per Bello (CJN) that the African Charter is a part of Nigeria's domestic law as "the Charter has become part of our domestic laws, the enforcement of its provisions like our laws fall within the judicial powers of the Court as provided by the Constitution and all other laws relating thereto". This position is also reiterated by the Supreme Court in *General Sani Abacha and Ors v Chief Gani Fawehinmi* (2000) 4 Federation Weekly Law Reports 533, where the Supreme Court held that the African Charter is a part of Nigerian laws and the provisions are enforceable by the courts as other laws in Nigeria.

127 Equality and Human Rights Commission, "Article 14".

128 *Mojekwu v Mojekwu* (1997) 7 NWLR 288.

if this brother dies, his own male child will inherit the property. The Court of Appeal condemned the practice as repugnant to natural justice, equity and good conscience.[129] More recently the courts have reaffirmed the principle of non-discrimination in similar female inheritance cases of *Ukeje v Ukeje*[130] and *Anekwe v Nweke*.[131] The courts ruled that inheritance laws and customs that exclude women from inheriting properties are contrary to the constitutionally guaranteed fundamental rights.[132] Indirect discrimination, on the other hand, occurs when a rule or policy supposedly applying to everyone equally actually works to the disadvantage of one or more groups.[133] Even where a law is non-discriminatory *per se*, if it is enforced in a discriminatory fashion the action can lead to a disadvantage.

The issue of discrimination features more prominently in the effect of criminal anti-adultery laws on women. Close scrutiny of criminal laws against adultery indicates that they could have a disproportionate discriminatory impact on women. The biased nature of the adultery law can also be gleaned from the procedural requirement for the prosecution of the offence. According to section 142 of the Criminal Procedure Code (CPC),[134] only the husband of a woman who has committed adultery or her father or guardian (in the case of unmarried women) and other persons can institute an action for adultery.[135] The law simply fails to empower a woman whose husband has committed adultery to make a complaint that the court can take cognizance of for prosecution. This provision reveals some elements of bias against a married woman whose husband has committed adultery, as she lacks the legal power to make

129 Ibid.

130 *Ukeje v Ukeje* (2014) 11 NWLR (Pt. 1418) 384.

131 *Anekwe v Nweke* (2014) 9 NWLR (Pt. 1412) 393.

132 Ibid.

133 Equality and Human Rights Commission, "Article 14".

134 Accordingly, "(1) No court shall take cognizance of an offence under section 387, 388 or 389 of the Penal Code except – / (a) upon a complaint made by the husband of the woman or in his absence by some person who had care of such woman on his behalf at the time when the offence was committed; or (b) in the case of the woman being unmarried upon a complaint made by her father or guardian or in his absence by some person who had care of such unmarried woman on his behalf at the time when the offence was committed. (2) Where the husband, father or guardian referred to in subsection (1) is under the age of eighteen years, or is an idiot or lunatic or is from sickness or infirmity unable to make a complaint some other person may, with the leave of the court, make a complaint on his behalf." Criminal Procedure Code, Cap C41, LFN 2004.

135 It is worth noting that there is no such provision in the Administration of Criminal Justice Act, 2015 which replaced the Criminal Procedure Code formerly applicable to the Federal Capital Territory, Abuja, where the Penal Code still applies.

the same complaint a man is empowered to. One may say that this provision is contrary to the spirit of equality and non-discrimination as embedded in the Constitution.

Even where the language of the law creating the offence is gender-neutral at face value, its enforcement is directed overwhelmingly against women and girls. In some countries, even rape could constitute adultery.[136] The cases of Safiya Husseini, Maryam Abubakar and Amina Lawal are practical examples of the social harms that befall women rather than men in adulterous situations. Only these women were charged with adultery, even when they allegedly committed the act with men. Amina, a single mother in Katsina State, was convicted of adultery and sentenced to death by stoning by a state Sharia court for conceiving a child out of wedlock. As in the case of Safiya Husseini, the alleged father of the child, Yahaya Abubakar, denied any involvement and was released without conviction for lack of evidence. Like Safiya, Amina's conviction was based largely on her pregnancy and confession (even after she withdrew the confession). The prosecutorial effect of adultery laws leads one to the belief that the law on adultery carries greater socio-cultural repercussions for women than for men.

5.6 *Adultery and the Right to Life*

The right to life is the most quintessential of all human rights. In the case of *Forum of Conscience v Sierra Leone,* the African Commission declared it to be the fulcrum of all other rights.[137] Section 33(1) of the Nigerian Constitution guarantees the right to life of every person and on this account, no one shall be deprived of his/her life unless it is legally permissible to do so in respect of a criminal offence by a competent court. The African Charter elegantly reaffirms this right in Article 4 by recognising that "every human being shall be entitled to respect for his life and the integrity of his person". Thus, people are not guaranteed merely the right to be alive but also the right to be respected and valued as human beings. The same can be said of the UDHR. It can be assumed that it emphasises the link between the right to life and respect for human liberty and security by making them part of the same provision in Article 3. The ICCPR also recognises and calls for the enhancement of the right to life in Article 6.

The "right to life" is a phrase that is commonly used to describe the belief that a human being has an essential right to a "life" and also the right to actually

136 Rhode, *Adultery*. In Pakistan, for example, a woman who has been raped has to prove it to avoid being accused of adultery.

137 *Forum of Conscience v Sierra Leone* (Communication No. 223/98) [2000] ACHPR 22 (6 November 2000).

live a full life without undue encroachment on this right by the state, its agents and oppressive laws.[138] This conceptualisation of the right to life is relevant to the discussion at hand because a far-reaching interpretation of this right would mean that it guarantees Nigerians the right not to be penalised for living the lives they choose to lead.[139] There is also the contention that the death penalty for adultery is a violation of the right to life, the most fundamental human right.[140]

In 2002 Amina Lawal was sentenced to death in Katsina State after being found guilty of having pre-marital sex.[141] In 2004 Daso Adamu in Bauchi State was sentenced to death by stoning after being found guilty of adultery.[142] Also in 2002 Hafsatu Adamu was sentenced to death by stoning in Sokoto State.[143] This clearly amounts to a gross violation of their right to life and the provisions of the Nigerian constitution.

6 Public Morality Counter-Debate

A counter-argument to these human rights arguments is that the provisions are not absolute. In Nigeria they can be limited by the sections creating them or the provisions of section 45 of the Constitution, which contains a wide ground for derogation in the interest of defence, public safety, order, morality or health or the purpose of protecting the rights and freedom of other persons. Thus, the argument for criminalising adultery may be justified in support of "morality", "health", "safety" and "order". The concept of public morality is vague, however, and subject to varying interpretations, depending on the perception of the majority and the location. Morality is a "system of principles and values concerning people's behavior, which is generally accepted by a society or by a particular group of people".[144] The standards of right or good conduct differ from one society to another and change over time. In Nigeria what is considered immoral in one part of the country may not necessarily

138 Olomojobi, *Human Rights and Civil Liberties in Nigeria*, 14.

139 See Olomojobi, *Human Rights and Civil Liberties in Nigeria*, 31–32 for more discussion on this.

140 See more discussions on capital punishment and the right to life in Center for Constitutional Rights, "The Death Penalty is a Human Rights Violation"; Riga, "Capital Punishment and the Right to Life," 23; Mumīsa et al., *Sharia Law and the Death Penalty*.

141 Weimann, *Islamic Criminal Law*, 177.

142 Ibid.

143 Weimann, *Islamic Criminal Law*, 176.

144 Collins English Dictionary, "Morality".

receive the same reprobation in another. For example, alcohol consumption is permissible in Southern Nigeria but unacceptable in the North, in line with the moral customs and traditions of the majority of Northerners. Indeed, several "morally justifiable" acts such as the disinheritance of females, forced marriages and wife kidnapping or abduction, wife inheritance, adverse widowhood practices, and female genital mutilation (FGM) have now been forbidden by the law and successfully challenged in the courts.[145] The invalidation of discriminatory exclusions and practices against women reflects the change in social and moral attitudes to the role and status of women. It is also worth noting that laws and policies were set up to prohibit these practices even when they enjoyed socio-cultural and traditional moral support.[146] A 2020 study has shown that the prevalence of FGM is gradually declining for women and girls above 15, however, it is increasing for girls below 14.[147] For the decriminalisation debaters, it may be that the law pre-empts changes in moral values.[148]

145 For example, in response to the problem of inheritance, some states in the Eastern States such as Anambra (e.g. the State Administration and Succession (Estates of Deceased Persons) Law, Cap 4, Laws of Anambra State, 1986) have adopted the succession laws in respect of real and personal estate on intestacy. Other laws such as the Administration of Estates Law, 1959 and Marriage Act, Cap 218, LFN 1990 have also stepped in to regulate inheritance. Cases such as *Asika and Ors v Atuanya* (2013) JELR 35731 (SC) and *Mojekwu v Ejikeme* (2000) 5 NWLR 402 have invalidated discriminatory practices against women as being incompatible with the principle of equity and natural justice. Also see Oni, "Right of Women to Inheritance," 44.

146 The Violence Against Persons (Prohibition) Act, 2015 (the VAPP Act) aims to eliminate gender-based violence in private and public life by criminalising and setting out the punishment for acts including rape (but not spousal rape), incest, domestic violence, stalking, harmful traditional practices and FGM (s. 6 of the VAPP Act). About thirteen states in Nigeria have put in place some form of law banning FGM. Some include: Bayelsa State – FGM (Prohibition) Law, 2004; Cross River State – the Girl-Child Marriages and Female Circumcision (Prohibition) Law, 2000; Ebonyi State – Law Abolishing Harmful Traditional Practices Against Women and Children, 2001; Edo State – Prohibition of Female Genital Mutilation Law, 1999; Enugu State – FGM (Prohibition) Law, 2004; Rivers State – Child Rights Act, 2009. For further information on FGM in Nigeria, see Thomas Reuter Foundation and 28 Too Many, "Nigeria: The Law and FGM".

147 Kandala et al., "Female Genital Mutilation/Cutting in Nigeria," 17–18.

148 Although a deeper moral argument for or against the morality of adultery is beyond the scope of this chapter, it is worth mentioning the controversy on whether or not the law should be involved in the regulation of morality, especially in matters that concern people's personal lives and their sexuality. The insightful arguments of Lord Devlin based on the Wolfenden Report and the response by Hart illustrate the contrasting positions on the issue. Contrary to the notion that issues of private morality and immorality are not the business of the law, Lord Devlin asserts that the law has a duty to uphold the morality of society. According to him, society has the right to protect and even punish conduct that are abhorred, even those that are not deemed injurious to others, as a society also serves

The human rights argument for depenalisation is made, bearing in mind that the right is not absolute. Although the law can regulate public morality, welfare, health and order and therefore limit the reliance on human rights, the limitations themselves are not absolute. The derogation of human rights in the interests of the public (section 45) requires that it is reasonably necessary in a democratic society and not to unduly oppress individuals, which could include their private choices. The state can protect the public from obviously offensive displays of sexual behaviour, violent and forced sexual behaviour, sexual abuse of all kinds, cruelty to animals, acts that spread diseases and non-consensual related offences. However, criminalising adults for how they conduct their private consensual non-harmful matters may be excessive and tantamount to invading an individual's privacy, especially as issues such as child marriages and marital rape are being condoned in the same society. Although human rights have limitations, an unjust restriction of them would invariably amount to an infringement.

Moreover, criminalising the act would not strengthen an already frail marriage nor would it repair any damage to the union. A criminal record may cause further damage to the family as a whole, especially where the adulterer is the breadwinner of the family or a caregiver of a child or younger children. In fact, having a criminal record can negatively impact on the family's wellbeing in terms of income potential, savings, assets, credit scores, healthy relationships, family strength and stability.[149] There are many professions and jobs that do not accept people with convictions. A person's inability to secure a job due to having a past criminal record can cause exceptional hardship to the innocent spouse and children in the union. According to a report, "the barriers associated with having a criminal record do not just result in lifelong punishment

---

the role of moral tutor and its criminal system has a proper tutorial function. Thus, he envisages a connection between law and morality, and argues for the majority's right to defend its social environment from a change that it despises. To him, common morality is the cement that binds a society and without it, it would disintegrate. Society, therefore, has the right to utilise the appropriate institutions and legal criminal sanctions to protect its moral principles. Hart, a leading academic, disagrees with this contention and argues that legalising moral codes was unnecessary, undesirable and morally wrong, as society is quite capable of accommodating different moral norms without disintegrating. He bases his argument on the contention that doing so will interfere with freedom of choice, liberty and the privacy of morality. Hart also disapproves of the law's interfering with issues of morality because it may punish behaviour that may not have proved harmful to another person. He strongly advocates the exercise of free choice by individuals, which is a moral value, and it is wrong to interfere with that right. See more at Dworkin, "Lord Devlin and the Enforcement of Morals," 986; Ward, *Introduction to Critical Legal Theory*, 19–27.

149 Love, "How a Parent's Criminal Record Limits Children".

for the parent with the record; they also can significantly limit a child's life chances".[150] A parent's conviction or even an arrest for adultery could affect the child's emotional stability and physical security, including the child's future economic and educational prospects. The point being made is that although the act of adultery is morally and socially unacceptable since it violates the core sanctity of a marriage, criminalisation of it could have a more devastating effect on the family than the discovery of the act itself. While acknowledging that adultery is reprehensible, perhaps, its regulation should be left to the private conscience of the person, the civil and divorce courts, and best of all, therapy and counselling – not criminal prohibitions that carry graver consequences.

In addition, the rights to liberty, thought, conscience and religion grant an individual the right to determine one's thoughts and conscience and decide one's own standard of what is right or wrong. When judging the standards of morality, the standards used to produce these moral norms should be honest, decent, unhypocritical and equitable. However, the standards of morality is not equal for men and women in Nigeria. Some may argue that fornication and adultery are "un-African",[151] yet a man is allowed to maintain as many wives as he likes while a woman is not. The prevalence of adultery also makes one wonder why many profess to have virtues, beliefs, and principles of morality yet flaunt them at will. The low rate of conviction and deterrence also raises the question of whether the law aims to actually serve a purpose or merely express the indignation of the people against the act.

7 Conclusion

Is the collateral consequence of criminalising adultery worth the affront of the act to society? Given the fact that having even a minor criminal record can be a life sentence to poverty, obstacles to employment, education and training, public assistance, financial empowerment, and family disruption, it is perhaps time to examine afresh the whole issue of criminalising adultery. This chapter has objectively laid bare the arguments for and against the penalisation of the act, calling for legislators to take another look at the law and possibly to decriminalise adultery or reframe the approach to it in the light of human rights.

150 Valla et al., "Removing Barriers to Opportunity for Parents with Criminal Records".

151 Cole, "Infidelity and Cheating in African Tradition".

On the one hand, the argument for the criminalisation of adultery goes down to the root of the principles of traditional Nigerian culture and religion, and in a society where acts and relationships are measured on the scale of moral values it is quite natural to find a deep concern for regulating sexual morality. On the other hand, it may be argued that the innate dignity, rights to liberty, privacy, thought, conscience, religion, association, dignity and other human rights that are available to every Nigerian citizen by virtue of their being subject to the Constitution of the Federal Republic of Nigeria may be undermined by the criminalisation of such sexual acts. These rights encompass protection from coercion and the freedom to live and lead one's life without unjustified restraint and limitation imposed by the public, the government or any of its agencies. They are among the founding principles of a democratic society. Whether or not such criminalisation falls under the permissible derogations is an interesting area for the courts to clarify.

Many people, even in societies that do not criminalise adultery, are intolerant of infidelity. Those who stray may also agree that cheating is wrong. People are born with internal filters of what is right or wrong, however, and criminalising the act may arguably run counter to the basic concept of human autonomy and freedom. This is in addition to the consequences of criminal incarceration on families and children. Further, the law accentuates the unequal power relations between men and women at the prosecutorial level.

Bibliography

Literature

Adewale, S. A. "Benin Crime and Traditional Africa." Accessed September 7, 2022. https://ihuanedo.ning.com/profiles/blogs/benin-crime-and-traditional.

Amnesty International. "Afghanistan: Reject Stoning, Flogging, Amputation and Other Taliban-Era Punishments." Accessed March 9, 2023. https://www.amnesty.org/en/wp-content/uploads/2021/06/pre016242013en.pdf.

Amnesty International. "My Life, My Health, My Education, My Choice, My Future, My Body, My Rights." Accessed March 9, 2023. https://www.amnesty.org/download/Documents/4000/act350012014en.pdf.

Ashaolu, Oluwafemi. "Man Beats Wife Up After Three Children's DNA Tests Come Out Negative." Accessed September 7, 2021. https://www.newsbreak.ng/man-beats-wife-up-after-three-childrens-dna-tests-come-out-negative/.

Baobab for Women's Human Rights. *Baobab for Women's Human Rights and Shari'a Implementation in Nigeria: The Journey So Far.* Lagos: Baobab for Women's Human Rights, 2003.

Barman, Bablu. "Concept of Hindu Marriage of India." *Journal of Emerging Technologies and Innovative Research* 5, no. 9 (2018): 426–30.

BBC. "Interview with Hillary Clinton." Accessed June 17, 2022. http://www.bbc.co.uk/programmes/b048033v.

Bello, Precious. "My Wife Cheats on Me – Pastor Tells Court." Accessed September 17, 2022. https://dailypost.ng/2019/09/12/wife-cheats-pastor-tells-court.

Butler, R. A. "Homosexual Offences and Prostitution (Report). H. C. Deb. (vol. 596, 26 November 1958)." Accessed March 9, 2023. https://api.parliament.uk/historic-hansard/commons/1958/nov/26/homosexual-offences-and-prostitution.

Carnegie Council for Ethics in International Affairs. "Cultural Relativism." Accessed May 16, 2022. https://www.carnegiecouncil.org/explore-engage/key-terms/cultural-relativism.

Center for Constitutional Rights. "The Death Penalty is a Human Rights Violation: An Examination of the Death Penalty in the U.S. from a Human Rights Perspective." Accessed March 9, 2023. https://ccrjustice.org/files/CCR%20Death%20Penalty%20Factsheet.pdf.

Chowbe, Vijaykumar Shrikrushna. "Adultery: A Conceptual and Legal Analysis." Accessed March 9, 2023. https://papers.ssrn.com/sol3/papers.cfm?abstract_id=1856991.

CNN. "A Chronology: Key Moments in the Clinton-Lewinsky Saga." Accessed September 17, 2022. https://edition.cnn.com/ALLPOLITICS/1998/resources/lewinsky/timeline/.

Cole, Patrick Dele. "Infidelity and Cheating in African Tradition." Accessed March 9, 2023. https://guardian.ng/opinion/infidelity-and-cheating-in-african-tradition/.

Collins English Dictionary. "Morality: Definition and Meaning." Accessed December 17, 2022. https://www.collinsdictionary.com/dictionary/english/morality.

Cornell Law School. "Privacy." Accessed December 6, 2022. https://www.law.cornell.edu/wex/privacy.

Crowley, Michael. "Lewinsky Scandal Still Affects Clintons." Accessed June 17, 2022. http://www.cbsnews.com/news/lewinsky-scandal-still-affects-clintons.

Daily Independent. "Woman Stabs Husband on Suspicion of Infidelity." Accessed June 20, 2022. https://www.independent.ng/woman-stabs-husband-on-suspicion-of-infidelity/.

Domingo, Rafael. "Restoring Freedom of Conscience." *Journal of Law and Religion* 30, no. 2 (2015): 176–93.

Dworkin, Ronald. "Lord Devlin and the Enforcement of Morals." *Yale Law Journal* 75, no. 6 (1966): 986–1003.

Emery, Robert E. *Cultural Sociology of Divorce: An Encyclopedia, Volume 1*. Thousand Oaks: SAGE, 2013.

Enyioha Opara, Minna. "I Killed My Wife for Committing Adultery: Suspect." Accessed June 20, 2022. https://punchng.com/i-killed-my-wife-for-committing-adultery-suspect/.

Equality and Human Rights Commission. "Article 14: Protection from Discrimination." Accessed March 9, 2023. https://www.equalityhumanrights.com/en/human-rights-act/article-14-protection-discrimination.

European Court of Human Rights. *Guide on Article 8 of the European Convention on Human Rights: Right to Respect for Private and Family Life, Home and Correspondence.* Strasbourg: Council of Europe and European Court of Human Rights, 2019.

Eweka, Iro. "Crime in Traditional Society." Accessed May 16, 2021. http://www.amicidilazzaro.it/index.php/crime-in-traditional-society/.

Folarin, Samson, and Afeez Hanafi. "Man Kills Wife in Benue, Woman Kills Husband in Lagos." Accessed June 17, 2022. https://punchng.com/infidelity-man-kills-wife-in-benue-woman-kills-husband-in-lagos/.

Fuller, Richard C. "Morals and the Criminal Law." *Journal of Criminal Law and Criminology* 32, no. 6 (1942): 624–30.

Glenn, Richard A. *The Right to Privacy: Rights and Liberties Under the Law.* Santa Barbara: ABC-CLIO, 2003.

Hakim, Catherine. *The New Rules: Internet Dating, Playfairs and Erotic Power.* London: Gibson Square, 2017.

Hermann, Henry R. *Dominance and Aggression in Humans and Other Animals: The Great Game of Life.* London: Elsevier Science, 2017.

Hirsch, Jennifer S., et al. "The Social Constructions of Sexuality: Marital Infidelity and Sexually Transmitted Disease – HIV Risk in a Mexican Migrant Community." *American Journal of Public Health* 92, no. 8 (2002): 1227–37.

Hölbl, G. *A History of the Ptolemaic Empire,* translated by Tina Saavedra. London: Routledge, 1994.

Human Rights Watch. "'Political Shari'a'? Human Rights and Islamic Law in Northern Nigeria." Accessed July 22, 2022. https://www.hrw.org/report/2004/09/21/political-sharia/human-rights-and-islamic-law-northern-nigeria.

I Reporter Online. "Meet the Nigerian Tribe Where Husband, Children Would Die if the Wife Commits Adultery." Accessed September 7, 2022. https://ireporteronline.com.ng/meet-the-nigerian-tribe-where-husband-children-would-die-if-the-wife-commits-adultery/.

Ibhawoh, Bonny. "Cultural Relativism and Human Rights: Reconsidering the Africanist Discourse." *Netherlands Quarterly of Human Rights* 19, no. 1 (2001): 43–62.

Igwe, O. W., and Enefaa Longjohn. "*Actus Reus* and Customary Criminal Law in Nigeria: An Appraisal of Context and Applicability." *African Journal of Law and Criminology* 4, no. 1 (2014): 77–88.

Inter-Parliamentary Union and United Nations Office of the High Commissioner for Human Rights. *Human Rights*. Geneva: Inter-Parliamentary Union, 2016.

Islam Online. "How Islam Views Adultery." Accessed June 13, 2022. https://archive.islamonline.net/1027.

Jones, Gareth H., ed. *The Sovereignty of the Law: Selections from Blackstone's Commentaries on the Laws of England*. London: Palgrave Macmillan, 1973.

Jones, Prudence J. *Cleopatra: A Sourcebook*. Norman: University of Oklahoma Press, 2006.

Kandala, Ngianga-Bakwin, et al. "Female Genital Mutilation/Cutting in Nigeria: Is the Practice Declining? A Descriptive Analysis of Successive Demographic and Health Surveys and Multiple Indicator Cluster Surveys (2003–2017)." Accessed March 9, 2023. https://knowledgecommons.popcouncil.org/departments_sbsr-rh/1077/.

Karst, Kenneth L. "The Freedom of Intimate Association." *Yale Law Journal* 89, no. 4 (1980): 624–92.

Kodama, Satoshi. "Bentham's Distinction Between Law and Morality and Its Contemporary Significance." *Bentham Studies in Japan Today* 16 (2019). https://doi.org/10.4000/etudes-benthamiennes.6378.

Langen, Tabitha T. "Gender Power Imbalance on Women's Capacity to Negotiate Self-Protection Against HIV/AIDS in Botswana and South Africa." *African Health Sciences* 5, no. 3 (2005): 188–97.

Long, Ryan. "Internet Encyclopedia of Philosophy: Egalitarianism." Accessed March 9, 2023. https://iep.utm.edu/egalitarianism/.

Love, Margaret. "How a Parent's Criminal Record Limits Children." Accessed September 7, 2022. https://ccresourcecenter.org/2016/01/06/6767/.

Marcus, Nancy C. "The Freedom of Intimate Association in the Twenty First Century." *George Mason University Civil Rights Law Journal* 16, no. 2 (2006): 269–328.

Marshall, Jill. *Personal Freedom Through Human Rights Law? Autonomy, Identity and Integrity Under the European Convention on Human Rights*. Leiden: Martinus Nijhoff, 2008.

Martin, Francisco Forrest, et al. *International Human Rights and Humanitarian Law: Treaties, Cases, and Analysis*. New York: Cambridge University Press, 2006.

Mattachine Society. *Mattachine Review, Volumes 5-6*. New York: Mattachine Society, 1959.

Mbosowo, Donald. "The Extent and Rate of Divorce in Plateau State, Nigeria 1980 to 1988." *Journal of Divorce and Remarriage* 21, 3–4 (1994): 147–70.

Meri, Josef W. *Medieval Islamic Civilization: A-K, Index*. London: Taylor & Francis, 2006.

Miller, Alyssa. "Punishing Passion: A Comparative Analysis of Adultery Laws in the United States of America and Taiwan and their Effects on Women." *Fordham International Law Journal* 41, no. 2 (2018): 425–71.

Minnesota Legislature. "Minnesota Statutes: 609.36 Adultery." Accessed March 9, 2023. https://www.revisor.mn.gov/statutes/cite/609.36.

Möller, Kai. "Two Conceptions of Positive Liberty: Towards an Autonomy-Based Theory of Constitutional Rights." *Oxford Journal of Legal Studies* 29, no. 4 (2009) 757–86.

Mumīsa, Michael, et al. *Sharia Law and the Death Penalty: Would Abolition of the Death Penalty Be Unfaithful to the Message of Islam?* London: Penal Reform International, 2015.

Nigerian Bulletin. "Igbo Culture and Tradition: 10 Things You Should Not Do in Igboland." Accessed September 7, 2022. https://www.nigerianbulletin.com/threads/igbo-culture-and-tradition-10-things-you-should-not-do-in-igboland.212996/.

Nwauche, E. S. "The Right to Privacy in Nigeria." *CALS Review of Nigerian Law and Practice* 1, no. 1 (2007): 63–90.

O'Reilly, James. "Marital Privacy and Family Law." *Studies: An Irish Quarterly Review* 66, no. 261 (1977): 8–24.

Ogbu, Osita Nnamani. *Human Rights Law and Practice in Nigeria, Vol 1.* 2 ed. Enugu: Snaap Press, 2013.

Ojo, Matthias Olufemi Dada. "Magun: The Traditional Juju for the Punishment pf Adultery Among Yoruba Natives." *Antropologija* 13, no. 3 (2013): 131–42.

Okon, V. S. "The Psychological Effects of Divorce on Children: A Case Study of Uyo Urban." BA thesis, University of Uyo, Nigeria, 2001.

Okorie, Albert. "An Assessment of the Traditional Penal Code for Adultery and the Operations of Women's Rights Instruments Among the Igbos, in South-Eastern Nigeria." *International Journal of Political Science* 6, no. 4 (2020): 32–45.

Olomojobi, Yinka. *Human Rights and Civil Liberties in Nigeria: Discussions, Analyses, and Explanations.* Lagos: Princeton and Associates, 2016.

Omotosho, Kehinde. "6 Weird Traditions You Probably Never Knew Existed." Accessed September 7, 2022. https://www.pulse.ng/lifestyle/food-travel-arts-culture/nigerian-cultures-6-weird-traditions-you-probably-never-knew-existed-id6662038.html.

Oni, B. "The Right of Women to Inheritance Under Native Law: An Evaluation." *Nigerian Journal of African Law* (2008): 44–48.

Oputa, C. A. *Human Rights in the Legal and Political Culture of Nigeria: Delivered at the 2nd Idigbe Memorial Lecture at the University of Benin on November 28, 1986.* Lagos: Nigerian Law Publications, 1988.

Parikh, Shanti A. "The Political Economy of Marriage and HIV: The ABC Approach, 'Safe' Infidelity, and Managing Moral Risk in Uganda." *American Journal of Public Health* 97, no. 7 (2007): 1198–208.

Perel, Ester. *The State of Affairs: Rethinking Infidelity.* New York: Harper, 2017.

Peters, R. "Zinā or Zinā." In *Encyclopaedia of Islam*, edited by Peri J. Bearman, et al. (online). 2 ed. Leiden: Brill, 2012.

Posner, Richard A. *An Affair of State: The Investigation, Impeachment, and Trial of President Clinton.* Cambridge, Mass.: Harvard University Press, 1999.

Quaraishi, Asifa. "Her Honor: An Islamic Critique of the Rape Laws of Pakistan from a Woman-Sensitive Perspective." *Michigan Journal of International Law* 18, no. 2 (1997): 287–320.

Rhode, Deborah L. *Adultery: Infidelity and the Law.* Cambridge, Mass.: Harvard University Press, 2016.

Riga, Peter J. "Capital Punishment and the Right to Life: Some Reflections on the Human Right as Absolute." *University of Puget Sound Law Review* 5 (1981): 23–46.

Roller, Duane W. *Cleopatra: A Biography.* Oxford: Oxford University Press, 2010.

Rundel, Martha. "Decisions Between Consenting Adults Made in Private – No Place for the Government to Tread." *Louisiana Law Review* 60, no. 3 (2000): 877–908.

Sagay, Itsejuwa Esanjumi. "Adultery." In *Nigerian Family Law: Principles, Cases, Statutes and Commentaries*, edited by Itsejuwa Esanjumi Sagay. Lagos: Malthouse Press, 1999.

Scheller, Arthur Jr. "Law and Morality." *Marquette Law Review* 36 (1953): 319–27.

Semerdjian, Elyse. "Zinah." In *The Oxford Encyclopedia of the Islamic World*, edited by John L. Esposito, 49–50. Oxford: Oxford University Press, 2009.

Shaman, Jeffrey M. *Equality and Liberty in the Golden Age of State Constitutional Law.* New York: Oxford University Press, 2009.

Shire, Emily. "How Monica Lewinsky Could Haunt Hillary Clinton." Accessed June 17, 2022. http://www.bustle.com/articles/156761-heres-how-monica-lewinsky-could-haunt-hillaryclintons- campaign-as-more-than-a-one-off-low-blow.

Smith, Daniel Jordan. "Modern Marriage, Men's Extramarital Sex, and HIV Risk in Southeastern Nigeria." *American Journal of Public Health* 97, no. 6 (2007): 969–1005.

Solove, Daniel J. "Understanding Privacy." *GWU Law School Public Law Research Paper No. 420*. Accessed March 9, 2023. https://ssrn.com/abstract=1127888.

Swaine, Lucas. "Freedom of Thought as a Basic Liberty." *Political Theory* 46, no. 3 (2016): 405–25.

Takala, Tuija. "Concepts of 'Person' and 'Liberty,' and Their Implications to Our Fading Notions of Autonomy." *Journal of Medical Ethics* 33, no. 4 (2007): 225–28.

Thomas Reuter Foundation and 28 Too Many. "Nigeria: The Law and FGM June 2018." Accessed December 17, 2022. https://www.28toomany.org/nigeria/.

Timm, Jane. "The Monica Lewinsky Jokes are Back." Accessed June 17, 2022. http://www.msnbc.com/msnbc/the-monica-lewsinksy-jokes-are-back.

Vallas, Rebecca, et al. "Removing Barriers to Opportunity for Parents with Criminal Records and their Children: A Two-Generation Approach." Accessed March 9, 2023. https://cdn.americanprogress.org/wp-content/uploads/2015/12/09060720/CriminalRecords-report2.pdf.

Van der Vossen, Bas. "Stanford Encyclopedia of Philosophy: Libertarianism." Accessed December 15, 2022. https://plato.stanford.edu/archives/spr2019/entries/libertarianism/.

Viator, Gabrielle. "The Validity of Criminal Adultery Prohibitions After *Lawrence v. Texas.*" *Suffolk University Law Review* 39 (2006): 837–61.

Wang, Hao. *Protecting Privacy in China: A Research on China's Privacy Standards and the Possibility of Establishing the Right to Privacy and the Information Privacy Protection Legislation in Modern China.* Berlin: Springer, 2011.

Ward, Ian. *Introduction to Critical Legal Theory.* 2 ed. London: Psychology Press, 2004.

Warren, Samuel D., and Louis D. Brandeis. "The Right to Privacy." *Harvard Law Review* 4, no. 5 (1890): 193–95.

Weimann, Gunnar J. *Islamic Criminal Law in Northern Nigeria: Politics, Religion, Judicial Practice.* Amsterdam: Amsterdam University Press, 2010.

Wolff, Jonathan. "Fairness, Respect, and the Egalitarian Ethos." *Philosophy & Public Affairs* 27, no. 2 (1998): 97–122.

Younkins, Edward. "Why the World is the Way It is: Cultural Relativism and It's Descendants." Accessed May 16, 2022. http://www.quebecoislibre.org/younkins26.html.

Case Law

African Commission on Human and Peoples' Rights

Forum of Conscience v Sierra Leone (Communication No. 223/98) [2000] ACHPR 22 (6 November 2000).

European Court of Human Rights

A. D. T. v the United Kingdom (Application no. 35765/97) July 31, 2000.

Case of X and Y v the Netherlands (Application no. 8978/80) March 26, 1985.

Dudgeon v the United Kingdom (Application no. 7525/76) October 22, 1981.

Niemietz v Germany (72/1991/324/396) December 16, 1992.

P. G. and J. H. v the United Kingdom (Application no. 44787/98) September 25, 2001.

Nigeria

Adam v Adam 3 PLR 1971, SUIT NO. M/196/1970.

Adewole v Jakande [1981] 1 NCLR 262.

AG *Federation v Atiku Abubakar* (2008) 2 CCLR SC 483.

Ajayi v Ajayi and Anor (HD/27/67) [1970] 10 (18 December 1970).

Anekwe v Nweke (2014) 9 NWLR (Pt. 1412) 393.

Asika and Ors v Atuanya (2013) JELR 35731 (SC).

General Sanni Abacha and Ors v Chief Gani Fawehinmi (2000) 4 Federation Weekly Law Reports 533.

Medical and Dental Practitioners Disciplinary Committee v Okonkwo (1968) 1 All NLR 306.

Medical and Dental Practitioners Disciplinary Tribunal v Okonkwo (2001) JELR 33516 (SC).

Mojekwu v Ejikeme (2000) 5 NWLR 402.
Mojekwu v Mojekwu (1997) 7 NWLR 288.
Ogudu v State (1994) 9 NWLR (Pt. 366) 1.
Peter Nemi v A. G. of Lagos [1994] ILRC 376.
Ukeje v Ukeje (2014) 11 NWLR (Pt. 1418) 384.

United Kingdom

Diane Pretty v Director of Public Prosecutions [2001] UKHL 61 (HL).

United States of America

Bamburg v Bamburg 386 S.W. 3d 31 (2011).
Bower v Bower 758 So. 2d 405 (Miss. 2000).
Campbell v Sundquist 926 S.W. 2d 250 (Tenn. Ct. App. 1996).
Eisenstadt v Baird 405 US 438 (1972).
Ex parte Pankey 848 So. 2d 963 (Ala. 2002).
Grisworld v Connecticut 381 US 479 (1965).
Hanby v Hanby 158 So. 727 (Ala. 1935).
Laurence v Texas 539 US 558 (2003).
Loving v Virginia 388 US 1 (1967).
Meyer v Nebraska 262 US 390 (1923).
Olmstead v United States 277 US 438 (1928).
Roberts v United States Jaycees 468 US 609 (1984).
Stanley v George (1969) 384 US 557.
State v Smith So. 2d 648 (La. App. 4th Cir. 1999).
White v White 166 So. 3d 574 (Miss. Ct. App. 2015).
Legislation and Government Publications.

Australia

Human Rights (Sexual Conduct) Act, 1994.

Nigeria

Administration of Criminal Justice Act, 2015.
Administration of Estates Law, 1959.
African Charter on Human and Peoples' Rights (Ratification and Enforcement) Act, Cap A9, Vol. 1, LFN 2004.
Constitution of the Federal Republic of Nigeria, 1979.
Constitution of the Federal Republic of Nigeria, 1999.
Criminal Code, Cap C38, LFN 2004.
Criminal Procedure Code, Cap C41, LFN 2004.
Marriage Act, Cap 218, LFN 1990.

Matrimonial Causes Act, Cap 220, LFN 1990.
Penal Code Act, LFN 1960.
Sharia Penal Code Law of Zamfara State of Nigeria 10 of 2001.
State Administration and Succession (Estates of Deceased Persons) Law, Cap 4, Laws of Anambra State, 1986.
Violence Against Persons (Prohibition) Act, 2015.

Pakistan

Offence of Zina (Enforcement of Hudood) Ordinance VII of 1979.

International Documents

UN Committee on Economic, Social and Cultural Rights. "General Comment No. 22 on the Right to Sexual and Reproductive Health (Article 12 of the International Covenant on Economic, Social and Cultural Rights)." E/C.12/GC/22. May 2, 2016. https://documents-dds-ny.un.org/doc/UNDOC/GEN/G16/089/32/PDF/G1608932.pdf?OpenElement.
UN Committee on the Rights of Persons with Disabilities. "General Comment No. 6 on Equality and Non-Discrimination." CRPD/C/GC/6. April 26, 2018. https://digitallibrary.un.org/record/1626976?ln=en.
UN Human Rights Committee. "CCPR General Comment No. 18: Non-Discrimination." November 10, 1989. https://www.refworld.org/docid/453883fa8.html.
UN Human Rights Committee. "CCPR General Comment No. 19: Article 23 (The Family) Protection of the Family, the Right to Marriage and Equality of the Spouses." July 27, 1990. https://www.refworld.org/docid/45139bd74.html.
UN Human Rights Committee. "CCPR General Comment No. 22: Article 18 (Freedom of Thought, Conscience or Religion)." CCPR/C/21/Rev.1/Add.4. July 30, 1993. https://www.refworld.org/docid/453883fb22.html.
UN Human Rights Committee. "CCPR General Comment No. 28: Article 3 (The Equality of Rights Between Men and Women)." CCPR/C/21/Rev.1/Add.10. March 29, 2000. https://www.refworld.org/pdfid/45139c9b4.pdf.

Treaties and Agreements

African Charter on Human and Peoples' Rights (1981).
European Convention on Human Rights (1950).
International Covenant on Civil and Political Rights (1966).
International Covenant on Economic, Social and Cultural Rights (1966).
Universal Declaration of Human Rights (1948).

CHAPTER 12

Limitations to the Application of Customary Law as Determinants of the Nature of Customary Law in Botswana

Bonolo Ramadi Dinokopila

Abstract

This chapter argues that the limitations and challenges to the application of customary law in Botswana are key determinants of the nature of customary law applicable in the country. Highlighting these challenges, as discernible from pre-independence and current laws, the chapter illustrates that these limitations and challenges have not only influenced the extent to which customary law is applicable but have also greatly influenced the nature and content of customary law in Botswana. Concomitantly, the chapter argues, customary law is being relegated, if it has not already, into a system of law that is undermined by the common law and statutory laws.

1 Introduction

The application of customary law in Botswana is best described by the words of Lord Tomlin in the case of *Pearl Assurance Co. v Union Government* when he had the opportunity to describe the application of Roman-Dutch Law in South Africa. He was of the following view:

> Roman-Dutch law … is a virile living system of law, ever seeking, as every such system must, to adapt itself consistently with its inherent basic principles to deal effectively with the increasing complexities of modern organised society.[1]

His words are, in the context of the place of customary law within the Botswana legal system, apt. This is because, customary law is forever in pursuit

1 *Pearl Assurance Co. v Union Government* [1934] AC 570, 579; see generally Rajak, "Virile System of Law".

 | DOI:10.1163/9789004696747_013

of finding its place within the modern society since the arrival of the British in Botswana, and the introduction of the dual legal system. Likewise, the society in Botswana is in search of ways of making sure that customary law continues to find application to the citizens. In fact, this is the case in Botswana and in many parts of Africa where customary laws continue to be secondary, marginalised and sometimes depicting indicators of social class stratification. This is notwithstanding that customary or traditional law is used by 80% of people in Sub-Saharan Africa as most of them do not have access to formal courts.[2]

In most countries, customary law exists alongside the received law. Its application is thus subject to several limitations imposed by the country's institutional, constitutional, and legal framework. In Botswana, these limitations can be located within the enabling legislation such as the Customary Law Act,[3] the Customary Courts Act[4] and the *Bogosi* (Chieftainship) Act[5] and the Constitution. These limitations are also discernible from the historical legislation that in many ways influenced the extent to which customary law is applicable.[6] Further, these limitations are manifested in the way that people deal with and apply customary law to their affairs.

The limits to the application of customary law in Botswana have in turn presented many challenges to the application of customary law. These challenges are presented when one deals with issues relating to the judicial ascertainment of customary law, customary law and human rights, ethnic equality and self-determination, codification, law reform, continuing conflicting situations as well as issues relating to colonialism and customary law. These challenges have persisted for many years and in many ways have influenced the nature of the applicable customary law norms. All aspects of customary law have been affected by these limitations in ways that may not be apparent. Worse, the areas affected by these laws concern matters that touch on the everyday lives of the ordinary *motswana* such as inheritance or succession, divorce, and chieftainship, among others.

Customary law's constant struggle for co-existence with the received law in Botswana also brings to the fore issues relating to the future of customary law. This is due to the impact of the limitations on the purview of customary law. As the courts continue to make pronouncements on the constitutionality of customary laws and practices, the reach of customary law is no doubt

2 Piron, "Donor Assistance to Justice Sector Reform," 9.
3 Customary Law Act, Cap. 16:01, Laws of Botswana (Customary Law Act).
4 Customary Courts Act, Cap. 04:05, Laws of Botswana (Customary Courts Act).
5 *Bogosi* (Chieftainship) Act, Cap. 41:01, Laws of Botswana (*Bogosi Act*).
6 For example, Bechuanaland Proclamations No. 74 and 75 of 1934.

reduced. Slowly being whittled down by these limitations, one cannot help but wonder what the nature and future of customary law is? This is an important question when one considers the country's constitutional review process that has just begun[7] and the position of customary law under the South African post-democratic dispensation. The latter does offer insights into the possibilities and further limitations on the application of customary law in a modern constitutional dispensation.

This chapter argues that these limitations and challenges are key determinants of the nature of customary law. They have, as aforementioned, not only influenced the extent to which customary law is applicable but have also greatly influenced the nature and content of customary law in Botswana. Concomitantly, customary law is being relegated, if it has not already, into a system of law that is undermined by the common and statutory laws. Of course, it can be argued that since the reception of foreign law, this was inevitable because of the changes that have come about due to dualism. Following this introduction, Part 2 of this chapter gives a brief historical account of the application of customary in law in Botswana. This is followed by a discussion of the current laws and practice on the application of customary law in Part 3. Parts IV and V discuss the limitation and challenges to the application of customary law in Botswana. This is followed by a discussion on the nature of customary law in part VI. Part VII concludes the chapter and provides some recommendations.

2 Customary Law in Botswana: A Brief Historical Perspective

A lot has been written on the nature and content of customary law in Botswana from a historical perspective.[8] There is thus no need to repeat the points made in the various works relating to customary law in Botswana. Most of these works, however, focused on the development of customary law in the years preceding independence. There is paucity of literature on the nature and content of customary law, for example, post-independence.

The available literature post-independence, for example, is largely focused on the various aspects of customary law. Molokomme's work on the nature of

7 The country's Constitution dates to 1966 to the time the country attained independence. The Constitution has not been subjected to any major review or reform. For the first time (in 2022), the country is undergoing a constitutional review/reform process.

8 Molokomme, "Reception of Roman Dutch Law," 121; Roberts, "Survival of the Traditional Tswana Courts," 103.

customary law is a good starting point for one's reflection on the nature of customary law in Botswana.[9] Firstly, she notes a valuable point that should underscore every discussion on the nature of customary law, which is that the nature of customary law is in fact problematic.[10] Secondly, she rightly notes that "customary law means different things to different people, at different points in time".[11] She then puts forward customary law as three dimensional: traditionalist, lawyers' and living customary law. "Traditionalist customary law" is understood as customary law in its purest form as was applicable in the precolonial era.[12] The "lawyers' customary law" is understood as the customary law that is "more technical or legal, as it is linked to the settlement of disputes in courts".[13] The body of rules making up "lawyers customary law" are those which emanate from the decisions of the colonial courts.[14] Finally, it is asserted that "living customary law" is made up of the "way of life of many people who live in both rural and urban Botswana".[15] It is true that the chameleonic nature of customary law makes it difficult to understand. The overlaps between the three conceptions of customary law described above is testament to this.

Prior to the arrival of the British, customary law in its purest form (traditionalist customary law) obtained. With the chiefs at the helm, it thrived and successfully operated across communities despite its plurality. It was the chief's decree and taboos, among others, that formed the basis of customary laws. Whilst the customs and practices (and therefore customary laws) of the various communities were similar in nature and content, the nuances did ensure the survival of each tribe's customary laws. It is the plurality of these customary laws that makes it difficult to assert that there is a single body of customary law in a particular country. This is not peculiar to Botswana. It characterises the nature of customary laws across the continent. Of course, the institution of chieftainship was central to the administration of these customary laws. This in part ensured that customary laws (the ethos, taboos, and customs) survived because they (customary laws) were in a way crucial to the survival of the institution of chieftainship.

9 Molokomme, "Customary Law in Botswana," 347–69.
10 Molokomme, "Customary Law in Botswana," 347.
11 Molokomme, "Customary Law in Botswana," 347.
12 Molokomme, "Customary Law in Botswana," 348.
13 Molokomme, "Customary Law in Botswana," 349; see also Woodman, "Legal Pluralism," 152–67; Woodman, "Some Realism About Customary Law," 128–52.
14 Molokomme, "Customary Law in Botswana," 349.
15 Molokomme, "Customary Law in Botswana," 350.

Botswana was proclaimed a Protectorate through Proclamation No. 1 of 1885.[16] However, it is through the 1891 Order-in-Council that Queen Victoria of Great Britain established "what was no more than a rudimentary form of governmental administration"[17] in the Bechuanaland Protectorate. The High Commissioner was, through this Order-in-Council, given the power to legislate for the Protectorate and on 10th June 1891, pursuant to that power, published a Proclamation regarding the administration of justice in the Protectorate.[18] The Proclamation, as later clarified by section 2 of the General Law Proclamation of 1909, further provided for the reception of Cape Colonial law which meant that Roman-Dutch Law, which was then Cape Colonial Law, became the common law of Botswana.[19] The 1891 Order-in-Council further provided as follows:

> The High Commissioner in issuing such Proclamations shall respect any native laws or customs by tribes or which the civil relations of any native chiefs, tribes or populations under Her Majesty's protection are now regulated, except so far as the same may be incompatible with the due exercise of her Majesty's power and jurisdiction.[20]

Thus, an undertaking was made by the British to respect native laws and customs. Following their arrival and the reception of foreign law, the application of customary law in its purest form (traditionalist customary law) continued. This period is commonly referred to as "a period of indirect rule" because the British Administration rarely interfered, or at least undertook not to interfere, with the application of customary law in the Protectorate. The understanding between the chiefs and the British Administration, as regards this indirect rule system, is captured by the then High Commissioner in the following words:

> the term "indirect rule"; or, in other words, a method of administration which preserves, – subject to the due exercise of the power and jurisdiction of the Crown, and subject to the requirements of peace, order and good government, – the tribal authority of the chiefs and the native laws

16 Ramsay, "Establishment and Consolidation of the Bechuanaland Protectorate," 118–33; Fombad, *Botswana Legal System*, 56.

17 Aguda, "Legal Development," 52–63.

18 Fombad, *Botswana Legal System*, 57.

19 *Silverstone (Pty) Ltd* v *Lobatse Clay Works (Pty) Ltd* [1996] BLR 190; Fombad, *Botswana Legal System*, 58.

20 Order-in-Council, May 9, 1891, cl. 4.

> and customs, without however derogating from the duty of supervision and supreme control entrusted to the High Commissioner.[21]

The position then was supposed to be that "the chiefs were to be allowed to continue to administer their internal affairs according to native law and custom".[22] It is important to note that the limits placed on the application of customary law at that time was that: customary law will not be applicable if it was "incompatible with the due exercise of her Majesty's power and jurisdiction".[23]

It appears that this understanding was not easy to comply with as there were instances where the Resident Magistrates wanted to intervene in the administration of customary laws. An example of such an instance is discernible from the case of *Chief Tshekedi Khama v Simon Ratshosa (Attorney General Intervening)*[24] in which the question was whether the Resident Magistrate had jurisdiction over a dispute in which the plaintiff's property was burnt as some form of punishment by the chief. The Judicial Committee of the Privy Council held that the Resident Magistrate had no jurisdiction as "the burning of the Plaintiff's houses and their contents was done in the ordinary course of native and tribal administration of justice".[25] Similarly, in the case of *Tshekedi Khama v the High Commissioner*[26] the Applicants challenged the implementation of proclamations billed to deal with the "jurisdiction and powers of the courts of the Chiefs in the Protectorates, when trying cases in accordance with native law and custom".[27] They argued, among others, that the High Commissioner through the said proclamations sought to make alterations to certain native laws and customs as specified in the Order-in-Council of May 1891. Further, that he had no power to make such alterations since the Order-in-Council from which he derived the powers required him to respect native law and custom.

Following this period of indirect intervention there were increased inroads into the application of native laws and customs by the British. Confrontation between the traditional leaders and the British administration was thus inevitable.[28] That notwithstanding, Proclamations No. 74 and 75 of 1934 are considered as having ushered in "a period of direct intervention" in the then

21 Stanley, "Explanatory Memorandum," 2.
22 Otlhogile, "*Tshekedi Khama and* ANO *vs. High Commissioner*," 29–38.
23 Order-in-Council, May 9, 1891, cl. 4.
24 [1931] AC 784 (*Simon Ratshosa* case).
25 *Simon Ratshosa* case, 796–7.
26 1926–53 HCLTR (BP).
27 Otlhogile, "*Tshekedi Khama and* ANO *vs. High Commissioner*," 29.
28 See generally Crowder, "Tshekedi Khama," 193–214.

Bechuanaland Protectorate. Serious changes, to which the chiefs objected to, were introduced as regards the application of customary law and the received law. In his lengthy explanatory memorandum, the High Commissioner to the Territory, H. J. Stanley, argued that the changes were necessary as "in the affairs of men nothing can remain stationery … and forms of government which do not adapt themselves to changing conditions, and progress with them, lose their vitality and sink into decay".[29] While the chiefs, during the period of indirect intervention, largely exercised their administrative and judicial functions with minimal interference from the British Administration, the proclamations proposed external checks and limits in the exercise of the powers of the chiefs. Further, the proclamations proposed ideas that were at variance with existing native laws and customs. The limits to the exercise of power by the chiefs were thus bound to become the limits to the application of customary law.

A few examples of the changes brought about by these two proclamations are therefore necessary. One of the most contentious changes proposed by the British through Proclamation No. 74 of 1934 was the recognition, suspension, deposition, and confirmation of chiefs.[30] Accordingly, the Commissioner was now given the power to refuse to recognise a chief despite that the person would be entitled to succeed to the throne as per the customary laws. Proclamation No. 74 of 1934 also proposed the introduction of tribal councils with chiefs now being required to consult the council in the exercise of their powers.[31] Proclamation No. 75 of 1934 also proposed significant changes to the administration of justice such as the introduction of the junior and senior native tribunals in the place of the *kgotla*.[32] Further, the jurisdiction of the native tribunals, and invariably that of the chiefs, were reduced. Specifically, the native tribunals could no longer preside over cases involving certain "serious" offences such as sedition, treason, murder, attempted murder, rape, attempted rape, and assault with intent to do grievous bodily harm among others.[33] The changes were quite substantial and contentious indeed. The High Commissioner to the Territory, H. J. Stanley, sought to allay the chiefs' concerns regarding these changes. He advised that the purpose of the two proclamations was not to abolish the principle of "indirect rule" but was "to provide for its continuance and its further development".[34]

29 Stanley, "Explanatory Memorandum," 2.
30 Proclamation No. 74 of 1934, cl. 2–12.
31 Proclamation No. 74 of 1934, cl. 5(1).
32 Proclamation No. 75 of 1934, cl. 7(1).
33 Proclamation No. 74 of 1934, cl. 8(1).
34 Stanley, "Explanatory Memorandum," 2.

The implementation of these proclamations was opposed by the traditional leaders, with Tshekedi Khama at the forefront of this crusade.[35] Rightly so because the changes suggested by the High Commissioner were far reaching despite the assertion that they were consistent with the "indirect rule" which was the general principle underlying the administration of the Bechuanaland Protectorate. Most importantly, a closer look at these changes meant that the reach of customary law was greatly reduced due to the limitations imposed on the powers of the chiefs by these two proclamations. Inevitably, the normative content of customary laws was modified. For example, customary criminal law offences were narrowed as they were obviously not going to be applied in their original form, if at all they were to be applied by colonial magistrates' courts. Further, the rules regarding succession of chieftainship were altered as a chief's ascension to the throne was no longer guaranteed only by the customary laws, norms and practices concerning chieftainship.

The Chiefs managed to resist these proposed changes until 1943 when new proclamations were promulgated by the High Commissioner. The 1943 Proclamations repealed the 1935 Proclamations but did not make any significant changes to what was set out in the 1935 Proclamations. Proclamation 33 of 1943 like the repealed Proclamation empowered the High Commissioner to recognise, suspend or dismiss a chief if they acted in a manner that was "a threat to good order, public, peace and good government".[36] It then reaffirmed the concept of a Tribal Council which was supposed to work with the chief and decisions on community affairs were now supposed to be arrived at through consensus or majority vote.[37]

The proclamations discussed above mark what is now commonly described as a "period of direct intervention" by the British. It can easily be concluded that the limitations imposed on the application of native laws and customs during this period have significantly impacted the nature and content of customary laws. This is so because what was applicable during this period was a confluence of the "traditionalist customary law" and "lawyers' customary law". This was borne out of the changes or limitations on the application of native laws and customs by the British.

The above historical account also evidences the birth of dualism. Dualism has in fact resulted in a situation in which customary law is treated as an adopted child within the country's legal system. Dualism, as will be illustrated below, has also nurtured an environment that might lead to the demise of

35 See generally Crowder, "Tshekedi Khama," 193–214.

36 Bechuanaland Proclamation No. 33 of 1942, cl. 7(1).

37 Ibid.

customary law. That is why this chapter argues that the limitations imposed on the application of native laws and customs should be looked at closely. As illustrated above, changes were proposed and implemented by the British Administration even though the changes had the potential to, and they did, alter the rubric and normative content of customary law.

3 The Application of Customary Law in Post-Colonial Botswana

Molokomme describes the customary law that mostly became applicable during the post-colonial era (or that is applicable in present-day Botswana) as the "living" or "contemporary" customary law which according to her:

> is reflected in the way of life of many people who live in both rural and urban Botswana. It is rather fluid, flexible, negotiable and dynamic, and represents the adaptations of people to the socio-economic changes taking place.[38]

Following the country's attainment of independence, customary law in its "purest form", the traditionalist customary law, even though in existence was mostly overshadowed by the "lawyers' customary law" and the "living customary law". The plurality of customary laws continued with various tribes still applying similar but different customary laws and practices.[39] As rightly observed by Molokomme, the customary law that is applicable is one that had to adapt to the modernised way of doing things. The "traditionalist customary law" or customary law in its purest form is now negligible owing to, among other things, the legislative changes that were introduced. That notwithstanding, there is great evidence of the desire or commitment by all stakeholders (chiefs, citizens, and the government) to preserve the application of what is considered as customary law at a given time.

One can therefore ask this important question: what about the commitment to preserve the nature and content of customary law in its purest form? Assuming that one can point out norms which may be described as customary

38 Molokomme, "Customary Law in Botswana," 350.

39 I am aware of the debate surrounding the use of the term "tribe" and the colonially influenced connotations that flow from the use of the term. However, and for purposes of this chapter, the use of the word "tribe(s)" is preferred. This is in part because of the prevalent use of the word in Botswana. Further, I have been persuaded by the arguments made in favour of this approach by Mensa-Bonsu, "Customary Law," 8–10.

law in its "pure form", the answer to this question will be that customary law in its purest form is not useful today. This is to the extent that such norms are unlikely to effectively regulate the current way of life of ordinary people. The impetus to preserve it, by way application to the affairs of people today, is therefore unlikely to exist. Further, and considering the legislative changes that have already taken place during the colonial era, innovative ways according to which customary law in its purest form may be successfully preserved are necessary. Certainly, this answer will be disappointing to the traditionalists, who, according to Molokomme, are more likely to be convinced that the current form of customary law is "a debased or corrupted form of customary law, which has been 'contaminated' by 'modernisation' and other western influences".[40]

At the time that Botswana attained independence, there was clear reluctance on the part of those involved in the design of the Republican Constitution[41] to have a bicameral national assembly. A bicameral parliament would have meant that the country's Parliament would have been made up of the national assembly, the President and the house of chiefs.[42] The refusal to embrace bicameralism as proposed by some of the chiefs inevitably led to the decline in the extent of control chiefs had over their constituents.[43] The position of chieftainship post-independence and their limited role in the governance of the country post-independence have also limited the sphere of influence and, by necessary extension, the nature, and the extent of application of customary law.[44] This, together with the various laws that have been adopted to regulate all matters concerning customary law and its administration will be discussed in the following section.

4 Limitations to the Application of Customary Law in Botswana

Pre-independence legislation discussed above contributed a great deal to the nature and content of customary laws post 1966 when Botswana attained its independence. The dualist nature of the country's legal system that was birthed also informed the nature and content of this customary law. That in some instances ordinary people viewed customary law as more important

40 Molokomme, "Customary Law in Botswana," 350.
41 Cap. 01:00, Laws of Botswana.
42 Proctor, "House of Chiefs," 62.
43 Proctor, "House of Chiefs," 62.
44 Ifezue, "Understanding Chieftainship in Botswana," 271–93.

than statutory or received law appears to not have made any significant difference. As will be illustrated by the following discussion, the laws that were later adopted also imposed further limitations on the application of customary law.

4.1 *The Constitution*

The Constitution of the Republic of Botswana does not make any reference to the place of customary law within the Botswana legal system. This however does not mean that the Constitution does not recognise customary law. On the contrary, there are various provisions in the Constitution that have been designed in such a way that, if interpreted properly, guarantees the application of customary law.[45] Some of these provisions even go to the extent of insulating customary law from being subjected to constitutional scrutiny. These are sections 10(12)(b), (d) and (e) as well as sections 15(4)(c) and (d) of the Constitution.[46] Further, the Constitution makes provision for the establishment of the *Ntlo ya Dikgosi* (House of Chiefs) under Part 3 and the involvement of the chiefs in the legislative process where the Constitution is being altered or the proposed enactment is likely to affect matters of customary law.[47]

The Constitution entrenches the concept of separation of powers that saw the African Advisory Council established during the colonial era translated into a *Ntlo ya Dikgosi* that would only play an advisory role.[48] The most obvious thing to note here is that the chiefs were now stripped of their legislative powers. Their judicial powers were, to some extent, left intact with the requirement that they should operate within the confines of the written law. Clearly, this framework was influenced by the changes that were first initiated through Proclamations 74 and 75 of 1934 discussed above. This has resulted in the weak application of customary law in that the chiefs are no longer able to freely come up with rules that respond to the immediate needs of their tribes. The case of *Kgafela Kgafela v The State*[49] (*Kgafela* case) illustrates this point. In that case, the 1st Appellant, who was a Chief of the *Bakgatla* tribe, together with others, were charged with various counts of assault occasioning bodily harm contrary to section 247 of the Penal Code.[50] The 1st Appellant was duly recognised as a

---

45 For a detailed discussion see Dinokopila and Kgoboge, "Customary Law and Limitations," 339–57.

46 For a detailed discussion on these exceptions see Dinokopila, "Unity Dow Case," 35–52; Fombad, "Constitutional Protection Against Discrimination," 139–70.

47 Constitution, s. 88(2).

48 Constitution, s. 85.

49 *Kgafela Kgafela v The State* (High Court) (unreported) case no. CLHLB-000148–10 (*Kgafela* case).

50 Cap 08:01, Laws of Botswana.

Chief by the Minister in terms of section 4 of the then Chieftainship Act.[51] The alleged acts of assault arose from the flogging of various individuals by several of the Appellants purporting to act on the authority of the 1st Appellant and his uncle, the third Appellant. The flogging on the bare back was carried out following what "was referred to as a rule of infraction, an offence allegedly said to exist under customary law of the appellants".[52] The Court was thus asked to decide whether a chief, the 1st Appellant in this case, had the power to inflict punishment, especially corporal punishment, on persons within his territory without invoking and complying with the applicable enabling statutory enactments. The Court answered the question in the negative holding that the Chief was expected to act within the limits of the Constitution and laws prescribed by Parliament. Specifically, a Chief was expected to follow due process before imposing any punishment and also, the alleged offence that people were being flogged for was unwritten and could not be imposed on his subjects. Therefore, corporal punishment could only be imposed by a Court acting in accordance with and within the parameters of the enabling Act of Parliament.[53] The Court acknowledged that that it may well have been that the chief, before the advent of colonial rule, could impose corporal punishment without regard to due process. However, that is no longer the case as customary law has changed because "[i]t is not a monolith that withstands the vicissitudes of time and change".[54]

The application of customary law has been greatly limited on account of the provisions of the Constitution. The first casualty in this instance being the now non-existent customary criminal offences. It should be noted that following the reception of the Cape Colonial Law, the customary courts continued to administer unwritten customary law.[55] The application of the unwritten customary criminal law was applicable only in so far as "it was not incompatible with the due exercise of Her Majesty's power and jurisdiction or repugnant to morality, humanity or natural justice or injurious to the welfare of the Africans".[56] There were changes made through various pieces of legislation on the application of customary criminal offences. However, the country's 1966 Constitution partly confirmed the subordination of this aspect of customary law. According to section 10(8) of the Constitution, "no person shall be convicted of a criminal

51 The Act has now been repealed by the *Bogosi* (Chieftainship) Act, Cap 41:01, Laws of Botswana.

52 *Kgafela* case, para. 15.

53 *Kgafela* case, para. 60.

54 *Kgafela* case, para. 42.

55 Brewer, "Sources of the Criminal Law," 24–36.

56 African Courts Proclamation, 1961, cl. 10; Brewer, "Sources of the Criminal Law," 34.

offence unless that offence is defined, and the penalty thereof is prescribed in a written law". There is an exemption, however, to section 10(8) which makes it possible to make room for customary criminal offences. Section 10(12) provides that a law should not be deemed to be contrary to section 10(8) of the Constitution if "it authorises a court to convict a person of a criminal offence under customary law to which, by virtue of that law, such person is subject".[57] That notwithstanding, the law[58] and the jurisprudence of the Botswana courts is that no person can be tried for any customary criminal offence. Sources of criminal law in Botswana are thus restricted to statutory enactments.[59] In *Bimbo* v *The State*[60] the Court held that no person could be prosecuted and punished for the crime of adultery as it was an unwritten offence.[61] This is despite the fact that adultery is, or was, in most tribes or societies in Botswana considered to be a customary criminal offence. In the case of *Tirelo v The Attorney-General*[62] (*Tirelo* case) Kirby J, as he then was, was of the view that:

> there are no longer any criminal offences under customary law. All of these have been superseded by the Penal Code and other penal statutes. But there so still remain ... a number of civil offences under customary law, which previously overlapped with criminal offences, but can no longer do so, since punishment must be prescribed by law. Such offences include, for example, adultery, seduction, cattle trespass, defamation and, as in this present case, 'go thuba lelwapa' (destroying someone's marriage).[63]

Lesetedi J, as he then was, in the *Kgafela* case discussed above was also of the view that:

> The penal laws passed by Parliament itself are written and published in the statutes ... They do not exist somewhere in the memories of sages to

57 Constitution, s. 10(12)(e).

58 Customary Courts Act, s. 12(6). The section provides that no person shall be charged with a criminal offence unless such an offence is created by the Penal Code or some other written law.

59 Brewer, "Sources of the Criminal Law," 24–36; Malila, "Reconciling Plural Legal Systems," 71–78.

60 *Bimbo v The State,* Criminal Appeal No. 56 of 1980 (unreported judgment) discussed in Frimpong, *Criminal Law of Botswana*, 35.

61 Frimpong, *Criminal Law of Botswana*, 35.

62 2008 (2) BLR 38 (HC) (*Tirelo* case).

63 *Tirelo* case, 48.

> be only ascertained and applied subject to the memories of those who claim to have a better memory of their content and the applicable punishments thereto.[64]

It suffices to point out that owing to the posture that was taken by the British, and evidently those who were involved in the design of the Republican Constitution, the overall scheme of the Constitution is designed in such a way that it places great restraints on the application of customary law. Where textually it appears not to do so, the courts have interpreted its provisions in such a way that it imposes very restrictive limitations on the application of customary law. The bill of rights under the Constitution, consistent with this approach, has also been interpreted to mean that customary law is subject to the provisions of the Constitution. This is despite the fact that the provisions so interpreted are couched in a manner that suggest the opposite. This aspect of the argument will be discussed in the later parts of this chapter.

4.2 *The Customary Law Act*

Himsworth[65] has reflected on the various aspects of the Customary Law Act in 1972. His observations are still relevant today as the Act has not seen any major changes. At the time that the Act was introduced, the common law courts only applied the common law to the exclusion of customary law. Customary law was then left to the preserve of the customary courts.[66] According to Himsworth, the Act answered three key questions relating to the application and use of customary law by the common law courts. Thus, the Act sets out principles according to which one can determine which system of law (common law or customary law) to apply,[67] which customary law to apply[68] and how to go about ascertaining the applicable customary law rules.[69] Were it not for the limitation imposed by section 2 of the Act, specifically the definition of customary law, one would have hailed such a move as progressive and as bound to secure a positive future for customary law in Botswana.

Section 2 of the Customary Law Act defines customary law as follows:

64 *Kgafela* case, para. 38.
65 Himsworth, "Botswana Customary Law Act," 4–18.
66 Ibid.
67 Customary Law Act, s. 4.
68 Customary Law Act, s. 10.
69 Customary Law Act, s. 11.

> means, in relation to any particular tribe or tribal community, the customary law of that tribe or tribal community so far as it is not incompatible with the provisions of any written law or contrary to morality, humanity or natural justice.

This is the standard definition of customary law and is found in every piece of legislation that deals or touches on issues of customary law.[70] This provision was known as the "repugnancy clause" and was generally applied by the British Administration to colonial subjects beyond Botswana. The above provision not only limits the application of customary law but also makes it overtly secondary to statutory law. There is ample literature on the nature of these clauses and their impact on customary law as well as the fact that they are a legacy of colonialism.[71] This provision is therefore crucial as any practice or custom falling below the standard set out therein will not be considered as customary law.

Interestingly, the limits imposed by this provision are to be applied by both the common law and the customary courts. Where the customary courts falter and apply customary law rules that fall short of the standard set out under section 2, their decisions will eventually be overturned if appealed. In the case of *Tidimalo Jokase v Gaelebale Mpho Seakgosing*,[72] Lesetedi J, as he then was, held that a customary law rule which disregarded the right of a widow not to be joined as a party at all in litigation affecting her property or property to which she has a substantial and direct interest, was not only contrary to the provisions of the Constitution but was also incompatible with the rule of natural justice and denied the applicant the right to be heard before an adverse decision is taken against her by a court of law. The case emanated from a customary court which had held that a woman whose husband was deceased had no locus standi and was supposed to be represented by a male member of the family.

4.3 *The Customary Courts Act*

The Customary Courts Act was preceded by the Native Administration Proclamation of 1943 and the African Courts Proclamation of 1961. According to section 15 of the Act, customary courts are empowered to administer

---

70 For example, Customary Courts Act, s. 2; Administration of Estates Act, s. 2; *Bogosi* Act, s. 2; Children's Act 8 of 2009, s. 2.

71 Demian, "On the Repugnance of Customary Law," 508–36; Thomas and Tladi, "Legal Pluralism or a New Repugnancy Clause," 354–63.

72 *Tidimalo Jokase v Gaelebale Mpho Swakgosing* (High Court) (unreported) case no. MAHLB-000661–10.

customary law[73] and any written law which they are authorised to administer by any written law.[74] The Penal Code is an example of the latter.[75] Like all legislation relating to customary law, the Act imposes limitations on the nature and content of customary law to be applied by the courts. Firstly, the customary law is subject to the provisions of the Act.[76] This essentially means that the civil and criminal jurisdiction, the constitution of the courts and the procedure of these courts, among others, are as set out under the Act. Secondly, the applicable customary law is subject to any written law.[77] The net effect of these provisions is that most customary law norms are most likely to contradict at least one written law, considering the numerous written laws given the breadth of statutory enactments.

Coupled with the above, is the fact that when the customary courts were introduced in 1966, the Act introduced various controls regarding the jurisdiction of the courts. It maintained some of the limitations that were imposed by the pre-independence legislation. The Act provides that chiefs cannot preside over serious criminal matters such as murder and treason.[78] Chiefs are also barred from presiding over cases that are technical in nature such as insolvency, company law[79] and matters of relationships to which customary law is inapplicable.[80] The power to preside over such matters has now been transferred to the magistrates courts and the High Court. In instances where the chiefs are allowed to preside over certain disputes, the nature and extent of the punishment is also provided for by the Act. For example, the Customary Courts (Corporal Punishment) Rules state the nature of the instrument to be used and further state that corporal punishment shall be administered on the buttocks only and on no other part of the body.[81] This is in fact a great deviation from the customary practice of *go kgwathisa* which formed the basis of the dispute in the *Kgafela* case discussed above. *Go kgwathisa* under most customary law rules and practice means flogging on the bare back. The Establishment and

---

73 Customary Courts Act, s. 15(a).

74 Customary Courts Act, s. 15(b).

75 Customary Courts Act, s. 12(3).

76 Customary Courts Act, s. 15.

77 Customary Courts Act, s. 15. There is further specific mention in this section that the applicable customary law is subject to the provisions of s. 10 of the Constitution and s. 32 of the Act. The former provisions deal with fair trial rights while the latter provides that lawyers do not have a right of audience before the customary courts.

78 Customary Courts Act, s. 13.

79 Customary Courts Act, s. 13(a)(ix).

80 Customary Courts Act, s. 13(c)(iv).

81 Cap 04:05, Laws of Botswana, Rules 1–3.

Jurisdiction of Customary Courts Order[82] also limits the extent to which a chief may impose punishment. These kinds of jurisdictional limits, both as to the crime and attendant punishment, did not exist under customary law in its purest form.

4.4 The *Bogosi* (Chieftainship) Act

Chiefs are instrumental in the administration of customary law in Botswana. In fact, they are the custodians of customary law and until the inroads that were made into their powers, the chief, the *kgotla* and customary law were co-extensive. To limit the sphere of operation of any, meant that the sphere of operation or influence of the other was also limited. This means that the centrality of the chief during the pre-colonial era, to the application of customary law largely informed the nature and content of customary law. Thus, the customary law rules and norms were informed by the decisions of the chiefs, more so that they were unwritten. The chiefs' law-making and judicial functions made it easier for them to have such great influence in what was deemed to be the customary law of that community. As aforementioned, the powers of the chiefs have been greatly limited by the Constitution, the Customary Law Act and the Customary Courts Act. The points made above as regards the limitations imposed on customary law by these statutory enactments are relevant to any reflection on the powers of the chiefs. The *Bogosi* (Chieftainship) Act, however, does not directly deal with the application of customary law as it is promulgated to address issues relating to chieftainship.

The approach taken by the *Bogosi* Act is not in any way different from the approach taken towards customary law in other statutes. It entrenches the limitations imposed by the country's legal system on the powers of the chief and inevitably the application of customary law. How can one expect a different approach when section 2 of the Act adopts the standard definition of customary law adopted by the legislature? Firstly, the application of customary law rules as regards matters of appointment of chiefs have been greatly abridged. In that sense, the Act provides for, among others, the functions,[83] recognition,[84] removal[85] and tenure[86] of chiefs all of which denotes a great deviation from the customary law rules of many tribes. For example, it is a widely accepted custom that a chief is born and successors to the title are as

82 Cap 04:05, Laws of Botswana, cl. 4.
83 *Bogosi* Act, s. 17.
84 *Bogosi* Act, s. 5.
85 *Bogosi* Act, s. 13.
86 *Bogosi* Act, s. 23.

per the various specific rules of each tribe. Unless contested by those within the chief's family, this usually admits of no conflict. When the time comes for the appointment of a new chief, the royal family announces the successor to the throne. In most instances, this is a mere formality as the tribe would have known who is supposed to ascend to the throne. The position under the *Bogosi* Act is now that it is the duty of the tribe assembled in the *kgotla* "to designate a rightful successor to the *Bogosi* according to customary law or according to the established norm and practice of that tribe". While this provision is inherently contradictory, it is an attempt by the legislature to "democratise" the appointment of chiefs that is even more puzzling. The objective of this provision, and many other provisions of this Act that have deviated from the common customary law rules relating to chieftainship, is not clear. What is clear though is that the provisions of this Act have significantly changed the normative content of the customary law rules relating to chieftainship in Botswana. At the very least, they have changed the extent to which such norms are applicable now and in the future.

According to the *Kgafela* case discussed above, the chief is obligated to perform his functions under the authority of the law and within the parameters set out by the law. Chiefs do not have the latitude to reform customary law in the same fashion as they did prior to the arrival of the British. This makes it clear that the development of customary and the nature of customary law are influenced by the written law more than the institution of *Bogosi*.

4.5 *Human Rights and Customary Law*

The relationship between customary law and human rights has always been a contentious one in many jurisdictions. Botswana has not escaped the challenges presented by the changes expected in a country that is committed to democracy, human rights, and the rule of law. A full discussion of the human rights-customary law dichotomy is beyond the scope of this chapter. It is sufficient to point out that it is a settled position of the law in Botswana that customary law is subject to human rights as protected by the Constitution, statutory human rights law[87] and in some instances, international human rights instruments.[88] The case of *Attorney General v Dow*[89] (*Dow* case) has

87 For example, the Children's Act of 2008 has a catalogue of human rights for the promotion and protection of children's rights.

88 This is largely because Botswana is a dualist state. Treaties do not become part of the domestic law and cannot be directly enforced unless they have been domesticated. See generally Quansah, "Examination of the Use of International Law," 46–48; Maripe, "Giving Effect to International Human Rights Law," 251–82.

89 1992 BLR 119 (CA) (*Dow* case).

been instrumental in ensuring that discriminatory customary law practices are outlawed and will continue to be outlawed.[90] Recent decisions of the Court of Appeal such as the *Ramantele v Mmusi*[91] in which the rule of ultimogeniture was declared unconstitutional, have followed the *Dow* case. In that sense, human rights are in fact a great limitation to the application of customary law in Botswana.

It is submitted that the human rights limitations imposed on customary law are as a result of the interpretation of the Constitution by the Courts and not due to the way the provisions have been couched or designed.[92] A closer look at section 3 and the relevant parts of section 15 of the Constitution reveals that they were designed in such a way that they are incapable of being used to impugn customary law.

Section 3 of the Constitution provides as follows:

> Whereas every person in Botswana is entitled to the fundamental rights and freedoms of the individual, that is to say, the right, whatever his or her race, place of origin, political opinions, colour, creed or sex, but subject to respect for the rights and freedoms of others and for the public interest to each and all of the following, namely –
> (a) life, liberty, security of the person and the protection of the law;
> (b) freedom of conscience, of expression and of assembly and association; and
> (c) protection for the privacy of his or her home and other property and from deprivation of property without compensation,
>
> the provisions of this Chapter shall have effect for the purpose of affording protection to those rights and freedoms subject to such limitations of that protection as are contained in those provisions, being limitations designed to ensure that the enjoyment of the said rights and freedoms by any individual does not prejudice the rights and freedoms of others or the public interest.

Section 15(4)(c) of the Constitution provides as follows:

90 See a detailed discussion of the *Dow* case in Dinokopila, "Unity Dow Case," 35–52; Fombad, "Constitutional Protection Against Discrimination," 139; Tshosa, "Application of Non-Discrimination," 190.

91 [2013] 2 BLR 658 (*Ramantele* case).

92 See generally Dinokopila and Kgoboge, "Customary Law and Limitations," 339–57.

(4) Subsection (1) of this section shall not apply to any law so far as that law makes provision-

[...]

(c) with respect to adoption, marriage, divorce, burial, devolution of property on death or other matters of personal law;

(*d*) for the application in the case of members of a particular race, community or tribe of customary law with respect to any matter whether to the exclusion of any law in respect to that matter which is applicable in the case of other persons or not.

In fact, the minority decisions of Schreiner JA and Puckrin JA in the *Dow* case are consistent with this position. They both held that a law that is based on customary laws of citizenship, according to which a woman could not pass citizenship to her children born to her and her non-citizen husband, was not *ultra vires* the Constitution.[93] Further, that a proper interpretation of the two provisions of the Constitution aforementioned leads one to conclude that customary law was insulated from constitutional scrutiny.[94] Even though Schreiner JA was hesitant to hold that the Constitution countenanced discrimination on the basis of gender, his conclusion impliedly does so.[95]

5 Other Limitations to the Application of Customary Law

Some of the contemporary challenges to the application of customary law in Botswana have been identified by Radijeng[96] to include, among others, issues relating to the ascertainment of customary law, the co-existence of customary law and human rights, possibilities of codification and law reform and continuing conflicting situations. To this, we can add failure to decolonise the laws in Botswana that has so far escaped scrutiny in the jurisdiction. Cumulatively, these challenges have affected the nature and content of customary law in Botswana as they greatly limited its sphere of application. They are continuing challenges, or problems, related to the application of customary law. They are really not new challenges.

Firstly, the Customary Law Act have set out elaborate principles relating to the application of customary law in Botswana. Among others, the Act sets out

93 *Dow* case, 190.

94 *Dow* case, 189.

95 Ibid.

96 Radijeng, "Customary Law (LAW 106) Course Outline" (2008) (available on file).

the principles relating to the following: to which cases will customary law be applicable,[97] instances where a question as to which customary law is applicable (conflict of customary laws),[98] and the ascertainment of customary law.[99] The question as to whether customary law is a question of law, or a question of fact has not raised any significant controversy. That notwithstanding, it is interesting to note that section 7 of the old Common Law and Customary Law Act provided that "customary law is a question of law for the court and not a question of fact".[100] However, and even though the rest of its content is exactly the same, a similar provision in the Customary Law Act,[101] the legislature has excised the part referring to whether customary law is question of fact or a question of law. This question has in fact indirectly come up in decisions of the courts relating to the application of customary law. In the case of *Kweneng Land Board v Kabelo Matlho*[102] (*Kabelo Matlho* case) the Court relied on section 7 of the Common Law and Customary Law Act and held that customary law is a question of law.[103] It further confirmed the use of literary works, such as Isaac Schapera's *Handbook of Tswana Law and Custom,* to prove the existence of a customary law rule but cautioned against elevating such texts to the status "of evidence or even as a binding authoritative statement of the law, which they are not".[104] The ascertainment should only be necessary where there is doubt as to the existence of a customary law rule. In the *Ramantele* case, Lesetedi J.A. indicated that in an instance where there is doubt or a dispute as to the existence of a custom, the party that alleges must prove the existence of that custom. He further set out the requirements that the Appellant had to satisfy to be successful. These included the requirement that the Appellant had to:

> show that such inheritance to the extent that it unfairly excluded the respondents, was in accordance with an [sic] ngwaketse custom which invariably only entitled a last born son to inherit the parents homestead to the exclusion of all the other children.[105]

---

97 Customary Law Act, ss. 4 and 5.
98 Customary Law Act, s. 10.
99 Customary Law Act, s. 11.
100 Common Law and Customary Law Act, s. 7. The Act appears to have been repealed and re-enacted as the Customary Law Act.
101 Customary Law Act, s. 11.
102 1992 BLR 292 (CA) (*Kabelo Matlho* case).
103 *Kabelo Matlho* case, 303.
104 Ibid.
105 *Ramantele* case, 670.

Lesetedi J.A further questioned:

> how, where no evidence was led before the Customary Court of Appeal, the High Court could rely on the papers filed on record in order to determine the nature, scope and justification, if any, for the application of the custom being impugned?[106]

He proceeded to also put forward the following remark:

> It is important to note that a court should not be too quick to consider the constitutionality of a customary law unless it is possessed of sufficient evidence regarding the existence and content of such custom, its application and the rationale thereof.[107]

The approach posited by Lesetedi J. A. does indicate a slight, and possibly realistic, shift when it comes to the ascertainment of customary law in Botswana. The new position seems to be that the existence and content of a rule of custom, if it is in doubt, must be proven before it is impugned by a court. This, Lesetedi J. A. argues, will save the court from "making decisions which have got no contextual and factual foundation, yet far-reaching consequences".[108] One cannot help though but wonder whether this approach brings back, through the backdoor, the rule in *Angu v Attah*.[109] The approach further begs the question, is the mode of ascertainment of customary law in Botswana now a question of both law and fact?[110] This is more or so that it is likely that the existence or the nature of some customs and norms is likely to be disputed. The shift though is realistic because of the disputes concerning the nature and content of the "dynamic and flexible" customary law that will come before the courts for determination. The common law courts are most certainly not able to assert knowledge of the various customary laws that are now applicable. There is no doubt though that through this process of ascertainment of customary law, the very rubric of customary law is likely to be altered.

Secondly, and connected to the above, is the fact that Botswana is likely to witness continuing conflicting situations concerning the application of customary law. The limits to the application of customary law put in place by the

106 *Ramantele* case, 669.
107 Ibid.
108 *Ramantele* case, para. 37.
109 (1909) Ren 550. See generally Korang, "Ascertainment of Customary Law," 93.
110 Korang, "Ascertainment of Customary Law," 95.

legislature and the courts, have ensured that most discriminatory customary law practices are excluded from application. Most customary law rules being patriarchal and discriminatory on the basis of status, are likely to fall short of the dictates of most written laws. This contestation will over the years become even more prominent as regards human rights issues, matters of succession, chieftainship, and punishment among others. As they continue to be struck down by the courts, the nature and content of customary law will continue to change.

Thirdly, it should be highlighted that the law reform process is court led and thus admits of a piecemeal approach. That is, in more instances there is anecdotal evidence to suggest that only aspects of customary law that are challenged before the courts will be subjected to reform. These will certainly be, among others, rules relating to status of women and children as well as issues relating to inheritance. Customary practices such *bogadi* (bride price) whose metamorphosis is bordering on it becoming a harmful cultural practice will remain in place. Additionally, this court led reform process is likely to lead to a parallel system of the applicable customary law as between the urban and rural populace. There is a great likelihood that the ordinary citizens in the rural parts of the country will continue to apply and conform to customary law rules in their purest form. The plurality of customary laws in Botswana is therefore likely to increase because different tribes are likely to continue to apply the various versions of customary law such as customs in their original nature (traditionalist customary law), or customs modified to or conform to the dictates of the written law (statutory customary law or living customary law). Such a dichotomy and plurality will be because this court led law reform usually takes a top-down approach. Speaking to a similar concern, Bekker and Koyana indicated that the judicial and legislative reforms of the customary law of succession in South Africa were undermined by the fact that "no account was taken of the social and monetary circumstances of the vast number of Africans that will have to live with the new law".[111]

The fourth thing to note about the application of customary law in Botswana is perhaps the most perplexing. Even though the decoloniality of laws conversation has taken centre stage in countries like South Africa, the topic has been ignored by the academia, the law makers, the judiciary and most importantly the public in Botswana. Yet it is beyond doubt that the country's legal history is underscored and is greatly influenced by British legal culture and Roman Dutch law. The absence of such an important conversation abounds despite that the limitations imposed on the application and operation of customary

111 Bekker and Koyana, "Judicial and Legislative Reform," 568–84.

law by the dual nature of the legal system engenders a culture of othering customary law. Modiri's words are apt when he observes (in the context of South Africa) that:

> The vaunted plurality of laws in the present constitutional dispensation conceals the marginalization and denigration of indigenous African law – which is marked as particular and frequently cast in a civilizational narrative as being in tension with progress, development and rights, being relegated and distorted from history into the present. Martin Chanock further points out that South African common law was central to the "creation of white memory and [the] racial and national identity" of European settlers.[112]

As the country embarks on a constitutional reform process, it becomes imperative that the country should have a conversation about decolonising the country's legal system. A constitution that is firm on the place of customary law within the country's legal framework is crucial to the nature and future of customary law in Botswana. Of course, the South African experience has revealed that "the constitutionally guaranteed legal pluralism"[113] will not be a panacea to the challenges that continue to bedevil the operation of the law and the application of customary law in Botswana. It will, however, place some limits to the limitations imposed on the application of customary law that continue to perpetuate the dominance of the received law within the country's legal system.

6 The Nature of Customary Law in Botswana

Diala has rightly observed that "the interpretation and application of customs by judges and litigants in intersecting social fields form part of indigenous norms' adaptation to socio-economic changes".[114] In his critique, he notes that the categorisation of customary law into "official" and "living" customary law is

112 Adebisi, "Decolonising the Law School," 471–74 citing the keynote address titled "Cacophony, Autocritique and Abolition: Impression Points on Decolonisation and the Law School" delivered by Joel Modiri, 13 September 2019, Law School, University of Bristol, published as Modiri, "Aporias of Decolonisation," 157–73.

113 Himonga, "Constitutional Court of Justice Moseneke," 101–23.

114 Diala, "Curriculum Decolonisation," 2–36.

misplaced.[115] Further that it sends judges on a wild goose chase as they try to "discover the living customary law". He argues:

> Rather, judges should focus on whether and to what extent litigants and communities utilise(d) the foundational values of indigenous law to adapt their customs to socio-economic changes. These values include "humaneness, family continuity, the duty of care owed to family members by the family head, the non-individual nature of marriage, and the preservation of the ancestral home."[116]

The approach in Botswana is nowhere near the one suggested by Diala. The approach is captured by the Court in the *Ramantele* case as involving an enquiry into the ascertainment of customary law, which it may be argued is the "living" customary law. The court will then have to confirm that the custom constituted a law in terms of the definition of customary law as defined in section 2 of the Customary Law Act. According to this provision, a custom is law only if it is not contrary to any enactment, morality, humanity, and natural justice. These factors, when looked at closely do confirm that the current legal framework is largely focused on achieving an equitable outcome on the resolution of dispute concerning customary law issues or aligning the customary practices with constitutional or statutory rights. While it may be argued that equity is one of the norms that the customary courts applied and continue to apply even today in the resolution of disputes, there were limits to the application of such equitable principles. Equity was not as pervasive as it is now explaining why customary law norms that were patriarchal in nature found their application. The Court in the *Ramantele* thus did not attempt to reconcile constitutional values approach with the customary law values or rationale underpinning the custom in issue.

The approach by the Botswana courts highlighted above has influenced the nature and content of customary law in many areas such as succession and inheritance, chieftainship, and marriage. For example, customs relating to the division of property following the dissolution of customary marriages have been greatly impacted by the requirements of fairness and equality. Previously, the property regime of customary law marriages was deemed to be largely out of community of property and was underlined by the principle of ensuring that family assets, such as the homestead, remained within the man's family. Thus,

115 Diala, "Curriculum Decolonisation," 5.

116 Diala, "Curriculum Decolonisation," 13.

it was rare to find the matrimonial home awarded to the woman upon divorce. However, over time this has changed, and customary courts have embraced the principles of equality and fairness in the distribution of matrimonial assets. The same can be said of principles of inheritance and succession as it can be observed that the customary courts have moved away from aspects of certain customs relating to succession. Customary courts have, in that respect, also embraced the principles of equality and non-discrimination in the resolution of these disputes.

As aforementioned, the customary law that is applied in this regard is not the "traditionalist" customary law but the customary law that is widely considered as the "living" customary law. The customary law that is being applied is almost free from the influences of the patriarchal order and nature synonymous with customary law. Kirby JP, as he then was, in his additional opinion in the *Ramantele* case has rightly noted "that the customary courts operate by and large as courts of equity".[117] This conclusion flows from his proper analysis of the nature and content of the "evolving and flexible rules of customary law".[118] Such rules, he restated, must not be contrary to morality, humanity or natural justice.[119] It is not hard, therefore, for ones to characterise the customary law that is being applied as amounting to principles of equity as informed by customary law. Customary law in that sense understood as traditional norms and customs in their purest form or, at the very least, referring to the "foundational values of indigenous law".[120]

Occasionally, one is then compelled to confront this important question: are the customs or customary laws that are applicable today, as emanating from the "evolving and flexible rules of customary law", really customary law(s)?[121] An answer to this question is in fact important to the overall debate on the nature or content and the future of customary law. Customary law in this respect should be understood as the "the rules people cite as traditionally governing their behaviour and which have been passed on from previous ages".[122] This is the customary law that Molokomme describes as the "traditionalist customary law"[123] and Bourdillon describes as "the law of the past".[124] This definition is apt

117 *Ramantele* case, 691.
118 Ibid.
119 Ibid.
120 Diala, "Curriculum Decolonisation," 2.
121 Bourdillon, "Is Customary Law Customary?" 140–49.
122 Bourdillon, "Is Customary Law Customary?" 140.
123 Molokomme, "Customary Law in Botswana," 348.
124 Bourdillon, "Is Customary Law Customary?" 140.

because if we adopt a definition that puts forward customary law as consisting of norms that are "flexible, adaptable and evolutionary",[125] how that customary law will fare in the future should not bother anyone so much because that customary law will adapt and will be applicable in its reformed nature and content. What in fact should be concerning is whether the customs and practices, from the past, that have been passed on from previous generations have any future considering the limitations discussed in the earlier parts of this chapter. It being known that the rationale and some of the values underpinning this "law of the past" have strong patriarchal and often discriminatory inclinations, it is crucial to establish whether such customs and practices have any future and are applicable today or are recognised as customary law.

The answer to this question is that the customary law that is mostly applied by the courts in Botswana, referred to as "statutory customary law by Bourdillion", has taken the form of principles of equity. It is not the "traditionalist customary law" or "the law of the past". This is to the extent that customs in issue have been forced to conform to the principles set out in the various statutory enactments, morality, humanity, or natural justice. This is the "customary law" that has partly evolved on its own accord but has been forced to conform to what the common law or the legislature – as well as the subjects or people, owing to the court led customary law reform process – insists should be deemed to be "customary law". This is perhaps the living customary law referred to above. Chances are that there will always be cases of an overlap between the "statutory customary law", "traditionalist customary law" and the customary law that has evolved on its own accord or living customary law. However, when one talks about customary law in Botswana, they are mostly referring to "statutory customary law" and not the unadulterated customs passed on from previous generations (customary law in its purest form) that still find application in some sections of the society and have not encountered the common or written law. They are also rarely thinking of the customary law that has evolved on its own accord in the not-so-distant past.

It is therefore apposite to conclude this discussion by highlighting that customary law in Botswana by its nature is not static. It is the living customary law.[126] This has been confirmed by the Court of Appeal in the *Kweneng Land Board* case and several other cases that followed. The *Kweneng Land Board* case does illustrate how customs can evolve in their own accord and when that happens, one should not be hesitant to refer to such evolved norms as customary

125 Morapedi, "Demise or Resilience," 250.

126 See generally Werbner and Werbner, *African Customary Justice*, 187.

law. In that case, the question was whether tribal land could be "held by any person in his personal and private capacity". The conclusion reached by the Court was that the conceptions of customary land as property which cannot be privately owned or sold were no longer accurate.[127] The Court also held that customary law had evolved to the extent that it recognised individual ownership of land.[128] Aguda J. A., as he then was, was of the view that there was sufficient evidence tendered to show that customary law had evolved to the extent that one could hold land in his personal and private capacity. The custom in issue, which was/is to the effect that customary land is allocated to and belonged to the family, was deemed to have undergone significant changes over time through the daily interactions and dealings of members of that tribe. The change did not come about due to the dictates of a statutory enactment or a judicial pronouncement.

7 Conclusion

This chapter has echoed the truism that pre-independence legislation has greatly informed the nature and content of much of the post-colonial legislation. In turn, the current legislation which no doubt bears the hallmark of British rule and Roman Dutch law influence have been used to further impose limitations on the application of customary law. The limitations imposed on customary law by the written law and the courts have over time shaped the nature and content of customary law in Botswana. These limitations are informed by what can only be described as a historical asymmetry that finds its genesis in the *Dow* case. While the Constitution had guaranteed the "constitutional plurality" that we now clamour for, the Court of Appeal in that case dealt away with such with the stroke of a pen. The courts have been instrumental in furthering this agenda and are beholden to the idea that customary laws should be immediately set aside if they exhibit any sign of failure to conform to the received laws. No attention is usually paid to the values underpinning the custom that is to be impugned.

The application of customary law having been limited in this fashion meant that it was easier for the legislature and the courts to make further inroads into its application. Examples of such inroads are contained in the statutory enactments discussed mostly under part IV of this chapter. Substantively, this

127 *Kabelo Matlho* case, 303.
128 Ibid.

means that customary law being limited in its application, its nature and content is invariably affected. This chapter has illustrated how such limitations have affected the nature and content of customary law.

The customary law that is largely applicable in Botswana is sometimes described as principles of equity that have been influenced by customary law. There might still be pockets of the society that apply unadulterated customs though. If that was not the case, how then do you explain recent decisions of the courts such as in the *Ramantele* case? Equally, the pervasive application of "statutory customary law" in Botswana is manifestly clear. The chapter has thus illustrated that the customary law that is now applicable in Botswana is still layered.

It is imperative however that the place of customary law within the Botswana legal system be constitutionally guaranteed. If at all there is commitment to the application of "customary law", it should not be subject to all written laws as this is likely to render inapplicable most customs simply because they do not conform to a standard that has so far failed to consider the rationale behind most customs. This conclusion does highlight the need for Botswana to engage in a serious conversation about decolonising the law and the search for true legal pluralism. It is timely because of the constitutional reform process that has been initiated.

Bibliography

Literature

Adebisi, Foluke. "Decolonising the Law School: Presences, Absences, Silences ... and Hope." *The Law Teacher* 54, no. 4 (2020): 471–74.

Aguda, Akinola. "Legal Development in Botswana from 1885 to 1966." *Botswana Notes and Records* 5, no. 1 (1973): 52–63.

Bekker, Jan C., and Digby S. Koyana. "The Judicial and Legislative Reform of the Customary Law of Succession." *De Jure* 45, no. 3 (2012): 568–84.

Bourdillon, Michael F. C. "Is Customary Law Customary?" *Nada: The Southern Rhodesia Native Affairs Department Annual* 11, no. 2 (1975): 140–49.

Brewer, I. G. "Sources of the Criminal Law of Botswana." *Journal of African Law* 18, no. 1 (1974): 24–36.

Crowder, Michael. "Tshekedi Khama and Opposition to the British Administration of the Bechuanaland Protectorate, 1926–1936." *Journal of African History* 26, no. 2–3 (1985): 193–214.

Demian, Melissa. "On the Repugnance of Customary Law." *Comparative Studies in Society and History* 56, no. 2 (2014): 508–36.

Diala, Anthony C. "Curriculum Decolonisation and Revisionist Pedagogy of African Customary Law." *Potchefstroom Electronic Law Journal* 22, no. 1 (2019): 2–36.

Dinokopila, Bonolo R., and Bonno Kgoboge. "Customary Law and Limitations to Constitutional Rights in Botswana." *Nordic Journal of Human Rights* 39, no. 3 (2021): 339–57.

Dinokopila, Bonolo R. "The Unity Dow Case and the Constitutional Protection of Women in Botswana." *Africa Nazarene University Law Journal* 3, no. 2 (2015): 35–52.

Fombad, Charles. "The Constitutional Protection Against Discrimination in Botswana." *International and Comparative Law Quarterly* 53, no. 1 (2004): 139–70.

Fombad, Charles M. *The Botswana Legal System*. Durban: LexisNexis, 2017.

Frimpong, Kwame. *Criminal Law of Botswana: Cases and Materials, Volume 1*. Gaborone: University of Botswana, 1988.

Himonga, Chuma. "The Constitutional Court of Justice Moseneke and the Decolonisation of Law in South Africa: Revisiting the Relationship Between Indigenous Law and Common Law." *Acta Juridica* 2017, no. 1 (2017): 101–23.

Himsworth, Chris M. G. "The Botswana Customary Law Act, 1969." *Journal of African Law* 16, no. 1 (1972): 4–18.

Ifezue, Godsglory O. "Understanding Chieftainship in Botswana: The Status and Powers of Chiefs in Present Day Botswana." *Journal of African Law* 59, no. 2 (2015): 271–93.

Korang, Daniel. "Ascertainment of Customary Law: A Question of Law or of Fact or Both?" *Journal of Law, Policy and Globalization* 38 (2015): 93–95.

Malila, Ikanyeng S. "Reconciling Plural Legal Systems: Between Justice and Social Disorder in Botswana." *Botswana Notes and Records* 42 (2010): 71–78.

Maripe, Bugalo. "Giving Effect to International Human Rights Law in the Domestic Context of Botswana: Dissonance and Incongruity in Judicial Interpretation." *Oxford University Commonwealth Law Journal* 14, no. 2 (2014): 251–82.

Mensa-Bonsu, Maame A. S. "Customary Law and 1992 Constitution of Ghana: A Comparative Theoretical Study." PhD diss., University of Oxford, 2021.

Modiri, Joel. "The Aporias of Decolonisation in the South African Academy." In *From Ivory Towers to Ebony Towers: Transforming Humanities Curricula in South Africa, Africa and African-American Studies*, edited by Oluwaseun Tella, and Shireen Motala, 157–73. Johannesburg: Jacana Media, 2020.

Molokomme, Athaliah. "Customary Law in Botswana: Past, Present and Future." In *Botswana in the 21st Century (Proceedings of a Symposium Organised by the Botswana Society, Gaborone)*, edited by Sue Brothers, 347–69. Gaborone: Botswana Society, 1994.

Molokomme, Athaliah. "The Reception of Roman Dutch Law in Botswana." *Lesotho Law Journal* 1, no. 1 (1985): 121–33.

Morapedi, Wazha G. "Demise or Resilience: Customary Law and the Changing Order in Africa: The Case of Chieftainship in Botswana." In *The Future of African Customary*

Law, edited by Jeanmarie Fenrich, et al., 247–65. New York: Cambridge University Press, 2011.

Otlhogile, Bojosi. "*Tshekedi Khama and ANO vs. High Commissioner*: The Making of the Court." *Botswana Notes and Records* 25, no. 1 (1993): 29–38.

Piron, Laure-Hélène. "Donor Assistance to Justice Sector Reform in Africa: Living Up to the New Agenda?" Accessed March 14, 2023. https://cdn.odi.org/media/documents/2309.pdf.

Proctor, Jesse Harris. "The House of Chiefs and the Political Development of Botswana." *Journal of Modern African Studies* 6, no. 1 (1968): 59–79.

Quansah, Emmanuel. "An Examination of the Use of International Law as in Interpretative Tool in Human Rights Litigation in Ghana and Botswana." In *International Law and Domestic Human Rights Litigation in Africa*, edited by Magnus Killander, 46–48. Preroria: PULP, 2010.

Radijeng, Godfrey. "Customary Law (LAW 106) Course Outline" (2008) (available on file).

Rajak, Harry. "A Virile System of Law: An Exploration of the South African Legal System – A Public Lecture Delivered at the University of the Free State,1 September 2009." Accessed March 14, 2023. https://hsf.org.za/publications/focus/focus-60-january-2011-making-south-africa-work-rules-of-the-game/HRajak.pdf.

Ramsay, Jeff. "The Establishment and Consolidation of the Bechuanaland Protectorate, 1870–1910." In *Botswana Politics and Society*, edited by Wayne Edge, and Mogopodi Lekorwe, 118–33. Pretoria: Van Schaik, 1998.

Roberts, Simon. "The Survival of the Traditional Tswana Courts in the National Legal System of Botswana." *Journal of African Law* 16, no. 2 (1972): 103–29.

Thomas, Philip J., and Dire D. Tladi. "Legal Pluralism or a New Repugnancy Clause." *Comparative and International Law Journal of Southern Africa* 32, no. 3 (1999): 354–63.

Tshosa, Onkemetse. "The Application of Non-Discrimination in Botswana in Light of *Attorney-General of Botswana v. Unity Dow*: Judicial Approach and Practice." *International Journal of Discrimination and the Law* 5, no. 2–3 (2001): 189–202.

Werbner, Pnina, and Richard P. Werbner. *African Customary Justice: Living Law, Legal Pluralism and Public Ethics*. London: Routledge, 2022.

Woodman, Gordon R. "Legal Pluralism and the Search for Justice." *Journal of African Law* 40, no. 2 (1996): 152–67.

Woodman, Gordon R. "Some Realism About Customary Law: The West African Experience." *Wisconsin Law Review* (1969): 128–52.

Case Law

Angu v Attah (1909) Ren 550.

Attorney General v Dow 1992 BLR 119 (CA).

Bimbo v The State, Criminal Appeal No. 56 of 1980 (unreported).

Chief Tshekedi Khama v Simon Ratshosa (Attorney General Intervening) [1931] AC 784.
Kgafela Kgafela v The State (High Court) (unreported) case no. CLHLB-000148–10.
Kweneng Land Board v Kabelo Matlho 1992 BLR 292 (CA).
Pearl Assurance Co. v Union Government [1934] AC 570.
Ramantele v Mmusi [2013] 2 BLR 658.
Silverstone (Pty) Ltd v Lobatse Clay Works (Pty) Ltd [1996] BLR 190.
Tidimalo Jokase v Gaelebale Mpho Swakgosing (High Court) (unreported) case no. MAHLB-000661–10.
Tirelo v The Attorney-General 2008 (2) BLR 38 (HC).
Tshekedi Khama v the High Commissioner 926–53 HCLTR (BP).

Legislation and Government Publications

Administration of Estates Act, Cap. 31:01, Laws of Botswana.
African Courts Proclamation, 1961.
Bechuanaland Proclamation No. 1 of 1885.
Bechuanaland Proclamation No. 74 of 1934.
Bechuanaland Proclamation No. 75 of 1934.
Bechuanaland Proclamation No. 33 of 1942.
Bogosi (Chieftainship) Act, Cap. 41:01, Laws of Botswana.
Chieftainship Act 19 of 1987.
Children's Act 8 of 2009.
Common Law and Customary Law Act, Cap. 16:01, Laws of Botswana (repealed).
Constitution of Botswana, Cap. 01:00, Laws of Botswana.
Customary Courts Act, Cap. 04:05, Laws of Botswana.
Customary Law Act, Cap. 16:01, Laws of Botswana.
Establishment and Jurisdiction of Customary Courts Order, Cap 04:05, Laws of Botswana.
General Law Proclamation, 1909.
Native Administration Proclamation, 1943.
Order-in-Council, May 9, 1891.
Penal Code, Cap. 08:01, Laws of Botswana.
Stanley, Hebert J. "Explanatory Memorandum on the Bechuanaland Protectorate Native Administration and Native Tribunals Proclamation by the then High Commissioner." Cape Town, 1934. Accessed April 13, 2023. https://www.botswanalaws.com/Bechuanaland/Subsidiary/1934/EXPLANATORY%20MEMORANDUM.pdf.

CHAPTER 13

Laws of Motion and Motions of Laws: Towards a Transformative Law-and-Political-Economy Framework for Customary Law in South Africa

Reshard L. Kolabhai

Abstract

How do we understand "customary law" in "post"-apartheid South Africa? The transformative 1996 Constitution recognises customary law as effectively "separate but equal" to the Western systems of common law and statute, with both customary law and ordinary Western law subject to the Constitution. This chapter instead argues that customs can be understood only in *motion*: that is, in a dialectic with the Western system of law, through both of their roles in shaping – and being shaped by – a shared system of political economy operating in space and time. Integrating insights from Critical Legal Realism and the growing field of Law and Political Economy (LPE), the chapter reconsiders Harold Wolpe's radical theorisation of the articulation of modes of production in the light of the Constitution and transformative constitutionalism. Such a reading points to an understanding of custom as generally coerced by capital's hegemony, with capital itself being constituted by the ordinary Western law and the State. In practice, then, custom is neither "separate" nor "equal" to common law and statute; at least not while the State upholds the latter, and while the latter constitutes capital. A Wolpean LPE framework thus points beyond the constitutional recognition of custom to the need for the systemic constitutional critique and transformation of ordinary Western law, for custom's sake.

1 Introduction*

the rise and fall of the sea yesterday
cast seeds far into the hinterland

* My deepest thanks go to William Matthewson and Anke Froehlich for reading and commenting on drafts; to Anthony Diala and Christa Rautenbach for their encouragement and patience; and to the two anonymous reviewers and Alan Brimer for their helpful feedback and suggestions. I especially thank the wonderfully warm and insightful people at the 2022

 | DOI:10.1163/9789004696747_014

while we stood scanning the horizon for more ships
today the red sun dances over the heads
of a multitudinous midday rush
our bulging eyes dimmed by a rage

SIPHO SEPAMLA, *To Makana and Nongqawuse* (1976)

Imagine, if you will, a major merger being concluded at a top South African law firm, in a *laani*[1] air-conditioned boardroom in the heart of the Sandton central business district in Johannesburg.[2] Imagine that, at precisely the same moment, a man in an impoverished rural area of the former Transkei[3] pays *lobola*[4] after having "carried away" a woman in *ukuthwala*.[5]

How do we think about these two legal acts? More importantly, how *should* we?

Customary law is taught and studied as a field separate from Western corporate law. These fields are practised, for the most part, by separate people. They are practised in worlds which are both physically and conceptually apart. It is difficult to hold the two images in one's head at the same time, in the same place: when thinking of one, it comes as a surprise to remember that the other does indeed occur contemporaneously, in the same country. And from a legal

International Initiative for Promoting Political Economy Annual Conference, in Bologna, Italy, where I presented a version of this chapter. Their political-economic expertise and support meant a great deal during this process. reshard.kolabhai@yale.edu.

1 A South African English term descended from an Isicamtho word meaning "white man". As a noun, it can also refer to "a boss or employer", or "a member of the upper classes". As an adjective, it means "uppercrust, 'posh', elegant, smart". Dictionary Unit for South African English, "larney".

2 Sandton has been dubbed "the richest square mile in Africa": Nyapokoto, "Road Between Sandton and Alexandra," 4, 101.

3 The Transkei was a nominally independent Bantustan, "homeland" or "Native reserve" for the AmaXhosa (Xhosa people), created by the apartheid government as part of its policy of "separate development". The area now falls within the poorest province in South Africa – the Eastern Cape – where 72.9% of the population was living below the upper-bound poverty line in 2015. Stats SA, *Poverty Trends*, 65.

4 An isiZulu and isiXhosa word; a custom amongst Southern African peoples of giving cattle, goods or (now usually) money to the parents of a women or girl to secure her hand in marriage; or such given as a traditional dowry. Also referred to as *lobolo*. Shope, "'Lobola is Here to Stay'," 64; Dictionary Unit for South African English, "lobola".

5 Literally "to carry off" in isiXhosa; a custom amongst some traditional Southern African peoples of abducting a girl or young woman with a view towards forcing through marriage negotiations. The girl or young woman or her relatives may consent to this, in which case the abduction and her resistance are forms of performance. Rice, "Understanding *Ukuthwala*."

point of view, as far as their constitutional recognition is concerned, we tend to think of these two legal acts as indeed equal, *but separate*.

South Africa's "Interim" Constitution of 1993, which formed the basis of the later recognition of "customary law" in the 1996 Constitution, phrased this separate equality as follows, in Constitutional Principle XIII: "Indigenous law, *like common law*, shall be recognised and applied by the courts, subject to the fundamental rights contained in the Constitution and to legislation dealing specifically therewith."[6] [Emphasis added.] In the "Final" Constitution of 1996 (hereafter "the Constitution"), "customary law" is protected in Chapter 12, but made subject to the Constitution:

Section 211: Recognition

(1) The institution, status and role of traditional leadership, according to customary law, are recognised, subject to the Constitution.

(2) A traditional authority that observes a system of customary law may function subject to any applicable legislation and customs, which includes amendments to, or repeal of, that legislation or those customs.

(3) The courts must apply customary law when that law is applicable, subject to the Constitution and any legislation that specifically deals with customary law.

Section 212: Role of traditional leaders

(1) National legislation may provide for a role for traditional leadership as an institution at local level on matters affecting local communities.

(2) To deal with matters relating to traditional leadership, the role of traditional leaders, customary law and the customs of communities observing a system of customary law –
   (a) national or provincial legislation may provide for the establishment of houses of traditional leaders; and
   (b) national legislation may establish a council of traditional leaders.

6 Constitutional Principle XIII of the Constitution of the Republic of South Africa, 1993. These principles – a result of negotiations primarily between the African National Congress and the apartheid government – were a set of constraints contained in the "Interim" Constitution, to which the "Final" Constitution had to conform before it could be certified and take effect.

The courts are now thus no longer left with any general discretion to prefer common law over "customary" law: where the latter is "applicable", it must be applied, subject only to the Constitution and relevant legislation. Meanwhile, filed away in Schedule 6 of the Constitution – the transitional arrangements – the existing system of common law and legislation shaped by colonialism and apartheid was preserved, to be transformed only gradually by constitutional mechanisms such as the new Bill of Rights:[7]

> **Item 2: Continuation of existing law**
> (1) All law that was in force when the new Constitution took effect, continues in force, subject to –
> (a) any amendment or repeal; and
> (b) consistency with the new Constitution.

How do we view this new, explicit recognition of "customary law" in the post-transition Constitution? How do we view the continuation of colonial and apartheid law? And what, if anything, do these have to do with each other? Indeed, they are both subject to the Constitution, and thus subject to being "transformed" by the Constitution – but is that all that is going on here? A central development in South Africa since 1994 has been the simultaneous introduction of liberal political democracy on the one hand, and neoliberal economic policies on the other.[8] How are these two directions linked – given that they are seemingly in tension as far as democracy is concerned – and what do they mean for "customary" law? What does "customary" law – perceived as "law-in-the-now", "law-close-to-people", "living law" – have to do with big commercial law firms, with financialisation, with globalisation, with rising inequality, with environmental collapse? While what may crudely be termed "conflict of laws" and "clash of cultures" approaches to "customary" law are critically important, on their own they seem unable to tackle this question.

This chapter asks if these two legal spheres – "Western" and "customary" law – really are worlds apart. It asks whether, like much of apartheid itself, their apartness may be merely conceptual. Above all, it asks how these legal spheres move, and how they move each other; how they articulate at the joint.

7 Klare, "Legal Culture," 146; Davis and Klare, "Transformative Constitutionalism," 403.

8 See generally Terreblanche, *Lost in Transformation*, 17–36, 59–123; Bond, *Elite Transition*; Ashman, Fine and Newman, "The Crisis in South Africa," 174; Fine, "Post-Apartheid South Africa," 75; Padayachee, "Harold Wolpe," 96.

South Africa's legal system is explicitly premised on some form of legal pluralism,[9] and Diala has rightly stressed that "customary" law develops in response to changes in socioeconomic contexts.[10] This chapter attempts to flesh out this dynamic, focussing on the mechanisms by which "Western" law shapes the context of "customary" law under a single national Constitution. The goal here is to move away from a static doctrinal legal analysis into the dynamism of the real world, to look at what the law does in motion, and then to look back at what this means for our approach to constitutional recognition.

A brief aside for definitions: by "custom" I broadly mean both ordinary social customs and those social customs which, in their communities, are elevated to the status and effect of law, regardless of their cultural background (although I focus here primarily on the customs of African peoples). Custom emanates from its particular socio-economic context; in turn, custom plays a role in shaping socio-economic contexts. This is a very wide definition, and unites countless varieties of customs across countless contexts – be they "indigenous" or "religious", "traditional" or "novel", "rural" or "urban". While this chapter focusses primarily on "traditional" African customs in general, its implications can largely be extended to customs of any other provenance, as will be seen.

I distinguish "custom" in this broad sense from the far narrower term "customary law", to which I give a particular meaning. I mean "customary law" to be that which the South African State factually recognises as "customary law," in terms of section 211 of the Constitution.[11] Both "custom" and "customary law" are thus descriptive, and are not mutually exclusive; the former is merely a reference to whatever is socially in practice, while the latter refers to the State's own legal construction. While there is some link and overlap between the two, the State's construction of "customary law" may be, and often is, in tension with custom as it is practised, experienced, reworked and reimagined.[12]

---

9 For an overview of legal pluralism in South Africa, see Rautenbach, *Introduction to Legal Pluralism*.

10 Diala, "Concept of Living Customary Law," 154–59.

11 I am deliberately avoiding the standard categorisations of "official customary law" and "living customary law", as my analysis is not centred on the question of how the State recognises customary law. Diala draws attention to the problems of the categories of "official" and "living", given the nature of legal-cultural exchange: Diala, "Concept of Living Customary Law". Siegel, with reference to Wicomb, also points to the philosophical and practical complexities arising from categorisation, especially in the light of neoliberalism: Siegel, "Boundaries of Customary Law," 357.

12 See for instance: Comaroff and Comaroff, "Chiefs, Capital, and the State"; Buthelezi and Skosana, "Salience of Chiefs"; Chanock, "Constitutionalism, Democracy and Africa," 126.

It is also important to note that traditional African "custom" and "customary law" were deliberately and directly reconfigured by the colonial and apartheid regimes, by subjecting them to European law.[13] This means that, while these customs retained some aspects of older African traditions, they are not wholly "traditional" in an untouched pre-colonial sense. Similarly, custom is today legally recognised only to the extent that it is consistent with the Constitution. The direct politico-legal regulation of custom by the State is thus nothing new – whether for exploitative ends under colonial-apartheid, or for ostensibly progressive, democratic and human rights ends under the post-1994 transition. The question we are considering here, rather, is this: what *indirect* constraints on custom and recognisable "customary law" arise from the simultaneous recognition and preservation of "all law that was in force when the new Constitution took effect"? In starting to explore this question, a framework must be built to allow for a political-economic critique of constitutional legal pluralism, mindful of South Africa's history of "racial" capitalism and its (neo)liberal "post"-apartheid[14] transition.

To get us moving here, I first prod our thinking with Harold Wolpe's seminal work on the subject on the articulation of modes of production in South Africa,[15] as a critique of the conceptual apartheid between these worlds. I then use this Wolpean lens to look at how the spheres of "Western" and "customary" law interact in the real world of political economy. While Wolpe has had a great impact on political-economic studies themselves, the value of his contributions for legal analysis have not yet been fully explored, especially in the realm

---

13 This included, for instance, the system of "indirect rule", where chiefs were able to retain and exercise their powers only at the pleasure of the ruling European power. As a result, much of African custom was permitted to be maintained and practised only to the extent that it did not interfere with or threaten the colonial-apartheid regimes. See Diala, "Concept of Living Customary Law," 144–58; Bennett and Murray, "Traditional Leaders," 26–1. This interference with cultural tradition as a means for traditional leadership to retain or even increase their political and economic power has continued to the present: Comaroff and Comaroff, "Chiefs, Capital, and the State"; Buthelezi and Skosana, "Salience of Chiefs".

14 I refer to "post"-apartheid in quotation marks deliberately, in order to disturb a common notion that apartheid amounted only to a narrow political system of formal statutory discrimination that ended in 1994. As is presented in this chapter, apartheid was inseparable from an extensive economic system of exploitation of "black" labour, and this system certainly did not end with the Interim or Final Constitutions. As Modiri puts it, "the fact of apartheid refuses to fade": Modiri, "Towards a '(Post-) Apartheid' Critical Race Jurisprudence," 237. See also Modiri, "Conquest and Constitutionalism"; Madlingozi, "Social Justice".

15 Wolpe, "Capitalism and Cheap Labour-Power," 425.

of constitutional law. I conclude by moving back to legal regulation, and consider what all of this might mean for how we reconfigure our approach to custom in the modern context of the South African Constitution, State and law.

I must be clear on what I am doing here: I am a legal academic interested in constitutional law and the developing field of Law and Political Economy (LPE),[16] which is in an especially early phase in South African legal studies. My interest lies in the legal interplay between the Constitution and "private law", and the effect thereof in our societal system of production and distribution. What I am not doing is attempting to contribute much new to the field of legal anthropology, which has explored these interplays for quite some time. In short, then, I am hoping to help move us forward in our legal understanding and analysis of the Constitution's simultaneous recognition of "customary law" alongside "all law that was in force when the new Constitution took effect". With a better understanding of what the Constitution is doing, and of how it came to do what it does, we will hopefully be better placed to imagine what it could and should do instead.

2 The Idea of Articulation: Wolpe's "Cheap Labour Thesis"

> I get my cue
> from the glint in the cop's eye.
> I have seen it before.
> So I have to find it.
> I pull away from Mono
> and hug myself in desperation.
> up, down, back, front, sides,
> like a crazed tribal dancer.
> I have to find it.
> Without it I'm lost, with it I'm lost,
> a cipher in Albert Street.
> I hate it. I nurse it,
> my pass, my everything. [...]
> The doors of the kwela-kwela[17] gape,
> I jabber at Mono.

16 See for instance Britton-Purdy et al., "Building a Law-And-Political-Economy Framework"; Mutua, "Introducing ClassCrits".

17 From "khwela", meaning "to climb on/in" in Nguni languages; refers to a police van. Dictionary Unit for South African English, "kwela-kwela".

> The doors swing lazy, sadistic like Jonah's whale.
> I take a free ride.
>
> STAN MOTJUWADI, *Taken for a Ride*

To begin thinking about the connected movement of legal worlds, we must first start in the world of political economy and struggle, with Harold Wolpe's theorisation of apartheid as the result of an articulation of modes of production. Wolpe's theory was extraordinarily academically influential in its time, and recent work has sought to revisit Wolpean analysis in both apartheid and "post"-apartheid South Africa.[18] This is not merely historical trivia. The predominant legal theory of the 1996 Constitution – accepted by the Constitutional Court[19] – is that of "transformative constitutionalism", "an enterprise of inducing large-scale social change through nonviolent political processes grounded in law".[20] This was a result of the politics of the transition from formal apartheid. The apartheid government had refused to simply concede power without certain concessions being made by the African National Congress; a negotiated compromise was thus reached to facilitate the hand-over of political power to the majority, but wide-reaching legal reform was to be left as an ongoing project of the 1996 "Final" Constitution, through both legislative action and adjudication. In his seminal article on transformative constitutionalism, Karl Klare identifies various transformative mechanisms in the Constitution's text: social rights and a substantive conception of equality; affirmative state duties; horizontality of the Bill of Rights; participatory governance; multiculturalism; and historical self-consciousness.[21] Wolpe's historical theory of apartheid is thus

18 Reynolds, Fine and Van Niekerk, *Race, Class and the Post-Apartheid Democratic State*; Friedman, *Race, Class and Power*.

19 *Mahlangu v Minister of Labour* 2021 (2) SA 54 (CC), para. 79; *Beadica 231 CC v Trustees for the Time Being of the Oregon Trust* 2020 (5) SA 247 (CC), paras. 74 and 100; *AB v Minister of Social Development* 2017 (3) SA 570 (CC), para. 126; *City of Tshwane Metropolitan Municipality v Afriforum* 2016 (6) SA 279 (CC), para. 165; *Print Media South Africa v Minister of Home Affairs* 2012 (6) SA 443 (CC), para. 97; *Road Accident Fund v Mdeyide* 2011 (2) SA 26 (CC), para. 125; *Hassam v Jacobs* 2009 (5) SA 572 (CC), para. 28.

20 Klare, "Legal Culture," 150 and generally; Davis and Klare, "Transformative Constitutionalism," 403; Roux, "Transformative Constitutionalism"; Van Huyssteen, "Constitutional Court and the Redistribution of Power"; Langa, "Transformative Constitutionalism"; Moseneke, "Transformative Adjudication," 313–14; Brickhill and Van Leeve, "Transformative Constitutionalism," 146–47; Ackermann, "South African Constitutional Revolution"; Van Marle, "Transformative Constitutionalism"; Liebenberg, *Socio-Economic Rights*, ch. 2.

21 Klare, "Legal Culture," 151–56.

critical, because it helps us better understand the mechanics of the dark past that the Constitution seeks to move us from. Without understanding apartheid, we cannot understand the Constitution.

Harold Wolpe was a prominent academic figure in the struggle against apartheid.[22] He studied sociology at the University of the Witwatersrand in Johannesburg, and joined the South African Communist Party in his second year before turning to law when the Party was banned in 1950. He became involved with uMkhonto we Sizwe[23] as an intelligence officer at Liliesleaf Farm in Rivonia. But the farm was raided by state police, leading to the arrests of leading struggle figures like Nelson Mandela, Walter Sisulu, Denis Goldberg, Govan Mbeki and Ahmed Kathrada. Wolpe attempted to flee the country, but was also arrested after being betrayed by a family member. The raid led to the infamous Rivonia Trial, when Mandela and others were sentenced to life imprisonment. But by the time the trial took place in 1963, Wolpe and three others had escaped Marshall Square police headquarters and prison in Johannesburg, in one of the most renowned escapes under apartheid. Wolpe went into exile in the United Kingdom, where he turned to academia and returned to sociology.

It was here that his most famous work was published, the 1972 article "Capitalism and Cheap Labour-Power in South Africa: From Segregation to Apartheid".[24] At the time, the two dominant critiques of apartheid were, respectively, liberal and communist. A mainstream liberal view was that racism in South Africa was irrational, and that racism improperly constrained the "freedom" of liberal capitalism through segregation, colour bars and so on. A mainstream communist view was that South Africa exhibited a certain kind of colonialism – known as Colonialism of a Special Type (CST)[25] – which was brought upon by capitalism. Unlike settler colonialism (which relied on the near-complete removal and genocide of indigenous populations, followed by the mass settlement of colonisers) or exploitation colonialism (which relied only on the colonial settlement necessary to achieve resource and labour exploitation), South Africa featured a significant minority of settlers living alongside, and exploiting the labour of, the indigenous majority. The

22 This is necessarily a summary of Wolpe, his context and work, his critics, and the underlying debates and theory; for a full account I recommend Friedman's excellent recent work on Wolpe: Friedman, *Race, Class and Power*, 1–45.

23 isiXhosa for "Spear of the Nation"; the paramilitary wing of the African National Congress, classified by the apartheid government as a terrorist organisation and banned.

24 See Friedman, *Race, Class and Power*, 2–7, 116–26, from which the background details here are given.

25 See Friedman, *Race, Class and Power*, 126–34 for the political and academic clashes between Wolpe's thought and the prevailing SACP analysis.

mainstream communist view held that all "white"[26] people, be they capitalist or working-class, benefited from this arrangement; and all "black" people, regardless of class, were victims of it. "Racial" oppression was held to simply be the manifestation of class oppression in South Africa, and so the primary political focus in South Africa for the communists would be the national struggle – the struggle for "racial" political equality under liberal democracy – rather than the class struggle. In short, both liberals and communists tended to adhere to the notion that "race" was external to capitalism; that "race" was distorting capitalism; and thus that the immediate priority in South Africa was political equality, rather than the achievement of economic class liberation.[27]

Wolpe breaks with the mainstream communist view, and seeks instead to theorise how apartheid worked beyond mere "racial" ideology or "race" reductionism. At the time, the increasing repressiveness of the National Party was seen as a result of its "racial" ideology, and as a response to increasing resistance to that ideology. Apartheid was thus merely segregation taken further – a difference of quantity in racism. But this approach could not explain why apartheid took the particularly distinct qualitative form it did. Wolpe seeks instead to explain apartheid in terms of the articulation of the modes of production in the territory of South Africa. The term "mode of production" refers to a particular society's collective productive forces (labour-power and means of production), coupled with the relevant social relations that link labour-power and the means of production, and which thus govern production and distribution. A "mode of production" is necessarily an abstraction, a theoretical generalisation. It aids in understanding the generalities of a particular political-economic system; but to be useful in a particular case, it must necessarily be concretised by refinement, through the application of specific insights from that case.

The dominant mode of production in South Africa in the 20th century and since has been capitalism. Capitalism is a mode of production with highly unequal control of the necessities for life and of the means of production.[28] This

26 "Race" and racial categories are historical and unscientific social constructs that arbitrarily group humans together for the purpose of discrimination, and are closely linked to political economy. See generally Smedley and Smedley, "Race as Biology is Fiction," 16; Fine, "Antimonies of Neo-Marxism," 92–94; Bunting, *Rise of the South African Reich*, 159–60, 189. Racial categories are accordingly referred to here with quotation marks, to problematise "race" realism and essentialism.

27 Also see Legassick, "Colonialism of a Special Type," 57.

28 This is necessarily a simplified presentation. For more detailed overviews of a Marxist analysis of capitalism, see Fine and Saad-Filho, *Marx's "Capital"*; Harvey, *Companion to Marx's Capital*. For an overview in the context of colonial-capitalist imperialism and the "civilising mission" of international law, see Tzouvala, *Capitalism as Civilisation*, 19–35.

unequal control is maintained via the law and enforced by the State, through numerous socio-legal institutions such as private property and contract. The vast majority of the affected population are unable to labour to produce the necessities of life to support themselves, as they have no access to the means of production. They are thus compelled to sell their labour-power in a labour market. Workers (usually male, as will be seen) must sell their labour-power to property-owners – "capitalists" – in exchange for a wage to sustain themselves. Their labouring with the capitalist's property is used to produce commodities, which also become the property of the capitalist, and then are exchanged (that is, sold) for money. This money is used to pay dividends to the capitalist; to reproduce and expand capital through reinvestment; and to reproduce labour-power through the payment of wages. The cycle repeats. Shareholders receive their dividends not by virtue of material work done, but by virtue of their status as property-owners; the workers who do the material work accordingly cannot be fully compensated for the material value of the work they do, as part of the value they add must instead be assigned to reinvestment and dividends. Capital is thus not merely a "thing"; rather, it is a social relation[29] which governs how labour interacts with the means of production – governing, therefore, production and distribution in a society – and which thereby gives rise to a particular mode of production.

Under capitalism, then, production and distribution are governed by a money-based market economy that requires constant financial movement and flow. In order for individual capitalists to succeed in such a system, they must remain competitive; if a business becomes unprofitable, the capitalists cannot support their own consumption, nor reproduce their capital (which necessarily degrades over time). Thus, capitalists are systemically required to re-invest in the means of production – to expand and accumulate their capital – and thereby reduce the percentage of their expenses directed to workers' wages relative to the business's gross income. This ultimately results in an economic mode where the means of production are overwhelmingly operated for the purposes of money-based market exchange, private profit and profit-driven reinvestment, rather than for the purpose of social need in and of itself.[30] In South Africa's context, capitalism as a mode of production in South Africa contrasted most clearly with the traditional "African redistributive economies" which operated in the "Native" reserves. According to Wolpe, these economies relied instead on the communal holding of land worked by an extended family,

29 Harvey, *Companion to Marx's Capital*, 303–04.

30 Kolabhai, "Private Property as Public Unhealth," 301.

with the product of labour distributed not by market exchange but by kinship units according to custom.[31]

This was the traditional abstract understanding of capitalism in European political-economic circles, which needed to be somewhat concretised to begin accurately describing the world. Thus, Marxist feminists would turn Marx on his head: as a result of particular historical social hierarchies, if certain dispossessed people are socially excluded from the labour market, they may be compelled to perform unwaged labour for workers who do receive a wage, in order to be able to share that wage. The historical unwaged labour of women in the home – working to support waged men and family units more broadly – was thus critical to the sustainment of capitalism, despite not even being perceived as "labour".[32] Capitalist oppression evidently intersected deeply with patriarchal oppression. The question amongst revolutionaries in South Africa in Wolpe's time was how, if at all, capitalist oppression intersected with "racial" oppression. This was the question Wolpe addressed.

Prevailing Marxist analysis in the Global South at the time held that capitalism had to constantly expand in search of greater profits, and that it would thus have to systematically destroy all other modes of production so that it could prevail everywhere. Wolpe challenges this hegemonic notion of capital by asserting instead that the situation in South Africa rather represented an articulation between two primary modes of production – capitalist and pre-capitalist – which together formed an economic system.[33] Wolpe holds that capitalism not only could survive alongside pre-capitalism, but that it had needed to. Under capitalism, labour-power must be reproduced; if the workforce is not maintained – through, for instance, wages – workers would be unwilling or unable to work. But wages come at a cost to the capitalist, who seeks to maximise profits and thus to reduce the cost of reproducing the labour force. (This is also one of the inherent contradictions of capitalism – the drive to produce commodities for sale ever more efficiently, while simultaneously lowering the wages of the workers who are unable to purchase those commodities, leads to cyclic crises of overaccumulation.)[34] Wolpe's insight is that the

31 Friedman, *Race, Class and Power*, 119; Wolpe, "Capitalism and Cheap Labour-Power," 432. See also Mafeje's critiques in Mafeje, "Articulation of Modes of Production," 123; Friedman, *Race, Class and Power*, 162–65.

32 See, for instance: Federici, *Revolution at Point Zero*, 91.

33 "Pre-capitalist" is a Marxist term. The "pre" is not a teleological value judgment of "backwardness", but rather reflects the tendency for capitalism to progressively remake all other modes of production in its image (as discussed below).

34 Bond, *Elite Transition*, 6–9.

pre-capitalist mode in the "reserves" fulfilled a role that capitalism "preferred" not to fulfil, in that the reserves were a site of social reproduction of labour-power.[35] The reserves allowed for the social support for the "black" migrant work force by providing subsistence and care to the young, the old, the sick, and the unemployed who lived there, without such subsistence and care being contingent on wages and capitalist labour relations. But as the reserves were unable to fully support the work force, labourers would still have to migrate to work in the cities. Their movements were most prominently regulated by the infamous administrative influx-control system known as the "pass laws", which required "black" men to carry a passbook on their person at all times. If their passbook did not show authorisation for their presence, they would be forcibly removed by the police and criminally charged. Wolpe argues that this system ultimately allowed the reserves to perform an indirect service for capital, as social reproduction in the rural reserves allowed urban wages to be pushed lower and profits to be raised higher. This was the "cheap labour thesis".

Wolpe was not alone in his belief. State policy-makers and analysts pre-apartheid also explicitly believed that the reserves were making "black" labour cheaper than "white"[36] – although, due to their racism, they viewed this as merely allowing the "black" labourer an unfair advantage in competing with their "white" counterparts. From the perspective of the State and capital, then, the reserves had to be protected to ensure that their pre-capitalist relations and their capacity for social reproduction were preserved. Thus, for instance, "white" people were forbidden from purchasing land in the reserves through the Native Land Act of 1913, while the Glen Grey Act of 1894 slowed the concentration of reserve land into the hands of a few "African" land-owners. The level of social reproduction in the reserves also had to be maintained at a healthy medium. If it moved too high, migrant workers would be under insufficient duress to become wage-labourers, as their existence could be viably sustained in the reserves alone. If the level of reproduction dropped too low,

35 See generally O'Laughlin, "No Separate Spheres".

36 See for instance the National Conference on the Poor White Problem – of which prominent apartheid prime ministers DF Malan and HF Verwoerd formed part – and which later informed the policy of the apartheid government concerning class and "race". Amongst other recommendations for legislative apartheid in the form of colour bars and the like, the Conference's 49th resolution reads: "The Conference is of the opinion that the tribal native from Native Reserves competes unfairly in urban employment with Poor Whites, the Coloured, and detribalised Natives, since their work is 'subsidised' as it were by their possessions in the Reserves, and they can therefore work for lower wages; and recommends the development of the Reserves as proposed by the Native Economic Commission." Du Toit, *Report of the National Conference*, 301.

capitalists' ability to profit off cheap labour reproduction would be threatened.[37] Importantly, however, Wolpe was not claiming that individual capitalists were intentionally scheming to maintain this delicate balance. Rather, he was simply presenting a descriptive observation of the way that the migrant labour system in South Africa must have been structurally operating given the two modes of production. As a result, while a hegemonic Western colonial conception of property was being used to justify and achieve dispossession by the State, this conception could never be hegemonic in practice in South Africa:[38] the State sought to preserve a legal space for custom, even if this form of custom was contorted and subsumed to suit the State's political and economic ends.

But the reserves could not last, as systemic contradictions within this articulation led to its own decline. Population growth and environmental degradation through land use decreased the relative productivity of the reserves. Moreover, as Wolpe puts it, capital disrupted the social relations upon which equitable distribution to migrant workers had been based, "by reason of the termination of the reciprocal social obligations of support between the migrant and his kin in the Reserve, even where the latter continues to produce sustenance. An important condition for this change is the permanent urbanisation of a substantial number of workers".[39] Capital needed to use the reserves, but using the reserves eventually made such use itself impossible. The systemic contradiction thus shifted from being primarily between modes of production to being primarily situated within capitalism itself, now operating more broadly in the relative absence of significant pre-capitalist relations. This gave rise to a "twofold effect of capitalist development", where impoverishment in rural areas led to impoverishment in urban areas, "[generating] conflict, not only about wages, but about all aspects of urban and rural life and [bringing] into question the structure of the whole society".[40] Workers had to plug the social reproduction gap with wages and thus fought for wage increases, leading to an increase in strikes and other actions in the 1940s. English-dominated capital in the cities, which supported the then Smuts government, sought liberal reforms to segregation that would quell the unrest. But such seemingly anti-"racial" reforms were not proposed for the sake of bettering the lot of

37 Friedman, *Race, Class and Power*, 135–38.

38 For a detailed account of the complex and sometimes contradictory interrelations between colonialism, "race", and property (both in its theory and practice) in other jurisdictions, see Bhandar, *Colonial Lives of Property*.

39 Wolpe, "Capitalism and Cheap Labour-Power," 443.

40 Wolpe, "Capitalism and Cheap Labour-Power," 444.

the exploited "black" workforce. Rather, such reforms would have maintained profits by putting "white" workers into greater competition with "black" workers, leading to decreases in pay and protection for "white" workers. The only way to protect the interests of both the "white" working class and the interests of capital, then, would be to keep "black" wages low through an increase in State force and repression even as the reserves deteriorated – indeed, *because* the reserves deteriorated.

This, Wolpe argues, is what apartheid was, as something qualitatively distinct from colonial segregation. The attempt to preserve profitably "cheap" labour for capitalists, while also protecting the "white" workforce in the face of their own deprivation by capital, formed the basis of apartheid as a political-economic system. Wolpe further argues that the later apartheid policy of "separate development" – which was "separate" in name only – was also premised on cheap labour, as was the creation of the "Bantustans" or "homelands" as supposedly separate States for "black" people. The homelands were now not to serve the role of subsistence, however. They instead kept the "traditional" structure of African societies, subject to the capitalist mode of production, as a means of "political, social, economic and ideological enforcement of low levels of subsistence"[41] for the benefit of capital situated near the borders. Rather than subsidising wages to reach a socially necessary level of reproduction, the homelands simply forcefully lowered what the socially necessary level of reproduction *was*.

There were many critiques raised against Wolpe's cheap labour thesis, some more valid than others.[42] One of Wolpe's more prominent critics, Archie Mafeje, raised several objections: that Wolpe neglected the role of cattle in the reproduction of cultural lineage, rather than their use for mere subsistence; that Wolpe's work neglected the role of culture as a self-standing drive alongside economic and political forces; and that Wolpe was too structuralist and formalist, underplaying the agency of the various actors in the system.[43] Feminist scholars pointed out that the reserves obviously did not spontaneously achieve social reproduction; rather, it was "black" women

41 Wolpe, "Capitalism and Cheap Labour-Power," 450.

42 See Friedman, *Race, Class and Power*, 135–75, for a full discussion. Some pro-capitalist critiques, for example, implied that migrant labour was not caused by systemic State-sponsored compulsion, but rather merely occurred as the result of discrete and uncoerced individual decisions to travel for work, taken by individual migrants: See Friedman, *Race, Class and Power*, 139–40. This position is evidently incorrect, especially from a Critical Legal Realist standpoint. See, most famously, Hale, "Coercion and Distribution," 470.

43 Mafeje, "Articulation of Modes of Production," 123; Friedman, *Race, Class and Power*, 162–65.

who were performing concrete acts of labour, including literal reproduction, under patriarchal social conditions in the reserves themselves. The social role and position of women – at the intersections of "race", class and gender, in both "capitalist" and "pre-capitalist" societies – could thus not be ignored.[44] Such an analysis resonates deeply with intersectional theory, which has been explicitly held by the South African Constitutional Court to be a core interpretive approach for South Africa's Constitution and transformative constitutionalism.[45]

In terms of orthodox political-economic theory, there is also the question whether the "reserves" actually resulted in wages being strictly "cheaper" over the long run, as "cheapness" itself is a very particular term with a narrow meaning. On this there seems to be little clarity, and authors seem to avoid the question.[46] Finally, Hindson sought to problematise the structural simplicity of Wolpe's analysis by pointing out that there was no neat division between "white capitalist" relations and "black pre-capitalist" relations.[47] Rather, the system of pass laws that facilitated the migrant labour system created *two* "black" groupings: a growing urban proletariat relying on increasing wages for their reproduction, and a shrinking migrant population increasingly unable to support itself in the reserves. On this, Hindson seems to have been prescient in describing the gradual shift from inter-racial to intra-racial economic inequality in South Africa since the 1980s, and the rapid growth of a "black" middle- and upper-class alongside the perennial poor "black" majority.[48]

While it is not clear whether, in a very narrow sense, Wolpe's thesis was true as to the systemic cheapness of "black" labour as a result of the reserves, his article provoked a revolution in thought for its use of articulation itself, and for the attention it drew to social reproduction in the reserves. It may be debateable to what extent the reserves specifically cheapened labour, but it is undeniably the case that "black" women in the reserves were doing something of fundamental systemic importance, fulfilling a crucial productive and distributive role in social reproduction for capital's migrant labourers via customary

44 Friedman, *Race, Class and Power*, 195–97. As discussed prior, this argument has also been raised more generally by Marxist-feminists; see for instance Federici, *Revolution at Point Zero*, 91.

45 *Mahlangu v Minister of Labour* 2021 (2) SA 54 (CC), paras. 73–109, especially para. 79; Crenshaw, "Mapping the Margins"; Mutua, "Introducing ClassCrits," 903–17; Conaghan, "Intersectionality and the Feminist Project in Law", 21–48; Van der Westhuizen, *Sitting Pretty*, 7–17.

46 For instance: Scully and Webster, "Countryside and Capitalism", 32–33.

47 Friedman, *Race, Class and Power*, 158–61.

48 World Inequality Lab, *World Inequality Report*, 147–50.

social relations. Over time these "black" women's ability to aid in labour reproduction decreased, and this made it all the more difficult for labourers to be supported, leading in turn to increasing strike and protest action and thus State repression. The apartheid government had worked very hard to present apartheid as a political programme of separateness, especially with regard to rural areas and the supposedly "independent" Bantustans; but Wolpe's work and its reception show that we should rather analyse apartheid systemically, in motion in space and time, in terms of the real economic forces it brought into play with politics and culture, and in how it plays out through "race" and class and gender. Our task now is to turn this same lens to law.

3 Capitalism against Custom: Constitutional Law and Political Economy

> There is no space to pack
> or unpack my histories or my selves
> I am trying to move
> without attracting too much attention
> to what I don't have
> or what I have lost
> or what has been stolen from me
>
> KOLEKA PUTUMA, *Local* (2017)

Wolpe's cheap labour thesis has primarily been of interest for sociologists, political-economists and the like. But his approach equally holds immense potential for constitutional legal analysis (which is perhaps unsurprising, given that he was himself a lawyer.) Two last theoretical steps are necessary to unleash Wolpe's analytical potential here.

The first theoretical step is something I have elsewhere referred to as a critical-systemic paradigm,[49] with influences drawn from Critical Legal Realism, Law and Political Economy, and political-economic theory more broadly. A traditional formalist approach to law focusses simply on asking what the law doctrinally says; on asking a pure mechanistic legal question relating to some specific formalistic field of law. This is descended from liberal Western legal scientism, which historically used abstract analysis to shield the law from critical scrutiny – especially where its racial, gender and class

49 See Kolabhai, "Private Property as Public Unhealth," 301.

effects are concerned. In such an approach, the law is fetishised: it appears natural, timeless, universal, outside of history and society, immobile. In such an approach, the law is taken as a given.

In contrast to such formalism about what the law says, I suggest we instead adopt a critical-systemic approach, by asking the following four questions: What is the law actually concretely *doing*? Why and how has it come to do this? What could it do instead? And what should it do instead?

In an article about the constitutional transformation of South Africa's common and customary law, Davis and Klare – writing from a Critical Legal Realist standpoint – explain that there is transformative possibility where legal rules are concerned.[50] If rules are recognised as rules, instead of merely acting as invisible norms, and if they are then understood as being socially contingent, they can be studied for their material effects and transformed if different material effects are sought. This, Davis and Klare argue, is core to the notion of transformative constitutionalism as adopted in South Africa. The four critical-systemic questions above attempt to target the various aspects of Davis' and Klare's point. The questions firmly set the law within history – as a historically contingent social relation which can be reimagined and changed, theoretically and through concrete political action. They allow us to move between law and the "real world". Such an approach is critical, in that it steps back to study the effects of the law, rather than merely accepting how the law or legal theory describes itself. And it is systemic, in that it looks beyond the formal categories of property rights, contracts and so on; beyond the dichotomy between the "Western" common law and statute on the one hand and "customary law" on the other; beyond the perceived divide between "public" and "private" law; and beyond such conceptual siloes as "law", "politics" and "the economy". The critical-systemic approach draws our attention to how the legal system moves as a whole; how it moves us; and how it is moved, and can be moved, and should be moved, in return. In Marxist terms, this is a dialectical relationship between agency and structure: humans, as shaped by their societies (and legal systems), continuously (re)shape their societies, which continuously (re)shape humans, and so on, across space and time.

The second theoretical step is then to ask what law is doing in terms of political economy, and thus to ask what political-economic insights may mean for legal regulation. This is a simple idea, but critical, and often overlooked in South African legal academia: legal systems play a constitutive role in creating

---

50 Davis and Klare, "Critical Legal Realism," 27–43; Davis and Klare, "Transformative Constitutionalism," 435–49.

and maintaining a certain mode of production, in that they form a core part of the social relations in a mode. For if there are certain "laws of motion of capital" (as Marx put it), these are underpinned by the existence of actual laws, enforced by the State. As geographer David Harvey puts it:

> The territorial units that emerge in the organization of capitalist space (everything from bounded individual and collective property rights on the land to the state itself) tend to fix things in space, which contrast with the fluid movement across space of capital in all of its forms (as money, as commodities, and as production activity).[51]

This is why it is necessary to "press play", to observe the world(s) set in motion by law. Viewing "laws in motion" thus does not simply mean that the legal practices themselves are changing – although this may well be the case. Rather, it refers to the real, complex, dynamic and material effects on human society and the world at large, occurring across the geographies of space and time, as a result of what we perceive to be merely static legal relations derived from abstract legal theory. In foregrounding these dynamics, the critical-system approach allows for the foregrounding of power relations, of an explicit commitment to meaningful democracy, and of substantive equality and freedom.[52] It also allows for substantive critique of the role of law in the economy, rather than taking economic relations as a given or as natural.[53] These aspects of the approach can indeed be derived from LPE, but have for some time also been strongly present in strands of transformative constitutionalism in South Africa.[54] For instance, in the recent ground-breaking Constitutional Court case of *Daniels v Scribante*[55] – where it was held that private actors can be under positive obligations to fulfil the fundamental socio-economic rights of others[56] – Froneman J wrote in a concurring judgment:

---

51 Harvey, *Companion to Marx's Capital*, 632. For a discussion of the time and space of capital, see Harvey, *Companion to Marx's Capital*, 617–36.

52 Britton-Purdy et al., "Building a Law-And-Political-Economy Framework," 1818–32.

53 Mutua, "Introducing ClassCrits," 866–70; Britton-Purdy et al., "Building a Law-And-Political-Economy Framework"; 1794–818.

54 The Constitutional Court has explicitly said that the right to equality in s 9 of the Constitution is founded on the notion of substantive equality: *Minister of Finance v Van Heerden* 2004 (6) SA 121 (CC), paras. 22–27; *Mahlangu v Minister of Labour* 2021 (2) SA 54 (CC), paras. 55, 79–88; Albertyn, "Substantive Equality"; Albertyn, "Contested Substantive Equality".

55 *Daniels v Scribante* 2017 (4) SA 341 (CC).

56 Liebenberg and Kolabhai, "Private Power," 263–67.

> Economic efficiency may be one important justification for legal rules. But economic growth can often blind us to the limits of market-based exchanges and the distributional assumptions that underlie them. [...] The right to dignity does not easily fit into the subject of a market exchange. [...] Protecting existing (skewed) patterns of allocation and distribution of resources cannot be justified with bland reliance on efficiency when such obvious inequality in bargaining power prevents citizens from not only enjoying the benefits of that efficiency, but from protecting their basic rights.[57]

Capitalism in South Africa, for instance, cannot exist but for the law of property, contract, companies, succession, and so on, as emerge from both common law and statute, and as enforced by the State.[58] Companies most evidently have no existence without the law that constitutes them,[59] but this observation applies equally to all lawful legal relations within the State's system. Property and contract, too, fundamentally rely on legal regulation and enforcement by the State.[60] Such law is generally referred to as "ordinary law", to distinguish it from "constitutional law"; I refer to it here as "ordinary Western law", to distinguish it from constitutional law (which in South Africa is also generally Western in tradition)[61] on the one hand, and from customary law on the other. To be more

57 *Daniels v Scribante* 2017 (4) SA 341 (CC), paras. 133–42.

58 Deakin et al., "Legal Institutionalism," 188; Pistor, *Code of Capital*; Deakin et al. also stress the interconnected nature of legal systems as comprising both State law (public ordering) and private or customary arrangements.

59 For a transformative examination of corporate regulation in South Africa, see Kolabhai, "Human Rights Obligations".

60 The exception would thus be where the State lacks effective *de facto* enforcement, such as in the case of unlawful activities or the black market; but the vast majority of South Africa's economic activity operates within the scope of the law.

61 There have, of course, been many "home-grown" African contributions to the system of South African constitutional law. The Constitution itself was the product of some prominent sectors of anti-apartheid and/or anti-colonial struggle. It would be inaccurate to simply equate the present constitutional system wholesale with a European constitutional tradition. However, the transition from the colonial-apartheid State and its legal institutions to those of the present has been a tale of continuity, rather than rupture. The apartheid bench was retained; the courts and litigation look and operate largely the same; Parliament, the Cabinet and the President, the State itself and the vast majority of its colonial-apartheid body of law have all remained. How we even interpret and assess the Constitution at all is still primarily shaped by Western epistemologies, whether inherited from colonialism or borrowed from jurisdictions like Germany and Canada. This has all given rise to several significant decolonial critiques of South Africa's constitutional project, including of transformative constitutionalism itself. It is possible that transformative constitutionalism – working "within the system" – still does not in fact contain the

precise, and following the Wolpean analogy, I refer to a particular set of legal relations that underpin a mode of production as a legal mode, with various legal modes interacting together as a legal system.

The legal forms that came to constitute the capitalist legal mode are ostensibly premised on ancient Western forms of property, contract and so on. But the substantive material operation of these forms has been a long tale not of continuity, but of repeated innovation, changing with the development of each mode of production. The ancient Western legal ideas of property and contract that are still claimed to be in operation today, for instance, could be traced at least as far back as the Romans; but the Roman Empire did not have a general wandering class of exploited wage-labourers selling their labour-power on a market – under the conditions of production for exchange, constant reinvestment and profit – springing from private ownership of the means of production. In other words, while legal forms may appear to have continuity through time and space, a critical-systemic approach can highlight the discontinuities in the substantive political-economic structures belied by those forms.[62] At the same time, a critical-systemic approach can draw attention to the political-economic similarities and connections between legal systems that appear to be disparate in form. The substantive legal regime giving rise to modern capitalism first arose in the West, but today, the reality created by capitalism – upheld by international law – has compelled legal systems worldwide to be reshaped to facilitate their own localised analogous forms of capitalism. Capitalism is thus effectively universally coded across almost all domestic legal systems, which in turns facilitates capital's globalised operation.[63] This means that capital cannot operate except through global State enforcement – through the worldwide (albeit varied) use of State law and force, in the form of courts, police, armies and so on.

Capitalist economic relations are fundamentally underpinned by socio-legal relations. But this is equally true of customary economic relations. Wolpe's argument notes that custom as a social relation also often forms part of a particular mode of production, and that it plays a significant role in social

necessary material tools to achieve meaningful social, economic and political transformation in South Africa. See, for instance: Modiri, "Conquest and Constitutionalism," 300; Madlingozi, "Social Justice," 123; Modiri, "Towards a '(Post-) Apartheid' Critical Race Jurisprudence," 231; Madlingozi, "South Africa's First Black Lawyers," 517. For a critique of the trend of Western constitutionalism in "post"-colonial Africa in general, and African states' general refusal to put responsive customary legal ordering at the heart of their constitutional projects, see Chanock, "Constitutionalism, Democracy and Africa," 126.

62 As will be noted later, this is just as true of custom as it is of common law.

63 See Pistor, *Code of Capital*; Tzouvala, *Capitalism as Civilisation*.

reproduction. Concerning the State and custom, then, Wolpe's article pokes us along with the following:

> The accessibility to the migrant-worker of the product of the Reserves depends upon the *conservation*, albeit in a restructured form, of the reciprocal obligations of the family […] It is no accident that the South African State has consistently taken measures, including the recognition of much of African law and custom, the recognition of and grant of powers to chiefs, the reservation of areas of land, etc., aimed at preserving the 'tribal' communities.[64]

A political-economist may read this and move on. A legal academic would immediately see that Wolpe is drawing attention to the role of custom in the face of capital – that is, to the role of custom in the face of the Western legal mode as enforced by the State. This is the heart of our use of articulation here, of this sense of movement by law.[65] Custom is shaped by its socio-economic context, and the ordinary Western legal mode and State create real-world implications in time and space for the context in which custom finds itself. Custom in turn creates real-world implications for the ordinary Western legal mode.

Such a reading of Wolpe shows that custom under segregation and apartheid was always being made to move, being made to do something useful for capital as a result of the migrants travelling between the two spheres – even when the custom itself still appeared to be in its "purest" form. And soon, capital's incursions led to custom itself changing. While customary relations were in some sense still preserved, they were now functioning in a more totalised capitalist mode. In other words, they had been forcibly economically integrated into, and subsumed under, the predominant Western system. People living by custom were forced either to abandon their customs, or to adapt them to the changing context mostly imposed from without.[66]

---

64 Wolpe, "Capitalism and Cheap Labour-Power," 435–36.

65 Incidentally, space, time and movement play a prominent role in the etymologies of the various English terms in this discussion. "Articulation" comes from "joint" (Latin *arcus*). "Constitution" descends from a verb meaning "to set in place", "establish", "decide" (Latin *constituo*). "Capital" once referred to "heads of cattle", from "head" (Latin *caput*). "Coerce" comes from a verb meaning "to surround, confine" (Latin *coerceo*). "Custom" comes from a verb meaning "to tend to, or become accustomed to (over time)"; to "set-in-place-for-oneself" (Latin *consuesco*). "Colonise" comes from a verb meaning "to cultivate land, to protect, to worship", from an earlier verb meaning "to move around, dwell" (from Latin *colo*); its participle form is *cultus*, whence also the English word "culture".

66 Diala, "Concept of Living Customary Law," 154–59.

Gradually, this shrank the sphere of custom that was able to govern production and distribution independent of capitalism. The economic aspects of life are naturally a significant part of an individual's and community's existence. Thus, while some customs were able to continue in some way, the material practices of customary communities were made to change. If we were to consider *lobola* as a single narrow cultural act, we would see that men still continued to give *lobola* in anticipation of marriage, even as the reserves deteriorated. But if we were to view *lobola* as part of a wider cultural tradition and practice of production and distribution, we would instead see that men now had to migrate to seek work in Western industries to be able to acquire money with which to acquire the *lobola* in the first place, because their prior customs of production and distribution had to be abandoned.[67] Production came not to be for traditional purposes, or for social reproduction itself, but both production and social reproduction came to be indirectly subsumed under the capitalist system of commodity production.[68] Indeed, Chanock argues that even the customary ties that led to the mutual support between migrant labourers and the women in the reserves – a social relation core to Wolpe's thesis – in fact eventually became little more than "desperate attempts to use all the resources of kin support", which "[owed] far more to circumstance than to [customary] communalist ethic".[69]

The shifting political economy of custom has continued into the present day. For instance, a rise in *ukuthwala* abduction marriages in some rural communities – despite declining rates of marriage overall – appears to be at least partly due to the fact that rural men are increasingly unemployed and marginalised in the neoliberalised South African economy. For these men, *ukuthwala* presents a means of achieving marriage without the higher wealth they believe would be necessary to attract women and pay for the wedding and *lobola*.[70] Older women, too, often play a role in orchestrating *ukuthwala*, as their own extremely fragile economic position means they would benefit from

67 Jeff Guy held there to be one particular primary distinction between truly pre-capitalist customs and those customs which had been reshaped in capital's image (even if they retained the trappings of tradition). If in the practice of *lobola* the community produced commodities in order to exchange them for the labour-power of women, it was pre-capitalist. If, however, the community aimed to produce and accumulate commodities as an end in itself, the community – and thus to some extent the nature of *lobola* – had been reconfigured by capitalism: Guy, "Pre-Capitalist Societies," 18.

68 Snyder, "Customary Law and the Economy," 34; Seidman and Seidman, "Political Economy of Customary Law," 44; Guy, "Pre-Capitalist Societies," 18.

69 Chanock, "Law, State and Culture," 63.

70 Rice, "Understanding *Ukuthwala*," 405–07.

"the companionship, labour, and status that the acquisition of a daughter-in-law would bring".[71] Younger women, meanwhile, are accordingly subjected to increasing levels of intersectional gender-based violence as a result of the wider changes in South Africa's political economy and its effects on the customs of their communities.

Thus, the outward form of a custom may appear unaltered, but its substance might well have changed in a wider political-economic context. In other words, wider customary cultural practices which constitute the social relations underpinning non-capitalist production and distribution are gradually destroyed, and certain narrow cultural practices are retained only to the extent that they remain possible under fundamentally different cultural political-economic conditions[72] – in much the same way as the continuity of Western legal forms belied major political-economic transformations over centuries. Custom was thus not merely made subject to the direct coercion of colonialism and legal impositions; it was made subject to the indirect coercion of the capitalist world created by Western law and the State. Apartheid rhetoric implied "separate but equal", but neither of these was true: there was, in an integrated system, a fundamental power imbalance between custom and the Western legal mode.

In fact, some degree of incursion into custom has always served as the basis for capitalism in South Africa, and the Western mode has thus consistently been put to this purpose through State force. Western law's role in constituting economic benefit is what first brought the West to Africa, and brought Western law and State power against communities living by custom: from the Dutch East India Company – a creature of law – landing on African shores;[73] to serfdom, slavery and the slave trade; to Britain conquering the Cape so that it could establish and maintain economic dominance over France; to British imperialist expansion in the territory, particularly over diamonds and gold in what were then foreign Afrikaner states; to the development of capitalism in the territory; and indeed, to the unification of the territory and the creation of the modern South African State from 1910. Western law and the State, in their myriad forms, were core to colonialism and capitalism, and necessarily had to disrupt custom for capital to succeed. Capital is not merely a pile of physical

71 Rice, "Understanding *Ukuthwala*," 400.

72 Berry, for instance, discusses the institution(s) of traditional leadership in South Africa as being constituted both by "tradition" and socio-economic control; the ongoing development of traditional leadership is thus tied to capitalism and economic geography: Berry, "Chieftaincy, Land, and the State," 79.

73 Miles, *Origins of International Investment Law*, 21–47.

things; rather, it is a social relation. A pile of physical things would be meaningless without waged workers labouring with it in production. Capital thus requires a corresponding labour market, which cannot be found if indigenous populations are happily living by traditional means and ways of life with no desire to perform exploitative labour for others' profit at great personal cost. The State thus historically used the law to confiscate land and institute money-based taxes – payable only through money earned from wage labour – in order to forcibly create a workforce.[74]

It is this separation of people from the means of production and their traditional non-capitalist ways of life, through Western law and State force, that leads to the laws of motion of capital. There is no law which generally forbids eating, or which forbids labouring to produce food, or which forbids one from owning and consuming the fruit of one's labour. But the laws of property, of contract, of employment all act together to constitute the laws of motion of capital. If the means of production are predominantly privately owned, the formalist approach to law presents this as an endless static sea of atomised and disconnected property rights, each of them justified in the abstract by the principles of property law. Yet the real result of such a sea of individual property rights, when aggregated, is that the propertyless are coerced into selling their labour-power to property-owners to live. There is no alternative, as the law prohibits access to the privately owned means of survival or production. Facially, such an employment contract may appear consensual – the worker may appear to willingly conclude the contract in exchange for the wage they require to avoid starvation. But this belies the significant coercion of the legal system as a whole.[75] Property law protects the means of production from being accessed by the dispossessed: if a dispossessed person were to attempt to gain access to privately owned means of survival or means of production, or to the products of their waged labour produced with such means of production, it would amount to trespassing or theft. The State would immediately intervene – be it with the police, the army or the courts – to protect the property, and thus the functioning of capital. This is the coercive power of capital. Workers are

74 Indeed, it was Australian colonialism that led Marx to observe that capital is not merely about some portion of the means of production being privately held by capitalists, but that it further requires the creation of a labour market to compel wage-labourers to work for capitalists. Colonists landing with their capital on indigenous shores would find no willing workers; the State had to artificially drive people into positions of need, as a matter of active policy, to compel them to become wage-labourers. Capital is thus not a thing, but a relation between people mediated by things: Harvey, *Companion to Marx's Capital*, 303–04; Friedman, *Race, Class and Power*, 119.

75 See, in the Legal Realist tradition, Hale "Coercion and Distribution," 470.

forced into work, not directly, but indirectly, as the law and State actively make survival impossible otherwise. As Terreblanche puts it:

> Capitalism is not a sovereign and self-regulatory system, and it does not operate in accordance with natural economic laws. Capitalism is not a natural construct. It is a human construct and a man-made phenomenon. It is a project always in the making. A capitalist system cannot exist in a political or constitutional vacuum.[76]

Capitalism is not a natural state, but is rather an active and continuous political project, requiring constant State intervention. Wherever capital goes, it encounters resistance, and for it to move things it must overcome this resistance by force. Broadly speaking, one could identify three such types of force. First, the direct force of the State in moving people. This includes enclosing the commons or communal land through confiscation, evicting people, quelling political uprisings and worker resistance, and endless other visible displays of State power in the courts and by the police. Second, the indirect force introduced by the State's prior use, or ongoing threat, of direct force. People moving to urban areas to find work and agreeing to pitiful wages under awful conditions are moved not directly by the State, but indirectly by the deprivation caused by the State's political-economic system. Of course, this direct and indirect force may be wielded "by the State", but in reality it is predominantly the result of labour performed in the service of the State by other wage-labourers, such as members of the police force. Movement in reality – as work, or force exerted over a distance – can be described in abstract terms, but is achieved by the concrete actions of people. The third "force" is that of internalised consciousness, ideology and culture. Over time, people internalise the norms imposed on them by active force, and lose their internal drive to resist, meaning that the State has less need of active force overall. This is the sort of "force" that the Black Consciousness movement – with such prominent leaders as Steve Biko – saw it necessary to overturn first in the struggle against apartheid.[77]

It would of course be reductionist to see the State as constantly and totally an instrument for the capitalist class – especially in South Africa, with its historical tensions between poorer rural "white" Afrikaners and wealthy urban "white" English capital. Indeed, these tensions played a core role in the political development of apartheid itself, and this is precisely why Wolpe's attempt

76 Terreblanche, *Lost in Transformation*, 37.

77 Biko, *I Write What I Like*, 21–25, 50.

at studying the linkages between "race" and class was so important. Thus, responding in part to Wolpe, Yudelman points out that the State does not unilaterally dominate capital (the traditional liberal position), nor vice versa (the traditional Marxist position).[78] Rather, there is a form of symbiosis between the State and capital, with the two often collaborating even if there are tensions within each and between the both of them. Nonetheless, capital in general has always held enormous, and most often predominant, sway.

The alignment between the State and economic interests runs deep through South African history, from the Dutch East India Company acting as government and corporation both, to mining magnate Cecil John Rhodes serving as Cape Prime Minister from 1890 (and instituting the Glen Grey Act of 1894, as discussed by Wolpe), and indeed through the 20th century to the present.[79] The drive for competition unique to capitalism means that capital must constantly expand in search of greater profits, and must constantly draw more and more of life into its orbit, subjecting everything and everyone to commodification. But capital has always relied on the force of the State to achieve this. Capital in turn sustains the State through tax revenue (which is itself also ultimately derived from workers' labour). There is thus a systemic synergy between capital and the State. At every turn, then, the promise of economic benefit upheld by Western law and the State brought Europeans into conflict with non-Europeans. On a very visceral level, this led to the original "conflict of laws" and "clash of cultures" – conflicts and clashes waged by steel against indigenous peoples. In short, colonial-apartheid was not merely a project of political discrimination: it was a project of economic exploitation driven by the Western system of law and the State. This was why the apartness of the "reserves" and "Bantustans" was merely illusory; the "white" minority continued to economically rely on the exploitation of "black" labour, as the "white" population could not perform the necessary labour themselves – both for deep-seated racist ideological reasons,[80] and because capital's demands were too high. As a result, as Marx and Engels famously put it:

---

78 Friedman, *Race, Class and Power*, 149–52. Others pointed out something similar regarding capital – that while all capitalists had an interest in the maintenance of the system in general, there were conflicting interests between specific fractions of capital in particular: Friedman, *Race, Class and Power*, 155–58. For a similar analysis of the present context of complex interactions between interest groups in the State, also see: Reynolds, "Challenging Hegemony," 125.

79 Terreblanche, *History of Inequality*, 51–65; Terreblanche, *Lost in Transformation*, 39–77, and generally.

80 Van Jaarsveld, *Afrikaner's Interpretation of South African History*, 22.

> The bourgeoisie, by the rapid improvement of all instruments of production, by the immensely facilitated means of communication, draws all, even the most barbarian, nations into civilisation. It compels all nations, on pain of extinction, to adopt the bourgeois mode of production; it compels them to introduce what it calls civilisation into their midst, i.e., to become bourgeois themselves. In one word, it creates a world after its own image. The bourgeoisie has subjected the country to the rule of the towns.[81]

Through the 20th century, the Minerals-Energy Complex – "a cluster of industries, heavily promoted by the State, around mining and energy"[82] – continued to exercise determinative sway over policy, even if often in tension with the "white" nationalist government. It continued to hold such sway into and through the liberal-democratic transition.[83] And today, the alignment of the State and capital can on the one hand be seen most visibly in the phenomenon of State capture and corruption, and on the other in the extraordinary wealth of current President Cyril Ramaphosa, who represents in one person a dramatic confluence of capital and State power. This confluence was at the heart of the Marikana massacre on 16 August 2012, when thirty-four striking mine-workers were extra-judicially killed by the State at a mine where Ramaphosa was non-executive director, and where his company Shanduka was a major shareholder.[84] Historical and political-economic analysis thus moves us away

81 Marx and Engels, *Communist Manifesto*, 40–41.

82 Ashman, Fine and Newman, "The Crisis in South Africa," 178.

83 Terreblanche, *Lost in Transformation*, 47–90.

84 Ramaphosa's estimated net worth in 2021 was R6 500 000 000. The average monthly income of an employed South African was R6 400 in 2019. If the average South African worker saved every cent and spent nothing, it would take 84 636 years to reach Ramaphosa's wealth. The mine-workers at Marikana were striking for a wage of less than double the average worker's income – R12 500, or 43 333 years. (Incidentally, it would take 50 years of saved income for the average worker to match one year of the President's official remuneration.) Richest, "Cyril Ramaphosa"; Matangira "Average Salary in SA"; Marinovich, *Murder at Small Koppie*; Magaziner and Jacobs, "Notes from Marikana," 137; Cairncross and Kisting, "Platinum and Gold Mining," 513; Parliament of South Africa, *2021 Estimates of National Expenditure*, 3.

The role of Black Economic Empowerment in creating a number of "black" capitalists and in developing the "black" middle class at the ongoing expense of the poor "black" majority thus renders a modern analysis of "race" and class in "post"-apartheid South Africa phenomenally complex. Yet Ramaphosa's wealth nonetheless still pales in comparison to that of South Africa's two richest men, who are both "white". In 2019, Oxfam reported that Nicky Oppenheimer's wealth amounted to $7,7 billion (R116 000 000 000), while Johann Rupert's amounted to $7 billion (R105 000 000 000). Oxfam found that Oppenheimer,

from merely evaluating Ramaphosa's legal powers as President, or his individual property rights, to viewing his power as part of South Africa's history of both political and economic oppression – to seeing how a "black" former union leader, too, can now also play a role in violently coercing the landless "black" majority of the country for personal profit.

In sum, this Wolpean lens presents a different way of thinking about the interactions between the Constitution, capitalism and custom in South Africa. It is not a "conflict of laws" approach, which looks at a static choice of which legal mode – for instance, *either* common *or* customary law – would be applicable in a single dispute. Such an approach would narrowly focus on the legal question of whether customary law is constitutionally recognised in a particular matter, with the systems considered "equal but separate". Nor is this a "clash of cultures" approach, which would look at how the two legal modes are subject to legal-cultural exchange of varying degrees of coercion, whether at the level of normative legal intervention (such as the Constitution or statutes regulating, overruling, or outlawing custom) or at the level of culture itself (such as customs developing following the influence of Western cultural norms). Both these approaches are critically important, but they do not themselves explain the material links between corporate law in Sandton and *lobola* or *ukuthwala* in a former "reserve" – the links which materially lead the modes into legal conflict, and the legal cultures into interaction, in the first place. These approaches also cannot fully examine the political-economic role of "customary law" through the liberal democratic and neoliberal economic transition, or through the ever-shifting dynamics of the present day.

A Wolpean lens of articulation accordingly focusses not merely on the legal or cultural interactions between legal modes, nor merely on the economic interactions between modes of production. Rather, the lens presents the two legal modes in a dialectic through their real-world effects. This does not at all mean that custom is solely determined by economic factors, but simply that the economic factors brought about by the Western legal mode play a significant role in how custom is shaped. Of course, there are countless varied forms of custom concretely operating in South Africa. The theoretical analysis here is focussed not on the concrete customs themselves; rather, it is on the more general interaction between capital and custom. Because of the ubiquity of capital, driven by its own systemic need for expansion, this analysis appears to be generally applicable to any custom outside of the Western legal mode

---

Rupert and Aliko Dangote of Nigeria – Africa's three richest men – had more wealth than the poorest 50%, or 650 million people. Oxfam, *Tale of Two Continents*, 9.

in South Africa, and indeed it may be applied by analogy to other jurisdictions as well.[85] Thus, while we can abstractly discuss "legal articulation" in the singular, and while it provides an effective theoretical framework, there are concretely as many articulations (in this sense) as there are customs, as each gives rise to particular political-economic relations. Each interacts with capitalism and the Western mode differently, and each is worthy of individual study. And, importantly, custom and its communities are never merely passive "victims" of capitalist incursion. Rather, custom always equally remains a site of contestation, resistance and agency, capable of being remade both for and against capital.

The relationship between custom and capitalism is thus phenomenally nuanced and complex. But the general point is this: the hegemonic drive of capitalism compels all customs to interact with the Western legal mode in some way, and this allows us to better understand the pattern and logic behind particular cases of interaction. The general coercive interaction between custom and capital, enabled by the Constitution, is thus deserving of our attention. If we do not study the political economy of Western and customary legal modes, we will not be able to see how the Constitution still perpetuates a system of deprivation, nor imagine how the Constitution could transform this system for the better.

4 Conclusion: Towards a Substantive Constitutional Critique of Capitalism

> O spirits of my father rejoice
> for the wisdom of your words has lingered
> in the air beyond our day
> we've seen the wars of the day
> demand briefcases and cotton ties
>
> SIPHO SEPAMLA, *To Makana and Nongqawuse* (1976)

85 Of course, the Western legal mode itself also relies on its own forms of custom, often invisibly. Indeed, there is a gap between the lived reality of law and its displayed "official" prescriptions in all societies: Chanock, "Law, State and Culture," 55. My distinction between "custom" and "ordinary Western law" does not mean that ordinary Western law somehow has no characteristics whatsoever that are also held by "custom"; rather, the distinction is made to discuss the articulation and structural power imbalance between the Western legal mode and other legal modes.

What then does all this mean for the Constitution, and for how we understand it? I believe a Wolpean Law and Political Economy framework holds great value for transforming our understanding of the present constitutional dispensation's transformative potential and pitfalls. The following are only some early insights.

First, the framework is particularly amenable to interdisciplinary study. The political economy of South Africa's transition has been deeply examined, both during the formal struggle against colonial-apartheid and since. South African legal studies, outside of legal anthropology, have remained relatively insulated from these insights. A critical-systemic lens allows us to consider how the law facilitates capitalist deprivation, and how the Constitution facilitated (or was at least complicit in) the neoliberal turn in the 1990s. Cook, for instance, discusses the complex intersections of the State, traditional leadership, and colonial and neoliberal capital on the platinum belt at the time of the Marikana Massacre in 2012.[86]

Second, the framework allows us to see the continuous alignment – even if nuanced and complicated – between the State and capital, even after the fall of formal apartheid. Rather than being a "normal" or "natural order", capital is a particular political and economic project that relies on State force and law. In particular, it relies on the ordinary Western common law and statute. The idea that capital and liberal democracy – both Western in origin – are somehow the "natural" way for humans to structure their society is also, of course, a deeply colonial one. A Wolpean framework helps us see that this ordinary Western legal system is not natural; on the contrary, that it would naturally collapse if not for the constant violence that upholds it. Although the common and customary law are ostensibly "separate but equal", they are in fact neither of these. Although the Constitution claims to recognize them equally, they do not, in practice, have equal State support; and as long as the State actively upholds capital, it simultaneously upholds an active and continuous attack on custom. The State has thus never been neutral in its treatment of custom and Western law. This also means that each individual incursion into custom – each case of a mining company abusing a local indigenous community and its environment, for instance – is not an isolated case. These cases are all connected by the systemic drive for profit, upheld by the State and law. They must thus be systemically addressed, through a transformation of the Western laws constituting capitalism.

---

86 Cook, "Corporate Kings," 211. Jean and John Comaroff observe that neoliberalism has in many ways strengthened traditional leadership in Africa generally, rather than sweeping it away as pre-modern: Comaroff and Comaroff, "Chiefs, Capital, and the State".

Third, the framework helps us to see that, while it is important to consider the legal question of customary recognition (the "conflict of laws" approach) in terms of sections 211 and 212 of the Constitution, this in fact misses half the story. It is not enough to ask whether a particular instance of custom should receive the legal recognition of the State in a particular matter, because this is an acontextual and ahistorical approach to what the custom itself is. By the time a claim for customary recognition gets to court, the custom itself has already been prefigured by capital. This is not to diminish the fact that the custom is important for its adherents, or to say that the custom is not worthy of recognition even when shaped by capital. Rather, it is to say that, without a critical-systemic view, the Constitution could for the next thousand years keep recognising various instances of custom without ever "noticing" that the customs themselves were being assaulted, transformed and diminished by capital. For custom to be meaningfully recognised, it must to some extent be meaningfully free to develop without the economic coercion of the ordinary Western system of law.

Ultimately, then, the meaningful constitutional recognition of customary law is reliant on an understanding and critique of the constitutional recognition of ordinary Western law. The Constitution recognises the common law and statute; the common law and statute constitute capitalism; capitalism coerces custom; and this coerced custom is then recognised by the Constitution. To break this chain, there must be a radical political-economic critique of ordinary Western common law and statute and its effects on custom. There must thus be a constitutional argument made to transform the laws underpinning capital. This could perhaps be on the basis of the fundamental human rights relating to culture and to cultural, religious and linguistic communities in sections 30 and 31 of the South African Bill of Rights. These possibilities must still be explored, but there is – at least in theory – some real potential in the Constitution for systemic critique and transformation.[87] The question is then whether this potential can be practically realised by social movements and lawyers. Very recently, for instance, environmental and indigenous activists won prominent legal victories against British oil multinational Shell's offshore seismic survey on the Wild Coast, in the Eastern Cape, partly on the basis of *prima facie* environmental and cultural rights.[88] This points to the potential for such rights to gradually disrupt capitalist relations, if put to this purpose. Perhaps

87 Kolabhai, "Human Rights Obligations," 133–51.

88 *Sustaining The Wild Coast NPC v Minister of Mineral Resources and Energy* 2022 (2) SA 585 (ECG); *Sustaining the Wild Coast NPC v Minister of Mineral Resources and Energy* 2022 (6) SA 589 (ECMk).

most importantly, then, a critical-systemic framework invites us to consider how – by reimagining and remaking legal pluralism in Africa – we could fundamentally reconfigure our social relations to allow for a more rational, just, democratic and human system of production and distribution.

There is much more to be said for an LPE approach to custom and customary law under South Africa's Constitution. The field is certainly deserving of further study, especially given the worsening global crises, and the growing global significance of political and intellectual movements critical of capitalism, coloniality, racism and patriarchy. This chapter's proposed Wolpean framework for understanding the South African constitutional system in its political-economic context is one of many tentative early steps on that journey. I do not pretend to have unpacked all the issues at play here. But I hope that starting to think more movingly about law, that articulating the reality of transformative constitutional law in its space and time and its real effects on real people, might help us move us forward. We will have to keep moving.

Bibliography

Literature

Ackermann, Lourens W. H. "The Legal Nature of the South African Constitutional Revolution." *New Zealand Law Review* 4 (2004): 633–80.

Albertyn, Catherine. "Contested Substantive Equality in the South African Constitution: Beyond Social Inclusion Towards Systemic Justice." *South African Journal on Human Rights* 34, no. 3 (2018): 441–68.

Albertyn, Catherine. "Substantive Equality and Transformation in South Africa." *South African Journal on Human Rights* 23, no. 2 (2007): 253–76.

Ashman, Sam, Ben Fine, and Susan Newman. "The Crisis in South Africa: Neoliberalism, Financialization and Uneven and Combined Development." *Socialist Register* 47 (2011): 174–95.

Bennett, Tom, and Christina Murray. "Traditional Leaders." In *Constitutional Law of South Africa*, edited by Stu Woolman, and Michael Bishop. 2 ed, ch. 26, OS 2005. Cape Town: Juta, 2004.

Berry, Sara. "Chieftaincy, Land, and the State in Ghana and South Africa." In *The Politics of Custom: Chiefship, Capital, and the State in Contemporary Africa*, edited by John L. Comaroff, and Jean Comaroff, 79–109. Chicago: University of Chicago Press, 2018.

Bhandar, Brenna. *Colonial Lives of Property: Law, Land and Racial Regimes of Ownership*. Durham: Duke University Press, 2018.

Biko, Steve. *I Write What I Like*. Oxford: Heinemann, 1987.

Bond, Patrick. *Elite Transition: From Apartheid to Neoliberalism in South Africa*. London: Pluto Press, 2014.

Brickhill, Jason, and Yana van Leeve. "Transformative Constitutionalism: Guiding Light or Empty Slogan?" *Acta Juridica* (2015): 141–71.

Britton-Purdy, Jedediah, et al. "Building a Law-and-Political-Economy Framework: Beyond the Twentieth-Century Synthesis." *Yale Law Journal* 129, no. 6 (2019): 1784–835.

Bunting, Brian. *The Rise of the South African Reich*. London: Penguin Books, 1969.

Buthelezi, Mbongiseni, and Dineo Skosana. "The Salience of Chiefs in Postapartheid South Africa: Reflections on the Nhlapo Commission." In *The Politics of Custom: Chiefship, Capital, and the State in Contemporary Africa*, edited by John L. Comaroff, and Jean Comaroff, 110–133. Chicago: University of Chicago Press, 2018.

Cairncross, Eugene, and Sophia Kisting. "Platinum and Gold Mining in South Africa: The Context of the Marikana Massacre." *New Solutions: A Journal of Environmental and Occupational Health Policy* 25, no. 4 (2016): 513–34.

Chanock, Martin. "Constitutionalism, Democracy and Africa: Constitutionalism Upside Down." *Law in Context* 28, no. 2 (2010): 126–44.

Chanock, Martin. "Law, State and Culture: Thinking About Customary Law After Apartheid." *Acta Juridica* (1991): 52–71.

Comaroff, John, and Jean Comaroff. "Chiefs, Capital, and the State in Contemporary Africa: An Introduction." In *The Politics of Custom: Chiefship, Capital, and the State in Contemporary Africa*, edited by John L. Comaroff and Jean Comaroff, 1–48. Chicago: University of Chicago Press, 2018.

Conaghan, Joanne A. F. "Intersectionality and the Feminist Project in Law." In *Intersectionality and Beyond: Law, Power and the Politics of Location*, edited by Emily Grabham, et al. 21–48. London: Routledge-Cavendish, 2008.

Cook, Susan. "Corporate Kings and South Africa's Traditional-Industrial Complex." In *The Politics of Custom: Chiefship, Capital, and the State in Contemporary Africa*, edited by John L. Comaroff and Jean Comaroff, 211–30. Chicago: University of Chicago Press, 2018.

Crenshaw, Kimberle. "Mapping the Margins: Intersectionality, Identity Politics, and Violence Against Women of Color." *Stanford Law Review* 43, no. 6 (1991): 1241–99.

Davis, Dennis M., and Karl Klare. "Critical Legal Realism in a Nutshell." In *Research Handbook on Critical Legal Theory*, edited by Emilio Christodoulidis, Ruth Dukes, and Marco Goldoni, 27–43. Cheltenham: Edward Elgar Publishing, 2019.

Davis, Dennis M., and Karl Klare. "Transformative Constitutionalism and the Common and Customary Law." *South African Journal on Human Rights* 26, no. 3 (2010): 403–509.

Deakin, Simon, et al. "Legal Institutionalism: Capitalism and the Constitutive Role of Law." *Journal of Comparative Economics* 45, no. 1 (2017): 188–200.

Diala, Anthony C. "The Concept of Living Customary Law: A Critique." *Journal of Legal Pluralism and Unofficial Law* 49, no. 2 (2017): 143–65.

Dictionary Unit for South African English. "kwela-kwela, n." *Dictionary of South African English*. Accessed September 1, 2022. https://dsae.co.za/entry/kwela-kwela/e04173.

Dictionary Unit for South African English. "larney, n. and adj." *Dictionary of South African English*. Accessed September 1, 2022. https://dsae.co.za/entry/larney/e04243.

Dictionary Unit for South African English. "lobola, n." *Dictionary of South African English*. Accessed September 1, 2022. https://dsae.co.za/entry/lobola/e04333.

Du Toit, P., ed. *Report of the National Conference on the Poor White Problem*. Cape Town: Nasionale Pers, 1934.

Federici, Silvia. *Revolution at Point Zero: Housework, Reproduction, and Feminist Struggle*. Oakland: PM Press, 2012.

Fine, Ben. "Post-Apartheid South Africa: It's Neoliberalism, Stupid!" In *Race, Class and the Post-Apartheid Democratic State*, edited by John Reynolds, Ben Fine, and Robert van Niekerk, 75–95. Scottsville: UKZN Press, 2019.

Fine, Ben, and Alfredo Saad-Filho. *Marx's "Capital"*. 6 ed. London: Pluto Press, 2016.

Fine, Robert. "The Antimonies of Neo-Marxism." *Transformation* 11 (1990): 92–103.

Friedman, Steven. *Race, Class and Power: Harold Wolpe and the Radical Critique of Apartheid*. Scottsville: UKZN Press, 2015.

Guy, Jeff. "Analysing Pre-Capitalist Societies in Southern Africa." *Journal of Southern African Studies* 14, no. 1 (1987): 18–37.

Hale, Robert L. "Coercion and Distribution in a Supposedly Non-Coercive State." *Political Science Quarterly* 38, no. 3 (1923): 470–94.

Harvey, David. *A Companion to Marx's Capital*. London: Verso Books, 2019.

Klare, Karl E. "Legal Culture and Transformative Constitutionalism." *South African Journal on Human Rights* 14, no. 1 (1998): 146–88.

Kolabhai, Reshard Lee. "Human Rights Obligations and South African Companies: A Transformative Approach." LLM diss., Stellenbosch University, 2020.

Kolabhai, Reshard Lee. "Private Property as Public Unhealth: A Critical-Systemic Paradigm in Times of Crises." In *Property and Pandemics: Property Law Responses to Covid-19*, edited by Zsa-Zsa Temmers-Boggenpoel, et al., eds, 301–28. Cape Town: Juta, 2021.

Langa, Pius. "Transformative Constitutionalism." *Stellenbosch Law Review* 17, no. 3 (2006): 351–60.

Legassick, Martin. "Colonialism of a Special Type and the Approach of the Marxist Workers' Tendency of the African National Congress to the National Question." In *Race, Class and the Post-Apartheid Democratic State*, edited by John Reynolds, Ben Fine, and Robert van Niekerk, 57–71. Scottsville: UKZN Press, 2019.

Liebenberg, Sandra, and Reshard Lee Kolabhai. "Private Power, Socio-Economic Transformation, and the Bill of Rights." In *Law, Justice and Transformation*, edited by Zsa-Zsa Temmers Boggenpoel, 245–83. Johannesburg: LexisNexis, 2022.

Liebenberg, Sandra. *Socio-Economic Rights: Adjudication Under a Transformative Constitution*. Cape Town: Juta, 2010.

Madlingozi, Tshepo. "Social Justice in a Time of Neo-Apartheid Constitutionalism: Critiquing the Anti-Black Economy of Recognition, Incorporation and Distribution." *Stellenbosch Law Review* 28, no. 1 (2017): 123–47.

Madlingozi, Tshepo. "South Africa's First Black Lawyers, amaRespectables and the Birth of Evolutionary Constitution: A Review of Tembeka Ngcukaitobi's *The Land is Ours*: South Africa's First Black Lawyers and the Birth of Constitutionalism." *South African Journal on Human Rights* 34, no. 3 (2018): 517–29.

Mafeje, Archie. "On the Articulation of Modes of Production." *Journal of Southern African Studies* 8, no. 1 (1981): 123–38.

Magaziner, Daniel, and Sean Jacobs. "Notes from Marikana, South Africa: The Platinum Miners' Strike, the Massacre, and the Struggle for Equivalence." *International Labor and Working-Class History* 83 (2013): 137–42.

Marinovich, Greg. *Murder at Small Koppie: The Real Story of the Marikana Massacre*. Cape Town: Penguin Books, 2016.

Marx, Karl, and Friedrich Engels. *The Communist Manifesto (1888 English Translation)*. London: Arcturus Publishing, 2017.

Matangira, Lungelo. "Study: Average Salary in SA is R6,400 and It's Not Enough to Live On." *EWN*. Last modified June 25, 2019. Accessed January 13, 2022. https://ewn.co.za/2019/06/25/study-reveals-average-salary-in-sa-is-r6-400-and-it-s-not-enough-to-live-on.

Miles, Kate. *The Origins of International Investment Law: Empire, Environment and the Safeguarding of Capital*. Cambridge: Cambridge University Press, 2013.

Modiri, Joel M. "Conquest and Constitutionalism: First Thoughts on an Alternative Jurisprudence." *South African Journal on Human Rights* 34, no. 3 (2018): 300–25.

Modiri, Joel M. "Towards a '(Post-) Apartheid' Critical Race Jurisprudence: 'Divining Our Racial Themes'." *Southern African Public Law* 27, no. 1 (2012): 231–58.

Moseneke, Dikgang. "The Fourth Bram Fischer Memorial Lecture: Transformative Adjudication (2002)." *South African Journal on Human Rights* 18 (2002): 309–19.

Mutua, Athena D. "Introducing ClassCrits: From Class Blindness to a Critical Legal Analysis of Economic Inequality." *Buffalo Law Review* 56, no. 4 (2008): 859–913.

Nyapokoto, Raimond. "The Road Between Sandton and Alexandra Township: A Fanonian Approach to the Study of Poverty and Privilege in South Africa." PhD diss., University of South Africa, 2014.

O'Laughlin, Bridget. "No Separate Spheres: The Contingent Reproduction of Living Labor in Southern Africa." *Review of International Political Economy* 29, no. 6 (2022): 1827–46.

Oxfam. *A Tale of Two Continents: Fighting Inequality in Africa.* Oxford: Oxfam, 2019.

Padayachee, Vishnu. "Harold Wolpe and the (Failed) Transformation of South African Capitalism." In *Race, Class and the Post-Apartheid Democratic State*, edited by John Reynolds, Ben Fine, and Robert van Niekerk, 96–121. Scottsville: UKZN Press, 2019.

Parliament of South Africa. *2021 Estimates of National Expenditure: Vote 1: The Presidency*. Pretoria: South African National Treasury, 2021.

Pistor, Katharina. *The Code of Capital: How the Law Creates Wealth and Inequality*. Princeton: Princeton University Press, 2019.

Rautenbach, Christa, ed. *Introduction to Legal Pluralism in South Africa.* 6 ed. Durban: LexisNexis, 2021.

Reynolds, John, Ben Fine, and Robert van Niekerk, eds. *Race, Class and the Post-Apartheid Democratic State*. Scottsville: UKZN Press, 2019.

Reynolds, John. "Challenging Hegemony within the South African State." In *Race, Class and the Post-Apartheid Democratic State*, edited by John Reynolds, Ben Fine, and Robert van Niekerk, 125–40. Scottsville: UKZN Press, 2019.

Rice, Kathleen. "Understanding *Ukuthwala*: Bride Abduction in the Rural Eastern Cape, South Africa." *African Studies* 77, no. 3 (2018): 394–411.

Richest. "Cyril Ramaphosa." Last modified October 25, 2021. Accessed January 13, 2022. https://www.richest.co.za/net-worth/cyril-ramaphosa-net-worth/.

Roux, Theunis. "Transformative Constitutionalism and the Best Interpretation of the South African Constitution: Distinction Without a Difference?" *Stellenbosch Law Review* 20, no. 2 (2009): 258–85.

Scully, Ben, and Edward Webster. "The Countryside and Capitalism: Rethinking the Cheap Labour Thesis in Post-Apartheid South Africa." In *Race, Class and the Post-Apartheid Democratic State*, edited by John Reynolds, Ben Fine, and Robert van Niekerk, 29–56. Scottsville: UKZN Press, 2019.

Seidman, Ann, and Robert B. Seidman. "The Political Economy of Customary Law in the Former British Territories of Africa." *Journal of African Law*, 28, no. 1–2 (1984): 44–55.

Shope, Janet Hinson. "'Lobola is Here to Stay': Rural Black Women and the Contradictory Meanings of Lobolo in Post-Apartheid South Africa." *Agenda* 20, no. 68 (2006): 64–72.

Siegel, Nica. "Thinking the Boundaries of Customary Law in South Africa." *South African Journal on Human Rights* 31, no. 2 (2015): 357–78.

Smedley, Audrey, and Brian D. Smedley. "Race as Biology is Fiction, Racism as a Social Problem is Real: Anthropological and Historical Perspectives on the Social Construction of Race." *American Psychologist* 60, no. 1 (2005): 16–26.

Snyder, Francis. "Customary Law and the Economy." *Journal of African Law* 28, no. 1–2 (1984): 34–43.

Stats SA. *Poverty Trends in South Africa*. Pretoria: Statistics South Africa, 2017.

Terreblanche, Sampie. *A History of Inequality in South Africa: 1652–2002*. Pietermaritzburg: University of KwaZulu-Natal Press, 2002.

Terreblanche, Sampie. *Lost in Transformation*. Johannesburg: KMM Review, 2012.

Tzouvala, Ntina. *Capitalism as Civilisation: A History of International Law*. Cambridge: Cambridge University Press, 2020.

Van der Westhuizen, Christi. *Sitting Pretty: White Afrikaans Women in Postapartheid South Africa*. Scottsville: UKZN Press, 2018.

Van Huyssteen, Elsa. "The Constitutional Court and the Redistribution of Power in South Africa: Towards Transformative Constitutionalism." *African Studies* 59, no. 2 (2000): 245–65.

Van Jaarsveld, Floris Albertus. *The Afrikaner's Interpretation of South African History*. Cape Town: Simondium Publishers, 1964.

Van Marle, Karin. "Transformative Constitutionalism as/and Critique." *Stellenbosch Law Review* 20, no. 2 (2009): 286–301.

Wolpe, Harold. "Capitalism and Cheap Labour-Power in South Africa: From Segregation to Apartheid." *Economy and Society* 1, no. 4 (1972): 425–56.

World Inequality Lab. *World Inequality Report: Part II – Trends in Global Income Inequality*. Paris: World Inequality Lab, 2018.

Case Law

AB v Minister of Social Development 2017 (3) SA 570 (CC).

Beadica 231 CC v Trustees for the Time Being of the Oregon Trust 2020 (5) SA 247 (CC).

City of Tshwane Metropolitan Municipality v Afriforum 2016 (6) SA 279 (CC).

Daniels v Scribante 2017 (4) SA 341 (CC).

Hassam v Jacobs NO 2009 (5) SA 572 (CC).

Mahlangu v Minister of Labour 2021 (2) SA 54 (CC).

Minister of Finance v Van Heerden 2004 (6) SA 121 (CC).

Print Media South Africa v Minister of Home Affairs 2012 (6) SA 443 (CC).

Road Accident Fund v Mdeyide 2011 (2) SA 26 (CC).

Sustaining The Wild Coast NPC v Minister of Mineral Resources and Energy 2022 (2) SA 585 (ECG).

Sustaining the Wild Coast NPC v Minister of Mineral Resources and Energy 2022 (6) SA 589 (ECMk).

Legislation and Government Publications

Constitution of the Republic of South Africa 200 of 1993.
Constitution of the Republic of South Africa, 1996.
Glen Grey Act 25 of 1894.
Native Land Act 27 of 1913.

Epilogue

Albie Sachs

Throughout the African continent, customary law has rich integrity and meaning for millions. It provides strong elements of human solidarity and interdependence, coupled with particularities of identity that give layered textures to people's lives. If evidence of the enduring significance of customary law were needed, the chapters in this book provide eloquent testimony. Some authors explain, however, that they are deeply disturbed by the fact that the full potential richness of customary law is constantly being undermined by attempts to force it into the mold of Western concepts.

They point to the incongruence of African countries gaining their independence and then adopting the legal principles of the European colonisers who had damaged their societies. They argue that colonialism disrupted indigenous culture, and communities didn't give themselves time to heal and return to their roots. In their view, the use of multiple legal systems has placed customary law in Africa in a significantly weakened position. They discuss legislative and judicial positions, which reflect Western notions, deprived customary law of its intrinsic vitality, adding that the rise of capitalism across Africa has deepened individualistic attitudes that manifest themselves powerfully in common and civil law.

They state further that under the influence of Western law, there has been a great weakening of the sense of belonging to a community and of the need to find consensus; that customary law doesn't fit into Western-type legal systems in any meaningful way, and that the status of women has also deteriorated because of Western thinking, alluding positively to the fact that customary law historically treated the status of men and women as being complementary. The authors go on to argue that combining Western and African law is "jurispathic", that is, it either destroys or negatively alters customary law. To add insult to injury, an already undermined customary law has been subjected to a further caveat that it should not be applied to the extent that it may be repugnant to what have been called "civilised values".

What remedy do the authors offer to the rampant jurispathology? Their answer is to call for what they term "adaptive legal pluralism". In their view, adaptive legal pluralism would be based on the notion of healing customary law from the manner in which it has been crimped and distorted in colonial and post-colonial societies. A key element of this healing would be restoring customary law's primary functions of enhancing social, economic and cultural

 | DOI:10.1163/9789004696747_015

interdependency by focussing on how its foundational values of communal welfare influence normative adaptations rather than individualistic Western-style forensic combat.

At this stage, let me make a disclosure. In my writings both off and on the Constitutional Court in South Africa, I have expressed views on customary law that place it in a substantially different matrix to the one the authors adopt. In particular, in their comprehensive introduction, they barely touch on the decisions of the Constitutional Court on customary law and, more significantly, the concept advanced by the Court of living customary law.[1] I had assumed that when this book's authors had asked me to write this conclusion, they had been well aware of my strong support for the notion of living customary law. But to make quite sure, I expressly asked them: knowing that many of my positions are dramatically different to yours, are you sure you want me to write this conclusion? Their answer was an emphatic yes. They added that if we end up in a "bee's nest", so be it.

From this, I infer that what they want from me is far from the usual bland, back-patting words contained in conclusions and prefaces. They invite something much more exciting! What they are challenging me to do is to engage seriously with the key issues they raise and provide candid, open comments on them. Their objective, I surmise, is that I would create a counterpoint to their texts and, hopefully, give added life and vitality to the book. If that is their dare, then I accept. Into the bees' nest, we go.

Let me start with the honey where I find myself in agreement with the authors. There is much of it. To begin with, I agree that notions of harsh individualism in African legal systems, introduced by Western-type legal thinking, have diminished strong African cultural and legal traditions of human interdependence and solidarity. I further agree that social solidarity and consensus-seeking have been unduly undermined by overemphasising adversarial forms of legal combat. Third, I fully endorse the strong stand the authors take against the choice of law or conflict of law paradigms that were retained and promoted in most post-independence African states. The dismally self-perpetuating result of the choice of law approach has been to divide the nation into what has come to be seen as a modern, dynamic, forward-looking, elite and urban-based section of the community, on the one hand, that appeared to be leading society into the future and, on the other hand, the rural and urban poor, regarded

1 Rautenbach explores the position of the Constitutional Court and delves somewhat into distinctions between "living" and "official" customary law within the framework of succession and inheritance in Ch 2. Unfortunately, however, the significance of this distinction doesn't feature at all in the intellectual scene-setting established by the 'Introduction'.

as being still stuck in and tenaciously clinging to the outmoded customs and values of the past. Fourth, I totally support the authors in their rejection of the repugnancy override. Indeed, it is hard to think of anything more repugnant than the repugnancy test itself. Finally, I would like to express my enthusiasm for the notion they have coined of "adaptive legal pluralism". I would, however, propose one change: to add the word "interactive" so that the phrase would read "adaptive, interactive legal pluralism". Later I will explain this addition.

And this is where the debate gets exciting, and the contrarian bees start to buzz, with several stings at the ready. The bees are not agitated by the need for adaptations to restore core principles of customary law relating to human interdependence and solidarity. Indeed, they support adaptations. But the actual adaptations for which they are willing to put their bodies on the line, are in fact very different to the ones the authors are calling for. As the bees would have it, the required adaptations should not be based on restoring an idealised and heavily patriarchal system of customary law that would be separated from and immunised against the generalised egalitarian law of the country. Nor should the adaptations be directed towards enabling customary law to evolve in its own space according solely to its own discreet, inherited and internal systemic logic. Rather, the adaptations should have the goal of allowing customary law to grow and flourish as an organic and enriching system of law that not only draws sustenance for itself from this new reality but also feeds into and influences the emerging socio-economic and constitutional reality. Far from being "jurispathic", congruence with this hard-won new Constitutional values will be "jurisalving".

As will become clear from what appears below, I identify strongly with these metaphorical bees. I do so on the basis of experience gained in the processes that led to customary law receiving full constitutional recognition in our new democracy. I also draw on my experience as a Justice of the Constitutional Court as we responded to a constitutional injunction to apply customary law as an original source of law and develop it in keeping with the egalitarian spirit of the Constitution and the Bill of Rights.[2] Although my focus will be on specific experiences in South Africa, my years of living in Mozambique and Kenya and working on the development of their respective legal systems lead me to believe that the perspectives that we have developed here on customary law have considerable relevance for the spectrum of possible developments in the rest of the African continent.

Let me start with Section 211 of the Constitution of South Africa. It declares:

2 Constitution of the Republic of South Africa, 1996.

(1) The institution, status and role of traditional leadership, according to customary law, are recognised, subject to the Constitution …
(2) *The courts must apply customary law when that law is applicable, subject to the Constitution and any legislation that specifically deals with customary law.*[3]

The implications of the latter provision for customary law are enormous. Customary law is given full status as an original source of law, equal in force and effect to the common law that had originally, in the colonial era, been derived in substance from Roman-Dutch law and in the process, from judicial review in England. It is worth repeating: customary law now has full constitutional force and effect for the millions of South Africans, in countryside and in town, who regulate their lives according to its norms and processes. What's more, all the courts of the land must entertain and deal with customary law where applicable.

At the same time, section 212 makes it clear that far from customary law, either being envisaged as operating outside of the country's general constitutional and legislative framework and far from it being treated as an autonomous system of law capable of being immunised against the principles of human dignity, equality and freedom, it is expressly made subject to these hard-fought-for and central values of the new constitutional order.

The core theme, then, is one of interaction rather than separation between customary law and other sources of law. This interactive relationship is further underlined by section 39 of the Constitution, which provides:

> When interpreting any legislation, and when developing the common law or customary law, every Court … must promote the spirit, purport, and objects of the Bill of Rights.

Please note: Customary law is not being singled out for therapeutic constitutional treatment as though it were some junior, immature system of law in need of vitamin injections. The exact same developmental injunction applies to the common law. And similarly, all legislation must be interpreted with the purpose of promoting the spirit of the Bill of Rights.

This broad, interactive, two-way relationship between the Constitution and customary law has had two significant consequences. In the first place, it has demonstrated how the core principles of human interdependence and

3 Emphasis added.

solidarity, so prominent in customary law, have in South Africa started to exert an influence well beyond the limited sphere of customary law itself. They have come to enrich the fabric of the whole of the country's legal system and, indeed, enable the Constitution to be better understood and applied in a manner that is deeply meaningful to the majority of the people. It might take some time before the full significance and operational ability of these principles is acknowledged in the lower courts, in Parliament, and in all of our law schools. But as I will show later, a meaningful start has been made. Indeed, it is striking to see how in many public controversies today, ancient traditions of human interdependence are conjoined with vigorous contemporary denunciations of what is called neoliberalism to critique the harsh individualism of much of contemporary life.

Secondly and conversely, it shows how the hard-won constitutional principles of equality and non-sexism, so tenaciously fought for by African feminists, have not been banished from customary law but, in fact, directed to flow into and provide continuing relevance and vitality to it. The central tenet of this epilogue, then, is as follows: What for the authors appears to be a source of lamentable Western-inspired assimilation of customary law, I see as a creative Africa-inspired initiative designed to ensure a long and invigorated life for its core elements. What is the source of my contrariness? My reflections on the U-word *ubuntu*, the P-word Patriarchy, the M and M-words Mix and Match, and the A-word Accountability. I will deal with each in turn.

1 Ubuntu

Let me start with the story of how core principles of customary law embodied in the term *ubuntu* came to be infused into our jurisprudence to humanise and enrich the general body of law in South Africa. It began with the insertion of the word *ubuntu,* a profound aspect of African philosophy, culture and law into the postamble of our country's Interim Constitution.[4] In poetic rather than technical language, the postamble underlined the need to confront and deal with the injustices of the past but to do so not in a spirit of retaliation and vengeance but in a spirit of reconciliation and *ubuntu*. These words opened the way for legislation by the new democratically elected Parliament to create a form of transitional justice by establishing the Truth and Reconciliation Commission. Headed by the late Archbishop Desmond Tutu, its hearings were

4 Constitution of the Republic of South Africa 200 of 1993.

conducted without the stiff formalities of a Western-type court of law. They were held in school and church halls in the community, frequently beginning with the people there singing hymns and saying prayers. Translators and comforters accompanied the witnesses, many of whom broke down and wept. The objective was to give voice to people who had suffered so much, speaking in their own language of the traumas to which they had been subjected.

Quite separately, in the context of formal Court proceedings, Justice Yvonne Mokgoro, the first African woman judge in the country, introduced the concept of *ubuntu* into South African jurisprudence. She did so in the *Makwanyane* case, the very first matter heard by the newly created Constitutional Court in 1995, which dealt with the constitutionality of the death penalty. She explained:[5]

> Generally, *ubuntu* translates as 'humaneness'. In its most fundamental sense it translates as personhood and 'morality'. Metaphorically, it expresses itself in *umuntu ngumuntu ngabantu*, describing the significance of group solidarity on survival issues so central to the survival of communities. While it envelopes the key values of group solidarity, compassion, respect, human dignity, conformity to basic norms and collective unity, in its fundamental sense it denotes humanity and morality. Its spirit emphasises a respect for human dignity, marking a shift from confrontation to conciliation.

Five of us joined her in referring to *ubuntu*. Justice Pius Langa stated that it was against a background of the loss of respect for human life and the inherent dignity which attaches to every person that a spontaneous call had arisen among sections of the community for a return to *ubuntu*. Justice Thole Madala similarly wrote that the concept of *ubuntu* permeated the Constitution generally and carried in it the ideas of humaneness, social justice and fairness.

Justice Ismail Mahomed declared that the need for *ubuntu* expressed the ethos of an instinctive capacity for and enjoyment of love towards our fellow men and women. In addition, the President of the Court [later called the Chief Justice] Arthur Chaskalson referred to the constitutional relevance of *ubuntu*, as did I in my concurring judgment. From the word go, then, even before the final Constitution came explicitly to grant full recognition of customary law as a source of law in South Africa, more than half the Justices on the Court were drawing on *ubuntu* as having a direct bearing on how the Bill of Rights had to be interpreted.

5 See *S v Makwanyane* 1995 (3) SA 391 (CC) para 308.

I should add that, at that stage, I did not regard *ubuntu* as an operational legal principle in and of itself but, rather, as an important value that would help with the interpretation of our Bill of Rights. Some years later, when writing the judgment for the Court in the *Port Elizabeth Municipality* case, I found myself changing my mind. I wrote that it was not only the dignity of the poor that was assailed when homeless people were driven from pillar to post in a desperate quest for a place where they and their family could rest their heads; our society as a whole was demeaned. The Constitution and the relevant statute confirmed that we were not islands unto ourselves. The judgment, concurred in by all my colleagues, then went on to say:[6]

> The spirit of *ubuntu*, part of the deep cultural heritage of the majority of the population, suffuses the whole constitutional order. It combines individual rights with a communitarian philosophy as a unifying motif of the Bill of Rights which is nothing if not a structured, institutionalised and operational declaration in our evolving new society of the need for human interdependence, respect and concern.

Later, in *Dikoko*,[7] a civil law matter, Justice Mokgoro invoked the spirit of *ubuntu* or *botho* to urge the Court to move away from awarding monetary damages for defamation towards encouraging and requiring an apology. Justice Mokgoro wrote that traditional law and culture had been related closely to *ubuntu* or *botho*, an idea based on a deep respect for the humanity of another; traditional law and culture had long considered that one of the principal objectives of the law was the restoration of harmonious human and social relationships where an infraction of community norms had ruptured them. The goal of civil courts in defamation matters should accordingly be to knit together shattered relationships in the community and encourage across-the-board respect for the basic norms of human and social interdependence.

In endorsing her approach,[8] I added that *ubuntu-botho* was intrinsic to and constitutive of our constitutional culture. Historically it was foundational to the spirit of reconciliation and bridge-building that enabled our deeply traumatised society to overcome and transcend the divisions of the past. In present-day terms it had an enduring and creative character, representing the element of human solidarity that bound together human dignity, equality and freedom to create an affirmative and mutually supportive triad of central

6 *Port Elizabeth Municipality v Various Occupiers* 2005 (1) SA 217 (CC) para 37.
7 *Dikoko v Mokhatla* 2006 (6) SA 235 (CC), para 68.
8 Ibid, para 113.

constitutional values. Deeply rooted in our society, it linked up with the world-wide striving to develop restorative systems of justice based on reparative rather than purely punitive principles. These concepts harmonised well with processes well-known to traditional forms of dispute resolution in our country. Recently, the principles had been applied creatively in the High Court[9] in a way that combined a suspended custodial sentence in a homicide case with an apology from a senior representative of the family of the accused, as requested and acknowledged by the mother of the deceased.

Finally, I will refer to the *Richtersveld* case[10] to show how in relation to property rights respect for customary law came to play a decisive role in how the Bill of Rights was to be interpreted. Section 25(7) of the Constitution provides that a person or community dispossessed of property after 9 June 1913 due to racially discriminatory laws or practices is entitled to restitution or alternative redress. The Richtersveld community had been squeezed off land in the Northern Cape after 1913 to make way for a State diamond mining company. The pattern of dispossession was clearly a racial one. They and their forebearers had occupied the land for centuries. Described in the past as a nomadic people, they had no title deeds to show ownership of any portions of the land. The critical legal question in the case was whether, in these circumstances, they had had any property rights of which they had been dispossessed. In a unanimous judgment, delivered in the name of the Court, it was stated that the nature and the content of the rights that the Richtersveld Community held in the land had to be determined by reference to indigenous law:[11]

> That is the law which governed its land rights. Those rights cannot be determined by reference to common law. … While in the past indigenous law was seen through the common law lens, it must now be seen as an integral part of our law. Like all law it depends for its ultimate force and validity on the Constitution. Its validity must now be determined by reference not to common law, but to the Constitutions.

Clearly, the Constitution acknowledged the originality and distinctiveness of indigenous law as an independent source of norms within the legal system. At the same time the Constitution, while giving force to indigenous law, made it clear that such law was subject to the Constitution and had to be interpreted

9 *S v Maluleke* 2008 (1) SACR 49 (T) referred to by myself in *Dikoko v Mokhatla* 2006 (6) SA 235 (CC), para 15 note 7.

10 *Alexkor Ltd v Richtersveld Community* 2004 (5) SA 460 (CC).

11 Ibid, paras. 50–51.

in the light of its values. Furthermore, like the common law, indigenous law was subject to any legislation consistent with the Constitution that specifically dealt with it: "In the result, indigenous law feeds into, nourishes, fuses with and becomes part of the amalgam of South African law".[12]

It was important in applying indigenous law to bear in mind that, unlike common law, indigenous law is not written. It is a system of law known to the community, practised and passed on from generation to generation. It is a system of law that has its own values and norms. Throughout its history, it had evolved and developed to meet the changing needs of the community. And it would continue to evolve within the context of its values and norms consistently with the Constitution. The dangers of looking at indigenous law through a common law prism were obvious. The two systems of law developed in different situations, under different cultures and in response to different conditions. The Court concluded that:[13]

> In the light of the evidence ... we are of the view that the real character of the title that the Richtersveld Community possessed in the subject land was a right of communal ownership under indigenous law. The content of that right included the right to exclusive occupation and use of the subject land by members of the community. The community had the right to use its water, to use its land for grazing and hunting and to exploit its natural resources, above and beneath the surface. It follows therefore that the Richtersveld Community had a right of ownership in the subject land under indigenous law.

2 Patriarchy

Having dealt with the impact traditional law concepts have had on how to interpret the South African Constitution and develop the common law, I now move to consider how the Constitution, in turn, not only impacted on the development of customary law, but contributed to recuperating its vigour and vitality. Crucial to this process is the fact that the warrior bees doing battle for introducing the principles of non-sexism and equality into customary law have not been Western human rights ideologues combatting gender discrimination

12 Ibid, para. 51.

13 Ibid, para. 62.

but African feminists fighting against what they termed the triple oppression of African women, as Africans, as African women and as workers.

I was witness to several angry spats during the constitutional negotiations at CODESA.[14] If the indignant exchange between Nelson Mandela and F W de Klerk was the most famous, and the row between Joe Slovo and Tony Leon the nastiest, for sheer barely controlled rage, nothing could compare with the standoff in an internal ANC (African National Congress) encounter between ANC Women's League feminists Baleka Mbete and Mavivi Mayakaka-Manzini, on the one hand, and CONTRALESA[15] male traditional leaders Phatekile Holomisa and Mvelo Nonkonyana, on the other. The background to the bottled-up rage was a debate inside the ANC on the future of Customary Law, which had reached a sticking point. The Women's League insisted on the supremacy of the principles of non-sexism and equality throughout the Constitution. For their part, the all-male CONTRALESA was adamant that customary law should have autonomous space within which to recover from the way its core elements had been undermined by Western law and then be allowed to develop in its own way according to its own time-honoured principles.

After long and heavy negotiations, an ANC task force crafted a compromise – traditional law would receive full constitutional recognition as an original source of law but would do so on the basis that it progressively moved towards full equality between men and women. A time and a place were then fixed for putting the compromise text to representatives of the Women's League and CONTRALESA for their acceptance. I had not been a party to the development of the compromise but was asked to attend the encounter as a member of the ANC Constitutional Committee and its National Executive.

As it turned out, the Women's League team, though profoundly unhappy, turned up for the meeting, but CONTRALESA decided to boycott it. We surmised that they could not stomach the idea of being seen to be agreeing to a future customary law that was not based on male leadership. No one was there to champion the compromise. The result was that the only position left on the table was that that had been forcefully advanced by the Women's League. The

14 CODESA (Convention for a Democratic South Africa) was a series of negotiations that took place in South Africa between 1991 and 1993. It played a crucial role in the transition from a system of racial segregation and discrimination to a democratic and non-racial society.

15 CONTRALESA (Congress of Traditional Leaders of South Africa) refers to a prominent organisation representing the interests of traditional leaders in South Africa. It was established in 1987 with the primary objective of uniting and advocating for the rights and concerns of traditional leaders and the communities they represent.

position of the Women's League, which had fought hard for many years to raise awareness of sexism inside the ANC, represented the overwhelming feeling of the ANC membership at the time, male and female. The principle of making customary law subject to the equality provisions of the Constitution was duly incorporated into the text of one of the Principles that would be binding on the drafters of the final Constitution and, as we have seen, ended up in the language used in section 211(3).

CONTRALESA was not yet done, however. When in 1996, the text of South Africa's final Constitution was forwarded to the Constitutional Court to be certified as complying with 34 Principles that had been agreed to in advance at CODESA, the public were given an opportunity to advance objections to it. CONTRALESA took this opportunity to challenge the subordination of customary law to the principles of equality, contending in their written submissions that this was not recognising customary law but destroying it.

I remember those moments well. I had been tasked with receiving, compiling and ordering all the objections. I received a message from Reception at the Court that Winnie Mandela wished to see me about the presentation of an objection. I wasn't enthusiastic about a personal meeting with an individual connected with litigants but was informed that she had a query about a purely procedural matter. I agreed to meet her, and felt even more uncomfortable when she came to my Chambers, flung her arms around me and explained that she was working with traditional leaders Phatekile Holomisa and Mvelo Nonkonyana. Both were advocates, and their query was not about the substance of their objection but about whether they should appear in Court in their capacity as advocates or as traditional leaders. I told her that only the President of the Court, Arthur Chaskalson, could answer their question and arranged for them to discuss the matter directly with him. When later that afternoon they arrived twenty minutes after the starting time allotted to them; a number of us assumed that Winnie Mandela caused the delay. But we were wrong. Apparently, Arthur Chaskalson had told them that it didn't matter in what capacity they addressed us; the argument would be the same. But in what he had intended to be taken as light-hearted banter of the kind frequently used by lawyers, he had suggested that they could shake up the heavy formalism of the proceedings by appearing in their traditional regalia. Taking his light-hearted comment seriously, they battled through the traffic to go home and change into traditional wear. And I must say, it produced one of the most memorable moments of my 15 years on the Bench. They looked resplendent in the crowded Court, addressing us eloquently not as smooth, heavily robed advocates but as proud African traditional leaders, with much more of their torsos exposed than counsel usually displayed. It reminded me of the famous day more than 30 years earlier when Nelson Mandela, dressed in traditional Xhosa regalia, asked the magistrate to recuse himself because he, Mandela, felt like he was a black man in a white man's court.

Their argument was simple. They told us that indigenous law is based both on custom and tradition; custom is the source of law while tradition is the basis of morality, the two fusing in the application and development of indigenous law; in their view, patriarchal principles which underlay much of indigenous law would be outlawed by the Bill of Rights, thereby undermining the core of indigenous law. They said this would jeopardise such hallowed institutions as lobola (bridewealth), open the way to allowing women to succeed in the monarchy on the same basis as men, and prevent a father from claiming damages for the seduction of his daughter.

The Court's judgment with respect to this argument was unanimous. It pointed out that the role of the Court was not to adjudicate on the merits of the text as drafted but simply to decide whether the text complied with the pre-requisites of the relevant Principle. The relevant Principle expressly stated that indigenous law, like common law, should be recognised and applied by the courts subject to the fundamental rights contained in the Constitution and to legislation dealing with it. The objection, in effect, appeared to be directed at the constitutional Principle rather than the text of section 211(3). Accordingly, the Court could not say that the text was in conflict with the relevant Principle and was obliged to reject the objection.

A decade later, exactly as CONTRALESA had feared, the matter of whether a woman could be a monarch came to the Court. Mrs Shilubana, who happened to be a Member of Parliament at the time, had been appointed by the government to assume the position of *Hosi* (Sovereign) of the Valoyi community. This happened after the Valoyi Royal Family had supported her taking up the role, as had a subsequent general meeting of the community. Shortly before his passing, however, her male cousin, who had then been the incumbent *Hosi*, had changed his mind and said that his son should succeed him. The son had then gone to court to challenge the appointment of Mrs Shilubana, claiming that, in terms of traditional law, women were not permitted to occupy the position of *Hosi*, saying that traditional leaders are born and not chosen. The High Court upheld the challenge.[16] The Supreme Court of Appeal agreed.[17] The matter was taken on further appeal to the Constitutional Court.[18] Two busloads of women journeyed through the night and took turns to sit in on the proceedings, eager

16 *Nwamitwa v Phillia* 2005 (3) SA 536 (T).
17 *Shilubana v Nwamitwa* 2007 (2) SA 432 (SCA).
18 *Shilubana v Nwamitwa* 2009 (2) SA 66 (CC).

to show their support for Mrs Shilubana and the rights of women generally. A smaller group of men and women were there to support her cousin. At the end of the day, it was wonderful to watch Chief Justice Pius Langa, with the aid of a Xitsonga-speaking law clerk, thanking the women for the patient and dignified manner in which they had listened to very technical proceedings in a language not their own.

After extensive deliberation, the Court in *Shilubana v Nwamitwa*[19] unanimously upheld the appeal. It declared that the Valoyi community had the right to develop the rules governing succession to the post of *Hosi* to enable a woman to do so. In doing so, the judgment underlined the fact that customary law was a living system of law capable of constant development.

The Court had articulated the theme of living customary law in the earlier case of *Bhe*.[20] The issue, in this case, was whether the principle of primogeniture (inheritance by the nearest male relative) was consistent with the foundational constitutional value of non-sexism and the equality clause in the Bill of Rights. In that case, the facts were as follows: Although not formally married under either civil or customary law, Nontupheko Bhe, a domestic worker, lived in a conjugal partnership with Vuyo Elius Ngolombane, a carpenter. When they received an RDP (Reconstruction and Development Programme) plot of land, they moved onto it with their young daughters, Anelisa and Nonkululeko. They created an informal dwelling, which they occupied while Mr Ngolombane set about constructing a house from their monthly savings. On the early death of Mr Ngolombane, the surviving family were shocked to discover that the deceased's father had come from the Eastern Cape, claimed ownership of the land, and sought to sell it to pay for the funeral expenses. The grandfather's position was that according to customary law, neither Nontupheko Bhe nor her two daughters, Anelisa and Nonkululeko, were eligible to inherit – the mother because she hadn't been legally married and the daughters, because they were girls, and only males could inherit.

With the support of the Women's Legal Centre, Nontupheko Bhe went to court on behalf of her daughters to get a declaration that they, and not their grandfather, were the rightful heirs of their father's estate. The matter eventually reached us at the Constitutional Court.[21]

In technical terms, the Bhe family brought two constitutional challenges. The first related to section 23 of the Black Administration Act 38 of 1927. Chief Justice Pius Langa dealt swiftly with this challenge while writing for a

19 Ibid.

20 *Bhe v Magistrate, Khayelitsha* 2005 (1) SA 580 (CC).

21 Ibid.

unanimous court on this issue. He pointed out that, although amended in many respects, that section still haunts many Africans subject to the parallel regime of intestate succession it created. Observing that it was a "relic of our racist and painful past that touched a raw nerve in most South Africans", he declared it unconstitutional.[22] He then turned to deal with the main issue before the Court, namely, the constitutionality of the customary law principle of primogeniture.

I will quote from his judgment at some length. I do so not only because I signed onto it but because I believe in what I would call the general Africanity of its overall reasoning, and more specifically, in the direct and upfront manner in which it dealt with an issue hardly touched upon by the authors of this book, namely, patriarchy.

He started by emphasising in general terms that specific provisions of the Constitution required that customary law be accommodated, not merely tolerated as part of South African law. It was both protected by and subject to the Constitution in its own right. Unfortunately, however, in the past, it had been seen through the prism of common law. This had partly led to the fossilisation and codification of customary law, which in turn led to its marginalisation. The result was to deny it of its opportunity to grow in its own right and to adapt itself to changing circumstances. In this regard, he cited the words of Justice Yvonne Mokgoro, "Customary law was lamentably marginalised and allowed to degenerate into a vitrified set of norms alienated from its roots in the community".[23] In words highly relevant to the themes raised in this book, he went on to say that the consequence of viewing customary law through the lens of the common law was that its many positive aspects had long been neglected. The inherent flexibility of the system was but one of its constructive facets. Customary law placed much store in consensus-seeking and naturally provided for family and clan meetings, which offered excellent opportunities to prevent and resolve disputes and disagreements. Nor were these aspects useful only in the area of disputes. They provided a setting which contributed to the unity of family structures and the fostering of cooperation, a sense of responsibility in and of belonging to its members, and the nurturing of healthy communitarian traditions such as *ubuntu*.[24]

Chief Justice Langa then turned to the specific constitutional challenge to what he called "the official customary law" approach to succession.[25] This

---

22 Ibid, para. 68.
23 Ibid, para. 43.
24 Ibid, para. 45.
25 Ibid, para. 86.

challenge, he said, was that the official approach was based on the rule of primogeniture. He pointed out that the Bhe family contended that the rule of primogeniture stopped (a) widows from inheriting as the intestate heirs of their late husbands; (b) daughters from inheriting from their parents; (c) younger sons from inheriting from their parents; and (d) extra-marital children from inheriting from their fathers. The family claimed these exclusions were part of a scheme underpinned by male domination. The judgment made it clear that the Chief Justice fully agreed with this contention. He pointed out that at a time when the patriarchal features of the common law were progressively being removed by legislation, customary law was being robbed of its inherent capacity to evolve in keeping with the changing life of the people it served, particularly women:[26]

> Thus customary law as administered failed to respond creatively to new kinds of economic activity by women, different forms of property and household arrangements for women and men, and changing values concerning gender roles in society. The outcome was formalisation and fossilisation of a system which by its nature should have functioned in an active and dynamic matter.

It was important to examine the context, the Chief Justice continued, in which the rules of customary law operated, particularly in relation to succession and the kind of society served by those rules. They were part of a system that fits the community's way of life. The system had its own safeguards to ensure fairness in the context of entitlements, duties and responsibilities. It was designed to preserve the cohesion and stability of the extended family unit and, ultimately, the entire community. This served various purposes, not the least of which was maintaining discipline within the clan or extended family: "Everyone, man, woman and child had a role and each role, directly or indirectly, was designed to contribute to the communal good and welfare".[27]

Implicitly rejecting the notion of gender complementarity in customary law extolled in this book, however, the Chief Justice went on to observe that the exclusion of women from heirship and consequently from being able to inherit property was in keeping with a system dominated by a deeply embedded patriarchy. This system reserved for women a position of subservience and subordination in which they were regarded as the perpetual minors under the

26 Ibid, para. 90.

27 Ibid, para. 75.

tutelage of the fathers, husbands, or the heads of the extended family. His conclusion was central to the way the Court looked at the customary law rule of primogeniture:[28]

> [T]he rules of succession in customary law have not been given the space to adapt and to keep pace with changing social conditions and values. One reason for this is the fact that they were captured in legislation, in text books, in the writings of experts and in court decisions without allowing for the dynamism of customary law in the face of changing circumstances. Instead, they have over time become increasingly out of step with the real values and circumstances of the societies they are meant to serve and particularly the people who live in urban areas … The role that women play in modern society and the transformation of the traditional African communities into urban industrialised communities with all their trappings, make it quite clear that whatever role the rule of male primogeniture may have played in traditional society, it can no longer be justified in the present day and age.

What needs to be emphasised, the judgment stated, was that because of the dynamic nature of society, official customary law, as it existed in the textbooks and the Act, was generally a poor reflection, if not a distortion of the true customary law:[29]

> True customary law will be that which recognises and acknowledges the changes which continually take place. … The official rules of customary law are sometimes contrasted with what is referred to as 'living customary law,' which is an acknowledgement of the rules that are adapted to fit in with changed circumstances.

The Chief Justice accordingly held that the principle of primogeniture was unconstitutional. His order declared that Anelisa and Nonkululeko Bhe were the true heirs of their father's estate and as such, the owners of the property on which they and their mother had lived. All of the judges who heard the matter signed on to this order. In addition, all of the judges agreed that, in practice, African families who wished to regulate their affairs in a customary manner

28 Ibid, para. 82.
29 Ibid, para. 86–87.

would continue to have family meetings to decide on questions of succession and inheritance.

There was one issue, however, on which the Court was divided. It was on whether Parliament should be requested and given time to pass a law dealing with how intestate estates should be dealt with under customary law. All except one of the judges agreed that the Court should do so and that, in the meanwhile, it should put interim arrangements in place. The one dissenter on this aspect was Justice Sandile Ngcobo. While fully accepting that the rule of primogeniture should go and agreeing that the daughters should inherit the property, he felt that the evolution of customary law in relation to intestate succession should be left to the families themselves and not be referred to Parliament. His judgment is a thoughtful one and has received a certain degree of support in academic circles. I would expect that many dissertations have been written and exam questions created because of the contrast between the majority and the minority decisions.

Finally, it should be pointed out that in practice, the main supporters of tradition are women. It is no accident that the first language people learn to use is called the mother tongue. The women maintain community culture through food, stories, and custom. They build homes in rural areas, till the field and show respect for the land, a communal way of doing things. They keep culture alive in the detailed daily activities of the community.

3 Mix and Match

I haven't studied the legislation from Parliament which followed as a result of the *Bhe* decision, so I would not wish to comment on it save to make three interconnected observations. The first is that one of the characteristics of customary law is that whatever the commentators might say at a theoretical level, its operation is not functionally dependent on references to statutes or regulations published in the government gazette or, for that matter, to law reports. Nor is it operationally reliant on references to documentary materials such as wills and title deeds. It functions according to evolving oral tradition in the community concerned. The second is that I would be surprised if the new statute hasn't given a central position to the practice of family meetings being held to decide on questions of the disposition of the property of the deceased family member. Indeed, even in the case of testate succession, where the terms of the Will are made public, there is nothing to prevent the heirs and legatees from getting together to pool and redistribute the properties in a way they believe would be best for all concerned.

Conversely, the opposite might be true as well. In a seemingly nostalgic gesture towards primogeniture, one of the authors of this book suggests that a traditionalist could use his "Last Will and Testament" to ensure that all his property goes to his nearest male heir, with the direction that he uses it to support the whole family. Once more, one can envisage many interesting exam questions on enforceability and the horizontal application of the Bill of Rights emanating from this suggestion.

The third observation is that although court decisions and national laws might have little direct impact on the ground where customary law is being applied, they might have great significance for the nature of the debates that rage within the family structures handling the issues in dispute. As Anika Claassens and Sindiso Mnisi, leading figures in the Land and Accountability Research Centre at the University of Cape Town Law School, have pointed out, they have a far-reaching impact on the power relations at a local level, which frames the context in which women struggle for change, and influence the possibilities they dare imagine:[30]

> A key insight of the legal pluralists is that, in practice, women mix and match claims derived from the overlapping legal and customary regimes of post-colonial society according to whichever best suits their specific interest in that instance.

These observations came to mind when reading an interesting chapter in the book based on research on an Eastern Cape community, concluding that there was considerable popular resistance to the statutory regime for intestate succession under customary law created by Parliament. I doubt that the word "resistance" is apposite. In the great majority of cases, the intestate regime created by Parliament is simply ignored because the family has agreed on what should be done, and it has not been necessary to resort to the statutory regime at all. The family proposes, and the family disposes. The inference I would draw from the answers that were given to the researchers' questionnaire is that the court decisions and the provisions of relevant statutes are not regarded as determinative texts to be either applied or defied. They simply don't enter into the picture at all as the normative foundations of the decision-making process. Their relevance is of a different order altogether. They carry significant normative weight as elements that the protagonists can use to further their

30 Claassens and Mnisi "Rural Women Redefining Land Rights in the Context of Living Customary Law", 491–516.

objectives in the family discussion about how to apply living, adaptive customary law to settle the disputes in issue. There might be times when the people on the ground will invoke court decisions and national law as determinative elements. For example, when an outrageous situation such as the one that occasioned the *Bhe* litigation arises, they can sue or threaten to sue in a state court. In less outrageous situations, however, they will refer in a generalised way to court decisions and consequential legislation as factors which weigh significantly in favour of ensuring meaningful protection for women, family members and younger children.

In their experience as researchers in various South African provinces, Claassens and Mnisi discovered that women used a range of arguments to advance their claims, many couched in terms of "customary" values. One such value was that all community members were entitled by birthright to land to fulfil their basic needs and support their children; women pointed to the fact that men were entitled to land only when they married and established families. Now that the family structure was changing and women were fulfilling the role of providing for the family, often without men, they contended that they were entitled to be allocated land on the same basis as men with families to support.

Often the principle of equality was asserted, and women referred to 'democracy' and the Constitution. They said that the times and the laws had changed and that discrimination was no longer legal. Arguments about the values underlying customary systems, such as the primacy of claims of need and entitlements of birth rights and belonging, were woven together with the right to equality and democracy.

These observations remind me of an incident involving the application of customary law in relation to criminal sanctions, brought to my attention by the Dutch lawyer and sociologist Barbara Oomen.[31] She had come to my Court Chambers to ask me to write a preface for a book she had written, based on her having learnt Sepedi and having spent a year living as a "curious outsider" in a modest style in the Sekhukhune area of Limpopo Province. In general terms, she told me of her disappointment about the scholarship on African customary law, pointing out that the general tendency was to submerge the lived reality into simplified ideological positions. On the one hand, tradition was trivialised as if it were a rather unfortunate relic of the past that stood in the way of progress and was doomed to disappear in a modern democracy. On the other hand, tradition was romanticised in a manner that gave it a pristine,

31 Oomen *Tradition on the Move.*

timeless, pure and sovereign character that was completely incompatible with its actual entanglement and functioning in contemporary society. As an example of this entanglement, she told me of a community discussion on the punishment to be applied under customary law to a person who had seriously violated community norms. The standard penalty was for the offender to be tied to a tree for a period of time, during which ants would crawl over and sting him. One of the speakers had intervened to say that we now had a Constitution, and such a penalty was no longer permissible in South Africa. The decision-makers accepted his argument and decided on another sanction that would not be against the Constitution.

4 Accountability

The proverb "A chief is a chief by the people", implies accountability by traditional leaders. However, it is said that traditional leaders claim to be legitimate and supportive of consensus-based leadership and decision-making, yet repeatedly act unilaterally and unaccountably in practice.The courts have rebuked traditional leaders for compelling rural families to pay rent for living on communal land. They have also been judicially criticised for entering into contracts to explore for and exploit minerals on land in the former homelands or off the coast of such land without seriously engaging with the people living in the communities on the affected land.

Commentators have observed that traditional leaders are demanding title deeds to all the land in the former homelands. In other words, they are resorting to Western constructs of exclusive ownership. Yet, rural people argue that customary property systems consist of relative and overlapping rights that coexist at different levels and are enforceable through layered decision-making processes. The irony would appear to be that the followers of Western ideas were the traditional leaders, and the believers in living customary law were the communities on the ground, frequently in women-headed families.

In conclusion: The authors are to be commended for undertaking this serious scholarly endeavour. They raise issues of great importance for hundreds of millions of people in our continent and do so on a pan-African scale. They underline the richness of core elements of customary law throughout the continent. They are also to be congratulated for their openness of mind in inviting me to write this contribution knowing full well that much of what I would say would be contrary to major propositions that they present. This is the way ideas advance. Thesis – antithesis – synthesis. The synthesis then becomes the foundation of further challenges, critiques, and so on. May the struggle for ideas continue!

Thank you, Anthony Diala and Christa Rautenbach, for sparking what I am sure will be an intense, rich and valuable debate for South Africa, the African continent, and the world.

Bibliography

Literature

Claassens, Anika, and Mnisi, Sindiso. "Rural Women Redefining Land Rights in the Context of Living Customary Law." *South African Journal on Human Rights* 25, no. 3 (2009): 491–516.

Oomen, Barbara: *Tradition on the Move: Chiefs, Democracy and Change in Rural South Africa.* Amsterdam: NiZA, 2005.

Case Law

Alexkor Ltd v Richtersveld Community 2004 (5) SA 460 (CC).

Bhe v Magistrate, Khayelitsha 2005 (1) SA 580 (CC).

Dikoko v Mokhatla 2006 (6) SA 235 (CC).

Nwamitwa v Phillia 2005 (3) SA 536 (T).

Port Elizabeth Municipality v Various Occupiers 2005 (1) SA 217 (CC).

S v Makwanyane 1995 (3) SA 391 (CC).

S v Maluleke 2008 (1) SACR 49 (T).

Shilubana v Nwamitwa 2007 (2) SA 432 (SCA).

Shilubana v Nwamitwa 2009 (2) SA 66 (CC).

Legislation

Constitution of the Republic of South Africa 200 of 1993.

Constitution of the Republic of South Africa, 1996.

Index

www.ingramcontent.com/pod-product-compliance
Lightning Source LLC
LaVergne TN
LVHW010622300926
849162LV00001B/35